CAN BANKS STI[L] KEEP A SECRET

C000047950

The duty to keep customer information confidential affects banks on a daily basis. Bank secrecy regimes around the world differ and multinational banks can find themselves in conflicted positions with a duty to protect information in one jurisdiction and a duty to disclose it in another. This problem has been heightened by the international trend promoting information disclosure in order to combat tax evasion, money laundering and terrorist financing. The US Foreign Account Tax Compliant Act (FATCA) is perhaps the most well-known. At the same time, data protection legislation is proliferating around the world. This book offers a holistic treatment of bank secrecy in major financial jurisdictions around the world, east and west, by jurisdictional experts as well as chapters by subject specialists covering the related areas of confidentiality in its broader privacy context, data protection, conflicts of laws, and exchange of information for the purposes of combatting international crime.

This project was financed by the Centre for Banking & Finance Law, Faculty of Law, National University of Singapore.

SANDRA BOOYSEN is an associate professor at the Faculty of Law, National University of Singapore and an executive committee member of the Faculty's Centre for Banking & Finance Law. Her teaching and research interests are in the fields of contract and transactional banking.

DORA NEO is an associate professor at the Faculty of Law, National University of Singapore and Director of the Faculty's Centre for Banking & Finance Law. Her teaching and research interests are in the fields of contract, banking law and secured transactions.

CAN BANKS STILL KEEP A SECRET?

Bank Secrecy in Financial Centres Around the World

SANDRA BOOYSEN

National University of Singapore

DORA NEO

National University of Singapore

CAMBRIDGE
UNIVERSITY PRESS

University Printing House, Cambridge CB2 8BS, United Kingdom

One Liberty Plaza, 20th Floor, New York, NY 10006, USA

477 Williamstown Road, Port Melbourne, VIC 3207, Australia

314-321, 3rd Floor, Plot 3, Splendor Forum, Jasola District Centre, New Delhi - 110025, India

79 Anson Road, #06-04/06, Singapore 079906

Cambridge University Press is part of the University of Cambridge.

It furthers the University's mission by disseminating knowledge in the pursuit of
education, learning and research at the highest international levels of excellence.

www.cambridge.org
Information on this title: www.cambridge.org/9781316508473
DOI : 10.1017/9781316535219

© Cambridge University Press 2017

First published 2017
First paperback edition 2018

A catalogue record for this publication is available from the British Library

Library of Congress Cataloging in Publication data
Names: Booysen, Sandra (Commercial law researcher) editor. | Neo, Dora Swee
    Suan, editor.
Title: Can banks still keep a secret? : bank secrecy in financial centres around the world /
    edited by Sandra Booysen, National University of Singapore, Dora Neo, National University
    of Singapore.
Description: First Edition. | New York : Cambridge University Press, 2017. | Includes
    bibliographical references and index.
Identifiers: LCCN 2017006679 | ISBN 9781107145146 (hardback)
Subjects: LCSH: Confidential communications—Banking. | Banks and banking—Records and
    correspondence—Law and legislation. | Disclosure of information—Law and legislation. | Data
    protection—Law and legislation. | BISAC: LAW / Banking.
Classification: LCC K1089 .C35 2017 | DDC 346.082—dc23 LC record available at
    https://lccn.loc.gov/2017006679

ISBN 978-1-107-14514-6 Hardback
ISBN 978-1-316-50847-3 Paperback

To Peter Ellinger – colleague, mentor, friend

CONTENTS

CONTRIBUTORS

SANDRA BOOYSEN,
Associate Professor, Faculty of Law,
National University of Singapore, Singapore

BEAT BRAENDLI,
Assistant Professor, Law School, University of St Gallen,
Switzerland

LISSA BROOME,
Wells Fargo Professor of Banking Law, University of North
Carolina School of Law, USA

STEFAN GANNON,
General Counsel, Hong Kong Monetary Authority, Hong Kong

GRAHAM GREENLEAF,
Professor, University of New South Wales, Australia

CHRISTOPHER HARE,
Travers Smith Associate Professor of Corporate and Commercial
Law, University of Oxford, UK

CHRISTIAN HOFMANN,
Assistant Professor, National University of Singapore, Singapore

CHIZU NAKAJIMA,
Emeritus Professor and formerly Head of Business and Law,
Guildhall Faculty of Business and Law, London Metropolitan
University, UK.

DORA NEO,
Associate Professor, Faculty of Law, National University of
Singapore, Singapore

PETER NOBEL,
Professor, Institute of Law, University of Zurich and Nobel & Hug,
Switzerland

MARTHA O'BRIEN,
Professor, University of Victoria, Canada

REIKO OMACHI,
Of Counsel, Morrison & Foerster (UK) LLP, UK

KEITH STANTON,
Professor, Bristol University, UK

ALAN TYREE,
formerly Landerer Professor of Information Technology and Law,
University of Sydney, Australia

WEI WANG,
Professor, Fudan Law School, China

FOREWORD

During the nineteenth and the first half of the twentieth centuries, the issue of bank secrecy remained of marginal importance. In early tomes on banking law, it was dealt with briefly and only in respect of the relationship between the bank and its customer.

The common law position was eventually clarified in *Tournier's* case, which recognised that, in certain circumstances, the bank was entitled to divulge customer information, *inter alia* when such disclosure was ordered by a court or was needed or required in the bank's own interest.

In many civil law jurisdictions, the issues related to bank secrecy were dealt with in specific statutes. These too were concerned mainly with the confidential nature of the relationship of banker and customer.

It would be mistaken to assume that bank secrecy was not used for purposes of tax evasion or illegal transactions in the nineteenth and early twentieth century. Numbered accounts, available in some European countries, enabled customers to avoid the declaration of revenues derived from deposits placed in such accounts or from securities (such as bonds) acquired through them. In some instances, bank secrecy enabled customers to hide some of their transactions even from their families.

Governments were aware of the situation but, in general, took the view that a customer's privacy – or the privacy of information – was of greater importance than enabling government bodies to access it. Indeed some bank secrecy laws were enacted with the express purpose of protecting customers from the searching eye of their own government. For instance, Swiss bank secrecy guarded the position of some German Jews who maintained accounts with Swiss banks during the World War II.

The perception of bank secrecy changed dramatically during the later years of the twentieth century. Three contributing factors are noteworthy. First, ever since the Bretton Woods Regime of 1945, countries started to repeal exchange control laws. Britain, for instance, repealed the Exchange Control Act 1946 in 1980. Inevitably, the increase in remittances meant an increase in money laundering. Some sectors were, and still are, particularly prone. For instance, the dramatic increase of prices of objects of art (which were sometimes accepted for sale without adequately checking the 'collector's' title) played fairly and squarely into the money launderers' hand.

The second development that led to a change in the perception of bank secrecy was the internationalisation of the banking sector. Many banks that used to be primarily domestic have turned themselves into international banking institutions. While their current emphasis is on wealth management and investment banking, many banks are also engaged in retail banking in foreign countries.

One significant consequence of this development was that, in the absence of a regulatory body, a customer could move his holdings from one of his bank's branches (or offices) to another branch of the same bank and actually from jurisdiction to jurisdiction. In certain cases, such a remittance could be issued by means of a telephone call or an email. The ensuing ease in remittances has, of course, facilitated the transfer of funds for purposes such as tax evasion and money laundering.

The third development that has led to a change in approaches to bank secrecy is the emergence of the web. Naturally, most banks acquired their own computer (or IT) facilities. In turn, this led to the advent of electronic banking and speeded up the decline in branch banking. Customers who used to effect their transactions by visiting the branches where they maintained their accounts, were able to effect money transfers and other types of banking business, from home or even while overseas.

In due course – mainly towards the end of the twentieth and in the twenty-first centuries – government tried to combat the protection afforded to customers through bank secrecy by finding alternative routes to obtaining information which they considered relevant. By way of illustration, consider a citizen of the United States who maintains an account with a Swiss bank. Until the compromises sparked by high profile cases involving UBS and Credit Suisse, an attempt by the American tax authorities to obtain from the Swiss bank information respecting his revenues (which would be taxable under American law) would have failed as the customer's information was protected by Swiss provisions respecting bank secrecy. As yet, no alternative routes were in place.

It is possible that at that stage governments were not too concerned. Tax evasions by individuals and by local corporations were disconcerting but did not call for instant attempts to combat them.

However, the position underwent radical changes in recent years. The globalisation of international trade entailed widespread tax evasion and tax fraud. Indeed, many international bodies shopped around for forums most suitable for their investments. The main objects were, invariably, to minimise tax and to ensure that information would be protected by local bank secrecy laws.

This situation became, in itself, a matter of concern. In addition, the activities of cross border crime syndicates became a menace. Throughout the entire Western World, governments searched for an arrangement which would require banks to supply customer information to local organisations which, in turn, would furnish it to appropriate authorities overseas.

The protocols and arrangements, instituted by organisations such as the G20, the OECD, the EU as well as specific strong arm tactics instigated by some economically leading countries, are discussed in detail in the excellent chapters of this book. Apart from the relevant overview of bank secrecy and treaties respecting the international exchange of tax information, the volume includes detailed analyses of the law prevailing in prominent jurisdictions.

Recent scandals that took place indicate that, in reality, any information supplied by means of alternative avenues ceases to be protected. In the first place, the confidentiality of such records may not meet with the customer's (or individual's) requirements. Secondly, the computer systems used by some countries are poorly protected and some (perhaps many) have been hacked into. A customer's details and personal information (which he readily supplied to his trusted bank) thereupon ceased to be private and protected.

The hacking incidents that took place in the course of the last two years suggests that bank secrecy, in its original form, may be a lesser evil than exposing bank customers' information to authorities with whom they are less safe than when kept solely by the bank.

The issue of finding the right balance between the customer's right of privacy and the right of the State to have his personal information may be an appropriate subject of future conferences. Indeed, political developments that may take place in the near future – such as a possible restructuring of the EU after Britain's exit – may lead to unforeseeable changes in the international scene, and many of the current treaties and arrangements may have to be re-examined.

Peter Ellinger
Emeritus Professor NUS,
Singapore

PART I

Bank Secrecy in Context

A Conceptual Overview of Bank Secrecy

DORA NEO

1.1 Introduction

Banks in many countries have a legal obligation not to disclose customer information, referred to as 'bank secrecy' or 'bank confidentiality'. This traditionally means that banks cannot reveal the state of a customer's account or information that they come to know in the course of a customer's banking relationship with them. However, bank secrecy is generally not an absolute obligation, and banks are allowed to reveal customer information in specific circumstances. The most common examples of exceptions to the duty of secrecy would be where there is customer consent, or where the law requires disclosure. Another example is where a bank is suing its customer. These exceptions have grown more prominent as banks have come under intense international pressure to reveal customer information in the fight against money laundering and terrorist financing, and to combat cross border tax evasion, as discussed in Chapters 4 and 5. The banking system is an indispensable, if generally unwitting, partner in the process of turning the proceeds of crime into 'clean' money, and in facilitating the financial support of terrorism. Offshore bank accounts provide safe havens for funds to be hidden from domestic tax authorities. Banks possess valuable information about their customers and their customers' transactions that could lead to the prevention of crime and terrorism, the recovery of unpaid taxes and the apprehension of wrongdoers. These developments have resulted in banks being faced with positive duties to disclose information about their customers in a growing number

Earlier versions of this paper were presented at the Bank Secrecy Symposium organised by the Centre for Banking & Finance Law at the National University of Singapore on 4–5 December 2014, and the NUS Law Faculty Research Seminar Series on 6 April 2016. I am grateful to the participants at these presentations and to my colleague, Sandra Booysen, for helpful comments on my drafts.

of situations. These situations tend to be subsumed under the general umbrella of bank secrecy law, and tend to be discussed as exceptions to the bank's duty of secrecy. However, we should recognise that there is a second contrasting and equally compelling aspect of bank secrecy law which emphasises disclosure rather than secrecy, under which banks have a mandatory obligation to provide customer information to government authorities. These situations, in addition to just being classified as exceptions to the duty of secrecy, should appropriately have a separate label that emphasises that the bank has a duty of disclosure.

This chapter examines conceptual aspects of a bank's duty of secrecy to its customer, of the exceptions to that duty and of the bank's obligation of mandatory disclosure of customer information. It analyses the bank's duties in the context of protection of privacy on the one hand and mandatory state regulation on the other, and suggest this as an appropriate conceptual framework for understanding the law of bank secrecy. This analysis will necessarily be general, with examples given where appropriate. Analyses of the substantive legal rules are provided by the eight jurisdictional chapters in this book (covering China, Germany, Hong Kong, Japan, Singapore, Switzerland, the United Kingdom and the United States), which examine the law of bank secrecy in each relevant jurisdiction. This chapter draws upon these substantive principles of bank secrecy law that apply in these eight jurisdictions to support and illustrate its conceptual analysis. These are just examples, and the observations and conclusions in this chapter are meant to apply more generally, and are not confined to the eight jurisdictions.

1.2   Bank's Duty Not to Reveal Customer Information

1.2.1   'Secrecy' versus 'Confidentiality'

The focus of the law of 'bank secrecy' or 'bank confidentiality' is on a bank's duty not to reveal its customers' information. Exactly who is considered to be a customer or what type of information is protected by the bank's duty of secrecy will vary in different jurisdictions. In the most straightforward sense, a customer is someone who has an account with the bank, and customer information is information about the customer's account. But questions might arise whether one might be regarded as a customer before the account has been opened or after it has been closed, and whether customer information may extend beyond account deposit information to information that comes to the bank's knowledge in its capacity as banker. Further, the obligation not to reveal information may extend, in some jurisdictions, beyond banks properly so called to cover also other types of financial institutions. These refinements of local law should be borne in mind when the terms 'bank' or 'customer' are used. The term 'financial information' will be used here generally as a convenient reference to information that is protected by the bank's obligation of secrecy in a particular jurisdiction.

For current purposes, the point to be emphasised is that the label attached to the duty, whether it is 'bank secrecy' or 'bank confidentiality', may not necessarily reflect the relative level of strictness of the bank's substantive duty not to reveal customer financial information.[1] These terms may be used interchangeably in some jurisdictions, while other jurisdictions may more commonly use one term rather than the other, probably as a matter of convention.[2] Although some may feel impressionistically that secrecy denotes a higher duty than confidentiality, this is not necessarily the case, as illustrated by the substantive chapters in this book. Indeed, the two words have the same meaning in the English language,[3] and it is unfortunate that the term 'bank secrecy' has acquired a negative association with illicit activity, particularly international tax evasion. The strictness of the bank's duty is in fact determined by the extent of the exceptions to the duty and the sanctions for its breach, and not by any difference in the terminology used. Further, foreign words that are used in various countries to refer to a bank's duty not to reveal customer information may

---

[1] For example, the discussion on Singapore by Booysen in Chapter 10 refers to 'bank secrecy', as did the heading in the Singapore Banking Act (Cap 19, 2008 Rev Ed Sing) before the coming into force of s 32(a) of the Banking (Amendment) Bill (No. 1/2016) (see *infra* note 2), whereas the discussion on Hong Kong by Gannon in Chapter 8 refers to 'bank confidentiality'. If there is to be any difference in strictness of the bank's duty based on the meaning of the two terms, one might expect this to be in the jurisdiction where the impressionistically stricter word 'secrecy' is used, but this is not the case. Instead, the exceptions in Schedule 3 of Singapore's Banking Act are arguably wider than those that apply under the common law in Hong Kong.

[2] See, for example, the discussion of the United Kingdom by Stanton in Chapter 12, where the author uses the term 'bank secrecy' in his chapter, although the conventional reference in the United Kingdom is to 'bank confidentiality', on the grounds that there is no difference in meaning between the two. In Singapore, a bill to amend the Banking Act, *supra* note 1 was passed on 29 February 2016, whereby the heading of s 47, which sets out the bank's obligation not to disclose customer information, was changed from 'banking secrecy' to 'privacy of customer information'. See s 32(a), Banking (Amendment) Bill, *supra* note 1.

[3] For example, the *Oxford English Dictionary*, 3rd edn (Oxford University Press, 2010) defines 'secrecy' as 'the action of keeping something secret or the state of being kept secret'. It defines 'confidentiality' in a similar way, as being 'the state of keeping or being kept secret or private'. The term 'secret' is defined as 'something that is kept or meant to be kept unknown or unseen others'.

themselves be nuanced, but if that is the case, they may not be susceptible to exact translation into English. It would be unproductive to investigate whether the label 'secrecy' or 'confidentiality' should be used in translation when the two words bear the same essential meaning. Ultimately, as the jurisdictional chapters in this book show, a bank's duty not to reveal customer information is not absolute, and countries that use either or both of these labels allow for exceptions to the bank's duty.

As mentioned, the terms 'bank secrecy' and 'bank confidentiality' are also conventionally used to encompass the bank's legal obligation to disclose customer information to the authorities in specific circumstances. This aspect of the bank's duty will be discussed later in this chapter. It may be observed that the use of the terms 'bank secrecy' or 'bank confidentiality' in this context is not only inaccurate, but also misleading, as what is in fact required is the opposite: 'bank disclosure'. Nevertheless, such wide usage of the two terms is well entrenched, and this chapter generally adopts it.

For consistency, the term, 'bank secrecy', will be used[4] to include an interchangeable reference to 'bank confidentiality'. This term will be used to refer to the bank's holistic obligations in relation to customer information, i.e. encompassing both the bank's traditional duty of secrecy/confidentiality as well as its growing duty of disclosure, or one or the other of these duties as the context requires. Where particular specificity is desired, this chapter refers either to the bank's duty not to reveal information (or to its duty of secrecy) on the one hand, or to its duty to disclose information on the other.

1.2.2   Conceptual Basis of Bank's Duty of Secrecy

1.2.2.1   Privacy and Confidentiality

The effect of the bank's duty not to reveal customer financial information is that the customer's privacy is protected. But is privacy protection the object of the imposition of this duty?

The Oxford English Dictionary defines privacy as 'the state or condition of being alone, undisturbed, or free from public attention, as a matter of choice or right; seclusion; freedom from interference or intrusion.'[5]

---

[4] This will also serve to minimise confusion between the term 'duty of confidentiality' and the term 'relationship of confidence' or 'confidential relationship' that will be introduced later in this chapter.

[5] *Oxford English Dictionary, supra* note 3, online: www.oed.com/view/Entry/151596?redirec tedFrom=privacy#eid

The Cambridge Dictionary Online defines it as 'someone's right to keep their personal matters and relationships secret'.[6] Simple as the process of definition may seem to a layperson from a linguistic point of view, privacy is an amorphous concept which scholars have found difficult to define with precision. One legally oriented conception of privacy that is relevant to the present discussion is that it is the 'claim of individuals, groups or institutions to determine for themselves when, how and to what extent information about them is communicated to others'.[7] Another sees it in terms of the extent to which an individual has control over information about himself or herself.[8] Both of these examples have been critiqued,[9] underlining the difficulty in defining privacy with exactness or comprehensiveness.[10] Another view[11] sees privacy as 'a state of voluntary physical, psychological and informational inaccessibility to others to which the individual may have a right and privacy is lost and the right infringed when without his consent others "obtain information about [the] individual, pay attention to him, or gain access to him"'.[12]

I suggest that privacy is something that is desired by human beings generally, and this would apply also to organisations, although in the latter case such desirability is likely to be usually for economic reasons alone. Even the most open person or organisation will have some matters that he, she or it would prefer not to share with others. Scholarly arguments have been made that privacy serves some important functions; for instance, it engenders personal autonomy (avoidance of 'manipulation or domination by others'); allows emotional release (removal of one's 'social mask'); facilitates self-evaluation and offers an environment where an individual can 'share confidences and intimacies' and 'engage in limited and protected

---

[6] Cambridge Dictionaries Online, online: http://dictionary.cambridge.org/dictionary/english/privacy

[7] A.F. Westin, *Privacy and Freedom* (London: Bodley Head, 1967) at 7.

[8] See e.g. C. Fried, 'Privacy', *Yale Law Journal*, 77 (1968) 475 and R. Parker, 'A Definition of Privacy', *Rutgers Law Review*, 27 (1974) 275 at 280–1.

[9] See e.g. N. MacCormick, 'Privacy: A Problem of Definition', *British Journal of Law & Society*, 1 (1974) 75 and R. Gavison, 'Privacy and the Limits of Law', *Yale Law Journal*, 89 (1980) 421.

[10] R. Gellman, 'Does Privacy Law Work?' in P. Agre and M. Rotenberg (eds.), *Technology and Privacy: The New Landscape* (Cambridge, MA: MIT Press, 1998). At 193, Gellman writes: 'Lawyers, judges, philosophers, and scholars have attempted to define the scope and meaning of privacy, and it would be unfair to suggest that they have failed. It would be kinder to say that they have all produced different answers.'

[11] R. Pattenden, *Law of Professional-Client Confidentiality* (Oxford University Press, 2003) at 9.

[12] *R* v. *Department of Health, ex p Source Informatics* [1999] 4 All ER 185 at 195 (Latham J).

communication'.[13] Privacy is often spoken of as a right. This could be meant in various senses, for instance, as a constitutional right, a legal right, a human right, an ethical right or a moral right. An examination of the philosophical foundations of privacy is beyond the scope of this chapter, and I will approach the discussion from the point of view that, apart from the language of rights, privacy is at least a desired value or a desired state.

Closely related to the concept of privacy is the concept of confidentiality. Confidentiality overlaps with privacy but is not identical to it. Both are based on the individual living in a community, but privacy rights are more fundamental in that they precede the obligations of confidentiality. Pattenden[14] explains it in this way: privacy rights require at least two people in a community, whereas confidentiality rights require at least three. Where A, B and C live in a community, confidentiality is achieved where A and B keep something from C, whereas privacy is attained where A is able to keep something from B and C. Confidentiality would require trust between individuals whereas privacy does not. 'Confidentiality requires some privacy, privacy requires no confidentiality'.[15] Therefore, confidentiality is less all-encompassing and is narrower than privacy protection. Broadly speaking, a duty of confidentiality could be seen to be an obligation on a person (such as a bank) not to reveal facts that are told to him or that he comes to know about by virtue of his confidential relationship with another person (such as a customer). Because of its more circumscribed ambit, and the values of privacy and trust related to it, courts and legislatures have been more willing to protect confidential relationships than to protect privacy rights in a more general way. This point will be illustrated later in this chapter.

1.2.2.2   Legal Basis of the Bank's Duty of Secrecy and Relevance to the Concepts of Privacy and Confidentiality

This section explores the legal basis of the bank's duty of secrecy with a view to establishing a link to privacy protection or otherwise.

Private Law   It would appear that a bank's duty not to disclose customer information is a generally applicable private law obligation. All eight jurisdictions covered in this book provide examples of banks' private law

---

[13] These are the four functions identified by A.F. Westin and summarised in R. Wacks, *Privacy and Media Freedom* (Oxford University Press, 2013) at 21.

[14] See *Law of Professional-Client Confidentiality, supra* note 11 at 6.

[15] *Ibid.*

duties of secrecy, even if sometimes in limited circumstances, as in the case of China. There may, in some countries, additionally be a public law duty of secrecy that applies to banks. This section focuses on the bank's duty of secrecy in private law, leaving public law duties to be examined later. A breach of a private law duty attracts only civil remedies, for example damages or an injunction. The bank will be liable to its customer, but it will not be subject to penal or regulatory sanctions.

Contract   Contract law is the most important source for the bank's duties of secrecy in private law. Where there is an express term in the contract between a bank and its customer requiring the bank not to reveal customer information,[16] this is clearly motivated by the parties' concern with privacy protection, particularly on the part of the customer. Where the contract is silent about the bank's duty of secrecy, this duty is implied in many countries.[17] Although the implied contractual duty approach is used in both common law and civil law countries, the common law analysis seems to be more developed and consistently applied across different common law jurisdictions, and will therefore be used to illustrate the connection with the concept of privacy.

The implied term approach in common law countries was first adopted in the influential UK case of *Tournier* v. *National Provincial and Union Bank of England*,[18] which today continues to be the basis for the bank's duty of secrecy not just in the United Kingdom but also in other common law countries such as Hong Kong, Australia and Canada.[19] It was also accepted by the Singapore courts before the Court of Appeal declared it to be supplanted by the statutory provision for bank secrecy in section 47

---

[16] An example can be seen in Germany, where the general terms and conditions included in every bank–customer relationship called 'AGB Banken' provide that the bank 'has the duty to maintain secrecy about any customer-related facts and evaluations of which it may have knowledge'. The bank may only disclose information concerning the customer if it is legally required to do so or if the customer has consented thereto or if the bank is authorised to disclose banking affairs. See Hofmann in Chapter 7 at p. 199.

[17] See the jurisdictional Chapters 6–13.

[18] [1924] 1 KB 461.

[19] See the discussion by Gannon on Hong Kong in Chapter 8 and Stanton on the United Kingdom in Chapter 12. See also chapters 2, 7, 13 and 19 in G. Godfrey (gen. ed.), *Neate and Godfrey: Bank Confidentiality*, 5th edn (London: Bloomsbury, 2015). *Tournier* was also accepted by the Singapore courts before the Court of Appeal declared in *Susilawati* v. *American Express Bank Ltd* [2009] 2 SLR (R) 737 at para. 67 that the statutory regime under s 47 of the Singapore Banking Act was the exclusive regime governing banking secrecy in Singapore. See the discussion by Booysen in Chapter 10.

of Singapore's Banking Act.[20] In the United States, a similar implied term approach was adopted by *Peterson* v. *Idaho First National Bank*[21] before it became overshadowed by the Right to Financial Privacy Act (1978) (RFPA),[22] which will be discussed later. When implying terms into a contract, common law courts are trying to give effect to the unexpressed intentions of the parties. The principles used in the process of implying terms are relevant to our conceptual analysis. The precise requirements (or at least the articulation of these requirements) that courts apply for the implication of contractual terms may vary in different countries. In *Tournier*, the court applied the principles that were established in the leading English case on implied terms at that time, *In re Comptoir Commercial Anversois and Power*.[23] Although other newer cases are now more commonly used as standard authorities for the implied term approach in the United Kingdom, *In re Comptoir Commercial Anversois and Power* provides useful general guidance. There, the court was of the view that a term should not be implied merely because it would be a reasonable term to include if the parties had thought about the matter, but that it must be such a necessary term that both parties must have intended that it should be a term of the contract, and have only not expressed it because its necessity was so obvious that it was taken for granted.[24] In *Tournier*, Scrutton LJ referred to this principle and stated:

> Applying this principle to such knowledge of life as a judge is allowed to have, I have no doubt that it is an implied term of a banker's contract with his customer that the banker shall not disclose the account, or transactions relating thereto, of his customer except in certain circumstances.[25]

While it might seem that a customer would typically be more concerned about secrecy than the bank, it must be emphasised that an implied term is one which a court considers that both parties would necessarily have agreed upon. A finding of an implied duty of secrecy shows the importance that the court thinks both the customer and the bank must have ascribed to secrecy. In *Tournier*, Atkin LJ specifically stated that he was 'satisfied that if [the bank] had been asked whether they were under an

---

[20] *Susilawati* v. *American Express Bank Ltd* [2009] 2 SLR(R) 737 at para. 67. See the discussion by Booysen in Chapter 10.

[21] 367 P. 2d 284 at 290 (Idaho, 1961). See the discussion by Broome in Chapter 13.

[22] 12 USC § 3402 (2013).

[23] [1920] 1 KB 868.

[24] *Ibid.* at 899–900, quoted in *Tournier*, *supra* note 18 at 483–4.

[25] *Tournier*, *supra* note 18 at 480–1.

obligation as to secrecy by a prospective customer, without hesitation they would say yes'.[26]

However, neither Scrutton nor Atkin LJJ elaborated specifically upon why it was seen as necessary to imply a term of secrecy in *Tournier*.[27] This is probably because, like the implied contractual term approach, the underlying conceptual basis of the bank's implied duty of secrecy was so obvious to them that they had taken it for granted. Although the word 'privacy' was never mentioned in *Tournier*, it seems clear, from the discussion of the implied term analysis above, that protection of the customer's privacy was precisely the unspoken conceptual basis of the bank's implied duty of secrecy.[28] Based on this analysis, the finding that the bank had an implied contractual duty of secrecy meant that the court found that both the bank and the customer must have intended that the bank should not reveal customer information, at least without the customer's consent or in the absence of other specific circumstances. Such concern with maintaining secrecy must obviously be linked with the desirability of privacy protection (whether as a primary or ancillary aim) to the parties.

Tort   Another potential source of the bank's duty of secrecy in private law is the law of tort. In Switzerland, for instance, Art. 28 of the Swiss Civil Code protects the privacy rights of any natural or legal person, and this has been recognised by the Swiss Supreme Court to include information relating to financial affairs.[29] An intrusion into these rights would also attract tortious liability under Art. 41 of the Swiss Code of Obligations.[30] A few other chapters of this book also mention tort law,[31] sometimes in a

---

[26] *Ibid.* at 483–4.

[27] *Ibid.* at 474.

[28] Bankes LJ, the third judge in *Tournier*, came closest to explaining why secrecy was important, stating that the 'credit of the customer depends very largely upon the strict observance of that confidence.' *Tournier, supra* note 18 at 474. This may have been true on the facts of the case, where the breach of the duty of secrecy by the bank manager would have revealed the weak financial position of the customer, but it can hardly be taken as a general rule, as a disclosure of a high credit balance in a customer's account may very well enhance his credit. A better general explanation is that it is important to protect the privacy of a client as revelation of his financial affairs may affect him adversely.

[29] See *Neate and Godfrey: Bank Confidentiality, supra* note 19 at 920. See also Nobel and Braendli in Chapter 11.

[30] *Ibid.* at 920. See also Nobel and Braendli in Chapter 11. Nobel and Braendli state that the law of personal rights as set out in the Swiss Civil Code are a source of the client's rights to secrecy in the banking relationship, and explain that an infringement would lead to tortious liability.

[31] See Booysen in Chapter 10, where the torts of defamation, breach of statutory duty and misuse of personal information were suggested as possible ways for a customer to seek

tentative manner[32] or as a matter of tangential relevance where the duties imposed are not specifically focused on bank secrecy.[33] Tort law imposes a duty on a person to respect certain interests of other persons, which does not depend on the existence of a contractual relationship. The interests protected by tort law have traditionally included, for example, bodily integrity (protected by the torts of assault and battery) and the interest in one's reputation (protected by the tort defamation). Another example of interests protected under tort law would be those arising under certain statutes: where a statute imposes a duty on someone to do something, breach of this duty may sometimes be actionable as the tort of breach of statutory duty.[34] While a bank's disclosure of customer information could amount to the commission of the tort of defamation or the tort of breach of statutory duty (assuming that the requisite elements of the relevant tort are made out), these torts generally have limited or no connection with bank secrecy, and are not helpful to our conceptual analysis. We have seen that tort law in Switzerland protects the customer's privacy. Modern tort law in some common law countries has expanded also to include the protection of privacy, although this may not always be relevant to bank secrecy. For example, many US states recognise the tort of invasion of privacy, which encompasses the public disclosure of private facts.[35] Under this tort, the disclosure of customer information by a bank would not be a breach of its tortious duty if the information is not given publicity by being communicated to the public at large, but is told to one person or

---

redress against a bank. The tort of breach of statutory duty was also mentioned by Stanton in Chapter 12, albeit in relation to the more general UK Payment Services Regulations 2009, SI 2009/209, which are not specifically directed at bank secrecy.

[32] Omachi in Chapter 9 states that in Japan, the legal basis for bank secrecy had not been much discussed lately, but that it was broadly understood that a bank would be liable in tort or for breach of contract.

[33] Wang in Chapter 6 suggests that in China, the Decision to Strengthen Network Information Protection made by the NPC Standing Committee and the Consumer Interests Protection Law both impose a tortious duty on banks to protect the personal information of the customers.

[34] An example is the UK Payment Services Regulations 2009, *supra* note 31 which requires an authorised payment institution to maintain arrangements sufficient to minimise the risk of loss through negligence or poor administration, and provides an action in tort for breach of statutory duty if this requirement is contravened. See Regs. 19(4) and 120. See the discussion by Stanton in Chapter 12, where it is suggested that a customer who loses money as a result of cybercrime (presumably because the bank has failed to keep its information secret) has an action in tort for its recovery under these regulations.

[35] See The American Law Institute, *Restatement (Second) of Torts*, § 652D.

a small group of persons.[36] A contrasting example to the United States is provided by the United Kingdom, where the tort of invasion of privacy is not generally recognised, and privacy is protected largely by the law of confidence, which is examined later.[37] Naturally, where it is easier to bring an action for breach of contract, the parties would prefer that to bringing a tort action.

Duty of Confidence   Another possible legal basis for the bank secrecy obligation in common law countries is the duty of confidence.[38] Both Cranston[39] and Ellinger[40] have noted that the banker–customer relationship is one of agency, which is a relationship of confidence that creates an obligation of secrecy.[41] This basis for bank secrecy has not been fully explored as the contractual approach is so dominant. Even where the contract does not provide for an express duty of bank secrecy, the bank's implied contractual duty of secrecy is well-established, and there is little need for an aggrieved customer to look beyond the law of contract. Nevertheless, a breach of confidence action has the advantage of being available where there is an absence of a contractual relationship. This might be useful, for example, where a potential customer does not proceed to enter into a contract with the bank.

The law of confidence imposes a duty to treat information as confidential. This duty of confidence arises from a relationship of confidence, where one party to the relationship is regarded as being legally bound to keep certain information about the other person confidential. The presence of an express or implied term of a contract is one of the ways of establishing a duty of confidence,[42] in the sense that one person cannot reveal information about another, and this has been discussed earlier. The duty

---

[36] See *ibid.*, comments to § 652D. For example, in the US case of *Peterson* v. *Idaho First National Bank*, *supra* note 21, the plaintiff's claim for the tort of invasion of privacy failed because there was no public dissemination of information regarding the plaintiff's account, and the case was decided on the bank's implied contractual duty of secrecy.

[37] In the United Kingdom, the law of confidence is part of equity law, although the second form of this action, the action for misuse of private information, has now been recognised as a tort: *Vidal-Hall* v. *Google* [2015] EWCA Civ 311.

[38] See Booysen, Chapter 10 at p. 288–9 and Stanton, Chapter 12 at p. 343–4.

[39] R. Cranston, *Principles of Banking Law*, 2nd edn (Oxford University Press, 2002) at 169–74.

[40] E.P. Ellinger, E. Lomnicka and C.V.M. Hare, *Ellinger's Modern Banking Law*, 5th edn (Oxford University Press, 2011) at 171–2.

[41] See the discussion by Stanton, Chapter 12 at p. 343–4.

[42] See R.G. Toulson and C.M. Phipps, *Confidentiality*, 3rd edn (London: Sweet & Maxwell, 2012) at 54.

of confidence could also arise from an equitable obligation where the circumstances import an obligation of confidentiality. It is in this context that the law of confidence is usually referred to, e.g. in connection with intellectual property law. The UK case of *Coco* v. *AN Clark (Engineers) Ltd*[43] provides an example of a typical fact situation that arises in such cases: Coco was developing a moped (motor-assisted cycle) and provided information to Clark in the course of negotiations to develop the moped. Clark decided not to proceed with the deal with Coco, and instead developed its own moped, allegedly using some of Coco's designs. The court in that case decided that three elements were necessary to establish a claim for breach of confidence: (i) the information to be protected had to have the necessary quality of confidence; (ii) the information was imparted in circumstances importing an obligation of confidence and (iii) there was an unauthorised use of the information by the defendant to the detriment of the party who originally communicated it. Therefore, if a reasonable person in the shoes of the recipient of the confidential information would have known that the information was confidential and imparted to him in confidence, there would be an implied equitable duty of confidentiality. In the House of Lords' judgement in *AG* v. *Observer Ltd*, Lord Goff stated: 'a duty of confidence arises when confidential information comes to the knowledge of a person (the confidante) in circumstances where he has notice, or is held to have agreed, that the information is confidential, with the effect that it would be just in all the circumstances that he should be precluded from disclosing the information to others.'[44] A second form of the action of breach of confidence has developed in the UK courts. In *Campbell* v. *MGN*, Lord Hoffmann stated that the second form of the action protects against misuse of information based on individual autonomy and dignity and the right to control the dissemination of information about one's private life, rather than the duty of good faith.[45] In the case, a newspaper published a story about the drug addiction of Naomi Campbell, a model, and included photos of her leaving the Narcotics Anonymous meeting. A majority of 3:2 in the House of Lords found in favour of Campbell. The court was of the view that a duty of confidentiality would exist when the facts gave rise to 'a reasonable expectation of privacy',[46] i.e. when a person knows or ought to know that the other can reasonably expect their privacy to be protected. In

---

[43] [1969] RPC 41.
[44] [1990] 1 AC 109 at 261.
[45] [2004] 2 AC 457 at para. 51.
[46] *Ibid.* at paras. 21, 96 and 134.

Douglas v. *Hello! Ltd*, Lord Nicholls stated, *obiter*, that the developed action of breach of confidence covered 'two distinct causes of action, protecting two different interests: privacy and secret (confidential) information', and was of the view that these two should be kept distinct and that information could qualify for protection on the grounds of privacy, confidentiality or both.[47] The English Court of Appeal has confirmed that later form of the action, misuse of private information, which protects a person's privacy and is available in the absence of an initial relationship of confidence, should be classified a tort and not an equitable wrong.[48]

On facts similar to those in *Tournier*, it would seem that the law of confidence overlaps with the law of contract. The widespread acceptance of the contractual analysis in this situation usually makes it unnecessary for the equitable analysis to be explored. But if the latter analysis was attempted, one could argue that the bank would owe the customer a duty of secrecy under the law of confidence, even in the absence of contract. The three principles stated in cases like *Coco* v. *AN Clark (Engineers) Ltd*[49] are capable of applying, with any necessary modification, to the bank–customer situation, although the confidential information concerned might not actually need to be imparted to the bank, as much of the information concerned, for example the customer's transactions or his account balance, would already be within its knowledge as a result of the banking services provided. It is hard to say whether it may be possible also for the customer to have a claim against the bank based on the second form of the action for breach of confidence, i.e. misuse of private information, as this area of the law is still developing.

Privacy, Confidentiality and the Private Law Bases of Bank Secrecy   The earlier discussion of the legal basis of the bank's duty of secrecy, particularly contract law and the law of confidence, sheds some light on the conceptual aspects of this duty. The underlying conceptual basis of privacy protection has been discussed earlier. The significance of the relationship of confidence between the bank and its customer as a factor leading to the imposition of the duty has also been discussed, in relation

---

[47] [2007] UKHL 21 at para. 255.
[48] *Vidal-Hall* v. *Google*, *supra* note 37. The form of action could be significant for procedural reasons (e.g. whether there could be service out of the jurisdiction, as well as to determine the type of damages that can be recovered).
[49] *Supra* note 43.

to the duty of confidence that might arise concurrently or independently with the contractual liability.

Cranston suggests that the decision in *Tournier* is based on the general principles governing breach of confidence.[50] This suggestion is not inconsistent with the contractual analysis seen in *Tournier*. Indeed, in *Tournier*, both Bankes and Scrutton LJJ referred to the confidentiality that existed in the relationship between the customer and the bank.[51] It might seem circular to say that the confidentiality of the bank–customer relationship led to implied contractual duties of confidentiality.[52] The connection between the nature of the relationship and the imposition of the duty would be clearer if we put this in another way. We could say that the close relationship of trust between the bank and its customer makes it obvious that it is necessary to imply a contractual term that the bank would not reveal information about its customer's financial affairs. In other words, the reason why courts see it as necessary to imply a term of bank secrecy is not just to protect the customer's privacy, but also to give effect to the expectations arising from the close relationship between bank and its customer. One of the factors that is relevant in the law of confidence is the nature of the information – that it must have the quality of confidence. This consideration is probably also applicable when the court considers the need to imply a term – that financial information is something that the customer would want to keep private. However, this is not vital: in some jurisdictions, it is not just the customer's account information that is protected, but also any information that has come to the bank's knowledge in the course of providing banking services to the customer.

A rough parallel can be drawn between the bank–customer relationship and professional relationships, such as lawyer–client and doctor–patient relationships, which have been long-accepted to impose duties of confidentiality.[53] In the nineteenth-century English case of *Taylor* v. *Blackburn*, Gaselee J stated that 'the first duty of an attorney is to keep the secrets of his client. Authority is not wanted to establish that proposition.'[54] The duty of secrecy may also be part of the ethical code of professionals. The medical profession, for instance, is bound by the Hippocratic Oath, which includes

---

[50] R. Cranston (ed.), *Legal Issues of Cross-Border Banking* (London: Bankers' Books Ltd, 1989).

[51] *Tournier, supra* note 18 at 474 (Bankes LJ) and 480–1 (Scrutton LJ).

[52] See Stanton in Chapter 12 at p. 343.

[53] This parallel is explicitly drawn by Bankes and Scrutton LJJ in *Tournier, supra* note 18 at 474 (Bankes LJ) and 480–1 (Scrutton LJ).

[54] (1836) 3 Bing (NC) 235.

the statement: 'I will respect the secrets which are confided in me, even after the patient has died.'[55] However, as Bankes LJ cautioned in *Tournier*,

> [T]he privilege of non-disclosure to which a client or a customer is entitled may vary according to the exact nature of the relationship between the client or the customer and the person on whom the duty rests. It need not be the same in the case of the counsel, the solicitor, the doctor, and the banker, though the underlying principle may be the same.[56]

While privacy is clearly the interest that is being protected by the bank's duty of secrecy, a key factor for such protection is the relationship of confidence between the bank and its customer. In the absence of a relationship of confidence, a contractual term of bank secrecy might not have been implied by the courts in various countries, and the law of confidence would not be applicable. Strangers are not bound to keep each other's secrets. Neither are contractual parties, in the absence of a special relationship of confidence or a contractual obligation to do so. A person who happens to catch sight of somebody else's account balance at an ATM is not required by law to keep this information to himself, and a car wash contractor who sees a bank account statement on the dashboard of a car that he is cleaning is unlikely to be bound to do so either.

The connection between confidentiality and the protection of privacy can be drawn by reference to the law of confidence, which serves to protect an individual's privacy in the specific context in which it operates. Gurry draws the connection between the action for breach of confidence and protection of the confider's privacy in this way: '[If] the confidential information is personal to the confider, the [legal] action for breach of confidence allows him the right to ensure that a confidante does not disseminate the information to others thereby granting greater access over

---

[55] The Hippocratic Oath was introduced as the 'Declaration of Geneva' at the 2nd General Assembly of the World Medical Association in Geneva in September 1948, and has undergone subsequent amendments without affecting the pledge of secrecy. For the full declaration, see WMA, 'WMA Declaration of Geneva' (September 1948), online: www.wma.net/en/30publications/10policies/g1/index.html

[56] *Tournier, supra* note 18 at 474. Indeed, the analogy between doctors, lawyers and bankers might not always be appropriate in every jurisdiction or for different types of liability. In Belgium for instance, the Supreme Court decided that bankers did not come under the scope of the application of Art. 458 of the Criminal Code, which provided that doctors, surgeons, health officers, pharmacists and all other persons who, because of their status or profession, are confided secrets will be fined or imprisoned if they reveal those secrets. Bankers were distinguished because they only had a duty of 'discretion'. See Cass, 25 October 1978, Pas. 1979, I, 237 discussed in *Neate and Godfrey: Bank Confidentiality, supra* note 19 at 85.

the confider to others and causing a loss to the confider's state of privacy.'[57] One could say that the concept of privacy underlies the obligation of bank secrecy, which is based on a confidential relationship created, *inter alia*, by contract.

Statute Providing Specifically for Private Law Duties of Bank Secrecy
The RFPA in the United States imposes limits on the power of the federal government to obtain customer financial records.[58] A bank that violates the RFPA may be subject to civil liability, including actual damages, punitive damages if the violation is wilful or intentional, and attorneys' fees.[59] It is notable for the current discussion that this is a statute which provides specifically for private law duties of bank secrecy, and that its name states unequivocally its concern with privacy protection. The RFPA and its relationship with the protection of customer privacy must be understood in context. Unlike the bank's contractual obligation of secrecy which applies generally, this statute is directed at disclosures made to the US government. This is because the RFPA was enacted in 1978 in response to the US Bank Secrecy Act of 1970,[60] which contrary to its name, required US financial institutions to report customer information to the government in certain circumstances. The RFPA was therefore needed as a counterbalance to this erosion of the customer's privacy.

Criminal Law The stakes are high when the bank's duty of secrecy is governed by a penal provision, as breach of the duty would render the bank liable to criminal sanctions such as a fine and/or imprisonment rather than just a private law action such as one for breach of contract. This criminal law duty might be over and above any of the private law duties discussed earlier. The motives for the imposition of criminal liability for a breach of the bank's duty of secrecy in any particular jurisdiction may

---

[57] F. Gurry, *Breach of Confidence* (Oxford: Clarendon Press, 1984) at 14.
[58] 12 USC (2013). Under this statute, any financial records sought must be 'reasonably described' and either (1) the customer authorised the disclosure, (2) there is an administrative subpoena, (3) there is a search warrant, (4) there is a judicial subpoena or (5) there is a formal written request from a federal government authority: 12 USC § 3402 (2013). If the government seeks information about a customer's account, the bank must notify the customer so that the customer has the opportunity to challenge the government's request: 12 USC § 3405(2) and (3) (2013). See further the discussion by Broome in Chapter 13.
[59] 12 USC § 3417(a) (2013).
[60] The formal name of this statute is the Currency and Foreign Transactions Reporting Act of 1970, 31 USC For a discussion of its provisions, see Broome in Chapter 13 at p. 375–7.

or may not be directly linked to the protection of privacy. Of the eight countries covered in this book, a duty of bank secrecy is imposed by the criminal law only in Singapore and Switzerland. In Switzerland, the penal law requirement for bank secrecy is found in Art. 47 of the Swiss Banking Act, while in Singapore, this is coincidentally found in section 47 of the Singapore Banking Act. It should be noted that in both these countries, the statutory provisions did not introduce the duty of bank secrecy, which already existed under private law.[61]

It is commonly believed that the criminal provision for Swiss bank secrecy, first implemented in 1934, was aimed to protect the interests and information of German citizens of Jewish origin, who were foreigners in Switzerland, from confiscation by the Nazi government in Germany, who attempted to gain control of these assets.[62] Two other reasons have been suggested.[63] One is that the Swiss bank secrecy provision was the result of pressure from French clients of Swiss banks after the names of some prominent French clients were found by the French police, and the French government made demands on the Swiss authorities in relation to tax evasion. The other is that increased government supervision on Swiss banks after a spate of bankruptcies in the 1930s led to Swiss banks, which had previously been subject only to light regulation, asking for a statutory guarantee of bank secrecy in exchange. These historical reasons do not specifically emphasise privacy rights, but the desirability of privacy in these situations must have been an important underlying consideration. In Chapter 11, Nobel and Braendli state that the Swiss Federal Court had always been of the opinion that bank secrecy was not a basic, constitutional, legal principle, but was merely a legal norm that may have to be withdrawn in the face of conflicting interests.[64]

In Singapore, there was no explanation for the inclusion of a bank secrecy provision when Singapore promulgated its first banking law statute

---

[61] There is some uncertainty in Singapore whether the implied term approach in *Tournier* still survives (see Booysen in Chapter 10). Even if it does not, there is still the possibility of an express contractual term providing for a duty of confidentiality that meets the statutory minimum standard.

[62] See Nobel and Braendli in Chapter 7 and *Neate and Godfrey: Bank Confidentiality*, *supra* note 19 at 922.

[63] See D. Chaikin, 'Policy and Fiscal Effects of Swiss Bank Secrecy', *Revenue Law Journal*, 15 (2005) 90 at 96–8, relying on the work of M. Perrenoud in 'Les fondements historiques du secret bancaire en Suisse', *Observatoire de la Finance*, 12 (Genève 2002) at 31–7. Available online: http://epublications.bond.edu.au/rlj/vol15/iss1/5

[64] Nobel and Braendli in Chapter 11 at p. 313–4.

in 1970 following its independence from Malaysia. This prohibited bank officers from disclosing customer account information to a non-resident person.[65] In 1983, the 1970 secrecy provision was amended to prevent disclosure to both residents and non-residents.[66] At the same time, this, as well as amendments in 1984,[67] expanded and refined the situations in which the bank's duty of secrecy in section 47 did not apply. Section 47 was repealed and re-enacted in 2001, with a long list of exceptions found in Schedule 3 of the Banking Act.[68] The parliamentary debates provide some insight into the thinking of the authorities. In the 1983 debate, a Member of Parliament raised the question of enhancing the competitiveness of the country's banking sector and supporting its growth as a financial centre as counterpoints in the parliamentary debate on the introduction of provisions that would allow banks to disclose customer information in more situations.[69] This question seemed to have stemmed from the Member's assumption that weaker bank secrecy would weaken competitiveness. In the 2001 debate, the then-Deputy Prime Minister stated that high standards of bank secrecy were a way to maintain customer confidence in the banking system.[70] However, he was speaking not in the context of justifying the existence of a duty of secrecy, but to push forward amendments that would provide greater exceptions to the bank's duty of secrecy, so too much should not be made of his statement. Given that these statements supporting a strict duty were made in the context of an amendment to expand the exceptions to the duty, perhaps the point to be taken is the importance of balancing the interests of secrecy with those of disclosure where appropriate. Privacy protection was not mentioned in any of the

---

[65] Banking Act (Act 41 of 1970). This replaced the Malayan Banking Ordinance No. 62 of 1958 which had hitherto continued to apply in Singapore post-independence.

[66] Banking (Amendment) Act 1983 (Act 6 of 1983).

[67] Banking (Amendment) Act 1984 (Act 2 of 1984).

[68] Banking (Amendment) Act 2001 (Act 23 of 2001). For the history of the statutory provisions relating to bank secrecy in Singapore, see S. Booysen, 'Bank Secrecy in Singapore and the Customer's Consent to Disclosure', *Journal of International Banking Law and Regulation*, 10 (2011) at 501, 502–3, and Booysen in Chapter 10.

[69] See speech of Member of Parliament, Dr Ow Chin Hock, on the second reading of the Banking (Amendment) Bill: *Parliamentary Debates Singapore: Official Report*, vol 61 at col 452 (30 August 1993). The unspoken assumption made by Dr Ow here was that a higher rather than a lower degree of confidentiality would enhance the competitiveness and growth of Singapore as a financial centre.

[70] See statement in parliament by Lee Hsien Loong on the second reading of the Banking (Amendment) Bill: *Parliamentary Debates Singapore: Official Report*, vol 73 at col 1689 (16 May 2001).

parliamentary debates, and it would appear that the aims for criminalising bank secrecy in Singapore were pragmatic.[71]

Even where the imposition of criminal liability for a breach of the bank's duty of secrecy may not be directly motivated by privacy protection, it is likely that this would at least be a relevant underlying consideration. Taking the example of Singapore, it would appear that the criminal law duty of bank secrecy was imposed for the economic reason of promoting competitiveness and building customer confidence in Singapore's financial system. That strong bank secrecy laws would promote such aims must be because of the value that bank customers would place on their privacy when selecting a jurisdiction in which to conduct their financial affairs.

Financial Sector Regulation and Voluntary Codes   Banks may be affected by general regulatory provisions in the financial industry that are not specifically directed at bank secrecy, but are relevant to it. An example from the United Kingdom is the power of the Financial Conduct Authority to regulate banks according to certain general principles under the Financial Services and Markets Act 2000, for instance to conduct business with integrity (Principle 1)[72] and with due skill, care and diligence (Principle 2),[73] and to take reasonable care to organise and control its affairs responsibly and effectively, with adequate risk management systems. If third parties obtain access to customer information because of a security breach, this might render the bank liable to an enforcement action under which a penalty is payable.[74]

An obligation to preserve customer confidentiality may also be imposed by voluntary codes of conduct adopted by the banking industry. One example is the Lending Code in the United Kingdom which states not only that personal information will be treated as private and confidential, but also that secure and reliable banking systems will be provided.[75] Another is the

---

[71] A bill to amend the Banking Act, *supra* note 1 was passed on 29 February 2016, whereby the heading of s 47, which sets out the bank's obligation not to disclose customer information, was changed from 'banking secrecy' to 'privacy of customer information'. See s 32(a) Banking (Amendment) Bill (No. 1/2016). No other changes were made to s 47 by this bill, and the change in heading was probably meant to move away from the pejorative associations with the word 'secrecy' and to state the factual effect of the section, rather than a reflection of a concern with protecting privacy per se.

[72] Financial Conduct Authority, 'Principles for Businesses', PRIN 2.1.1.1, online: www.handbook.fca.org.uk/handbook/PRIN.pdf

[73] *Ibid.*, PRIN 2.1.1.2.

[74] See Stanton in Chapter 12 at p. 347.

[75] *Ibid.* at p. 345.

Association of Banks in Singapore's Code of Consumer Banking Practice (2009) which states that banks will obey their duty of secrecy required by the Banking Act.[76]

In these instances, the aim of the regulation or code would generally be to maintain the general stability of the financial system and to ensure high standards of service and ethical conduct. The bank's duty regarding the secrecy of customer information and records is one of the features that supports these aims.

1.3   Exceptions to Bank's Duty of Secrecy – Conceptual Aspects

The bank's duty of secrecy is not absolute, but is subject to exceptions. Many examples of these exceptions can be found in the jurisdictional chapters of this book. Situations where the bank is permitted to disclose customer information, discussed in this section, must be distinguished from those in which the bank is required to disclose customer information, which is discussed in the next section. There is usually an overlap between the two situations, because a situation where a bank is required to disclose customer information would also usually be a situation where such disclosure would be permitted as an exception to the bank's duty of secrecy. However, situations where the bank is required to disclose customer information impose a positive duty of disclosure on the bank that is not present where the bank is merely excused from its duty of secrecy.

Allowing exceptions to the bank's duty of secrecy is in keeping with the nature of the concept of privacy, and therefore also of the related concept of confidentiality. Privacy is not an absolute concept, and 'its protection must always be sought against conflicting values or interests.'[77] Article 8 of the European Convention for the Protection of Human Rights and Fundamental Freedoms provides:

> Right to respect for private and family life

1. Everyone has the right to respect for his private and family life, his home and his correspondence.
2. There shall be no interference by a public authority with the exercise of this right except such as is in accordance with the law and is necessary

---

[76] Association of Banks in Singapore, 'Code of Consumer Banking Practice' (November 2009), cl 3.c.ii.

[77] N. Witzleb, D. Lindsay, M. Paterson and S. Rodrick (eds.), *Emerging Challenges in Privacy Law* (Cambridge University Press, 2014) at 1.

in a democratic society in the interests of national security, public safety or the economic well-being of the country, for the prevention of disorder or crime, for the protection of health or morals or for the protection of the rights and freedoms of others.[78]

The precise details of this provision are more applicable to the discussion in the next section relating to the bank's mandatory duty of disclosure. For now, it should be noted that even under the European Convention, which acknowledges the human right to privacy, exceptions to this right are provided. It would follow that it is perfectly consistent conceptually to have exceptions to the bank's duty of secrecy, even where privacy is being protected in the sense of being a desirable value falling short of a legally protected right.

Two exceptions to the bank's duty of secrecy are common across various countries. The first is where disclosure is made with the consent of the customer. This exception underlines the fact that the customer can always waive his right to secrecy.[79] The second is where disclosure is made under compulsion of law. The latter exception is particularly relevant in the implied term situation, where it is assumed that the parties could not have intended the bank to contravene the law in seeking to adhere to its contractual obligations. The applicability of these two broad exceptions means that the implied term approach remains conceptually intact despite the onslaught of pressures leading to the so-called erosion of the bank's duty of secrecy, because the implied term of secrecy is envisaged to be only as strict as the parties intend it to be, and the law allows it to be.

Other examples of exceptions to the bank's duty of secrecy are provided by Schedule 3 of the Singapore Banking Act, which lists a total of more than twenty specific situations where disclosure of customer information is allowed, subject to the conditions set out in the schedule.[80] The exceptions deal with a wide range of situations, including the commonly

---

[78] Available at Council of Europe, 'European Convention on Human Rights' (4 November 1950), online: www.echr.coe.int/Documents/Convention_ENG.pdf. That there are exceptions to the concept of privacy is also acknowledged by academic writings, for example, the seminal article by Warren and Brandeis entitled 'The Right to Privacy', published in *Harvard Law Review*, 4 (1890) at 193.

[79] Clauses providing for customer consent to disclosure of information by the bank in certain circumstances are commonly included in the standard terms and conditions of banks, and the question arises whether such clauses will be binding if the customer is not aware of these terms. See for example, the discussion by Booysen in Chapter 10 and Nobel and Braendli in Chapter 11.

[80] See the discussion by Booysen in Chapter 10.

occurring exceptions mentioned earlier, namely where the written consent
of the customer has been obtained, or law enforcement situations such as
where disclosure is in compliance with an order to furnish information for
investigating an offence. There are also exceptions to facilitate the operational requirements of the bank. For example, disclosure is permissible
in connection with an internal audit of the bank and for the outsourcing
of its operations. Disclosure is also permitted to facilitate the workings of
features of the financial system, for example the collation of information
by the credit bureau.[81] These operationally inclined exceptions are more
extensive than those allowed under common law. From a conceptual point
of view, these exceptions promote the efficient functioning of the bank and
the financial system, and are consistent with the pragmatic aims of the
Singapore bank secrecy provision.

1.4   Conceptual Aspects of the Bank's Duty of Mandatory Disclosure

In certain situations, the law imposes a mandatory duty on the bank to disclose customer information. Three prominent examples are where disclosure is required in relation to anti-money laundering (AML), countering
the financing of terrorism (CFT) and combatting international tax evasion. These matters are discussed in detail in Chapters 4 and 5, and are also
touched upon in the jurisdictional chapters of this book. Where mandatory disclosure coincides with an exception to the bank's duty of secrecy,
the analysis in the previous section will apply. Ultimately, the existence of
exceptions to the bank's duty of secrecy is consistent with the non-absolute
nature of the concept of privacy. In this section, an additional aspect of the
situation is considered, and that is the active interference with the customer's privacy by the state authorities. Public authorities have to justify this
interference by invoking competing interests such as national security, the
economic well-being of the country and the prevention of crime, which
are among those set out in Art. 8 of the European Convention of Human
Rights, extracted in the previous section. Countervailing protections may
have to be set out to limit the extent of the interference. For example, as
mentioned earlier, the US Bank Secrecy Act[82] which required banks to

---

[81] The exceptions in Schedule 3 of the Singapore Banking Act are merely permissive, and
the bank and its customer are allowed to agree to stricter standards of confidentiality than
required by the statute, see s 47(8).
[82] Also known as the Currency and Foreign Transactions Reporting Act of 1970, 31 USC.

provide customer information in certain circumstances was counter-balanced by the RFPA which instituted safeguards such as the proper procedure to be followed and the requirement to inform the customer about the information request.[83]

The imposition of mandatory duties on banks to disclose customer information may be problematic in countries like Germany, where bank secrecy is protected by the Constitution.[84] From the customer's point of view, this guarantees the right of 'informational self-determination', which is the right to decide 'whether and to what extent one wishes to disclose personal information'.[85] Just as the bank's mandatory duty of disclosure infringes on the customer's right of privacy, it also infringes on the bank's constitutional right to exercise freedom of occupation, i.e. the freedom to choose and perform one's occupation.[86] However, limitations may be imposed on these constitutional rights 'to the extent that they pursue a legitimate public interest, are based on statute and respect the principle of appropriateness'.[87] These constitutional rights are therefore 'subject to legislative overrides' and do not offer absolute protection from state intervention, but 'a disproportionate use of the legislative incursions by the German state' may be challenged by the customer or the bank in the Constitutional Court.[88]

In the law relating to AML and CFT, if a bank suspects that funds are the proceeds of a criminal activity, or are related to terrorist financing, it is required to report its suspicions to the financial intelligence unit in its country.[89] In relation to taxation, banks must disclose customer information to tax authorities as a result of the sweeping developments to counter international tax evasion, particularly as a result of the US Foreign Accounts Tax Compliance Act (FATCA), and the widespread acceptance of the OECD's common standard for the automatic exchange of information in tax matters.[90] Banks are exempted from their duties of secrecy when they disclose customer information pursuant to AML, CFT and international taxation laws. These incursions into customer

[83] 12 USC (2013). See the discussion by Broome in Chapter 13.
[84] See generally Hofmann in Chapter 7.
[85] See Hofmann in Chapter 7 at p. 206 and chapter 16 in *Neate and Godfrey: Bank Confidentiality, supra* note 19 at 384.
[86] *Ibid.*
[87] *Ibid.* at 384.
[88] Hofmann in Chapter 7 at p. 207.
[89] See Nakajima in Chapter 4 on the international pressures on banks to disclose information.
[90] See O'Brien in Chapter 5 on international developments in exchange of tax information.

privacy are largely based on internationally agreed standards set by the Financial Action Task Force (FATF) and the OECD, and do not seem to be controversial as being undue interference. The FATF recommendations are endorsed by more than 190 countries[91] and more than 100 countries have committed to implementing the OECD standard for the automatic exchange of information by 2018.[92] Even FATCA, which is the result of the unilateral action of the US government, has many subscribers,[93] as the economic consequences of not cooperating – the imposition of a 30 per cent withholding tax in certain payments made from the United States to non-compliant financial institutions – would be devastating.

The disclosure requirements imposed on banks by the laws relating to AML, CFT and the prevention of international tax evasion must be looked at beyond the lens of bank secrecy. The objectives of the AML and CFT regimes are to combat money laundering and terrorist financing by preventing these activities and bringing to justice the perpetrators of these offences as well as those who aid their commission. In the case of money laundering, there is also the aim of preventing the underlying predicate offences in relation to which funds are being laundered, such as drug trafficking, corruption and other serious crimes. Issues of bank secrecy arising from the duty to report suspicious transactions are just part of the big picture. Another important element is the 'know your customer' (KYC) requirements of the AML and CFT regime, which impose an equal burden on banks. Further, the KYC and suspicious transactions reporting requirements are not confined to the financial industry but applicable also to other designated businesses and professionals such as lawyers and accountants. Similarly, the disclosure of information for tax purposes can be seen as an extension of the international cooperation in tax matters that has been taking place for years, even if its scope is unprecedented.

---

[91] See FATF, 'Countries' (2016), online: www.fatf-gafi.org/countries

[92] See OECD, 'Global Forum on Transparency and Exchange of Information for Tax Purposes: Status of Commitments' (9 May 2016), online: www.oecd.org/tax/automatic-exchange/commitment-and-monitoring-process/AEOI-commitments.pdf

[93] More than 110 countries have signed intergovernmental agreements with the United States under FATCA. See US Department of the Treasury, 'Foreign Account Tax Compliance Act (FATCA)' (11 July 2016), online: www.treasury.gov/resource-center/tax-policy/treaties/Pages/FATCA.aspx

1.5   Privacy Protection in Perspective

The developments in relation to bank secrecy since the 1990s have largely been to curtail its scope and to allow or to require banks to disclose customer information in an increasing number of situations in response to modern challenges and situations as discussed in Chapters 4 and 5 and the jurisdictional chapters of this book. In particular, the bank's duties of disclosure for AML, CFT and prevention of tax evasion purposes have been alluded to earlier. Protection of the customer's privacy in financial matters is gradually being reduced and sacrificed. This might seem inconsistent with other aspects of privacy which seem to be enjoying increased protection, such as personal data protection, which has seen active development internationally. This has been triggered by technological advances and social changes. With the rise of computerisation and e-commerce, massive amounts of data about individuals are now easily stored and retrieved. An increasing number of countries have adopted data protection laws to regulate the collection and use of such data,[94] and such laws are applicable to banks (in addition to their secrecy obligations), as they are to other businesses. This increased protection of privacy in the sphere of data protection might appear diametrically opposed to the erosion of privacy that is happening in the sphere of bank secrecy, but this development must be seen in context. The relative novelty of data protection laws has led to attention being focused on the new privacy rights that it provides rather than on its limitations. Like bank secrecy, data protection is not absolute. Taking the example of Singapore, the Monetary Authority of Singapore (MAS) has clarified that for the purposes of meeting the AML and CFT requirements, such as in the course of performing customer due diligence, financial institutions can collect, use and disclose personal data of an individual customer without the respective individual's consent.[95] More generally, the Singapore statute provides for situations where collection, use or disclosure of information without consent is permitted, for instance where it is clearly in the interest of the individual, where there is

---

[94] For a discussion of data protection and its relationship with bank secrecy, see Greenleaf and Tyree in Chapter 2.

[95] See e.g. Monetary Authority of Singapore, 'MAS Notice 626 on Prevention of Money Laundering and Countering the Financing of Terrorism – Banks' (24 April 2015), at para. 13, online: www.mas.gov.sg/~/media/MAS/Regulations%20and%20Financial%20 Stability/Regulatory%20and%20Supervisory%20Framework/Anti_Money%20 Laundering_Countering%20the%20Financing%20of%20Terrorism/MAS%20Notice%20 626%20%20April%202015.pdf

an emergency, where it is necessary in the national interest or otherwise authorised by law.[96] These exceptions, particularly the open-ended exception that applies to a disclosure authorised by law, might potentially be as wide as those applying to bank secrecy.

Privacy is a multifaceted concept, and different aspects may require different treatment, depending on the existing state of the law and the circumstances calling for protection or erosion of privacy. Data protection law and bank secrecy law are examples of the regulation of informational privacy. Other aspects include laws on health privacy and online privacy. Privacy also involves being free from observation or disturbance. Contemporary phenomena, like the rise of terrorism, are relevant not just to banking but also to other spheres and may pose similar challenges. For example, the requirement for disclosure of banking information where it is suspected that a transaction is connected with terrorist financing has a parallelism in the need for surveillance or monitoring of private citizens without heeding their privacy rights.

Because of the broadness of the concept of privacy, courts may be wary of allowing a general right of action based on privacy. The example of the United Kingdom is a case in point where the courts were unwilling to recognise the legal right of privacy although they had for many years developed the law of confidence, which protects aspects of privacy.[97] In the UK House of Lords case of *Wainwright* v. *Home Office*,[98] Lord Hoffmann distinguished between privacy as a value underlying the existence of some legal right, and privacy as a legal right in itself,[99] and expressed the view that any protection of privacy as such must come from the legislature. The House of Lords held in *Wainwright* v. *Home Office* that there was no action in the United Kingdom for invasion of privacy and that the Human Rights Act 1998 and Art. 8 of the European Convention[100] did not create such

---

[96] Singapore Personal Data Protection Act 2012 (No. 26 of 2012), Schedules 2–4. The balance that must be struck between individual rights and wider societal interests can be seen in the Singapore's Personal Data Protection Act 2012, which provides in section 3 that: 'The purpose of this Act is to govern the collection, use and disclosure of personal data by organisations in a manner that recognises both the right of individuals to protect their personal data and the need of organisations to collect, use or disclose personal data for purposes that a reasonable person would consider appropriate in the circumstances.'

[97] See Toulson and Phipps, *Confidentiality, supra* note 42, especially chapter 6.

[98] [2004] 2 AC 406.

[99] *Ibid.* at para. 31.

[100] Article 8(1) of the ECHR, *supra* note 78 states, *inter alia*, that 'everyone has the right to respect for his private and family life, his home and his correspondence.'

a cause of action. In *Campbell* v. *MGN*,[101] the House of Lords gave effect to the Convention by interpreting the common law duty of confidence to take into account the Art. 8 right to privacy, resulting in two forms of the action for breach of confidence, one based on the traditional principles of confidentiality and the second based on privacy.[102]

1.6   Conclusion

A bank's obligation to keep its customer's information secret rests ultimately on the concept of privacy. It is an aspect of privacy protection that is well established, as in other confidential relationships such as the solicitor–client and doctor–patient relationships. Such protection has been conveniently facilitated in some jurisdictions by the willingness of the courts to find an implied contractual term imposing such a duty. Privacy, in the sense of being able to keep one's information private, and confidentiality, in the sense of being able to trust another person to do so, are both relevant underlying concepts. The bank's duty of secrecy to its customer is based mainly on private law, but some jurisdictions impose criminal sanctions for breach of the duty of bank secrecy. Even where the reasons for such criminalisation are pragmatic, for example to build an attractive financial centre or to promote stability in the banking system, privacy protection is likely to be an underlying consideration. These motivations capitalise on the customer's desire for privacy, and take advantage of the trust in a financial system that tends to result when financial privacy is protected. Exceptions to the duty of bank secrecy are growing, and positive duties of disclosure are being imposed in an increasing number of situations. This erosion of the obligation of secrecy is consistent with the idea that privacy is not an absolute right, and must be balanced against competing interests. Similar trade-offs are being made in other areas, for instance where individuals are subject to electronic surveillance in the fight against crime, which is made possible by technological advances. The rise of information technology has led to the enactment of data protection laws, which can serve to protect individual privacy. However, like bank secrecy laws, data protection laws are generally subject to exceptions. The growing obligation of banks to disclose customer information must be seen in perspective. The erosion of bank secrecy is largely in relation to

---

[101] *Supra* note 45.
[102] These are explained by Lord Nicholls in *Douglas* v. *Hello! Ltd*, *supra* note 47 at para. 255.

disclosures to government authorities, and the duty of disclosure arises in the context of state intervention for purposes that go beyond bank secrecy law, such as crime prevention, national security, international cooperation and economic advancement. Customer privacy is still protected in cases where there are no overriding competing interests, an example in many countries being the disclosure to private persons without the consent of the customer.

Bankers' Duties and Data Privacy Principles: Global Trends and Asia-Pacific Comparisons

GRAHAM GREENLEAF AND ALAN TYREE

2.1 Introduction – The Uncomfortable Obligations of Modern Banking

An examination of the relationship between the traditional duties of banks to their customers and data privacy laws is of increasing international relevance because of the growing ubiquity of data privacy laws. As is explained in other chapters,[1] at the end of the 1980s the Vienna Convention required state parties to criminalise money laundering, and the Financial Action Task Force (FATF) started development of its '40 recommendations' including 'suspicion-based reporting' to a state authority, exemption of banks from any consequent breaches of bank–customer confidentiality and similar exemption of international requests for mutual assistance. The enactment by legislatures across the world of those recommendations, and subsequent recommendations concerning measures for reporting of 'suspicious transactions', counter-terrorist financing, anti-sanctions avoidance and anti-corruption have led to the global retreat of the banker's traditional duty of confidentiality in an increasingly wide and complex range of circumstances, beyond the acronym 'AML-CTF'.[2]

However, since the 1970s a somewhat inconsistent development to which banks (among other entities) were subject gradually became 'globalised': the development of 'data privacy' laws (also called 'data protection' and 'information privacy' laws), which imposed on banks an overlapping but very different range of obligations from the traditional duties owed by banks to their customers.

This chapter was first presented at the Banking Secrecy Symposium, 4–5 December 2014, Centre for Banking and Finance Law, National University of Singapore.

[1] See in particular Nakajima, Chapter 4.
[2] Anti-Money Laundering Counter-Terrorism Financing.

This chapter first explains both the contours of the increasingly global phenomenon of data privacy laws, and that these laws have considerable uniformity in their content. The core principles of data privacy laws are then examined, using examples from jurisdictions in the Asia-Pacific,[3] comparing those principles with the duties of bankers. Conclusions are drawn about the extent to which the two differ or are similar, and the overall approach that banks might take to dealing with the diversity of data privacy laws.

Banks everywhere will increasingly have to take into account data privacy laws, in addition to their traditional duties. The breadth of obligations imposed by these laws, while often in parallel with traditional duties, is generally of much broader scope, and will require new accommodations in banking practice, particularly for banks with multinational operations. However, the statutory exceptions to data privacy laws, particularly in relation to law enforcement and revenue protection, will very often apply to banks, and the specific statutory provisions concerning AML-CTF will usually override the requirements of data privacy laws. The standards imposed by data privacy laws, and penalties for their breach[4] are becoming stronger, and that is likely to continue to occur.

2.2 The International Trajectory of Data Privacy Legislation

Over forty years ago, Sweden's *Data Act 1973* was the first comprehensive national data privacy law, and the first such national law to implement what we can now recognise as a basic set of data privacy principles.[5] As of April 2016 there were 110 such laws, an average rate of increase of 2.6 additional countries per year for the last forty-two years. The picture that emerges from analysis of the growth of these laws over time[6] is that data privacy laws are spreading globally, and their number and geographical diversity accelerating since 2000. Before further analysing this global growth, it is necessary to clarify what is meant by a 'data privacy law'.

---

[3] Parts of this chapter are based on G. Greenleaf, *Asian Data Privacy Laws: Trade and Human Rights Perspectives* (Oxford University Press, 2014), chapters 3.1, 3.2 and 17.

[4] There is no scope in this chapter to demonstrate the rising enforcement standards, see *ibid.*, chapter 18.

[5] In 1970, both the United States's *Fair Credit Reporting Act* and a data protection law for public sector in the Lander of Hessen, Germany, had included sets of data protection principles, but did not have the scope required for laws considered here.

[6] This analysis is presented in greatest detail in G. Greenleaf, 'Sheherezade and the 101 Data Privacy Laws: Origins, Significance and Global Trajectories', *Journal of Law, Information & Science*, 23(1) (2014), online: SSRN, http://ssrn.com/abstract=2280877

2.2.1   *The Minimum Standard for a 'Data Privacy Law'*

The privacy principles in the two earliest international instruments on data privacy, the OECD privacy Guidelines of 1980[7] (the OECD Guidelines) and the Council of Europe (CoE) data protection Convention 108 of 1981[8] (Convention 108) can be summarised as the following ten principles (the minimum principles):

1. *Data quality* – relevant, accurate and up-to-date
2. *Collection* – limited, lawful and fair; with consent or knowledge
3. *Purpose specification* at time of collection
4. *Notice* of purpose and rights at time of collection (implied)
5. *Uses and disclosures limited* to purposes specified or compatible
6. *Security* through reasonable safeguards
7. *Openness* regarding personal data practices
8. *Access* – individual right of access
9. *Correction* – individual right of correction
10. *Accountable* – data controller with task of compliance.

In a series of analyses since 2011 and accompanying tables of data privacy laws,[9] Greenleaf has charted which countries have data privacy laws.[10] The assumption on which the analysis is based is that a data privacy law must include (i) as a minimum, access and correction rights (individual participation), (ii) some 'finality' principles (limits on use and disclosure based on the purpose of collection), (iii) some security protections and (iv) overall, at least eight of the ten principles identified above (i.e. at least five others).[11] These comprise a basic or minimum set of data privacy principles with some pedigree in international agreements and

---

[7]   OECD, 'OECD Guidelines on the Protection of Privacy and Transborder Flows of Personal Data' (23 September 1980), online: www.oecd.org/sti/ieconomy/oecdguidelinesonthepro tectionofprivacyandtransborderflowsofpersonaldata.htm

[8]   Council of Europe, 'Convention for the Protection of Individuals with Regard to Automatic Processing of Personal Data', ETS No. 108 (28 January 1981), online: www.coe.int/en/web/ conventions/full-list/-/conventions/rms/0900001680078b37

[9]   See 'Sheherezade and the 101 Data Privacy Laws', *supra* note 6.

[10]   For this purpose, a country (including any independent legal jurisdiction) is considered to have a 'data privacy law' if it has one or more laws covering the most important parts of its private sector, or its national public sector, or both.

[11]   The published analyses take a slightly more complex approach, breaking the ten listed principles into fifteen, and requiring eleven of the fifteen overall, but this equates approximately to eight of the ten listed here.

academic scholarship.[12] The minimum standard for a data privacy law also requires some methods of officially backed enforcement (i.e. not only self-regulation). The most recent analysis (February 2015) showed that the number of countries meeting such minimum requirements had expanded by 10 to 109 since mid-2013.[13]

2.2.2   Patterns of Global Growth of Data Privacy Laws

The global rate of expansion of countries with data privacy laws has averaged approximately 2.6 laws per year for forty-two years. Viewed by decade, growth has been: 9 (1970s), +12 (1980s), +20 (1990s), +39 (2000s) and +30 (5.25 years of the 2010s), giving the total of 110. Such laws are now found in all geographical regions except the Pacific Islands.[14] Since 2015, for the first time, the majority of data privacy laws are found outside Europe (now fifty-six to fifty-four). European laws will increasingly be in the minority, as there is almost no room for their expansion within Europe, since Europe now has near-full adoption.[15] Growth is likely to continue, with at least twenty-one more countries currently having official bills working their way through political and legislative processes.[16] Other new developments such as the African Union's 2014 Convention on cybercrime, e-commerce and data protection[17] are likely to promote further growth. On current projections, by 2020 there are likely to be at least

---

[12] Principles concerning minimal collection, retention limits and sensitive information are not included, as they only became common requirements in the 'second generation' of data privacy laws and agreements from the 1990s onwards (as discussed later).

[13] G. Greenleaf, 'Global Data Privacy Laws 2015: 109 Countries, with European Laws now in a Minority', *Privacy Laws & Business International Report*, 133 (2015), 14–7, online: SSRN, http://ssrn.com/abstract=2603529. The additional ten countries are: South Africa, Kazakhstan, Mali, Ivory Coast, Lesotho, Brazil and the Dominican Republic, plus three small former Dutch colonies (Curaçao, the BES Islands and St Maartens). The 110th country is Turkey, which enacted its law in March 2016.

[14] EU (28); Other European (25); (sub-Saharan) Africa (17); Asia (12); Latin America (10); Caribbean (7); Middle East (4); North America (2); Australasia (2); Central Asia (2); Pacific Islands (0).

[15] The exception is Belarus.

[16] See the Global Table of Data Privacy Bills in 'Global data privacy laws 2015', *supra* note 13, which lists known official Bills for new Acts, both those which have been introduced into legislatures and those which are under official consideration by governments. Information is included about the current known state of a Bill.

[17] G. Greenleaf and M. Georges, 'The African Union's Data Privacy Convention: A Major Step Toward Global Consistency?' *Privacy Laws & Business International Report*, 131 (2014), 18–21.

140 countries with such laws,[18] including most of the world's economically significant countries. Countries without comprehensive private sector laws may well have significant e-commerce or consumer sector privacy laws with similar effects on the banking sector, as do China, Indonesia, Turkey and the United States at present. Laws which have a strong 'family resemblance' to at least the minimum data privacy principles listed earlier will be close to ubiquitous by the end of the decade. This ubiquity will require changes to banking practices.

2.2.3 'European' Data Privacy Standards and Beyond

The 'minimum' data privacy principles of the early 1980s, discussed earlier, are no longer the prevailing international standard, including outside Europe. From the early 1990s an extended set of principles were developed for the EU Data Protection Directive adopted in 1995,[19] but they were based on, and incorporated, the 1980s minimum principles described earlier.[20] The following list[21] of the most significant differences in relation to privacy principles between these 'European' instruments and the minimum 1980s instruments is not comprehensive[22] but is sufficient to demonstrate the higher, stricter standards the former require. There are eight 'European' content principles[23] that may be found in national privacy

---

[18] If the current rate of expansion for 2010–15 continues in a linear fashion, over 50 new laws would result in this decade, bringing the total to 140. However, the growth of data privacy laws since the 1970s has been one of continued acceleration, not linear growth, which if it continues would result in between 140 and 160 (i.e. 60 to 80 new laws this decade).

[19] EC, *Directive 95/46/EC of 24 October 1995 on the Protection of Individuals with Regard to the Processing of Personal Data and on the Free Movement of such Data* (1995) O.J. L. 281 at 31 *et seq.*

[20] They also included some additional elements already found in the CoE Convention, which was itself 'updated' in 2001 via its Additional Protocol, to reflect principles from the EU Directive. See Council of Europe, 'Additional Protocol to the Convention for the Protection of Individuals with regard to Automatic Processing of Personal Data regarding supervisory authorities and transborder data flows', ETS No. 181 (8 November 2001), online: www.coe.int/en/web/conventions/full-list/-/conventions/treaty/181

[21] This was first argued in G. Greenleaf, 'The Influence of European Data Privacy Standards Outside Europe: Implications for Globalisation of Convention 108', *International Data Privacy Law*, 2(2) (2012), 68–92, online: SSRN, http://papers.ssrn.com/abstract_id=1960299

[22] Other 'European' elements could be added to the list, for example the right to prevent further processing, but it was decided to keep the list to a manageable size. A choice was then made of the most important distinguishing elements.

[23] The original analysis also included two 'European' enforcement requirements ((ix) requirements of a DPA and (x) access to court remedies), and so was put in terms of how many out of ten principles (not eight) a law embodied.

laws, called in summary[24]: (i) Data export restrictions based on destination; (ii) Minimal collection; (iii) 'Fair and lawful processing'; (iv) 'Prior checking' of some systems; (v) Deletion; (vi) Sensitive data protections; (vii) Automated processing controls and (viii) Direct marketing opt-out. None of the aforementioned eight elements is required, or even recommended, by the OECD Guidelines.[25]

It is a common but mistaken assumption that only the minimum standard of data protection is achieved by the laws of most countries outside Europe.[26] An analysis was undertaken of the laws of thirty-three countries outside Europe[27] with data protection laws as on December 2010.[28] It showed that in relation to ten principles that were more strict than the OECD/CoE minimum principles (the above eight, plus two concerning enforcement), the thirty-three non-European laws examined on average included seven out of the ten above-mentioned 'European' principles. Some of these additional 'European' principles occurred in more than 75 per cent of the thirty-three countries assessed, including (i), (ii), (v) and (vi) earlier.

No post-2010 global comparison has yet been done. However, further analysis in 2014 of eleven Asian countries with data privacy laws (including China for this purpose) showed that, on average, each of the eight 'European' principles described earlier is implemented in five of the eleven Asian jurisdictions, and on average each jurisdiction implements almost four of these principles.[29] These Asian jurisdictions could therefore, on average, be described as 'halfway' between the minimum principles and the 'European' principles. This generalisation probably holds true for most other regions outside Europe.

The strengthening of data protection laws is far from complete. The European Union (EU) is in the final stages of reform of the Data Protection Directive, almost certainly by replacing it with a Regulation (the General

---

[24] For more details see *Asian Data Privacy Laws, supra* note 3 at 56; alternatively 'The Influence of European Data Privacy Standards Outside Europe', *supra* note 21.

[25] Nor are they required or recommended by the APEC Privacy Framework (2004), which is based substantially on the OECD Guidelines of 1980.

[26] Laws in European countries can be assumed to exhibit generally higher standards, because of the requirements of the EU Directive, and the Additional Protocol to the CoE Convention.

[27] Copies, or translations, of six of the thirty-nine laws were not available, so only thirty-three were examined.

[28] 'The Influence of European Data Privacy Standards Outside Europe', *supra* note 21.

[29] *Asian Data Privacy Laws, supra* note 3 at 502–3.

Data Protection Regulation, GDPR), and has finalised. The EU is likely to strengthen most of its standards, but nothing can be considered final until all negotiations are complete. At least fifteen new elements have been identified as possible components of such enhanced principles,[30] but those finally adopted may differ considerably. The enforcement provisions after reform of the Directive may also set a much stronger standard.

2.2.4   Implications of Ubiquitous 'European' Privacy Standards for Banks

If something close to the content of the GDPR drafts under discussion is enacted, this will constitute, in conjunction with an ongoing 'modernisation' of CoE Convention 108,[31] a 'third generation' of data privacy principles, again of primarily European origin. Like the 'second generation' European principles, they can be expected to gradually but strongly influence the shape of non-European data privacy laws.

Whether we are talking about the near-future of global privacy laws embodying something close to 'second generation' European standards, or about future embodying 'third generation' standards, the global reality for banks will be a world that requires compliance with something resembling European privacy laws. It will therefore be prudent and practical for banks with multinational operations, if they wish to have consistent privacy practices across their countries of operation, to consider adopting a set of privacy standards which are considerably higher than the 1980s minimum principles, and which adopt the most significant and widely enacted

---

[30] These may include more explicit consent (opt-in) requirements, and obligations to prove same; more explicit requirements of data minimisation at collection; a 'right to be forgotten'; a right to data portability, including a right to obtain a copy of personal data in a portable format; regulation of automated 'profiling'; demonstrable implementation of privacy principles (stronger 'accountability'); implementation 'by design'; implementation 'by default'; liability of local European representatives of a processor; mandatory data breach notification; the ability to require privacy impact assessments; data protection officers required; more specific requirements in relation to data exports; EU rules to apply to extra-territorial offering of goods, services or monitoring and a right to online subject access. This summary is derived substantially from an early analysis in February 2012: C. Kuner, 'The European Commission's Proposed Data Protection Regulation: A Copernican Revolution in European Data Protection Law', *Bloomberg BNA Privacy and Security Law Report* (6 February 2012), 1–15, online: SSRN, http://ssrn.com/abstract=2162781. Some elements will probably be dropped in the final Regulation.

[31] G. Greenleaf, '"Modernising" Data Protection Convention 108: A Safe Basis for a Global Privacy Treaty?' *Computer Law & Security Review*, 29 (2013), online: SSRN, http://ssrn.com/abstract=2262296

'European' standards. They will then have to adjust these data privacy
obligations according to their local AML-CTF obligations.

2.3   Principles in Data Privacy Laws
Compared with Bankers' Duties

The principal obligation of a bank which is relevant for comparison with
data privacy laws is the bank's duty of secrecy which, in common law countries, received its classic exposition in *Tournier* v. *National Provincial &
Union Bank of England* as an implied term in the contract between bank
and customer.[32] There are also statutory sources of the obligations of
bank secrecy, as in Singapore[33] and Switzerland,[34] but these appear to
have a less consistent conceptual basis across jurisdictions.[35] The contractual duty as described in *Tournier* is therefore used as the main point
of comparison in this chapter, although this does result in a necessary
oversimplification.

The most important thing about data privacy laws, compared with the
specific legal rules concerning bank secrecy (whether from statutory
banking laws or at common law), is the much wider range of obligations that they impose on banks concerning personal data, and that they
are not limited to customer data. They encompass, as well as disclosure
restrictions (where comparisons with bank secrecy laws may be readily drawn), collection limitations, limits on internal use by banks, limits
on overseas transfers, obligations concerning access and correction, data
quality and security. Some of these obligations may also arise from banking statutes.

To explain this wider range of obligations, this section summarises and
compares the data privacy laws in Asia[36] plus, in some cases, Australia
but not other Asia-Pacific countries with data privacy laws.[37] It assesses

[32] [1924] 1 KB 461. See A. Tyree, *Banking Law in Australia*, 8th edn (Chatswood, NSW: LexisNexis, 2014).
[33] See Booysen, Chapter 10.
[34] See Nobel and Braendli, Chapter 11.
[35] For a conceptual discussion of bank secrecy, see Neo, Chapter 1.
[36] This comparison is derived in part from chapter 17 of *Asian Data Privacy Laws*, *supra* note 3. For the details of the laws of each jurisdiction, see the relevant country chapters in Part II of that book. For the sake of readability of these comparisons, legislative citations are not given. They may be found in the relevant chapters of the book. The relevant legislation is listed in the following note.
[37] New Zealand, Canada, the United States, Mexico and various South American countries.

how far beyond the requirements of banking law these privacy obligations extend, and to what extent these laws are similar and consistent, once
we go beneath the generalisation that all are in the family of 'data privacy
laws'. The exceptions to these principles which are of particular relevance
to banks are often not detailed here, because they vary so much between
jurisdictions.

We will focus on the following comparisons between data privacy laws
and bank's secrecy duties:

1. 'Personal data' vs. 'customers' data', and other differences in scope
2. Minimum collection vs. 'know your customer' (KYC)
3. Use and disclosure restrictions vs. *Tournier* exceptions
4. International dimensions of banking disclosures
5. Security and data breach vs. safe custody duties.
6. Access, correction and other new customer rights

2.3.1   Data Privacy Laws in Asia and Australia,
and Complaints Concerning Banks

Twelve Asian jurisdictions have significant data privacy laws affecting their private sectors.[38] Six of these laws are comprehensive, covering
both the public and private sectors: Hong Kong,[39] Japan,[40] South Korea,[41]
Macau,[42] the Philippines[43] (not yet in force) and Taiwan.[44] Three others

---

[38] This paper does not consider Nepal and Thailand, the laws of which cover their public sectors only. A Bill dealing with the private sector was before the previous Thai legislature in
2013: *Asian Data Privacy Laws, supra* note 3, chapter 12.

[39] Personal Data (Privacy) Ordinance 1995 (Hong Kong SAR); see *Asian Data Privacy Laws,
supra* note 3, chapter 4.

[40] Act on the Protection of Personal Information 2003 (Japan) and related legislation; see
Asian Data Privacy Laws, supra note 3, chapter 8. The Japanese law has now been reformed
comprehensively, but the reforms are not yet in force: see G. Greenleaf, 'Japan: Toward
International Standards – Except for "Big Data"', *Privacy Laws & Business International
Report*, 135 (2015), 12–4, online: SSRN, http://ssrn.com/abstract=2649556

[41] Personal Information Protection Act 2011 (South Korea); see *Asian Data Privacy Laws,
supra* note 3, chapter 5.

[42] Personal Data Protection Act 2005 (Macau SAR); see *Asian Data Privacy Laws, supra*
note 3, chapter 9.

[43] Data Privacy Act 2012 (Philippines); see *Asian Data Privacy Laws, supra* note 3, chapter 12.

[44] Personal Data Protection Act 2010 (Taiwan); see *Asian Data Privacy Laws, supra* note 3,
chapter 6.

cover most of the private sector (India,[45] Malaysia[46] and Singapore[47]), and a further three (China,[48] Vietnam[49] and Indonesia[50]) have data privacy laws which cover their e-commerce and consumer sectors. Any of these countries may also have data privacy laws specific to the banking sector[51] or other related financial sectors (e.g. credit reporting),[52] which go beyond being only bank secrecy rules, and include the other minimum elements of a data privacy law.

There are few examples of court actions being taken to enforce data privacy principles against banks. There are examples, in the available data, of complaints of breaches of these principles by banks reported by the data protection authorities (DPAs) or Privacy Commissioners in the databases of the International Privacy Law Library.[53] From Asian jurisdictions, significant numbers of complaint examples are available from Hong Kong SAR, Macau SAR and South Korea (though generally only in Korean).[54] However, significant numbers of complaint examples are available from Australia, New Zealand, Canada and the (US) FTC's jurisdiction.

---

[45] Information Technology (Reasonable Security Practices and Procedures and Sensitive Personal Data or Information) Rules 2011 (India); see *Asian Data Privacy Laws*, *supra* note 3, chapter 15.

[46] Personal Data Protection Act 2010 (Malaysia); see *Asian Data Privacy Laws*, *supra* note 3, chapter 11.

[47] Personal Data Protection Act 2012 (Singapore); see *Asian Data Privacy Laws*, *supra* note 3, chapter 10. See also G. Greenleaf, 'Regulations Bring Singapore's Data Privacy Law into Force', *Privacy Laws & Business International Report*, 130 (2014), 1–4.

[48] SC-NPC Decision on Internet Information Protection 2012 (China), SC_NPC Amendments to the Consumer Law 2013 (China), and subsidiary legislation; see *Asian Data Privacy Laws*, *supra* note 3, chapter 7.

[49] Law on Information Technology 2006 (Vietnam); see *Asian Data Privacy Laws*, *supra* note 3, chapter 13.

[50] Regulation on the Operation of Electronic Systems and Transactions 2012 (Indonesia); see *Asian Data Privacy Laws*, *supra* note 3, chapter 13.

[51] For example, Indonesia has various provisions on privacy in its banking laws, but no general data privacy law: see DLA Piper, 'Data Protection Laws of the World: Indonesia' (March 2012), online: EDRM, www.edrm.net/resources/data-privacy-protection/data-protection-laws/indonesia

[52] This paper does not cover the requirements of specific data privacy laws relating to credit reporting, though their implications for banks are substantial, or banking-sector-specific laws. In Malaysia, credit reporting practices are largely exempt from its general data privacy law.

[53] WorldLII, 'International Privacy Law Library' (4 July 2016), online: www.worldlii.org/int/special/privacy. It is located on the World Legal Information Institute (WorldLII).

[54] No complaint examples are yet available from the newly established DPAs in Singapore or Malaysia, or the yet-to-be-established DPA in the Philippines. Because the laws of Japan, Taiwan, China, Vietnam and Indonesia do not establish any central DPA, examples are more difficult to find from those jurisdictions.

2.3.2   Differences in Scope: 'Personal Data' vs. 'Customers' Data'

Data privacy laws have generally wider scope than banking laws. Banks do not usually have general exemptions from data privacy laws, but statutory requirements may in effect exempt them from particular data privacy principles in some situations.

2.3.2.1   Banks are Generally Not Exempt

Where data privacy laws do exist and cover the private sector, it is very unusual to find any wholesale exemptions for the banking or financial sector *per se*, and none are found in Asian data privacy laws at present. Banks are therefore 'data controllers' (or similar terms) in relation to all persons whose personal data they hold or otherwise control, not only their customers. The application of the laws to persons, data and transactions may differ somewhat between countries.

However, powers to create banking exemptions sometimes exist, even though not yet used. Singapore allows the Minister of Communications and Information to completely exclude any class of organisation or class of data. Singapore's DPA can do likewise, with ministerial approval, granting complete or partial exemptions. Singapore's Act is also subordinate to any other Act, or any other legal requirements, to the extent of any inconsistency. In Malaysia, there is a similar ministerial capacity to exempt, on the advice of the Commission, and such exemptions may be partial or complete. Such blanket powers to create exemptions are foreign to EU law, which specifies the permissible grounds of exemption,[55] and are not found in other Asian jurisdictions.

Any blanket exemptions in data privacy laws for government access to banking records, including for security agencies, may cause problems for countries outside Europe that wish to have their data protection laws regarded as 'adequate' by the EU.[56] Even when such access is supported by specific legislation, the decision by the European Court of Justice in *Schrems*[57] underlines that they must be proportionate to the objectives to be achieved. Although the lack of 'adequacy' status for the data privacy

---

[55] EU Directive, *supra* note 19, Art. 13.

[56] To put it simply, an 'adequacy' finding concerning country X by the European Commission, made under Art. 25 of the Data Protection Directive of 1995, allows businesses in EU member states to export personal data to country X without taking any protective measures specific to the transaction (e.g. Standard Contractual Clauses). Such additional protective measures are often considered onerous.

[57] *Maximillian Schrems* v. *Data Protection Commissioner*, C-362/14 (CJEU).

laws of Asian countries has not yet caused major problems for their companies, but may have increased the costs of transfers from EU countries, the *Schrems* decision shows that such problems may arise in future.[58]

2.3.2.2   Persons Protected: 'Customers' and 'Personal Data'

In most jurisdictions, only natural persons have data privacy rights. In Asia and Australia, legal entities are never protected by data privacy laws, but only by natural persons. In most cases, they must also be living persons.[59] In contrast, a bank's duties are to the 'customer' in banking law, irrespective of whether the customer is a natural or legal person. In this respect, the bank's duty of secrecy is normally broader than data privacy rights.

However, the requirement that a bank is acting in its role as a bank imposes limitation on the scope of the banks' duties, although *Tournier* may extend to non-bank financial institutions, and has been held to apply to merchant banks and credit unions.[60] *Tournier* was an action for breach of contract. The New South Wales Court of Appeal has held that it only applies to the banker–customer contract.[61] The result is very unsatisfactory. In *Brighton*, four guarantors were claiming a right of confidentiality. Two were customers of the bank, two were not. The two bank customers were held to have the benefit of *Tournier* in spite of the fact that their status as customers was wholly incidental to their status as guarantors. The application of *Tournier* was extended dramatically beyond the banking context in an English High Court case.[62] The relationship between the parties was client and sex worker. The client sought to restrain the sex worker from divulging certain information. The Court held that *Tournier* applied and that the disclosure was justified under the 'self-interest' exception to the duty of confidentiality. This decision would extend the *Tournier* principles

---

[58] The *Schrems* decision invalidated the Safe Harbor agreement between the United States and the European Union which allowed 'blanket' transfers of personal data from the EU to US companies participating in the Safe Harbor scheme. It is unresolved at the time of writing how future EU–US personal data transfers will take place.

[59] The Philippines and Singapore are unusual in providing that the estate of a deceased person may exercise some rights after a person's death.

[60] For examples, see *Banking Law in Australia, supra* note 32 at 6.2.1.

[61] *Brighton v. Australia and New Zealand Banking Group Ltd* [2011] NSWCA 152; see A. Tyree, 'Tournier unbound', *Journal of Banking and Finance Law and Practice*, 26 (2015), 207 for a criticism of this decision.

[62] *AVB v. TDD* [2014] EWHC 1442 (QB); see also *Jackson v. Royal Bank of Scotland* [2005] UKHL 3 where a duty of confidentiality was implied into a transferable letter of credit transaction.

to contracts between the bank and other parties who are not necessarily customers.

However, where a bank holds a person's personal data, both 'bank' and 'customer' status are irrelevant to data privacy law. All Asian data privacy laws take the approach, conventional since the minimum principles of the 1980s and adopted in European laws,[63] that what is personal data is determined by its capacity to identify a person (not actual identification).[64] Whether the conventional definition is now sufficient for privacy protection is very questionable, but that is not the purpose of this discussion. Data privacy laws are therefore broader in the extent of the persons to whom they may apply than the *Tournier* duty of secrecy, irrespective of how broad an interpretation of *Tournier's* application is taken.

2.3.2.3   Data Types Protected

The bank's duty of secrecy applies at least in respect of transactions that go through the customer's account, and in relation to any securities taken by the banker, although some members of the court in *Tournier* suggested that the duty extended to any information arising out of the banking relations of the bank and its customer.

There is no *Tournier* requirement that the information must be recorded in some way. In this respect, the bank's duty of secrecy is normally broader than data privacy rights, because in data privacy laws (in all jurisdictions except the Philippines) information must be embodied in a document before it is regulated. 'Document' is given a very wide definition, sometimes on the basis of capacity to reproduce the data (Hong Kong), or its inclusion in a database or otherwise being systematically organised (Japan and Malaysia). Information held only in a person's mind is therefore exempt, with the exception of the Philippines, which specifies that it refers to personal information 'whether recorded in a material form or not'. No Asian laws are restricted to data processed by automated means, except that of India. Other Acts include organised manual filing systems, as in Europe.[65]

---

[63] Christopher Kuner, *European Data Protection Law*, 2nd edn (Oxford University Press, 2007), 91–8.

[64] India is the only exception to the conventional approach, because many of its principles only apply to 'sensitive' data, which is very narrowly defined but does include financial information. The application of India's law to banks is complex.

[65] *European Data Protection Law, supra* note 63 at 99.

2.3.2.4　'Sensitive Data' Principles

The European-influenced principles of additional protection for 'sensitive' personal data are found in about half of the Asian laws, notably South Korea, Macau, Malaysia, the Philippines and Taiwan. Singapore, Hong Kong, India, Vietnam and China do not have special protections for sensitive data. The definitions of 'sensitive data' vary considerably across jurisdictions, everywhere, but do not usually include financial data (except in India). Although the EU Directive has specified categories[66] of sensitive data, EU 'Member States differ substantially in their definitions of sensitive data, and in the permissible grounds for processing them,'[67] and do not include financial information. The Philippines has the broadest categories that could affect banks, as it adds to the EU categories: marital status, age, 'education' and genetic information and (in effect) legally privileged information. Malaysia's categories would be of limited application to banks. Banks and other businesses dealing with personal information across a range of Asian jurisdictions will need to be aware of these differences in the meaning, and administration, of sensitive personal information to avoid potential problems.

Aside from these general data protection laws, most jurisdictions are likely to have specific laws dealing with particular categories of sensitive information, particularly financial and credit information, and medical information. Japan has various separate laws dealing with such data, and a number of ministry guidelines. Hong Kong also has specific laws dealing with such matters as old criminal records, and Singapore has a number of laws dealing with 'sensitive' categories. Such sectoral laws are not covered here.

2.3.3　Minimum Collection vs. 'Know Your Customer'

All Asian jurisdictions under consideration impose some data collection limitations based on the purpose of collection, but the majority go further and allow only minimal or necessary collection.

2.3.3.1　Minimal Collection

The majority of jurisdictions in Asia (China, Hong Kong, India, South Korea, Macau, Taiwan and Singapore) implement the stricter European

---

[66] EU Directive, *supra* note 19, Art. 8 protects 'personal data revealing racial or ethnic origin, political opinions, religious or philosophical beliefs, trade-union membership, and the processing of data concerning health or sex life'; see *European Data Protection Law, supra* note 63 at 101–3.

[67] *European Data Protection Law, supra* note 63 at 103–6 provides many examples.

approach of 'minimal' collection – that personal data should only be collected where it is necessary for a (legitimate) specified purpose,[68] rather than the weaker minimum (OECD and APEC) limitation that collection should be 'not excessive'. Japan, Malaysia, the Philippines and Vietnam (only by implication) adopt the less strict 'not excessive' approach. Only South Korea takes the further step in data minimisation, requiring that, wherever possible, transactions should be anonymous.[69] It also requires the business to prove that it only collected the minimum necessary information.

In contrast, traditional bankers' duties do not require any such minimisation of data collection. To the contrary, it is a standard element of AML-CTF legislation for banks to be required to accurately identify customers (KYC). As a result, these statutory obligations will usually prevail over those in data privacy laws, whether of the 'not excessive' or 'minimal' varieties, at least to the extent specified by the relevant AML-CTF law. However, excessive collection beyond what is justified by these laws could still in theory be in breach of data privacy laws.

South Korea's data privacy law also has a very unusual explicit 'no denial of service' principle that goods and services cannot be refused because a person refuses to provide more than the minimum necessary information. Singapore is similar in the provision prohibiting organisations, as a condition of providing a product or service, from requiring an individual to consent to the collection, use or disclosure of their personal data beyond what is reasonable to provide the product or service. These provisions give strong support to minimal collection requirements, and are not yet found in the European principles. At best, such restrictions are only implied in other laws. There are no equivalents in banking laws, and these provisions could easily conflict with 'KYC' requirements in other laws.

2.3.3.2   Purpose of Collection and Notice Required

The minimum principles only require that the purposes must be 'specified' by the time of collection but are ambiguous about what notice is required to the person who is the subject of the data (the data subject). The European principles require that notice of such purposes must be given to the data

---

[68] *Ibid.* at 73–4.

[69] The 'anonymity principle' is rare in data privacy laws, having originated in German legislation, and also found in Australia's private sector law since 2001, but now weakened by 2012 reforms. See *ibid.* at 74 concerning the German law.

subject,[70] as do the APEC principles. All Asian jurisdictions require that the purpose of collection be specified by the time of collection from the data subject, but in the Philippines it may be specified as soon as possible thereafter (as allowed by the minimum principles). All jurisdictions except the Philippines and Japan require notice of such purpose, and other matters, to be given to the data subject by the time of collection of personal data from the data subject. In Japan, the requirement of individual notice can be avoided by a public announcement of a purpose of collection.

The content of the notice that must be given to data subjects is specified in greatly differing detail.[71] At the very specific end are China's Guidelines (but not its laws). For example, Macau requires data subjects to be informed (unless they already have the information) of the purposes of processing, the recipients of the data, the consequences of not providing the information and rights of access and correction. Hong Kong requires much the same.

When personal data is collected from third parties (i.e. concerning, but not from, the data subject), there is a requirement to provide notice to the data subject in three laws only (South Korea, Macau and Taiwan). This is not required in the minimum principles. Macau requires the notice to be given when the data is recorded, or not later than when it is used or disclosed. No law explicitly requires notice to be given when data is collected by observation or from documentary sources, but where laws require consent of the data subject as a condition for processing to be legal, this may have the same effect. Malaysia seems to only require such notice where the data user proposes to change the purpose of use to one different from the original purpose of collection.

2.3.3.3   Consent to Collection and Definitions of Consent

Half of the Asian laws explicitly require consent for collection from the data subject, and other forms of processing. Others do not, even though they usually require notice. Notice requirements to data subjects may often mean that there is implied consent to the purpose of collection. South Korea, Taiwan, Macau and Malaysia do explicitly require consent before collection, with few and relatively narrow exceptions. The Philippines's law, while ostensibly requiring consent, has so many exceptions that consent is just one of many methods by which processing may be legitimate. China and Vietnam require consent (in the consumer and e-commerce

---

[70] Kuner says 'the data controller must specifically inform the data subject of the purposes for which data are being collected': *ibid.* at 100.

[71] See details in the country chapters in Part II of *Asian Data Privacy Laws, supra* note 3.

contexts). It is not part of the banker's duty of secrecy to obtain consent from the customer before collecting information about him or her.

Definitions of consent vary greatly, affecting not only collection, but also use and disclosure of personal data. Macau requires 'unambiguous consent'. Taiwan requires written consent. The Philippines requires that consent be a 'freely given, specific, informed indication of will' and that it be 'evidenced by written, electronic or recorded means', which leaves open the possibility of an express 'opt out' but not implied consents. Hong Kong often requires 'prescribed consent', which must be expressed, and can be withdrawn. The South Korean law concerning consent is unusually strict in that it requires not only writing but also (i) separating consents for each item requiring consent (i.e. 'unbundling' of consents) and (ii) segregating consent forms of those items that require consent and those that do not ('unbundling' non-consents). Malaysia also requires unbundling of consents. This lack of consistency, even though express consent is most commonly required, is likely to cause difficulty for companies attempting to do business across multiple Asian jurisdictions, and it might be easier to adopt a standard approach of explicit unbundled consents.

The fourth exception to *Tournier* (discussed later) allowing disclosures by a bank (not internal uses) is express or implied consent by a customer. Consent need not be written; it can be implied, for example, from notorious banking practice or a practice that the customer is made aware of.[72] Under the statutory bank secrecy regime of Singapore, consent must be written but there is some debate about what qualifies as written consent.[73] As discussed earlier, the forms of consent required by data privacy laws will often be more strict than bank secrecy laws, and in such cases banks will have to comply with both standards prevailing in their jurisdictions.

2.3.3.4 Lawful, Fair and Non-intrusive Collection

Laws in almost all Asian jurisdictions follow the minimum requirements that collection must be by lawful means, and by fair means (which is a substantive limitation going beyond other existing laws), with only India and Malaysia omitting these minimum requirements. China only includes them explicitly in its Guidelines, but some of its laws refer to general principles of fairness and good faith. In Hong Kong, 'fair' has been interpreted by a tribunal to include 'non-intrusive' means in a case concerning paparazzi.

---

[72] *Turner v. Royal Bank of Scotland plc* [1998] EWCA Civ 529.
[73] See Booysen, Chapter 10.

The scope of the fair processing requirements in other jurisdictions is less clear. There are no equivalent requirements in the bank's duties to customers.

2.3.3.5   'Openness' Requirements – Particularly Privacy Policies

The minimum requirement of the principle of 'openness' (as the OECD described it) is that any person should be able to find out about personal data processing practices, whether or not they are a data subject. It is found in an explicit form in the legislation of only seven of the eleven Asian jurisdictions. However, all Asian laws except those of the Philippines and Japan require a published privacy policy.

2.3.4   Use and Disclosure Restrictions vs. Tournier Exceptions

The banker's common law, contractual duty of secrecy is not absolute, and its exceptions were said by Bankes LJ in *Tournier* to be classified under four heads: '(a) where disclosure is under compulsion by law; (b) where there is a duty to the public to disclose; (c) where the interests of the bank require disclosure; (d) where the disclosure is made by the express or implied consent of the customer'. These exceptions will be compared below to their equivalents in data privacy laws. The compulsion by law (statutory) exceptions in data privacy laws to the use and disclosure principles is most likely to be of relevance to banks, because they go beyond the question of 'compatible uses' which is first discussed.

2.3.4.1   Secondary Uses/Disclosures based on 'Compatibility' and Others

The bank's duties under *Tournier* limit only disclosures (secrecy), not internal uses by the bank which may be different from the purposes for which they originally collected the information. Data privacy laws go further, limiting internal uses (as well as disclosures) in various ways linked to the purpose of collection. In other words, the original purpose of collection of personal data is the starting point in determining what uses may be made of the data, including disclosures of it. This is sometimes called the 'finality' principle of data privacy laws, and exceptions to it are expressed in various ways.[74] All Asian data privacy laws start from requiring personal data to be

---

[74] Both the basic and European principles allow additional (secondary) uses/disclosures that are 'not incompatible' with the purpose of collection. In the EU, this very general criterion for secondary uses has been interpreted differently between member states, but is usually

used or disclosed only for the purpose for which the personal data was collected, but then allow a spectrum of 'secondary uses' (of varying widths) to be added, by formulae such as 'not incompatible' or 'reasonably expected' uses or disclosures. All of the Asian data privacy laws therefore include to some extent the principle of 'finality', meaning a limit to the uses that can be made of collected data based on the original purpose of collection.

The main issue becomes what exceptions to collection-purpose-based 'finality' are allowed, described as 'secondary' uses or disclosures. In Asia, quite a range of wordings are used to indicate allowed secondary uses.[75] The differences (if any) between the meanings of these terms is speculative in the absence of decisions interpreting them, but it seems likely that a considerable range of differences will emerge.

For example, the Canadian Privacy Commissioner determined that a couple's personal information (closure of an account and reasons for closure) was disclosed by one bank to another for a purpose that a reasonable person would not find appropriate in the circumstances, even though the customer had signed a broad document consent to such disclosures.[76] A bank that sold details of its credit card accounts (information and liabilities) to another bank was in breach where it had not obtained the customer's consent – but another bank was not because it had obtained consent through an assignment clause in an agreement.[77]

---

accompanied by requirements that data subjects be informed very specifically for the purpose of collection, thus limiting what can be regarded as 'compatible'. See *European Data Protection Law*, *supra* note 63 at 99–100.

[75] These include (from potentially least restrictive to potentially most restrictive) the wordings of 'not incompatible' (Macau), 'compatible' (the Philippines), 'reasonably expected' (Singapore), 'duly related' (Japan), 'directly related' (Hong Kong, Malaysia), 'in conformity with' (Taiwan), 'within the scope' (South Korea), for the 'purpose and scope announced' (Vietnam) and 'for the purpose for which it has been collected' (but with limited application) (India). China's more recent laws use a variety of wordings. In the Philippines, mere 'compatibility' does not seem sufficient unless the use/disclosure is also for 'legitimate interests' or within another exception. At the other end of the spectrum, in Malaysia, secondary disclosures are allowed and 'directly related' (and for other reasons), but secondary uses do not have to be 'directly related'. Singapore's Act does allow secondary use on the basis of purposes that a reasonable person would consider appropriate, but secondary uses will more often be based on 'deemed consent', lengthy schedules of exceptions and other legislation. The overall position is too complex to be clear.

[76] *PIPEDA Case Summary #2003-211: Bank accused of improperly disclosing overdraft information to another bank* [2003] CAPrivCmr 113 (4 September 2003), online: www.worldlii.org/ca/cases/CAPrivCmr/2003/113.html

[77] *PIPEDA Case Summary #2006-350: Customers allege that sale of personal information by one bank to another occurred without knowledge and consent* [2006] CAPrivCmr 17 (9 June 2006), online: www.worldlii.org/cgi-bin/sinodisp/ca/cases/CAPrivCmr/2006/17.html

Other examples of breaches include a Canadian bank which breached collection limitations (over collection) by requiring a tax return and assessment[78]; an Australian bank allegedly used credit card transaction details to check on staff sick leave[79]; a Canadian bank inadvertently but wrongly disclosed details to a customer's mother (with the same name).[80]

2.3.4.2   Statutory Exceptions to Use and Disclosure Principles

Tournier provides that the contractual duty of confidentiality is overridden by the duty of both parties to submit to other legal requirements, including statutory requirements. There must be a legal requirement involving compulsion, not merely a demand or request from a government body. Such duties can arise outside statutes, such as the common law duty of a banker who is a witness in court to disclose in response to questions asked. Normally, only the requirements of local laws, not foreign laws, are relevant.[81] Statutory bank secrecy regimes tend to have similar qualifications, for example in Singapore and Switzerland.[82]

The statutory exceptions in data privacy laws vary too widely to cover fully here.[83] Hong Kong has a typical range of statutory exemptions relevant to banks. There are exemptions from the principles of use limitation, and of subject access, where it is considered necessary to protect various public and social interests such as the prevention and detection of crime, and the remedying of unlawful[84] conduct. The exemptions only apply where complying with the privacy principles would prejudice the interests concerned. In Korea, there are limited exceptions to the need for

---

[78] PIPEDA Report of Findings #2013-009: Bank over-collects client's personal information for credit increase [2013] CAPrivCmr 13 (28 May 2013), online: www.priv.gc.ca/cf-dc/2013/2013_009_0528_e.asp

[79] *Bank allegedly using credit card transaction details to check on staff sick leave* [1997] NSWPrivCmr 4 (1 January 1997), online: www.austlii.edu.au/au/cases/nsw/NSWPrivCmr/1997/4.html

[80] PIPEDA Case Summary #2002-100: *Woman accuses bank of telling her mother about her bank account* [2002] CAPrivCmr 94 (19 December 2002), online: www.worldlii.org/ca/cases/CAPrivCmr/2002/94.html

[81] See, for example, *XAG* v. *A Bank* [1983] 2 All ER 464 and *FDC Co Ltd* v. *Chase Manhattan Bank NA* [1984] HKCA 260 where foreign court orders were held not to be justification for disclosing customer's account details.

[82] As discussed by Booysen in Chapter 10 and Nobel and Braendli in Chapter 11.

[83] Details are in the relevant country chapters in Part II of *Asian Data Privacy Laws, supra* note 3.

[84] 'Unlawful' in this context includes civil wrongs. For example, witness statements collected for the purpose of possible criminal proceedings were permitted to be disclosed to plaintiffs in a civil suit: *Lily Tse Lai Yin & Others* v. *The Incorporated Owners of Albert House & Others* [2001] HKCFI 976.

consent: where special provisions exist in other laws; where the data subject (or legal representative) is not in a position to give consent, or their
address is unknown, and it is necessary to protect the interests of the data
subject or a third party (but not the interests of the bank, the data controller). Taiwan allows broad exemptions from obtaining consent or informing
persons where collection, processing or use is made for purposes of public
interest (undefined) and also meets other criteria. Malaysia provides a very
broad exemption for any processing by commercial organisations 'for the
purpose of carrying out regulatory functions' where application of the Act
would be likely to prejudice those functions. It also has six general exceptions from the requirement of consent, which result in a broad 'authorised
by law' type of exception for all forms of processing (except where sensitive data is concerned). The Philippines has very similar exemptions relating to functions of public authorities and assisting investigations.

While there is some degree of consistency across Asia in relation to
these statutory exceptions, particularly where uses to assist law enforcement are concerned, this should not be exaggerated, and each country has
substantial differences from the next.

2.3.4.3   Broad Exceptions based on the Public Interest or the Interests of Others

The most poorly defined of the *Tournier* exceptions is 'where there is a
duty to the public to disclose'. Suggestions have been made that this would
include where the customer's dealings indicated 'dealing with the enemy
in time of war' or where there is a 'danger to the state'.[85] Lord Denning took
a broader view that the exception 'should extend to crimes, frauds and
misdeeds, both those actually committed as well as those in contemplation, provided always – and this is essential – that the disclosure is justified in the public interest'.[86] In 1989, the UK Court of Appeal tentatively
accepted that such an exception could excuse a disclosure by a bank in the
United Kingdom to the US Federal Reserve that Libyan parties appeared
to be moving funds in breach of US decrees freezing Libyan funds.[87] After
the subsequent quarter-century of legislation requiring 'suspicion-based'
bank reporting of money-laundering, potential terrorism, sanctions-
avoidance, etc., it is easy to imagine that the *Tournier* duty would be readily
found to include exceptions for such purposes.

---

[85] See *Banking Law in Australia, supra* note 32 at 6.2.4 for discussion.
[86] *Initial Services* v. *Putterill* [1967] 3 All ER 145 at 148.
[87] *Libyan Arab Foreign Bank* v. *Banker's Trust Co* [1989] QB 728, per Staughton J.

In data privacy laws, similar exceptions are often found. The examples of Hong Kong and Taiwan are given earlier. Macau and the Philippines have narrower exceptions based on the EU exception for protection of the legitimate interests of others (as distinct from the public interest), but only if they are not overridden by interests in protecting the fundamental rights of the data subject.[88]

2.3.4.4   Exceptions based on the Interests of the Bank

Another *Tournier* exception is 'where the interests of the bank require disclosure'. This is regarded as including where the bank has initiated legal proceedings, and where a guarantor seeks information about the account of a primary debtor, although the extent of this exception is unclear.[89] In data privacy laws, such exceptions based on the interests of the data controller (the bank in this instance) are very unusual.

2.3.4.5   Exceptions based on Consent

One of the *Tournier* exceptions is 'where the disclosure is made by the express or implied consent of the customer'. Consent must be informed, so customers must be aware of the banking practice relied upon.[90] The practice of 'banker's references' has led to considerable dispute concerning when such references can be said to be based on implied consent, and one point of view is that such practices are more safely based on express consent, or at least on the giving of notice to the customer.[91]

In data privacy laws, although consent is always an allowed ground for change of use or for new types of disclosure of personal data, the extent of disclosure and other conditions for valid consent vary, as discussed earlier. The South Korean requirements for such consent are strict and require disclosure of identity of recipients, and of the consequences of refusing consent.

2.3.4.6   Exceptions based Merely on Notice

The minimum principles for data privacy laws require that every change of purpose must be 'specified'. South Korea has detailed notice requirements when consent is sought for change of purpose. The minimum principles do not state that giving notice is sufficient in itself (as an exception to the

---

[88]   FRA, 'Handbook on European Data Protection Law' (April 2014) at 84–90, online: http://fra.europa.eu/sites/default/files/fra-2014-handbook-data-protection-law-2nd-ed_en.pdf; see EU Directive, *supra* note 19, Art. 7(f).

[89]   See *Banking Law in Australia, supra* note 32 at 6.2.5 for discussion.

[90]   *Turner* v. *Royal Bank of Scotland, supra* note 72.

[91]   See *Banking Law in Australia, supra* note 32, 6.3.

finality requirement) to be the basis of a change of purpose. However, Japan allows new disclosures (unrelated to the purpose of collection) after notice is given on a website, with an opt-out allowed, but this does not apply to new secondary uses by the data user. It is therefore questionable whether Japan's law complies with the basic principles. Malaysia has exceptions for disclosure which depend on notice, but also require being 'directly related' to the purpose of collection. *Tournier* and statutory regimes, such as Singapore's, do not include an exception based merely on notice.

2.3.4.7   Restrictions on Direct Marketing Uses

Tournier does not impose restrictions on a bank's internal uses of information it holds, but data privacy laws will usually do so where the use is for marketing purposes. Singapore's bank secrecy regime was, notably, amended after the passing of its data protection law, to stop the marketing exception.[92] In the EU, the right to object to personal data being used for direct marketing is required to be able to be exercised before data is transferred to third parties,[93] not only as the data subject's *ex post facto* response to a direct marketing communication. Seven Asian laws take an approach at least as strong as that of the EU.[94] Overall, this is one of the strongest implementations of a 'European' principle across Asian jurisdictions. Hong Kong (after the 2012 amendments) and South Korea now go further: if consent to collect data is being obtained for any marketing purposes, the data subject must be told this, and their consent to that use obtained, so 'opt-in' is in fact required. Complaints of breaches are common. In Hong Kong, putting opt-out requirements in small print at the back of an advisory letter was not sufficient notice[95] in a case where a Hong Kong bank failed to follow the opt-out procedures in the HK law.[96]

---

[92] As discussed in Booysen, Chapter 10.

[93] FRA, 'Handbook on European Data Protection Law', *supra* note 88 at 119; see Art. 14(b) of the EU Directive, *supra* note 19.

[94] The European-influenced principle of a right to opt-out from direct marketing is found in Macau, Hong Kong, South Korea, Malaysia, Taiwan and Vietnam. China's highest level laws may require a similar right. India has a weak form of opt-out through withdrawal of consent, and Japan a different but equally weak opt-out through notices on websites. Only Singapore and the Philippines do not require either opt-out or opt-in procedures (no matter how weak), so in those countries the only limit (other than do-not-call telemarketing regimes) is whether a particular form of marketing is allowed as a secondary use of the personal data.

[95] *A and Financial Institution* [2012] AICmrCN 1 (1 May 2012), online: www.austlii.edu.au/au/cases/cth/AICmrCN/2012/1.html

[96] *Collection and Use of Customers' Personal Data by Industrial and Commercial Bank of China (Asia) Limited in Direct Marketing* [2011] HKPCPDIR 5 (20 June 2011), online: www.worldlii.org/eng/hk/other/pcpd/IR/2011/5.html

2.3.5   International Dimensions of Banking Disclosures

The issues surrounding the transfer of personal data between countries, and the overseas operation of data privacy laws, are very contentious, and have generated a substantial literature.[97] The issues can only be summarised here but are discussed elsewhere at length.[98] Overall, in Asia, it has been argued that only in South Korea and Macau can the overall requirements be described as somewhat strict on businesses involved in data exports, and protective of data subjects.[99] Almost everywhere else data subjects are generally in a very weak position, although the position in Singapore is complex.[100]

Does the law of the controller's jurisdiction assert extraterritorial operation? In Asia, explicit assertions of extraterritorial application are found in only four data privacy laws, but it is a more difficult question whether there are implied assertions of extraterritorial application. Only in South Korea, China and Vietnam does there seem to be no likely extraterritorial scope.

Under what conditions are transfers to a foreign jurisdiction allowed, whether to contracted data processors, or to third parties? Four jurisdictions, Hong Kong, Japan, Vietnam and the Philippines, have no effective limitations, and China's restrictions are based only on Guidelines as yet. Overall, the other Asian jurisdictions with data privacy laws have a fairly low level of restrictions on personal data exports, but with much variation.

In most Asian jurisdictions data subjects can (in theory) enforce contracts made between a local data controller and a foreign processor which are expressed to be for the benefit of data subjects, such as are required (for example) in Standard Contract Clauses for data exports from EU countries.[101] Even where such enforcement is permitted, enforcement against a foreign recipient (processor) is likely to raise additional problems such as the proper law of the contract, and the enforcement of foreign judgements. However, some common law jurisdictions have a doctrine of privity of contract which, subject to exceptions, prevents third parties (data subjects) for whose benefit contracts are made from enforcing those contracts.

---

[97] For leading examples, see C. Kuner, *Transborder Data Flows and Data Privacy Law* (Oxford University Press, 2013) and D. Svantesson, *Extraterritoriality in Data Privacy Law* (Copenhagen: Ex Tuto Publishing, 2013).

[98] See *Asian Data Privacy Laws, supra* note 3, chapter 17, part 6: 'Comparing the international dimensions of data privacy laws' at 497–501.

[99] See *ibid.* at 499–500.

[100] 'Regulations Bring Singapore's Data Privacy Law into Force', *supra* note 47.

[101] See *Asian Data Privacy Laws, supra* note 3, chapter 2, section 3.1.

Any form of 'standard contractual clauses' may, therefore, be useless as a form of protection providing rights to data subjects, in relation to exports from those jurisdictions. Singapore and Hong Kong have reformed the doctrine of privity of contract along the lines of the UK reforms, to allow for such enforcement unless it would conflict with the parties' express or implied intentions.

2.3.6 Security and Data Breach Notification vs. Safe Custody Duties

One of the most likely areas of vulnerability with serious consequences for banks regarding data protection is breaches of the security of customer information, with possible additional liabilities to notify data breaches, and even to pay mandatory compensation to each customer whose details are disclosed.

Banks' duties of secrecy of account information and other information about account-holders, and duties of safe custody of documents (as a bailee), are each capable of breach. In some countries the duty may be absolute, but in other countries, such as Australia, negligent breach may be required, with the probable standard of care being that of a 'reasonable banker in all the circumstances'.[102]

Data privacy laws in all jurisdictions require security safeguards, which must usually be against 'loss or unauthorised access, destruction, use, modification or disclosure' (minimum requirements), and only state the requirements in such abbreviated form. The standard of care required is sometimes phrased as requiring 'appropriate' measures, which is the European terminology[103] (Macau and Taiwan), or to take 'reasonable' steps, which is the OECD terminology. Some jurisdictions have an arguably stronger formulation such as 'necessary and proper steps' (Japan), 'whatever is necessary' to secure data (South Korea) or other formulations such as 'practical steps' (Malaysia). Detailed security requirements may also be specified (e.g. South Korea, Malaysia and Macau), and are likely to be more important than the words used to specify a standard. The Philippines has special security provisions for government agencies holding sensitive data (such as data pertaining to ethnicity, religion and health), and requirements that contractors holding such data must register with the DPA.

---

[102] See *Banking Law in Australia, supra* note 32 at 6.6.
[103] FRA, 'Handbook on European Data Protection Law', *supra* note 88 at 95–6.

Two examples concerning banks are illustrative. In the United Kingdom, a monetary penalty notice was served on the Bank of Scotland after customers' account details were repeatedly faxed to the wrong recipients. The information included payslips, bank statements, account details and mortgage applications, along with customers' names, addresses and contact details.[104] In an Australian case, the complainant and his wife applied for a loan with a bank, and provided the bank with all their financial details (including tax returns). The bank's branch office then faxed these details (plus comments on the credit worthiness of the complainants) in a nineteen-page fax to its head office. Unfortunately, the fax was incorrectly sent to an unrelated third party. The bank responded to the complaint by directing all its branch offices to ensure that the head office fax number was stored in the autodial memory of every branch fax machine and paid A$500 each to the complainant and his wife for their embarrassment.[105]

2.3.6.1   Data Breach Notification

The traditional duties of banks have not explicitly required them to advise their customers, or governments, if the security of customer information is compromised. Under data privacy laws, requirements to issue compulsory data breach notification (DBN) can be a considerable sanction because of their potential effects on the reputation and financial situation of a bank or other data controller. Various jurisdictions in the United States have had DBN requirements for some years. They exist in the laws of some European jurisdictions, and are compulsory under EU law for telecommunications providers.[106] They are now required under the revised 2013 OECD Guidelines.[107] In Asia, DBN is required by four laws. In South Korea, the Philippines and Taiwan, individuals likely to be affected must be notified of data breaches. In China, the Philippines and South Korea (when affecting more than 10,000 data subjects), the DPA or relevant ministry must be notified. There are no DBN provisions in the comparatively recent Singaporean and Malaysian laws, the revised

---

[104] *Bank of Scotland (Monetary penalty Notice)* [2013] UKICO 2013-7 (5 August 2013), online: www.bailii.org/uk/cases/UKICO/2013/2013-7.html

[105] *Bank faxes details to wrong number – Section 18N* [1995] PrivCmrA 12 (1 July 1995), online: www.austlii.edu.au/au/cases/cth/PrivCmrA/1995/12.htm

[106] FRA, 'Handbook on European Data Protection Law', *supra* note 88 at 96–7.

[107] See *Asian Data Privacy Laws, supra* note 3, chapter 19, section 3.3.

Hong Kong law,[108] Macau's law (which reflects the state of EU law a decade ago), India's legislation or Japan's newly revised law.[109] The Australian government released a discussion draft Bill for mandatory DBN in December 2015. An Australian example that prompted notification under its existing voluntary scheme is where a superannuation provider allowed data on 568 members to be downloaded from a website as a result of lack of adequate security measures.[110]

2.3.6.2   Compulsory Compensation for Data Breaches

Under the common law bank secrecy regime of *Tournier*, damages are recoverable for breach of the duty of secrecy.[111] Under statutory regimes, the availability of damages will depend on the legislation, although in some cases, this may be unclear.[112] Data privacy laws in Asia are highly variable in whether data subjects are able to seek compensation through court proceedings,[113] and none allow compensation to be awarded by DPA (in contrast with Australia). The most liberal compensatory provisions where damage results from data breaches are in amendments to Korea's *Credit Information Act* in March 2015, which provide for punitive damages of up to three times the damage caused by personal credit information being lost, stolen, leaked, fabricated or damaged due to the relevant business' wilful misconduct or gross negligence. More significantly, they provide for statutory damages of up to US$3,000 (KRW 3 million) per data subject whose personal credit information was stolen, lost, leaked, fabricated or damaged due to the relevant business' wilful misconduct or negligence, without need for proof of damage. Such provisions are likely to be extended in Korea to all data controllers. It is possible that this approach may spread to other jurisdictions.

---

[108] In Hong Kong, government agencies have reached agreement with the privacy commissioner to notify him immediately of such breaches, but this does not apply to the private sector, despite the recent revisions to its law.

[109] G. Greenleaf, 'Japan: Toward International Standards – Except for "Big Data"'. In Japan, ministerial guidelines require notification to the relevant ministry, the basis of a quasi-voluntary data breach notification system.

[110] *First State Super Trustee Corporation: Own motion investigation report* [2012] AICmrCN 4 (1 June 2012), online: www.austlii.edu.au/cgi-bin/sinodisp/au/cases/cth/AICmrCN/2012/4 .html: no compensation available for Own Motion Investigations until 2014.

[111] See Stanton, Chapter 12.

[112] See, for example, Booysen, Chapter 10.

[113] See *Asian Data Privacy Laws*, *supra* note 3, chapter 18, part 3.5: 'Access to judicial remedies by data subjects'.

2.3.7   Access, Correction and Other New Customer Rights

Banker–customer law does not generally give customers a right to access the files banks hold on them. In data privacy laws, user access and correction rights are found in all Asian jurisdictions except China.[114] Taiwan has an unusual and strong provision that user rights 'may not be waived in advance nor limited by special agreement', and other jurisdictions are also reluctant to allow such rights to be waived or restricted. For example, a New Zealand bank's claim of 'trade secret' was rejected as a basis for limiting statutory access.[115] A Canadian bank has also failed in its attempts to rely on exemptions to limit access rights of employees.[116]

2.3.7.1   Access and Data Portability

South Korea exemplifies the broadest access rights, requiring access not only to the content held, but also to the purpose of collection and use, the retention period, details of disclosures to third parties and details of consents by the data subject. At least Singapore, Hong Kong, the Philippines and Taiwan also require disclosures to third parties in access requests (requiring specific request in Singapore). The Philippines' novel contribution to Asian data privacy laws is the right to obtain a copy of your file in a commonly used machine-readable form, anticipating proposals for reform of the EU Directive. Macau requires the DPA to be informed of some types of refusal of access. Exceptions to rights of access and correction vary a great deal.[117]

Some jurisdictions such as Hong Kong allow a data user to charge a reasonable but not excessive fee for complying with a data access request. Its DPA has held some fees to be excessive,[118] such as where a bank set up a new fee structure intending to charge all customers a flat-rate fixed fee of

---

[114] All of China's data privacy laws primarily address the obligations of the administrator of personal information, and do not clearly state the rights of data subjects. The 2013 Guidelines (not a law), for the first time, clearly assume and imply rights of access and correction.

[115] *Bank Refuses Couple Access To File Claiming Trade Secret – (Case Note 36631)* [2003] NZPrivCmr 14 (1 July 2003), online: www.nzlii.org/nz/cases/NZPrivCmr/2003/14.html

[116] *PIPEDA Report of Findings #2013-004: Bank provides former employee with insufficient access to his personal information* [2013] CAPrivCmr 17 (18 July 2013), online: www .worldlii.org/ca/cases/CAPrivCmr/2013/17.html

[117] The details are in the relevant country chapters in Part II of *Asian Data Privacy Laws, supra* note 3.

[118] See PCPD, 'Data Protection Principles in the Personal Data (Privacy) Ordinance – From the Privacy Commissioner's Perspective' (2010), at 87–8, online: www.pcpd.org.hk/ english/resources_centre/publications/books/files/Perspective_2nd.pdf   for   detailed considerations.

HK$200 (US$25) for complying with a data access request to obtain copies of their personal data in the custody of the bank. The bank was held to be permitted to recover only the labour costs and actual out-of-pocket expenses incurred in locating, retrieving, reproducing and sending the requested data to the requestor based on the work involved being done by clerical or administrative staff. The bank failed to establish it had taken this approach, and was found to have imposed a fee structure that was liable to be excessive. The Bank abandoned the proposed fee structure before implementing it.[119]

2.3.7.2   Corrections and Notifications

All Asian laws allow data subjects to obtain corrections to their records, and half of them also require notification of corrections to third parties who have had access to the data subject's file: Hong Kong, Singapore, Macau, Taiwan and the Philippines. Macau extends this to blocking and erasure, and requires third parties to do likewise. In South Korea, correction (and deletion) requests must be decided within ten days, and if denied the reasons (including information about how to appeal) must be provided in a standard outcome notice, but leave it up to the data subject to inform third parties. Where a correction is refused, the data subject is explicitly entitled to add their own version of the situation to their file, in Hong Kong, Malaysia and Taiwan, although there is variation in what may be added. Other laws may allow this by implication of the data quality principle. This does not seem to occur in Japan.

2.3.8   Accuracy and Completeness

All Asian data privacy laws impose duties on the bank to the data subject that personal data must be accurate and complete (relative to the use of the data), with wording varying considerably between jurisdictions. In banking law, there is a contractual duty on the bank to exercise reasonable care and skill to give accurate and complete information, when giving 'bank references' (or similar disclosures to third parties like credit bureaus).[120] The duty under data privacy laws is not restricted to such situations, and could apply in situations where there is, for example, a statutory duty to

---

[119] PCPD, 'Bank Imposing Fee at a Flat Rate for Complying with a Data Access Request', Report R10-5528 (24 February 2010), online: www.pcpd.org.hk/english/enforcement/commissioners_findings/investigation_reports/files/R10_5528_e.pdf

[120] See *Banking Law in Australia*, *supra* note 32 at 6.3.2. The *Hedley Byrne* principles only protect the recipient of a bank reference against negligence, not the data subject: see 6.3.3.

disclose to a government body, but the personal data held by the bank is inaccurate or incomplete, and harm to the customer results.

2.3.8.1   Deletion and Blocking of
Use – Automatic and on Request

Automatic (i.e. non-request) deletion or anonymisation of data once the reason for its collection is completed is required in all Asian jurisdictions except Japan, Vietnam and China.[121] The Philippines provisions have many exceptions and are ill-drafted. In Singapore the provision for deletion of data will be difficult to enforce, due to the complexity of proving that all legitimate business purposes have expired.[122] India's provision has multiple defects.[123] There is often ambiguity, as in Taiwan, about whether data must be deleted or can be anonymised.

Deletion of data on request, including data provided by third parties, is provided in South Korea. This is close to a 'right to be forgotten' in its implementation. In Japan there is a vague provision allowing data subjects to request deletion, but it is not clear when the data controller can refuse to do so. A right to block the use of data is found in South Korea, Macau, Malaysia, the Philippines and Taiwan. India allows consent to use information to be withdrawn, which implies that use is blocked, but not deletion. Hong Kong allows 'prescribed consent' to collect data to be withdrawn, implying a right to block use of data originating from the data subject. There are no such provisions in China or Vietnam. South Korea is also unusual in having a specific provision that data subjects must be informed of the transfer of their personal information as the result of sale of a business in whole or part, and that they have a right to opt-out (withdraw consent) from their personal information being transferred.

2.4   Conclusion

There is common ground between bank secrecy and data privacy regimes, but the differences are complex and occur at many points, resisting any simple comparisons. In a few respects, *Tournier* duties of banks may be

---

[121] It is not required by the minimum data privacy principles, but is required by European principles.

[122] See *Asian Data Privacy Laws, supra* note 3 at 301.

[123] It only applies to sensitive information and only prohibits retention of information beyond when it may lawfully be used, which is not the same as when its purpose of collection has expired.

broader than those arising from data privacy laws, such as in their application to nonnatural persons, and their duties of safe custody. In most respects, however, it is data privacy laws that impose more strict obligations, including limits on personal data collected; a narrower range of allowed disclosures; DBN requirements and access and correction regimes. Usually, banks will have to comply both with traditional duties of secrecy and with data privacy regimes and their stricter and broader requirements, subject to specific statutory exceptions. Both regimes are subject to the overriding requirements of AML-CTF laws.

Now that data privacy laws are becoming ubiquitous across the world, and with relatively consistent standards, as suggested earlier, banks everywhere will increasingly have to take into account data privacy laws, in addition to their traditional duties. The breadth of obligations imposed by these laws, while often in parallel with traditional duties, is generally of much broader scope, and will require new accommodations in banking practice, particularly for banks with multinational operations.

Bank Secrecy and the Variable Intensity of the Conflict of Laws

CHRISTOPHER HARE

'A secret remains a secret until you make someone promise never to reveal it.'

(Fausto Cercignani)[1]

3.1 Introduction

The cross-border nature of modern banking business has made the conflict of laws increasingly important for banks across a broad range of activities. This is no less the case when one considers the scope of the bank's basic duty to keep its customers' information 'secret' or 'confidential',[2] since

---

An earlier version of this chapter was presented at the Bank Secrecy Symposium hosted by the Centre for Banking and Finance Law at the Faculty of Law, National University of Singapore on 4–5 December 2014. My thanks to the symposium organisers and participants for their helpful comments. As this chapter was finalised after the United Kingdom's referendum vote on 23 June 2016 to leave the European Union, but before the triggering of Art. 50 of the Treaty of Lisbon, O.J. C. 306/01 or the conclusion of any agreement on the precise terms of 'Brexit', it is written on the basis of EU law still having full effect in the United Kingdom. The future position may well be radically different: consider *R (on the application of Miller)* v. *Secretary of State for Exiting the European Union* [2017] UKSC 5.

[1] B. Morris (ed), *Simply Transcribed: Quotations from Fausto Cercignani*, 2nd edn (Milan: e-book, 2014) at 26.

[2] This chapter uses the terminology of 'secrecy', rather than 'confidentiality', to refer to the bank's core obligation, arising out of the account contract, not to disclose its customers' information. There are three reasons for this. First, the language of 'bank secrecy' reflects the statutory terminology adopted in some jurisdictions: see *Banking Act*, para. 47 (Switzerland); *Criminal Code*, s 156 (Argentina); *Banking and Financial Institutions Act 1989*, s 97 (Malaysia). That said, Singapore plans to abandon the language of 'secrecy' in favour of 'privacy': see *Banking Act* (Cap 19, 2008 Rev Ed Sing), s 47 (Singapore). Secondly, referring to 'bank secrecy' emphasises that the bank's duty of non-disclosure (at least as traditionally conceived in the United Kingdom) extends to information that is not actually confidential at all. For example, the fact that a person holds his account with a particular bank would traditionally be information that is protected by the bank's duty of secrecy, yet

different jurisdictions vary quite significantly in the way that they define the information caught by that core duty and its qualifications.[3] To a large extent, this is the consequence of each jurisdiction enacting an increasingly large body of legislation (often with little similarity in drafting) that trenches upon the duty of secrecy in ever more expansive ways. The point was lucidly put by Clarke J (on behalf of a unanimous Irish Supreme Court) in *Walsh* v. *National Irish Bank Ltd*:

> There have been many developments in the law relating to both disclosure obligations and confidentiality in recent years. It is fair to say that the law has developed in different ways in different jurisdictions. Given the cross-border nature of many of the issues with which courts in various jurisdictions are concerned, it is hardly surprising that conflicts may arise between disclosure obligations owed in one jurisdiction and potential duties of confidence or obligations to respect privacy owed in other jurisdictions. What are the courts to do when a clear disclosure obligation in one jurisdiction potentially or arguably conflicts with a possible duty to retain confidentiality or to respect privacy in another jurisdiction?[4]

---

the bank customer reveals that information to third parties every time he draws a cheque, presents a debit card for payment or makes an electronic funds transfer. Information that has been voluntarily put in the public domain is difficult to describe as confidential in the truest sense of that word. Thirdly, and related to the previous point, the language of 'bank secrecy' helpfully distinguishes the duty owed by banks specifically from the more general form of equitable liability for breach of confidence, which arises in any situation involving the disclosure of confidential information: see *Coco* v. *AN Clark (Engineers) Ltd* [1968] FSR 415 at 419–21; *Attorney-General* v. *Observer Ltd* [1990] 1 AC 109 at 281. That said, the traditional action for breach of confidence has recently been expanded to protect the misuse of private information (see, for example, *Douglas* v. *Hello! Ltd (No 3)* [2008] 1 AC 1 at paras. 255, 272–8; *Campbell* v. *Mirror Group Newspapers Ltd* [2004] 2 AC 457 at paras. 14, 21, 51, 96, 134; *Vestergaard Frandsen A/S* v. *Bestnet Europe Ltd* [2013] 1 WLR 1556 at paras. 23–8), which might nowadays encompass the bank's duty of secrecy: see Neo, Chapter 1. See also R. Cranston, *Principles of Banking Law*, 2nd edn (Oxford: Oxford University Press, 2002) at 171–4. It remains to be seen whether such extended notions of confidentiality will continue to be necessary in future given the arguably more extensive recognition of privacy rights in *PJS* v. *News Group Newspapers Ltd* [2016] UKSC 26. For recognition that duties of secrecy, confidentiality and privacy may overlap in the banking context, see *Slattery* v. *Friends First Life Assurance Co Ltd* [2013] IEHC 136 at paras. 100–12, rev'd on a different point: [2015] IECA 149 at paras. 90–3.

[3] For example, jurisdictions may differ as to what amounts to a customer's consent to disclosure: see *Re ABC Ltd* [1984] CILR 130.

[4] *Walsh* v. *National Irish Bank Ltd* [2013] IESC 2 at para. 4. Similar conflicts between duties of disclosure and obligations of secrecy arise in the context of arbitration (see R. Mosk and T. Ginsburg, 'Evidentiary Privileges in International Arbitration' (2001) 50 *International and Comparative Law Quarterly* 345) and regulation (see H. Erbstein, 'Bank Secrecy Law and its Implications for American Securities Regulation' (1995) 16 *Company Lawyer* 133).

This chapter attempts to provide an answer by examining Clarke J's final question through a conflict of laws lens.[5] In some respects, the task has been made easier in recent years by three broad legal trends that are likely to diminish the scope and difficulty of the conflict of laws issues arising out of disputes concerning bank secrecy (and indeed the same is likely to be true of banking law disputes more generally). First, banking and financial arrangements increasingly contain provisions that purport to settle any jurisdictional or choice of law disputes between the parties. While there may still be legal issues concerning a particular clause's interpretation or validity, such contractual provisions certainly reduce (if not eliminate entirely) any potential sphere for the conflict of laws' operation. Indeed, banks may be able to sidestep cross-border litigation concerning breaches of bank secrecy entirely by including contractual provisions whereby customers give general consent in advance to all forms of disclosure (although the validity of such a step remains questionable). Secondly, there has been significant harmonisation of the rules relating to jurisdiction (such as in the recast *Brussels I Regulation*[6] and, to a lesser degree, the Trans-Tasman scheme for civil jurisdiction and judgments),[7] recognition of judgments and arbitral awards (such as in the recast *Brussels I Regulation* and the New York Convention)[8] and choice of law (such as in the *Rome I*[9] and *II Regulations*).[10] This has contributed significantly to predictability in this area,[11] as jurisdictional and choice of law issues ought then to be

---

[5] For an interesting recent (albeit non-banking) case that highlights the international limits of rights to secrecy, confidentiality or privacy, see *PJS* v. *News Group Newspapers Ltd* [2016] EWCA Civ 393 at paras. 39–50, *rev'd* [2016] UKSC 26, at paras. 45, 57–66, 70.

[6] *Regulation (EU) No 1215/2012 of the European Parliament and of the Council of 12 December 2012 on Jurisdiction and the Recognition and Enforcement of Judgments in Civil and Commercial Matters* (2012) O.J. L. 351 [*Brussels I Regulation*].

[7] *Agreement between the Government of Australia and the Government of New Zealand on Trans-Tasman Court Proceedings and Regulatory Enforcement*, 24 July 2008 [2013] ATS 32 (entered into force 11 October 2013). See also *Trans-Tasman Proceedings Act 2010* (Cth) and *Trans-Tasman Proceedings Act 2010* (NZ), 2010/108.

[8] *Convention on the Recognition and Enforcement of Foreign Arbitral Awards*, 10 June 1958 [*New York Convention*].

[9] *Regulation (EC) No 593/2008 of the European Parliament and of the Council of 17 June 2008 on the Law Applicable to Contractual Obligations* (2008) O.J. L. 177 [*Rome I Regulation*].

[10] *Regulation (EC) No 864/2007 of the European Parliament and of the Council of 11 July 2007 on the Law Applicable to Non-contractual Obligations* (2007) O.J. L. 199 [*Rome II Regulation*].

[11] There is the promise of a worldwide convention on the enforcement of judgments in civil matters in the *Hague Convention on the Recognition and Enforcement of Foreign Judgments in Civil and Commercial Matters* (concluded on 1 February 1971), which entered into force

decided in the same way irrespective of the court actually seized of the conflicts issue. At least in theory, this should remove some of the perceived vagaries and biases of the conflict of laws process. Thirdly, there has been a degree of international harmonisation of the substantive principles applicable to particular types of banking transaction, which diminishes the significance of the conflict of laws because the homogeneity of domestic law means that litigants are much less concerned about where they litigate or what domestic legal system will apply. The fight against money laundering and terrorist financing provides the most obvious example[12] of such harmonisation (indeed one that has particular relevance to bank secrecy, since (reasonable) suspicion of such activities usually requires banks to disclose account-related information). In this regard, the Financial Action Task Force (FATF) – an intergovernmental body tasked with developing and promoting international and domestic policy to combat money laundering and terrorist financing – has developed a framework of minimum standards that national legislatures should implement in order to combat such activity effectively.[13] To this end, FATF operates a 'mutual evaluation programme' by which member states are monitored for their progress towards implementing the various FATF standards into their domestic legal order. The upshot is that most jurisdictions will have broadly similar legislation as to the conduct that amounts to money laundering and terrorist financing, and accordingly the circumstances in which banks will be required to disclose information about their customers in that regard.

The impact of such harmonisation measures should not, however, be overstated: where harmonisation initiatives simply impose minimum standards, there will continue to be variations in the manner of domestic

---

on 20 August 1979. Unfortunately, at the date of writing, there remain only five contracting states, namely Albania, Cyprus, Kuwait, the Netherlands and Portugal.

[12] Further examples of harmonisation relevant to the bank's duty of secrecy arise in the context of data protection (such as *Directive (EC) 95/46 of the European Parliament and of the Council of 24 October 1995 on the Protection of Individuals with regard to the Processing of Personal Data and on the Free Movement of such Data* (1995) O.J. L. 281/31) and administrative assistance in tax matters (such as OECD, *Multilateral Convention on Mutual Administrative Assistance in Tax Matters: Amended by the 2010 Protocol* (1 June 2011), online: www.oecd .org/ctp/exchange-of-tax-information/ENG-Amended-Convention.pdf; *Directive (EU) 2011/16 of the European Council of 15 February 2011 on the Administrative Co-operation in the Field of Taxation* (2011) O.J. L. 64). For further discussion of data protection in the banking context, see Greenleaf and Tyree, Chapter 2. On exchange of tax information, see O'Brien, Chapter 5.

[13] Financial Action Task Force, 'FATF Standards: FATF 40 Recommendations' (October 2003) (www.fatf-gafi.org/media/fatf/documents/FATF%20Standards%20-%2040%20Recom mendations%20rc.pdf) [FATF 40 Recommendations].

implementation and, in other cases, harmonisation may depend in some way upon the consent of the parties to the transaction[14] or may leave certain specific issues to national law.[15] Where harmonisation measures are partial, consent-based or based upon minimum standards, their potential impact upon the banks' duty of secrecy will still differ from jurisdiction to jurisdiction, leaving scope for the conflict of laws to operate. Accordingly, despite the ameliorations described earlier, it remains true that there are often (to use Clarke J's own words) 'no easy answers' to the question posed in *Walsh* (as set out in the quote earlier).[16] It is suggested that the reason for the perceived difficulty of providing a satisfactory answer to that question stems from a failure to distinguish between the different situations in which cross-border conflicts between obligations of confidentiality and disclosure can arise. In this regard, there appear to be three key scenarios, each of which will be considered in a separate section below: judicial proceedings between a bank and its customer concerning whether the former was justified in disclosing the latter's account-related information; judicial proceedings initiated by a private third party, public authority or state against a bank seeking the disclosure of its customer's account-related information for use in other judicial, regulatory or criminal proceedings abroad to which the bank is not a party; and direct legislative, executive or regulatory action in one jurisdiction that seeks to compel the disclosure of account-related information in another jurisdiction.

The role that the conflict of laws plays certainly alters (and arguably diminishes) as one moves from the first of these scenarios to the last.

---

[14] An example of legal rules that are reasonably well harmonised, but that nevertheless depend upon the parties' consent before they are effective to govern a particular documentary or standby letter of credit, is the International Chamber of Commerce's *Uniform Customs and Practice for Documentary Credits* (1 July 2007), online: www.fd.unl.pt/docentes_docs/ma/mhb_MA_24705.pdf (UCP 600), effective from 1 July 2007. As the UCP 600 must be incorporated into the letter of credit to be effective, this raises the possibility (maybe more theoretical than real) that some letters of credit may not be governed by the UCP 600 at all. Another (more likely) possibility is that some letters of credit may be issued subject to an earlier version of the UCP, which would similarly undermine the harmonising nature of the instrument.

[15] For example, although the UCP 600 contains harmonised rules for most issues that might affect letters of credit, certain matters (such as the exceptions to the autonomy principle; the determination of the law applicable to the various letter of credit relationships; and the obligations of confidentiality owed by participant banks) are governed by the principles of national law: see *United City Merchants (Investments) Ltd* v. *Royal Bank of Canada* [1983] 1 AC 168; *Jackson* v. *Royal Bank of Scotland* [2005] UKHL 3; *Marconi Communications International Ltd* v. *PT Pan Indonesia Bank Ltd* [2005] 2 All ER (Comm) 325; *Trafigura Beheer BV* v. *Kookmin Bank Co* [2006] CLC 643.

[16] *Walsh* v. *National Irish Bank, supra* note 4 at para. 4.

The first scenario, involving litigation between banks and their customers, is staple fare for the conflict of laws, which can assist in determining not only where the dispute can or should be resolved and whether any resulting monetary judgment can be enforced,[17] but also the law that governs the scope and content of (as well as qualifications to) the bank's duty of secrecy. In contrast, the role played by the conflict of laws is somewhat lessened in the second scenario: whether a court seized of proceedings will help a litigant by requesting a foreign court's assistance to obtain account-related information from a bank located in that foreign jurisdiction, or whether a court should accede to such a request, is a matter that the conflict of laws (by virtue of the jurisdictional question generally having been settled by that stage of the process[18] and by virtue of the choice of law process' self-denying ordinance in favour of the *lex fori* in matters of evidence and procedure)[19] generally leaves to the procedural laws of the court seized of the issue (albeit that international instruments have nowadays introduced a degree of procedural harmonisation in this regard).[20] That said, the conflict of laws does perform a residual role in such cases by limiting a court's extraterritorial application of those procedural laws[21] or by

---

[17] Placing 'can' and 'should' in opposition is intended to contrast the generally non-discretionary nature of the European jurisdictional and choice of law regimes and the significant exercise of discretion that traditionally accompanies the common law approach to jurisdiction and choice of law.

[18] The jurisdictional rules of the conflict of laws determine where proceedings can or should be brought, but do not purport to regulate the substantive issues or the conduct of those proceedings once initiated.

[19] See, for example, *Rome I Regulation, supra* note 9, Arts. 1(3), 18; *Rome II Regulation, supra* note 10, Arts. 1(3), 15(c), 22. See also *Boys* v. *Chaplin* [1971] AC 365 at 379, 382–3, 389, 394; *Harding* v. *Wealands* [2007] 2 AC 1 at paras. 13–84; *Cox* v. *Ergo Versicherung AG* [2014] AC 1379 at paras. 12–6, 40–4.

[20] See generally *Hague Convention on the Taking of Evidence Abroad in Civil or Commercial Matters*, 18 March 1970, 23 UST 2555 [*Hague Evidence Convention*]; *Regulation (EC) 1206/2001 of the European Council of 28 May 2001 on the Co-operation between Member States in the Taking of Evidence in Civil or Commercial Matters* (2001) O.J. L. 174 [*European Evidence Regulation*].

[21] In *Belhaj* v. *Straw* [2017] UKSC 3 at para. 236, Lord Sumption indicated that it is 'a fundamental principle of English private international law' that a state should not apply its laws extraterritorially. In that regard, the interpretative presumption against the extraterritorial application of domestic legislation applies regardless of whether that legislation is classified as procedural or substantive for choice of law purposes: see, for example, *In re Sawers* (1879) 12 Ch D 522 at 526; *Clark* v. *Oceanic Contractors Inc* [1983] 2 AC 130 at 145; *Agassi* v. *Robinson (Inspector of Taxes)* [2006] 1 WLR 1380 at paras. 16, 20; *Lawson* v. *Serco Ltd* [2006] ICR 250 at paras. 1, 6; *Al-Skeini* v. *Secretary of State for Defence* [2007] UKHL 26 at paras. 11, 44–7, 137; *Office of Fair Trading* v. *Lloyds TSB Bank plc* [2008] AC 316 at paras. 4, 11, 25; *Duncombe* v. *Secretary of State for Children, Schools and Families (No 2)* [2011] ICR 1312 at

denying their use to enforce a foreign jurisdiction's penal, revenue or other public laws.[22] Even this limited function seems, however, to evaporate in the third scenario, since the conflict of laws has not (at least tradition-ally) been conceived as being capable of regulating or resolving clashes between the exercise of legislative, executive or regulatory power of dif-ferent states. This realm of politics, diplomacy, international relations and public international law has traditionally been a no-go area for the con-flict of laws. While this view has recently been challenged academically by those advocating an altogether more ambitious role for the conflict of laws,[23] for now, at least, the orthodoxy persists that conflicts between legis-lative or executive acts must be resolved either by treaty-making (or some other less formal, supranational, consent-based mechanism)[24] or through an unseemly tit-for-tat exchange of legislation and counter-legislation enacted at domestic level.[25]

---

para. 16; *Ravat* v. *Halliburton Manufacturing and Services Ltd* [2012] ICR 389 at para. 27; *Cox* v. *Ergo Versicherung AG*, *supra* note 19 at paras. 27–34.

[22] See, for example, *Regazzoni* v. *Sethia* [1958] AC 301 at 319–21; *Attorney-General of New Zealand* v. *Ortiz* [1984] 1 AC 1 at 20–2; *Williams & Humbert Ltd* v. *W&H Trade Marks (Jersey) Ltd* [1986] AC 368 at 428; *QRS 1 ApS* v. *Frandsen* [1999] 1 WLR 2169 at 2171; *The Republic of the Philippines* v. *Maler Foundation* [2013] SGCA 66 at paras. 106–7; *Shergill* v. *Khaira* [2015] AC 359 at para. 41; *Belhaj* v. *Straw*, *supra* note 21 at para. 65.

[23] See further Section 3.4.

[24] See, for example, *United Nations Monetary and Financial Conference*, July 1944 [Bretton Woods Agreement]; FATF 40 Recommendations, *supra* note 13; Basel Committee on Banking Supervision, 'Basel III: A Global Regulatory Framework for More Resilient Banks and Banking Systems' (December 2010, revised June 2011), online: www.bis.org/publ/bcbs189_dec2010.pdf.

[25] See, for example, *Protection of Trading Interests Act 1980* (UK), c 11, s 1, which gives the Secretary of State the power to give directions to any person carrying on business in the United Kingdom not to comply with any measures 'taken by or under the law of any over-seas country for regulating or controlling international trade . . . in so far as [those meas-ures] apply or would apply to things done or to be done outside the territorial jurisdiction of that country by persons carrying on business in the United Kingdom' if those measures 'are [also] damaging or threaten to damage the trading interests of the United Kingdom'. Among the various forms of extraterritorial legislation targeted by this provision, a particu-lar concern was the extraterritorial application of US antitrust legislation, with the result that judgments for multiple damages (which are common in US antitrust proceedings) are rendered unenforceable in the United Kingdom as a matter of public policy: *ibid.*, ss 5–7. At a European level, there has also been blocking legislation designed to deal with the extrater-ritorial impact on the European Union of economic and trade sanctions imposed (usually by the United States) on third party states, such as Cuba, Libya and Iran: see *Regulation (EC) No 2271/96 of the European Council of 22 November 1996 Protecting against the Effects of the Extraterritorial Application of Legislation Adopted by a Third Country, and Actions Based Thereon or Resulting Therefrom* (1996) O.J. L. 309 [*European Blocking Regulation*]. See also *Proposal for a Regulation of the European Parliament and of the Council Protecting against*

Each of these three scenarios will be considered in turn in the following sections, starting with the role of the conflict of laws in banker-customer disputes concerning bank secrecy (considered in Section 3.2); then moving on to how the conflict of laws regulates judicial requests by litigating parties for account-related information from non-party banks (considered in Section 3.3); and finally discussing the extraterritorial application of one jurisdiction's bank disclosure legislation or executive orders against entities located in other jurisdictions (considered in Section 3.4). While reference will be made to conflict of laws principles in other jurisdictions when this proves instructive, the analysis and discussion will be distinctly Anglo-centric to avoid an already unwieldy topic becoming unmanageable. Nevertheless, the key ideas and central thesis in this chapter are capable of transposition *mutatis mutandis* to other jurisdictions.

3.2   Bank Secrecy and the Conflict of Laws in Bank-Customer Disputes

When there is a dispute between a bank with its head office in one jurisdiction and a customer with his account held by a branch in another (regardless of whether the dispute concerns a breach of bank secrecy or some other banking law issue), the conflict of laws will determine not only where any subsequent proceedings can or should be commenced,[26] but also the law applicable to the dispute and the enforceability of any resulting judgment. Indeed, such is the importance of these preliminary issues for banking (and other commercial) disputes that litigants not infrequently settle the substantive claim once the conflict of laws issues have been resolved. That said, the fact that these issues arise at all in bank-customer disputes (whether generally or in the specific context of bank secrecy) is largely the product of banking enterprises' fragmentation across a network of branches. It may be unsurprising, therefore, that the branch concept has cast a long shadow over the resolution of conflict of laws issues in bank-customer disputes. Often, the location of the particular customer's branch will provide a basis not only for assuming jurisdiction over the banking

---

the *Effects of the Extraterritorial Application of Legislation Adopted by a Third Country and Actions Based Thereon or Resulting Therefrom* (6 February 2015) COM/2015/048 (considered by the European Union Council on 27 April 2016).

[26] In non-bank-customer disputes, the jurisdiction in which the proceedings are brought can often be a matter of some significance, since the coercive powers of a court to order the other party to the proceedings, or even third parties such as banks, to provide information differ between jurisdictions: see further Section 3.3.

entity as a whole, but also for enforcing a judgment against the assets of the bank's head office or other branches or for determining the law applicable to the bank's duty of secrecy to its customer. Accordingly, this section will in turn consider the development of the branch concept as the basis for conflict of laws analysis in each of the areas of jurisdiction, recognition of foreign judgments and choice of law. The essential thesis of this section is that, in each of those conflict of laws areas, the courts have over-relied on a single connecting factor and that the constant harking back to the jurisdiction where a particular branch is established may no longer be justified, as it does not reflect the reality of modern banking business. In searching for more appropriate connecting factors in the application of conflict of laws principles to banking disputes, the most obvious and straightforward candidate is the jurisdiction of the bank's head office, but (as will be further discussed subsequently) there may be other suitable alternatives when one is considering the bank's duty of secrecy in particular.

3.2.1   Jurisdiction

The jurisdiction in which the customer sues his or her bank may be critical to the likelihood of success on the merits: in claims alleging breach of the bank's duty of secrecy, the customer will wish to sue in the jurisdiction whose choice of law rules apply a law that defines the exceptions to that duty in the narrowest manner possible; whereas, in other types of banker-customer claim, the choice of jurisdiction will determine the extent of the court's coercive powers to order disclosure of information or discovery of documents that the customer may find useful in pursuing his or her claim. Given the customer's clear motivation to shop (where possible) for the most favourable forum for the litigation, it becomes critical to ascertain the bases upon which jurisdiction can be assumed over proceedings against a bank. From the bank's perspective, assuming that the account contract does not contain an exclusive jurisdiction clause (which is obviously the most straightforward way of a bank protecting itself), the most troubling aspect of the jurisdictional rules' structure is that, in addition to the place of its head office, a bank may potentially be sued in any jurisdiction where it has a branch.[27] Certainly, at common law, an English court has been prepared

---

[27] It is flawed to suggest that banks can benefit as claimants (such as when they are suing for the recovery of an overdraft facility or loan) from any jurisdictional rule based upon the location of the branch that has dealt with the particular customer or borrower, since the latter would generally have to be sued according to his or her presence in the jurisdiction

to assume jurisdiction over an individual defendant on the basis of the most fleeting presence within the jurisdiction,[28] and jurisdiction may be taken over a foreign-incorporated company by serving proceedings upon 'any place of business' in the United Kingdom,[29] even if that place has little other connection with the subject matter of the proceedings.[30] It is clear that a foreign bank's English branch, which will usually have established operations, fixed business premises and a permanent staff, would qualify as that bank having 'a place of business' within the United Kingdom, since such a degree of permanence would be tantamount to a form of 'residence',[31] although a much lesser degree of presence may also suffice.[32]

While mere fleeting or temporary presence may appear to be an exorbitant basis of jurisdiction, the English courts at least (and indeed other common law jurisdictions) may well invoke the self-denying ordinance to refuse to hear proceedings on the grounds that the court is *forum non conveniens*[33] (which is similar to the *forum conveniens* jurisdiction employed

---

(at common law) or in his or her domicile (under the *Brussels I Regulation, supra* note 6 at Arts. 62–3). Accordingly, the focus on the branch concept tends only to operate to the banks' detriment.

[28] *Colt Industries Inc* v. *Sarlie* [1966] 1 WLR 440; *HRH Maharanee Seethadevi Gaekwar of Baroda* v. *Wildenstein* [1972] 2 QB 283; *SSL International plc* v. *TTK LIG Ltd* [2011] EWCA Civ 1170 at para. 57. See also *Carrick* v. *Hancock* (1898) 12 TLR 59 at 60; *Adams* v. *Cape Industries plc* [1990] Ch 433 at 518.

[29] *Companies Act 2006* (UK), c 46, s 1139(2); *Civil Procedure Rules 1998*, No. 1998/3132, r 6.9(2)(7). See also *Goldman Sachs International* v. *Novo Banco SA* [2015] EWHC 2371 (Comm) at para. 74.

[30] *Teekay Tankers Ltd* v. *STX Offshore & Shipping Co* [2014] EWHC 3612 (Comm) at paras. 31–42; *Chopra* v. *Bank of Singapore Ltd* [2015] EWHC 1549 (Ch) at paras. 96–8. See also *South India Shipping Corporation Ltd* v. *Export-Import Bank of Korea* [1985] 1 WLR 585; *Saab* v. *Saudi American Bank* [1999] 1 WLR 1861 at paras. 7, 12–15, 18.

[31] Indeed, the defendant's residence is increasingly recognised as a basis for international jurisdiction: see *State Bank of India* v. *Murjani* (Unreported, 27 March 1991, CA); *Motorola Credit Corporation* v. *Uzan* [2004] EWHC 3169 (Comm) at paras. 21–9; *Relfo Ltd* v. *Varsani* [2011] 1 WLR 1402. Consider L. Collins (ed), *Dicey, Morris and Collins on The Conflict of Laws*, 15th edn (London: Sweet & Maxwell, 2016) at para. 11-110.

[32] Consider *Dunlop Pneumatic Tyre Co Ltd* v. *Cudell & Co* [1902] 1 KB 342 (exhibition stand); *Saccharin Corporation Ltd* v. *Chemische Fabrik Von Heyden Aktiengesellschaft* [1911] 2 KB 516 (sole agent's office); *South India Shipping Corporation Ltd* v. *Export–Import Bank of Korea, supra* note 30 (correspondent office). It is also possible to commence proceedings against a company by leaving the claim form with a person holding a senior position in the company: see *Civil Procedure Rules 1998, supra* note 29, r 6.5(3)(b). Such personal service requires that the company be carrying on business in England: see *SSL International plc* v. *TTK LIG Ltd, supra* note 28.

[33] See generally *Spiliada Maritime Corporation* v. *Cansulex Ltd* [1987] AC 460; *Lubbe* v. *Cape plc* [2000] 1 WLR 1545; *Berezovsky* v. *Michaels* [2000] 1 WLR 1004; *VTB Capital plc* v. *Nutritek International Corporation* [2013] 2 AC 337.

by the courts when giving permission to serve proceedings on a defendant outside the jurisdiction).[34] Accordingly, if, for example, a personal customer commenced proceedings in England against a Canadian bank (on the basis that it had an English branch) in respect of a dispute concerning the customer's only account with the bank's New York branch, the English courts might well decline to hear the claim on *forum non conveniens* grounds. In contrast, where a personal customer has dealt with his or her bank almost exclusively through its English branch, the English courts are likely to reject any suggestion that it is *forum non conveniens*. Indeed, given that an English branch will have a more stable and permanent connection with that jurisdiction than an individual who is fleetingly present, that very sense of permanence potentially diminishes the significance of *forum non conveniens* in the bank-customer context. Equally, where a customer, who has commenced proceedings against its bank in England, has dealings with that bank through its English head office and/or a mix of various branches in different jurisdictions (as may well occur with large corporate customers), the English courts may well refuse to stay the proceedings on *forum non conveniens* grounds, as it is unlikely that the bank will be able to demonstrate the existence of 'another available forum which is *clearly or distinctly* more appropriate than the English forum',[35] given

---

[34] In such 'service out' cases, as well as showing that England is the *forum conveniens*, it is also necessary for the putative claimant to demonstrate that there is a serious issue to be tried on the merits and a good arguable case that the intended proceedings fall within one of the jurisdictional heads in *Civil Procedure Rules 1998*, *supra* note 29, Practice Direction 6B at para. 3.1: see *Seaconsar Far East Ltd* v. *Bank Markazi Jomhouri Islami Iran* [1994] 1 AC 438 at 453–7; *Altimo Holdings and Investment Ltd* v. *Kyrgyz Mobil Tel Ltd* [2012] 1 WLR 1804 at para. 71. Claims for breach of bank secrecy might be brought within the contractual head of jurisdiction, when the account contract is concluded through the bank's English branch, is governed by English law, is subject to an English jurisdiction clause or is breached in England (*ibid.*, para. 3.1(6)–(7)); or, within the tortious head of jurisdiction, when the customer sustains damage in England or the bank commits the acts constituting a breach of bank secrecy in England (*ibid.*, para. 3.1(9)): see *Vidall-Hall* v. *Google Inc* [2016] QB 1003 at paras. 43–51. In addition, there is a distinct head of jurisdiction for claims involving a 'breach of confidence' or 'misuse of private information' (see *Civil Procedure Rules 1998*, *supra* note 29, Practice Direction 6B at para. 3.1(21)), but whether this is available for claims based upon breaches of a bank's duty of secrecy depends upon how one conceives of that duty: see *supra* note 2. The exercise of such a long-arm jurisdiction to serve proceedings on defendants abroad ought not to create significant unfairness or difficulties for banks, as that jurisdiction is premised upon England being 'the forum in which the case can be suitably tried for the interests of all the parties and for the ends of justice': see *Spiliada Maritime Corporation* v. *Cansulex Ltd*, *supra* note 33 at 480. Accordingly, this particular jurisdictional basis is not considered further in this chapter.

[35] *Spiliada Maritime Corporation* v. *Cansulex Ltd*, *supra* note 33 at 477 (emphasis added).

that the connecting factors relevant to the dispute will be spread across a number of jurisdictions. It follows that, despite possessing a discretionary power not to hear jurisdictionally inappropriate cases, an English court might nevertheless remain seized of proceedings that actually have little connection with England. By enabling a customer to choose the jurisdiction in which to sue the bank on the sole basis that the bank happens to have a branch in that jurisdiction (at least in circumstances where the courts seized of the jurisdictional dispute will not exercise their *forum non conveniens* discretion to decline jurisdiction), a customer is able to engage in a degree of forum shopping in order to litigate in the jurisdiction that is most protective of bank secrecy and that accordingly is most likely to result in success for the customer, or that, alternatively, is likely to grant the most generous form of disclosure against the defendant bank.[36] The consequence of allowing such forum shopping is that a bank, through its branches, may be exposed to bank secrecy regimes of differing strengths and to a range of different disclosure regimes varying in form and extent from the disclosure regime applicable in its head office's jurisdiction.

While the possibility of forum shopping in the banking context might be attributed (despite the existence of a *forum non conveniens* discretion) to the relaxed common law jurisdictional rules based solely upon the defendant's presence within the jurisdiction, the risk of forum shopping is little diminished in jurisdictions that employ a more stringent basis for the assumption of international jurisdiction than mere presence (such as residence, habitual residence or domicile, all of which would arguably be readily satisfied by a bank branch), but do not employ any countervailing discretion for the staying of jurisdictionally inappropriate proceedings.[37]

---

[36] For example, where a bank is party to civil proceedings in England and Wales, no distinction is made between the disclosure of documents within and without the jurisdiction provided they are within the possession, custody or power of the bank: see *The Consul Corfitzon* [1917] AC 550 at 555–6; *MacKinnon* v. *Donaldson, Lufkin & Jenrette Corporation* [1986] 1 Ch 483 at 494–5; *Masri* v. *Consolidated Contractors International Co SAL (No 4)* [2008] EWCA Civ 876 at paras. 38–54, rev'd on a different issue: [2010] AC 90; *National Grid Electricity Transmission plc* v. *ABB Ltd* [2013] EWHC 822 (Ch) at paras. 20–31, 50, 56; *Secretary of State for Health* v. *Servier Laboratories Ltd* [2013] EWCA Civ 1234 at paras. 99–101. See also R.G. Toulson and C.M. Phipps, *Confidentiality*, 3rd edn (London: Sweet & Maxwell, 2012) at para. 10-004. Similarly, in non-bank-customer disputes, forum shopping may be driven by the need to secure the greatest possible disclosure rights against a non-party bank, which will lead to a litigant choosing a jurisdiction in which the courts have broad coercive powers against third parties and generous exceptions to the bank's duty of secrecy: see further Section 3.3.

[37] Civil law jurisdictions frequently provide for some more significant connecting factor, but do not generally recognise the ability to stay proceedings on *forum non conveniens* or other

An example of just such a regime is the recast Brussels I Regulation,[38] which is inspired by the stricter civil law approach to jurisdiction. The primary basis of jurisdiction under the Brussels regime is the defendant's domicile,[39] which equates to a company's statutory seat, central administration or principal place of business.[40] For the purposes of English law, this means the corporate defendant's registered office or, where there is no such office, its place of incorporation or formation,[41] in other words, the bank's head office. In addition, however, the recast Brussels I Regulation provides a number of alternative heads of 'special jurisdiction' that would enable a customer to sue their bank somewhere other than its head office, such as the Member State where the 'obligation in question' is to be performed[42] or, if the customer qualifies as a 'consumer',[43] in the place of his or her domicile.[44] In practice, both of these heads of 'special jurisdiction' are likely to point towards the customer's local branch as the alternative

---

discretionary grounds: see *re Harrods (Buenos Aires) Ltd (No 2)* [1992] Ch 72; *Owusu v. Jackson*, C-281/02 [2005] ECR I-1383.

[38] *Brussels I Regulation, supra* note 6. On the issue of forum shopping within the Brussels regime, see generally B. Davenport, 'Forum Shopping in the Market' (1995) 111 *Law Quarterly Review* 366; P. De Vareilles-Sommières, *Forum Shopping in the European Judicial Area* (Oxford: Hart Publishing, 2007). See further *The Tatry*, C-406/92 [1994] ECR I-5439; *The Alexandros T* [2013] UKSC 70.

[39] *Brussels I Regulation, supra* note 6, Art. 4(1).

[40] *Ibid.*, Art. 63(1).

[41] *Ibid.*, Art. 63(2).

[42] *Ibid.*, Art. 7(1). Originally, the autonomous notion of the 'obligation in question' referred to the obligation on which the claimant's claim was based (see *Etablissements A. de Bloos Sprl v. Etablissements Bouyer SA*, C-14/76 [1976] ECR 1497 at paras. 7–17; *Martin Peters Bauunternehmung GmbH v. Zuid Nederlandse Aanemers Vereniging*, C-34/92 [1983] ECR 987 at paras. 9–10; *Öfab, Östergötlands Fastigheter AB v. Koot*, C-147/12 [2015] QB 20 at para. 27), but in relation to a bank account the position is now governed by Art. 7(1)(b), which provides that the place of performance of the 'obligation in question' is 'in the case of the provision of services, the place in a Member State where, under the contract the services were provided or should have been provided'. Even where the relevant legal system views the bank's duty of secrecy as tortious or equitable, the contractual head of jurisdiction will nevertheless generally continue to apply (see *Kalfelis v. Bankhaus Schröder Munchmeyer Hengst & Co*, C-189/87 [1988] ECR 5565 at paras. 16–20; *Kolassa v. Barclays Bank plc*, C-375/13 [2015] IL Pr 14 at para. 44) when there exists between the customer and bank an 'obligation freely entered into with regard to another' (see *Jakob Handte & Co GmbH v. Traitements Mécano-Chimiques des Surfaces SA*, C-26/91 [1992] ECR I-3967 at para. 15) and the conduct complained of 'may be considered a breach of the terms of the contract, which may be established by taking into account the purpose of the contract' (see *Brogsitter v. Fabrication de Montres Normandes EURL*, C-548/12, ECLI:EU:C2014:148 at paras. 18–29).

[43] *Brussels I Regulation, supra* note 6, Art. 17(1)(c).

[44] *Ibid.*, Art. 18(1).

jurisdictionally relevant place.[45] Moreover, as a further alternative basis of jurisdiction,[46] Art. 7(5) of the recast Brussels I regime explicitly entitles a claimant/customer to bring proceedings before the courts of a Member State where the defendant has a 'branch, agency or other establishment', which phrase 'implies a centre of operations which has the appearance of permanency'.[47] While this notion would clearly encompass a bank branch, it would even extend to the circumstances where the bank has established a banking subsidiary company with apparent authority to bind the parent bank.[48] That said, Art. 7(5) does contain an inbuilt limitation that the proceedings must be 'as regards a dispute arising out of the operations' of the relevant branch. In *Somafer SA* v. *Saar-Ferngas AG*,[49] the European Court of Justice interpreted this limitation as requiring that the proceedings relate to either the management of the bank branch, some business contracted by the branch on behalf of the principal entity, or some non-contractual liability arising from the operations of the branch itself. While the dispute must, therefore, have *some* degree of connection with the branch, this does not have to be significant.[50] Moreover, the operations about which complaint is made need not take place in the same Member

---

[45] When the customer is a consumer, the likelihood is that they will have chosen to open an account at his or her local branch, so that the jurisdiction indicated by *Brussels I Regulation*, *supra* note 6, Arts. 17–18 will usually be the same as the jurisdiction where the relevant branch is located. Similarly, for the purposes of special jurisdiction under Art. 7(1), the customer's branch is likely to be the place where 'the services were provided or should have been provided'. For the difficulties when a customer has accounts in different Member States, see *Wood Floor Solutions Andreas Domberger GmbH* v. *Silva Trade SA*, C-19/09 [2010] 1 WLR 1900 at paras. 21–43.

[46] Even where the consumer protection provisions of the *Brussels I Regulation*, *supra* note 6, Arts. 17–18 apply, the jurisdictional rules based upon branches in Art. 7(5) continue to apply and are reinforced: *ibid.*, Arts. 17(1)–(2).

[47] *Mahamdia* v. *People's Democratic Republic of Algeria* [2012] IL Pr 41 at para. 48. The phrase 'branch, agency or other establishment' has been given an autonomous definition and does not include an exclusive distributor (see *Etablissements A. de Bloos Sprl* v. *Establissements Bouyer SA*, *supra* note 42 at paras. 13, 20–3), a sales representative without a fixed place of business or the power to bind the defendant (see *Somafer SA* v. *Saar-Ferngas AG*, C-33/78 [1978] ECR I-2183 at para. 13), or an independent commercial agent (see *Blanckaert & Willems PVBA* v. *Trost*, C-139/80 [1981] ECR I-819 at para. 13).

[48] *SAR Schotte GmbH* v. *Parfums Rothschild Sàrl*, C-218/86 [1987] ECR I-4905; *Anton Durbeck GmbH* v. *Den Norske Bank ASA* [2003] QB 1160 at paras. 27, 40-1, 46–51; *Mahamdia* v. *People's Democratic Republic of Algeria*, *supra* note 47.

[49] *Somafer SA* v. *Saar-Ferngas AG*, *supra* note 47 at para. 13. See also *Mahamdia* v. *People's Democratic Republic of Algeria*, *supra* note 47 at para. 48.

[50] Consider generally *Saab* v. *Saudi American Bank* [1999] 1 WLR 1861 at paras. 14–27.

State as where the relevant branch is located.[51] This means that, where a customer has had dealings with a number of branches in different Member States, the customer will be able to choose the jurisdiction with the most liberal disclosure regime as against his or her bank. From the bank's perspective, this is particularly problematic, given that the European Court of Justice in *Owusu* v. *Jackson*[52] has now clearly indicated that the English courts have no discretion to decline to hear proceedings where jurisdiction has initially been allocated on the basis of the provisions of the recast *Brussels I Regulation*. Accordingly, the Brussels regime does not permit jurisdiction to be declined purely on the basis of the lack of connection between the dispute and the jurisdiction in which the relevant bank branch is established. Like the common law, therefore, the *Brussels I Regulation* leaves banks jurisdictionally exposed by virtue of their branch operations (although it might well be argued that this is simply the price that the bank pays for doing business in a particular place).

3.2.2   Recognition and Enforcement of Foreign Judgments

An important consequence of a customer relying upon a bank's branch network in order to found jurisdiction against that bank as defendant is the possibility that the resulting judgment can then be enforced against the assets of the bank's head office or branches in other jurisdictions. Given that each jurisdiction defines the principles for the recognition of foreign judgments in a different manner, the focus will be on the English conflict of laws approach to the recognition and enforcement of foreign judgments.

At common law, foreign judgments will be recognised and enforced where the defendant in the foreign proceedings submits to the foreign jurisdiction or is present in that jurisdiction when the judgment is issued. According to the English Court of Appeal in *Adams* v. *Cape Industries plc*,[53] 'presence' for these purposes will encompass where a bank has its head office or a branch. This means that, where a customer is able to sue a bank in respect of a breach of its duty of secrecy in a foreign jurisdiction where that bank has a branch, any resulting judgment can be enforced against

---

[51]   *Lloyd's Register of Shipping* v. *Société Campenon Bernard*, C-439/93 [1995] ECR I-961.

[52]   *Owusu* v. *Jackson*, *supra* note 37. See also *Schmid* v. *Hertel* [2014] 1 WLR 633 at paras. 41–5; *Comité d'Entreprise de Nortel Networks SA* v. *Rogeau*, C-649/13 [2016] QB 109 at para. 36. Consider the limits introduced by the notion of 'reflexive effect' in *Ferrexpo AG* v. *Gilson Investments Ltd* [2012] EWHC 721 (Comm) at paras. 117–98.

[53]   *Adams* v. *Cape Industries plc*, *supra* note 28 at 518. See also *Rubin* v. *Eurofinance SA* [2012] UKSC 46 at paras. 8, 108–32; *Vizcaya Partners Ltd* v. *Picard* [2016] UKPC 5 at para. 2.

the bank's assets in England (and possibly other jurisdictions that enforce judgments on the same basis). Similarly, where jurisdiction is founded upon Art. 7(5) of the recast *Brussels I Regulation*, any judgment will be freely enforceable against any bank assets within the European Union.[54] Undoubtedly, by allowing jurisdiction to be founded upon the presence of a particular branch, banks become more susceptible to having their assets subject to enforcement proceedings in England (and potentially other jurisdictions).

3.2.3   Choice of Law

The law applicable to (or governing)[55] the bank's obligation of secrecy[56] will depend in the first instance upon the source of that obligation and its characterisation for choice of law purposes. Accordingly, in those jurisdictions where the bank's duty of secrecy arises by virtue of contractual, tortious/delictual or equitable obligations,[57] its scope for the purposes of a particular dispute will largely depend upon the operation of the choice of law principles in the jurisdiction seized of the proceedings.[58] In some jurisdictions, however, the bank's duty of secrecy has a statutory origin,[59]

---

[54] *Brussels I Regulation*, *supra* note 6, Art. 52. There are limited grounds for the non-recognition of a Member State's judgment in Art. 45(1).

[55] For the sake of simplicity and consistency, reference will be made to 'applicable law' (to reflect the language of the *Rome I Regulation*, *supra* note 9) rather than 'governing law' (a term synonymous with the common law approach to choice of law), although the discussion is equally relevant to both choice of law regimes.

[56] For the justifications for using the language of 'secrecy' rather than 'confidence' or 'confidentiality', see *supra* note 2.

[57] For consideration of the possible overlap between these different sources of liability, see *Slattery* v. *Friends First Life Assurance Co Ltd*, *supra* note 2 at paras. 100–12, *rev'd* on a different point: [2015] IECA 149 at paras. 90–3.

[58] Of these possibilities, the most common source of obligation is the banker-customer contract itself, as in, for example, England (see *Tournier* v. *National Provincial and Union Bank of England* [1924] 1 KB 461), Ireland (see *National Irish Bank Ltd* v. *Radió Telefís Éireann* [1998] 2 IR 465 at 494; *O'Brien* v. *Radió Telefís Éireann* [2015] IEHC 397 at paras. 63–7), Hong Kong (see *FDC Co Ltd* v. *The Chase Manhattan Bank NA* [1990] 1 HKLR 277; *Australia and New Zealand Banking Group Ltd* v. *Chen* [2016] HKCU 1116 at para. 75), Belize (see *Re Diaz* [1992] 51 WIR 51 at 59–60), China (see *Luomou* v. *Yi Bank* [2011] *huyizhong minliu (shang) zhongzi* No 198 [3 February 2012]) and Germany (see *Bürgerliches Gesetzbuch*, ss 241, 311). For the existence of a non-statutory duty of secrecy in Mauritius, see *State Bank International Ltd* v. *Pershing Ltd* (1996) 1 OFLR 170 at 173–4. That said, in other contexts, English law has recognised that issues of privacy and confidentiality may also be protected by tortious and equitable obligations: see further *supra* note 2.

[59] See, for example, *Banking Act*, *supra* note 2, s 47 (Singapore); *Banking and Financial Institutions Act 1989*, *supra* note 2, ss 97, 104 (Malaysia); *Banking Act*, *supra* note 2 at para.

such that the international reach of that duty will potentially be limited in two ways:[60] by the application of the choice of law principles of the court seized of the dispute and by the domestic principles of statutory interpretation that determine the territorial limits (as well as the limits *ratione materiae* and *personae*) of the legislation in question.

The additional complexity (from a conflict of laws perspective at least)[61] that arises out of the duty of secrecy being statutory is exemplified by s 47 of the Singaporean Banking Act. In terms of the (first) choice of law question, that provision appears to apply irrespective of any law chosen by the parties as applicable to the issue before the court, since s 47 provides that '[f]or the avoidance of doubt, nothing in [that section] shall be construed to prevent a bank from entering into an express agreement with a customer of that bank for a higher degree of confidentiality than that prescribed in this section'. The strong implication is that banks in Singapore may not insert clauses into their customers' contracts *lowering* standards of bank secrecy, which would also potentially include attempts to circumvent Singaporean bank secrecy by means of a foreign choice of law clause.[62] What remains unclear, however, is whether the legislative intent is also to apply s 47 where a foreign law applies by virtue of objective connecting factors, rather than the parties' own choice. One suspects that this problem could be sidestepped relatively easily by applying the relevant choice of law principles with a homewards bias. As regards

---

47 (Switzerland); *Criminal Code, supra* note 2, s 156 (Argentina); *Right to Financial Privacy Act*, 12 USC (1978), §§ 3401–22 (the United States). For a common law analysis of Swiss bank secrecy laws, see *Suzlon Energy Ltd* v. *Bangad* [2011] FCA 1152 at paras. 30–9. For the suggestion that the Singaporean statutory duty of secrecy displaces the traditional duty arising by way of a contractual implied term, see *Susilawati* v. *American Express Bank Ltd* [2009] 2 SLR (R) 737 at paras. 65–7. See further Booysen, Chapter 10.

[60] See F.A. Mann, 'Statutes and the Conflict of Laws' (1972–3) 46 *British Yearbook of International Law* 117 at 127: 'Two questions must be clearly distinguished: does English law apply? If so, does the internal English statutory provision extend to the circumstances in issue?' See also S. Dutson, 'The Conflict of Laws and Statutes: The International Operation of Legislation Dealing with Matters of Civil Law in the United Kingdom and Australia' (1997) 60 *Modern Law Review* 668 at 673.

[61] In other respects, the Singaporean position is arguably more straightforward. For example, a bank may find reliance upon *Banking Act, supra* note 2, s 47 (Singapore) particularly attractive, as the exceptions to bank secrecy are clearly defined, in contrast to those jurisdictions that still rely upon a contractual obligation of bank secrecy, where the exceptions to that obligation are stated in a far more generalised manner: see *Tournier* v. *National Provincial and Union Bank of England, supra* note 58.

[62] For an example of legislation that was intended to apply even if the parties attempt to evade its operation by means of a choice of law clause, see the *Unfair Contract Terms Act 1977* (UK), c 50, s 27(2).

the (second) statutory interpretation question, the territorial reach of the obligation not to disclose 'customer information'[63] is defined in s 47 by reference to the fact that the obligor must be a 'bank *in Singapore*',[64] which is defined as either 'a bank incorporated in Singapore' or 'in the case of a bank incorporated outside Singapore, the branches and offices of the bank located within Singapore'.[65] Accordingly, s 47 of the Banking Act (at least on its face) purports to have both an 'outward-looking' effect (as it applies extraterritorially to Singapore-incorporated banks' dealings with customers abroad) and an 'inward-looking' effect (as it applies to the dealings of foreign-incorporated banks through branches in Singapore).

Despite the provision's clear wording, however, the 'outward-looking' effect of s 47 may well be curbed. Certainly, in a dispute between a Singaporean bank and a foreign customer heard outside Singapore, the foreign court would likely refuse to apply that provision, as it would be tantamount to the direct or indirect enforcement of a foreign penal law.[66] Indeed, a foreign court's attitude to s 47 is unlikely to change, even where the customer is also Singaporean or where the issue involves the enforcement of a Singaporean judgment against assets within that foreign court's jurisdiction.[67] Furthermore, regardless of whether the proceedings concerning the obligation of secrecy in s 47 take place in Singapore or abroad, there is a strong presumption against the extraterritorial application of legislation,[68] particularly when it is intended to have penal effect.[69] In practice, this should limit the application of s 47 to bank dealings within

---

[63] *Banking Act, supra* note 2, s 40A (Singapore).

[64] *Ibid.*, s 47 (emphasis added).

[65] *Ibid.*, s 2.

[66] *European Bank Ltd* v. *Citibank Ltd* [2004] NSWCA 76 at para. 51. For the exclusively penal nature of *Banking Act, supra* note 2, s 47 (Singapore), see *Susilawati* v. *American Express Bank Ltd, supra* note 59 at paras. 65–7. For the public policy against enforcing foreign penal laws, see, for example, *QRS 1 ApS* v. *Frandsen, supra* note 22 at 2171; *Belhaj* v. *Straw, supra* note 21 at para. 65.

[67] See generally *Attorney-General of New Zealand* v. *Ortiz, supra* note 22.

[68] See, for example, *In re Sawers, supra* note 21 at 526; *Clark* v. *Oceanic Contractors Inc, supra* note 21 at 145, 152; *Lawson* v. *Serco Ltd, supra* note 21 at para. 6; *Agassi* v. *Robinson (Inspector of Taxes), supra* note 21 at paras. 16, 20; *Al-Skeini* v. *Secretary of State for Defence, supra* note 21 at paras. 11, 44–7, 137; *Office of Fair Trading* v. *Lloyds TSB Bank plc, supra* note 21 at paras. 4, 11, 25; *Masri* v. *Consolidated Contractors International Company SAL (No 4)* [2010] AC 90 at para. 10; *Cox* v. *Ergo Versicherung AG, supra* note 19 at paras. 27–9; *Bilta (UK) Ltd* v. *Nazir (No 2)* [2016] AC 1 at paras. 212–4. See also *Walsh* v. *National Irish Bank Ltd, supra* note 4 at para. 50.

[69] See *Air-India* v. *Wiggins* [1980] 1 WLR 815 at 818; cf *In re Paramount Airways Ltd (in administration)* [1993] Ch 223 at 236–8.

Singapore, although a Singaporean court would probably be more sympathetic than its foreign counterparts to an argument involving the extraterritorial application of its own legislature's will. In contrast, recourse to s 47 is most likely to succeed when the 'inward-looking' effects of that provision are litigated before the Singaporean courts (as this would effectively be equivalent to an entirely domestic situation), although foreign courts hearing an equivalent dispute might remain concerned about the penal nature of that provision.

The conflict of laws issues are more straightforward in the increasingly usual case where the bank's duty of secrecy or confidentiality arises out of a contractual relationship.[70] While an increasing number of banking transactions (such as the provision of wealth management services to high-networth individuals[71] or the provision of information by a borrower to the arranging bank in a syndicated loan[72]) may be subject to express undertakings of confidentiality, the issue of bank secrecy has classically arisen in the context of the provision of account and associated services to retail customers and corporate clients. In this context, the bank's duty of secrecy (together with its limitations) takes the form of a term implied in law[73] into the banker-customer contract[74] arising out of the account-holding

---

[70] A duty of secrecy, confidentiality or privacy may also arise by virtue of tortious or equitable principles: see *supra* note 2. Where the duty is tortious in nature, the applicable law is determined by the *Rome II Regulation, supra* note 10, for European Union Member States or (usually) by the *lex loci delicti* or double actionability principles in other common law jurisdictions. Where the obligation is equitable in nature, there is controversy as to whether the applicable law is the *lex fori* (see T.M. Yeo, 'Choice of Law for Equity', in S. Degeling and J. Edelman (eds), *Equity in Commercial Law* (Pyrmont, NSW: Lawbook Co, 2005) at chapter 7) or the same law that would apply to tortious claims (see L. Collins (ed), *Dicey, Morris and Collins on The Conflict of Laws, supra* note 31 at paras. 34-083–34-086).

[71] *Mannesman AG v. Goldman Sachs International* (Unreported, EWHC (Ch D), 18 November 1999, Lightman J); *Primary Group (UK) Ltd v. Royal Bank of Scotland plc* [2014] EWHC 1082 (Ch) at paras. 180–260.

[72] See, for example, *United Pan-Europe Communications NV v. Deutsche Bank AG* [2000] 2 BCLC 461.

[73] *Vizcaya Partners Ltd v. Picard, supra* note 53 at para. 57.

[74] *Tournier v. National Provincial and Union Bank of England, supra* note 58. See further *Primary Group (UK) Ltd v. Royal Bank of Scotland plc, supra* note 71 at para. 180; For a detailed discussion of this implied duty and its limitations, see E.P. Ellinger, E. Lomnicka and C. Hare, *Ellinger's Modern Banking Law*, 5th edn (Oxford: Oxford University Press, 2011) at 171–207; Stanton, Chapter 12. See also *An Inspector of Taxes v. A Firm of Solicitors* [2013] IEHC 67 at para. 10; *Slattery v. Friends First Life Assurance Co Ltd, supra* note 2 at paras. 100–12, *rev'd* on a different point: [2015] IECA 149 at paras. 90–3. For a critique of the justification (given in *Tournier*) that the customer's credit depends upon a strict observance of the bank's duty of secrecy, see R. Cranston, *Principles of Banking Law, supra* note 2 at 169.

relationship.[75] Irrespective of whether the duty of secrecy or confidentiality arises by virtue of an express or implied term, a different analysis is required to the situation where the duty is statutory in nature, since concerns relating to extraterritoriality and the penal nature of the legislation are much less likely to be significant.

Assuming, therefore, that one conceives of the banker-customer relationship as creating a single debtor-creditor contract containing a number of implied terms,[76] rather than a debtor-creditor relationship with a 'number of implied superadded obligations',[77] the law applicable to that contract will determine the scope of (and exceptions to) the bank's duty of secrecy (at least to the extent of 'the private law rights and obligations of the bank and customer concerned').[78] Accordingly, the starting point is to determine whether the parties have chosen an applicable law.[79] While traditionally there was an absence of choice of law clauses in banking contracts (most usually explained on the basis that banks were content with the default choice of law rules that the courts would apply in the absence of choice,[80] considered next), this has changed significantly in recent years. Such choice of law clauses are now boiler-plate in individually negotiated, high-level financial transactions and in industry-wide standard-form

---

[75] There are other circumstances, besides the opening of a bank account, that may give rise to an implied duty of secrecy or confidentiality, such as in the context of transferable letters of credit: see *Jackson v. Royal Bank of Scotland, supra* note 15 at para. 20.

[76] *Joachimson v. Swiss Bank Corporation* [1921] 3 KB 110 at 127 (Atkin LJ).

[77] *Ibid.* at 119 (Bankes LJ). Atkin LJ's approach in *Joachimson* was subsequently preferred to that of Bankes LJ in *Tai Hing Cotton Mill Ltd v. Liu Chong Hing Bank Ltd* [1985] 2 All ER 947 at 956.

[78] *Walsh v. National Irish Bank Ltd, supra* note 4 at para. 61.

[79] The courts have been reluctant to allow the choice of a non-state law: see *Halpern v. Halpern* [2007] EWCA Civ 291. As well as an express choice of law, it is possible for the parties impliedly to choose an applicable law, where this is 'clearly demonstrated by the terms of the contract or the circumstances of the case': see *Rome I Regulation, supra* note 9, Art. 3(1). Such an implied choice may be demonstrated by the use of a particular standard-form contract associated with a particular legal system, the parties' prior course of dealing, the reference to the legal rules of a particular jurisdiction or the inclusion of a jurisdiction or arbitration clause in the contract: see, for example, *Oldendorff v. Libera Corporation* [1996] CLC 482 at 504.

[80] When there is no choice of law expressed in the agreement, the default approach is to apply the law of the branch where the customer's account is held, an approach that banks are likely to favour since it will often result in claims for repayment of overdraft facilities or loans being governed by the customer's local law where those liabilities were incurred. Accordingly, the default branch rule minimises the risk of a bank's right of repayment being in some way detrimentally affected by an unanticipated foreign law.

banking contracts.[81] More significantly for present purposes, as it becomes increasingly common for account contracts to be governed by detailed, standardised terms and conditions in the mandate document,[82] so banker-customer contracts are more frequently subjected to express choices of law (albeit that the choice is invariably imposed unilaterally by the bank requiring the customer to sign its standard terms and conditions).[83] It is not always the case, however, that the contract contains an express choice of law clause and, even when such a clause does exist, it may prove to be legally invalid,[84] insufficiently wide to cover the dispute in question or may be subject to certain controls relating to 'evasive' choices of law.[85]

In such circumstances, when there was no (effective) choice of law, the courts at common law developed default rules that would operate to determine the governing law in the absence of choice. As a customer's account is (notionally at least) held with a particular branch and his or her dealings with a bank have traditionally been effected through that branch, Staughton J, in *Libyan Arab Foreign Bank* v. *Bankers Trust Co*,[86] held that '[a]s a general rule

---

[81] See, for example, Loan Market Association, 'Senior Multicurrency Term and Revolving Facilities Agreement for Leveraged Finance Transactions' (14 June 2016).

[82] *BMP Global Distribution Inc* v. *Bank of Nova Scotia* [2009] 1 SCR 504 at paras. 47–8.

[83] See, for example, National Westminster Bank, 'NatWest Personal & Private Current Account Terms' (6 April 2016), cl. (v)–(vi), which provides that '[i]f [the customer's] address is in Scotland . . . Scots law applies to these Terms and to any overdraft made available on the account' and '[i]f your address is in England or elsewhere . . . English law applies to these Terms and to any overdraft made available on the account'. This form of clause is common among English-incorporated banks and involves a mix of branch-based and head office-based approaches to choice of law.

[84] A choice of law may be invalidated at common law on the basis that it was not 'bona fide and legal' (see *Vita Food Products Inc* v. *Unus Shipping Company Ltd* [1939] AC 277), that there was no consent to the clause or that it infringes the *Unfair Contract Terms Act 1977* (UK), *supra* note 62, or the *Consumer Rights Act 2015* (UK).

[85] *Rome I Regulation*, *supra* note 9 at Arts. 3(4), 6(2). A choice of law clause cannot be used to deprive a 'consumer' of the protections afforded by the mandatory rules of his or her habitual residence (*ibid.*, Art. 6(2)), including statutory protections afforded to the consumer's data or private information: see *Verein für Konsumenteninformation* v. *Amazon Sàrl* C-191/15 ECLI:EU:C:2016:612 at paras. 58–9. This decision would also arguably protect a consumer bringing a claim for breach of bank secrecy when his habitual residence is in a Member State that enshrines in legislation the obligation upon banks to maintain secrets. See generally *Bankers Trust International plc* v. *RCS Editori SpA* [1996] CLC 899; *Caterpillar Financial Services Corporation* v. *SNC Passion* [2004] EWHC 569 (Comm); *Emeraldian LP* v. *Wellmix Shipping Ltd* [2010] EWHC 1411 (Comm); *Spar Shipping AS* v. *Grand China Logistics Holding (Group) Co Ltd* [2015] EWHC 718 (Comm); *Banco Santander Totta SA* v. *Companhia de Carris de Ferro de Lisboa SA* [2016] EWCA Civ 1267.

[86] *Libyan Arab Foreign Bank* v. *Bankers Trust Co* [1989] QB 728 at 746. See also *Clare & Co* v. *Dresdner Bank* [1915] 2 KB 576 at 578; *X AG* v. *A Bank* [1983] 2 All ER 464.

the contract between a bank and its customer is governed by the law of the place where the account is kept, in the absence of agreement to the contrary'. This statement of principle has been confirmed on a number of occasions[87] and is based on the notion that a bank's branches should (at least for some purposes) be treated as separate entities from its head office,[88] such that a distinct and separate law should govern a particular branch's dealings with its customers. Applying the law of the particular branch to the banker-customer relationship can also be justified as according with the traditional view, established in *Joachimson v. Swiss Bank Corporation*,[89] that the bank's obligation to repay account funds only crystallises when the customer has made demand at the branch where his or her account is held and that the bank's obligation is to repay at the branch in question. Moreover, given that the customer will generally open an account with a branch in his or her own jurisdiction (and thereafter ordinarily deal with the bank through that particular branch), the application of the law of that branch (rather than the bank's head office) might be further justified as according with the reasonable expectations of the parties, particularly those of the customer who ultimately exercised a free choice to open an account with the branch in question. Indeed, such is the significance attached to this 'default branch principle' that, in *Sierra Leone Telecommunications Co Ltd v. Barclays Bank plc*,[90] Cresswell J stated that '[i]t is a rule of the greatest commercial importance, and there is a risk of grave difficulty and confusion if some other law is the governing law'. This sentiment finds echoes in the fact that the default principle to a large extent reflects the position adopted by banks in drafting their choice of law clauses.[91]

This common law default position was similarly adopted under the Rome Convention,[92] which originally determined the law applicable, in the absence of an express or implied choice, to contractual disputes commenced

---

[87] *Libyan Arab Foreign Bank v. Manufacturers Hanover Trust Co* [1988] 2 Lloyd's Rep 494 at 502; *Attock Cement Co Ltd v. Romanian Bank for Foreign Trade* [1989] 1 WLR 1147 at 1159; *Libyan Arab Foreign Bank v. Manufacturers Hanover Trust Co (No 2)* [1989] 1 Lloyd's Rep 608; *Bank of Credit & Commerce Hong Kong Ltd v. Sonali Bank* [1994] CLC 1171 at 1178; *Walsh v. National Irish Bank Ltd* [2007] IEHC 325 at paras. 26–34; *Fairfield Sentry Ltd v. Citco Bank Nederland NV* [2012] IEHC 81 at paras. 53–60.

[88] *R v. Grossman* (1981) 73 Cr App 302 at 308; *Libyan Arab Foreign Bank v. Bankers Trust Co*, *supra* note 86 at 747–8.

[89] *Joachimson v. Swiss Bank Corporation*, *supra* note 76 at 127; *Libyan Arab Foreign Bank v. Bankers Trust Co*, *supra* note 86 at 746.

[90] *Sierra Leone Telecommunications Co Ltd v. Barclays Bank plc* [1998] CLC 501 at 505.

[91] See *supra* note 83.

[92] *Convention (EC) 80/934 of 19 June 1980 on the Law Applicable to Contractual Obligations* [1980] O.J. L. 266 [*Rome Convention*].

before the courts of a European Union Member State. According to that
Convention, the default law applicable to a banking contract was 'the law
of the country with which it is most closely connected',[93] which was presumed to be 'the country where the party who is to effect the performance
which is characteristic of the contract has, at the time of conclusion of the
contract . . . in the case of a body corporate or unincorporate, its central
administration'[94] or 'where under the terms of the contract the performance is to be effected through a place of business other than the principal place of business, the country in which that other place of business is
situated'.[95] According to Cresswell J, in *Sierra Leone Telecommunications*,[96]
it is the bank that provides the characteristic performance 'in the case of
a bank account', so that, when a particular branch opens an account for a
customer, the applicable law is presumed to be the law of the place where
the branch is located. While it was possible under the Rome Convention
to displace this presumption where 'the contract is more closely connected
with another country',[97] this would only occur in circumstances where the
contract was 'predominantly connected with another country',[98] such that
it would not often be possible to displace the law of the particular branch
in favour of some other applicable law.[99] Similarly,[100] under the Rome I

---

[93] *Ibid.*, Art. 4(1).

[94] *Ibid.*, Art. 4(2).

[95] *Ibid.*

[96] *Sierra Leone Telecommunications Co Ltd* v. *Barclays Bank plc, supra* note 90 at 505. See also
Walsh v. *National Irish Bank Ltd (HC), supra* note 87 at paras. 35–7.

[97] *Rome Convention, supra* note 92, Art. 4(5).

[98] *Intercontainer Interfrigo SC (ICF)* v. *Balkenende Oosthuizen BV* [2010] QB 411 at paras. 50,
59–64; *Haeger & Schmidt GmbH* v. *MMA IARD* [2015] QB 319 at para. 23. See also *Samcrete
Egypt Engineers and Contractors SAE* v. *Land Rover Exports Ltd* [2002] EWCA Civ 2019 at
paras. 41, 45; *Gard Marine & Energy Ltd* v. *Glacier Reinsurance AG* [2010] EWCA Civ 1052
at paras. 46–7; *British Arab Commercial Bank plc* v. *Bank of Communications* [2011] EWHC
281 (Comm) at paras. 33–4; *Golden Ocean Group Ltd* v. *Salgaocar Mining Industries Pvt Ltd*
[2012] EWCA Civ 265 at paras. 52–4; *Lawlor* v. *Sandvik Mining and Construction Mobile
Crushers and Screens Ltd* [2012] EWHC 1188 (QB) at para. 16; *Deutsche Bank (Suisse) SA*
v. *Khan* [2013] EWHC 482 (Comm) at paras. 359–60; *Sax* v. *Tchernoy* [2014] EWHC 795
(Comm) at paras. 121–2; *Molton Street Capital LLP* v. *Shooters Hill Capital Partners LLP*
[2015] EWHC 3419 (Comm) at para. 93.

[99] The English courts have sometimes been overzealous in disapplying the presumptively
applicable law in the banking law context: see *Marconi Communications International Ltd*
v. *PT Pan Indonesia Bank Ltd, supra* note 15, criticised C. Hare, 'The Rome Convention and
Letters of Credit' [2005] *Lloyd's Maritime and Commercial Law Quarterly* 417.

[100] In *Molton Street Capital LLP* v. *Shooters Hill Capital Partners LLP, supra* note 98 at para.
94, Popplewell J noted, however, that '[t]he text and architecture of Article 4 of the Rome I
Regulation is very different from that of the Rome Convention'.

Regulation,[101] which has since replaced the Rome Convention and now provides the rules for choice of law in contract within the European Union, the law applicable to the account contract (unless the customer qualifies as a 'consumer')[102] is the law of the jurisdiction where the bank has its 'habitual residence',[103] which means 'the place where the branch . . . is located' in circumstances '[w]here the contract is concluded in the course of the operations of a branch'.[104] Moreover, this presumptive position can only be departed from 'where it is *clear* that the connection is *manifestly* closer to [another] country',[105] which, on the current approach at least, would be rather rare in the banking context.[106]

Accordingly, whether one applies the English choice of law rules at common law or under the harmonised European regime, the law applicable to the bank's duty of secrecy, in the absence of choice, is (and always has been) *prima facie* the law of the place where the relevant branch is located. Despite the apparent dominance of this 'default branch principle', it is submitted that, as its origins are arguably faulty[107] and as it is

---

[101] *Rome I Regulation, supra* note 9.

[102] A 'consumer' for these purposes means a 'natural person' who concludes a contract falling 'outside his trade or profession' with another 'acting in the exercise of his trade or profession': see *Rome I Regulation, supra* note 9, Art. 6(1). A customer falling within this definition would be entitled to commence proceedings against his or her bank in the jurisdiction of the former's habitual residence provided that the bank 'pursues [its] commercial or professional activities in the country where the consumer has his habitual residence' or the bank 'by any means, directs such activities to that country or to several countries including [the country of the consumer's habitual residence]': *ibid.*, Art. 6(1)(a)–(b). This latter requirement will be satisfied if the bank has a branch in the place of the customer's habitual residence, which will often be the case as a consumer is likely to open his or her account with the local branch. This means that the consumer provisions of the *Rome I Regulation, supra* note 9, are likely to point towards the location of a particular bank's branch as being the jurisdictionally relevant place. It is important to note, however, that not all personal bank accounts will attract the operation of these consumer jurisdiction provisions.

[103] Assuming that an account contract is a 'contract for the provision of services', Art. 4(1)(a) provides that the contract should be governed by the law of the country where the service provider (in other words, the bank) has its 'habitual residence'. Even if this provision were not to apply, Art. 4(2) would lead to the same result, as the bank would be providing the 'characteristic performance': see *Sierra Leone Telecommunications Co Ltd* v. *Barclays Bank plc, supra* note 90 at 505.

[104] *Rome I Regulation, supra* note 9, Art. 19(2).

[105] *Molton Street Capital LLP* v. *Shooters Hill Capital Partners LLP, supra* note 98 at para. 94.

[106] L. Collins (ed), *Dicey, Morris and Collins on The Conflict of Laws, supra* note 31 at para. 33-308.

[107] The foundational common law decisions supporting the 'default branch principle' (namely, *Libyan Arab Foreign Bank* v. *Bankers Trust Co, supra* note 86; *Libyan Arab Foreign Bank* v. *Manufacturers Hanover Trust Co, supra* note 87; *Libyan Arab Foreign Bank* v. *Manufacturers Hanover Trust Co (No 2), supra* note 87) concerned the impact of a US freezing order on funds deposited with English branches of foreign banks. As this might be conceived as a

nowadays increasingly an anachronism,[108] there are strong justifications for its abandonment. That is not to say that the location of the customer's particular branch should be irrelevant to ascertaining the account contract's (and duty of secrecy's) applicable law (and, indeed, it will continue to be largely determinative where the Rome regime applies[109]), but rather that the weight accorded to the branch's location ought to be lessened, so that it is neither the presumptive starting point nor the automatic end-result. In essence, the location of the customer's branch should simply be one connecting factor among many, its precise weight depending upon the particular circumstances. In this regard, the normative argument for abandoning the 'default branch principle' can be put in either of two ways: the broader, more radical suggestion is that the law of the branch's place of business should no longer operate as the default choice of law rule for *any aspect* of the banker-customer contract; the narrower, more limited suggestion is that, while that default rule might continue to apply to the banker-customer contract in general, there are additional considerations peculiar to the bank's duty of secrecy that justify adopting a different approach to that issue by a process akin to *dépeçage*.[110] Support for a more fact-sensitive and less rigid approach to choice of law in this context may be derived from comments in *Walsh* v. *National Irish Bank Ltd*, where, in the context of deciding the law applicable to the account relationship between a customer and the Manx branch of an Irish bank, Clarke J stated:

> It may well be that many, indeed possibly all, of the relevant banking contracts, have, as their proper law, the law of the Isle of Man, although it is possible that, in all the circumstances, and particularly where a relevant

---

proprietary (rather than a contractual) issue, the emphasis on the 'default branch principle' for choice of law purposes could be explained as little more than the application of the *lex situs* principle to bank accounts (although this suggestion has itself become problematic in light of subsequent developments: see *Raiffeisen Zentralbank Österreich* v. *Five Star Trading LLC* [2001] 1 QB 825; *The Republic of the Philippines* v. *Maler Foundation*, *supra* note 22 at para. 92). On a proprietary analysis, these cases should not be interpreted as establishing a presumptive rule for choice of law in contract.

[108] The leading decisions establishing the 'default branch principle' (see *supra* note 107) were all decided before the advent of the Internet and modern methods of communication and conducting business. That said, in *Fairfield Sentry Ltd* v. *Citco Bank Nederland NV*, *supra* note 87 at paras. 53–60, Geoghehan J in the Irish High Court accepted the continued validity of the 'default branch principle' in the internet age.

[109] Although the *Rome I Regulation* applies in the United Kingdom at the time of writing, the referendum vote to leave the European Union on 23 June 2016 may provide an opportunity for thinking afresh about the current English approach to choice of law in banking disputes.

[110] See, for example, *Rome I Regulation*, *supra* note 9, Art. 3(1).

customer is Irish resident, the banking contract concerned might be governed by Irish law.[111]

Just as there might be strong reasons for disapplying the 'default branch principle' in circumstances where the customer happens to be resident in the same jurisdiction as the bank's head office, there might also be an equally strong argument for falling back onto some other law (such as that of the place where the bank has its central administration) in circumstances where the customer has a number of accounts with different branches of the bank located in different jurisdictions. Unfortunately, in *Libyan Arab Foreign Bank* v. *Bankers Trust Co*,[112] Staughton J preferred the somewhat strained notion that the bank's relationship with a customer who held accounts in London and New York involved a single contract with different aspects being governed, respectively, by English and New York law.[113] Even if it were possible to achieve a similar result on the current wording of the *Rome I Regulation*,[114] its artificiality merely strengthens the case for reducing the reliance upon the location of the branch as the default position for choice of law purposes.

More generally, the principal justifications for the 'default branch principle' no longer appear as convincing as they might once have been. First, the reliance for this default rule upon the notion of legal separation between a bank's various branches and its head office has been gradually eroded – in *Walsh* v. *National Irish Bank Ltd*,[115] the Irish Supreme Court made clear that the courts would only maintain the distinction when it was appropriate to do so (although the court gave little guidance as to when that might be the case). Indeed, it must be stressed that the notion of branch separation in the banking law context is even more artificial than the equivalent principle that applies to subsidiaries in the context of corporate groups.[116] Unlike a subsidiary company, which has a distinct legal personality that separates that entity from its directors and shareholders, thereby shielding

---

[111] *Walsh* v. *National Irish Bank Ltd, supra* note 4 at para. 53.

[112] *Libyan Arab Foreign Bank* v. *Bankers Trust Co, supra* note 86 at 747.

[113] While the 'single contract' approach is consistent with the orthodox view concerning the nature of the banker-customer account relationship in *Joachimson* v. *Swiss Bank Corporation, supra* note 76 at 127, it is unclear whether this view can be said to accord with either the parties' expectations or commercial reality.

[114] For the view that this is not possible, see L. Collins (ed), *Dicey, Morris and Collins on The Conflict of Laws, supra* note 31 at para. 33-307.

[115] *Walsh* v. *National Irish Bank Ltd, supra* note 4 at para. 30. See also *Libyan Arab Foreign Bank* v. *Bankers Trust Co, supra* note 86 at 748.

[116] See generally *Adams* v. *Cape Industries plc, supra* note 28.

a parent company from liabilities incurred by its subsidiary, a branch has never been treated as a separate legal person from the rest of the bank. Rather than being automatically afforded the liability-shielding and asset-partitioning protections associated with a full-blown separate legal personality,[117] the bank as an entity is generally liable for the contractual and tortious obligations incurred by its authorised agents, regardless of whether those agents happen to be working at branch or head-office level. Similarly, English law makes the bank's head office ultimately responsible for the repayment of deposits made with a particular branch following that branch's closure[118] (although US banks may be liable for branch deposits without the branch needing first to close[119]), and the bank's head office is entitled to combine a customer's accounts even if they are held at different branches.[120] Equally, when it comes to applying conflict of laws principles to the network of bank branches, the notion of separation between a bank head office and its branches comes under strain. As discussed previously,[121] a customer or other third party claimant, who has been dealing with a particular bank branch, can normally bring proceedings against the bank in the jurisdiction where that branch is located and, indeed, may sometimes even have the option of commencing proceedings in a number of different jurisdictions where the defendant bank's other branches are located. In such circumstances, it is not just the branch that is subject to the relevant jurisdiction, but the entire bank as a legal entity. Indeed, as Staughton J accepted in *Libyan Arab Bank* v. *Bankers Trust Co*,[122] if

---

[117] While the separate corporate personality principle does not operate as a default rule to protect the head office from depositor claims, banks can include a 'ring-fencing' clause in their account contracts stipulating that repayment of funds will only be effected at the counters of the relevant branch: see *Libyan Arab Foreign Bank* v. *Manufacturers Hanover Trust Co (No 2)*, supra note 87; *Wells Fargo Asia Ltd* v. *Citibank NA*, 936 F. 2d 723 (2d Cir., 1991).

[118] *R* v. *Lovitt* [1912] AC 212 at 219; *Sokoloff* v. *National City Bank*, 224 NYS 102 (1927), aff'd 227 NYS 907, aff'd 164 NE 745 (1928). See also *Lloyd Royal Belge Société Anonyme* v. *L Dreyfus & Co* (1927) Lloyd's LR 288; *Richardson* v. *Richardson* [1927] All ER Rep 92, explaining *Leader, Plunkett & Leader* v. *Direction der Disconto-Gesellschaft* (1914) 31 TLR 83, rev'd [1915] 3 KB 154. See further W. Blair, 'Liability for Foreign Branch Deposits in English Law', in R. Cranston (ed), *Making Commercial Law: Essays in Honour of Roy Goode* (Oxford: Oxford University Press, 1997) at chapter 13.

[119] *Vishipco Line* v. *Chase Manhattan Bank*, 660 F. 2d 854 (2d Cir., 1981); *Garcia* v. *Chase Manhattan Bank*, 735 F. 2d 645 (2d Cir., 1984); *Wells Fargo Asia Ltd* v. *Citibank NA*, supra note 117.

[120] *Garnett* v. *M'Kewan* (1872) LR 8 Ex 10 at 13–4. See also *Good Property Land Development Pte Ltd* v. *Société Genérale* [1996] 2 SLR 239 at 249–50; *Pertamina Energy Trading Ltd* v. *Crédit Suisse* [2006] 4 SLR 273 at para. 43.

[121] See Section 3.2.1.

[122] *Libyan Arab Foreign Bank* v. *Bankers Trust Co*, supra note 86 at 748.

judgment is secured against a bank in a jurisdiction where a branch is located, that judgment can be enforced against *all* the bank's assets, not just against the assets of the particular branch in question. Moreover, as will be discussed subsequently,[123] the courts have sometimes been prepared (albeit cautiously) to collapse the distinction between a bank's head office and its branches when it comes to taking evidence abroad or producing evidence in support of foreign proceedings.

Secondly, the justification for the 'default branch principle', based upon the notion that demand and repayment of account funds must be made at the particular branch where the account is kept, is increasingly at odds with modern banking practice. As well as the fact that demand is not necessary in relation to all types of account[124] or in all circumstances,[125] the requirement that a demand for repayment must be made at the branch where the current account is located is nowadays, more often than not, overridden by contrary agreement.[126] This is usually the explanation for banks permitting their customers to withdraw cash from the ATMs of other branches or banks, or enabling customers to pay for purchases by debit card. More dramatically, in *Damayanti Kantilal Doshi* v. *Indian Bank*,[127] the Singapore Court of Appeal went much further, suggesting that the principle requiring demand at the customer's own branch was nowadays obsolete *as a matter of law*, not just banking practice, in the light of technological developments.

Thirdly, to the extent that the 'default branch principle' was based in any way upon customer expectations regarding their likely dealings with their bank, it probably no longer reflects the course of the modern bank-customer relationship. This is largely the consequence of the increasingly remote banking relationship that results from customers' use of internet and mobile phone banking,[128] and their ability to withdraw any cash

---

[123] See Section 3.3.

[124] For the position regarding fixed deposits maturing at a predetermined date, see *Standard Chartered Bank* v. *Tiong Ngit Ting* [1998] 5 MLJ 220 at 228; *Damayanti Kantilal Doshi* v. *Indian Bank* [1999] 4 SLR 1 at paras. 44–5.

[125] No demand by the customer is needed to withdraw funds from an account when the bank is wound up: see *Re Russian Commercial and Industrial Bank* [1955] 1 Ch 148; *Proven Development Sdn Bhd* v. *Hong Kong and Shanghai Banking Corporation* [1998] 6 MLJ 150 at 155. That said, a demand may still be required when deposits have been nationalised or expropriated: see *Lazard Brothers* v. *Midland Bank Ltd* [1932] 1 KB 617 at 667.

[126] *Bank of Scotland* v. *Seitz* (1990) SLT 584 at 590.

[127] *Damayanti Kantilal Doshi* v. *Indian Bank*, *supra* note 124 at para. 28.

[128] Consider United Kingdom Competition and Markets Authority, *Retail Banking Market Investigation: Summary of Final Report*, 9 August 2016.

required from a network of ATMs, other than an ATM based at their own branch. The modern reality is that customers, unless they happen to be high-net-worth individuals targeted for wealth management services, rarely have any need to enter a branch and rarely have any face-to-face contact with bank employees there. This trend is reflected in the structure of the retail banking market (at least in the United Kingdom) where the large 'high street' banks have engaged in a significant programme of branch closures; where competitors for banking services (such as the Post Office, department stores and supermarkets) have increasingly developed other points of contact with customers (such as in-store kiosks); and where there is increased competition from 'online banks' without any physical presence or branches. Indeed, to the extent that there is still personal contact with banks, it is increasingly via chat functions operating through online banking or mobile phone applications or via call centres outsourced to jurisdictions in which employees can be hired at a fraction of the cost of the bank's home jurisdiction. In this respect, the arm's-length manner in which banks deal with their personal customers nowadays is to a large degree the way in which banks have dealt with corporate and commercial customers for some time, since these latter customers tend to deal directly with the head office, a number of different branches or a particular department within the bank (such as the trade finance department).

While the above factors undermine the application of the 'default branch principle' to all aspects of the banker-customer contract, there are additional factors that make it even more inappropriate nowadays to adopt such an approach with respect to the bank's contractual duty of secrecy to its customer. First, where a customer deals with a bank by phone or through the chat function on the bank's website, the call centre employees/chat operatives may well access the customer's bank information in a jurisdiction (frequently India) that is far removed from the bank's head office or branches. On this basis, there may be a credible argument that the scope of the bank's duty of secrecy to its customer should accordingly be determined by reference to the laws of the jurisdiction where the call centre/chat operatives are located, rather than by the law of a branch that the customer may never have visited. Not only does this accord with the manner in which the customer's bank information is accessed, but it also accords with the basic notion that a commercial entity seeking to take the advantages of establishment in a particular jurisdiction (such as, for example, cheap labour) should also abide by the legal limitations associated with conducting business in that place. The position is *a fortiori* when there is no human intermediation whatsoever, such as when a customer accesses his account through internet or mobile banking. Secondly, however the customer chooses to access its account information, the commercial reality is that customer information is no longer physically recorded in bank ledgers that are held at a particular branch, but instead the data are stored electronically. Certainly, in *Libyan Arab Bank* v. *Bankers Trust Co*, Staughton J appeared to accept that the electronic storage of information might be a factor in reducing the significance of the branch as the touchstone for determining the law applicable to the banker-customer contract and the duty of secrecy in the absence of choice:

> In the age of the computer it may not be strictly accurate to speak of the branch where the account is kept. Banks no longer have books in which they write entries; they have terminals by which they give instructions; and the computer itself with its magnetic tape, floppy disc or some other device may be physically located elsewhere. Nevertheless it should not be difficult to decide where an account is kept for this purpose.[129]

Now that devices such as magnetic tape and floppy discs have been replaced by centralised computer databases storing all customer information (and located either at the bank's head office or, increasingly commonly, at special off-site secure facilities or data centres), the position is *a fortiori*, since it will no longer necessarily be possible to locate any physical device at a particular branch on which customer information is stored. Indeed, the dematerialisation and delocalisation of customer information has continued apace with the advent of 'cloud computing'[130] in the banking world,[131] since, with the appropriate passwords and access rights, account-related information can be accessed from a computer terminal located anywhere in the world. While the Irish High Court, in *Walsh* v. *National Irish Bank Ltd*,[132] suggested recently that the 'default branch principle' should be retained, despite the move from branch ledgers to centralised data storage and computing networks, it is difficult to see how this can be correct, whether from a customer-expectation perspective (as they would probably expect their information to be protected by the laws

---

[129] *Libyan Arab Foreign Bank* v. *Bankers Trust Co*, *supra* note 86 at 746.

[130] 'Cloud computing' has been defined judicially as 'the capacity of Internet-connected devices to display data stored on remote servers rather than on the device itself': see *Riley* v. *California*, 134 S. Ct. 2473 at 2491 (2014).

[131] See, for example, 'Silver Linings', *The Economist*, 20 July 2013. See also P. Crosman, 'Why Banks are Finally Embracing Cloud Computing', *American Banker*, 12 August 2013; 'Six Reasons Why Cloud Computing will Transform the Way Banks Serve Clients', *Banking Technology*, 28 July 2014.

[132] *Walsh* v. *National Irish Bank Ltd (HC)*, *supra* note 87 at para. 26.

where the bank's central computer system or local data centres are located
or where the information is readily accessed by the bank's call centre or
other employees) or from a bank-efficiency perspective (as the bank's
position would probably be made immeasurably more straightforward if it
did not have to juggle a multitude of different laws applicable to its duty of
secrecy). Accordingly, the courts in England and abroad should, in appropriate circumstances, be entitled to ignore the 'default branch principle' in
favour of more suitable alternative connecting factors, whether the location of the bank's head office, its data storage facility or its call centre, to
determine the law applicable to banks' secrecy obligations.

There is one final point worth noting. Even if there is no stomach at
present to downgrade the 'default branch principle' itself,[133] there are nevertheless other mechanisms currently available to the courts whereby they
can apply a different law to the dispute before them, other than the law
of the relevant bank branch. These techniques could enable a progressive
court to achieve a functionally equivalent result to that suggested above.
Accordingly, even where a foreign law is applicable to a dispute pending
before it, a court may displace the applicable law entirely if that would contravene the forum's public policy,[134] or the court may overlay the applicable
law with any 'overriding mandatory provisions of the law of the forum',[135]
which (at least for the purposes of the *Rome I Regulation*) are defined as
'provisions the respect for which is regarded as crucial by a country for
safeguarding its public interests, such as its political, social or economic
organization'.[136] Even more significantly for the purposes of the present
analysis is that the *Rome I Regulation* has now introduced the concept of a
'third state mandatory rule', whereby a court may apply the overriding provisions 'of the law of the country where the obligations arising out of the
contract have to be or have been performed'.[137] The concept of the 'third
state mandatory rule' could well be used by a court that was so minded
to displace some or all of the law of the relevant bank branch in favour of
the law of the bank's head office, computer storage facility or call centre, as
considered appropriate.

---

[133] Banks may be concerned, for example, about whether the application of a law, other than
the law of the branch where the account is held, may make the recovery of overdrafts and
loans more difficult: see *supra* note 80.
[134] See, for example, *Rome I Regulation, supra* note 9, Art. 21.
[135] *Ibid.*, Art. 9(2).
[136] *Ibid.*, Art. 9(1). Consider *Régie Nationale des Usines Renault SA* v. *Maxicar SpA*, C-38/98
[2000] ECR I-2973.
[137] *Rome I Regulation, supra* note 9, Art. 9(3).

3.3 Bank Secrecy and the Conflict of Laws in Third Party Disclosure Requests

Where proceedings arise between a customer and his or her bank, as stated previously,[138] one of the motivations behind choosing one jurisdiction over another may be the more extensive forms of discovery available against the other party. In England at least, discovery can be extensive since no distinction is made between the disclosure of documents within and without the jurisdiction provided they are within the possession, custody or power of the defendant bank.[139] The position is more complicated, however, when a bank is not party to the proceedings, but a claimant wishes to obtain a third party disclosure order against that bank, as a non-party, on the basis that it possesses account-related information or has custody of account documents needed to bring or strengthen the claimant's case. In such cases, it will be important to commence the proceedings in a jurisdiction to which the third party bank is amenable for the purposes of obtaining the necessary disclosure. Whether this is possible is a conflict of laws question answered by applying the jurisdictional rules considered above.[140] Assuming the court has international jurisdiction over the matter, the nature and extent of third party disclosure available is purely a matter for the domestic procedural law of the court seized of the main proceedings.

In that regard, the English principles regulating third party disclosure provide a good sense of the broad range of coercive powers frequently available to courts in different jurisdictions,[141] although clearly there is little uniformity in that regard. For example, where proceedings are pending in England, Part 34 of the Civil Procedure Rules 1998 (CPR 1998) introduced the power on the part of the English courts to issue a 'witness summons' requiring a witness (including potentially a bank) to attend court to give evidence or to produce documents to the court.[142] Moreover, the CPR

---

[138] See Section 3.2.1.

[139] R.G. Toulson and C.M. Phipps, *Confidentiality, supra* note 36 at para. 10-004. It is also irrelevant that the information relates to foreign transactions: see *Clinch* v. *Inland Revenue Commissioners* [1974] QB 76.

[140] See Section 3.2.1.

[141] For detailed analysis of the various common law and statutory forms of compulsory disclosure in England, see A. Malek and J. Odgers (eds), *Paget's Law of Banking*, 14th edn (London: LexisNexis, 2014) at chapter 33.

[142] *Civil Procedure Rules 1998, supra* note 29, r 34.2(1). See also *Assistant Deputy Coroner for Inner West London* v. *Channel 4 Television Corporation* [2007] EWHC 2513 (QB) at paras. 3–4; *JSC Mezhdunarodniy Promyshlenniy Bank* v. *Pugachev* [2015] EWCA Civ 139 at para. 55; *Bromfield* v. *Bromfield* [2015] UKPC 19 at para. 26.

1998 introduced a new procedure whereby a claimant,[143] who has already commenced the substantive proceedings, may obtain documentary disclosure from non-parties.[144] Where proceedings are intended, but not yet commenced, the English courts, pursuant to the jurisdiction recognised in *Norwich Pharmacal Co* v. *Customs & Excise Comrs*,[145] may compel a bank to make pre-action disclosure of its customer's confidential information to a third party who requires that information in order to be able to commence proceedings against the customer. This type of order is particularly useful when a claimant is attempting to trace the proceeds of a fraud through one or more of the defendant's bank accounts and requires details of those accounts' operations in order to complete that exercise successfully.[146] Finally, beyond these general bases for third-party bank disclosure, there is

---

[143] The term 'claimant' is used in preference to that of 'plaintiff' due to the change in terminology introduced by the *Civil Procedure Rules 1998, supra* note 29.

[144] *Civil Procedure Rules 1998, supra* note 29, r 31.17. See generally *American Home Products* v. *Novartis* [2001] EWCA Civ 165; *Three Rivers DC* v. *Bank of England (No 4)* [2002] 4 All ER 881; *Tajik Aluminium Plant* v. *Hydro Aluminium AS* [2005] EWCA Civ 1218; *Ixis Corporate and Investment Bank* v. *WestLB AG* [2007] EWHC 1852 (Comm); *Flood* v. *Times Newspapers Ltd* [2009] EWHC 411 (QB); *Fanmailuk.com Ltd* v. *Cooper* [2010] EWHC 2647 (Ch); *Lampert* v. *Lloyds TSB Bank plc* [2012] EWHC 2312 (Ch); *Global Energy Horizons Corporation* v. *Gray* [2014] EWHC 2925 (Ch); *B* v. *Goldsmith Williams Solicitors* [2014] EWHC 4520 (Ch).

[145] *Norwich Pharmacal Co* v. *Customs & Excise Comrs* [1974] AC 133 at 175–6, 182, 188, 190, 199; *British Steel Corporation* v. *Granada Television Ltd* [1981] AC 1096 at 1175, 1197, 1200; *X Ltd* v. *Morgan-Grampian (Publishers) Ltd* [1991] 1 AC 1 at 54; *Ashworth Hospital Authority* v. *MGN Ltd* [2002] 1 WLR 2033 at paras. 2, 36, 57, 66; *R* v. *Secretary of State for Foreign and Commonwealth Affairs (No 1)* [2009] 1 WLR 2579 at para. 94; *Rugby Football Union* v. *Consolidated Information Services Ltd* [2012] UKSC 55 at paras. 14–8. In *Koo Golden East Mongolia* v. *Bank of Nova Scotia* [2007] EWCA Civ 1443 at para. 37, Sir Anthony Clarke MR described the situation where a bank account holds the proceeds of wrongful activity as being the 'classic case' for *Norwich Pharmacal* relief against a bank. Nevertheless, the Court of Appeal (at para. 49) emphasised that '[a] court should be very reluctant to make a *Norwich Pharmacal* order which involves a breach of confidence as between a bank and its customer'. Where a *Norwich Pharmacal* order is made, the bank's obligation is to provide 'full information', so that the bank must potentially disclose its customer's personal details and any information relating to its involvement in the commission of the relevant wrong: see *RCA* v. *Reddingtons Rare Records* [1974] 1 WLR 1445. For the equivalent position in Singapore, see *UMCI Ltd* v. *Tokyo Marine & Fire Insurance Co (Singapore) Pte Ltd* [2006] 4 SLR(R) 95; *Michael* v. *World Sport Group Pte Ltd* [2014] 2 SLR 208; *La Doce Vita Fine Dining Co Ltd* v. *Deutsche Bank AG* [2016] SGHCR 3.

[146] See generally *Bankers Trust Co* v. *Shapira* [1980] 1 WLR 1274; *Arab Monetary Fund* v. *Hashim (No 5)* [1992] 2 All ER 911. For recent applications in the tracing context, see *Santander UK plc* v. *National Westminster Bank plc* [2014] EWHC 2626 (Ch); *Santander UK plc* v. *Royal Bank of Scotland plc* [2015] EWHC 2560 (Ch); *BDW Trading Ltd* v. *Fitzpatrick* [2015] EWHC 3490 (Ch); *Ramilos Trading Ltd* v. *Buyanovsky* [2016] EWHC 3175 (Comm).

a plethora of narrower statutory bases.[147] Whichever of the various afore-mentioned bases of disclosure is used, the Bankers' Books Evidence Act 1879 (BBEA 1879) establishes a special procedure for producing evidence of a person's bank account to a court.[148] This procedure was originally introduced to avoid the inconvenience caused to banks by the common law rule that the *originals* of bank ledgers and books had to be physically produced to the court by a bank employee.[149] Accordingly, the BBEA 1879 renders *copies* of any entry in a 'banker's book' admissible as evidence 'in all legal proceedings'[150] against any party to the proceedings (including the party who has called for the copies),[151] and provides that such copies are to be received as *prima facie* evidence of the relevant entry and any matters recorded therein.

The operation of the above principles, however, assumes two key matters: first, that the third party bank is amenable to the court's personal jurisdiction and, secondly, that the information and/or documents are within the territorial jurisdiction of the relevant court. Where either assumption is falsified, the position is much more complex for litigants, since courts are generally reluctant either to order domestic banks to disclose customer information in support of foreign proceedings or to request such disclosure from a foreign court or bank in support of domestic proceedings.[152] In that regard, there are broadly two routes by which a claimant can seek to obtain such information or evidence. First, if the relevant bank does not

---

[147] See, for example, *Police and Criminal Evidence Act 1984* (UK), c 60, s 9; *Companies Act 1985* (UK), c 6, ss 431–453D; *Insolvency Act 1986* (UK), c 45, s 235; *Criminal Justice Act 1987* (UK), c 38, s 2; *Terrorism Act 2000* (UK), c 11, ss 15–8, 21A; *Proceeds of Crime Act 2002* (UK), c 29, s 330; *Income Tax Act 2007* (UK), c 3, s 748.

[148] It is clear that the *Bankers' Books Evidence Act 1879* (UK), c 11, and its foreign equivalents do not provide an independent basis for disclosure against banks, but merely deal with *how* disclosure should occur once the court has dealt with the 'logical prior question' of *whether* disclosure should be ordered: see *La Doce Vita Fine Dining Co Ltd v. Deutsche Bank AG, supra* note 145 at para. 91.

[149] *Wheatley v. Commissioner of Police of the British Virgin Islands* [2006] 2 Cr App Rep 21 at para. 14. See also *Wee Soon Kim Anthony v. UBS AG* [2003] 2 SLR (R) 91 at para. 17; *La Doce Vita Fine Dining Co Ltd v. Deutsche Bank AG, supra* note 145 at para. 86.

[150] According to the *Bankers' Books Evidence Act 1879* (UK), *supra* note 148, s 10, the notion of proceedings includes 'any civil or criminal proceeding or inquiry in which evidence is or may be given' and arbitration, but not a commission of inquiry: see *Douglas v. Pindling* [1996] AC 890 at 901. See also *La Doce Vita Fine Dining Co Ltd v. Deutsche Bank AG, supra* note 148 at paras. 95–6.

[151] *Harding v. Williams* (1880) 14 Ch D 197.

[152] It is precisely because attempts to obtain disclosure against foreign banks are so fraught with legal difficulty that it is important for litigants to position themselves jurisdictionally at the outset, so as to secure the necessary third party evidence to support their case.

have any presence in the jurisdiction where the proceedings in question are taking place, or if the bank does have a branch in that jurisdiction, but the evidence is held abroad at the bank's head office or relates to foreign banking operations, then the claimant may apply (at least in England) for 'letters of request' or 'letters rogatory'. This procedure involves the court before which proceedings are pending (the requesting court) sending a request to the foreign court where the relevant banking records are maintained (the requested court) for the production of those records. As the 'letters of request' procedure depends upon the requested court's assistance, it enables the requesting court to obtain the relevant information without committing, directly or indirectly, any infringement of the other jurisdiction's sovereignty, and is accordingly largely unobjectionable. Secondly, and much more problematically, if the foreign bank that holds the relevant information has a branch within the jurisdiction where the proceedings are taking place, then the claimant may apply to the court that is hearing the dispute for a witness summons that can then be served on the bank officers at the branch within the jurisdiction.[153] The witness summons effectively orders those bank officers to testify in court or produce documents (wherever they might be located) to the court. This type of order is frequently problematic, however, as the bank may face the unenviable choice between being held in contempt of court if it defies the witness summons or being liable to its customer if obeying the witness summons would infringe bank secrecy in the jurisdiction where the information is held.

The following sections consider in particular the approach of the English courts and English law to such requests for information, albeit that comparative material will be considered where appropriate. Unsurprisingly, the English courts have adopted a different approach according to whether the information or evidence is being sought from an English bank in support of proceedings abroad or whether an English court is seeking equivalent information from a foreign bank in support of English proceedings. Both situations will be considered in turn.

3.3.1   Evidence Sought in England in
Support of Foreign Proceedings

As regards the first route mentioned previously, namely the 'letters of request' procedure, where another European Union Member State (except

---

[153] *Civil Procedure Rules 1998, supra* note 29, r 34.2(1).

Denmark) requests evidence in the United Kingdom in relation to a 'civil or commercial matter',[154] then the position is governed by Council Regulation (EC) 1206/2001 on the Co-operation between Member States in the Taking of Evidence in Civil or Commercial Matters (Regulation 1206/2001).[155] The request must relate to evidence that is intended for use in judicial proceedings,[156] must be transmitted directly to the competent court in the United Kingdom[157] and must be in the prescribed form.[158] The requested court in the United Kingdom must acknowledge receipt of the request within seven days,[159] unless the request is incomplete or in an incorrect form,[160] and must execute the request in accordance with its own procedural laws within ninety days of its receipt.[161] In that regard, the requesting court cannot generally question the procedures adopted by the requested court[162] (although where the evidence in question is supplied by a witness providing evidence directly to the requesting court, this must be effected in

---

[154] Consider *In re New Cap Reinsurance Corporation Ltd* [2012] Ch 538 at paras. 42–7. For requests for assistance from foreign courts in criminal matters, see *Crime (International Co-operation) Act 2003* (UK), c 32, ss 13–5. This may be relevant to the present context if a bank regulator or data protection authority is seeking to impose criminal or regulatory penalties on a bank for breaches of the duty of secrecy or other infringements. For assistance in the liquidation context, see *Singularis Holdings Ltd* v. *PricewaterhouseCoopers* [2015] AC 1675.

[155] *European Evidence Regulation, supra* note 20, Art. 1(1). It is mandatory to follow the procedures in the Regulation where the order made in one Member State affects 'the powers of the [other] Member State', but otherwise a Member State may rely upon its own national procedural laws when seeking evidence in another Member State: see *Masri* v. *Consolidated Contractors International Co SAL (No 4), supra* note 36 at paras. 38–54, *rev'd* on a different issue: [2010] AC 90; *ProRail BV* v. *Xpedys NV*, C-332/11 [2013] IL Pr 18 at paras. 37–53; *National Grid Electricity Transmission plc* v. *ABB Ltd* [2013] EWHC 822 (Ch) at paras. 50–7; *Secretary of State for Health* v. *Servier Laboratories Ltd, supra* note 36 at paras. 99–104, 111–6.

[156] *European Evidence Regulation, supra* note 20, Art. 1(2). See *Re MF Global UK Ltd* [2015] EWHC 2319 (Ch) at paras. 37–41.

[157] *European Evidence Regulation, supra* note 20, Art. 2(1). A requesting court can take evidence directly without the assistance of the requested court, but this procedure is not available where coercive measures are necessary: *ibid.*, Art. 17.

[158] *Ibid.*, Art. 4. There is no obligation on the requesting court to pay an advance to the requested court for the witness' expenses: see *Werynski* v. *Mediatel 4B Spólka z o.o.*, C-283/09 [2012] QB 66 at paras. 47–69.

[159] *European Evidence Regulation, supra* note 20, Art. 7(1).

[160] *Ibid.*, Art. 8(1). The requested court must inform the requesting court of any incompleteness within thirty days.

[161] *Ibid.*, Art. 10. The foreign litigants and/or their representatives can request to be present when the evidence is taken in the United Kingdom: *ibid.*, Arts. 11–2.

[162] *Breslin* v. *Murphy* [2013] NICA 75 at paras. 65–6.

accordance with the procedural laws of that court).[163] Moreover, a requested court in the United Kingdom can decline a request that a particular person give evidence if that person is entitled to refuse to do so by virtue of either English law or the law of the requesting court.[164] Arguably, this provision would entitle an English bank to resist a request for evidence from the court of another European Union Member State on the ground that compliance would infringe the duty of secrecy owed to one of its customers.

In contrast, where the requesting court is not located in another Member State, any letter of request is governed by the Hague Convention on the Taking of Evidence Abroad in Civil or Commercial Matters 1970,[165] and, where the requested court is in the United Kingdom, the position is governed by the Evidence (Proceedings in Other Jurisdictions) Act 1975. Indeed, this legislation provides the *only* basis upon which an English court can deal with such a letter of request from a non-EU requesting court.[166] Where such a request is made, comity requires that the English court trust to the requesting court's judgement as to what evidence is relevant to the foreign proceedings,[167] and accordingly requires the court to accede to the request in a pragmatic and timeous manner, unless there is good reason not to do so.[168] That said, there are statutory limitations upon an English

---

[163] *Lippens v. Kortekaas*, C-170/11 [2012] IL Pr 42 at para. 39. For the situation where the evidence is actually to be taken in the foreign jurisdiction, consider *ProRail BV v. Xpedys NV*, supra note 155 at paras. 37–53.

[164] *European Evidence Regulation, supra* note 20, Art. 14(1).

[165] *Hague Evidence Convention, supra* note 20.

[166] *Re Pan American Airways Inc's Application* [1992] QB 854; *Smith v. Philip Morris Companies Inc* [2006] EWHC 916 (QB) at para. 30; *R (on the application of Omar) v. Secretary of State for Foreign and Commonwealth Affairs* [2014] QB 112 at paras. 22–3; *Ramilos Trading Ltd v. Buyanovsky, supra* note 146 at paras. 111–34; cf *Tchenguiz v. Director of the Serious Fraud Office* [2014] EWHC 2379 (Comm) at paras. 21–2. The legislative scheme displaces any inherent jurisdiction that the English courts might previously have possessed to assist foreign courts in obtaining evidence: see *Goncharova v. Zolotova* [2015] EWHC 3061 (QB) at para. 38.

[167] A court also exercises a discretion as to the most appropriate manner in which the evidence can be furnished: see *Evidence (Proceedings in Other Jurisdictions) Act 1975* (UK), c 34, s 2(2). See also *Breslin v. Murphy, supra* note 162 at para. 68. For these purposes, 'evidence' does not include points of claim and skeleton arguments from an earlier London arbitration demonstrating that a party to that arbitration is running inconsistent arguments in subsequent foreign proceedings: see *Emmott v. Michael Wilson & Partners Ltd* [2008] 1 Lloyd's Rep 616 at paras. 109, 122. Where the evidence is given by a witness in person, they are entitled to 'conduct money' and payment for expenses and loss of time: see *Evidence (Proceedings in Other Jurisdictions) Act 1975*, s 2(5).

[168] *Rio Tinto Zinc v. Westinghouse Electric* [1978] AC 547 at 654; *Vale SA v. Livingstone & Co Ltd* [2015] EWHC 1865 (QB) at para. 11; *Goncharova v. Zolotova, supra* note 166 at para. 53. In *Land Rover North America Inc v. Windh* [2005] EWHC 432 (QB) at paras. 11, 18, 19,

court's ability to respond to such a request. First, an English court will not require any particular steps to be taken in response to the letter of request unless 'they are steps which can be required to be taken by way of obtaining evidence for the purposes of civil proceedings in the court making the order'.[169] Secondly, an English court will not make a general order requiring the global production of any documents that might potentially be relevant to the foreign proceedings,[170] but instead will only order the production of documents specified by the requesting court[171] – 'fishing trips' for relevant documents are impermissible.[172] Accordingly, a general request for all bank statements received by a particular person during a given period is unacceptable, while a request for all the statements given to that person during that period by a single, nominated bank may be granted.[173] Thirdly, a court

---

Treacy J stated that an English court should apply the following two-stage test in deciding whether to accede to a foreign court's request: 'In summary, in considering the letters of request . . . the court should, in my opinion, ask first whether the intended witnesses can reasonably be expected to have relevant evidence to give on the topics mentioned in the amended schedule of requested testimony, and second whether the intention underlying the formulation of those topics is an intention to obtain evidence for use at the trial or is some other investigatory, and therefore impermissible intention.'

[169] *Evidence (Proceedings in Other Jurisdictions) Act 1975, supra* note 167, s 2(3). For example, requests under the legislation may not be used for the purpose of obtaining pre-trial disclosure in accordance with US civil procedure: see *Vale SA v. Livingstone & Co Ltd, supra* note 168 at para. 12. See also *Smith v. Philip Morris Companies Inc, supra* note 166 at para. 30.

[170] An impermissibly wide request may be subject to a 'blue pencil' deleting the aspects of the request that are objectionable: see *Refco Capital Markets v. Crédit Suisse (First Boston) Ltd* [2001] EWCA Civ 1733 at paras. 30–2; *Vale SA v. Livingstone & Co Ltd, supra* note 168 at para. 12.

[171] *Evidence (Proceedings in Other Jurisdictions) Act 1975, supra* note 167, s 2(4). The documents requested can be 'compendiously described', but only if that description clearly identifies the exact category of document to be produced: see *Vale SA v. Livingstone & Co Ltd, supra* note 168 at para. 12. See also *Genira Trade & Finance Inc v. Refco Capital Markets Ltd* [2001] EWCA Civ 1733 at paras. 32, 35.

[172] An application for the oral examination of a witness cannot be described as 'fishing' if there are sufficient grounds for believing that the intended witness might have evidence relevant to the trial (*First American Corp v. Sheikh Zayed Al-Nahyan* [1998] 4 All ER 439), although the letter of request must not 'oppress' the witness, which would be the case if the witness were at risk of subsequently being joined as a party to litigation (*ibid.* at 449). An English court should give the requesting court the benefit of the doubt where possible (*Smith v. Philip Morris Companies Inc, supra* note 166 at paras. 30, 36), but a statement in a letter of request that evidence is to be used at trial is not necessarily conclusive of the purpose for which the evidence will be used (*United States of America v. Philip Morris* [2003] EWHC 3028 (Comm) at para. 76). See also *Genira Trade & Finance Inc v. Refco Capital Markets Ltd, supra* note 171 at paras. 28–32; *Land Rover North America Inc v. Windh, supra* note 168 at paras. 13, 17–8, 26.

[173] *Re Asbestos Insurance Coverage Cases* [1985] 1 WLR 331.

cannot accede to a request for evidence if this would involve the compulsion of a witness who is not compellable either by virtue of English law or by the law of the requesting court.[174] Accordingly, as the House of Lords made clear in *Re Westinghouse Uranium Contract*,[175] the English courts may resist a request when this would infringe a litigant's privilege against self-incrimination or involve the extraterritorial application of the foreign state's penal, revenue or other public laws. Moreover, of especial relevance to the present discussion is the fact that an English court could use this third statutory limitation as a basis for resisting the disclosure of information that is subject to an obligation of confidentiality or, more particularly, the bank's duty of secrecy. Alternatively, such a refusal might be justified on the more straightforward basis that the English courts ultimately exercise a discretion as to whether to accede to the foreign court's request.[176] Certainly, in *Vale SA v. Livingstone & Co Ltd*,[177] Andrews J recently reiterated that a 'relevant consideration' for an English court when deciding whether to accede to a letter of request is whether such a step will require a party 'to breach a confidence in giving evidence or providing documents'.

Indeed, the interplay between the English court's discretion to accede to letters of request and any potential breaches of the bank's duty of secrecy was considered in *Re State of Norway's Application*,[178] where, at the request of the Norwegian tax authorities, the Norwegian courts issued letters rogatory seeking the oral examination of two bank officers in relation to the affairs of a trust. The English Court of Appeal declined to assist the foreign court on the ground, *inter alia*, that ordering the witnesses to give evidence would involve the bank in a breach of its duty of secrecy owed to its customer. As the bank's duty of secrecy is qualified, however, the existence of such a duty does not *automatically* preclude an English court from assisting a foreign court. There may be circumstances where disclosure is justified. According to Kerr LJ in *State of Norway* (with whom Glidewell and Gibson LJJ agreed), the court 'must carry out a balancing exercise' between 'the desirable policy of assisting a foreign court' and the 'great weight' to be given 'to the desirability of upholding the duty of

---

[174] *Evidence (Proceedings in Other Jurisdictions) Act 1975, supra* note 167, s 3(1). See also *Civil Procedure Rules 1998, supra* note 29, r 34.20.

[175] *Re Westinghouse Uranium Contract* [1978] AC 547.

[176] *Smith v. Philip Morris Companies Inc, supra* note 166 at para. 30.

[177] *Vale SA v. Livingstone & Co Ltd, supra* note 168 at para. 13.

[178] *Re State of Norway's Application* [1987] QB 433, *aff'd* [1990] 1 AC 723. See also *Honda Giken Kogyo Kabushiki Kaisha v. KJM Superbikes* [2007] EWCA Civ 313.

confidence'[179] – an approach subsequently confirmed by Lord Goff on appeal.[180] It would appear that 'one of the most critical factors in the complex balancing exercise' is 'the importance and degree of relevance of the confidential information',[181] so that, 'when that information is of central importance to the issues in the underlying case',[182] the English courts are particularly likely to accede to the foreign court's request for evidence (even when this involves a breach of a bank's duty of secrecy). This is likely to be the case when the account information is required in order to trace the proceeds of fraud[183] or where the foreign proceedings arise out of an international banking fraud.[184] Where the balance does tip in favour of providing foreign assistance, Kerr LJ in *State of Norway* indicated that the necessary disclosure could be justified under the first *Tournier* qualification, namely that disclosure is compelled by law.[185] In contrast, Glidewell LJ preferred to justify any disclosure under the second *Tournier* qualification, namely that there is a public interest in the English courts assisting foreign courts.[186]

It is precisely because the success of the 'letters of request' or 'letters rogatory' procedure depends upon the exercise of the requested court's discretion, that some requesting courts (particularly in the United States) have used the second route mentioned earlier for obtaining evidence abroad

---

[179] *Re State of Norway's Application (CA)*, supra note 178 at 486–7. See also *Vale SA* v. *Livingstone & Co Ltd*, supra note 168 at paras. 13–4, citing *Science Research Council* v. *Nasse* [1980] AC 1028. Consider further *Crédit Suisse Fides Trust SA* v. *Cuoghi* [1998] QB 818. For a similar balancing exercise in other jurisdictions, see *Unilever plc* v. *Procter and Gamble* (1990) 38 FTR 319; *Comaplex Resources International Ltd* v. *Schaffhauser Kantonalbank* [1990] IL Pr 319; *Bank Valetta plc* v. *National Crime Authority* [1999] 164 ALR 45; *Arab Banking Corporation* v. *Wightman* (1997) 70 ACWS 3d 50.

[180] *Re State of Norway's Application (HL)*, supra note 178 at 810.

[181] *Vale SA* v. *Livingstone & Co Ltd*, supra note 168 at para. 39.

[182] *Ibid.*

[183] *Ibid.*

[184] *First American Corp* v. *Sheikh Zayed Al-Nahyan*, supra note 172 at 448–9. An English court will assist the foreign court by remedying any defects in a letter of request, but will not rewrite the letter of request so that it strays 'too far away from the original': see *Smith* v. *Philip Morris Companies Inc*, supra note 166 at paras. 30, 41–5; *Refco Capital Markets* v. *Crédit Suisse (First Boston) Ltd*, supra note 170 at paras. 30–2; *Vale SA* v. *Livingstone & Co Ltd*, supra note 168 at para. 12. See also *State of Minnesota* v. *Philip Morris Inc* [1998] IL Pr 170 at para. 69. In *Pharaon* v. *Bank of Credit and Commerce International SA (in liquidation)* [1998] 4 All ER 455, Rattee J emphasised that such disclosure should be limited to what is reasonably necessary to satisfy the public interest in disclosure.

[185] *Re State of Norway's Application (CA)*, supra note 178 at 485.

[186] *Ibid.* at 489–90.

more expeditiously,[187] namely by ordering bank officers based at *local* branches in the requesting jurisdiction (frequently the United States) to disclose account-related information arising out of that bank's international or overseas operations.[188] In this regard, the relevant bank officer (in the United States) may be ordered by the local court either to give oral testimony or to produce documents to the court and, if he refuses to obey the order, he may face contempt-of-court proceedings.[189] That said, if the circumstances are such that disclosure would not have been ordered in the foreign jurisdiction had the case been a purely domestic one (so that disclosure would constitute a breach of those foreign secrecy laws), a US court will give weight to those foreign laws.[190] Since the US Supreme Court decision in *Société Nationale Industrielle Aérospatiale* v. *United States District Court for the Southern District of Iowa*,[191] the modern trend in the United States is to balance a number of factors before compelling disclosure that might breach such foreign bank secrecy laws,[192] namely the importance of the documents concerned to the US proceedings; the degree of specificity in identifying relevant documents; the location of the relevant information; the availability of alternative means for securing the information; the extent to which non-disclosure would undermine US

[187] R. Cranston, *Principles of Banking Law, supra* note 2 at 182. In the United States, the courts have stressed that the *Hague Evidence Convention, supra* note 20, is not the sole means of obtaining evidence located abroad: see *Société Nationale Industrielle Aérospatiale* v. *United States District Court for the Southern District of Iowa*, 482 US 522 at 539–43 (1987).

[188] Consider *Marc Rich & Co* v. *United States*, 707 F. 2d 663 (2d Cir., 1983).

[189] *United States* v. *Field*, 532 F. 2d 404 (1976), *cert denied*: 429 US 940 (1976) (although on the facts there was no breach of foreign secrecy laws, as the Cayman Islands banking authorities could compel disclosure of the relevant information in comparable circumstances). Similarly, a foreign bank secrecy law that contains an absolute prohibition on disclosure will be accorded more respect than laws that are subject to qualifications: see *United States* v. *First National City Bank*, 396 F. 2d 897 at 903 (2d Cir., 1968).

[190] Some US decisions have treated a prohibition under the law of the place where the information is located as a sufficient reason in itself for refusing to make a disclosure order: see *First National City Bank of New York* v. *IRS*, 271 F. 2d 616 (1959), *cert denied*: 361 US 948 (1960); *Ings* v. *Ferguson*, 282 F. 2d 149 (1960); *Application of Chase Manhattan Bank*, 297 F. 2d 611 (2d Cir., 1962); *United States* v. *Rubin*, 836 F. 2d 1096 at 1102 (8th Cir., 1998).

[191] *Société Nationale Industrielle Aérospatiale* v. *United States District Court for the Southern District of Iowa, supra* note 187.

[192] *Strauss* v. *Crédit Lyonnais SA*, 249 FRD 429 at 438–9 (SDNY, 2008); *Lantheus Medical Imaging Inc* v. *Zurich American Insurance Co*, 841 F. Supp. 2d 769 at 791–7 (SDNY, 2012); *Motorola Credit Corporation* v. *Nokia Corporation*, 73 F. Supp. 3d 397 at 399–404 (SDNY, 2014). For similar issues in the context of sovereign immunity, see *Republic of Argentina* v. *NML Capital Ltd*, 134 S. Ct. 2250 (2014). For further aspects of that litigation, consider *NML Capital Ltd* v. *Republic of Argentina* [2011] UKSC 31.

interests or disclosure would undermine the interests of the jurisdiction where the information is located; any hardship that might be caused to the party compelled to disclose; and the good faith or otherwise of that party.[193]

This last factor in particular has often proved to be determinative. Thus, in *Société Internationale pour Participations Industrielles et Commerciales SA v. Rogers*,[194] where the issue concerned whether a Swiss bank's action should be dismissed for failure to comply with a US production order, the US Supreme Court refused to impose sanctions against the bank as there was no evidence that it had 'deliberately courted legal impediments' under Swiss law to avoid making disclosure and accordingly had not acted in bad faith by deliberately using the foreign law to evade compliance with US law. By way of contrast, in *SEC v. Banca della Svizzera Italiana*,[195] where there was evidence that a Swiss bank had participated in, and profited from, insider trading activity and had deposited funds in a US bank account 'fully expecting to use foreign law to shield it from the reach of [United States] laws', the US District Court ordered the bank to respond to certain interrogatories despite the risk of breaching Swiss bank secrecy laws. Similarly, where the evidence indicates that a bank has not taken any *bona fide* steps in the foreign jurisdiction to obtain permission to disclose the relevant information (assuming of course such steps are available), a US court is unlikely to allow a bank to rely on foreign bank secrecy laws to resist disclosure of confidential information.[196] In contrast, where a foreign bank has made a genuine, albeit unsuccessful, attempt to seek the permission of relevant foreign authorities to obtain the information in

---

[193] *Restatement (Second) of Foreign Relations Law of the United States* (St Paul, MN, 1965), § 40; *Restatement (Third) of Foreign Relations Law of the United States* (St Paul, MN, 1986), § 442; *Restatement (Fourth) of Foreign Relations Law of the United States* (St Paul, MN, 2016), § 306.

[194] *Société Internationale pour Participations Industrielles et Commerciales SA v. Rogers*, 357 US 197 at 208–9 (1958).

[195] *SEC v. Banca della Svizzera Italiana*, 92 FRD 111 at 118–9 (SDNY, 1981). See also *United States v. Field*, *supra* note 189; *Arthur Andersen & Co v. Finesilver*, 546 F. 2d 338 (1976); *United States v. Vetco*, 644 F. 2d 1324 at 1331 (9th Cir., 1981); *In re Grand Jury Subpoena*, 218 F. Supp. 2d 544 at 554 (SDNY, 2002).

[196] *United States v. First National City Bank*, *supra* note 189. See also *United States v. Bank of Nova Scotia*, 691 F. 2d 1384 at 1389 (11th Cir., 1982); *United States v. Bank of Nova Scotia*, 740 F. 2d 817 at 825–6 (11th Cir., 1984); *United States v. Davis*, 767 F. 2d 1025 at 1035 (2d Cir., 1985); *Cochran Consulting Inc v. Uwatec USA Inc*, 102 F. 3d 1224 at 1227 (1996); *Weiss v. National Westminster Bank plc*, 242 FRD 33 at 56 (EDNY, 2007). The US courts do not regard the *Hague Evidence Convention*, *supra* note 20, as precluding the making of a direct order against local branches of foreign banks, the principle of comity notwithstanding: see *Murphy v. Reifenhauser KG Maschinenfabrik*, 101 FRD 360 (1984).

question, a subpoena against the bank will be refused,[197] or, if the order has already been granted, the court will refuse to impose sanctions against the bank for non-compliance.[198]

While the multifactorial approach in the *Aérospatiale* decision certainly reveals a degree of sensitivity to the difficulties faced by banks in complying with disclosure orders with extraterritorial effects, the judicial concern over impermissible extraterritoriality appears in recent times to have heightened in the United States. For example, in *Morrison* v. *National Australian Bank Ltd*,[199] which concerned allegations that an Australian bank had breached US securities laws, the US Supreme Court strongly reasserted the (long-recognised)[200] presumption against the extraterritorial application of federal legislation by stressing that '[w]hen a statute gives no clear indication of an extraterritorial application, it has none.'[201] The view that legislation must give an 'affirmative indication'[202] of its extraterritorial intent, if it is to have such an effect, has been twice confirmed by the same court subsequently.[203] While this approach has arguably produced the unintended consequence of causing more recent US legislation to become more explicitly and aggressively extraterritorial, a more positive outcome might be found in the important recent (non-banking) decision in *Microsoft Corporation* v. *United States*.[204] In this decision, the Second Circuit Court of Appeals quashed a warrant issued under the Stored Communications Act,[205] which was served on the offices of Microsoft in the United States and which required the company to seize, 'import' and produce in the United States a particular customer's emails located at Microsoft's Irish data storage facility. Even though the email account was accessible through Microsoft's cloud computing services, the Court

---

[197] *Trade Development Bank* v. *Continental Insurance Co*, 469 F. 2d 35 (2d Cir., 1972); *United States* v. *Bank of Nova Scotia*, supra note 196; *Minpeco SA* v. *Conticommodity Services Inc*, 116 FRD 517 (SDNY, 1987).

[198] A party in breach of a US court's disclosure order may raise a defence of 'substantial justification': see *United States Federal Civil Judicial Procedure Rules*, r 37(b)(5)(g)(3). See also *Pharaon* v. *Bank of Credit and Commerce International SA*, supra note 184 at 460.

[199] *Morrison* v. *National Australian Bank Ltd*, 561 US 247 (2010).

[200] *Equal Employment Opportunity Commission* v. *Arabian American Oil Co*, 499 US 244 at 248, 256 (1991), citing *Foley Bros Inc* v. *Filardo*, 336 US 281 at 285 (1949).

[201] *Morrison* v. *National Australian Bank Ltd*, supra note 199 at 255.

[202] *Ibid.* at 265.

[203] *Kiobel* v. *Royal Dutch Petroleum Co*, 133 S. Ct. 1659 at 4–5 (2013); *RJR Nabisco Inc* v. *European Community*, 136 S. Ct. 2090 at 7–10 (2016).

[204] *Microsoft Corporation* v. *United States*, US App Lexis 12926 (2016).

[205] Stored Communications Act, 18 USC § 2703.

concluded that the warrant operated extraterritorially, since it required the seizure of data stored in Dublin, and violated the customer's 'expectation of privacy' that he enjoyed by virtue of Irish law. Although the Court of Appeals indicated that there might be an important distinction between the kind of warrant under consideration in *Microsoft* and the type of disclosure order in cases like *Aérospatiale*, the *Microsoft* decision may herald a new era of judicial self-restraint on the part of the US courts.[206]

Until the US Supreme Court confirms that the approach in *Microsoft* extends beyond just warrants, however, the US practice of compelling local bank officers to disclose information about their employer's foreign activities will probably continue. Pursuing such a course is not without its practical difficulties, however, since there may be cases in which the US courts will still require the cooperation and assistance of the foreign court to enforce their disclosure orders. In such cases, no matter how much restraint the US courts purport to exercise (in light of the *Aérospatiale* and *Microsoft* decisions[207]) when granting such disclosure orders, foreign courts are still likely to view such extraterritorial orders with suspicion and accordingly prioritise their own domestic interests.[208] Indeed, when faced with such exercises of long-arm jurisdiction, the English courts have even been prepared to grant pre-emptive countermeasures to prevent banks in England disclosing information pursuant to such orders. In *X AG v. A Bank*,[209] the US Department of Justice, which was conducting an investigation into the crude oil industry, served a subpoena on the head office of a US bank for the production in the United States of documents relating to accounts held with the bank's London branch by a group of companies, one of which had had dealings on the US crude oil market. As the bank intended to comply with the subpoena, the corporate customers obtained an interim injunction from the English courts restraining the bank from disclosing the relevant records. Subsequently, Leggatt J had to decide whether to continue or vacate the injunction. Despite the fact that

---

[206] A petition for rehearing has been filed with the Second Circuit Court of Appeals: see *Microsoft Corporation v. United States of America* (Docket No. 14-2985, 13 October 2016).

[207] *Société Nationale Industrielle Aérospatiale v. United States District Court for the Southern District of Iowa, supra* note 187; *Microsoft Corporation v. United States, supra* note 204.

[208] *State Bank International Ltd v. Pershing Ltd, supra* note 58 at 177–8.

[209] *X AG v. A Bank, supra* note 86. For a case where the shoe was on the other foot, see *State Bank International Ltd v. Pershing Ltd, supra* note 58 at 177–8. For the possibility of a US court enjoining a foreign party from seeking an injunction abroad that would prevent disclosure in the United States, see P. Roth, 'Reasonable Extraterritoriality: Correcting the "Balance of Interests"' (1992) 41 *International and Comparative Law Quarterly* 245 at 250.

the US District Court had, since the initial granting of the English interim injunction, ordered the bank to obey the subpoena, Leggatt J continued the injunction restraining the bank from passing information concerning the corporate group's affairs to the bank's head office in the United States or to any other person or branch. Although his Lordship had to weigh all the relevant factors in determining whether the balance of convenience favoured the vacation or continuation of the injunction, he considered that two factors in particular favoured its continuation: first, that compliance with the US order would potentially render the bank liable to its English customers for breaching its duty of secrecy (which duty was governed by English law as the relevant accounts were maintained in London); and, secondly, that the US District Court would be unlikely to commence contempt proceedings if an English court were to enjoin the bank from making disclosure. A similar approach is evident in Hong Kong,[210] although in cases of international fraud, the English courts have shown less reluctance about enforcing disclosure orders of the US courts to the extent necessary to satisfy the public interest justifying disclosure.[211]

3.3.2   Evidence Sought Abroad in Support of English Proceedings

Although the position is not identical to that considered in the previous section, broadly similar principles apply when an English court assists a litigant to obtain evidence from a bank located abroad or from the foreign branch of an English bank for the purpose of proceedings before the English courts.[212] When the documents are maintained, or the witnesses located, in another European Union Member State, the English courts can

---

[210] *FDC Co Ltd* v. *Chase Manhattan Bank* [1985] 2 HKC 470 at 477, where Huggins VP stated that '[t]he Hong Kong courts could enjoin the [b]ank against disclosing the information to the United States Government in Hong Kong', since '[a]ll persons opening accounts with banks in Hong Kong, whether local or foreign banks, are entitled to look to the Hong Kong courts to enforce any obligation of secrecy that is, by Hong Kong law, implied by virtue of the relationship of banker and customer'. Moreover, his Honour stated that 'the obligation of secrecy is not subject to territorial limits' and that disclosure in *FDC* could not be justified on the basis of the 'compulsion of law' exception to the *Tournier* doctrine. See also *Nam Tai Electronics Inc* v. *PricewaterhouseCoopers* [2008] 1 HKC 427 at para. 47; cf *Jim Beam Brands Co* v. *Kentucky Importers Pty Ltd* [1994] 1 HKLR 1 at 9.

[211] *Pharaon* v. *Bank of Credit and Commerce International SA (in liquidation), supra* note 184 at 465, citing *First American Corp* v. *Sheikh Zayed Al-Nahyan, supra* note 172 at 448–9.

[212] For the position where the English proceedings are criminal in nature, see *Crime (International Co-operation) Act 2003* (UK), *supra* note 154, ss 13–5.

make a request for assistance from the foreign court under the procedure in Regulation 1206/2001.[213] That legal regime also governs the situation where the English courts wish to take evidence directly in another Member State without the foreign court's assistance. The key aspects of this regime were considered previously.[214] In contrast, when the foreign court is located outside another Member State, then neither Regulation 1206/2001 nor the Evidence (Proceedings in Other Jurisdictions) Act 1975 applies to the English court's letter of request. Originally, the English courts relied upon their inherent jurisdiction to issue a letter of request in such circumstances,[215] but the CPR 1998 now expressly confers such a power on the English courts.[216]

As an alternative route to using the 'letters of request' procedure, when relevant information is held abroad by a foreign bank or by the foreign branch of an English bank, litigants have sometimes requested that an English court make an order for disclosure *directly* against the bank's officers within the jurisdiction, requiring those officers to obtain the relevant information from the bank's foreign office and disclose it to the applicant. Like the US courts following the *Aérospatiale* decision,[217] which was considered above, the English courts have generally been unwilling to grant such orders on the ground that it might be viewed as an extraterritorial infringement of the foreign court's jurisdiction. Thus, in *R v. Grossman*,[218] the Court of Appeal discharged an order under s 7 of the BBEA 1879, which was granted to the Inland Revenue for the purpose of prosecuting tax offences. The order directed Barclays Bank's head office in London to obtain the bank records of a particular corporate account held with its Manx branch and to enable the Inland Revenue to inspect those records.

---

[213] *European Evidence Regulation, supra* note 20. This Regulation does not apply to an English court's order that an English judgment debtor identify the location of his assets wherever situated: see *Masri* v. *Consolidated Contractors International Co SAL (No 4), supra* note 36 at paras. 39–45, 53–4, *rev'd* on a different issue: [2010] AC 90. See also *Re MMR and MR Vaccine Litigation (No 10)* [2004] All ER (D) 67 (request to Irish courts granted).

[214] See Section 3.3.1.

[215] *Panayiotou* v. *Sony Music Entertainment (UK) Ltd* [1994] Ch 142.

[216] *Civil Procedure Rules 1998, supra* note 29, r 34.13(1)–(2).

[217] *Société Nationale Industrielle Aérospatiale* v. *United States District Court for the Southern District of Iowa, supra* note 187.

[218] *R v. Grossman, supra* note 88. See also *United Company Rusal plc* v. *HSBC Bank plc* [2011] EWHC 404 (QB) at paras. 67–73. *Grossman* does not, however, govern the issue of jurisdiction over substantive proceedings brought against an English bank's foreign branch, as this is governed by the recast *Brussels I Regulation, supra* note 6: see *Mahme Trust Reg* v. *Lloyds TSB Bank plc* [2004] 2 Lloyd's Rep 637 at para. 32.

Lord Denning MR's vacation of the order was motivated by the jurisdictional conflict that would arise if it were allowed to stand, and by the fact that the appropriate course for inspecting the bank records in the Isle of Man was to make an application to the Manx courts in accordance with their legislation and procedures.[219] This was also the appropriate solution to the 'comity' problem suggested by the Irish Supreme Court more recently in *Walsh v. National Irish Bank Ltd*.[220] Similarly, in *MacKinnon v. Donaldson Lufkin & Jenrette Securities Corporation*,[221] Hoffmann J declined to issue a witness summons[222] (requiring an officer at a Bahamian bank's London branch to attend trial in order to produce all the relevant documents held by the bank's New York branch) on the basis that this infringed US sovereignty. His Lordship considered that the bank's duty of secrecy should be regulated by the jurisdiction where the particular account was kept, otherwise '[i]f every country where a bank happened to carry on business asserted a right to require the bank to produce documents relating to accounts kept in any other such country, banks would be in the unhappy position of being forced to submit to whichever sovereign was able to apply the greatest pressure.'[223]

In *Masri v. Consolidated Contractors International Company SAL (No 2)*,[224] however, Lawrence Collins LJ stressed more recently that there is no absolute rule that 'the court will never have jurisdiction to make orders [under the BBEA 1879] against the London branch of a foreign bank in relation to

---

[219] *R v. Grossman, supra* note 88 at 307–8. See further *Chemical Bank v. McCormack* [1983] ILRM 350 at 354.

[220] *Walsh v. National Irish Bank Ltd, supra* note 4 at paras. 62–7. If an application is made to the US courts for assistance, the relevant procedure is contained in 28 USC §1782, which provides a speedy and efficient way of obtaining the necessary information. Some US Circuits allow for potentially unlimited jurisdiction; others will not grant disclosure to an extent greater than would be ordered in the foreign jurisdiction. See generally M. Jarrett, 'Assistance from the United States for Litigants Abroad' (2000) 151 *New Law Journal* 390.

[221] *MacKinnon v. Donaldson, Lufkin & Jenrette Securities Corporation, supra* note 36, discussed with approval in *Bilta (UK) Ltd v. Nazir (No 2), supra* note 68 at para. 212. Cf *Re Mid East Trading Ltd* [1998] 1 All ER 577 (liquidator's application under the *Insolvency Act 1986* (UK), *supra* note 147, s 236, for disclosure of documents situated abroad).

[222] *Civil Procedure Rules 1998, supra* note 29, Pt 34.

[223] *MacKinnon v. Donaldson, Lufkin & Jenrette Securities Corporation, supra* note 36 at 494. See also *Parbulk II AS v. PT Humpuss Intermoda Transportasi TBK* [2011] EWHC 3143 (Comm) at paras. 92–3; *National Grid Electricity Transmission plc v. ABB Ltd* [2013] EWHC 822 (Ch) at para. 20; *Deutsche Bank AG v. Sebastian Holdings Inc* [2015] EWHC 2773 (QB) at para. 26.

[224] *Masri v. Consolidated Contractors International Company SAL (No 2)* [2008] EWCA Civ 303 at paras. 32–5.

papers held by head office, nor that it will never be possible to issue a witness summons against the bank's London branch officer in respect of head office transactions'. According to his Lordship, such disclosure orders or witness summonses would only be made when the circumstances of the particular case demonstrated 'a sufficient connection with England to justify an order'. In particular, his Lordship suggested that *Donaldson Lufkin* might have been decided differently if the papers that were held by the foreign bank's head office in that case had related to English transactions instead.[225] Some doubt has, however, been cast upon these views by *Masri v. Consolidated Contractors International Company SAL (No 4)*,[226] in which Sir Anthony Clarke MR stated that Lawrence Collins LJ may have 'somewhat understated' the current relevance of the presumption against extraterritoriality, a view with which Lawrence Collins LJ also agreed in the later case.[227] In that regard, the traditional, more conservative approach in *Grossman* and *Donaldson Lufkin* – that only in exceptional circumstances should a court hearing proceedings compel a bank to produce books or records held by a branch or its head office outside the jurisdiction – was preferred by Lord Mance when *Masri* was subsequently appealed,[228] and has been endorsed in Australia[229] and Ireland.[230] It is also consistent with the approach adopted recently in the *Microsoft* decision.[231] Accordingly, using the 'letters of request' procedure whenever possible must be the preferable route for a litigant given the riskiness and unattractiveness of trying to obtain the requisite evidence through a direct local order.

---

[225] *Ibid.* at para. 34. See also *Parbulk II AS* v. *PT Humpuss Intermoda Transportasi TBK*, *supra* note 223 at paras. 92–3. For these purposes, there might also be a 'sufficient connection' with England if the foreign bank has registered as a foreign company in the United Kingdom: see *Mitsui & Co Ltd* v. *Nexen Petroleum UK Ltd* [2005] 3 All ER 511 at paras. 30–2.

[226] *Masri* v. *Consolidated Contractors International Company SAL (No 4) (CA)*, *supra* note 36 at paras. 15–6, *rev'd* on a different issue: [2010] AC 90, discussed with approval in *Bilta (UK) Ltd* v. *Nazir (No 2)*, *supra* note 68 at para. 212.

[227] *Masri* v. *Consolidated Contractors International Company SAL (No 4) (CA)*, *supra* note 36 at para. 80, *rev'd* on a different issue: [2010] AC 90.

[228] *Masri* v. *Consolidated Contractors International Company SAL (No 4) (SC)*, *supra* note 68 at paras. 19, 26. See also *AB Bank Ltd* v. *Abu Dhabi Commercial Bank PJSC* [2016] EWHC 2082 (Comm) at para. 34. See further *Société Eram Shipping Co Ltd* v. *Compagnie Internationale de Navigation* [2003] 3 WLR 21 at paras. 22–3, 31, 67, 70, 113, applying similar principles when refusing a third party debt order over a foreign account's credit balance.

[229] *Suzlon Energy Ltd* v. *Bangad*, *supra* note 59 at paras. 40–7.

[230] *Walsh* v. *National Irish Bank Ltd (HC)*, *supra* note 87 at paras. 44–8.

[231] *Microsoft Corporation* v. *United States*, *supra* note 204.

3.4   Bank Secrecy, the Conflict of Laws and Non-judicial Disclosure

As traditionally (and broadly) conceived, the conflict of laws provides a system of principles whereby judicial bodies (usually national courts, but potentially also arbitral tribunals) can determine the forum and legal system best suited to resolving an extant dispute and the consequences of any ensuing judgment (or award). In essence, these principles are reactive (only applying once a dispute between individuals has arisen), specific (dealing only with the particular dispute) and judicial (being invoked by national courts to resolve international disputes). It is for this reason that the conflict of laws has a role (albeit one of varying intensity) in resolving some of the international challenges to the maintenance of bank secrecy in the previous two sections.[232] In contrast, the present section concerns the situation where one state enacts legislation or issues an executive order that purports to regulate foreign activity directly, such as imposing obligations on banks and other financial entities to disclose their customers' account-related information not only if those banks and customers are within the relevant jurisdiction, but also if one or both are beyond that state's territorial reach. Such extraterritorial legislative or executive action has usually been taken in the name of detecting financial crime, identifying the proceeds of crime, preventing terrorist activity or uncovering tax evasion. Indeed, a particularly controversial recent example of such legislation is the Foreign Account Tax Compliance Act 2010 (FATCA), which requires foreign financial institutions to enter into an agreement with the US tax authorities to disclose the details of account-holders who are suspected of being US taxpayers, together with details of account-related activity.[233] Where a foreign bank or other financial institution has failed to enter into such an agreement, any US payer, who makes a payment to such

---

[232] See Sections 3.2 and 3.3.

[233] *Foreign Account Tax Compliance Act 2010*, 26 USC § 1471(c)(1). A further example of the possible extraterritorial application of US legislation might be if the parties to a foreign-currency swap transaction between a US and foreign bank, or a dollar-denominated swap between two foreign banks, were required to report details of that transaction to US regulators by virtue of the *Dodd-Frank Wall Street Reform and Consumer Protection Act* (Pub. L. 111-203, H.R. 4173) § 722(d): see H. Ying, 'Report of Proceedings' March 2015 at 38, online at http://law.nus.edu.sg/cbfl/pdfs/reports/CBFL-Rep-HY1.pdf. Consider also *Regulation (EU) No 648/2012 of the European Parliament and of the Council of 4 July 2012 on OTC Derivatives, Central Counterparties and Trade Repositories* (2012) O.J. L. 201/1. See further the long-arm jurisdiction and extraterritorial forfeiture powers in *Uniting and Strengthening America by Providing Appropriate Tools Required to Intercept and Obstruct Terrorism (USA Patriot Act) Act 2001*, 115 Stat. 272 §§ 317–19.

a non-compliant entity, must 'deduct and withhold from such payment a tax equal to 30 percent of the amount of such payment'.[234]

Traditionally, this form of legislative or executive conflict has fallen within the purview of public international law or international relations rather than the conflict of laws,[235] and has usually been resolved by bilateral or multilateral treaties[236] or other forms of supranational accord;[237] through political, diplomatic or other less formal channels;[238] or, as a last resort, by passing domestic 'blocking' legislation.[239] Increasingly, however, there is academic recognition that the conflict of laws has suffered from 'tunnel vision',[240] which is the result of its isolation from political discourse and its subordination to public international law concerns.[241] According to this new approach, the conflict of laws should be more ambitious in

[234] *Foreign Account Tax Compliance Act 2010, supra* note 233, § 1471.

[235] Domestic courts will not generally give effect to another jurisdiction's penal, revenue or other public laws (see *supra* note 22) and the act of state doctrine prevents the courts in one jurisdiction sitting in judgment over the sovereign acts of another state (see *Buttes Gas & Oil Co v. Hammer* [1982] AC 888 at 931; *Attorney-General v. Nissan* [1970] AC 179 at 237; *R v. Bow Street Metropolitan Magistrate, ex parte Pinochet Ugarte (No 3)* [2000] 1 AC 147 at 286; *Kuwait Airways Corporation v. Iraqi Airways Co (Nos 4 and 5)* [2002] 2 AC 883 at paras. 24, 112, 135; *Lucasfilm Ltd v. Ainsworth* [2012] 1 AC 208 at para. 87; *The Republic of the Philippines v. Maler Foundation, supra* note 22 at paras. 46–58; *Belhaj v. Straw, supra* note 21 at paras. 1–112).

[236] To a large extent, the extraterritorial concerns associated with the *Foreign Account Tax Compliance Act 2010, supra* note 233, have been resolved by the United States entering into a series of intergovernmental agreements with affected jurisdictions that purport to regulate the disclosure of account-related information by banks and financial institutions in those jurisdictions. For the current list of the different models of intergovernmental agreement between the United States and other jurisdictions, see US Department of the Treasury, 'FATCA' (2010), online: www.treasury.gov/resource-center/tax-policy/treaties/Pages/FATCA.aspx.

[237] See, for example, the Bretton Woods Agreement, *supra* note 24; FATF 40 Recommendations, *supra* note 13; Basel Committee on Banking Supervision, *supra* note 24.

[238] Consider generally A.-M. Slaughter, *A New World Order: Government Networks and the Disaggregated State* (Princeton: Princeton University Press, 2004).

[239] See, for example, *Protection of Trading Interests Act 1980* (UK), *supra* note 25, ss 1, 5–7; *European Blocking Regulation, supra* note 25. See further L. Collins, 'Blocking and Clawback Statutes: The United Kingdom Approach' (1986) *Journal of Business Law* 452; W. Haseltine, 'International Regulation of Securities Markets: Interaction between United States and Foreign Laws' (1987) 36 *International and Comparative Law Quarterly* 307 at 312–4.

[240] H. Muir Watt, 'Private International Law Beyond the Schism' (2011) 2 *Transnational Legal Theory* 347 at 356. See also *The Republic of the Philippines v. Maler Foundation, supra* note 22 at para. 55: 'Private international law is concerned with both executive/legislative sovereignty and adjudicative sovereignty'.

[241] H. Muir Watt, 'The Relevance of Private International Law to the Global Governance Debate', in H. Muir Watt and D. Fernandez Arroyo (eds), *Private International Law and Global Governance* (Oxford: Oxford University Press, 2014) at chapter 1.

its reach, moving beyond its current court-limited role (since 'there is nothing that limits Conflicts thinking to the judicial sphere'[242] and 'Conflicts-style reasoning need not be the province of courts alone')[243] and metamorphosing into a more proactive and generalised set of principles (as 'an instrument for global governance' that seeks to regulate 'the transnational exercise of private power').[244] At present, if one jurisdiction purports to exercise legislative, executive or regulatory control over the disclosure of account-related information by banks in other jurisdictions (as under FATCA), the conflict of laws will largely prefer the interests of the latter jurisdiction by virtue of the twin principles against extraterritoriality and the enforcement of penal, revenue or other public laws (a form of 'public law taboo').[245] The 'global governance' approach, however, would enable the conflict of laws to provide a more nuanced response to FATCA-type situations than simply denying effect *tout court* to the legislation in question. This more sophisticated approach is justified in the bank secrecy context, since extraterritorial disclosure legislation, such as FATCA, is often passed in response to bank customers engaging in legal or regulatory arbitrage, by taking advantage of the fact that legal systems protect bank secrecy to differing degrees and accordingly opening accounts with financial institutions affording the greatest protection to account-related information.[246] This is effectively one of the techniques that Switzerland has used to attract banking business. Accordingly, conflict of laws techniques, such as the multifactorial approach of *forum non conveniens*[247] or the public policy-based 'government interest analysis' from choice of law in tort,[248] might be invoked to determine the appropriate balance between

---

[242] A. Riles, 'Managing Regulatory Arbitrage: A Conflict of Laws Approach' (2014) 47 *Cornell International Law Journal* 63 at 104.

[243] *Ibid.* at 105.

[244] See generally H. Muir Watt, 'Private International Law Beyond the Schism', *supra* note 240; G. Saumier, 'PILAGG in Practice: Two Examples of Concrete Steps' (2012) *PILAGG e-series GG/1*, online: http://blogs.sciences-po.fr/pilagg/files/2013/09/PILAGG-e-series-GG-1-Saumier.pdf.

[245] H. Muir Watt, 'The Relevance of Private International Law to the Global Governance Debate', *supra* note 241.

[246] Consider K. Pistor, 'A Legal Theory of Finance' (2013) 41 *Journal of Comparative Economics* 315 at 329.

[247] See generally *Spiliada Maritime Corporation* v. *Cansulex Ltd, supra* note 33; *Lubbe* v. *Cape plc, supra* note 33; *Berezovsky* v. *Michaels, supra* note 33; *VTB Capital plc* v. *Nutritek International Corporation, supra* note 33.

[248] See, for example, *McGhee* v. *Arabian American Oil Co*, 871 F. 2d 1412 at 1424 (9th Cir., 1989); *Grosshandels-und Lagerei-Berufsgenossenschaft* v. *World Trade Center Properties LLC*, 435 F. 3d 136 at 139–40 (2006); *CRS Recovery Inc* v. *Laxton*, 600 F. 3d 1138 at 1141–2 (9th Cir., 2010).

one jurisdiction's desire to protect its fundamental domestic interests from being undermined by foreign activity, on the one hand, and bank customers' commercial freedom to 'shop' for the most amenable foreign jurisdiction, on the other.[249] It is arguably time to transform the conflict of laws into something more subtle and aspirational.[250]

3.5   Conclusion

This chapter's fundamental thesis is that the conflict of laws' difficulty in dealing effectively with international disputes concerning bank secrecy and disclosure is largely attributable to the failure to distinguish properly between three different situations, namely bank-customer litigation about breaches of bank secrecy, attempts to secure disclosure judicially from non-party banks and attempts to secure disclosure directly from foreign banks by legislative, executive or regulatory means. The reality is that the conflict of laws applies with varying intensity in each of these situations. While it has been suggested that the conflict of laws might be more ambitious in dealing with non-judicial conflicts, even in that area where the conflict of laws applies most intensely (in bank-customer litigation concerning the breach of the secrecy duty), a significant change has been advocated above, namely the loosening of the iron grip exercised by the place of the customer's branch over conflict of laws issues involving banks, whether as a basis for founding jurisdiction, recognising and enforcing judgments or determining the applicable law. Not only does this approach expose banks and their assets to an unnecessarily wide range of jurisdictions between which a customer may choose freely in order to maximise his or her litigation advantages, but also, in choice of law terms, the location of the relevant branch has increasingly little to do with the manner in which banking business is conducted or in which customers engage with their banks. Both suggested changes require the conflict of laws to adapt to technological advances, developments in banking practice and the challenge of increased globalisation.

---

[249] For a judicial rejection of the view that 'an underlying governmental interest' might be used to displace concerns over extraterritorial sovereign acts, see *Peer International Corporation* v. *Termidor Music Publishers Ltd* [2004] 2 WLR 849 at paras. 46, 65; *The Republic of the Philippines* v. *Maler Foundation, supra* note 22 at paras. 59–63. Contrast the more imaginative (and less territorially fixated) approach to the clash of regulatory competences in *A* v. *B Bank* [1992] 1 All ER 778 at 792. See also *Lorentzen* v. *Lydden & Co Ltd* [1942] 2 KB 202; *Bank of Crete SA* v. *Koskotas (No 2)* [1992] 1 WLR 919 at 925.

[250] H. Muir Watt, 'Future Directions?', in H. Muir Watt and D. Fernandez Arroyo (eds), *Private International Law and Global Governance, supra* note 241 at chapter 18.

The International Pressures on Banks
to Disclose Information

CHIZU NAKAJIMA

4.1 Introduction

In 2009, at the London Summit, the G20 famously declared that '[t]he era of banking secrecy is over.'[1] Since then the Organisation for Economic Co-operation and Development (OECD) has been continuing to lead the initiative, which it launched in 1998,[2] to improve countries' capacity to tackle tax evasion that, in its view, has been facilitated by offshore financial centres and bank secrecy.[3] This initiative has received greater support from those governments around the world that have found themselves in serious need of securing tax revenues to restore the health of the public finances as they came under particular strain after the financial crisis.[4] This has culminated in the G8 countries stating in their Lough Erne Declaration in 2013, 'Tax authorities across the world should automatically share information to fight the scourge of tax evasion.'[5]

While the international initiatives to tackle tax evasion are pertinent to the discussion of the international pressures on banks to disclose information and their impact on bank secrecy, this chapter focuses primarily on

A version of this chapter was presented at the Bank Secrecy Symposium hosted by the Centre for Banking and Finance Law at the National University of Singapore, Faculty of Law on 4–5 December 2014.

[1] G20, 'London Summit – Leaders' Statement' (2 April 2009), at para. 15, online: www.imf .org/external/np/sec/pr/2009/pdf/g20_040209.pdf
[2] OECD, 'Harmful Tax Competition: An Emerging Global Issue' (1998), online: www.oecd .org/tax/transparency/44430243.pdf. See also OECD, 'Towards Global Tax Co-operation' (2000), online: www.oecd.org/tax/harmful/2090192.pdf
[3] OECD, 'The Era of Bank Secrecy is Over: The G20/OECD Process is Delivering Results' (26 October 2011), online: www.oecd.org/ctp/exchange-of-tax-information/48996146.pdf
[4] See, for example, *ibid.* at 5, stating '[h]igh levels of tax evasion are particularly hard to tolerate at a time of strong pressure on public finances.'
[5] G8, 'G8 Lough Erne Declaration' (18 June 2013), at para. 1, online: www.gov.uk/government/ publications/g8-lough-erne-declaration/g8-lough-erne-declaration-html-version

the measures to combat money laundering and terrorist financing that impose duties on banks to disclose information, which, in turn, may directly conflict with their duties of confidentiality owed to their customers.[6] Nevertheless, it is worthy of note that what has laid the vital foundation for the development of 'information sharing' between tax authorities, endorsed by the G8 nations, are the information disclosure and sharing mechanisms that have been established worldwide through the introduction and implementation of anti-money laundering (AML) and combating the financing of terrorism (CFT) regimes.[7] The issues are intrinsically linked as the laundering process is a necessary element in tax evasion, which in turn is recognised as one of the predicate offences of money laundering. Furthermore, there are international initiatives to facilitate closer cooperation between tax and AML/CFT authorities, as will be discussed later.[8]

This chapter, therefore, examines the various international initiatives, with particular attention to those by the Financial Action Task Force (FATF), which have led jurisdictions around the world to the establishment of measures to facilitate information disclosure by banks in the form of AML and CFT measures, and the resulting conflicting demands put upon these banks which, at the same time, owe a duty of confidentiality to their customers.

4.2   The Global Fight against Money Laundering and Terrorist Financing

The advent of AML regulation has had an enormous impact on the way in which banking and financial services are conducted worldwide,[9] and

---

[6] For detailed discussion on tax-related issues, see O'Brien, Chapter 5.

[7] See OECD, 'Standard for Automatic Exchange of Financial Account Information' (5 November 2015), at 4, online: www.oecd.org/ctp/exchange-of-tax-information/automatic-exchange-financial-account-information-common-reporting-standard.pdf (21 July 2014) at 44, acknowledging contributions that 'global anti-money laundering standards' have made to the move towards automatic exchange of information on a multilateral basis.

[8] See OECD, 'Improving Co-operation between Tax and Anti-Money Laundering Authorities: Access by Tax Administrations to Information Held by Financial Intelligence Units for Criminal and Civil Purposes' (September 2015), online: www.oecd.org/ctp/crime/report-improving-cooperation-between-tax-anti-money-laundering-authorities.pdf

[9] On the international and regional efforts to combat money laundering, see, for example, W.C. Gilmore, *Dirty Money: The Evolution of International Measures to Counter Money Laundering and the Financing of Terrorism* (France: Strasbourg: Council of Europe Publishing, 1995), FATF, '25 Years and Beyond' (2014), online: www.fatf-gafi.org/media/fatf/documents/brochuresannualreports/FATF%2025%20years.pdf, and IMF and World Bank, 'Enhancing Contributions to Combating Money Laundering: Policy Paper' (April 2001), online: www.imf.org/external/np/ml/2001/eng/042601.PDF

it has been observed that its impact is considerably more significant than other measures promulgated in the context of financial regulation in the European Union.[10] Indeed, financial institutions have been made to stand on the front line to protect the global financial system from use by criminal and terrorist organisations.

It can be said that even before the international move against money laundering began, there had been signs that it was 'the declared policy of many regulatory authorities, including most significantly the US Securities and Exchange Commission, to "ring fence" probity in the financial services industry by imposing significant and onerous obligations, on those who handle other people's money or who facilitate transactions, to take steps in the exercise of due diligence to ensure that their contribution is both lawful and proper.[11] Indeed, as early as 1963, the US Securities and Exchange Commission's (US SEC) administrative enforcement programme converted professional intermediaries into 'reluctant policemen' by placing them on a first line of defence against securities fraud.[12] It has, thus, been observed that '[p]rofessionals, the ubiquitous middle men in today's complex society, will often be required to yield up information for the purpose of litigation in courts, and with increasing frequency, for administrative hearings and determinations. The courts have wide powers in their inherent jurisdiction to order, and regulate, the disclosure of confidential information.'[13]

The global fight against money laundering began in earnest with the United Nations Convention against Illicit Traffic in Narcotic Drugs and Psychotropic Substances (Vienna Convention) in December 1989, which obligated the party states to criminalise money laundering. In the context of this chapter, what is most significant is the establishment of the FATF in June 1989 at the Economic Summit of the Group of Seven, at which the G7 countries considered measures to protect the global financial system from money laundering.[14]

---

[10] C. Nakajima, *Conflicts of Interest and Duty – A Comparative Analysis of Anglo-Japanese Law* (London: Kluwer Law International, 1999) at 180. See also EC, *Directive 2005/60/EC of the European Parliament and of the Council of 26 October 2005 on the Prevention of the Use of the Financial System for the Purpose of Money Laundering and Terrorist Financing* [2005] O.J. L. 309/15, and Council of Europe, *Convention on Laundering, Search, Seizure and Confiscation of the Proceeds from Crime* (8 November 1990), CETS No. 141.

[11] Nakajima, *Conflicts of Interest and Duty, supra* note 10 at 182.

[12] *Ibid.* See also C. Nakajima, 'The Cost of Laundry', *Journal of Financial Crime*, 3 (1995), 172.

[13] D.F. Partlett, *Professional Negligence* (Sydney: The Law Book Company, 1985) at 150.

[14] See the Economic Declaration made by the G7 countries at the Paris Summit, G7 Information Centre, 'Economic Declaration' (16 July 1989), online: www.g8.utoronto.ca/summit/1989paris/communique/index.html#drugs

In April 1990, the FATF announced Forty Recommendations for member countries pertaining to fighting money laundering. Following the '9/11' terrorist attacks in the United States, the FATF's remit was expanded beyond AML to cover CFT and eight special recommendations, which later became nine, were adopted in 2001. The FATF's mandate was further extended to include the financing of proliferation of weapons of mass destruction in 2008. The recommendations were updated in 2012, incorporating these three components to form the existing consolidated Forty Recommendations.[15] The FATF states that these Recommendations have been endorsed by over 180 countries and have come to be 'universally recognised as the international standards' for AML and CFT.[16]

The original 1990 FATF Recommendation 16 introduced the notion of suspicion-based reporting by financial institutions to the competent authority. It states:

> If financial institutions suspect that funds stem from a criminal activity, they should be permitted or required to report promptly their suspicions to the competent authorities. Accordingly, there should be legal provisions to protect financial institutions and their employees from criminal or civil liability for breach of any restriction on disclosure of information imposed by contract or by any legislative, regulatory or administrative provision, if they report in good faith, in disclosing suspected criminal activity to the competent authorities, even if they did not know precisely what the underlying criminal activity was, and regardless of whether illegal activity actually occurred.[17]

As mentioned earlier, the current FATF Recommendations were updated and consolidated into a single body of Forty Recommendations in 2012. Section D, 'Preventive Measures', Recommendation 20 on 'Reporting of suspicious transactions' states:

> If a financial institution suspects or has reasonable grounds to suspect that funds are the proceeds of a criminal activity, or are related to terrorist financing, it should be required, by law, to report promptly its suspicions to the financial intelligence unit (FIU).[18]

---

[15] Unless otherwise stated, FATF recommendation numbers mentioned in this chapter refer to the 2012 version of the recommendations.

[16] FATF, 'International Standards on Combating Money Laundering and the Financing of Terrorism and Proliferation' (February 2012) at 7, online: www.fatf-gafi.org/media/fatf/documents/recommendations/pdfs/FATF_Recommendations.pdf. Indeed, on inside cover, it is stated: 'The FATF Recommendations are recognised as the global anti-money laundering (AML) and counter-terrorist financing (CFT) standard.'

[17] FATF, 'The Forty Recommendations of the Financial Action Task Force on Money Laundering' (1990) at 3, online: www.fatf-gafi.org/media/fatf/documents/recommendations/pdfs/FATF%20Recommendations%201990.pdf

[18] 2012 FATF Recommendations, *supra* note 16 at 19.

In regard to the establishment of an FIU in each country and its function within the jurisdiction, Recommendation 29 states:

> Countries should establish a financial intelligence unit (FIU) that serves as a national centre for the receipt and analysis of: (a) suspicious transaction reports; and (b) other information relevant to money laundering, associated predicate offences and terrorist financing, and for the dissemination of the results of that analysis. The FIU should be able to obtain additional information from reporting entities, and should have access on a timely basis to the financial, administrative and law enforcement information that it requires to undertake its functions properly.[19]

The FATF addresses issues pertaining to bank secrecy in the following two Recommendations. Section D, Recommendation 9 on 'Financial institution secrecy laws', states:

> Countries should ensure that financial institution secrecy laws do not inhibit implementation of the FATF Recommendations.[20]

Furthermore, Recommendation 21(a) addresses confidentiality issues pertaining to bank secrecy, thus, stating that financial institutions, their directors and officers should be:

> [P]rotected by law from criminal and civil liability for breach of any restriction on disclosure of information imposed by contract or by any legislative, regulatory or administrative provision, if they report their suspicions in good faith to the FIU, even if they did not know precisely what the underlying criminal activity was, and regardless of whether illegal activity actually occurred.[21]

The FATF attaches great importance to international cooperation and addresses the issue of bank secrecy by stating in its Recommendation 37 that countries should not refuse to execute a request for mutual legal assistance on the grounds of bank secrecy.[22]

These FATF Recommendations reflect the situations in the past where banks might have found themselves caught in conflicting duties of confidentiality and disclosure. Reporting by banks has been challenged in the past. However, US courts, for example, have found that the rights protected under the legislation requiring reporting and disclosure outweighed the inconvenience caused to financial institutions.[23] In many cases pertaining

---

[19] *Ibid.*, at 24.
[20] *Ibid.*, at 14.
[21] *Ibid.*, at 19.
[22] *Ibid.*, at 27.
[23] See, for example, *California Bankers Association* v. *Shultz*, 416 U.S. 21 (1974).

to the extraterritorial application of the US law, the US courts have chosen to take a 'balancing approach', which requires the weighing of 'the importance of the US interest in disclosure against the interest of the target state in retaining the confidentiality of the information or documents in question'.[24] While 'weighing the public interest in maintaining confidence against a countervailing public interest favouring disclosure'[25] may be a sound balancing approach in a domestic context, when applied in an extraterritorial context, understandably, it has triggered negative reactions from foreign courts[26] and protests from foreign governments.[27] It has been argued that the adoption of 'shared values' approach could prevent such conflicts pertaining to the extraterritorial application of internal economic law.[28] Taking this approach, in a situation where, for example, the US courts wish to apply extraterritorially the US internal economic law and if the law expresses values that are shared with the country to which they wish to apply it, it is argued that the courts of the country concerned should apply the said law. However, this still leaves open the possibility of the foreign courts declining to apply the law on the grounds that it poses a threat to national interests. Furthermore, 'shared values' may not be so easily found among different states as their economic policies may not necessarily be converging, notwithstanding the globalisation of business and commerce.[29]

Having said this, as it has been observed, the global economic system is governed by a complex legal network, consisting of treaty-based intergovernmental organisations such as the International Monetary Fund (IMF) and the World Bank, regional agreements and private legal systems.[30] Let us now turn our attention to the measures, at national, regional and

---

[24] P.T. Muchlinski, *Multinational Enterprises and the Law* (Oxford: Oxford University Press, 2007) at 166.

[25] Lord Goff in *Attorney-General* v. *Guardian Newspapers (No. 2)* [1990] 1 AC 109 at 282.

[26] See, for example, in England, *XAG and Others* v. *A Bank* [1983] 2 All ER 464 (QBD Com Ct); in Germany, *Krupp Mak Maschinenbau GmbH* v. *Deutsche Bank AG* (Landgericht Kiel 6/30/82) 22 ILM 740 (1983), discussed in Muchlinski, *Multinational Enterprises and the Law, supra* note 24 at 167.

[27] For example, the Japanese Government's strong protest against the findings in *United States* v. *Toyota Motor Corporation*, 569 F. Supp. 1158 (C.D. Cal. 1983).

[28] See B. Grossfeld and C.P. Rogers, 'A Shared Values Approach to Jurisdictional Conflicts in International Economic Law', *ICLQ*, 32 (1983) 931.

[29] See, for example, Muchlinski, *Multinational Enterprises and the Law, supra* note 24 at 175.

[30] O. Perez, 'The Many Faces of the Trade-Environment Conflict: Some Lessons for the Constitutionalisation Project', in C. Joerges, I. Sand and G. Teubner (eds), *Transnational Governance and Constitutionalism* (Oxford: Hart Publishing, 2004) at 239.

international levels, to facilitate information disclosure by banks to relevant authorities and information exchange between the authorities.

4.3   National Legislative Measures and Bilateral and Multilateral Agreements

According to the survey,[31] conducted by the Anti-Fraud and Anti-Money Laundering Committee and the Fiscal Committee of the European Banking Federation, of all EU member states, other European countries and three countries outside Europe, namely the United States, Australia and Japan, had in place measures to enable reporting by financial institutions to domestic competent authorities without breaches of bank secrecy laws. This is the case regardless of whether bank secrecy is established on a statutory basis, as in most civilian systems of law, or as an implied term of contract, as in many common law jurisdictions.[32] The findings of this survey suggest that bank secrecy laws are not obstacles to disclosure obligations under the AML/CFT regime in those countries studied.

Furthermore, the initiatives by intergovernmental organisations have led to the signing of bilateral agreements, facilitating mutual legal assistance and cross-border disclosure of information not only in the context of AML/CFT but also now increasingly in tax-related matters. It has been suggested that by facilitating information exchange between the competent authorities of various countries, these bilateral agreements are reducing the need to resort to extraterritorial application of internal laws. The OECD, for example, is pushing for multilateral agreements in tax matters, in order to close any loopholes, by encouraging countries to become signatories to the Multilateral Convention on Mutual Administrative Assistance in Tax Matters.[33] Indeed, scholars have found that after the signing of a bilateral agreement, some funds were moved out by their owners to other jurisdictions where no bilateral agreements existed between those jurisdictions and their home countries. For example, a study of bilateral bank deposit data provided by the Bank for International Settlements (BIS) concludes that the signing of bilateral agreements led to the relocation of bank deposits from jurisdictions which have signed bilateral

---

[31] European Banking Federation, 'Report on Banking Secrecy' (April 2004), online: www.ebf-fbe.eu/wp-content/uploads/2014/03/Bk_secrecy_Report04-2004-02083-01-E.pdf

[32] See, *ibid.*, the annex to the report which provides a useful comparison chart between the jurisdictions studied in the survey.

[33] OECD, 'The Era of Bank Secrecy Is Over', *supra* note 3 at 6.

agreements with their home countries to those without such agreements, and that they have not resulted significantly in the repatriation of funds to the home countries.[34] Therefore, it can be observed that the OECD's eagerness to promote multilateral agreements is driven by the perceived need to create a level playing field in order to discourage such regulatory arbitrage.

The OECD's efforts to facilitate exchange of financial information between jurisdictions on the basis of the aforementioned Multilateral Convention have gone a step further whereby, as of 16 February 2016, 80 jurisdictions have signed the multilateral competent authority agreement which allows the automatic exchange of information between competent authorities in tax matters, to be implemented from September 2017 onwards.[35] The OECD states that 'the intergovernmental implementation of the US Foreign Account Tax Compliance Act (FATCA) . . . acted as a catalyst for the move towards automatic exchange of information in a multilateral context', and equally acknowledges the progress made by 'global AML standards'.[36]

Nevertheless, it is to be noted that in tax matters, 'competent authorities' between which information exchange is to be facilitated are tax authorities, whereas in regard to AML and CFT, information exchange is to be facilitated between the FIU established in each jurisdiction. Therefore, banks are required not only to disclose information but also to disclose this to different competent authorities, depending on whether it is in regard to AML/CFT or tax matters.

While the OECD's ongoing efforts to facilitate automatic information exchange reflect the need for the authorities to secure tax revenues to help public finances, as it has been noted earlier, the establishing global standards that require financial institutions to disclose information to the authorities were achieved by the FATF in regard to AML and CFT. And it should also be noted that the revision of the FATF Recommendations in 2012 resulted in the inclusion of tax evasion as one of the predicate offences of money laundering, and, as a result, the FATF will, no doubt, continue to play a significant role in the fight against tax evasion.

---

[34] See N. Johannesen and G. Zucman, 'The End of Bank Secrecy? An Evaluation of the G20 Tax Haven Crackdown', *American Economic Journal: Economic Policy*, 6 (2014) 65.

[35] OECD, 'Signatories of the Multilateral Competent Authority Agreement on Automatic Exchange of Financial Account Information and Intended First Exchange Date' (27 January 2016), online: www.oecd.org/ctp/exchange-of-tax-information/mcaa-signatories.pdf

[36] See OECD, 'Automatic Exchange of Financial Account Information: Background Information Brief', *supra* note 35 at 3.

4.4   The Implementation of 'Global Standard' through Mutual Evaluation and Black Listing

The FATF regards itself as 'the global standard-setter'[37] in AML and CFT,[38] and as such has developed an assessment mechanism to ensure that those over 180 jurisdictions, which have endorsed the FATF Recommendations, are compliant with what they have signed up to. The mechanism is based on the so-called mutual evaluation, comprising self-assessment and peer review, led by the FATF and FATF-style regional bodies (FSRBs), and other assessment bodies such as the World Bank and the IMF.[39]

The most recent round of mutual evaluation began in 2014, using a new methodology,[40] which not only continues with the evaluation of each country's compliance with the FATF Recommendations as before, but also adds to the mutual evaluation exercise 'a systematic assessment of the effectiveness of national systems ... The future assessments will determine how well countries achieve the objective of fighting Money Laundering and Financing of Terrorism.'[41]

The process under the new methodology comprises the following two interlinked components. First, the technical compliance assessment, which 'addresses the specific requirements of each of the FATF Recommendations, principally as they relate to the relevant legal and institutional framework of the country, and the powers and procedures of competent authorities', which, in turn, 'represent the fundamental building blocks of an AML/CFT system'.[42] The second component, the effective assessment, focuses on the extent to which the country's

---

[37] FATF, 'International Standards on Combating Money Laundering and the Financing of Terrorism and Proliferation', *supra* note 16.

[38] FATF, 'FATF issues new Mechanism to Strengthen Money Laundering and Terrorist Financing Compliance' (22 February 2013), online: www.fatf-gafi.org/documents/documents/fatfissuesnewmechanismtostrengthenmoneylaunderingandterroristfinancingcompliance.html

[39] See FATF, 'Procedures for the FATF Fourth Round of AML/CFT Mutual Evaluations' (October 2013) at 17, online: www.fatf-gafi.org/media/fatf/documents/methodology/FATF-4th-Round-Procedures.pdf

[40] See FATF, 'Methodology for Assessing Technical Compliance with the FATF Recommendations and the Effectiveness of AML/CFT Systems' (February 2013), online: www.fatf-gafi.org/media/fatf/documents/methodology/FATF%20Methodology%2022%20Feb%202013.pdf

[41] FATF, 'FATF Issues New Mechanism to Strengthen Money Laundering and Terrorist Financing Compliance', *supra* note 38.

[42] FATF, 'Methodology for Assessing the Technical Compliance with the FATF Recommendations and the Effectiveness of AML/CFT Systems', *supra* note 40 at 4.

AML/CFT-related legal and institutional framework is delivering the expected outcomes. By combining the two components, the evaluation process is designed to analyse the extent of the country's compliance with 'the FATF standards' and its success in maintaining 'a strong AML/CFT system, as required by the FATF recommendations'.[43]

What makes these jurisdictions take the FATF mutual evaluation seriously and with much apprehension is the fact that the findings on each jurisdiction are published and are made public. The FATF has used 'the carrot and the stick' methods to induce and coerce countries into implementing the FATF Recommendations whereby the FATF 'has succeeded in supranationalising money laundering law'.[44] The 'carrot' element has been offered by the World Bank and the IMF[45] through the provision of technical assistance and the increased incorporation of AML/CFT assessment into 'loan/development packages'.[46] The 'stick' element has been delivered through the FATF's own mechanism to list those jurisdictions, which are deemed to be lacking in adequate AML measures in place, as 'Non-Cooperative Countries and Territories' (NCCTs). The FATF launched the NCCTs exercise in 1998 and initially listed 23 jurisdictions as NCCTs. By 2006, the FATF delisted the last jurisdiction. The NCCTs have been replaced by the list of 'High-risk and non-cooperative jurisdiction' in which the FATF currently includes 15 jurisdictions.[47] Furthermore, the publication of unfavourable results of the mutual evaluation may not only embarrass the country concerned but also have detrimental effects on its economy and businesses therein, as based on the FATF findings, some banks may well decide to de-risk themselves by withdrawing their business from the jurisdiction in question.

Notwithstanding the efforts and resources that have been devoted to ensuring that jurisdictions around the world comply with AML/CFT standards, the effectiveness of AML/CFT measures, in terms of successful prosecutions, let alone the seizure of proceeds of crime or even the disruption of the money flow of criminal enterprises or terrorist organisations,

---

[43] *Ibid.*

[44] D.A. Leslie, *Legal Principles for Combatting Cyberlaundering* (New York: Springer, 2014) at 14.

[45] IMF and World Bank, 'Anti-Money Laundering and Combating the Financing of Terrorism: Observations from the Work Program and Implications Going Forward' (31 August 2005), online: www.imf.org/external/np/pp/eng/2005/083105.pdf

[46] O. Bures, *EU Counterterrorism Policy: A Paper Tiger?* (Farnham: Ashgate, 2011) at 178.

[47] FATF, 'High-Risk and Non-Cooperative Jurisdictions' (2016), online: www.fatf-gafi.org/countries/#high-risk

has been questioned.[48] Indeed, it has been argued that the disruption of money flow would only be effective against those enterprises that require regular flow of funds.[49]

While the effectiveness of AML/CTF measures in combating money laundering and terrorist financing may be questionable, what is certain is that in terms of obtaining financial intelligence as a tool to aid law enforcement or intelligence agencies, the FATF has created a global network of FIUs, which receive globally standardised information through suspicion-based reporting. As a result, not only these FIUs are in a position to exchange information among themselves but also such information can now be accessed by tax authorities.[50] Considering the fact that since the announcement of the Forty Recommendations in 1990, the FATF has managed to lead countries around the world to the introduction of AML/CFT measures, the FATF's achievement not only in global standard setting but also in its implementation must be worthy of recognition, particularly given the potential usefulness of these developments to supervisory, law enforcement and tax authorities around the world.

Nevertheless, concerns have been raised on many occasions in regard to whether it is appropriate to place banks and other commercial entities on the front line in the fight against organised crime, terror, corruption and now tax evasion, and whether compliance costs, as well as legal, regulatory and reputational risks to which these banks and other entities are exposed, are proportionate or justifiable.[51]

Having said this, given the aforementioned value to various authorities of access to a global network of financial intelligence, it is highly unlikely that the clock could be turned back or any attempts would be made to undo the process.

4.5   Institutional Perspective

The twenty-first century has seen a further paradigm shift from the sole focus on economic goals to the recognition of the importance of balancing

---

[48] See, for example, M. Levi and P. Reuter, 'Money Laundering', *Crime and Justice*, 34(1) (2006) 289–375.

[49] B. Rider, 'Strategic Tools – For Now and Perhaps the Future?', in B. Rider (ed), *Research Handbook on International Financial Crime* (Cheltenham: Edward Elgar Publishing, 2015) at 726–54.

[50] See OECD, 'Improving Co-operation', *supra* note 8.

[51] See, for example, B. Rider, 'Proceeds of Crime – A Bridge Too Far?', *Journal of Money Laundering Control*, 19 (2016) 1.

economic and social goals.[52] This has moved not only the social goals higher up on the agenda of intergovernmental organisations but also that of governments around the world. The paradigm shift has seen the development of an unprecedented number of international instruments which, in turn, have resulted in the governments around the world introducing legislative measures in the areas that had previously been regarded as the domain of corporate social responsibility (CSR). This has significant implications, particularly to those who regard CSR as 'voluntary' action on the part of corporations,[53] as opposed to a legal requirement.[54] As a result of international developments in measures to combat money laundering, which some had previously identified as one of the issues covered by standards in CSR,[55] it can no longer be regarded as an area in which banks and other regulated entities have the choice to decide whether to comply or not. In contrast, notwithstanding much criticism levelled at the failure of corporate governance after the financial crisis, in most countries it continues to operate on a 'comply or explain' basis, which is arguably not suited to dealing with matters of criminal nature.[56]

As I have observed, we cannot ignore the consensus reached at an international level, to tackle financial crime and money laundering in particular, and the recognition of the need to improve '[e]ffective

---

[52] See, for example, M. Iskander and N. Chamlou, 'Corporate Governance: A Framework for Implementation' (May 2000), online: www-wds.worldbank.org/servlet/WDSContent Server/WDSP/IB/2000/09/08/000094946_00082605593465/Rendered/PDF/multi_page.pdf

[53] See, for example, the definitional change in the European Commission's statements on 'CSR' – in its Green Paper published in 2001, at 6, it defined CSR as 'a concept whereby companies integrate social and environmental concerns in their business operations and in their interaction with their stakeholders on a voluntary basis' whereas ten years on in 2011 it defined as 'the responsibility of enterprises for their impacts on society', see *Communication from the Commission to the European Parliament, the Council, the European Economic and Social Committee and the Committee of the Regions: A Renewed EU strategy 2011–14 for Corporate Social Responsibility* [2011] COM/2011/0681 final.

[54] See C. Nakajima and W. Harry, 'Is the Desire to Embed Corporate Social Responsibility within Organizations at a Crossroads?', *International Studies of Management and Organizations*, 42 (2012) 3.

[55] See, for example, W. Cragg and K. McKague, 'Compendium of Ethics Codes and Instruments of Corporate Responsibility' (January 2007), online: www.yorku.ca/csr/_files/file.php?fileid= fileCDOICwJiei&filename=file_Codes_Compendium_Jan_2007.pdf. This compendium was compiled as a companion to the book, W. Cragg (ed), *Ethics Codes, Corporations and the Challenge of Globalization* (Cheltenham: Edward Elgar Publishing, 2005).

[56] See, for example, C. Nakajima, 'Corporate Governance and Responsibility' in B. Rider (ed), in *Research Handbook on Financial Crime* (Cheltenbalm: Edward Elgar Publishing, 2015), 155–65.

co-operation between financial regulators and law enforcement authorities'.[57] Furthermore, in 1998 the G7 countries announced an initiative to 'enhance the capacity of anti-money laundering systems to deal effectively with tax related crimes'.[58] According to the then Economic Secretary to HM Treasury of the United Kingdom, one of the G7 countries, 'The [G7] initiative is designed to ensure that financial institutions report suspicions of tax-related crime and that this information is shared both domestically and internationally'.[59] It is, therefore, arguable that the case for a wider interpretation of 'the duty to the public to disclose' must be considerably stronger than it was in 1924 when the case of *Tournier* v. *National Provincial and Union Bank of England* (hereinafter *Tournier*)[60] was decided in England, and that similar consideration must have gained significance in other jurisdictions, given the increasing emphasis on disclosure and sharing of information at an international level, let alone 'domestically'.[61]

The so-called tax havens which have been the targets of the OECD's initiative against 'Harmful Tax Competition'[62] are no exceptions to the rule. Through mutual legal assistance treaties, jurisdictions such as the Cayman Islands, would allow disclosure of confidential information without the danger of triggering bank secrecy laws. Notwithstanding this, the US Treasury Department's advisory notice, issued in 2000, calls for extra vigilance when doing business in the Cayman Islands by stating: 'The Cayman Islands remains committed to strict bank secrecy, outside of a limited suspicious transaction reporting and international cooperation regime'.[63] In the light of such warning, it is not surprising that the Cayman

---

[57] See the conclusions of the meeting of G7 Finance Ministers and the representatives of the European Commission who met prior to the G7 Summit held in Birmingham, UK, in May 1998, 'Conclusions of G7 Finance Ministers' (9 May 1998) at para. 7, online: University of Toronto G8 Information Centre, www.g8.utoronto.ca/finance/fm980509.htm

[58] *Ibid.*, at para. 16.

[59] Keynote speech given by Mrs Helen Liddell MP, the then Economic Secretary to HM Treasury, at the Joint Meeting of Commonwealth Finance and Law Officials of Money Laundering, 1 June 1998, quoted in M. Bridges, 'The Nexus between Money Laundering and Tax Evasion', in G. Funnell (ed), *HMRC Investigations and Enquiries 2011/12* (London: Bloomsbury Professional Ltd., 2011), 139–62 at 147.

[60] [1924] 1 KB 461.

[61] For discussion of the *Tournier* case, see, for example, C. Nakajima, *Conflicts of Interest and Duty*, *supra* note 10, Chapter 8.

[62] OECD, 'Harmful Tax Competition', *supra* note 2.

[63] S. Said, 'Banking Secrecy in the Cayman Islands', see US Department of Treasury Financial Crimes Enforcement Network, 'Transactions involving the Cayman Islands', Advisory Issue 14, July 2000: www.fincen.gov/news_room/rp/advisory/pdf/advis14.pdf

Islands is one of the signatories to the Multilateral Competent Authority Agreement, which will facilitate automatic exchange of information in tax matters, starting in September 2017.

Another aspect of financial crime that has been vigorously pursued by the OECD is corruption. The international fight against corruption began in earnest with the adoption in 1997 of the OECD Convention on Combating the Bribery of Foreign Public Officials in International Business Transactions. This was followed by the United Nations Convention against Corruption, which entered into force in 2005.[64] Corruption is one of the predicate offences stipulated in the FATF Recommendations and proceeds of corruption would need to be laundered if the ill-gotten gains were to be enjoyed without fear of detection or prosecution. Recognising that '[c]orruption and money laundering are intrinsically linked',[65] the G20 have mandated the FATF to assist in the fight against corruption. The FATF Recommendation 12 requires banks to apply enhanced customer due diligence to the so-called politically exposed persons (PEPs). Parallel to this are the various AML standards in private banking, set by the Wolfsberg Group, a group of private banking institutions, coming together in the aftermath of a scandal which revealed that the former President of Nigeria, Sani Abacha, had been laundering the funds that he and his family had syphoned off his country through the private banking arms of leading international banking groups.[66]

While tackling corruption and tax evasion continues to be high on the agenda in the global arena, escalating conflicts in the Middle East and the rise and expansion of terrorist activity and the resulting real and perceived threats to many countries not only in the region but also on a global scale have necessitated the leaders of the G20 to deal with terrorism as a matter of urgency. Indeed, at the recent G20 Summit, held in

[64] For further discussions on international initiatives to fight corruption, see C. Nakajima and P. Palmer, 'Anti-corruption: Law and Practice', in A. Stachowicz-Stanusch (ed), *Organizational Immunity to Corruption: Building Theoretical and Research Foundations* (Charlotte: Information Age Publishing, 2010) at 99–110.

[65] FATF, 'Corruption: A Reference Guide and Information Note on the Use of the FATF Recommendations to Support the Fight against Corruption' (2010) at 2, online: www.fatf-gafi.org/media/fatf/documents/reports/reference%20guide%20and%20information%20note%20on%20fight%20against%20corruption.pdf

[66] For the case study, see FATF, 'Specific Risk Factors in the Laundering of Proceeds of Corruption: Assistance to Reporting Institutions' (June 2012) at 16–7, online: www.fatf-gafi.org/media/fatf/documents/reports/Specific%20Risk%20Factors%20in%20the%20Laundering%20of%20Proceeds%20of%20Corruption.pdf. See also, Nakajima and Palmer, 'Anti-corruption: Law and Practice', *supra* note 64 at 103.

Turkey in November 2015, the G20 countries resolved to fight terrorism and affirmed their commitment to 'tackling the financing channels of terrorism' through various measures, including the enhancement of cooperation in information exchange among others.[67] Against this background, the FATF submitted a report to the G20 leaders on its actions against terrorist financing.[68]

The paradigm shift in the context of international initiatives to fight financial crime and resulting measures to tackle global issues, including money laundering, terrorist financing, tax evasion and corruption, is an ongoing process, even though the shift may be subtle and somewhat inconspicuous. Indeed, those who have come into contact with this area recently may be forgiven for thinking that the present-day AML/CFT measures have little or nothing to do with the drugs trade. It is, therefore, appropriate to acknowledge here that because the 'drug issues' which, G7 countries declared in 1989, had 'reached devastating proportions',[69] G7 countries mandated a task force drawn from the G7 countries and other interested countries 'to assess the results of cooperation already undertaken in order to prevent the utilization of the banking system and financial institutions for the purpose of money laundering, and to consider additional preventive efforts in this field, including the adaptation of the legal and regulatory systems so as to enhance multilateral judicial assistance'.[70] This task force formed the basis of the establishment of the FATF in 1990.

Given the nature of the international fora in which these issues of mutual concern are discussed, the issues themselves are highly politically influenced and therefore the issues which receive most attention and thus the allocation of necessary resources are the ones which are perceived to be sufficiently pressing at the relevant times to command the requisite political will for action to be taken. It is, therefore, arguable that priorities change and issues on the agenda may appear somewhat cyclical, as it

---

[67] G20, 'Statement on the Fight against Terrorism' (16 November 2015), online: European Council, www.consilium.europa.eu/en/press/press-releases/2015/11/16-g20-leaders-antalya-statement-terrorism/

[68] FATF, 'Terrorist Financing FATF Report to G20 Leaders – Actions Taken by the FATF' (November 2015), online: www.fatf-gafi.org/media/fatf/documents/reports/Terrorist-financing-actions-taken-by-FATF.pdf

[69] See the Economic Declaration made by the G7 countries at the Summit meeting held in Paris on 16 July 1989, *supra* note 14 at para. 52.

[70] *Ibid.*

has been observed in regard to the cyclical nature of a crisis followed by a reform in corporate governance.[71]

4.6   Unintended Consequences

I have observed earlier that, as a result of global consensus building led by major industrial nations,[72] such as the G7, G8 and more recently G20, and assisted by intergovernmental organisations such as the World Bank, the IMF and the European Commission, global standards in AML/CFT have been set and, in turn, they have been implemented in jurisdictions around the world. It may be useful, at this juncture, to take stock of some of the unintended consequences resulting from this 'one-size-fits-all' approach to standardisation in this area. I will limit my discussion within the purview of this chapter which is to examine the pressures on the banks to disclose information in compliance with AML/CFT regulation.

At the organisational level, banks are faced not only with the proliferation of legal and regulatory requirements with which to comply but also the resulting increasing costs of human and financial resources. Furthermore, banks are required to disclose information to a number of different authorities and in different jurisdictions as banking business is most unlikely to be confined within one single jurisdiction. As I have observed, while banks are required to submit suspicious activity/transaction reports to the FIUs in regard to money laundering and terrorist finance, they are, at the same time, required to submit financial account information to the competent tax authorities.

OECD has set out the 'Common Reporting Standards', aimed at 'maximizing efficiency and reducing costs for financial institutions'.[73] OECD is also leading work to improve cooperation between tax and AML authorities.[74] Nevertheless, while these initiatives may facilitate better exchange of information between these authorities domestically and internationally, it will not help the banks which are, nevertheless, required to disclose different types of information, which need to be kept confidential other than in the context of reporting, to different relevant authorities.

---

[71] See, for example, T. Clarke, *International Corporate Governance: A Comparative Approach* (Oxford: Routledge, 2007) at 13.

[72] See, for example, the Economic Declaration made by the G7 countries at the Summit meeting held in Paris on 16 July 1989, *supra* note 14.

[73] OECD, 'Standard for Automatic Exchange of Financial Account Information', *supra* note 7 at 6.

[74] OECD, 'Improving Co-operation', *supra* note 8.

Another example of unintended consequence is de-risking 'significant regions or sections of the public', leading to financial exclusion, which, the FATF acknowledges, is a growing problem.[75] The FATF has been working on 'financial inclusion' as it recognises that 'applying an overly cautious approach to AML/CFT safeguards can have the unintended consequence of excluding legitimate businesses and customers from the formal financial system.'[76] Indeed, de-risking continues to be high on the FATF's agenda, as it has the potential to 'drive financial transactions underground which creates financial exclusion and reduces transparency, thereby increasing money laundering and terrorist financing risks'.[77] While the FATF recognises that banks' propensity to de-risk is understandable in the light of huge fines imposed on banks around the world, it is, nevertheless, at pains to point out that those were imposed in the context of 'egregious cases involving banks who deliberately broke the law, in some cases for more than a decade, and had significant fundamental AML/CFT failings'.[78] Against this background, the FATF has published the *Guidance for a Risk-Based Approach: Effective Supervision and Enforcement by AML/CFT Supervisors and Law Enforcement*,[79] reiterating that 'when failures are detected, the regulator or supervisor should apply actions that are appropriate and proportionate, taking into account the nature of the failure.'[80]

It is worthy of note that the FATF emphasises that it is important for the supervisory and enforcement actions to remain 'appropriate and proportionate'. A spate of regulatory sanctions imposed on banks by the supervisor in one jurisdiction may trigger a chain reaction of sanctions on the same banks imposed by supervisors in other jurisdictions, as witnessed in recent years. In the light of this, the FATF's reiteration of appropriateness

---

[75] See, for example, the speech given by the FATF President, Roger Wilkins A.O., 'The danger of driving both illicit markets and financial exclusion', at the 6th Annual International Conference on Financial Crime and Terrorism Finance (8 October 2014), online: www.fatf-gafi.org/publications/fatfgeneral/documents/danger-illicit-markets-financial-exclusion.html

[76] FATF, 'Anti-Money Laundering and Terrorist Financing Measures and Financial Inclusion' (February 2013) at 5, online: www.fatf-gafi.org/media/fatf/documents/reports/AML_CFT_Measures_and_Financial_Inclusion_2013.pdf

[77] See 'FATF Takes Action to Tackle De-risking' (23 October 2015), online: www.fatf-gafi.org/publications/fatfrecommendations/documents/fatf-action-to-tackle-de-risking.html

[78] See 'FATF Clarifies Risk-based Approach: Case-by-Case, Not Wholesale De-risking' (23 October 2014), online: www.fatf-gafi.org/publications/fatfgeneral/documents/rba-and-de-risking.html

[79] (October 2015), online: www.fatf-gafi.org/media/fatf/documents/reports/RBA-Effective-supervision-and-enforcement.pdf

[80] See 'FATF Takes Action to Tackle De-risking', *supra* note 77.

and proportionality may be of small comfort to banking groups operating in multiple jurisdictions.

4.7   Multilayered Competing/Conflicting Demands

In order to gain a better understanding of the international pressures that are brought onto banks to disclose information in the increasingly globalised world in which we live, the existence of multilevel competing/conflicting institutional pressures need to be recognised and to be taken into consideration. Indeed, more studies need to be conducted in the context of globalisation to fully appreciate the phenomenon where institutional pressures at international or regional levels result in the creation of national legislation which in turn lead to competing/conflicting demands brought upon commercial entities operating transnationally or even domestically.

Current limitations in research in this area are due to the fact that there is relatively little cross-disciplinary research conducted and, indeed, very few vehicles are perhaps available to facilitate and promote it, at least in the countries in which the present author has worked or has collaborated.[81] Nevertheless, such research is much needed to fully understand the impact of institutional pressures at the international level, which, in turn, will create or influence institutional pressures at the national level to which banks need to respond. Furthermore, in order to avoid negative or unintended consequences of regulatory measures, such multilevel institutional analysis may become a useful tool.

It seems to me that certain social issues of global scale have necessitated global standard setting, such as in regard to AML/CFT, which, in turn, has created competing regulatory demands at different levels – *inter alia*, confidentiality versus transparency at the governmental level. Governments are not immune from these institutional pressures. Therefore, governments will respond to institutional pressures set by international instruments or even soft laws comprising statements of best practice, and, as in the case of the FATF Recommendations, will implement what is required through national legislation.

---

[81] One exception is the long-standing annual International Symposium on Economic Crime, held at Jesus College, University of Cambridge, which draws together participants from the public sector, ranging from government ministers, policy makers, regulators, supervisors, members of the judiciary and law enforcers, and the relevant professions as well as a cross section of academic disciplines, to discuss issues of mutual concern pertaining to the prevention and control of economic crime.

It may be arguable that conflicting demands can be reconciled at an international level. Some scholars observe that bank secrecy will not necessarily be an obstacle to the increasing need for governments to pursue tax revenues, as some jurisdictions will impose withholding tax across the board on non-resident account holders.[82] It is also observed that, on the one hand, some jurisdictions may choose to comply with transparency demands as they see the advantage of obtaining other business as a result of their acceptability globally. On the other hand, some jurisdictions will gain more customers because of the lack of transparency.[83] Therefore, it may be that superficial compliance, referred to by some scholars as 'decoupling', will happen in certain jurisdictions, just as it has been observed among companies when faced with conflicting demands.[84]

4.8   Conclusion

While, post-financial crisis, there may not be much sympathy for banks, particularly in those countries where many were bailed out by the governments, and for bankers generally, the pressures which banks are under as a result of the conflicting demands imposed on them in the global fight against financial crime are not insignificant. And those conflicting demands invariably result in exposing banks to increasing legal, regulatory and reputational risks.

While the conflict between the requirements under the AML/CFT regulatory framework and bank secrecy may well be addressed through the exceptions to bank secrecy, established in *Tournier*, of disclosure under compulsion of law and under a duty to the public,[85] and legislative reform introducing exceptions to strict bank secrecy laws, there may well be occasions when banks will be exposed to legal risk, for example, civil actions taken by their customers. In other words, not every aspect of conflicts of duty resulting from conflicting legal and regulatory requirements has necessarily been addressed. It should be noted that the statutory provisions,

---

[82] See, for example, H. Huizinga and S.B. Nielsen, 'Withholding Taxes or Information Exchange: The Taxation of International Interest Flows', *Journal of Public Economics*, 87(1) (2003) 39–72, and Johannesen and Zucman, 'The End of Bank Secrecy?', *supra* note 34.

[83] *Ibid.*, at 89–90.

[84] See, for example, C. Clark, J. Grosvold and S. Hoejmose, 'Corporate Governance and Board Diversity Strategy: An Empirical Test of Decoupling', *Academy of Management Proceedings* 2013(1) (2013) 15273.

[85] See the discussion and comments on the *Tournier* case by Gannon (Chapter 8), Booysen (Chapter 10) and Stanton (Chapter 12).

based on the FATF Recommendations, may only protect banks against liability arising directly from breach of the obligation of confidentiality, and may not, therefore, protect them from liability for defamation, malicious prosecution or third-party claims.[86]

In the global fight against tax evasion, 'bank secrecy' has been somewhat demonised, particularly given the negative connotation of the word, 'secrecy' that has been used in the context of various initiatives by the OECD to tackle tax evasion. For example, the OECD's report, entitled 'The Era of Bank Secrecy Is Over', opens by stating, 'In April 2009, G20 Leaders took action to end the era of bank secrecy. The Global Forum report on exchange of information . . . sets out how this initiative radically improved countries' capacity to tackle tax evasion carried out through the exploitation of offshore financial centres and banking secrecy.'[87] In the context of this chapter, in which I have attempted to examine the conflicting demands on banks resulting from legal and regulatory requirements for information disclosure in the facilitation of fight against financial crime, the use of the term 'confidentiality' may be more appropriate.

As for the dynamics between confidentiality and disclosure in this context, with record fines being imposed by the US and other regulatory authorities on banks for compliance failures, banks' propensity to information disclosure will only become greater.

---

[86] The discussion of such liability is beyond the scope of this chapter but see, in the context of English law, C. Nakajima, *Conflicts of Interest and Duty*, *supra* note 10 at 191–3 and 226–7. It is worthy of note that s. 37 of the *Serious Crime Act 2015* (UK), c 9 inserted a new subsection, 4A, into s. 338 of the *Proceeds of Crime Act 2002* (UK), c 29 which provides, 'Where an authorised disclosure is made in good faith, no civil liability arises in respect of the disclosure on the part of the person by or on whose behalf it is made.' Nevertheless, it is also to be noted that Lord Bates, introducing the amendment stated that 'immunity from civil proceedings will apply only where a suspicious activity report is submitted in good faith, and those in the regulated sector responsible for submitting such reports will continue to be liable for any negligent or malicious conduct', House of Lords, *Parliamentary Debates* (2 March 2015), col. 45 (Lord Bates, Parliamentary Under-Secretary of State, Home Office).

[87] OECD, 'The Era of Bank Secrecy Is Over', *supra* note 3 at 2.

International Developments in Exchange of Tax Information

MARTHA O'BRIEN

5.1 Introduction

The goal of this chapter is to provide a survey of recent developments in international exchange of tax information and the impact these have had, or potentially will have, on bank secrecy. Each country has its own rules for when its tax authorities may collect information about its own tax-payers from domestic financial institutions, the requirements for judicial authorisation to obtain such information, the line between audits and criminal investigations and constitutional and privacy protection limits on access by the revenue authorities to such information. This contribution will not attempt to examine how the international regimes now being implemented will affect any particular jurisdiction's bank secrecy rules, which is addressed in other chapters.

5.2 Overview

Developed countries with functioning income and capital taxation systems began to be concerned about the effects of globalisation on their tax bases and ability to collect tax revenue in the mid- to late 1980s. With the international liberalisation of trade, investment and capital movements came offshore financial centres, with strict bank secrecy rules and prohibitions on disclosure of ownership and control of entities such as corporations, trusts and foundations. It became easier for individuals to hide capital, and the income from that capital, in anonymous offshore bank and investment accounts, using corporations or trusts to further obscure the source and ownership of the unreported assets and earnings. Globalisation also made it easier and more advantageous for multinational enterprises (MNEs), advised by clever professionals specialising in global tax minimisation, to shift income to low tax jurisdictions, encouraged by incentives to locate certain activities in low tax foreign financial centres. As financial services came to be delivered electronically, such avoidance and evasion[1] of taxation were facilitated.

The non-reporting of taxable income and assets by individuals, and the aggressive minimisation of global tax bills by MNEs are distinct problems. They are often conflated in public discourse however, as both have negative impacts on the ability of national tax authorities to collect tax on the worldwide income of their residents in accordance with their national laws. Both have led to concerted international efforts to reduce the revenue drain. The increasingly common strategies of MNEs to reduce their global tax liability through legal, though sometimes unduly aggressive or artificial structures and transactions, are the target of the Organisation for Economic Cooperation and Development's (OECD) ambitious Base Erosion and Profit Shifting (BEPS) project, commenced in 2013.[2] BEPS includes measures to enhance international transparency of tax positions, but that is not its primary objective, and BEPS will not be examined further in this chapter.

The other group of initiatives, the subject of this chapter, is more narrowly directed at taxpayers' exploitation of the tax authorities' inability to obtain information about their resident taxpayers' assets and income in foreign jurisdictions, and specifically information about ownership and control of bank accounts in foreign financial centres. These initiatives began slowly and in an unfocussed manner, but are now maturing, spurred by the US Foreign Accounts Tax Compliance Act (FATCA) into a multilateral system of automatic exchange of all financial account information among many jurisdictions, including some that have long been regarded as bastions of banking secrecy, if not outright tax havens.[3] If the

---

[1] The meaning of the terms 'avoidance' and 'evasion' in this chapter requires clarification, as they are used to mean different things in different jurisdictions. I use 'avoidance' to refer to legal tax planning, even where the effect is to avoid large amounts of tax. 'Evasion' is used to refer to illegal acts including false reporting and deliberate failure to report transactions, income or assets and the use of artificial transactions intended to conceal real transactions and relationships.

[2] The Final BEPS package for reform of the international tax system to tackle tax avoidance was presented to the G20 Finance Ministers and endorsed at their meeting on 8 October 2015 in Lima, Peru: OECD, 'BEPS 2015 Final Reports' (October 2015), online: www.oecd .org/tax/aggressive/beps-2015-final-reports.htm

[3] A tax haven has been defined by the OECD in OECD, 'Harmful Tax Competition, An Emerging Global Issue' (April 1998), online: www.oecd.org/tax/transparency/44430243.pdf [OECD, 'Harmful Tax Competition']. The characteristics of tax havens identified by the OECD are set out in note 21. In addition, the refusal to enter into tax treaties or Tax Information Exchange Agreements (TIEA) is often mentioned as a characteristic of a tax haven.

implementation of the Multilateral Convention on Mutual Assistance in Tax Matters, discussed below, proceeds as designed, banking secrecy in tax matters will, as they say, be history.

The landscape of international tax information exchange (exchange of information, EOI) has changed utterly since the twenty-first century began, although the evolution still has some way to progress. The next several sections describe how bilateral action, i.e. tax conventions and TIEAs between two countries, and early multilateral initiatives of the European Union, the Council of Europe,[4] the OECD, G-20 and others, were of limited effectiveness. However, these instruments and initiatives both laid the groundwork for, and revealed the necessity of, compelling foreign and domestic financial institutions to collect and report account information in order to construct an effective, multilateral, automatic system of exchange of tax information. Now, in September 2015 with FATCA and the OECD's Common Reporting Standard close to implementation, it remains to be seen how well they will operate in reality.

5.3   Methods of Exchange of Tax Information

EOI can occur between two countries in any of three ways: on request, spontaneously or automatically. Formal EOI began under the bilateral double taxation conventions (tax treaties) that have proliferated since approximately 1950. It seems that under these conventions only EOI on request was originally contemplated – i.e. when one country's tax authority made a specific request for information about a particular taxpayer that it believed the tax authorities of the other country either already had, or could obtain through its normal tax information gathering powers. However, spontaneous EOI, that is, when one tax authority realises it has information about a taxpayer that would be of use to the other country's tax authority in determining the taxpayer's liability in the latter country and accordingly delivers that information, has become widespread at least among some OECD member countries. EOI on request and spontaneous EOI are effective when there is sufficient information already available to one or both tax authorities to identify probable non-reporting or other inconsistencies or concerns about specific taxpayers or groups

---

[4] The Council of Europe is an international organisation of forty-seven European states, originally formed in 1949. It promotes human rights, democracy and the rule of law, and is probably best known for the European Convention on Human Rights and the European Court of Human Rights, located in Strasbourg, France.

of taxpayers. Automatic (sometimes called 'routine') EOI requires much more sophisticated legal frameworks, and harmonised information-gathering, transmission and receiving systems.

Exchange of tax information must be differentiated from assistance in the enforcement of foreign tax laws, including in the collection of foreign taxes.[5] Historically, the courts in England,[6] the United States[7] and other countries[8] refused to enforce the tax laws of a foreign state on principles of national sovereignty. More recent tax treaties may contain a provision for reciprocal assistance in enforcement and collection of the contracting states' taxes, although this is still relatively uncommon.

5.4   Exchange of Tax Information under Double Taxation Conventions

The tax treaty provisions between contracting states represent the baseline for EOI from which more recent initiatives to broad EOI have emerged since approximately 2000. The practice of concluding tax treaties dates from the early twentieth century.[9] The number of bilateral tax treaties multiplied after the Second World War, and there are now estimated to be over 3000 in force. Model tax treaties were published by the OECD in 1963 and by the United Nations in 1980.[10] The OECD's Model was updated in 1977

---

[5] This distinction is well established. Countries have, in the past, agreed to exchange information, but rarely, until recently, did they agree to assist in tax collection. These two distinct issues are reflected separately in the model and actual treaties. In the recent Canadian challenge to FATCA, *infra* note 71, the court specifically distinguished between EOI and enforcement obligations.

[6] *Attorney General* v. *Lutwydge* (1729) 145 ER 674 (Ex Ct). For an erudite and interesting history of the 'revenue rule', that one state will not allow its courts to be used to collect tax on behalf of another state, see D.B. Debenham, 'From the Revenue Rule to the Rule of the "Revenuer": A Tale of Two Davids and Two Goliaths', *Canadian Tax Journal*, 56(1) (2008), 1–66.

[7] *Moore* v. *Mitchell*, 30 F. 2d 600 (2d Cir. 1929).

[8] The Supreme Court of Canada denied a claim by the United States to enforce a tax judgment of the US courts in Canada in *United States of America* v. *Harden* [1963] SCR 366.

[9] The League of Nations conducted the first study by experts of the requirements for a model bilateral tax treaty, reporting in 1927, followed by a draft Model tax treaty in 1928.

[10] The UN Model is very similar to the OECD Model, but seeks to provide an alternative allocation of taxing jurisdiction between contracting states where one is a developed economy and the other is developing or emerging. The UN Model was updated in 2001 and 2010 and can be found at: UN, 'Model Double Taxation Convention between Developed and Developing Countries' (May 2012), online: www.un.org/esa/ffd/documents/UN_Model_2011_Update.pdf

and 1992, and is now revised more or less continuously.[11] Both Models are accompanied by voluminous commentary to assist tax authorities, advisors and courts with interpretation and application. Almost all bilateral tax treaties now in force follow closely the provisions of one of the Models, with limited divergences to meet specific policy objectives of one or the other of the contracting states. With respect to EOI, both UN and OECD Models contain recently revised and very similar provisions, as well as extensive commentary.

The Committee on Fiscal Affairs (CFA) of the OECD prepared a report surveying member countries' laws on bank secrecy and brought forward recommendations to ensure greater access to bank records for tax purposes in 2000.[12] The report's recommendations were carried through to the model TIEA of 2002, discussed below, and the 2005 update to OECD Model Article 26(1), which was further updated in 2012.[13]

The current OECD Model Article 26(1) provides in part:

> The competent authorities of the Contracting States shall exchange such information as is foreseeably relevant for carrying out the provisions of this Convention or to the administration or enforcement of the domestic laws concerning taxes of every kind and description imposed on behalf of the Contracting States, or of their political subdivisions or local authorities.[14]

While the obligation to supply information under para. 26(1) is not restricted to EOI on request, a further agreement or developed practice between the competent authorities of the contracting states would normally be required before information would be exchanged spontaneously or automatically. For example, the Canadian competent authority has,

---

[11] The OECD Model assumes that the contracting states are both developed economies with relatively equal flows of investment and capital between them. The OECD Model is, however, used in negotiations beyond the OECD members. A condensed version of the current OECD Model and Commentary is available at: OECD, 'Model Tax Convention on Income and on Capital' (15 July 2014), online: www.keepeek.com/Digital-Asset-Management/oecd/taxation/model-tax-convention-on-income-and-on-capital-condensed-version-2014_mtc_cond-2014-en#page6. The United States has its own Model, which is similar to the OECD Model.

[12] OECD, 'Improving Access to Bank Information for Tax Purposes' (24 March 2000), online: www.oecd.org/tax/exchange-of-tax-information/2497487.pdf

[13] A TIEA is used when there is no reason for one or both jurisdictions to enter into a full-blown tax treaty. The OECD Model Article 26(1) was updated in 2005 to reflect the fact that the model TIEA, adopted in 2002, was actually more demanding of the agreeing jurisdictions than Model Treaty Article 26(1).

[14] OECD, Update to Article 26 of the OECD Model Tax Convention and its Commentary (17 July 2012), online: www.oecd.org/ctp/exchange-of-tax-information/120718_Article%2026-ENG_no%20cover%20(2).pdf

apparently for some years, agreed to provide the following information to the US Inland Revenue Service (IRS) automatically:

> (a) [t]he names and addresses of all persons whose addresses are within the US and who derive from sources within Canada dividends, interest, rents, royalties, salaries, wages, pensions, or other fixed or determinable annual or periodical profits and income, showing the amount of such profits and income in the case of each addressee[;][15]

The commentary that accompanied the 2005 revisions to Art. 26(1) states:

> The standard of 'foreseeable relevance' is intended to provide for exchange of information in tax matters to the widest possible extent and, at the same time, to clarify that Contracting States are not at liberty to engage in 'fishing expeditions' or to request information that is unlikely to be relevant to the tax affairs of a given taxpayer.[16]

The distinction between a valid request for very wide-ranging information and a fishing expedition has been a matter of ongoing discussion, and the OECD commentary on this specific issue runs to five pages, including several examples. Contracting states may interpret the parameters of 'foreseeable relevance' and 'fishing expeditions' quite differently. The issue of what details the request for information must specify before the requested state is obligated to accept the request and act on it has also not been fully resolved in the commentary on OECD Model Article 26 or the *Manual on the Implementation of Exchange of Information Provisions for Tax Purposes*.[17] It has been noted that a state that receives a request (the 'requested state') may demand so much, and such specific, information about a taxpayer before it will accept the request and act on it that the process becomes one of confirming information the requesting state already had, rather than assisting it to investigate suspected civil or criminal tax avoidance more fully. This may be a strategy to prevent 'fishing expeditions', and thus expedite the location and exchange of information by the state receiving the request, but can also be used to obstruct a request.[18]

---

[15] Canada Revenue Agency, *Income Tax Treaties Reference Manual*, 94 ITC 100, 94 ITC 364, 'Automatic (or Routine) Exchange' as quoted in N.P.J. Johnston, 'Overview of the Foreign Account Tax Compliance Act and the Definition of Financial Institution', *2013 Conference Report* (Toronto: Canadian Tax Foundation, 2014), 17: 1–33 at 9.

[16] Update to Article 26 of the OECD Model Tax Convention and its Commentary, *supra* note 14 at 3, para 5.

[17] Dated 23 January 2006, online: www.oecd.org/tax/exchange-of-tax-information/36647823.pdf

[18] See the discussion of the acceptable standard for identifying the taxpayer and the holder of the requested information in G. Larin and A. Diebel, 'The Swiss Twist: The Exchange of Information Provisions of the Canada-Switzerland Protocol', *Canadian Tax Journal*, 60 (2013), 28–40.

Model Article 26(2) provides for protection of information received pursuant to para. 26(1), requiring that it be 'treated as secret in the same manner as information obtained under the domestic laws of that State'. Disclosure to persons concerned with tax administration or adjudication, including courts and administrative bodies, or oversight of these is permitted, with the proviso that the information may only be used for these purposes. An optional final sentence allows the receiving state to use the information for other purposes that are permitted under the laws of both states and where the supplying state authorises this. The commentary explains that this permits sharing of the exchanged information 'with other law enforcement agencies and judicial authorities in that State on certain high priority matters (e.g. to combat money laundering, corruption, terrorism financing)'.[19]

Paragraph 26(3) ensures that a contracting state is not obliged to carry out measures that are not in accordance with its own, or the other contracting state's laws and administrative practices, to supply information that could not be obtained under its own or the other contracting state's laws or normal administration or to supply information that reveals trade, business, industrial, commercial or professional secrets or which would be contrary to public policy. However, para. 26(5), added in 2005, specifies that para. (3) does not allow a contracting state to decline to supply information solely because it 'is held by a bank, financial institution, nominee or person acting in an agency or a fiduciary capacity or because it relates to ownership interests in a person'. This ensures a contracting state may not refuse to supply information that is protected by domestic bank secrecy laws, or other confidentiality rules preventing the collection by or disclosure to domestic tax authorities of the identities of shareholders, beneficiaries, trustees, agents or nominees.

Paragraph 26(4) was added in 2005 to make clear that a requested state may not refuse to obtain or supply information on the basis that it has no interest in the information for its own tax purposes. The requirement imposed by some countries, that the information be relevant to behaviour that would constitute tax evasion under the law of the requested state, is no longer a permitted condition of providing the information.

The OECD Model revisions of 2005 led to the signing of numerous protocols updating existing tax treaties. Most new tax treaties negotiated after 2002 contain the language of the 2005 revisions, which also reflects

---

[19] Update to Article 26 of the OECD Model Tax Convention and its Commentary, *supra* note 14 at 11, para 12.3.

the provisions of the Model TIEA discussed below, which upgraded the international standard for EOI. Retroactivity of the EOI obligation may be restricted to providing information related to years following the entry into force of the treaty or protocol.

5.5   Tax Information Exchange Agreements

In 1996 the OECD's 'CFA' began its investigation of 'harmful tax competition', originally aimed at laws and practices of OECD members, such as preferential tax regimes intended to draw capital and investment away from other developed economies. The CFA's 1998 report[20] identified the distinguishing features of tax havens[21] and harmful preferential tax regimes,[22] described the problems these cause to national tax systems and made numerous detailed recommendations to combat their harmful effects. The report also set out guidelines for OECD members to mitigate harmful practices in their own systems and internationally, and proposed the creation of the 'Forum on Harmful Tax Practices' composed of both OECD and non-member countries. The proposed Forum was to serve as an organisation for the continued discussion of the problems posed by tax havens and harmful preferential tax regimes, and to identify solutions. Solutions included promoting principles of good tax administration to combat harmful tax practices, monitoring the implementation of the Report's recommendations and guidelines for preventing the adoption of new harmful tax practices and eliminating existing ones and making a list of jurisdictions judged to be tax havens.

The Forum was established in 2000 by OECD member countries and certain participating non-members with a plan to develop dialogue with non-member countries. It was restructured as the Global Forum on

---

[20] OECD, 'Harmful Tax Competition', *supra* note 3.

[21] *Ibid.*, at 21–5. These features are: no or nominal taxation; laws or administrative practices that allow taxpayers to exploit strict secrecy rules and protections from scrutiny by tax authorities to prevent effective exchange of information about their assets, financial accounts or activities in the low tax jurisdiction, lack of transparency in the way laws and administrative practices are applied or operate to various entities and activities; lack of any requirement of substantive activity in the jurisdiction in order to avoid taxation and benefit from the secrecy rules.

[22] *Ibid.* at 25: 'Four key factors assist in identifying harmful preferential tax regimes: (a) the regime imposes a low or zero effective tax rate on the relevant income; (b) the regime is "ring-fenced"; (c) the operation of the regime is non-transparent; (d) the jurisdiction operating the regime does not effectively exchange information with other countries.'

Transparency and Exchange of Information in Tax Matters in 2009 (the 'Global Forum'), and has, as of 2015, 127 members.[23]

The Global Forum has made very significant contributions to international tax transparency[24] and EOI. In 2002, the Global Forum produced a model TIEA adopting a new international standard for EOI on request. The international standard for EOI is essentially the same as that in Art. 26 of the OECD Model convention described above, and indeed the 2005 revision of Art. 26 followed the adoption of the model TIEA. A TIEA may be used where one or both contracting jurisdictions have no need for, or interest in, negotiating a comprehensive tax treaty.[25] A model protocol to the TIEA to provide for automatic and spontaneous exchange of tax information was published by the OECD in 2015.[26]

Also in 2002, the Global Forum published a list of thirty-eight 'uncooperative tax havens', meaning those that were unwilling to provide tax information in accordance with the new international standard. OECD member countries were encouraged to enter into TIEAs with countries and jurisdictions with which they had no tax treaties, and offshore financial centres (the polite term for tax havens) were also firmly pressured towards accepting requests for tax information and eliminating barriers, such as laws protecting bank secrecy and nominee ownership of shares and other assets.

Over time, the language has become more conciliatory as the membership of the Global Forum has expanded, and a clear process for meeting the tax transparency standard has been put in place. The Global Forum conducts a two-phase peer review of each member jurisdiction to determine its progress in adopting the Global Forum's standards for tax transparency. The first phase is an evaluation of the participating jurisdiction's

---

[23] There are also fifteen observer jurisdictions. For a more detailed history and activities of the Global Forum, see OECD, 'Global Forum on Transparency and Exchange of Information for Tax Purposes' (2016), online: www.oecd.org/tax/transparency/

[24] 'Transparency' in tax matters generally refers to tax authorities' access to information regarding ownership of company shares, company accounts or details of trust ownership, control and beneficial entitlement, and not to bank and other financial account confidentiality or secrecy.

[25] This may be due to the fact that the parties have little or no bilateral direct investment, one (or sometimes both) imposes no income, profits, wealth or capital tax and therefore has no interest in allocating tax jurisdiction between the parties, or preventing double taxation or tax evasion, which are the primary objectives of tax treaties.

[26] OECD, 'Model Protocol for the Purpose of Allowing the Automatic and Spontaneous Exchange of Information Under a TIEA' (2015), online: www.oecd.org/ctp/exchange-of-tax-information/Model-Protocol-TIEA.pdf

legal and regulatory framework and the second evaluates the practical implementation of the transparency standards. A jurisdiction must have passed the first phase before it can go on to the second, although for some countries the reviews of the two phases are conducted simultaneously. On completion of the Phase 2 peer review, a jurisdiction receives a rating of 'compliant', 'largely compliant', 'partially compliant' or 'non-compliant'. The results of the peer reviews are published on the Global Forum's site. The most recent report on progress, from April 2015, shows ratings for seventy-seven jurisdictions.[27] Several jurisdictions had not yet passed from Phase 1 to Phase 2, and four have been rated non-compliant: British Virgin Islands, Cyprus, Luxembourg and Seychelles. Supplementary reviews have been requested by all of these other than Seychelles. As of September 2015, Switzerland has proceeded to Phase 2 after making changes to its laws to allow it to pass Phase 1.

As the Multilateral Convention on Mutual Assistance in Tax Matters (discussed below) has become a widely adopted instrument for tax information exchange by both OECD and non-OECD members, the TIEAs in place between jurisdictions with standard income tax regimes and those that used to be tax havens required updating to incorporate the Convention's broader obligations. Accordingly, the OECD released a model protocol for TIEAs in 2015 which can be used to implement the Multilateral Convention's provisions for spontaneous and automatic EOI.[28]

5.6 EU Contributions to Exchange of Tax Information

5.6.1 Mutual Assistance Directive

The EU's guarantee of a single market based on the free movement of persons, services, enterprise and capital between member states increased the need for common rules on EOI. Directive 77/799/EEC,[29] the 'Mutual Assistance Directive' of 1977, was the first multilateral instrument imposing obligations on states to exchange tax information automatically, spontaneously and on request. The European Court of Justice has

---

[27] The report is available at OECD, 'OECD Secretary-General Report to the G20 Finance Ministers and Central Bank Governors' (April 2015), online: www.oecd.org/tax/transparency/about-the-global-forum/g20/2015-April-GF-report-G20.pdf

[28] Model Protocol for the Purpose of Allowing the Automatic and Spontaneous Exchange of Information under a TIEA, *supra* note 26.

[29] EC, *Council Directive 77/799/EEC of 19 December 1977 concerning mutual assistance by the competent authorities of the Member States in the field of direct taxation* [1977] O.J. L. 336/20.

confirmed that the 1977 Directive's purposes were as set out in its Sixth Recital, that is, the correct assessment of taxes on income and on capital and the exchange of any information which appears relevant for that purpose, as well as to combat tax evasion and avoidance.[30] However, it did not require member states to exchange tax information that was subject to domestic bank secrecy rules.[31] By the early 2000s, the 1977 Directive was clearly obsolete, particularly in view of the developments in international EOI, including the OECD Model tax treaty Art. 26. A new Directive adopted in 2011,[32] to be implemented by the member states as of 1 January 2013, eliminated bank secrecy on the basis for refusing to collect or exchange tax information. It also brought organisational uniformity, requiring member states to identify a competent authority and a liaison office for the purpose of ensuring administrative cooperation. Increased efficiency is achieved by requiring the use of harmonised electronic means of exchange using the EU's Common Communication Network (CCN), already in use for value-added tax cooperation. Also of note is Art. 24 of the 2011 Directive on exchange of information with third countries, which contemplates spontaneous sharing of information received from third countries with other EU member states, and sharing of information received from other EU member states with third countries.

5.6.2   The Savings Tax Directive

In the European Union, the liberalisation of capital movements, especially after 1990,[33] and the advent of the euro as a common currency exacerbated concern that each member state could effectively serve as a tax haven for the residents of all other member states. The established lore was of legions of German dentists driving to Luxembourg on their holidays to deposit cash in interest-bearing accounts, never intending to report the interest income to the German tax authorities. Of course, the

---

[30] Case C-420/98, *W.N. v. Staatssecretaris van Financiën* [2000] ECR I-02867.

[31] Case C-451/05, *Européenne et Luxembourgeoise d'investissements SA (ELISA) v. Directeur Généneral des Impôts* [2007] ECR I-8287.

[32] EC, *Council Directive 2011/16/EU of 15 February 2011 on administrative cooperation in the field of taxation and repealing Directive 77/799/EEC* [2011] O.J. L. 64/2.

[33] The free movement of capital lagged the other freedoms in time, and was not substantively achieved until the implementation in the member states of *Council Directive 88/361/EEC of 24 June 1988 for the implementation of Article 67 of the Treaty* [1988] O.J. L. 178/5. Member states were required by Art. 1(1) read with Art. 6(1) of the Directive to 'abolish restrictions on movements of capital taking place between persons resident in Member States' by 1 July 1990.

proliferation of cross-border bank accounts was not confined to Germans and Luxembourg, as any member state could potentially serve as a location for a secret bank account for residents of any other state.

The Savings Tax Directive[34] of 2003 was the first multilateral attempt at mandatory automatic exchange of financial account information. In simple terms, this directive required 'paying agents', for the most part financial institutions located in EU Member States, to report interest earned on accounts of which the beneficial owner was an individual resident in another EU Member State to the paying agent's national tax authorities. The reporting requirements included the paying agent's name and address, the account number, the identity and residence of the beneficial owner of the account and the amount of interest paid. The tax authority of the paying agent would then report that information to the tax authority of the EU Member State of residence of the individual. The tax authorities of three EU member states, Austria, Belgium and Luxembourg, were temporarily exempted from the automatic exchange of information by reason of their banking secrecy rules. These countries were instead obliged to withhold tax on interest payments made to residents of other member states, initially at a rate of 15 per cent, rising to 35 per cent over time. Seventy-five per cent of the revenue collected was to be transferred to the EU member state of residence of the beneficial owners of the interest. Further, agreements were negotiated between the European Union and Switzerland, Andorra, Liechtenstein, San Marino and Monaco according to which these jurisdictions were bound to apply the same withholding rates and share the revenue on the same basis. The names of account holders and amounts of interest earned by each account were not transmitted to the tax authorities where the account holders were resident so that the banking secrecy laws of the withholding country were observed.

The Savings Tax Directive was significant in that its reporting obligations were automatic, multilateral and imposed on the paying agents rather than tax authorities. It was, however, disappointingly ineffective, and the European Commission and independent researchers soon noted the deficiencies in coverage, the ease by which the reporting could be evaded, and the failure of the withholding tax to collect the anticipated revenue, based on the amount of EU residents' capital held in Swiss banks

[34] EC, *Council Directive 2003/48/EC of 3 June 2003 on taxation of savings income in the form of interest payments* [2003] O.J. L. 157/38.

and other foreign accounts.[35] Although attempts were made to amend the directive to remedy these deficiencies, the implementation of automatic exchange of financial account information among member states in accordance with Council Directive 2014/107/EU, which adopts the OECD's common reporting standard, discussed below, is now overtaking the Savings Tax Directive, which will be repealed at the end of 2015.[36]

5.6.3   The Platform for Tax Good Governance

The European Union undertook a parallel study of harmful tax practices at the same time as the OECD, in 1996. The initial result was adoption of a 'Code of Conduct for Business Taxation' under which EU member states made a political commitment not to introduce new harmful tax measures and to roll back their tax laws identified as harmful. Improvement of tax transparency, that is, the ability of tax authorities to determine owner- ship and control of assets and entities such as corporations and trusts, was apparently left to the Global Forum. Taxation of foreign financial accounts and EOI regarding such accounts was pursued partially and separately, under the Savings Tax Directive.

More recently, the 'Platform for Tax Good Governance'[37] has taken over the task of 'naming and shaming' tax havens, following a 2012 EU Commission Recommendation that included criteria for identifying tax havens, and a recommendation that EU member states identify and publish blacklists of third countries that met those criteria.[38] At a meeting of the Platform in December 2014, the criteria applied by various member states in deciding which countries to blacklist were reviewed in detail and a wide divergence

---

[35] T. Rixen and P. Schwarz, 'How Effective is the European Union's Savings Tax Directive? Evidence from Four EU Member States', *Journal of Common Market Studies*, 50(1) (2012), 151–68; A.M. Jiménez, 'Loopholes in the EU Savings Tax Directive', *IBFD Bulletin for International Taxation* (2006), online: http://ssrn.com/abstract=2471813

[36] See the announcement at EC, 'Repeal of the Savings Directive and the New EU–Switzerland Agreement' (2015), online: http://ec.europa.eu/taxation_customs/taxation/personal_tax/savings_tax/revised_directive/index_en.htm

[37] The Platform is a section of the Commission Directorate-General Taxation and Customs Union. Its public documents can be found at EC, 'Platform for Tax Good Governance' (2016), online: http://ec.europa.eu/taxation_customs/taxation/gen_info/good_governance_matters/platform/index_en.htm

[38] EC, *Commission Recommendation of 6 December 2012 regarding measures intended to encourage third countries to apply minimum standards of good governance in tax matters* [2012] C-8805.

in national policies and practices was documented.[39] For example, the larg-est group, eighteen member states (of twenty eight) used compliance with standards of tax transparency and EOI standards in assessing tax systems of other countries; thirteen used these criteria for determining whether a jurisdiction should be on a blacklist. The presence of harmful tax measures in a country's tax system was also important as a criterion for twelve member states, used in combination with indicators of transparency and availability of EOI. Eight member states used the level of taxation for blacklisting pur-poses, six of them in combination with transparency and EOI.

In June 2015 the EU's controversial list of thirty 'uncooperative jurisdic-tions' was published, based on a minimum of ten member states having identified a particular jurisdiction as uncooperative.[40] Some countries reacted very strongly to being listed as uncooperative.[41] For example, Bermuda noted that it has a TIEA with five of the eleven EU member states that listed it as uncooperative, and that two of the eleven are in the process of removing Bermuda from its list. The Cayman Islands, also on the EU list, pointed out that it has a TIEA with all the EU member states, other than Bulgaria, that blacklisted it. Many of the jurisdictions on the EU's list are members of the Global Forum, and some are even among the early adopters of automatic EOI under the Multilateral Convention on Administrative Assistance in Tax Matters discussed below.[42] Criticism of the lack of clarity as to what criteria contribute to blacklisting by member states, and the arbitrariness and lack of transparency in some cases have undermined the credibility of this particu-lar mechanism for applying pressure to exchange tax information.

5.7   The United States: The Foreign Accounts Tax Compliance Act

FATCA is the true game-changer in the universe of EOI initiatives, although, as will be described below, it is by no means the last word.

---

[39] EC, 'Discussion paper on criteria applied by EU Member States to Establish Lists of Non-Cooperative Jurisdictions' (19 December 2014), online: http://ec.europa.eu/taxation_customs/resources/documents/taxation/gen_info/good_governance_matters/platform/meeting_20141219/discussion_paper_criteria_lists.pdf

[40] The list can be found at EC, 'Tax Good Governance in the World as Seen by EU Countries' (31 December 2015), online: http://ec.europa.eu/taxation_customs/taxation/gen_info/good_governance_matters/lists_of_countries/index_en.htm?wtdebug=true

[41] S.S. Johnston, 'Targeted Countries Slam EU Tax Haven Blacklist', *Tax Notes International* (2015), 1159–61.

[42] OECD, 'Joint Statement by the Early Adopters Group' (October 2014), online at: www.oecd.org/tax/transparency/AEOI-early-adopters-statement.pdf

Two events have been identified as the instigators for FATCA: the prosecution of the largest Swiss bank, UBS, commenced by the US Federal Department of Justice in 2008[43] and the global financial crisis of 2008–9,[44] with its consequent increased federal deficit and debt, and thus the need to collect more of the tax that was apparently being evaded by US taxpayers. The UBS affair, subsequent actions by the US authorities against other banks in Switzerland and elsewhere[45] and the consequences for tax enforcement and bank secrecy have been described in numerous scholarly articles[46] as well as in reliable journalism. The prosecutions of the foreign banks revealed that the earlier programmes under which the IRS collected information about foreign financial accounts and other assets held by US persons were inadequate to prevent the non-reporting of such, and indeed that some foreign financial institutions (FFI) had actively assisted US taxpayers to exploit loopholes in these programmes.[47]

FATCA was enacted by the US Congress as a subtitle of the Hiring Incentives to Restore Employment Act (HIRE Act) of 2010.[48] The new law lengthened the Internal Revenue Code by only ten pages, but by one estimate[49] the regulations released by 2014 filled over 700 pages. There is limitless professional, academic and technical literature on the FATCA. The following is only the most basic description of the extremely complex regime.[50]

Under the FATCA regime participating FFIs enter into an agreement with the IRS under which they agree to report annually to the IRS certain

---

[43] A. Turina, 'Ex Uno Plura: How Unilateral FATCA May Contribute to Reshaping Administrative Cooperation in Tax Matters Along Multilateral Lines', *Bocconi Legal Papers*, 2 (2013), 121 at 134–5 and B.J. Bondi, 'Don't Tread on Me: Has the United States Government's Quest for Customer Records from UBS Sounded the Death Knell for Swiss Bank Secrecy Laws?', *Northwestern Journal of International Law & Business*, 30(1) (2010), online: http://ssrn.com/abstract=1573982

[44] Joshua D. Blank and Ruth Mason, 'Exporting FATCA', NYU Law and Economics Research Paper No. 14-05, (2014), online: http://ssrn.com/abstract=2389500 [Blank and Mason].

[45] An official summary of such activities is found at US Department of Justice, 'Offshore Compliance Initiative' (5 February 2016), online: www.justice.gov/tax/offshore-compliance-initiative

[46] See for example, Bondi, *supra* note 43.

[47] M.A. Dizdarevic, 'The FATCA Provisions of the Hire Act: Boldly Going Where No Withholding has Gone Before', *Fordham L Rev*, 79 (2010–11), 2967.

[48] (2010) 26 USC §§1471–4.

[49] R.A. Berg and P.M. Barba, 'FATCA in Canada: The Restriction on the Class of Entities Subject to FATCA', *Canadian Tax Journal*, 62(3) (2014), 587 at 598 [Berg and Barba], online: www.ctf.ca/CTFWEB/EN/Publications/CTJ_Contents/2014CTJ3.aspx

[50] I am particularly indebted to the work of N.P.J. Johnston, *supra* note 15, for this brief description of the main aspects of the FATCA. See also Blank and Mason, *supra* note 44 and Berg and Barba, *supra* note 49.

identifying information of the holders of each account held by a 'specified US person' or by a foreign (non-US) entity with one or more substantial US owners.[51] The definition of 'specified US person' includes individuals who are citizens of or residents in the United States and US entities, such as corporations, partnerships and trusts organised under US law. US publicly traded corporations, banks, Real Estate Investment Trusts (REITs), regulated investment companies and certain other US entities are excluded from the definition of specified US person. Accounts at FFIs with cumulative balances under US$50,000 in the case of individual account holders, and US$250,000 in the case of accounts held by entities are not required to be reported, although an FFI may report the information listed above in respect of these accounts. The participating FFI agrees to report to the IRS the specified US person's name, address, tax information number (TIN), the account number, the value or balance in the account annually, all payments into and out of the account and other information. For accounts held by US entities, the FFI agrees to report the same details in respect of any substantial US owner of the entity. Participating FFIs also agree to employ particularised acts of due diligence to identify their specified US person account holders, and collect documentation in respect of account holders that have indicia of status as a US person, such as an address in the United States or a US place of birth. An account holder that fails to provide information to allow a determination of US status is dubbed 'recalcitrant' and is treated as a specified US person. A specified US person account holder must provide a waiver of local confidentiality laws that would otherwise prevent the FFI from reporting, or the FFI must close the account.

A nonparticipating FFI is subject to withholding of 30 per cent of US source 'withholdable payments', including the gross amount of dividends, interest, salary, wages, proceeds of disposition of property that could produce US source interest or dividends, and other amounts to it, or to its account holders. Participating FFIs must withhold 30 per cent of 'passthru payments' (withholdable payments of which it is not the beneficial owner) to its recalcitrant account holders or to nonparticipating FFIs. US withholding agents, that is, US persons who make a withholdable payment, must also withhold in respect of payments to non-financial foreign entities (NFFEs) unless the NFFE or beneficial owner of the payment certifies that it has no substantial US owner or provides the name, address, TIN of each

---

[51] Substantial ownership consists of 10 per cent direct or indirect ownership by votes or value.

substantial US owner to the withholding agent, and the withholding agent has no reason to suspect such information is incorrect and provides it to the IRS. A US withholding agent who fails to withhold where required becomes liable for the amount that should have been withheld. Participating FFIs may elect to have the US withholding agent make the withholding on passthru payments in lieu of the participating FFI making the withholding. Participating FFIs that fail to withhold as required on passthru payments are liable to termination of the agreement with the IRS, so that they become subject to withholding on US source withholdable payments.

The innovation of FATCA is not the reliance on foreign banks and other financial institutions to collect and report the account holder information to the IRS on an automatic basis, as the EU's Savings Tax Directive had done this multilaterally through harmonisation of Member State rules, albeit in a much more limited and less effective way. It is the enforcement of these obligations through the withholding tax on nonparticipating FFIs (and passthru payments) that makes FATCA much more effective. The size and importance of the US economy makes it necessary for all FFIs (other than small, purely local institutions with no US account holders and no US source income, direct or indirect) to submit to FATCA's reporting regime, rather than suffer withholding on their US source payments. Those FFIs that were also subject to domestic privacy or banking secrecy laws prohibiting disclosure of account holder information were placed in an untenable situation, and some began to close accounts or turn US persons away, so-called 'de-risking'.[52] Many countries found the unilateral, extraterritorial reach of FATCA to enforce US tax law to be abusive, especially since the United States uniquely taxes not only its residents but also its citizens, including those who have never lived in the United States and have no US assets, income or tax liability.[53]

There are some potential gaps in the FATCA regime. For example, an US person who is an individual may split their foreign accounts among FFIs so that no FFI holds more than US$50,000, and is therefore not obliged to report the account (though it may). For a US entity, the threshold for mandatory reporting is US$250,000 held in one or more accounts at a particular FFI.

---

[52] The reaction to FATCA in the form of account closures was reported at: Bloomberg Business, 'US Millionaires Told Go Away as Tax Evasion Rule Looms' (8 May 2012), online: www.bloomberg.com/news/articles/2012-05-08/us-millionaires-told-go-away-as-tax-evasion-rule-looms

[53] See Blank and Mason, *supra* note 44 at 1246, and their footnotes 15 through 21.

As details of the regulations implementing FATCA were published, alternatives to individual agreements between each FFI and the IRS were sought. In February 2012, the five largest EU countries[54] and the US Treasury Department issued a joint statement of their commitment to create 'an intergovernmental approach to improving international tax compliance and implementing FATCA'.[55] In July 2012, these six jurisdictions and the European Commission published the first model intergovernmental agreement (IGA), now the Model 1A IGA.[56] This version allows FFIs in the partner jurisdiction to provide the account information to their home tax authorities; these then provide the information automatically to the IRS under the tax treaty or TIEA provisions between the United States and that partner jurisdiction. This overcomes any conflict between disclosure of account information and home country privacy laws, if necessary by legislatively exempting such disclosure from privacy and bank secrecy laws. The FFIs covered by the IGA are not required to enter into a FATCA agreement with the IRS and, most significantly, are not subject to FATCA withholding. Model 1A IGAs are in principle reciprocal; this is discussed further below.

Model 1B IGAs are non-reciprocal, but otherwise the same as Model 1A IGAs.[57] A country that does not impose an income tax would have no reason to participate in reciprocal reporting of financial accounts held by its residents in US financial institutions. Model 2 IGAs are also non-reciprocal. The affected FFIs are required by the Model 2 IGA to enter into an agreement with, and report account holder information directly to, the IRS.

Although Model 1A IGAs are described as reciprocal, the obligations of the United States and its financial institutions to identify accounts held by residents of the partner jurisdiction and to report amounts paid into such accounts are neither clearly stated nor as extensive as those of the partner jurisdiction. The lack of reciprocity in the obligations to exercise due diligence to identify foreign account holders and exchange

---

[54] The members of the 'G5' are France, Germany, Italy, Spain and the United Kingdom.

[55] The text of the joint statement is found at: HM Treasury, 'Joint Statement regarding an Intergovernmental Approach to Improving International Tax Compliance and Implementing FATCA' (8 February 2012), online: www.gov.uk/government/news/joint-statement-regarding-an-intergovernmental-approach-to-improving-international-tax-compliance-and-implementing-fatca

[56] Blank and Mason, *supra* note 44 at 1247 amusingly refer to the United Kingdom's 2012 legislation to provide for EOI agreements, modelled on the IGA, with its crown dependencies and overseas territories such as the Channel Islands, as a 'son of FATCA'.

[57] There are two versions of the Model 1B IGA, one for countries that have an existing TIEA or tax treaty with the United States and one for those that do not. The Singapore Model 1B IGA is an example of the latter. The same holds true for Model 2 IGAs. Berg and Barba, *supra* note 49, provide a fuller description of the IGAs.

information under Model 1A IGAs is portrayed graphically by Allison Christians.[58] In particular, Annex I to the Model 1A IGA sets out details of due diligence obligations to identify accounts of US persons that apply only to the partner jurisdiction, and not to US financial institutions. Model 1 IGAs run to forty-eight pages with annexes, and while they undoubtedly simplify and make less onerous the application of the FATCA regime in the partner jurisdiction, they do not eliminate it. Partner jurisdictions must ensure that their domestic legislation correctly implements the obligations in the IGA, which may result in additional legal and interpretation issues.[59]

Model 1A IGAs nevertheless purport to impose some obligations on the United States and its financial institutions. For example, Art. 2(2)(b) of the Canada–US IGA requires the IRS to report automatically to the Canada Revenue Agency (CRA) with respect to Canadian Reportable Accounts held at Reporting US Financial Institutions starting in respect of calendar year 2014:

1. the name, address and Canadian TIN of any person who is a resident of Canada and is an account holder of the account;
2. the account number (or the functional equivalent in the absence of an account number);
3. the name and identifying number of the Reporting US Financial Institution;
4. the gross amount of interest paid on a Depository Account;
5. the gross amount of US source dividends paid or credited to the account; and
6. the gross amount of other US source income paid or credited to the account, to the extent subject to reporting under chapter 3 of subtitle A or chapter 61 of subtitle F of the US Internal Revenue Code.

The amounts of US source income that are subject to reporting and withholding under subpara. (6) include:

> Interest (other than original issue discount as defined in section 1273), dividends, rent, salaries, wages, premiums, annuities, compensations, remunerations, emoluments, or other fixed or determinable annual or periodical gains, profits, and income.[60]

---

[58] A. Christians, 'What You Give and What You Get: Reciprocity Under a Model 1 Intergovernmental Agreement on FATCA', *Cayman Financial Review* (2013), online: http://ssrn.com/abstract=2292645

[59] For example, in Berg and Barba, *supra* note 49, the authors describe features of the Canadian statutory regime implementing the IGA that create uncertainty, if not confusion, as to which entities are subject to it.

[60] This is the most pertinent portion of IRS 26 USC § 1441 – withholding of tax on non-resident aliens.

Accordingly, under the IGA the amounts that US financial institutions must report and that the IRS must share with the CRA are quite extensive. However, it seems that the necessary domestic regulations to make the reciprocal IGA obligations of US financial institutions enforceable and create the powers the IRS requires to share information have yet to be put in place.[61]

The IGA programme has proved extremely popular. As of 31 August 2015, ninety jurisdictions have entered into Model 1A IGAs, eight countries have signed a Model 1B IGA and fourteen have signed Model 2 IGAs.[62] As of 27 August 2015, 171,109 FFIs had registered with the IRS and received a Global Intermediary Identification Number (GIIN) which allows the FFI to avoid the 30 per cent withholding tax.[63] The IRS estimates that fewer than 500,000 entities will have to register as FFIs, which implies that there is still some progress to be made.[64] It has been reported that there are still 131 jurisdictions that have not signed an IGA, and that those jurisdictions account for only 6,579 of the issued GIINs.[65]

Model 1 IGAs clearly contemplate broader multilateral cooperation to improve automatic exchange of taxpayer information. Article 6(3) of the Model 1A provides:

> Article 6(3). Development of Common Reporting and Exchange Model.
> The Parties are committed to working with other partners and the Organisation for Economic Co-operation and Development [and the

---

[61] See Christians, *supra* note 58 at 2 where she cites the rather weak commitment to future reciprocity in Art. 6(1) of the Model: 'The [Government of the] United States acknowledges the need to achieve equivalent levels of reciprocal automatic information exchange with [FATCA Partner]. The [Government of the] United States is committed to further improve transparency and enhance the exchange relationship with [FATCA Partner] by pursuing the adoption of regulations and advocating and supporting relevant legislation to achieve such equivalent levels of reciprocal automatic exchange.'

[62] The numbers of Model 1A, Model 1B and Model 2 IGAs, and numbers of GIINs are reported by William Byrnes at William Byrnes, 'Has There Been a Prohibition on New GIIN Joints?' (27 August 2015), online: Kluwer International Tax Blog, www.kluwertaxlawblog .com/blog/2015/08/27/has-there-been-a-prohibition-on-new-giin-joints/. The full list of all IGAs signed, awaiting local ratification, and agreed in substance is available at US Department of the Treasury, 'Additional FATCA Documents' (15 January 2016), online: www.treasury.gov/resource-center/tax-policy/treaties/pages/fatca-archive.aspx. Links to the texts of all signed IGAs may also be found at this site.

[63] See William Byrnes, 'Byrnes and Perryman's FATCA Update of July 2015' (27 July 2015), online: www.kluwertaxlawblog.com/blog/2015/07/27/byrnes-perrymans-fatca-update-of-july-2015. The writers note that the Cayman Islands has the highest number of registered FFIs at 31,533.

[64] See the answer to Question 8 on the FFI list at US IRS, 'IRS FFI List FAQs' (19 November 2015), online: www.irs.gov/Businesses/Corporations/IRS-FFI-List-FAQs#ListQ7

[65] Byrnes and Perryman's FATCA Update of July 2015, *supra* note 63.

European Union] on adapting the terms of this Agreement to a common model for automatic exchange of information, including the development of reporting and due diligence standards for financial institutions.[66]

However, as will be discussed more fully below, the hub-and-spoke system of bilateral agreements created by FATCA and the IGAs is very much a one-way transfer of information unless and until the United States undertakes the same obligations as the countries whose governments have entered into IGAs.

The compliance costs associated with FATCA and the IGAs are obviously enormous. Some have questioned whether the increased revenue the IRS expects to collect from taxpayers who can no longer conceal their assets and income abroad justifies the costs for FFIs,[67] withholding agents, NFFEs, the IRS and the tax authorities in other countries.[68]

The effects of FATCA are amplified by the fact that the United States, unlike any other jurisdiction, subjects its citizens, wherever reside, as well as its residents, to worldwide taxation. The US Department of State Bureau of Consular Affairs estimates that there are up to 8,700,000 US citizens living outside the United States.[69] US citizens are 'specified US persons', and though they may never have lived in the United States or earned any income from US sources, their accounts at FFIs are subject to disclosure under the numerous IGAs that have been concluded. Legal

---

[66] The same clause is present in Model 1B IGAs, such as that between Singapore and the United States, but without the reference to the European Union which obviously only applies to EU member states.

[67] A 2014 *Wall Street Journal* article estimated the compliance costs for Canada's five largest banks at C$750 million and counting: Rita Trichur, 'Canada Banks Tally Their Tax-Compliance Tab' (27 July 2014), online: *Wall Street Journal*, www.wsj.com/articles/canada-banks-tally-their-tax-compliance-tab-1406504252. If the estimated cost of US$100 million per FFI quoted in a 2011 article in Forbes magazine turns out to be fairly accurate, the cost of FFIs alone will be far in excess of what is collected: Robert Wood, 'FATCA Carries Fat Price Tag' (30 November 2011), online: Forbes, www.forbes.com/sites/robertwood/2011/11/30/fatca-carries-fat-price-tag/

[68] The Joint Committee on Taxation, a non-partisan committee of the US Congress, estimated in 2010 that a total of US$8.7 billion would be collected as a result of FATCA by 2020: Joint Committee on Taxation, 'Estimated Revenue Effects of the Revenue Provisions Contained in Senate Amendment 3310, The 'Hiring Incentives to Restore Employment Act', under Consideration by the Senate' (23 February 2010), online: www.jct.gov/publications.html?func=startdown&id=3649. See also Reuven S. Avi-Yonah and Gil Savir, 'Find It and Tax It: From TIEAs to IGAs', University of Michigan Public Law Research Paper No. 443 (2015), online: http://ssrn.com/abstract=2567646

[69] This estimate is found at US Department of State, 'By the Numbers' (April 2015), online: http://travel.state.gov/content/dam/travel/CA%20by%20the%20Numbers-%20May%202015.pdf

and constitutional challenges to FATCA and the IGA have been launched in the United States,[70] Canada[71] and other countries.[72] The number of US citizens with dual nationality renouncing their US citizenship has increased greatly in recent years, undoubtedly in many cases to allow the individual to avoid the consequences of FATCA.[73]

5.8   The Convention on Mutual Administrative Assistance in Tax Matters, the OECD Common Reporting Standard and Competent Authority Agreement

The Convention on Mutual Administrative Assistance in Tax Matters (the 'Convention') may be the ultimate solution for combatting tax evasion that relies on the inability of tax authorities to obtain access to foreign account information. A joint initiative of the Council of Europe and the OECD, the Convention was first opened for signature by member states of these two organisations in 1988. It entered into force in 1995, with only eight countries having ratified it, and only gradually gained further adherents.[74]

---

[70] *Crawford et al.* v. *US Dept of the Treasury et al.*, No. 3:15-cv-250 (SD Ohio 2015) in the US District Court for the Southern District of Ohio Western Division. The challenge is supported by Senator Rand Paul: Leslie Kellogg, 'Lawsuit by US Presidential Candidate Challenges the Constitutionality of FATCA' (24 July 2015), online: Jdsupra Business Advisor, www.jdsupra.com/legalnews/lawsuit-by-u-s-presidential-candidate-81901/

[71] *Virginia Hillis and Gwendolyn Louise Deegan* v. *Attorney General of Canada and Minister of National Revenue*, 2015 FC 1082: a motion by the plaintiffs for judgment by summary trial for a declaration that the Canada–US IGA was invalid under Canadian law and the Canada–US tax treaty was dismissed by the Federal Court of Canada on 16 September 2015. The constitutionality of the IGA under Canada's Charter of Rights and Freedoms will be determined at a later date following a full trial in this case.

[72] The Economist reports that a dual Dutch–US national resident in the Netherlands successfully sued a Dutch lender that had closed his account: *The Economist*, 'Dropping the Bomb: America's Fierce Campaign against Tax Cheats is Doing More Harm than Good' (28 June 2014), online: www.economist.com/news/finance-and-economics/21605911-americas-fierce-campaign-against-tax-cheats-doing-more-harm-good-dropping

[73] Perhaps the most famous is Boris Johnson, the mayor of London: *The Guardian*, 'London Mayor Boris Johnson to Renounce US Citizenship' (14 February 2015), online: www .theguardian.com/politics/2015/feb/14/london-mayor-boris-johnson-to-renounce-us-citizenship. See also: Catherine Bosley and Richard Rubin, 'A Record Number of Americans Are Renouncing Their Citizenship' (10 February 2015), online: *Bloomberg Business*, www .bloomberg.com/news/articles/2015-02-10/americans-overseas-top-annual-record-for-turning-over-passports and R.A. Berg, 'FATCA in Canada: The "Cure" for a U.S. Place of Birth', Report of the *Proceedings of the Sixty-Sixth Tax Conference* (Toronto: Canadian Tax Foundation, 2015), 1–38.

[74] The failure of the 1988 Convention to require adequate protection for the confidentiality of taxpayer information has been cited as a reason for its tepid reception.

The 1988 Convention provided for exchange of tax information between the parties' tax authorities, mutual assistance in collection of taxes and assistance in service of documents; some signatories did not undertake the obligation to assist in collection of taxes owed to another signatory country.

In April 2009, the G20 leaders called for updating of the Convention to reflect the new international standard[75] for exchange of tax information and for it to be open to all countries. A protocol was opened for signature on 27 May 2010, and the amended Convention incorporating the protocol was opened for signature on 1 June 2011.[76] As of 31 August 2015, the amended convention or the protocol is in force in 71 jurisdictions, including numerous nonstate dependencies of the United Kingdom, the Netherlands and Denmark.[77] Some of these, such as the British Virgin Islands, the Cayman Islands, the Channel Islands and the former members of the Netherlands Antilles, have long been regarded as tax havens. The United States signed the protocol in 2010, but has still not brought it into force. [78]

Although the 2011 Convention allows parties to reserve their positions in respect of certain taxes or, for example, to refuse to provide assistance in collection, jurisdictions may not opt out of the core obligations to exchange tax information automatically, spontaneously[79] and on request. Implementation of the Convention between Parties is to be achieved, according to Art. 24,

[75] The current international standard is essentially the same as Art. 26 of the OECD Model.

[76] OECD, 'Convention on Mutual Administrative Assistance in Tax Matters' (1 June 2011), online: www.oecd.org/ctp/exchange-of-tax-information/ENG-Amended-Convention.pdf

[77] For the current status of the Convention, see OECD, 'Jurisdictions Participating in the Convention on Mutual Administrative Assistance in Tax Matters' (1 September 2015), online: www.oecd.org/ctp/exchange-of-tax-information/Status_of_convention.pdf. Nonstate dependencies are not independent parties to the Convention but under Art. 29 it may be extended to them when a state signatory declares the dependency as part of its territory.

[78] Switzerland signed the Protocol in 2013. As of September 2015 Switzerland had not brought the Convention into force, but has signalled its intention to do so; see *infra* note 83.

[79] Article 7: A Party shall, without prior request, forward to another Party information on which it has knowledge in the following circumstances:

  (a) the first-mentioned Party has grounds for supposing that there may be a loss of tax in the other Party;
  (b) a person liable to tax obtains a reduction in or an exemption from tax in the first-mentioned Party which would give rise to an increase in tax or liability to tax in the other Party;
  (c) business dealings between a person liable to tax in a Party and a person liable to tax in another Party are conducted through one or more countries in such a way that saving in tax may result in one or the other Party or in both;
  (d) a Party has grounds for supposing that a saving of tax may result from artificial transfers of profits within groups of enterprises;
  (e) information forwarded to the first-mentioned Party by the other Party has enabled information to be obtained which may be relevant in assessing liability to tax in the latter Party.

through agreement between the Parties' competent authorities. This could have meant that the Convention remained an unimplemented aspirational instrument, if the further steps were not taken by each country's tax administration. However, in February 2014 the OECD, working with G20 countries and the European Union, issued the Standard for Automatic Exchange of Financial Account Information (the 'Standard'), composed of the Common Reporting and Due Diligence Standard (CRS) and the Model Competent Authority Agreement (CAA).[80] The Standard aims to prevent a proliferation of different due diligence and reporting requirements for financial institutions, including banks, custodians, brokers, certain collective investment vehicles and certain insurance companies. Accounts held by individuals, corporations, trusts, foundations and other entities are reportable, and there are look-through rules for passive entities so that individuals who control them can be identified. All investment income, account balances and sales proceeds from financial assets are to be reported.

The CAA facilitates implementation of automatic exchange of financial account information, either under Art. 6 of the Convention or under exchange of information provisions of an existing tax treaty. The CRS, designed as an annex to the CAA, is obviously and admittedly inspired by, and modelled on the FATCA Model 1 IGAs, but it is reciprocal, and there are no 'FATCA-esque' withholding obligations. A detailed commentary on the CRS, intended to assist in interpretation and application, was published with the final version of the Standard in July 2014.

By October 2014, it was clear that jurisdictions were choosing overwhelmingly to implement automatic EOI with each other through a multilateral version of the CAA.[81] As of 4 June 2015, sixty-one countries had signed a declaration of commitment to exchange financial account information automatically in accordance with the CRS, although some had yet to sign or bring into force the Convention.[82] It is evident that countries

---

[80] These are available online at: OECD, 'Standard for Automatic Exchange of Financial Account Information in Tax Matters' (21 July 2014), online: www.oecd.org/tax/exchange-of-tax-information/standard-for-automatic-exchange-of-financial-information-in-tax-matters.htm

[81] OECD, 'Multilateral Competent Authority Agreement of Automatic Exchange of Financial Account Information', online: www.oecd.org/ctp/exchange-of-tax-information/multilateral-competent-authority-agreement.pdf

[82] OECD, 'Signatories of the Multilateral Competent Authority Agreement on Automatic Exchange of Financial Account Information and Intended First Information Exchange Date' (4 June 2015), online: www.oecd.org/tax/exchange-of-tax-information/MCAA-Signatories.pdf. The declarations of Switzerland and Liechtenstein are perhaps the most notable. Absent, among many others, is the United States.

have realised that if they must disclose this information to the IRS under FATCA, they can share such information with other jurisdictions on a reciprocal basis and receive the same or similar benefits to those the US anticipates with FATCA. There is also no doubt a measure of peer pressure between countries that are keen to collect tax that may be hidden abroad to enter into reciprocal AEOI, and pressure to participate is also exerted on jurisdictions that were once viewed as tax havens.

The multilateral CAA (MCAA) allows for non-reciprocal AEOI, as some jurisdictions will be senders but not receivers. It is understood that the latter are jurisdictions that have no or very low income or corporate taxes, and therefore no concerns that their residents are evading, and for whom this information has therefore no purpose. The MCAA specifies that information will be automatically exchanged annually within nine months of the end of the calendar year. Annex B to the CAA will list one or more methods for data transmission and encryption standards.

Notwithstanding the high number of countries committing to the MCAA process, there are still numerous nonparticipating jurisdictions where only the FATCA will apply, whether or not an IGA is in place. The United States will receive information or impose withholding, but its IGA partner jurisdictions will have to wait for full, or even some, reciprocity. It has been noted that the United States may in fact be playing the role of tax haven to the rest of the world by requiring other countries' FFIs to report and withhold in respect of US taxpayers, but failing to reciprocate.[83] Moreover, it seems likely that nonparticipating jurisdictions will receive an influx of funds as those taxpayers who relied on bank secrecy rules to evade taxation close their accounts in participating jurisdictions and transfer their funds to nonparticipating jurisdictions.

5.9   Conclusion

Offshore tax evasion is difficult to quantify accurately for obvious reasons, but just as obviously it results in very significant revenue loss for many countries.[84] Evasion undermines the fairness of a country's tax system,

---

[83] See the discussion of US legislators' expressed reluctance to reciprocate, and their support for making the United States a haven for capital from other countries in Christians, *supra* note 58 at 5–8.

[84] The US Senate Subcommittee on Investigations has estimated that tax evasion amounts to US$100 billion annually (although not all of this is connected to offshore evasion). See Jane G. Gravelle, 'Tax Havens: International Tax Avoidance and Evasion' (15 January 2015), online: Congressional Research Service, www.fas.org/sgp/crs/misc/R40623.pdf at 1, fn 1.

and can cause taxpayers who would willingly pay their legal share of the tax burden to become cynical and distrustful if they believe others are evading. On the other hand, a case can be made that undue access by tax authorities to what is normally considered private information can violate public standards of privacy protection, and that EOI regimes, especially for automatic exchange, may not sufficiently protect against information being disclosed to persons who are not entitled to it. In the context of EOI on request or spontaneous EOI, a country that places a high value on protection of confidential information may require that a taxpayer whose information is to be provided to a foreign tax authority be notified and has the opportunity to challenge the decision. However, such procedural safeguards could not play a part in a regime where information is exchanged electronically and automatically, without review before the 'send' button is pressed. As AEOI becomes a reality, taxpayers will undoubtedly challenge the laws that allow it.

As of September 2015, there are two AEOI regimes being implemented: the US FATCA regime and the OECD's multilateral system. The FATCA's effectiveness is likely to be greater due to the withholding requirements, but only the US revenue benefits from it. The recent efforts by the OECD to create an effective, multilateral, automatic information exchange regime are to be applauded, as this is the most promising way to reduce tax evasion where bank secrecy and lack of transparency as to ownership and control of assets and entities have facilitated the hiding of capital abroad. To be effective, however, the regime must be universal or near universal, so that the hiding places are obvious because they are so few. It is difficult to see how the OECD's emerging regime can be truly effective without US participation. The OECD's system, created from the reactive momentum generated by FATCA, and even with so many jurisdictions participating, cannot command the same compliance from evaders from those jurisdictions. It is to be hoped that before long the United States will sign on to the multilateral system, and remove any possibility that the original driver of change will become the newest and safest tax haven for evaders from the rest of the world.

PART II

Bank Secrecy in Financial
Centres Around the World

6

China

WEI WANG

6.1 Introduction

Historically, China has not recognised bank secrecy. Today, there are laws and regulations that provide for bank secrecy, but overall the protection is weak. The National Secrecy Law [*baoshou guojia mimifa*][1] protects national secrets[2]; it does not cover banking, individual or institutional secrets. Generally speaking, Chinese legislation prefers national secrecy to individual privacy. For example, Art. 53 of PRC Constitution[3] provides that Chinese citizens must guard national secrets, while Art. 40 of the Constitution only protects citizens' freedom and privacy of correspondence [*tongxin mimi*]. To date, China has not passed a formal privacy law for individuals or institutions, and has no legislative plan to do so. This does not mean that China fails to provide any protection of privacy (including, *inter alia*, of bank information) for individuals or institutions. There are a few articles in the Chinese civil law concerning the protection of general privacy for individuals and institutions. While the term 'privacy' [*yinsi*] cannot be found in the General Principle of Civil Law of 1987, in 2009 China published a law using the specific term 'privacy', i.e. the Tort Law [*Qinquan Zerenfa*].[4]

A version of this chapter was presented at the Bank Secrecy Symposium hosted by the Centre for Banking and Finance Law at the National University of Singapore, Faculty of Law on 4–5 December 2014.

[1] National Secrecy Law [*Baoshou Guojia Mimifa*] (1988), online: www.gov.cn/flfg/2010-04/30/content_1596420.htm

[2] Article 2 of the National Secrecy Law, *ibid.*, states that national secrets refer to the matters related to national security and interests, ascertained by law procedures and known by people within a specific period and scope. Theoretically it is possible that under some special circumstances, individual secrets may also constitute national secrets.

[3] Constitution of the People's Republic of China [*Zhonghua Renmin Gongheguo Xianfa*] (1982).

[4] See Tort Law [*Qinquan Zerenfa*] (2009), Art. 2, online: www.gov.cn/flfg/2009-12/26/content_1497435.htm

Likewise, one of the earliest Chinese banking laws, the General Banking Regulation [*Yinhang Tongxing Zeli*] published in 1908 by the late Qing Dynasty, did not contain any article relating to a bank's duty of keeping their customers' banking affairs secret. Another earlier banking law, the Regulation on Saving Banks [*Chuxu Yinhang Zeli*], also published in 1908, had nothing to do with bank secrecy. On 24 April 1931, China published its first Banking Act, which had no bank secrecy article. The lack of a bank secrecy article continued in the second Banking Act of 1947. After 1949, the people's government adopted the policy of encouraging people to make deposits.[5] On 28 July 1956, the People's Bank of China (PBC), the central bank of the People's Republic of China, established three principles for depositing: voluntary depositing, free withdrawal and maintaining secrecy for depositors.[6] But the principles were totally destroyed by the Cultural Revolution which broke out in 1966. Voluntary depositing became 'voluntary' turning over (to the government), and free withdrawal became free withdrawal by 'revolutionary organisations', while depositors' privacy was neglected.[7] Such neglect was consistent with the emphasis on collectivism and contempt for individualism during the period of the Cultural Revolution. On 18 February 1968, the Central Committee of the Chinese Communist Party, the State Council, the Central Military Committee and the Central Cultural Revolution Panel jointly issued an urgent notice[8] to freeze the deposits of ten kinds of people: 'traitors, spies, capitalist roaders in the communist party, landlords, rich peasants, counterrevolutionaries, bad elements, rightists who have not been well reformed, counterrevolutionary bourgeois, and counterrevolutionary intellectuals'.[9] This is the notorious Notice of February 18.

In order to redress the chaos in banking, in 1972, the PBC issued the Tentative Rule on Savings Deposits [*Chuxu Cunkuan Shixing Zhangcheng*], and this rule restated the three principles of 1956 and added a fourth – 'interest bearing deposits'.[10] The PBC also issued a notice as an annex to

---

[5] Common Creed of the Chinese People's Political Consultative Conference [*Zhongguo Renmin Zhengzhi Xieshanghui Yigong Tonggangling*] (1949), Art. 37, online: www.cppcc .gov.cn/2011/09/06/ARTI1315304517625199.shtml

[6] *Sixty Years of the PBC: 1948–2008* (Beijing: China Finance Press, 2008) at 363.

[7] See generally W. Zhipan, *Legal Affairs of Commercial Banks* [*Shangye Yinhang Fawu*] (Beijing: China Finance Press, 2005) at 209.

[8] 'An Urgent Notice on Further Carrying Out Thrifty Revolution and Retrenchment' [*Guanyu Jinyibu Shixing Jieyue Naogeming, Jianjue Jieyue Kaizhi de Jinji Tongzhi*], Zhongfa [68] No. 31, in *Financial System Digest* [*Jinrong Zhidu Zhaibian*] (PBC Guangdong Branch, 1974), at 10–14.

[9] *Ibid.* at para. 10.

[10] 'The Tentative Rule on Savings Deposits' [*Chuxu Cunkuan Shixing Zhangcheng*] (1972), Art. 2, in *Financial System Digest, supra* note 8, at 176.

the rule of 1972, providing that only public security organs and judicial organs could inquire into savings deposits.[11] However, the situation was not fundamentally changed until the end of the 1970s when China adopted the reform and open policy. In 1980, the PBC published the Rule on Savings Deposits [*Chuxu Cunkuan Zhangcheng*],[12] which succeeded the four 1972 principles for depositing. Since then, Chinese people have gradually realised the significance of the protection of privacy (including bank account information) of individuals and institutions, and there are now some laws, regulations and rules relating to bank secrecy.

This chapter focuses on relevant laws, regulations, rules or treaties relating to bank secrecy in China. It is divided into three sections. Section 6.2 discusses the bank's duty of secrecy. Section 6.3 analyses the duty to disclose information. Section 6.4 is about Chinese attitudes to different aspects of bank secrecy. This chapter ends with concluding remarks.

6.2   Bank's Duty to Keep Secret

The bank's duty of secrecy (referred to in this chapter as 'the duty to keep secret') appears in a number of administrative laws, regulations and rules. Additionally, the duty to keep secret may also be created by a contract. The former can be regarded as a public law duty, and the latter a private law duty. The obligation for wrongful disclosure of bank information may also be subject to tort law, which is part of private law.

6.2.1   Administrative Duty to Keep Secret

Administrative Rules and Regulations on Banks' Duty to Keep Secret   The 1980 Rule on Savings Deposits was replaced by the Administrative Regulation on Savings [*Chuxu Guanli Tiaoli*], published by the State Council in December 1992, which took effect in March 1993 and was amended in 2010. Article 32 of the Administrative Regulation on Savings states as follows:

> Savings Institutions have the duty of keeping depositors' savings secret. Savings Institutions do not help any units or individuals inquire, freeze or appropriate savings deposits, unless otherwise provided by national laws, administrative regulations.

---

[11] 'Some Issues to be Internally Controlled in the Tentative Rule on Savings Deposits' [*Chuxu Cunkuan Zhangcheng Zhong Xu Neibu Zhangwo de Yixie Wenti*], para. 1, in *Financial System Digest, supra* note 8 at 179.

[12] PBC Rule on Savings Deposits [*Chuxu Cunkuan Zhangcheng*] (28 May 1980), (80) *Yinchuzi* No. 10.

The definition of 'savings deposits' [*chuxu cunkuan*] is clarified in a rule made by the PBC in 1993 to mean 'RMB or foreign currency deposits owned by individuals in savings institutions within the territory of China'.[13]

In 1988, the PBC issued the Bank Settlement Rules [*Yinhang Jiesuan Banfa*]. Article 11 of the Rules provides that banks shall keep deposits secret. In 1997, the PBC issued Payment and Settlement Rules [*Zhifu Jiesuan Banfa*]. The 1997 Rules replaced the 1988 rules, but the duty to keep deposits secret was preserved.[14] Around the same time, in 1996, the PBC published the General Rules on Lending [*Daikuan tongze*]. Paragraph 4 of Art. 23 states that 'a lender shall keep a borrower's debts, finance, production and operations secret, with the exception of an inquiry based on laws.' Similar articles appear in other banking rules, such as Rules on RMB Settlement Accounts (2003) [*Renminbi Jiesuan Zhanghu Guanli Banfa*],[15] and Provisions on True Names of Individual Deposit Accounts [*Geren Cunkuan Zhanghu Shimingzhi Guiding*].[16]

Commercial Banking Law In 1995, the Standing Committee of the National People's Congress (NPC) enacted the Commercial Banking Law, which was amended in 2004 and 2015. Two articles in the Commercial Banking Law are directly related to bank secrecy.

Article 29 of the Commercial Banking Law is designed for individual savings deposits. It states:

> For the business of individual savings deposits, a commercial bank shall abide by the principles of voluntary depositing, free withdrawal, interest-bearing deposits, and keeping secret for depositors.
>
> For individual savings deposits, a commercial bank has the right to refuse the request from any units or any individuals to inquire, freeze or deduct, unless otherwise provided by laws.

It must be noted that Art. 29 of the Commercial Banking Law uses the term 'right' and not 'duty' to describe the legal basis for a bank to

---

[13] Relevant Provisions of the PBC for Fulfilling Administrative Regulation on Savings (1993), Art. 1, *Yinfa* No. 7.

[14] See Payment and Settlement Rules [*Zhifu Jiesuan Banfa*] (1997), Art. 19, online: http://kzp .mof.gov.cn/content.jsp?infoid=249&class_id=01_10_01_07

[15] Administrative Rules on RMB Settlement Accounts [*Renminbi Jiesuan Zhanghu Guanli Banfa*] (1 September 2003), online: www.pbc.gov.cn/zhifujiesuansi/128525/128535/128620/ 2898144/index.html

[16] Provisions on True Names of Individual Deposit Accounts [*Geren Cunkuan Zhanghu Shimingzhi Guiding*] (1 April 2000), online: www.pbc.gov.cn/publish/tiaofasi/584/1420/14200/14200_.html

refuse requests from third parties to disclose information relating to depositors.

Article 30 of the Commercial Banking Law is designed for institutional deposits. It states as follows:

> For institutional savings, a commercial bank has the right to refuse the request from any units or any individuals to inquire, unless otherwise provided by laws or regulations. A commercial bank has the right to refuse the request from any units or any individuals to freeze or deduct, unless otherwise provided by laws.

Due to the fact that 'laws' in China usually means the laws enacted by the NPC or its standing committee, while 'regulations' in China mean the rules made by the State Council,[17] the degree of protection of bank secrecy in individual savings deposits is higher than in institutional deposits since the latter is subject to laws and regulations while the former is subject only to laws. For institutional deposits, the duty of bank secrecy on *inquiry* is lower than that on *freezing and deduction*.

> Article 73 of the Commercial Banking Law states as follows:
> A commercial bank shall assume liability for payment of default interest and other civil liability if the property of depositors or other clients is damaged as a result of the commercial bank's:
>
> ...
>
> (3) illegal inquiry, freezing, or deduction of the savings deposits of individuals or the deposits of units
>
> ...
>
> If a commercial bank commits one of the acts specified in the preceding paragraph, it shall be instructed by the banking regulatory authority under the State Council to rectify and its unlawful gains shall be confiscated; if the unlawful gains exceed 50,000 yuan, it shall, in addition, be fined not less than the amount of such gains but not more than five times that amount; and if there are no unlawful gains or such gains are less than 50,000 yuan, it shall be fined not less than 50,000 yuan but not more than 500,000 yuan.

It must be noted that Art. 73 of the Commercial Banking Law does not contain a criminal law penalty clause,[18] which makes it different from Art. 74 of the same law which clearly provides that, for eight stipulated events,

---

[17] According to Art. 88 of the PRC Legislation Law, laws have a higher status than regulations: [*Lifa Fa*] (2000), Art. 88, online: www.gov.cn/test/2005-08/13/content_22423.htm

[18] The banking regulatory authority is an administrative organ. The nature of a fine imposed by it is an administrative penalty, not a criminal penalty. For the seven kinds of administrative penalties, see Art. 8 of PRC Administrative Penalties Law (1996), English translation available online: www.china.org.cn/english/government/207306.htm

such as establishing a branch without approval, criminal responsibility shall be investigated according to law.[19]

Comparing Arts. 73 and 74 of the Commercial Banking Law, one can arrive at the conclusion that 'illegal inquiry, freezing or appropriation of the savings deposits of individuals or the deposits of units' is not as serious as the eight events which may constitute crimes. At this point, it may be noted that Art. 73 of the Commercial Banking Law is different from Art. 47 of the Swiss Banking Act or section 47 of the Singapore Banking Act, both of which contain penal clauses.[20]

6.2.2 Criminal Penalties for Disclosing Bank Secrets

Although Art. 73 of the Commercial Banking Law does not have a criminal penalty like Art. 74, it is still possible for the act of illegal disclosure of deposit information to be penalised by the Criminal Law in a broad sense. Such a conclusion is supported by a PBC notice in 2011.[21]

In 2009, the Standing Committee of the NPC amended the Criminal Law (7th Amendment). A clause was added to Art. 253 of the Criminal Law, providing that, if a staff member of a financial institution sells or illegally provides personal information collected by the institution during the period of performing its duty or providing services, and if the circumstances are serious, he or she shall be imprisoned for less than three years, be put into criminal detention or be fined. But the definition of serious circumstances is unclear.

---

[19] Commercial Banking Law [*Shangye Yinhangfa*] (1995), English translation available online: www.china.org.cn/english/DAT/214824.htm. The eight illegal events in Art. 74 are:

1. establishing a branch without approval;
2. dividing or merging without approval;
3. raising or lowering interest rates in violation of relevant regulations or taking in deposits or granting loans by other illegitimate means;
4. leasing out or lending its business license;
5. buying and selling foreign exchange without approval;
6. buying or selling government bonds without approval, or issuing, buying or selling financial bonds without approval;
7. violating relevant State regulations, engaging in trust investment and the business of securities, investing in real property not for private use or investing in nonbanking financial institutions or enterprises;
8. granting credit loans to its connections or granting guaranteed loans to its connections on conditions that are more preferential than those for granting the same to other borrowers.

[20] See Booysen, Chapter 10 and Nobel and Braendli, Chapter 11.
[21] PBC *Yinfa* (2011), Art. 10 (5). It must be noted that a PBC notice has no *de jure* legal force, but has *de facto* effect.

6.2.3 Contractual Duty to Keep Secret

Compared with the rare use of the term 'privacy', Chinese civil law does use the term 'secret' [*mimi*] in a contractual context. For example, an employer and an employee may agree upon confidential matters in their labour contract (or in a separate confidential agreement) in order to protect the employer's business secrets and intellectual property rights.[22] However, the Contract Law of 1999, which contains fifteen kinds of agreements (e.g., a sales agreement, a loan agreement, etc.), does not include a confidentiality agreement. Article 124 of the Contract Law leaves room for the existence of an innominate contract. Therefore, it is possible for a bank and its customer to make a confidentiality agreement. Even if there is not a confidentiality agreement or a confidentiality clause between a bank and its customer, a contractual duty to keep bank information secret may still exist.

In a notice issued by the PBC in 2011,[23] if a banker illegally provides customers' personal financial information and causes damage to the customer, the banker shall be liable.[24] Although the PBC notice does not mention the nature of the legal liability, it could be implied that such liability is contractual liability (or at least civil liability) between the banker and its customers.

According to Art. 43 of the Contract Law of 1999, contractual parties shall have the duty of maintaining business secrets whether the contract has been concluded or not. Even if there is not a secrecy clause in the contract, both parties still have to abide by the *bona fide* principle of keeping secret based on the nature and aim of the contract, or based on trade custom.[25] Here, the duty to keep information secret is called a collateral obligation [*fusui yiwu*], a legal concept from German civil law.

In a contractual dispute on savings deposits, the Shanghai No. 1 Intermediate People's Court stated that 'keeping depositors' information secret is an important contractual obligation',[26] although there was not a formal confidentiality agreement or clause in that case. This judgment does

---

[22] The Labour Contract Law [*Laodong Hetongfa*] (2008), Art. 23, English translation available online: www.npc.gov.cn/englishnpc/Law/2009-02/20/content_1471106.htm

[23] PBC *Yinfa* (2011) No. 17, 21 January 2011.

[24] PBC *Yinfa* (2011) No. 17, Art. 12.

[25] See The Contract Law [*Hetongfa*] (1999), Art. 60, English translation available online: www.npc.gov.cn/englishnpc/Law/2007-12/11/content_1383564.htm. According to this article, besides the duty of keeping secret, there are at least two duties with the same nature, the duty of notice and the duty of assistance.

[26] *Luomou v. Yi Bank, et al., Huyizhong Minliu (Shang) Zhongzi*, 2011 No. 198. The judgment was made on 3 February 2012.

not mention whether such a duty is a collateral obligation (from German civil law) or an implied duty as found in common law jurisdictions.

In the opinion of Chinese courts, the contractual duty of keeping secret relating to banking information is bilateral, not unilateral. This is also the opinion of the main Chinese banking supervisor, China Banking Regulatory Commission (CBRC). Article 89 of Administrative Measures for E-banking[27] provides as follows:

> If the damages are made by hidden safety troubles of the E-banking system, illegal internal operations, or other non-customer reasons, the financial institution shall undertake proper liability.
>
> If the damages are made by customer's intentional disclosure of transaction code, or failure to fulfill his/her safety and confidentiality duty in service agreement, the financial institution may exempt from proper liability according to the service agreement, unless otherwise provided by laws or regulations.

In *Wu Jianbing* v. *Agriculture Bank* (*Xianju Subbranch*),[28] Wu Jianbing (Wu) (the plaintiff), after getting a debit card from Agriculture Bank (defendant), revealed the card number to an unknown business partner. Although Wu did not admit that he also told the password to his partner, someone withdrew money from Agriculture Bank and the bank's ATM machines by using the correct password. In the retrial, the Zhejiang Higher People's Court held that Wu failed to keep his card information secret by telling the card information to an unknown person. Agriculture Bank had no fault, so the bank should not undertake any liability.

In a bank card case raised by a card holder against a bank (also the card issuer), evidence showed that someone had cloned the bank card, swiped the fake card and used a true password. The card holder asked the bank to pay the loss arising from the cloned card. Guangdong Higher People's Court held that both parties had the duty of properly keeping information relating to the bank card a secret, so the bank should undertake 70 per cent of liability, and the card holder 30 per cent.[29]

---

[27] Administrative Measures for E-banking [*Dianzi Yinhang Yewu Guanli Banfa*], (1 March 2006) CBRC Order [2006] No. 5, online: www.cbrc.gov.cn/govView_EAB589F936AD446 DA3F711CEEA97F2D9.html

[28] *Wu Jianbing* v. *Agriculture Bank* (*Xianju Subbranch*), *Zheshang Tizi*, 2009 No. 27.

[29] *Dinghuogui* v. *Agriculture Bank of China* (*Sihui Bihaiwan Sub-branch*), *Yuegaofa Miner Tizi*, 2013 No. 19. The judgment was made on 28 February 2014.

In *Liang Yanfen* v. *ICBC* (*Guangzhou Dananlu Subbranch*),[30] Liang Yanfen (the plaintiff) was the debit card holder and ICBC (the defendant) was the card issuer. The records of the card transactions showed three purchases by e-payment, and four fund transfers through a third-party payment platform (Gripay). All of the transactions only needed the card numbers, password, mobile phone numbers and SMS verification codes. So this case was not a traditional bank card clone case, but a case of internet banking and mobile banking. Liang Yanfen claimed that her mobile phone had never received the SMS verification codes from ICBC, but ICBC proved that the bank had sent out SMS verification codes. The court held that Liang Yanfen was at fault for the leakage of her card number and passwords, while ICBC was at fault for not effectively making the SMS verification codes reach Liang Yanfen's mobile phone (it was possible that those SMS verification codes were intercepted by computer virus). In the end, the court held that the bank should undertake 70 per cent liability, while the card holder 30 per cent.

It must be noted that, according to a case published by the Supreme People's Court, the duty of keeping secrets for depositors covers not only personal information, but also a safe and confidential environment for depositors when they go to a bank for transactions. If the bank fails to fulfil the duty, this will constitute a breach of contract, and it will incur civil liability for such breach.[31] In that case, Zhou Peidong (the plaintiff), did not know how to use the ATM machine in the lobby of the bank (the defendant), so he asked the bank staff for help, but the bank staff asked him to read and operate according to the notice on the ATM machine. During the process of operation and another round of asking for help, Zhou's debit card was switched with another card by a fraudster, and it was highly possible that his password was also seen by the fraudster. When Zhou reported the loss of his card, he found that the deposits in his account had been withdrawn. The court held that the bank failed to provide safe facilities for the ATM machine to prevent third parties getting access to Zhou or catching sight of his password, so the bank broke its duty of keeping secret, and should undertake all liability.

---

[30] *Liang Yanfen* v. *ICBC* (*Guangzhou Dananlu Subbranch*), *Suizhong Fajin Minzhongzi*, 2015 No. 1066. The judgment was made on 26 October 2015.

[31] *Zhou Peidong* v. *Jiangdong Agriculture Bank* (a savings contract case), *Zuigao Renmin Fayuan Gongbao*, 2006 (Issue no. 2).

In another case also published in the Gazette of the Supreme People's Court,[32] Wang Yongsheng (the plaintiff), the holder of a debit card issued by Bank of China (BOC) (Nanjing Hexi Subbranch), withdrew cash from an ATM machine in a network of BOC. Wang's card information and password were captured by a fraudster who had tampered with the system. By cloning two cards, the fraudster withdrew, in two different cities, most of the money in Wang's account. The defendant, BOC (Nanjing Hexi Subbranch) argued that, according to the debit card contract between Wang and the bank, Wang as the card holder shall properly keep his password, and the risk or loss of leaking the password shall be undertaken by the card holder himself. The court (Nanjing Gulou District People's Court) held that the loss of password was caused by the bank's failure to provide a safe environment that was conducive to the preservation of secrecy. Card holders usually do not have professional knowledge, and do not have the ability to tell whether the system has been tampered with. It is the bank's duty to conduct necessary maintenance of its ATM machines so as to provide its customers a safe and secure environment. Therefore, the court held that BOC should undertake all civil liability. The court further pointed out that the criminals did not directly infringe *Wang's* property, but infringed the bank's property, and the obligations in the relationship between Wang and the bank still existed. Another case, *Gujun v. Shanghai Bank of Communications* (a savings contract case), reached a similar conclusion.[33]

6.2.4 Tort Obligation under Chinese Law

Although there is no personal information protection law in China, the Chinese legislature (NPC or its Standing Committee) has taken some measures to protect personal information. The efforts are reflected in the Decision to Strengthen Network Information Protection made by the NPC Standing Committee,[34] stating that network service providers and other units or their staff shall, in the process of collecting personal electronic information for business, strictly keep secret, and never leak, distort,

---

[32] *Wang Yongsheng v. Bank of China (Nanjing Hexi Subbranch)* (a savings contract case), *Zuigao Renmin Fayuan Gongbao*, 2009 (Issue no. 2).

[33] *Gujun v. Shanghai Bank of Communications* (a saving's contract case), *Zuigao Renmin Fayuan Gongbao*, 2005 (Issue no. 4) at 41–5.

[34] Decision to Strengthen Network Information Protection [*Guanyu Jiaqiang Wangluo Xinxi Baohu de Jueding*] (28 December 2012), online: www.gov.cn/jrzg/2012-12/28/content_2301231.htm

destroy, sell or illegally provide the information to others.[35] In violation of the above duty, an infringer may incur administrative liability, criminal liability and civil liability (tort).[36]

In 2013, China amended the Consumer Interests Protection Law,[37] introducing personal information into the consumer protection system for the first time. Article 29 of the amended Consumer Interests Protection Law provides that business operators and their staff shall strictly keep consumers' personal information secret, and never leak, sell or illegally provide such information to others. Certainly, 'consumers' include financial consumers, and 'business operators' include banks. The Consumer Interests Protection Law does not state the legal nature of violating the duty of keeping consumers' personal information secret, but it can be inferred from Art. 50 of the law that it is a tort, not breach of contract. The countermeasures for infringing consumers' personal information are, *inter alia*, cessation of infringement and compensation for loss.[38]

6.3   Duty to Disclose Information

From Section 6.2, it is obvious that, in China, the duty to keep secret in banking is not absolute. Almost every relevant law, regulation or rule has an exception clause in which information disclosure is allowed. This part discusses these laws, regulations and the agencies empowered to ask banks to disclose information.

In 2002, the PBC issued the Administrative Rules for Financial Institutions to Assist the Work of Inquiry, Freezing and Deduction [*jinrong jigou xiezhu chaxun dongjie kouhua gongzuo guanli guiding*].[39] Article 2 of the rule interprets the definition of 'assist to inquire' [*xiezhu chaxun*] as follows:

> 'Assist to inquire' means that financial institutions, according to relevant provisions of laws and administrative regulations and the requirements to make inquiry from the competent authorities [*youquan jiguan*], disclose the amount, currency and other information of deposits of units or individuals to the competent authorities.

---

[35] *Ibid.* at para. 3.
[36] *Ibid.* at para. 11.
[37] Consumer Interests Protection Law [*Xiaofeizhe Quanyi Baohufa*] (31 October 1993), online: www.npc.gov.cn/npc/xinwen/2013-10/26/content_1811773.htm
[38] *Ibid.* (as amended in 2013), Art. 50.
[39] *Yinfa* (2002) No. 1, issued on 15 January 2002 by the PBC, effective from 1 February 2002, online: www.pbc.gov.cn/rhwg/020505f.htm

Article 4 of the rule defines 'competent authorities' as:

> Judicial organs, administrative organs, military organs, and other institu-
> tions [*shiye danwei*] engaging in administrative affairs, which are empow-
> ered to inquire, freeze, appropriate deposits of units or individuals in
> financial institutions.

The list of competent authorities with the power of inquiry includes the
following: (1) people's courts; (2) taxation organs; (3) customs; (4) people's
procuratorates; (5) public security organs; (6) state security organs; (7) military security departments; (8) prisons; (9) investigation organs for smuggling; (10) supervision organs (including military supervision organs); (11)
auditing organs; (12) administrative organs for industry and commerce
and (13) regulatory organs for securities. A brief discussion of each follows.

6.3.1   Civil Procedure Law (People's Courts)

The Civil Procedure Law allows people's courts to inquire into deposits in
civil cases.[40] Article 242 (Art. 221 in the English translation) of the Civil
Procedure Law states as follows:

> If the person subject to enforcement [*bei zhixingren*] fails to fulfill its obli-
> gations in the legal document according to the enforcement notice, the
> people's court shall be empowered to make inquires to relevant units about
> savings deposits, bonds, shares, funds or other properties.

Undoubtedly, banks are included in 'relevant units'. However, in order
to ask banks to assist to make inquiry, courts must satisfy some procedural
conditions. Otherwise banks can refuse to provide assistance.

6.3.2   Tax Collection Law (Administration of Taxation)

The Tax Collection Law [*shuishou zhengshou guanlifa*] empowers tax
authorities to inquire into deposit accounts.[41] Paragraph 6 of Art. 54 of the
Tax Collection Law states:

> Upon approval of the commissioner of a tax bureau (or a sub-bureau
> thereof) above the county level, the tax authority has the power to inquire
> the deposit accounts that a taxpayer engaged in production or business

---

[40] Civil Procedure Law [*Minshi Susongfa*] (1991), English translation available online: www
.china.org.cn/english/government/207339.htm

[41] Tax Collection Law [*Shuishou Zhengshou Guanlifa*] (1992), English translation available
online: www.china.org.cn/business/laws_regulations/2007-06/22/content_1214782.htm

operations or a withholding agent (*koujiao yiwuren*) has opened with banks or other financial institutions, on presentation of a permit for the inspection of deposit accounts which is of a nationally unified form. When a tax authority investigates a tax case relating to violation of law, it may, upon approval of the commissioner of a tax bureau above the city level, to inquire the savings deposits of suspects in the case.

The Tax Collection Law makes a distinction between taxpayers (withholding agents) and suspects. The procedure to inquire into deposit accounts of the former is not as rigid as that of the latter.

6.3.3   Customs Law (Customs)

The Customs Law [*haiguanfa*] also empowers customs authorities to inquire into deposits in banks.[42] Paragraph 5 of Art. 6 of the Customs Law provides:

> When investigating a smuggling case, customs may, upon approval of the commissioner of a regional customs [*zhishu haiguan*] or of the commissioner of its subordinate customs [*lishu haiguan*] authorized by the former, inquire deposits, remittances of the suspected units and suspected individuals in financial institutions and postal services.

The investigation organ for smuggling is the Anti-Smuggling Bureau of General Administration of Customs (GACC).

6.3.4   Criminal Procedure Law (Procuratorates, Public Security Organs, State Security Organs, Military Security Departments and Prisons)

The Criminal Procedure Law allows several authorities to inquire into financial information in criminal cases.[43] Article 142 (Art. 117 in the English translation) of the Criminal Procedure Law states as follows:

> Public security organs [*gongan jiguan*] or people's procuratorates [*renmin jiancha jiguan*] may, based on the need to investigate crimes, inquire or freeze criminal suspects' deposits, remittances, bonds, shares, funds or other properties according to law.

The Criminal Procedure Law also empowers state security organs [*guojia anquan jiguan*] and military security departments [*jundui baowei*

---

[42] Customs Law [*Haiguanfa*] (1987), English translation available online: www.china.org.cn/english/government/207292.htm

[43] Criminal Procedure Law [*Xingshi Susongfa*] (1979), English translation available online: www.china.org.cn/english/government/207334.htm

bumen] to enjoy the same power with public security organs in relevant criminal cases,[44] which means that those organs and departments also have power to make inquiry into deposit accounts.

Article 60 of the Prison Law empowers prisons to investigate crimes committed by criminals in prisons.[45] The Prison Law itself does not empower prisons to ask banks to disclose personal information. However, Art. 290 of the Criminal Procedure Law covers prisons pursuant to which they also enjoy the power of making inquiry and freezing deposits, like public security organs and people's procuratorates.

On 29 December 2014, the CBRC, the Supreme People's Procuratorate, the Ministry of Public Security and the Ministry of State Security jointly issued the Provisions of the Work of Inquiry and Freezing for Banking Financial Institutions to Assist People's Procuratorates, Public Security Organs and State Security Organs.[46] The new provisions have detailed procedures for inquiry and freezing initiated by People's Procuratorates, Public Security Organs and State Security Organs.

6.3.5   Administrative Supervision Law (Supervision Organs)

Article 21 of the Administrative Supervision Law [*Xingzheng Jianchafa*] states as follows:

> In investigating corrupt, bribery, misappropriation or other violations of administrative disciplines, a supervision organ may inquire the deposits of the suspected in banks or other financial institutions. When necessary, it may ask a people's court to take conservancy measures, freeze the deposits of the suspected in banks or other financial institutions.[47]

Procedurally, it is easier for a supervisory organ to inquire into the deposits than to freeze the deposits, because it will have to rely on a court for freezing deposits.

---

[44] *Ibid.*, Arts. 4, 290 (Art. 225 in the English translation).

[45] Prison Law [*Jianyufa*] (1994), English translation available online: www.npc.gov.cn/ englishnpc/Law/2007-12/12/content_1383784.htm

[46] Provisions of the Work of Inquiry and Freezing for Banking Financial Institutions to Assist People's Procuratorates, Public Security Organs and State Security Organs [*Yinhangye Jinrong Jigou Xiezhu Renmin Jianchayuan Gong'an Jiguan Guojia Anquan Jiguan Chaxun Dongjie Gongzuo Guiding*] (1 January 2015) *Yinjianfa* [2014] No. 53, online: www.cbrc.gov .cn/chinese/home/docView/F24D3D019B8B4987AD74826D2FBDF01B.html

[47] Administrative Supervision Law [*Xingzheng Jianchafa*] (1997), English translation available online: www.npc.gov.cn/englishnpc/Law/2007-12/11/content_1383546.htm

6.3.6   Audit Law (Audit Organs)

Article 33 of the Audit Law states:

> An audit organ has the power to inquire the accounts of the audited in financial institutions, with the approval of the person in charge of the audit organ at the county level or higher.[48]

Article 34 provides that the audit organ shall apply to a people's court in order to freeze the deposits in financial institutions.

6.3.7   Regulation on the Prohibition of Pyramid Selling (Administrative Organs for Industry and Commerce)

Article 14(7) of the Regulation on the Prohibition of Pyramid Selling [*Jinzhi Chuanxiao Tiaoli*] empowers administrative organs for industry and commerce to inquire into accounts and deposits of the organisers or operators who are suspected of pyramid selling. If there is evidence to prove the transference and concealment of illegitimate funds, they may apply to judicial organs to freeze the fund.[49]

6.3.8   Securities Law (CSRC)

Article 180(6) of the Securities Law empowers regulatory organs for securities to inquire into bank accounts of investigated or related parties, and if necessary, they may freeze the accounts.[50] The current Chinese securities regulator is China Securities Regulatory Commission (CSRC).[51]

6.3.9   PBC, CBRC and CIRC

In the Administrative Rules for Financial Institutions to Assist the Work of Inquiry, Freezing and Deduction (PBC 2002), there are thirteen governmental organs empowered with the functions of inquiry, freezing and/or deduction. Among the thirteen organs, there is only one financial

---

[48] Audit Law [*Shenjifa*] (1994), English translation available online: www.china.org.cn/china/ LegislationsForm2001-2010/2011-02/14/content_21917188.htm

[49] Regulation on the Prohibition of Pyramid Selling [*Jinzhi Chuanxiao Tiaoli*] (10 August 2005) No. 444, English translation available online: www.asianlii.org/cn/legis/cen/laws/ropops432/

[50] Securities Law [*Zhengquanfa*] (1998), English translation available online: www.china.org.cn/english/government/207337.htm

[51] The CSRC website is available at: www.csrc.gov.cn/pub/newsite

regulator, i.e. CSRC. However, the other three Chinese financial regulators (PBC, CBRC and China Insurance Regulatory Commission (CIRC)) also have the power to inquire into bank accounts.

Article 23 of the Anti-Money Laundering Law provides as follows:[52]

> Where the administrative department of anti-money laundering of the State Council or its dispatched organ at provincial level finds any doubtful transaction, and if an investigation is therefore required, it may conduct an investigation into relevant financial institutions, and the latter shall cooperate and faithfully provide relevant documents and materials.
>
> In the investigation into any doubtful transaction, there shall be no fewer than 2 investigators, who shall show their legal certificates and investigation notice issued by the administrative department of anti-money laundering of the State Council or by its dispatched organ at provincial level. Otherwise, the financial institution under investigation has the right to refuse the investigation.

The administrative department of anti-money laundering of the State Council is the PBC.

In addition to the PBC, according to the Banking Supervision Law (2003),[53] the CBRC also has the power of inquiring into accounts of relevant financial institutions and their staff, and linked persons, and if necessary, it will apply to a people's court to freeze their accounts.[54] It is the duty of banks to disclose information to the CBRC, otherwise the banks may be punished.[55]

Furthermore, according to the Insurance Law,[56] the CIRC has the power of inquiring into bank accounts of insurance companies, insurance agents, insurance brokers, insurance asset management companies, representative offices of foreign insurance institutions and other entities and individuals who are suspected of engaging in or being involved in illegal business, and if necessary, it will apply to a People's Court to freeze the accounts.[57]

---

[52] Anti-Money Laundering Law [*Fanxiqianfa*] (2006), English translation available online: www.npc.gov.cn/englishnpc/Law/2008-01/02/content_1388022.htm. The PBC Rules were made in 2002, while the Anti-Monday Laundering Law was made in 2006. When the PBC made the list in 2002, the PBC did not have such a power authorised by a law. Perhaps that is the reason why the PBC itself is not in the list of the PBC Rules of 2002.

[53] Banking Supervision Law [*Yinhangye Jiandu Guanlifa*] (2003), English translation available online: www.npc.gov.cn/englishnpc/Law/2007-12/05/content_1381962.htm

[54] *Ibid.*, Art. 41.

[55] *Ibid.*, Art. 45.

[56] Insurance Law [*Baoxianfa*] (1995), English translation available online: www.npc.gov.cn/englishnpc/Law/2007-12/12/content_1383720.htm

[57] *Ibid.*, Art. 155(6), 155(7).

In sum, there are at least sixteen institutions with the power of making inquiry into bank accounts.

It is worth noting that the PBC Rule of 2002 sets up two primary principles for banks to assist an inquiry, i.e. (1) to abide by law and rules and (2) not to harm the lawful rights and interests of customers.[58] The scope of banks' assistance is only limited to deposit materials, including materials pertaining to the opening of bank accounts, deposits status, accounting documents, accounting books, bank statements relating to deposits.[59] If an authority only provides the name of the institution under inquiry (without account numbers) to the bank, the bank shall positively assist the authority to make inquiry into the institution based on archives of account management.[60] There is an obvious distinction between institutions and individuals in respect of the degree of assistance. For example, even if an auditing organ cannot provide a precise account name or account number of the audited unit/institution, the bank still has a duty to assist the inquiry. However, if the auditing organ cannot provide the name, account number or ID number of the audited individual, it seems that the financial institution has no duty to assist the inquiry.[61] This special protection of individual accounts is consistent with Art. 11 of the PBC Rules 2002.[62]

6.4   A Mixture of Conservatism, Activism and Pragmatism

6.4.1   External Conservatism: Limitations to Disclosure of Financial Information to Overseas Territories

The Chinese government is always prudent when it comes to disclosing financial information abroad. In 2011, the PBC issued a notice on protection of individual financial information [*Renmin Yinhang Guanyu Yinhangye Jinrong Jigou Zuohao Geren Jinrong Xinxi Baohu Gongzuo de Tongzhi*].[63] Individual financial information covers personal ID information, property information, account information, credit

---

[58] PBC Rule of 2002, Art. 5.
[59] *Ibid.*, Art. 14.
[60] *Ibid.*, Art. 15.
[61] See the 'Notice on Relevant Issues of Inquiring Accounts and Deposits of Audited Units in Financial Institutions by Auditing Organs' (8 July 2006), online: www.csrc.gov.cn/pub/newsite/flb/flfg/bmgf/zh/dcycf/201012/t20101231_189606.html. Issued by National Audit Office, PBC, CBRC and CSRC.
[62] Article 11 of the PBC Rule of 2002, *supra* note 58 provides that an authority shall provide the ID number of the individual if it cannot provide his account number.
[63] PBC *Yinfa* [2011] No. 17.

information, financial transaction information, derivative information (including personal consumption habit, investment intention) and other personal information.[64] This notice provides that individual financial information collected in the territory of China shall be stored, dealt with and analysed in the territory of China, and such financial information shall not be provided to overseas territories, unless otherwise provided by Chinese laws, regulations or PBC rules.[65]

On 6 July 2015, the Standing Committee of NPC promulgated a draft Network Security Law for public opinion.[66] Network Operators[67] shall establish a customer-information-protection system, enhancing the protection of customer personal information, privacy and commercial secrets,[68] keep information secret and shall not sell or illegally provide such information to others.[69] The operators of key information infrastructure (including, *inter alia*, the financial industry) shall store, in the territory of the PRC, the important personal information. If it is necessary to store it outside the PRC or provide such information to organisations or individuals outside the PRC, a security evaluation shall be carried out according to the rules made by the national cyberspace administration and relevant agencies under the State Council.[70]

For foreign-funded banks, their e-banking operation systems and business processing servers may be established either in the territory of the PRC or outside.[71] If it is necessary in business or management for foreign-funded banks to transfer e-banking data to their overseas headquarters, the foreign-funded banks shall abide by laws and regulations, adopt necessary measures to protect customers' lawful rights and abide by the rules of data exchange and transference.[72] Furthermore, all banks shall take appropriate measures to guarantee that their e-banking business conforms to the rules of protecting customer information and privacy.[73]

---

[64] *Ibid.*, Art. 1.
[65] *Ibid.*, Art. 6.
[66] Network Security Law (draft) [*Wangluo Anquanfa*] (2015), online: www.npc.gov.cn/npc/ xinwen/lfgz/flca/2015-07/06/content_1940614.htm
[67] Internet operators refer to the owners, managers and other internet service providers using internet owned or managed by others. See Art. 65(3) of the draft of Network Security Law of the PRC, *ibid.*
[68] *Ibid.*, Art. 34.
[69] *Ibid.*, Art. 36.
[70] *Ibid.*, Art. 31.
[71] Administrative Measures for E-banking, *supra* note 27, Art. 10(5).
[72] *Ibid.*, Art. 60.
[73] *Ibid.*, Art. 52.

It is possible for a foreign court to ask China to assist to obtain evidence for the foreign proceedings, but only based on an international convention, or a bilateral judicial aid treaty.[74] China is not prepared to allow a foreign court to directly obtain evidence in China or to force a Chinese company located in China to disclose information overseas. Chinese reluctance for disclosure of banking information to overseas territories is reflected in a US federal case, *Gucci America, Inc.* v. *Weixing Li*.[75]

In 2010, Plaintiffs (Gucci America and others) sued Weixing Li and others for selling counterfeit products to American consumers. The US District Court for the Southern District of New York (Richard and Sullivan JJ) granted the plaintiff's motion to freeze the defendants' assets and enjoin the defendants from selling counterfeit goods. The plaintiff had evidence that certain defendants wired proceeds of their counterfeit sales to accounts with BOC, so they served BOC with an Asset Freeze Injunction and subpoena requesting all documents (including information on accounts at BOC held by defendants) at its New York City branch. BOC is headquartered in Beijing, China. It has only four branches in the United States. BOC contended that its American branches could not search the records of the China-based offices, nor could they ascertain whether the defendants had accounts at BOC branches outside of the United States. The District Court ordered BOC to comply with the injunction and subpoena. When BOC failed to comply, the District Court held BOC in civil contempt and ordered BOC to pay fines and fees. BOC appealed. In September 2014, the appellate court partly supported BOC, vacated the orders of the District Court and remanded the case. In October 2015, the District Court reordered BOC to hand over the account information of the defendants.[76]

It is beyond the scope of this chapter to review the judgments of the District Court and appellate court for or against BOC, but the attitude of the Chinese authorities towards disclosure of financial information

---

[74] China is a member state of the Hague Evidence Convention (The Convention on the Taking of Evidence Abroad in Civil or Commercial Matters), and China has bilateral judicial aid treaties with 49 countries. For the details of the judicial aid treaties, see Department of Judicial Assistance and Foreign Affairs, 'Foreign Judicial Assistance Treaties Concluded' [*Zhongguo Yu Waiguo Sifa Xiezhu Tiaoyue Dijie Qingkuang*] (26 August 2009), online: www.moj.gov.cn/sfxzws/content/2009-08/26/content_1144120.htm?node=7382

[75] *Gucci America, Inc.* v. *Weixing Li*, 2011 WL 6156936 (SDNY, 2011), not reported in F. Supp. 2d; *Gucci America, Inc.* v. *Weixing Li*, 768 F. 3d 122 (2d Cir., 2014).

[76] Erika Kinetz, 'A Blow to Chinese Bank Secrecy? Bank of China Ordered to Disclose Counterfeiters' Records' (7 October 2015), online: US News, www.usnews.com/news/business/articles/2015/10/06/bank-of-china-ordered-to-release-counterfeiters-records

abroad is reflected in this case. On 3 November 2011, two banking regulators in China, PBC and CBRC, wrote a letter to the District Court, stating that Chinese laws prohibit commercial banks from freezing accounts
or turning over account records pursuant to foreign court orders. The letter also showed that the Chinese banking regulators had issued a severe
warning to BOC and were evaluating appropriate sanctions.[77] BOC also
introduced a declaration from a Chinese banking law professor asserting
that Chinese banking laws prohibit BOC from freezing bank accounts
pursuant to a foreign court order, and that doing so could render it civilly
and criminally liable.[78] The common rationale of the regulatory letter and
expert declaration is that China's sovereign interest in Chinese banking
laws is to 'engender client confidence in the banking system and therefore
promote the further development of the banking system.'[79] The reason for
China's unwillingness to disclose information about the defendants to the
District Court of the United States is not to protect the counterfeiters, but
to protect China's sovereignty and the dignity of Chinese law when this is
in conflict with American law.

As a principle of Chinese law, under no circumstances shall a Chinese
company incorporated and headquartered in China abide by or follow an
American court order or judgment, regardless of whether this Chinese
company has a branch in the United States or not, unless there is a judicial aid or cooperation agreement between China and the United States
or there is a convention with such a duty to which both countries are
members. According to the principle of reciprocity, an American company incorporated and headquartered in the United States has no duty
to abide by or follow a Chinese court order or judgment, whether this
American company has a branch in China or not, unless there is a treaty
obligation. China and the United States are both members of the Hague
Convention,[80] so it is possible to use the channel of the Hague Convention

[77] *Gucci America, Inc.* v. *Weixing Li*, supra note 75 at 128.
[78] *Ibid.* at 138.
[79] *Ibid.*
[80] In the judgment of the district court of the United States, the Hague Convention in this
      case refers to the Hague Convention on Service Abroad of Judicial and Extrajudicial
      Documents in Civil or Commercial Matters (Hague Service Convention). China rati-
      fied the Hague Service Convention on 2 March 1991 (National People's Congress of the
      PRC, 'Ratification of the Hague Service Convention' (2 March 1991), online: www.npc
      .gov.cn/wxzl/gongbao/2000-12/16/content_5002519.htm), and the United States rati-
      fied the Hague Service Convention on 24 August 1967 (Hague Conference on Private
      International Law, 'Convention of 15 November 1965 on the Service Abroad of Judicial
      and Extrajudicial Documents in Civil or Commercial Matters: Status Table' (13 June 2016),

to get relevant documents in China. Indeed, in the case, BOC did suggest that the American plaintiffs use a discovery request under the Hague Convention.[81] However, in the opinion of the District Court of the United States, a Hague Convention request in this case would be unduly time-consuming and expensive, as well as less certain to produce the needed evidence than direct use of the US federal rules.[82]

The worries of Judge Richard Sullivan about the difficulties of taking of evidence in China are understandable. Perhaps, even if the United States requested China to provide account information in BOC, China would refuse to do so based on the reason that China's sovereignty or security would be prejudiced,[83] as clearly stated in the Regulatory Letter by PBC and CBRC to the District Court of the United States. However, there are a number of other questions worth considering: is a Hague Evidence Convention request more time-consuming and expensive than the process of the US federal rules? In other words, is the process based on the US federal rules more effective in taking account information from China than a Hague Evidence Convention request? Furthermore, is the jurisdiction in the United States for such a case more effective in taking account information and freezing bank accounts in China than the jurisdiction in China? From the perspectives of taking evidence, freezing property and executing judgment, is it more convenient to initiate the case in a Chinese court? Is it a time-consuming, expensive and ineffective decision to choose a US court as the forum in such a case? It is interesting to note that the case using US federal rules has been ongoing for more than five years, and no evidence has been obtained from China. It is highly possible that, during five years, the counterfeiters in China had transferred their illicit money from Chinese banks into 'safe' places with ease, or squandered all

---

online: www.hcch.net/en/instruments/conventions/status-table/?cid=17). However, in my opinion, Judge Richard Sullivan of the district court of the United States mistook the Hague Service Convention with the Hague Evidence Convention (The Convention on the Taking of Evidence Abroad in Civil or Commercial Matters). The Hague Service Convention has nothing to do with taking evidence abroad. China ratified the Hague Evidence Convention on 3 July 1997 (National People's Congress of the PRC, '26th Meeting of the 8th NPC' (26 December 2000), online: www.npc.gov.cn/npc/cwhhy/content_6015.htm), while the United States ratified the Hague Evidence Convention on 8 August 1972 (Hague Conference on Private International Law, 'Convention of 18 March 1970 on the Taking of Evidence Abroad in Civil or Commercial Matters: Status Table' (16 March 2016), online: www.hcch.net/en/instruments/conventions/status-table/?cid=82).

[81] *Gucci America, Inc.* v. *Weixing Li (DC)*, *supra* note 75.
[82] *Ibid.*
[83] See Art. 12(b) of the Hague Evidence Convention, *supra* note 74.

the money. To make it worse, no one can predict the cost of the litigation (especially attorney fees) for such a case, nor can anyone foresee the length of such a litigation war between the plaintiff and the non-party (BOC), let alone a potential tension and the effect on diplomatic relations between the two countries. The case reminds us of what Lord Denning said in 1983: 'As a moth is drawn to the light, so is a litigant drawn to the United States.'[84]

6.4.2   Internal Activism: Omnipresent People's Courts

In contrast to external conservatism, there is a manifest internal activism in disclosing financial information in China. In addition to the numerous governmental agencies with the power of inquiring into, freezing or deducting from bank accounts, as discussed earlier, recently People's Courts have been combining almost all information investigation powers into one by way of internet technology. In 2014, the Supreme People's Court and the CBRC jointly announced the establishment of a national, internet-based system for enforcement of judgments and orders [*quanguo wangluo zhixing chakong jizhi*].[85] The first model is the network connection between the Supreme People's Court and the headquarters of banks through the special network of the CBRC. Every People's Court may inspect and control information through the network of the Supreme People's Court. It is called 'head to head' [*zong dui zong*]. The second model is the network connection between a higher People's Court and provincial branches of banks through the special network of a CBRC local bureau. It is called 'point to point' [*dian dui dian*].[86] Such network connections should have been established before December 2015, and the network check and control function should have been online before February 2016.[87]

In 2013, prior to the joint announcement referred to in the previous paragraph, the Supreme People's Court issued Provisions on Network

---

[84]   *Smith Kline & French Labs Ltd.* v. *Bloch* [1983] 2 All ER 72.
[85]   Opinions of People's Courts and Banking Financial Institutions on the Work of Network Enforcement Check and Control and the Joint Work of Credit Punishment [*guanyu renmin fayuan yu yinhangye jinrong jigou kaizhan wangluo zhixing chakong he lianhe xinyong chengjie gongzuo de yijian*] (24 October 2014), Fa [2014] No. 266, online: www.chinacourt .org/law/detail/2014/10/id/147981.shtml
[86]   *Ibid.* at para. 5.
[87]   Provisions on the Work of Network Enforcement Check and Control between People's Court and Banking Financial Institutions [*renmin fayuan yinhangye jinrong jigou wangluo zhixing chakong gongzuo guifan*] (17 December 2015), Fa (2015) No. 321, online: www .huye.cn/News/Show.asp?id=320

Inquiring and Freezing Deposits of Enforcees (i.e. persons against whom judgments or rulings have been issued) [*Guanyu Wangluo Chaxun Dongjie Beizhixingren Cunkuan de Guiding*].[88] In order to enhance the network cooperation between courts and banks, the Supreme People's Court and several commercial banks signed MOUs on Network Enforcement Inspection, Control and Information Sharing.[89]

Now it is very easy for a People's Court to inspect and control the bank account and other banking information of the enforcee, without stepping out of the court door. Similarly, a People's Court may also check and control the shares, securities account and real estate of the enforcee, through network connections with administrations of industry and commerce, securities regulators and real estate bureaus.[90] Besides the cooperation between courts and administrative agencies, the Supreme People's Court is trying to cooperate with credit investigation and service companies. On 24 July 2015, the Supreme People's Court signed an MOU with Zhima Credit in order to sanction dishonest enforcees [*shixin beizhixingren*] through the third-party credit investigation and service company. As of 17 December 2015, under the MOU, Zhima Credit has prevented dishonest enforcees from buying flight tickets, renting cars, making loans and booking hotels through several network consumption platforms around 130,000 times.[91] It must be noted that the inquiry and freezing of bank accounts through the network connections between courts and banks are not only limited to those of the enforcee (*beizhixingren*), but also applied to those of a person (*beibaoquanren*) whose property has been frozen by a court.[92] One may ask whether this is a step forward or going too far.

For People's Courts, the network connections with banks or credit companies can significantly reduce enforcement costs. For the losing parties,

---

[88] Provisions on Network Inquiring and Freezing Deposits of Enforcees (29 August 2013), *Fashi* [2013] No. 20.

[89] A Reply of the Supreme People's Court to Suggestions of Allowing People's Courts to Inquire Banking Deposits for People's Banks (28 May 2014), online: www.court.gov.cn/hudong-xiangqing-6423.html

[90] *Ibid.*; see also the Notice of Enhancing Information Cooperation, Regulating Enforcement and Assistance of Enforcement [*Guanyu Jiaqiang Xinxi Hezuo Guifan Zhixing yu Xiezhu Zhixing de Tongzhi*] (10 October 2014), *Fa* [2014] No. 251, online: http://file.chinacourt.org/f.php?id=2417&class=file. Jointly issued by the Supreme People's Court and the State Administration for Industry and Commerce.

[91] Sharing the information of Enforcees between Supreme People's Court and Zhima Credit (4 January 2016), online: www.court.gov.cn/zixun-xiangqing-16431.html

[92] Provisions on the Work of Network Enforcement Check and Control between People's Court and Banking Financial Institutions, *supra* note 87 at para. 21.

the network connections leave them (and their properties) few hiding places. But the problem is whether People's Courts are always trustworthy. Unfortunately, a lot of negative news of reckless actions by some People's Courts have aggravated public concerns. In 2003, a People's Court asked a bank to disclose account information of customer A without telling the bank the ID number or other details of customer A. The bank provided the account information of customer B with the same name as customer A. The court then held that the deposit in the bank account of customer B belonged to the plaintiff.[93] This Chinese case is a typical case of 'putting Zhang's hat on Li's head' [zhangguan lidai]. Today such kind of abuse of judicial power still exists. In July 2015, a person named Xue Zhangbing found that the money in his bank account had disappeared. The bank told him that a local People's Court (Huaibei Xiangshan District People's Court, Anhui Province) deducted his money by a judgment against him. After investigation, Xue Zhangbing claimed that the court made a mistake in identifying the true defendant, so he asked for a retrial and compensation.[94] In less than one month, the court corrected the error against the innocent Xue Zhangbing, and returned the deducted money to his bank account.[95] A similar mistake also took place in a local court of Shandong Province.[96]

6.4.3   Pragmatism: International Tax Cooperation

Faced with increased awareness of the importance of antiterrorism financing, and the new round of anticorruption, anti-money laundering and anti-tax evasion measures,[97] the Chinese government has strengthened international cooperation in the field of exchange of information. In order to get overseas financial information, especially to trace money hidden

---

[93] See Liu Xiaoyong, 'A Study of Relevant Legal Issues on Assistance of Financial Institutions for Inquiry, Freezing and Deduction' [jinrong jigou xiezhu jinxing chaxun, dongjie, kouhua xiangguan falv wenti yanjiu] (20 September 2004), online: www.chinacourt.org/article/detail/2004/09/id/133002.shtml

[94] Zhang Angao, 'A Person of Huainan Claimed a Mistake in a Trial and Deduction of His Deposit by Court' (22 July 2015), online: Anhui News, http://ah.anhuinews.com/system/2015/07/22/006883332.shtml

[95] Zhang Angao, 'Huaibei Court Formally Withdrew the Judgment of "Xue Zhangbing Case"' (5 August 2015).

[96] 'Agriculture Bank (Jiangsu Yixing Subbranch) Helped a Customer to Recover Fund Wrongfully Deducted by a Court' (1 July 2010), online: China Financial Network News, www.zgjrjw.com/news/bgdkb/201071/16203265886.html. The court is Shandong Feixian People's Court.

[97] See Nakajima, Chapter 4 and O'Brien, Chapter 5 on international developments in these areas.

abroad by corrupt officials who fled abroad, China has realised the importance of exchange of information with foreign countries.

6.4.3.1   Bilateral Tax Treaties

In a bilateral tax treaty, there is usually an article on exchange of information. The best example is Art. 25 of the Sino-American Agreement for
the Avoidance of Double Taxation and the Prevention of Fiscal Evasion
with respect to Taxes on Income (1984).[98] Up to December 2015, China
has concluded 101 agreements for the avoidance of double taxation with
foreign countries, with 97 agreements effective.[99] The Chinese mainland
has also concluded arrangements and agreements for avoidance of double
taxation with Hong Kong,[100] Macao[101] and Taiwan.[102] In 2009, China
successfully used the mechanism of information exchange in a tax treaty
to determine a linked trade.[103]

6.4.3.2   Bilateral TIEAs

From 2009 to 2015, China signed bilateral tax information exchange agreements (TIEAs) with ten offshore financial centres or tax havens, which are
shown in Table 6.1.

---

[98] Available online at the IRS website: www.irs.gov/pub/irs-trty/china.pdf. Article 25 of this
     agreement states:

> The competent authorities of the Contracting States shall exchange such
> information as is necessary for carrying out the provisions of this Agreement
> or of the domestic laws of the Contracting States concerning taxes cov-
> ered by this Agreement insofar as the taxation thereunder is not contrary to
> this Agreement, in particular for the prevention of fraud or evasion of such
> taxes. The exchange of information is not restricted by Article 1. Any infor-
> mation received by a Contracting State shall be treated as secret and shall
> be disclosed only to persons or authorities (including courts and admin-
> istrative bodies) involved in the assessment, collection, or administration
> of, the enforcement or prosecution in respect of, or the determination of
> appeals in relation to, the taxes covered by this Agreement. Such persons or
> authorities shall use the information only for such purposes. They may dis-
> close the information in public court proceedings or in judicial decisions.

[99] State Administration of Taxation, 'Tax Treaty' [*Shuishou Tiaoyue*], online: www.chinatax
     .gov.cn/n810341/n810770
[100] Signed on 21 August 2006, effective on 8 December 2006.
[101] Signed on 27 December 2003, effective on 30 December 2003.
[102] Signed on 25 August 2015, not effective yet.
[103] State Administration of Taxation, 'China's First Successful Use of Information Exchange
     to Achieve Tax Adjustments' (9 December 2009), online: www.chinatax.gov.cn/n810214/
     n810641/n810697/n813233/c1089184/content.html

Table 6.1. *Sino-foreign tax information exchange agreements (as of 2015)*

Serial No.	Jurisdiction	Signed on	Effective from	Applicable since
1	Bahamas	2009-12-01	2010-08-28	2011-01-01
2	British Virgin Islands	2009-12-07	2010-12-30	2011-01-01
3	Isle of Man	2010-10-26	2011-08-14	2012-01-01
4	Guernsey	2010-10-27	2011-08-17	2012-01-01
5	Jersey	2010-10-29	2011-11-10	2012-01-01
6	Bermuda	2010-12-02	2011-12-31	2012-01-01
7	Argentina	2010-12-13	2011-09-16	2012-01-01
8	Cayman	2011-09-26	2012-11-15	2013-01-01
9	San Marino	2012-07-09	2013-04-30	2014-01-01
10	Liechtenstein	2014-01-27	2014-08-02	2015-01-01

Source: www.chinatax.gov.cn/n810341/n810770 (accessed 10 January 2016).

The scope of taxes covered by such agreements is very broad. Sometimes it covers all taxes except customs tariffs, e.g. the Sino-Jersey Agreement for Exchange of Information relating to Taxes. Sometimes it covers income tax, payroll tax and/or property tax.[104] The Sino-Isle of Man Agreement covers income tax, land appreciation tax, value-added tax, excise tax and business tax.[105]

Information gathering measures are also broad enough to include judicial, regulatory or administrative laws and procedures enabling a Contracting Party to obtain and provide the information requested.

It must be noted that there are possibilities to decline requests. One example is Art. 7 of the Sino-Jersey Agreement for Exchange of Information Relating to Taxes:

The competent authority of the requested party may decline to assist:

(a) where the request is not made in conformity with this Agreement;

(b) where the requesting party has not pursued all means available in its own territory to obtain the information, except where recourse to such means would give rise to disproportionate difficulty;

---

[104] Sino-British Virgin Islands Agreement for the Exchange of Information Relating to Taxes, Art. 3 (7 December 2009), online: www.chinatax.gov.cn/n810341/n810770/c1152709/part/1152711.pdf

[105] Sino-Isle of Man Agreement for the Exchange of Information relating to Taxes, Art. 3 (30 April 2014), online: www.chinatax.gov.cn/n810341/n810770/c1152723/content.html

(c) where the disclosure of the information requested would be contrary to the public policy (public order) of the requested party or
(d) where the competent authority of the requesting party would not be able to obtain the information under its laws or in the normal course of administrative practice if the requested information were within the jurisdiction of the requesting party.

It is interesting to note a national treatment obligation in such an agreement, which usually takes the following expression:

> The requested party may decline a request for information if the information is requested by the requesting party to administer or enforce a provision of the tax law of the requesting party, or any requirement connected therewith, which discriminates against a national of the requested party as compared with a national of the requesting party in the same circumstances.[106]

However, there is no most-favoured-nation (MFN) treatment clause in the TIEAs. The lack of a MFN treatment clause makes those TIEAs separate and independent, and applicable only between the parties, which also shows the limitations of TIEAs. In order to broaden the scope of international cooperation for tax information exchange, the best way is to conclude multilateral conventions.

6.4.3.3   Multilateral Conventions

On 27 August 2013, China became the fifty-sixth signatory state of the Multilateral Convention on Mutual Administrative Assistance in Tax Matters.[107] It is the first multilateral tax convention signed by China. On 1 July 2015, the Standing Committee of NPC ratified this multilateral convention.[108] The focus of the multilateral convention is the automatic exchange

---

[106] Sino-Jersey Agreement for Exchange of Information Relating to Taxes, Art. 7(4), online: www.chinatax.gov.cn/n810341/n810770/c1152749/part/1152753.pdf
[107] OECD, 'China Joins International Efforts to End Tax Evasion' (27 August 2013), online: www.oecd.org/ctp/china-joins-international-efforts-to-end-tax-evasion.htm. For the whole text of the multilateral convention, see OECD, 'Joint Council of Europe/OECD Convention on Mutual Administrative Assistance in Tax Matters', online: www.oecd.org/ctp/exchange-of-tax-information/Convention_On_Mutual_Administrative_Assistance_in_Tax_Matters_Report_and_Explanation.pdf. This Convention is discussed by O'Brien, Chapter 5.
[108] National People's Congress of the PRC, 'Decision of the NPC on Ratification of the Multilateral Convention on Mutual Administrative Assistance in Tax Matters' (2 July 2015), online: www.npc.gov.cn/npc/xinwen/2015-07/02/content_1940459.htm

of information.[109] This multilateral convention also covers all forms of compulsory payments to the general government, except customs duties.[110]

It must be noted that there are a few important statements (reservations) made by the Chinese government when ratifying the Convention. For example, China will not provide any form of assistance in relation to the taxes listed in Art. 2(1)(b), including *inter alia*, taxes on income, profits, capital gains or net wealth, which are imposed on behalf of political subdivisions or local authorities of a Party; compulsory social security contributions payable to general government or to social security institutions established under public law. China will not provide assistance in the recovery or conservancy of any tax claim for all taxes. China will not provide assistance in the service of documents for all taxes. China will not permit the service of documents through the post.[111]

6.5   Concluding Remarks

Although there are secrecy provisions in some Chinese laws or regulations, they are not coherent or persistent, and are seldom seriously enforced. There are many governmental organs who can easily inquire into the financial information concerning deposits belonging to Chinese citizens or foreigners in the territory of the PRC, while there is not any case raised by depositors against those governmental organs for abuse of inquiry or against banks for wrongful disclosure of account information in China. More importantly, depositors do not even know (or do not have a chance to know) that their bank accounts have been or are being investigated by a powerful government agency. Chinese bank secrecy rules are composed of general and abstract principles which neither impose a duty to reasonably notify the depositors about an inquiry, nor provide an opportunity for depositors to challenge the legality of such inquiry. If there is no specific procedure, law or rule to protect the lawful interests of depositors, how can the depositors exercise their civil right or constitutional/administrative right against banks or governmental organs based on substantive law

---

[109] See Art. 6 of the Multilateral Convention on Mutual Administrative Assistance in Tax Matters, *supra* note 107.

[110] For the status of the Multilateral Convention on Mutual Administrative Assistance in Tax Matters, see OECD, 'Jurisdictions Participating in the Convention on Mutual Administrative Assistance in Tax Matters Status' (9 January 2016), online: www.oecd.org/ctp/exchange-of-tax-information/Status_of_convention.pdf

[111] Decision of the Standing Committee of the NPC on Ratification of the Multilateral Convention on Mutual Administrative Assistance in Tax Matters, *supra* note 108.

(e.g. contract law, commercial banking law)? Current Chinese law is not concerned about the rights of depositors, nor does it empower depositors to challenge the legitimacy of the order to make inquiry issued by an administrative agency, or by a court. At this point, a lesson can be learnt from the Financial Privacy Act of 1978 of the United States which requires a bank to notify its customer of requests for information.[112]

Considering that China does not allow a purely free flow of capital, the Chinese tax burden is quite heavy and public powers of government are overwhelmingly stronger than private rights, it is impossible for this country to become a tax haven. As a consequence, few foreigners transfer large amounts of capital to China for the purpose of tax evasion. So the direction of capital flow is outward, not inward. This is the reason why China is supportive of information exchange and not information secrecy. China (as a member of the G20) has reached an unprecedented consensus with OECD countries for information disclosure. China's extremely open and positive participation in the international efforts for information exchange contrasts sharply with her conservatism in some other international fields (e.g., international human rights). This attitude is understandable. For a country emphasising centralisation of state powers for a long time, any measure strengthening central powers, domestic or international, is generally welcome. Personal privacy (including privacy of bank account information) can hardly withstand even a single blow from governmental powers.

Historically, China neglected private rights while public power has been emphasised for many centuries. Even today, China has not established a complete system of personal privacy protection or a reliable system of bank secrecy. In the current social and political climate, it is very difficult for bank secrecy law to be rooted, or to thrive. In the history of the modernisation of the Chinese legal system, China introduced a large number of Western laws, but bank secrecy law was one of the last to be introduced and it came at the wrong time. A bank secrecy clause first appeared in Chinese banking law in the 1950s, but it was written in water. Due to movements such as the cultural revolution, individuals had almost no privacy or secrets. Only in the 1980s did bank secrecy reappear in China. But with the global financial crisis and the necessity of antiterrorism measures, the legal position of bank secrecy has suffered again. Undeniably, strengthening the duty to disclose information (rather than the duty to keep secret) has a positive side, especially for the struggles against terrorism, money

---

[112] See Broome, Chapter 13.

laundering, financial crimes and tax evasion. The concern is whether these measures will go to the other extreme and mark the end of bank secrecy. In China, however, it is too early to worry about the death of bank secrecy, because whether there is true bank secrecy to start with is highly debatable. How can we discuss the demise of someone before his birth? This is similar to a classic Chinese idea expressed in The Analects of Confucius: [*lunyu*] – *wei zhisheng, yan zhisi*? How can you know what death is before you know what life is?

Germany, with References to the European Union

CHRISTIAN HOFMANN

7.1 Introduction

From a transnational perspective, bank secrecy may be understood as the attempt of banks – and even governments – to shield data of customers from foreign authorities. If the veil of bank secrecy is pierced at the transnational level, foreign authorities gain access to confidential data about bank customers. In most cases, such data access is sought by the authorities in the customers' countries of tax residence (or citizenship in the case of the United States) for the enforcement of taxation, in other instances to prevent and prosecute money laundering, bribery, fraud and other crimes. Transnational cooperation among national authorities therefore aims to provide principles and mechanisms that support or even coerce the cross-border exchange of information collected by banks to foreign authorities.

At the national level, however, the notion of bank secrecy encompasses a much wider range of legal issues as argued here for the case of Germany. Bank customers do not only wish to shield their information from the state, its institutions and agents, but also – and perhaps even more so – from other private parties. But banks are interested in forwarding confidential data about their customers to other financial institutions, customers or data collection agencies. A national regime for the protection of private data must therefore provide answers as to how conflicts in interests between banks and their customers are resolved, i.e. under what conditions banks may disclose customers' data not only to authorities, but also to private entities and persons.

A version of this chapter was presented at the Bank Secrecy Symposium hosted by the Centre for Banking and Finance Law at the National University of Singapore, Faculty of Law on 4–5 December 2014.

This chapter discusses the German approach to such a regime. It distinguishes between situations in which customers seek to defend their data against disclosures by banks and instances where authorities, especially bank supervisors and tax authorities, access the information held by banks. It will show that customers are in a strong position against voluntary disclosures by banks, whereas the state has very far-reaching authority to gain access to confidential data (see Section 7.2.3). The term 'bank secrecy' rather than 'bank confidentiality' is preferable here because it corresponds best to the German term 'Bankgeheimnis'; it is also the term recently used by the European Commission.[1]

Germany's membership in the European Union (EU) inevitably influences its rules of bank secrecy. Details are mentioned throughout the entire chapter, but the main impact of data transfer among EU member states for tax purposes is discussed in a separate section because recent developments of cross-border information exchange on the global and EU level (the EU rules about automated data exchange and the Single Supervisory Mechanism (SSM) in the Euro area) have led to substantial changes in EU law (see Section 7.3).

7.2   The Bank Secrecy Regime in Germany

Bank secrecy is often reduced, in the media and from the layman's perspective, to tax evasion and enforcement of tax claims. There is much more to it, of course. Rooted in the relationship of the bank and its customer is the obligation of the bank to keep what it knows about the customer secret (as will be explained in Section 7.2.2.2). But this principle is not without exceptions. Numerous entities may seek to gain access to this information, and in each instance the issue arises whether, and to what extent, such requests for information sharing are justified. In this, on the one hand, the customers' interests are generally clear: bank secrecy serves the customers' interests in preventing the bank from sharing their information. The bank, on the other hand, may have conflicting interests stemming from its intention to forward customer information to other financial institutions for business development purposes or other customers, especially to issue warnings about the financial situation of business partners of its

---

[1] See European Commission, 'Fighting Tax evasion: EU and Switzerland Sign Historic Tax Transparency Agreement' (27 May 2015), online: http://europa.eu/rapid/press-release_IP-15-5043_en.htm.

customers. In addition, it may be obliged to reveal customer information to the authorities.

Resulting from these considerations, the two aspects that will be distinguished in this chapter are: firstly, an analysis of the rights of the bank to share information with other private parties, in particular other banks and other customers, and the rights of the customer to prevent such disclosure (Section 7.2.2); secondly, the interference of the state in this bank–customer relationship, its demands for disclosure and the rights of banks and customers to defend their shared information against such intrusion (Section 7.2.3). These discussions are preceded by an introduction to the general legal framework of German law as relevant to bank secrecy (Section 7.2.1).

7.2.1 *The Relevant Legal Framework for Bank Secrecy in Germany*

With respect to (broadly understood) banking law, the (stereo-)typical distinction between codified rules in civil law jurisdictions and judge-made law in common law countries is of little help to understand the legal regime in a particular jurisdiction. In practically all jurisdictions, whether they follow civil or common law principles, the rules applying to banks consist of a broad mixture of statutory provisions in highly specific legislation and regulation and a long tradition of judge-made principles. Differences become visible when turning to principles in more general fields of relevance to banking such as contract law principles. Here, civil law jurisdictions rely predominantly on codifications, common law jurisdictions on case law.

With regard to bank secrecy, as this volume explains, some common law jurisdictions have overarching statutory provisions on bank secrecy, for example Singapore[2], while others do not, for example the United Kingdom.[3] Similar diversity exists in the civil law world: Switzerland relies on statutory provisions,[4] while such are non-existent in German law.

---

[2] See s. 47 of the Banking Act (Cap 19, 2008 Rev Ed Sing): 'Customer information shall not, in any way, be disclosed by a bank in Singapore or any of its officers to any other person except as expressly provided in this Act.' See also Booysen, Chapter 10.

[3] Although various statutory enactments may affect the UK's bank secrecy regime, see Stanton, Chapter 12.

[4] Article 47 of the Swiss Banking Act. See also Nobel and Braendli, Chapter 11. Austria is similar with its s 38 Bankwesengesetz (Banking Act); see S. Tiefenthaler and E. Welten, 'Chapter 3: Austria' in F. Neate and G. Godfrey, *Neate and Godfrey: Bank Confidentiality*, 6th edn (London: Bloomsbury Professional, 2015) at 59.

The German legislator has generally given little attention to contractual banking law. When the Civil Code 'Bürgerliches Gesetzbuch' or BGB came into force on 1 January 1900, it contained only rudimentary provisions on loans and deposits, and this status remained unaltered for almost a hundred years. The German legislator has shown surprising reluctance to 'interfere' in the bank–customer relationship and left it to courts and commentators in legal literature to develop the framework for issues that unavoidably arose in the course of a century of banking practice in Germany. Academic writing is highly influential in Germany and courts commonly – if not close to always – refer extensively to literature in their rulings.

The situation has, however, changed dramatically in some fields of banking law in the recent past. The European legislator has been very active in the fields of consumer and investor protection law, and as a result, the German legislator has been forced to implement such rules into German codes. Germany now has detailed rules on consumer credit contracts and payment transactions, all included in the BGB, and detailed rules on investor protection in the German Acts for the regulation of capital markets and financial services providers.[5]

But the fact remains that there is no comprehensive banking or financial legislation providing rules for all or at least a multitude of aspects of banking law. The existing Banking Act, the 'Kreditwesengesetz' (KWG), is limited to the regulation of banks and other financial institutions and therefore does not contain rules applicable to the bank–customer relationship.[6] As a result, for bank secrecy the 'traditional' rule applies: no legislative provision deals with the issue of confidentiality in the bank–customer relationship in Germany. The rules are derived from court decisions and academic writing.[7]

It has long been accepted by the German courts and legal scholars that customers have a contractual right against the bank to keep information stemming from their relationship confidential. A collection of cases and academic

---

[5] See ss 488–510 BGB, ss 675c–676c BGB and the Securities Trading Act (Wertpapierhandelsgesetz).

[6] For more detail on the KWG, see A. Gläser, 'Chapter Three: Prudential Supervision of Banks in Germany and in the European Economic Area' in N. Horn (ed), *German Banking Law and Practice in International Perspective* (Berlin: Walter de Gruyter, 1999) at 38–41.

[7] There is very limited 'case law' in Germany as only the decisions of the Federal Constitutional Court have the status of 'law' whereas all other court decisions including those of the different federal high courts decide the case at stake – and nothing more. They provide guiding principles for the same and other courts on how to rule on similar cases in the future, but no principle of precedent or *stare decisis* exists.

comments provide guidelines in this field: courts and authors refer to general principles of the law of obligations and apply them to the legal relationship of banks and their customers (see Section 7.2.2). In contrast, explicit statutory provisions entitle the authorities, especially bank regulators and tax authorities, to access confidential information held by banks (see Section 7.2.3).[8]

The criminal law is of little relevance for German bank secrecy, unlike in other jurisdictions such as Switzerland and Singapore.[9] Breaches of obligations to keep confidential information secret may result in criminal liability in many relationships that typically involve the sharing of sensitive information, such as doctors and patients or lawyers and clients.[10] In contrast, no criminal sanctions result from breaches of bank secrecy obligations in Germany. The only exception applies to representatives of state-owned banks who qualify as public officials or persons entrusted with special public service functions, which is less and less the case nowadays in Germany.[11] Criminal law becomes more relevant for the right to withhold information if disclosing it would lead to self-incrimination (see Section 7.2.3.3).

7.2.2 Bank Secrecy and Disclosure to Private Parties

7.2.2.1 Bank Secrecy as a Contractual Principle

As there is no statutory provision addressing bank secrecy in the relationship of banks and their customers in Germany, general principles of the law of obligations (as generally applied in a private party context, not just in the bank–customer relationship) set the framework for the duty of the bank to treat the customer's information confidential.[12] Such duty of confidentiality does not require a valid contract and the bank is similarly restricted when agreements are invalid or when the parties decide not to conclude a

---

[8] The following analysis focuses on statutory provisions. While these are available in English, and can therefore be used by the readers of this book, judgments are usually available in German only. Relevant literature is also predominantly in German. Some references to such sources in German are therefore unavoidable.

[9] See Booysen, Chapter 10 and Nobel and Braendli, Chapter 11, respectively.

[10] Section 203 of the German Criminal Code (Strafgesetzbuch (StGB)).

[11] Section 203(2) no. 1, 2 StGB. On criteria for determining whether criminal sanctions apply to bank representatives, see the decision of the Federal High Court in civil and criminal law matters of 27 October 2009 – XI ZR 225/08, BGHZ 183, 60 at 63 (matter ultimately left undecided).

[12] In civil law traditions, contract law is defined differently from common law jurisdictions, and German law is no exception. For civil law jurisdictions, the focus is on the obligations that persons/entities owe to each other, and contracts are an important, but not the only, way to create obligations between private parties.

contract, i.e. when the relationship remains pre-contractual. German law generally expands contractual obligations into the pre-contractual phase. While originally developed by the courts, the principles governing pre-contractual duties have found their way into the civil code. The legislator explicitly embraced the principles stemming from decades of rulings by the Federal High Court in civil and criminal law matters (Bundesgerichtshof or BGH) in its 2002 reform of the law of obligations and inserted new provisions in the civil code. These provisions are now found in ss 241, 311 BGB.[13] As a result, the bank is held to the rule that all information obtained during the contractual and pre-contractual phase is covered by a general obligation of confidentiality. Even the pre-contractual phase constitutes a bank–customer relationship and consequently, information shared in this phase is protected whether or not the pre-contractual stage leads to a contractual agreement.[14]

The inclusion of the pre-contractual phase is important since customers are routinely required to disclose extensive information in the stage before an agreement is reached. Banks wish and need to know the sources of funds before accepting them as deposits, above all to comply with regulatory requirements stemming from anti-money laundering rules and prudential regulation.[15] If customers borrow money or have access to overdraft facilities, banks also need to assess their creditworthiness, both in their own interest and to be able to comply with requirements of capital to debt ratios[16] and consumer protection provisions.[17]

---

[13] German law is exceptional among civil law traditions in its application of pre-contractual obligations. The concept of 'culpa in contrahendo' as now reflected in ss 241, 311 BGB results in pre-contractual obligations that are generally unknown in other civil law jurisdictions, especially those rooted in the French tradition. For more detail, see H. Beale, B. Fauvarque-Cosson, J. Rutgers, D. Tallon and S. Vogenauer, *Cases, Materials and Text on Contract Law*, 2nd edn (Oxford: Hart Publishing, 2010) at 372–426 in general and more specifically at 374, 383–5, 407 seq., 419–24 on German law.

[14] T. Schulz and T. Fett, 'Chapter 16: Germany' in *Neate and Godfrey: Bank Confidentiality*, *supra* note 4 at 389.

[15] The nature of bank's liabilities impacts the High Quality Liquid Assets (HQLA) requirements under Basel III and therefore requires banks to have very detailed knowledge about their customers and the nature of their deposits or other debts owed by the bank. For these HQLA requirements, see Basel Committee on Banking Supervision, 'Basel III: The Liquidity Coverage Ratio and Liquidity Risk Monitoring Tools' (January 2013), online: www.bis.org/publ/bcbs238.pdf

[16] Creditworthiness is an essential factor in the process of risk-weighing the bank's assets, resulting in the determination of the amount of capital required by banks for their financing.

[17] If the borrower is a consumer, the bank must assess his creditworthiness in order to protect the customer from a situation of unsustainable debt, see s 509 BGB that implements the provisions in Art. 8 of EC, *Directive 2008/48/EC of 23 April 2008 on credit agreements for consumers and repealing Council Directive 87/102/EEC* (2008) O.J. L. 133/66.

7.2.2.2   Protection by Bank Secrecy and Its Limits

The Federal High Court has defined bank secrecy as the obligation of the bank to keep all information secret that the customer wishes to remain confidential.[18] It has also agreed with academic commentators that bank secrecy is only one of many facets of the special relationship between a bank and its customers from which a multitude of obligations result, including obligations to respect the other party's interests, to protect the other side's assets and to show some degree of loyalty to each other.[19]

The general terms and conditions included in every bank–customer relationship in Germany and called 'AGB Banken' provide that the bank 'has the duty to maintain secrecy about any customer-related facts and evaluations of which it may have knowledge'. An example of a typical provision, taken from the terms of Deutsche Bank is as follows: the bank 'may only disclose information concerning the customer if it is legally required to do so or if the customer has consented thereto or if the Bank is authorized to disclose banking affairs'.[20] These AGB are prepared by the three associations under which all banks operating in Germany are organised: the association of private commercial banks, the association of public banks, which includes the savings banks, and the association of cooperative banks. This division of the German banking sector is commonly referred to as the 'three-pillar structure' of the banking system.[21] The member banks adopt these pre-drafted terms and conditions and include them in the contracts with their customers.

What information the customer wishes to remain secret is decided by him as expressly declared or implied in statements or conduct.[22] If the customer's intentions on the issue cannot be determined, the bank must respect the customer's assumed intent as decided by his objective interests.[23] In doing so, the bank must take into account that its statements about

---

[18] BGH of 12 May 1958, II ZR 103/57, BGHZ 27, 241; BGH of 24 January 2006, XI ZR 384/03, BGHZ 166, 84, 91 seq. See also Schulz and Fett, *supra* note 14 at 389.

[19] BGH of 24 January 2006 – XI ZR 384/03, *supra* note 18. These are typical terms featured in all kinds of legal relationships in German law, be they of a contractual, pre-contractual or quasi-contractual nature.

[20] The cited text stems from the English version of Deutsche's AGB banken, available at https://www.deutsche-bank.de/fk/de/docs/2016_DB_AG_GTB_General_Business_Conditions_ENG_effective_5th_June_2016.pdf.

[21] Deutsche Bundesbank, 'Structural Developments in the German Banking Sector' (April 2015) at 36, online: www.bundesbank.de/Redaktion/EN/Downloads/Publications/Monthly_Report_Articles/2015/2015_04_structural.pdf?_blob=publicationFile

[22] Schulz and Fett, *supra* note 14 at 389.

[23] *Ibid.*, at 390; P. Schantz, 'Bankgeheimnis' in H. Schwintowski, *Bankrecht*, 4th edn (Cologne: Carl Heymanns, 2014), s 3 at 25.

the financial situation of customers in general or details about their business relationship with a customer carry substantial weight. Third parties assume that such comments are made on a well-informed basis, i.e. are based on insider knowledge that goes beyond common knowledge and information already circulated by the (financial) press. Resulting from this, such statements can do significant harm to the customer, be they true or not. They may even lead to financial ruin if creditors start to question the customer's solvency (see the 'Kirch Media case' discussed as a part of Section 7.2.2.4).[24]

The obligation to keep customers' information confidential applies to the entire bank. Every organ and its members, agents and employees of the bank are bound by it, regardless of whether such person has received the relevant information from the customer directly or internally from other bank representatives or data on file.[25] The internal dissemination of sensitive information and aggregation of information is also restricted. Commentators have correctly pointed out that internal systems of data sharing that grant all bank employees access to all or sensitive information are incompatible with customer interests and therefore in breach of bank secrecy.[26]

Banks are interconnected. Their close ties are unavoidable for many reasons, be it for the execution of payment orders, in order to jointly shoulder large syndicated loans or to finance each other on the interbank lending market. Such interconnectedness sometimes requires that customers' data is shared. Banks that receive information in this way are also subject to the bank secrecy principles. They are bound by the declared or implied will or assumed intentions of the persons to whom the information applies as if these people were their customers.[27]

These principles lead to a wide understanding of bank secrecy and, generally speaking, to effective protection of bank customers. The courts have, however, restricted the scope of application of bank secrecy in one respect. Only information that stems from the business relationship of the bank and the customer is protected by the secrecy rules. The criterion has been called an 'inner connection' between the business relationship and the way in which the bank finds out about the information.[28]

---

[24] G. Bitter, 61 Wertpapiermitteilungen 1953 (1957) (2007); Schantz, *supra* note 23 at 16.

[25] H. Krepold, in H. Schimansky, H. Bunte and H.J. Lwowski, *Bankrechts-Handbuch*, 4th edn (Munich: C.H. Beck, 2011), § 39 at 21.

[26] Krepold, *supra* note 25 at 24; Schantz, *supra* note 23 at 20.

[27] Bundesgerichtshof (Federal High Court in Civil and Criminal Matters) of 12 May 1958, II ZR 103/57, *supra* note 18.

[28] BGH of 24 January 2006 – XI ZR 384/03, *supra* note 18.

7.2.2.3   Protection of Bank Customers
by the Data Protection Act

In addition to these general rules on bank secrecy stemming from general principles of the law of obligations, bank customers' information is protected by the data protection laws. Both mechanisms apply alongside each other,[29] and consequently bank secrecy rules are of the greatest practical significance in situations where data protection laws do not apply.[30] Such is the case when the bank customer is a legal person since the laws of data protection only cover natural persons.[31] The most relevant provisions of Germany's data protection laws are s 28 and s 28a of the Federal Data Protection Act (Bundesdatenschutzgesetz or BDSG).[32]

7.2.2.4   Requirements for Information Sharing

Bearing in mind the principles of bank secrecy and data protection laws, the principle of customer consent is essential for any information sharing by the bank. With his explicit or implied consent to the transfer of data, the customer waives his right to confidentiality. Without such consent, the bank may only share information if, based on good reasons and after weighing all relevant aspects, it comes to the conclusion that the information sharing is in the best interest of the customer and if there is no time to seek the customer's prior approval.[33] Typical examples of disclosures made with the customer's consent are set out as follows.

Transfer of Data to the Credit Rating Agency 'SCHUFA'   Banks generally require the consent of their customers for disclosure to the German credit rating agency 'SCHUFA' as a prerequisite for entering into the bank–customer relationship. They seek permission to receive information from and to forward data to SCHUFA.[34] This agency collects data about all debtors in Germany and shares the collected information

---

[29] BGH of 27 February 2007, XI ZR 195/05, BGHZ 171, 180 at 188 (in German). For a general discussion of how data protection laws and bank secrecy laws compare with each other, see Greenleaf and Tyree, Chapter 2.

[30] Schantz, *supra* note 23 at 11. Banks must comply with the requirements of the BDSG at all times since breaches constitute criminal or administrative offences, see ss 43, 44 BDSG and Schulz and Fett, *supra* note 14 at 386.

[31] On all these criteria see Schantz, *supra* note 23 at 385.

[32] The provisions are available online at: www.gesetze-im-internet.de/englisch_bdsg/englisch_bdsg.html#p0383.

[33] BGH of 19 September 1985 – III ZR 213/83, BGHZ 95, 362, 365.

[34] SCHUFA is short for 'Schutzgemeinschaft für allgemeine Kreditsicherung'; see online: www.schufa.de/en/en/home/index.jsp.

with existing and future creditors. Banks, trading companies and other sectors of the German economy qualify as such creditors and they can apply for access to the agency's database.[35] SCHUFA collects information on a person's credit history, and records positive and negative facts relating to any debtor's payment conduct. Payment defaults or delays result in negative records in its database.

Creditors have access to this database on the basis of reciprocity. If they themselves report data collected about their debtors to SCHUFA, they are entitled to access all information that was provided by other creditors. Such access is most important for creditors who extend credit, especially lenders, credit card issuers, as well as telecommunication companies and suppliers who do not insist on prepaid services or payment on the spot.[36]

In the past, any transfer of data to SCHUFA used to require the consent of the debtor. The practice of the banks, however, under which they demanded every future customer to agree to the free transfer of all data in all instances as a prerequisite for any bank–customer relationship, rendered this requirement of consent meaningless. As a result, the legislator now regulates such data transfers in s 28a BDSG. Independent from the customer's consent, each transfer of sensitive information relating to a natural person requires justification. The justifying criteria are laid down in s 28a BDSG and must be met prior to any disclosure of information to SCHUFA.

The criteria are: data referring to a claim may only be transferred if the customer-debtor does not render performance on time and if the transfer of data is necessary to protect the reasonable interests of the collector of the data or a third party. While these criteria sound like substantial safeguards effectively protecting the interests of debtors, banks have diluted them in their practical application, with the approval of the courts. The criterion of 'reasonable interests' has been rendered meaningless. The courts derive such interests from the principle of reciprocity. Since every creditor is required to provide data in order to obtain data, the courts have considered every data transfer necessary in the justified interests of the transferor.[37]

Consequently, only the following further requirement provides some protection: the law restricts data transfers to an exclusive number of instances,[38] the common theme of which could be summarised as those

---

[35] According to SCHUFA's own representation, the database contains 682 million records collected from 663 million people and 4.2 million companies.

[36] Schantz, *supra* note 23 at 70.

[37] OLG Frankfurt of 16 March 2011 – 19 U 291/10; KG Berlin of 23 August 2011, 4 W 43/11.

[38] These scenarios are further requirements for the transfer of data according to s 28a(1) BDSG.

situations in which the debtor's default on payment debt is evident and that he had sufficient opportunity to adhere to his obligations.

The same shift in principles has occurred for the access to data stored by SCHUFA. Here again, the mere consent of natural persons to such data access is no longer a sufficient criterion. Potential future creditors of natural persons such as banks prior to contracting with a customer may access the database to find out more about the person's financial situation under the conditions set out in s 29(2) BDSG. It requires the creditor to show a legitimate interest in accessing the data base combined with the lack of a legitimate interest of the natural person in preventing such data access.

Disclosure of Information to Other Third Parties The principle of consent remains the decisive criterion in all other situations where the bank wishes to disclose information to anyone other than SCHUFA. It is common practice of banks to provide other banks with general information about a customer. For most of these purposes, especially for the execution of payment transactions, such disclosure generally does not require and include detailed information about the customer's holdings in bank accounts and overall financial situation, and is therefore non-sensitive. The sensitive cases are those in which the bank reveals information about the customer's financial situation, creditworthiness and solvency. This kind of disclosure requires a distinction to be made between private parties, defined as natural persons and non-professional associations, and professional parties, defined as companies and merchants.[39] While any transfer of information referring to private parties requires their consent, such consent is presumed for professional parties in all matters that relate to their sphere of business. As a result, professional parties must explicitly object to the transfer of information to prevent such disclosure. As an additional safeguard, banks' common practice is to require the recipients of information to credibly explain their justified interests in the information.[40]

These requirements prevail in situations of conflicts of interest for banks. Under German law, a bank is not the fiduciary of its customers and

---

[39] The term merchant refers to a certain group of professionals defined in the German Commercial Code. This special category of merchants, in French called commercaux, in German called Kaufleute, is common in civil law traditions, but no equivalent exists in common law jurisdictions. For a definition of activities that constitute a commercial business see ss 1–7 Handelsgesetzbuch (HGB).

[40] Based on the terms and conditions of banks as approved by German courts (AGB Banken). In this respect and generally, see Schantz, *supra* note 23 at 57 seq.; also Schulz and Fett, *supra* note 14 at 391 seq.

therefore not generally required to shield them from potential harm.[41]
As a result, under normal circumstances a bank may grant a loan to one
customer without issuing a warning even though it is aware that the proceeds of the loan will be used for a contractual relationship with another
bank customer whose financial difficulties are known to the bank, but not
the borrower. However, such incidents will sour the relationship with the
customer whose losses could have been prevented. Banks are therefore
genuinely interested in disclosing such confidential information to third
parties, but they may only do so if the affected customer has consented.[42]
Exceptions apply if one customer attempts to defraud the other. When
the bank knows that its customer is developing or executing a fraudulent
scheme under which other customers are likely to incur losses, the bank
owes the latter customers a contractual obligation to protect them from
losses, generally by issuing a warning or by revealing information about
the former customer and his scheme.[43]

The 'Kirch Media' Case   The most prominent case in Germany in which
the principles of bank secrecy were tested was the action for compensation
brought by Leo Kirch on behalf of two of the companies belonging to his
insolvent, but formerly influential, media empire against Deutsche Bank
and its former head of the executive board, Rolf Breuer.[44]
    Deutsche Bank was one of the main lenders to the Kirch group. When,
in 2002, media reports about the financial difficulties of the media group
were circulating, Rolf Breuer was asked in an interview how he assessed
the financial situation of the group. He did not address the question as the
official representative of Deutsche Bank, but said that under the current

---

[41] This follows from BGH of 11 February 1999 – IX ZR 352–97, 52 Neue Juristische
Wochenschrift (NJW) 2032 (at 3a) (1999).
[42] Schulz and Fett, *supra* note 14 at 403. Other authors suggest that the bank may decide in
favour of one or the other customer by weighing the conflicting interests, see B. Müller-
Christmann in K. Langenbucher, D.H. Bliesener and G. Spindler, *Bankrechts-Kommentar*
(Munich: C.H. Beck, 2013), chapter 1 at 54.
[43] BGH of 6 May 2008 – Xl ZR 56/07, 8 Zeitschrift für Bank- und Kapitalmarktrecht (BKR)
381 (2008).
[44] The head of the executive board is called 'Vorstandsvorsitzender'. His function is comparable
to that of a chief executive officer, stemming from the two-board structure of German stock
corporations. On these principles of German company law, see P.L. Davies and K.J. Hopt,
'Boards in Europe – Accountability and Convergence', *American Journal of Comparative
Law*, 61 (2013), 301 at 310–2; see also T. Baums and K.E. Scott, 'Taking Shareholder
Protection Seriously? Corporate Governance in the United States and Germany', *American
Journal of Comparative Law*, 53 (2005), 31 at 54–6; G.H. Roth and P. Kindler, *The Spirit of
Corporate Law* (Munich: C.H. Beck, 2013) at 74.

circumstances, he (personally) doubted the financial sector in general would support the media group with further loans.

This announcement was understood by the public as a judgment by someone who knew the media group's financial situation well and as an indication that Deutsche Bank would not provide any further financial support to the group. The result was that many creditors lost confidence in the group and its rescue efforts – which in retrospect seemed far from hopeless prior to Breuer's statement – failed, resulting in the insolvency of the entire group and the downfall of its media empire and its formerly powerful controlling shareholder and chief executive, Leo Kirch.

The Federal High Court held that Rolf Breuer had breached the duties that Deutsche Bank owed to the Kirch group under the contractual relationship stemming from the loan agreements between Deutsche Bank and the group.[45] The Court reasoned that statements by the head of the executive board of one of the dominant lenders were destined to be understood as negative signals about the debtor's future, about Deutsche's willingness to provide further help and could be expected to result in drastic reactions by other creditors.[46]

Whether or not Deutsche Bank was liable to pay damages to the plaintiff depended on the further issue of whether the insolvency of the Kirch group would have been prevented without Breuer's statements. This was to be decided in further proceedings; however, after a twelve-year-long legal battle, Kirch and Deutsche Bank settled in 2014 for 925 million EUR.[47]

7.2.3   Bank Secrecy as Safeguard against Information Access by Public Authorities

Whereas the prior discussion focused on conflicting interests of the bank and its customer, this following section deals with situations in which the interests of banks and customers are aligned or, at least, are not opposed.

---

[45] Under German law, companies are liable for the acts, omissions and knowledge of their organs and (executive) employees. This is derived from ss 31, 166 BGB.

[46] See BGH of 24 January 2006 – XI ZR 384/03, *supra* note 18.

[47] See Reuters, 'Deutsche Bank Seeks Compensation from ex-CEO in Kirch Case: Newspaper' (2 August 2014), online: www.reuters.com/article/2014/08/02/us-deutsche-bank-idUSK-BN0G20AR20140802. The legal disputes are, however, far from over because Deutsche Bank, unhappy about Breuer's comments back in 2002 and the following dispute with the Kirch Group, is currently suing Rolf Breuer for breach of director's duties. Furthermore, investigations against Breuer and other top executives of Deutsche Bank, including the two top executives whose terms recently ended, Anshu Jain and Jürgen Fitschen, have started because prosecutors suspect that Breuer and his colleagues lied when giving testimony in preceding court proceedings.

In these instances, the state requires banks to disclose information about their customers. Customers wish to shield their information shared with banks from attempts by tax authorities and other public agencies to 'pierce the veil of bank secrecy'. The banks are neutral to such demands or indirectly share the reluctance of their customers: bank supervisors may see the need for interference in the bank–customer relationship in situations of accumulated risk and, more generally, dissemination of such information comes with the potential risk that competitors learn facts that the bank does not want to publicise.

While German law, as discussed earlier (Section 7.2.2), offers substantial protection for confidential bank data against access by interested private parties, the opposite is true for data access demanded and initiated by the authorities. As explained in this section, German law enables authorities to access confidential information to a remarkably large extent. This has led to the commonly used denomination of German bank customers as the 'transparent customers'.[48]

The starting point, however, is the limitation on the power of the state, its institutions and agents, to interfere in the private sphere of individuals as provided in the German Constitution that protects individuals, i.e. natural persons and, to a limited extent, legal persons from acts of sovereign power. The German constitution is called 'Grundgesetz' (GG), and is often (but arguably misleadingly) translated literally into English as the 'Basic Law'. The provisions relevant for the protection of confidential information are Art. 1(1) in combination with Art. 2(1). These articles guarantee the right of the so-called 'informational self-determination', meaning the right to decide individually whether and to what extent one wishes to disclose personal information.[49] Banks are protected by Art. 12 of the constitution,

---

[48] The German term is 'gläserne Kunden', used by, for instance, M. Tolani, 'Existiert in Deutschland ein Bankgeheimnis? – Das Bankgeheimnis gegenüber dem Staat unter Berücksichtigung der jüngsten gesetzlichen Veränderungen', *Zeitschrift für Bank- und Kapitalmarktrecht (BKR)*, 7 (2007), 275.

[49] Decided by the constitutional court ('Bundesverfassungsrericht' (BVerfG)) in several decisions, in particular in BverfG of 15 December 1983, BVerfGE 65, 1 (42 seq.); BVerfG of 11 June 1991, BVerfGE 84, 192 (194); BVerfG of 13 June 2007 – 1 BvR 1550/03 E, 60 Neue Juristische Wochenschrift (NJW) 2464 (2465) (2007). See also A. Rust, 'Chapter 10: Data Protection as a Fundamental Right' in A. Rust and E. Fort (eds), *Exchange of Information and Bank Secrecy* (Alphen aan den Rijn: Wolters Kluwer Law & Business, 2012), 177 at 178. Relevant personal information is understood broadly. Whether the person to whom the information relates is interested in protecting it from access depends on the circumstances, see BVerfG of 13 June 2007 – 1 BvR 1550/03 E.

which applies to legal as well as natural persons and protects the freedom to exercise one's individual profession and occupation of choice.[50]

Although these constitutional rights are subject to legislative overrides and therefore do not offer absolute protection from state intervention,[51] what they do is to allow a bank customer or a bank to challenge in court a disproportionate use of the legislative incursions by the German state. Restrictions to the right of 'informational self-determination' must pursue a legitimate objective, must not go beyond what seems required to achieve an identified objective and are required to take sufficient account of the individual's interests in keeping confidential information private.[52]

How these mechanisms protect financial data held by banks is best explained by analysing the powers of bank supervisors (Section 7.2.3.1) and tax authorities (Section 7.2.3.2) to coercive information access.

7.2.3.1   Access to Information by Bank Supervisors and Financial Regulators

The most far-reaching authority to access data held by banks has been granted to the financial regulators and supervisors.[53] The supervision of banks is exercised in Germany jointly by a federal agency charged with the supervision (and to some extent regulation) of all financial institutions and other significant providers of financial services in Germany, the federal financial supervisory authority called the 'Bundesanstalt für Finanzdienstleistungsaufsicht' (BaFin), and the 'Deutsche Bundesbank', the German central bank.

While these principles have remained unaffected in most instances, on 1 November 2014 the situation became more complicated for German banks

---

[50] On the constitutional law aspects of bank secrecy in Germany, see also Schulz and Fett, *supra* note 14 at 384.

[51] On the additional, yet also restricted protection by EU fundamental rights law, see Rust, *supra* note 49 at 189–93.

[52] For more detail, see *ibid.*, at 178.

[53] Regulation is here understood as the establishment of specific rules of behaviour, whereas supervision is understood as the monitoring of the behaviour of banks, including compliance with rules and regulations. This understanding corresponds to the general usage of these terms, see for instance the communication by the Monetary Authority of Singapore, 'Tenets of Effective Regulation' (June 2010, revised in April 2013) at 4, fn 1, online: www.mas.gov.sg/~/media/MAS/About%20MAS/Monographs%20and%20information%20papers/Tenets%20of%20Effective%20Regulationrevised%20in%20April%202013.pdf. See also R.M. Lastra, 'The Role of the IMF as a Global Financial Authority' in C. Herrmann and J.P. Terhechte (eds), *2011 European Yearbook of International Economic Law*, vol II (Berlin: Springer, 2011), 121 at 122.

that are of systemic importance to the Euro zone financial market (Euro zone 'SIBs'). Such banks are supervised jointly by the European Central Bank (ECB) and (under its lead role) the above-mentioned German institutions as well as other national competent authorities in Euro zone member states in which these SIBs operate.[54]

Regardless of which agency is competent in any given scenario, the powers of supervision are exercised under the KWG (German Banking Act).[55] The core provision in this respect is s 44 KWG. It requires all banks[56] and several other types of financial institutions to provide requested information to the supervisory authorities, the BaFiN and the Deutsche Bundesbank. s 44 KWG grants the banking supervisors substantial authority to require information from supervised institutions and to carry out inspections.[57] This authority leads to practically unlimited disclosure duties on the supervised institutions. A significant exception is contained in s 44(6) KWG: 'A person obliged to furnish information may refuse to do so in

---

[54] On this new regime for Euro zone SIBs called the SSM, see in detail Council Regulation (EU) No 1024/2013 of 15 October 2013 conferring specific tasks on the European Central Bank concerning policies relating to the prudential supervision of credit institutions (2013) O.J. L. 287/63 (SSRM Regulation); E. Ferran and V.S.G. Babis, 'The European Single Supervisory Mechanism', *Journal of Corporate Law Studies*, 13 (2013), 255.

[55] The German legislator is required to constantly align the KWG with relevant EU legislation. It is required to implement all relevant provisions of EU directives in the KWG. In addition, directly applicable EU law, i.e. EU regulations, are directly applied by the national authorities. The authority of supervisors discussed here stem from the KWG and partially reflect harmonised EU rules.

[56] Banks are called 'credit institutions' by EU legislation and therefore also in the German KWG. Credit institutions are defined as institutions 'undertaking the business of which is to take deposits or other repayable funds from the public and to grant credits for its own account' in Art. 4(1) point (1) of *Regulation (EU) No. 575/2013 of the European Parliament and of the Council of 26 June 2013 on prudential requirements for credit institutions and investment firms and amending regulation (EU) No. 648/2012* (2013) O.J. L. 176/1, referred to in Art. 3(1) point (1) of EC, *Directive 2013/36/EU of the European Parliament and of the Council of 26 June 2013 on access to the activity of credit institutions and the prudential supervision of credit institutions and investment firms, amending Directive 2002/87/EC and repealing Directives 2006/48/EC and 2006/49/EC (text with EEA relevance)*, (2013) O.J. L. 176/338 (commonly referred to as 'CRD IV').

[57] Section 44 KWG reads (in excerpts): '(1) An institution or a superordinated enterprise, the members of its governing bodies and its employees shall, upon request, provide information about all business activities and submit documentation to BaFin, the persons and entities which BaFin uses in performing its functions and the Deutsche Bundesbank. BaFin may perform inspections at the institutions and superordinated enterprises, with or without a special reason, and may entrust the Deutsche Bundesbank with the task of carrying out such inspections.'

respect of any questions, the answering of which would place him/her or one of his/her relatives (. . .) at risk of criminal prosecution.'[58]

In addition to the disclosure requirements under s 44 KWG, the institutions are required to report large loans to the Deutsche Bundesbank, based on ss 13a(1), 14(1) KWG. The most intrusive effect for bank customers, however, stems from s 24c(1) KWG that requires all supervised institutions to keep permanently updated lists with the name and date of birth of every account holder, their account numbers and the dates when the accounts were opened and, if applicable, closed. Amounts and transaction details, however, are not included in these lists.

The supervisory authorities may access individual data in this database if necessary to perform their prudential tasks under the Money Laundering Act ('Geldwäschegesetz' or GwG). For purposes of money laundering prevention, banks are required to monitor suspicious activities of customers and to report them to the authorities.[59] This obligation in the German Money Laundering Act implements the provisions of EU legislation,[60] and the European as well as German legislator adhere to the recommendations of the Financial Action Force on Money Laundering.[61] The courts have interpreted these obligations widely and require banks to immediately report any suspicious activities, even in instances where the facts are still inconclusive,[62] and the supervisors monitor the banks' compliance with these principles. In addition, the supervisors exercise all tasks assigned to them under the KWG and seek access to the lists if considered necessary to evaluate the bank's compliance with regulatory requirements such as minimum capital adequacy or leverage ratios or reporting requirements for large loans.

Such automated data access by the supervisory authorities seems justified by the fact that the need for information for supervisory purposes occurs in a multitude of cases. To request such information on an individual basis would take too long and entail the risk of selective disclosure

---

[58] On this exception, see Section 7.2.3.3.
[59] See s 11 of the Money Laundering Act (Geldwäschegesetz or GwG). See Nakajima, Chapter 4, on the role of banks as 'reluctant policemen'.
[60] The relevant EU legislation was recently amended and will lead to changes of the German Money Laundering Act, but not affect any of the principles discussed here. See *Directive 2015/849 of 20 May 2015 on the prevention of the use of the financial system for the purposes of money laundering or terrorist financing* (2015) O.J. L. 141/73.
[61] Schulz and Fett, *supra* note 14 at 398.
[62] See the decision of the Regional High Court in Frankfurt am Main (OLG), decision of 17 December 2012 – 19 U 210/12, BeckRS 2013, 06607.

by the banks. The extraordinary and questionable aspect, however, is that such access of data takes place in secret. According to s 24c(1) sentence 2 KWG,[63] the bank is required to ensure that the BaFin has automated access at all times to these data files by means of a procedure of BaFin's choice and to provide the technical means and organisational measures that such data access goes unnoticed. The bank itself is not allowed to monitor such data retrievals. It must ensure that it – and consequently no customer – can and will ever find out when such data access has taken place.[64]

As a result, no affected party can assess whether the requirements for the data access have been met, i.e. whether the access seemed necessary for the purposes of prudential supervision or prevention of money laundering, challenge intrusions into the privacy sphere and seek protection from current and future violations. This renders, factually speaking, any

---

[63] Section 24(c) KWG reads (in excerpts):

(1) Credit institutions shall maintain a data file in which they must store the following data without delay (. . .), the name – and for natural persons the date of birth – of the holder and of any party authorised to draw on the account. (. . .) The credit institution shall ensure that BaFin has automated access at all times to the data entered in the data file pursuant to sentence 1 by means of a procedure of BaFin's choice. The institution shall ensure by means of technical and organisational measures that it cannot monitor such data retrievals.

(2) BaFin may access individual data entered in the data file pursuant to subsection (1) sentence 1 insofar as this is necessary to enable it to perform its prudential functions under this Act or the Money Laundering Act, in particular with respect to unauthorised banking business and financial services or the misuse of the institutions by means of money laundering or fraudulent activities to the detriment of the institutions, and if there is particular urgency in individual cases.

(3) Upon request, BaFin will provide information entered in the data file pursuant to subsection (1) sentence 1 to the supervisory authorities pursuant to section 9 (1) sentence 4 number 2 insofar as this is necessary to enable them to perform their prudential functions under the conditions set out in subsection (2),

 1. the authorities or courts responsible for providing international judicial assistance in criminal cases, and otherwise for the prosecution and punishment of criminal offences, insofar as this is necessary to enable them to perform their statutory functions,

 2. the national authority responsible for imposing restrictions on capital transfers and payment transactions pursuant to the Foreign Trade and Payments Act insofar as this is necessary to enable it to perform its functions ensuing from the Foreign Trade and Payments Act or from legal instruments of the European Union in connection with restrictions on economic and financial relations.

BaFin will access the data stored in the data files by means of an automated procedure and transmit them to the authority making the request. BaFin will verify the permissibility of such transmission only if it has particular grounds for doing so. The responsibility for the permissibility of the transmission shall lie with the authority making the request.

[64] See the discussion of s 24c KWG by M. Brender, 'Rechtspolitische Problematik des automatisierten Kontenabrufs', *Zeitschrift für Rechtspolitik*, 42 (2009), 198 (in German).

restrictive requirements for such secret data accesses redundant. Critical commentators have pointed out that in spite of restrictive requirements in the law, factually speaking the legislator has granted the authorities unlimited and uncontrolled access to all data contained in the bank files.[65]

Such hidden access to sensitive personal information stands in stark contrast to the constitutionally guaranteed principles of post-war Germany, in particular enshrined in Art. 19 of the constitution, especially in subpara 4 which provides: 'Should any person's rights be violated by public authority, he may have recourse to the courts. If no other jurisdiction has been established, recourse shall be to the ordinary courts.' Whereas, formally speaking, this constitutional guarantee of recourse to the courts is respected because administrative courts will hear cases of alleged violations of rights to privacy, such jurisdiction of the courts is of no practical value unless customers (and banks) are aware of such intrusive actions.

Nevertheless, the Federal Constitutional Court has found some of the provisions in s 24c KWG compatible with basic rights guaranteed by the constitution.[66] The Court noted that the competence of the bank supervisor under s 24c(3)(No 2) KWG to access and forward information to authorities and courts is 'for the prosecution and punishment of criminal offences, insofar as this is necessary to enable them to perform their statutory functions' or 'for providing international judicial assistance in criminal cases'.[67] The court discussed the aspect that neither the bank nor – and this is the more relevant aspect – the account holder learned about the data access before a situation of *fait accompli* had occurred, i.e. the transfer of information to prosecutors and courts had taken place. The court ruled that the provisions in question were nevertheless compatible with the requirements of the GG, particularly with its Art. 19(IV). The court reasoned that the permitted access was limited to core elements of the account information, namely the account numbers, the dates on which the accounts were opened and (if applicable) closed, the names and (if applicable) dates of birth of account holders and of parties authorised to draw on the accounts. The court emphasised that the authorities were not permitted to access and forward further information such as detailed transactions leading to credits and debits on the accounts.

---

[65] See the criticism made by Tolani, *supra* note 48. See also the critical note struck by Schulz and Fett, *supra* note 14 at 409.
[66] BVerfG of 13 June 2007 – 1 BvR 1550/03 E, *supra* note 49 at 2468 (paras at 109–27).
[67] See the full wording of s 24c(3)(No 2) KWG, *supra* note 63.

The court also assumed that all authorities involved would strictly adhere to the rules provided in s 24c KWG and concluded that the permitted data access seemed of low intrusive quality. Furthermore, it assumed that the affected parties would sooner or later learn about such data access from the authorities who were using the data for their purposes, especially in criminal investigations.[68] Based on this, it upheld the legality of the provisions.

The ruling of the court boils down to the following: if the secret access does not result in any consequences for the account holder such as criminal investigations, the court sees no reason for disclosure to the customer that the access occurred. The principle of *nemo iudex sine actore* is obviously of no concern to the court because supervisors have only had access to basic information about the bank customer and potential investigations have not reached the stage where the customer would be required to be informed of criminal investigations against him. Such disclosure is required under the principles of criminal procedure when investigators suspect an individual directly of a breach of the law, i.e. when they proceed from general fact seeking, directed against nobody in particular, to formal investigations against an individual. The court also accepts the outcome of a fait accompli. When disclosure about the data transfer from supervisors to further authorities is made, a potentially unlawful data access and transfer can neither be stopped nor be reversed. It will be left to the courts in criminal proceedings to decide about the legality of the supervisors' data access and transfer and whether illegally acquired data can be used against defendants, but the access itself and the dissemination of information will already have taken place at that stage.[69]

Taking a step back: as regards such information access and, more generally, any disclosure of customer-related information to the supervisors, some level of protection for banks and their customers stems from the confidentiality obligations to which all organs and employees of the supervisor are subject. This requirement follows from s 9 KWG. However, the rule is subject to a wide list of exceptions, also provided in s 9(1) KWG, permitting the employees of BaFin and Bundesbank to forward the information to practically any national and a wide range of foreign (predominantly in, but not confined to the Euro zone and EU) authorities, agencies or persons requiring the information for the pursuit of official tasks. Dissemination of confidential information is thereby easily facilitated; banks and customers

---

[68] BVerfG of 13 June 2007, *supra* note 49 at 2474 (at para 174).
[69] It seems impossible to say with certainty whether courts would reject such information based on the fact that the information was acquired illegally. The 'fruit of the poisonous tree' doctrine is not generally accepted by German courts.

have little control or knowledge of where their information goes and the above-discussed ruling of the constitutional court is an example of such information transfers from supervisors to further authorities.

Here again, an important safeguard applies. The supervisors are only permitted to share data with their counterparts and other agencies from other countries if and insofar as they are subject to similar confidentiality requirements. The German provision addressing this principle of mutual confidentiality is found in s 9(1) KWG,[70] but it is of course a generally understood global standard.[71]

The cross-border dissemination of information has become systematic with the establishment of the centralised supervisory regime under the SSM. The SSM centralises the supervision over significant banks (in simplified terms: over big, systemically important banks) operating in the Euro zone and tasks the ECB to cooperate with the national supervisors in Euro zone countries to jointly establish a cross-border operating supervisor for such banks. Each bank affected by the SSM is supervised by a Joint Supervisory Team (JST) that consists of representatives of the ECB and each national supervisor. It seems evident that such JSTs can only function as permanent fully informed and cross-border operating monitors of banks if they have unrestricted access to all relevant data about the supervised banks. While formerly the cross-border exchange of confidential data used to take place upon request and was therefore subject to the decision of the national competent authority and based on a case-by-case assessment, the SSM requires the permanent, full and automated data exchange among all participating national authorities and the ECB.

---

[70] The provision reads (in excerpts): 'If the authority is located in another state, the facts may be passed on only if that authority and the persons commissioned by it are subject to a confidentiality requirement corresponding to that specified in sentence 1.' Sentence 1 referred to here reads (in excerpts): 'Persons employed by BaFin (. . .) and persons employed by the Deutsche Bundesbank, insofar as they are acting to implement this Act, may not disclose or use without authorisation facts which have come to their notice in the course of their activities and which should be kept secret in the interests of the institution or a third party (especially business and trade secrets), not even after they have left such employment or their activities have ended.' Section 9(1) KWG continues (in excerpts): 'The foreign authority is to be informed that it may use information solely for the purpose for which it has been passed on to it. Information from another state may be passed on only with the express permission of the competent authorities providing this information and only for such purposes as have been agreed by these authorities.'

[71] See, from a very different part of the world, the Monetary Authority of Singapore, 'Explanatory Brief: Monetary Authority of Singapore (Amendment) Bill 2015' (14 April 2015) at para. 15(c), online: www.mas.gov.sg/news-and-publications/media-releases/2015/explanatory-brief-monetary-authority-of-singapore-amendment-bill-2015.aspx.

Such new modalities are possible under s 9 KWG as all its requirements are met. Section 9(1) KWG permits data transfers to other supervisors in countries of the European Economic Area[72] (in no. 9) and to the ECB (in no. 10) for as long as they are subject to confidentiality requirements comparable to those applying to the German supervisors. The provisions do not contain any further restrictions so that regular and even permanent and automated transfers of data are covered.

7.2.3.2   Access to Information by Tax Authorities

Germany taxes all types of income, and earnings from deposits and financial investments are no exception. Income tax rates are high, among the highest in the world (49.3 per cent for childless single employees at the income level of an average worker),[73] and vigorously enforced. This state of affairs has been the impetus for a number of German tax residents to evade taxation by putting their money in bank accounts in countries that neither tax foreign depositors nor report their holdings to the competent foreign authorities.

This explains Germany's perspective on tax evasion. Germany has not tried to increase its competitiveness by lowering taxes, but has joined other nations in their attempt to close loopholes for their tax residents. This has resulted in high profile incidents of German authorities buying data revealing the names of German account holders in Switzerland from employees of Swiss banks for millions of Euros, thereby bypassing official routes of data exchange, enticing breaches of Swiss law of data privacy and damaging diplomatic relations.[74] While such incidents could not have more clearly underlined the need for a new tax treaty between the two countries, the German and Swiss governments and legislators failed to agree on new

---

[72] The European Economic Area includes all EU members and three of the EFTA states: Iceland, Liechtenstein and Norway.

[73] See OECD, 'Tax Burdens on Labour Income Continue to Rise across the OECD' (11 April 2014), online: www.oecd.org/tax/tax-burdens-on-labour-income-continue-to-rise-across-the-oecd.htm.

[74] Germany was joined in this questionable practice by France, and officials in both countries insist that no laws were breached, rather legitimate claims to taxes were being pursued, while Switzerland complained about serious violations of its laws, see E. Kristoffersson and P. Pistone, 'General Report' in E. Kristoffersson, M. Lang, P. Pistone et al. (eds), Tax Secrecy and Tax Transparency, Part 1 (Frankfurt: Peter Lang, 2013) at 8 seq. See also media reports at Spiegel Online International, 'The "Singapore Connection": German Tax Investigators Set Their Sights on UBS' (10 August 2012), online: www.spiegel.de/international/germany/german-authorities-investigate-ubs-in-relation-to-tax-evasion-a-849366.html.

rules in 2012.[75] The recently concluded taxation agreement between the EU and Switzerland, however, will resolve the issue when it enters into effect in 2018. In this agreement, Switzerland agrees to an automatic exchange of financial account information with EU member states.[76]

Financial earnings, be they in the form of interest paid for deposits, dividends paid for shareholdings in companies or any other form of income stemming from investments in financial products, are subject to withholding tax in Germany. The bank deducts the tax amount from the income and transfers the tax to the state while crediting the remainder to the customer's account.

Tax authorities are authorised to require all relevant information from tax subjects, and if they fail to comply with their duties, the authorities have means to acquire information without their assistance. The German Fiscal Code 'Abgabenordnung' (AO) regulates administrative procedures in tax matters and vests competences in tax authorities to enable them to acquire relevant information if tax subjects fail to comply with their duties to declare income. This includes the authority to investigate financial earnings. The authorities can bypass the tax payer and request data directly from the bank, i.e. account records and other documents for inspection.[77] Such information access is not based on the authority of bank supervisors under the provisions of the KWG to forward information to other national (and foreign) authorities (as discussed in Section 7.2.3.1),[78] but stems from authorizations found in the provisions of the AO.

---

[75] See media reports at M. Hesse and B. Schmid, 'Penalties and Profits: Illicit Tax-Cheat CDs May Endanger Swiss-German Treaty' (16 July 2012), online: Spiegel Online International, www.spiegel.de/international/germany/tax-authorities-might-torpedo-german-swiss-treaty-on-tax-evaders-a-844455.html.

[76] *Amending Protocol to the Agreement between the European Community and the Swiss Confederation providing for measures equivalent to those laid down in Council Directive 2003/48/EC on taxation of savings income in the form of interest payments*, Council of the European Union document 8297/15 of 21 May 2015.

[77] Section 93(1) AO provides that the tax authorities shall obtain the relevant information primarily from the tax subject and from other sources only if necessary to assess and verify the tax situation of the tax subject. Section 97(2) AO contains the requirements for bypassing the tax payer: failure to furnish the requested information, provision of insufficient information or authorities' suspicion that the information may be incorrect. See further, Schantz, *supra* note 23 at 51, 64; Krepold, *supra* note 25 at 245.

[78] Section 9(1) KWG does not include the tax authorities in the catalogue of authorities, state agencies and public institutions to which the German bank supervisors may transfer data. Section 9(5) KWG clarifies that the bank supervisors are only authorised to support the tax authorities when their authority is established by and exercised in accordance with the provisions of the AO.

Section 93b AO contains a powerful authorization. It allows the tax authorities to make use of s 24c KWG (the provision discussed in detail in Section 7.2.3.1). It authorizes them to access bank files that contain basic information about all the banks' customers. Such access is, however, more restricted for tax authorities than for bank supervisors. They must first unsuccessfully seek to obtain the information from the bank customer directly, and – in contrast to the covert access by bank supervisors – inform the bank customer about their data access.[79] It seems likely that the main reasons for such different procedural requirements can be found in the different roles of bank supervisors and tax authorities. Bank supervisors have no executive powers vis-à-vis bank customers. Their regulatory targets are banks, and data access of bank supervisors predominantly serves the purposes of assessing whether banks comply with regulatory requirements. In contrast, tax authorities are investigating the compliance of banks and their customers with fiscal law, and can issue administrative acts (Verwaltungsakte) addressed at either of them. As a result, the requirements to access such data is, and should be, higher for tax authorities than bank supervisors.

The scope of application of such direct data access has recently been further restricted by s 93(7) AO as a result of the flat tax of 25 per cent on all capital income that was introduced in 2009. Banks transfer the flat tax automatically to the tax authorities, further declarations by tax subjects are not required and, as a result, automated data access by fiscal authorities has since become rare.[80] However, the Federal Minister of Finance recently announced plans to replace the flat tax by a capital income tax subject to the individual tax rate as it applies to all other sources of income.[81] In such a case, the automated access of tax authorities would regain substantial relevance since taxation of tax subjects would again depend upon their honest and complete disclosure of capital income, and it will reignite the interest of authorities in access to detailed information about bank customers.

---

[79] These restrictions stem from s 97(7), (8) AO and further guidelines provided by the Ministry of Finance, see the 'Anwendungserlass zur Abgabenordnung – Regelungen zu ss 92 und 93 AO', Gz. IV A 4-S 0062-1/0 of 10 March 2005. See further Schantz, *supra* note 23 at 35–40.

[80] Compare Schulz and Fett, *supra* note 14 at 393 seq.

[81] As reported by the German media, see V.M. Schäfers, 'Schäuble rückt von der Abgeltungsteuer ab' (10 November 2015), online: Frankfurter Allgemeine Zeitung, www.faz.net/aktuell/wirtschaft/recht-steuern/schaeuble-rueckt-von-der-abgeltungsteuer-ab-13904823.html.

Apart from such direct investigations into the financial circumstances of taxpayers, tax authorities may incidentally retrieve data about bank customers in the course of auditing banks. In such instances, bank customers are protected by s 30a AO. It requires the authorities to 'take special account' of the confidential relationship between banks and their customers (ss 1). Also significant is ss 3: 'Deposit accounts or securities accounts in relation to which an identity check (...) has been carried out may not on occasion of the external audit of a credit institution be identified or copied for the purpose of verifying correct payment of taxes.'

The provisions seem to prohibit tax authorities from using any information acquired on occasion of external audits for purposes different from those that justified the audit. However, this is not how the authorities have read and applied them, and the German courts have had to clarify where the line between general interest in efficient enforcement of tax obligations and right to protection of sensitive data of individuals must be drawn.

The Federal High Court in Fiscal Matters[82] decided that data found incidentally may be used if 'sufficient reasons' exist for further investigations. This is the case if the authorities come across data referring to a bank customer whom they are also investigating. The court was referring to cases in which the concrete data access was not triggered by investigations against this person, but either directed against the bank or its other customers. The court also permitted authorities to use data incidentally retrieved for further investigations if they find evidence that a bank customer engaged in bank transactions that, as the court puts it, seem susceptible to the temptation of tax evasion in a more than average way and make it seem more likely that upon further investigations instances of tax evasion will be discovered.[83] The courts have not clarified which circumstances can lead to such 'temptations', but have ruled that the practice of tax authorities

---

[82] The German court system consists of state and federal courts. The Federal Court in Fiscal Matters, called 'Bundesfinanzgerichtshof', ranks highest in fiscal matters, i.e. its judgments can only be appealed on allegation of breach of constitutional law and referred to the Federal Constitutional Court.

[83] High Court in Fiscal Matters of 9 December 2008 – VII R 47/07, BFH 62 Neue Juristische Wochenschrift (NJW) 1437 (1440)(2009). The wording here is translated from the German original which reads: 'wenn das zu prüfende Bankgeschäft Auffälligkeiten aufweist, die es aus dem Kreis der alltäglichen und banküblichen Geschäfte hervorheben oder eine für Steuerhinterziehung besonders anfällige Art der Geschäftsabwicklung erkennen lassen, die – mehr als es bei Kapitaleinkünften aus bei Banken geführten Konten und Depots stets zu besorgen ist – dazu verlockt, solche Einkünfte dem Finanzamt zu verschweigen, wenn also eine erhöhte Wahrscheinlichkeit der Entdeckung unbekannter Steuerfälle besteht'.

to instigate investigations against customers for whom the bank executes capital markets transactions is illegal.[84]

7.2.3.3 Disclosure by Banks in Criminal Proceedings and for Criminal Investigations

In criminal proceedings against bank customers, bank secrecy does not protect the bank–customer relationship. This rule applies regardless of the nature of the charge, i.e. whether the alleged criminal acts are a direct result of the bank–customer relationship such as in instances of money laundering or tax evasion, or whether access to account information helps to collect evidence in cases of fraud, bribery, etc. Banks and their organs, agents and employees are required, if called upon, to give full testimony in court and before investigative judges and prosecutors.[85] Vis-a-vis the police, however, such obligations do not exist.[86] A bank employee may legally remain silent when enquiries are made by the police. Only if prosecutors and judges see sufficient reason to order the bank employee to appear before them and answer their questions, is the employee required to disclose all information about the bank's customer under investigation. However, the bank's directors, agents or employees are entitled to remain silent even when ordered to appear before a prosecutor or judge if disclosing information about the bank customer would incriminate themselves.[87] This exemption becomes relevant in cases in which the bank's representatives or employees have provided assistance to the customer's attempts to launder money or avoid taxation.

In civil proceedings, the bank's obligation to keep its customers' data confidential aligns with its agents' entitlement to refuse testimony in court. Banks are understood as legal 'persons to whom facts are entrusted, by virtue of their office, profession or status, the nature of which mandates their confidentiality', and their testimony in court about their customers' data as a situation in which 'their testimony would concern facts to which the

---

[84] *Ibid.*

[85] See ss 162, 161a German Code of Criminal Procedure ('Strafprozessordnung' or StPO).

[86] This is an undisputed principle of German criminal law, see Müller-Christmann, *supra* note 42 at 47; Schantz, *supra* note 23 at 28. See also Schulz and Fett, *supra* note 14 at 397.

[87] Section 44(6) KWG: 'A person obliged to furnish information may refuse to do so in respect of any questions, the answering of which would place him/her or one of his/her relatives as designated in s 383(1) numbers 1 to 3 of the Code of Civil Procedure at risk of criminal prosecution 142 or proceedings under the Act on Breaches of Administrative Regulations (Gesetz über Ordnungswidrigkeiten)'.

confidentiality obligation refers.[88] Unless released from its secrecy obligation by the customer, the bank is not permitted to reveal any information in court.[89]

7.3   The Current and Future EU System on Information Exchange

Bank secrecy is a timely topic in all financial centres around the globe, particularly in Europe. In October 2014, the finance ministers of the EU agreed to tackle the transnational issues stemming from bank secrecy with EU legislation. Such plans for harmonisation became possible when the remaining strongholds of resistance against cross-border data exchange about foreign account holders in the EU, in particular Luxembourg[90] and Austria,[91] agreed to drop their resistance to uniform rules. While Switzerland[92] and Liechtenstein are not members of the EU (Liechtenstein is a member of the European Economic Area), their approaches to bank secrecy have been of high relevance to bank secrecy in the EU. Their willingness to cooperate with EU countries in matters of automated data exchange has terminated resistance by Austria and Luxembourg, and led to the EU consensus.[93]

Taxation in the EU is not harmonised. It has to a large extent remained an area of exclusive competence of the member states. But since obstacles to cross-border trade and services, labour and capital have been removed in the EU's inner market,[94] collaboration among EU member states, to enable

---

[88] This wording stems from s 383(1) no 6 of the Zivilprozessordnung (Civil Procedure Code).

[89] Müller-Christmann, *supra* note 42 at 32; Schulz and Fett, *supra* note 14 at 402.

[90] On bank secrecy in Luxembourg, see the contributions by A. Steichen, 'Chapter 1: Information Exchange in Tax Matters: Luxembourg's New Tax Policy' in *Exchange of Information and Bank Secrecy, supra* note 49 at 9; on bank secrecy and data protection, J. Winandy, 'Chapter 12: Legal Protection against the Transfer of Information (Luxembourg)', *ibid.*, at 221; E. Fort, P. Hondius and J. Neugebauer, 'Chapter 5: Development of the International Information Exchange and Domestic Implementation', *ibid.*, at 99–117; P. Reckinger, 'Chapter 26: Luxembourg' in *Neate and Godfrey: Bank Confidentiality, supra* note 4 at 635–68; E. Chambost, *Bank Accounts: A World Guide to Confidentiality* (Hoboken, NJ: John Wiley & Sons, 1983), chapter 28 at 175–80.

[91] On bank secrecy in Austria, see the contribution by Tiefenthaler and Welten, *supra* note 4 at 59–81.

[92] On Switzerland, see Nobel and Braendli, Chapter 11.

[93] Tiefenthaler and Welten, *supra* note 4 at 59.

[94] Resulting from the fundamental freedoms under the Treaty on the Functioning of the European Union (TFEU), the free movement of goods (Art. 28 seq. TFEU), freedom of movement for workers (Art. 45 TFEU), freedom of establishment (Art. 49–54 TFEU), free movement of services (Art. 56–62 TFEU) and free movement of capital (Art. 63 TFEU). See in detail C. Barnard and S. Peers (eds), *European Union Law* (Oxford University Press, 2014), chapters 12–15; P. Craig and G. de Búrca, *EU Law: Text, Cases and Materials*, 6th edn (Oxford University Press, 2015), chapters 18–22.

them to enforce their tax claims, is unavoidable.[95] Such existing collaboration consists predominantly in information exchange among EU members.

Several legislative acts of the EU (and its predecessors, the EC and EEC), including regulations and directives, provide the framework for such cooperation.[96] They require member states to fight money laundering and organised crime by controlling the activities of their financial institutions. In particular, member states are obliged by EU law to put in place legislation that requires financial institutions to report suspicious activities to the authorities (as already referred to in Section 7.2.2.3).[97]

The Mutual Assistance Directive[98] provides the basis for automated exchange of information about income from employment, director's fees, life insurance products, pensions and immovable property.[99] While the directive prevents member states from declining information exchange on the grounds that the information is held by a bank or other financial institution,[100] i.e. it is not permissible to rely on principles of bank secrecy to oppose such data exchange, other sources of income, such as interest stemming from deposits, are not included in the automated exchange stemming from the Directive.

Such sources of income and the exchange of information about them are subject to the Savings Directive.[101] It requires all member states to recognise the tax claims of other member states by reporting all interest earned by foreign depositors to the competent foreign tax authorities[102]

---

[95] In this respect, from a broader – global – perspective, see K. Drüen, 'Chapter 4: The Mutual Assistance Directive' in *Exchange of Information and Bank Secrecy, supra* note 49, 77 at 78.

[96] See in detail EC, 'Administrative Co-operation and Mutual Assistance – Overview', online: http://ec.europa.eu/taxation_customs/taxation/tax_cooperation/gen_overview/index_en.htm, and further information at EC, 'Taxation and Customs Union: General Overview', online: http://ec.europa.eu/taxation_customs/taxation/vat/how_vat_works/index_en.htm#vat_overview.

[97] See *Directive 2015/849 of 20 May 2015 on the prevention of the use of the financial system for the purposes of money laundering or terrorist financing, supra* note 60. See also Stanton, Chapter 12. See also the recommendations of the Financial Action Task Force (FATF) of February 2012 that impacted the Commission's proposal for amendments to the 2005 directive and led to the new 2015 directive and Nakajima, Chapter 4.

[98] EC, *Council Directive 2011/16/EU of 15 February 2011 on administrative cooperation in the field of taxation and repealing Directive 77/799/EEC* (2011) O.J. L. 64/1. For further detail on the directive, see Drüen, *supra* note 95 at 79–81.

[99] *Directive 2011/16/EU, supra* note 98, Art. 8(1).

[100] *Ibid.*, Art. 18(2). See also Fort, Hondius and Neugebauer, *supra* note 90 at 98.

[101] EC, *Council Directive 2003/48/EC of 3 June 2003 on taxation of savings income in the form of interest payments* (2003) O.J. L. 157/38.

[102] *Ibid.*, Art. 8.

by way of automatic exchange of such information.[103] Austria, Belgium[104] and Luxembourg, however, were initially exempted from these obligations for a transitional period. The exemption for Austria, Belgium and Luxembourg allowed these three nations to replace the requirement of information sharing with a payment of withholding tax. They were allowed to impose a withholding tax of (ultimately) 35 per cent on foreign EU account holders and transfer 75 per cent of the withheld amount to the member state of residence of the beneficial owner of the account.[105]

It was initially contemplated that the transitional period would not come to an end before several non-EU countries, known for their low taxes and high standards of privacy on earnings, would comply with demands for automatic cross-border data exchange. These non-EU countries are the Swiss Confederation, the Principality of Liechtenstein, the Republic of San Marino, the Principality of Monaco and the Principality of Andorra.[106] While Belgium chose to terminate its exceptional status and opted into the system of automatic information exchange in 2010, Austria and Luxembourg have continued to operate under the withholding tax option.[107]

Until recently, it seemed unlikely that Austria and Luxembourg would lose their privileged status anytime soon. Switzerland, Liechtenstein, Monaco, San Marino and Andorra seemed determined to defend their privileges of privacy granted to financial institutions and their customers. But the turning point came rather suddenly in 2008 when the G20 nations embraced the OECD standards on exchange of information as laid down in the Convention on Mutual Administrative Assistance in Tax Matters

---

[103] *Ibid.*, Art. 9.

[104] On bank secrecy in Belgium, see J. Richelle and F. Mareels, 'Chapter 4: Belgium' in *Neate and Godfrey: Bank Confidentiality, supra* note 4 at 83–8.

[105] *Directive 2003/48/EC, supra* note 101, Arts. 11 and 12.

[106] *Directive 2003/48/EC, supra* note 101, Art. 10. See also J. Schröder, 'Chapter 3: Savings Taxation and Banking Secrecy' in *Exchange of Information and Bank Secrecy, supra* note 49 at 60.

[107] The Savings Directive 2003/48/EC was amended in March 2014 by EC, *Council Directive 2014/48/EU of 24 March 2014 amending Directive 2003/48/EC on taxation of savings income in the form of interest payments* (2014) O.J. L. 111/50. The amendments have closed loopholes opened by narrow definitions of beneficial owners under the original Directive that had led to circumventions of the requirements for reporting of income and payment of withholding tax, see Recital 3 of *Directive 2014/48/EU*. However, the privileges for Austria and Luxembourg remain under the new Directive which must be implemented by 1 January 2016. On the continued existence of the privileges, see Art. 1 in combination with the amended wording of Arts. 8(a), (b), 9(a) and on the implementation deadline, Art. 2(1) of *Directive 2014/48/EU*.

and decided to push for their global adoption.[108] Following this consensus, the progress on information sharing of financial data has been immense.[109] The G8 countries declared in 2013 that authorities around the world should automatically share information to fight tax evasion and corruption.[110] In the years since then, the majority of countries around the globe have agreed to participate in an automated exchange of information, including all big financial centres and important economies, and the above-named non-EU countries with which Austria and Luxembourg traditionally compete over financial customers.[111]

Impressed by these remarkable developments, Austria and Luxembourg dropped their resistance to an EU-wide regime of automated data exchange.[112] In October 2014, the finance ministers of the EU member states agreed to extend the existing administrative cooperation in tax matters to the sensitive field of bank accounts in order to achieve full tax transparency in the EU and to comply with the OECD standards. As a result, the EU Directive on administrative cooperation in the field of taxation will apply to bank accounts in the entire EU.[113] Twenty-seven EU countries – including Luxembourg – have agreed to have the new information exchange regime implemented by 2017 whereas Austria has requested an extension until 2018.[114]

In response to these developments it has been said that bank secrecy was coming to an end in the EU,[115] presumably inspired by the statement of former EU tax commissioner Algirdas Šemeta that Bank secrecy

---

[108] See Schröder, *supra* note 106 at 61; Fort, Hondius and Neugebauer, *supra* note 90 at 95 seq.

[109] Drüen, *supra* note 95 at 78. See also Fort, Hondius and Neugebauer, *supra* note 90 at 98.

[110] See the 'G8 Lough Erne Declaration' (18 June 2013), online: UK Government, www.gov.uk/government/publications/g8-lough-erne-declaration/g8-lough-erne-declaration-html-version. See also Nakajima, Chapter 4.

[111] See the list of jurisdictions at OECD, 'Jurisdictions Participating in the Convention on Mutual Administrative Assistance in Tax Matters Status' (4 November 2015), online: www.oecd.org/ctp/exchange-of-tax-information/Status_of_convention.pdf

[112] For Luxembourg see Reckinger, *supra* note 90 at 635 seq.; for Austria, see Tiefenthaler and Welten, *supra* note 4 at 59 seq.

[113] *Council Directive 2011/16/EU, supra* note 98, as amended by EC, *Council Directive 2014/107/EU of 9 December 2014 amending Directive 2011/16/EU as regards mandatory automatic exchange of information in the field of taxation* (2014) O.J. L. 359/1.

[114] European Commission, 'Automatic Exchange of Information: Frequently Asked Questions' (15 October 2014), online: http://europa.eu/rapid/press-release_MEMO-14-591_en.htm

[115] See, for instance, Peter Spiegel, 'EU Agrees Laws to End Banking Secrecy' (14 October 2014), online: Financial Times, www.ft.com/cms/s/0/0ca39924-53b3-11e4-929b-00144feb7de.html.

was dead.[116] Such statements are, however, oversimplifying the matter. They refer to only one aspect of bank secrecy: the disclosure of relevant information about financial activities of foreign tax residents to their competent foreign tax authorities. While this is undoubtedly the most debated aspect of bank secrecy on the international level, this chapter has shown that there are other equally important facets of bank secrecy on the national level. The new regime of information exchange will not reduce the factual and legal relevance of the national issues, thereby leaving bank secrecy, understood as a principle that applies to parties in a bank–customer relationship, intact.

7.4   Conclusion

Bank secrecy in Germany is relevant as a protective mechanism for customers against disclosure of information to any third party, be it the state, a private company or person. In its practical effect, however, the protection provided against the state is feeble. The general principle of bank secrecy is of no relevance since the competences of the authorities, predominantly the bank supervisors and tax authorities, are based on legislative provisions and give the authorities far-reaching powers to collect information from banks. This will increase with the new EU rules on cross-border data exchange.

The predominant practical relevance of bank secrecy is therefore restricted to situations in which the bank seeks to disclose confidential information to private parties. This is particularly relevant for data transfers to the credit rating agency SCHUFA, other banks and business entities. While data transfer to SCHUFA is regulated by statute, disclosures to other banks and customers are subject to contractual principles. The general principles of the law of obligations decide what information is protected by bank secrecy and under what requirements such information may be disclosed.

On the EU level, the automated cross-border exchange of data on bank customers will be expanded and include income stemming from deposits, savings accounts and other forms of financial investments. It will enter into force in two stages leading to the elimination of the potential to hide holdings in bank accounts from tax authorities by 2018.

---

[116] See Algirdas Šemeta, 'Speaking Points by Commissioner Šemeta at the ECOFIN Press Conference' (14 October 2014), online: European Commission, http://europa.eu/rapid/press-release_SPEECH-14-693_en.htm?locale=en.

8

Hong Kong

STEFAN GANNON

8.1 Introduction

'Bank secrecy', better described in the Hong Kong context as 'bank confidentiality', has attracted a good deal of attention over recent years. Much of the debate has been focussed on finding the appropriate balance between public and private interests. On the one hand, most people would, I think, accept that a person, corporate or individual ought to have the right to have his/its bank handle his/its private affairs in a confidential manner. On the other hand, it is also commonly acknowledged that such a duty cannot be absolute – there have to be qualifications to facilitate the prevention and detection of crime, terrorist activity, tax evasion, etc.

Financial and economic crime knows no borders. In the sphere of financial services regulation, the model of national authorities regulating parts of global entities with purely domestic regulation is outdated. Many jurisdictions have enacted legislation opening windows of disclosure for banks in order to combat crime and facilitate effective prudential regulation. The ability to exchange information for such purposes across borders to give the authorities global reach where appropriate is key to success. As a significant international financial centre and a member of the Financial Stability Board, Hong Kong has enacted a number of major legislative changes in recent years to align with best international practice in these areas.

The views expressed herein represent my own views and not those of the Monetary Authority appointed pursuant to s 5A(1) of the Exchange Fund Ordinance (Cap 66, Laws of Hong Kong) (the 'Monetary Authority'), the Hong Kong Monetary Authority or the Government of the Hong Kong Special Administrative Region of the People's Republic of China. I alone am responsible for any errors. A version of this chapter was presented at the Bank Secrecy Symposium hosted by the Centre for Banking and Finance Law at the National University of Singapore, Faculty of Law on 4–5 December 2014.

8.2   Bank Confidentiality Regime in Hong Kong

8.2.1   Basis of the Bank Confidentiality Regime in Hong Kong

In Hong Kong, the existence of a bank's legal duty to maintain the confidentiality of its customers' affairs is based on common law and is well-established. English authorities and decisions from other common law jurisdictions are persuasive precedents in the Hong Kong courts. The leading authority remains the English Court of Appeal's decision in *Tournier* v. *National Provincial and Union Bank of England* (*Tournier*).[1] In this well-known case, a bank had disclosed to its customer's employer the fact that the customer was not paying off his overdraft but had instead indorsed a cheque in his favour to a bookmaker. The English Court of Appeal held that the bank had breached its duty of confidentiality to the customer, and that such duty is an implied term of a bank's contract with its customer. The court held, however, that the duty of confidentiality is subject to various qualifications, which are explored later. Additionally, the duty of confidentiality must be considered in the light of common sense, for example in the English case of *Christofi* v. *Barclays Bank Plc*,[2] it was held that it was neither sensible nor necessary to impose a duty on a bank not to disclose information to a person who was taken to have that information already under a statutory scheme. In my view, the Hong Kong courts would follow the same line of reasoning.

The principle set out in *Tournier* was applied in the Hong Kong Court of Appeal decision in *FDC Co Ltd and Others* v. *The Chase Manhattan Bank NA* (the *FDC* case)[3] which will be discussed later in this chapter.

8.2.2   Bank–Customer Relationship

According to *Tournier*, the duty of confidentiality arises when a bank–customer relationship is established, and it is an implied term of the contract between a bank and its customer. The right to confidentiality belongs to the customer and not to the bank. The question of who is the 'customer' is therefore relevant.

Whilst there is no statutory definition of 'customer' in the Banking Ordinance (BO),[4] 'customer' is defined in a number of bank merger

---

[1] [1924] 1 KB 461.
[2] [1999] 4 All ER 437.
[3] [1990] 1 HKLR 277.
[4] Cap 155, Laws of Hong Kong.

Ordinances[5] as any person having a banking account, a loan account or other dealing, transaction agreement or arrangement with the relevant merging bank. In the non-statutory code entitled 'Code of Banking Practice'[6] issued jointly by the HKAB[7] and the DTC Association (The Hong Kong Association of Restricted Licence Banks and Deposit-taking Companies, DTCA), and endorsed by the Monetary Authority,[8] the terms 'customers' and 'personal customers' are used interchangeably and both mean a private individual who: (i) maintains an account in Hong Kong (including a joint account with another private individual or an account held as an executor or trustee, but excluding the accounts of sole traders, partnerships, companies, clubs and societies) with, or who receives other services from an authorized institution (AI) as defined in the BO[9] or (ii) acts as guarantor or provider of third-party security (whether or not the guarantor or provider of third-party security is a customer of the institution) for a borrower who is an individual or otherwise.[10]

The term 'customer' has also been considered in a number of overseas cases. In *The Great Western Railway Company* v. *The London and County Banking Company Limited*,[11] the English House of Lords held that a customer of a bank was someone who had an account with the bank and the fact that the bank had for many years been accustomed to cashing cheques made payable to a person did not make that person a customer. In *Woods* v. *Martins Bank Ltd*,[12] the defendant bank had accepted instructions from the plaintiff customer to collect monies from the account of the plaintiff at

---

[5] See, for example, the Bank of China (Hong Kong) Limited (Merger) Ordinance (Cap 1167, Laws of Hong Kong).

[6] Hong Kong Association of Banks (HKAB) and the DTC Association, 'Code of Banking Practice' (February 2015), online: HKAB, www.hkab.org.hk/DisplayArticleAction .do?sid=5&ss=3

[7] The HKAB is a statutory industry body which promotes the interests of licensed banks in Hong Kong and makes rules for the conduct of banking business, in consultation with the Financial Secretary of Hong Kong.

[8] The 'Monetary Authority' is a person appointed by the Financial Secretary under s 5A of the Exchange Fund Ordinance (Cap 66, Laws of Hong Kong) to assist the Financial Secretary in the performance of his functions under the Ordinance, and to perform such other functions as the Financial Secretary may direct or which may be assigned to the Monetary Authority under any other Ordinance.

[9] Under s 2(1) of the BO, *supra* note 4, an AI means '(a) a bank; (b) a restricted licence bank or (c) a deposit-taking company'.

[10] See the definition of 'Customer' in 'Annex I – Useful Definitions' of the Code of Banking Practice, *supra* note 6.

[11] [1901] AC 414.

[12] [1959] 1 QB 55.

a building society, to pay a substantial part of such monies to a company which the plaintiff wished to finance and to retain the balance of the same to the order of the plaintiff. Notwithstanding the fact that the plaintiff had not established an account at the bank at the time, the court held that the relationship of bank and customer existed between the parties from the date those instructions were accepted. These are well-established principles which the courts in Hong Kong would be likely to apply.

The above cases, albeit relevant, may not shed much light on the issue in the context of what can be described as 'nontraditional' banking services. They are not conclusive as to whether a person becomes a customer of a bank only in relation to services provided by the bank that constitutes 'banking business' as defined in the BO,[13] or whether a person can become a customer of a bank in relation to any service provided by that bank that involves maintaining an account of any sort.

8.2.3   Duration and Scope of the Duty

An implied duty of confidentiality arises when a bank–customer relationship commences. However, the duty does not cease when a customer closes his account[14] and it probably continues after a customer's death.[15] In other words, information gained during the currency of the account remains confidential unless one of the qualifications to bank confidentiality discussed later applies to such information.

The duty of confidentiality is not confined to the actual state of the account (i.e. whether there is a debit or credit balance, and the amount of

---

[13] The term 'banking business' is defined in s 2(1) of the BO, *supra* note 4, as:

> The business of either or both of the following:
>
> (a) receiving from the general public money on current, deposit, savings or other similar account repayable on demand or within less than the period specified in item 1 of the First Schedule [of the BO] or with a period of call or notice of less than that period, other than any float or SVF deposit as defined by s 2 of the Payment Systems and Stored Value Facilities Ordinance (Cap 584);
>
> (b) paying or collecting cheques drawn by or paid in by customers.

[14] Bankes LJ stated in *Tournier, supra* note 1 at 473, that:

> I certainly think that the duty does not cease the moment a customer closes his account. Information gained during the currency of the account remains confidential unless released under circumstances bringing the case within one of the classes of qualification I have already referred to.

[15] M. Hapgood QC, *Paget's Law of Banking*, 13th edn (London: LexisNexis Butterworths, 2007) at para. 8.2.

the balance) but extends to information derived from the account itself (i.e. transactions that go through the account).[16] The duty should also extend to other information which is itself in some way referable to the bank–customer relationship even if it is received from persons other than the customer, at least provided that the information is received by the bank in its capacity as banker to the customer.[17]

8.2.4 Consequences of Breach of the Duty

A breach of an express or implied duty of confidentiality by a bank is a breach of a term of the contract between the bank and its customer for which the customer can bring a contractual claim for damages. In addition, the court may grant equitable remedies such as an injunction against the bank and/or its staff prohibiting disclosure of customer information, a breach of which could result in penalties for contempt of court including fines and/or imprisonment.

8.2.5 Other Provisions

Apart from there being an implied contractual duty of confidentiality under common law, banks may choose to enter into confidentiality agreements or undertakings with their customers to create an express contractual obligation of confidentiality.

In addition, a bank's duty of confidentiality is supplemented by, among other things, (i) the Personal Data (Privacy) Ordinance (PDPO)[18] insofar as the customer is a living individual and (ii) the Code of Banking Practice, mentioned earlier.

The PDPO protects the privacy of individuals in relation to their personal data. Personal data is defined in s 2(1) of the PDPO as any data: (i) relating directly or indirectly to a living individual; (ii) from which it

---

[16] See the judgment of Atkin LJ in *Tournier*, *supra* note 1 at 485, and *Christofi* v. *Barclays Bank Plc* [1998] 2 All ER 484 at 488 (upheld on appeal, [1999] 4 All ER 437).

[17] Support for this position can be found in the judgment of Atkin LJ in *Tournier* [1924] 1 KB 461 at 485 where he stated:

> I further think that the obligation extends to information obtained from other sources than the customer's actual account, if the occasion upon which the information was obtained arose out of the banking relations of the bank and its customers – for example, with a view to assisting the bank in conducting the customer's business, or in coming to decisions as to its treatment of its customers.

[18] Cap 486, Laws of Hong Kong.

is practicable for the identity of the individual to be directly or indirectly ascertained and (iii) in a form in which access to or processing of the data is practicable. Among other provisions of the PDPO which protect the personal data privacy of individuals, s 4 provides that a 'data user'[19] shall not do any act, or engage in any practice, that contravenes a data protection principle, of which there are six set out in Schedule 1 to the PDPO. The Office of the Privacy Commissioner for Personal Data in Hong Kong (PCPD), which is an independent statutory body set up to oversee the enforcement of the PDPO, has recently published a guidance note entitled 'Guidance on the Proper Handling of Customers' Personal Data for the Banking Industry'[20] (Banking Industry Guidance) to assist the banking industry in understanding and complying with the relevant requirements under the PDPO as well as promoting good practices in relation to the collection, accuracy, retention, use, security of and access to customers' personal data. According to the Banking Industry Guidance, there is no doubt that a bank is a 'data user' in relation to the personal data of its customers which it holds and, accordingly, banks must observe all the requirements under the PDPO to protect the personal data privacy of their customers.[21]

The six data protection principles in the PDPO set out what the PCPD considers to be fair information practices with which data users must comply in the handling of personal data. These regulate the collection, accuracy, retention, use, security, transparency of policies and practices, as well as access to and correction of personal data. For example, Data Principle 3 provides that personal data shall not be used for any purpose other than the purpose for which the data was collected or a directly related purpose, unless prior 'prescribed consent' has been obtained from the individual who is the subject of the personal data, where 'prescribed consent' means an express consent given voluntarily and which has not been withdrawn in writing.

The Code of Banking Practice provides that banks should treat their customers' and former customers' banking affairs as private and confidential and should at all times comply with the PDPO in the collection, use and holding of customer information.[22] Although the Code of Banking

---

[19] The term 'data user' is defined in the PDPO to mean, in relation to personal data, a person who, either alone or jointly or in common with other persons, controls the collection, holding, processing or use of personal data: s 2(1), PDPO, *supra* note 18.

[20] See Office of the Privacy Commissioner for Personal Data, 'Guidance on the Proper Handling of Customers' Personal Data for the Banking Industry' (October 2014), online: www.pcpd.org.hk/english/publications/files/GN_banking_e.pdf

[21] *Ibid.* at para. 2.2.

[22] Sections 8.1 and 8.2 of the Code of Banking Practice, *supra* note 6.

Practice does not have the force of the law, it has been endorsed by the Monetary Authority which expects all members of HKAB and DTCA in Hong Kong to comply with it. Breaches of the Code of Banking Practice, or indeed the PDPO and the common law duty of confidentiality, may give rise to questions of fitness and propriety and may therefore lead the Monetary Authority to consider supervisory action.

8.3   Qualifications to the Duty of Confidentiality

As mentioned earlier, the duty of confidentiality is not absolute but qualified.[23] The qualifications to the duty of confidentiality are: (i) where disclosure is under compulsion by law; (ii) where there is a duty to the public to disclose; (iii) where the interests of the bank require disclosure and (iv) where the disclosure is made by the express or implied consent of the customer.

8.3.1   Disclosure under Compulsion by Law

This qualification can be dealt with in two categories: (i) compulsion by an order of a court and (ii) compulsion by statute.

8.3.1.1   Compulsion by an Order of a Court

A court may compel a bank to disclose information relating to its customer's account in legal proceedings. Such a court order usually requires a bank official to attend court and to bring with him specified books, documents or letters relating to a customer's affairs. Courts in criminal proceedings generally adopt a cautious approach when exercising this jurisdiction, taking into account matters such as whether there is other evidence in the possession of the prosecution to support the charge.[24] They generally limit the period of the disclosure of the bank account to a period that is strictly relevant to the charge before them. In civil proceedings in Hong Kong, the rule is that the statutory power to order inspection should not be inconsistent with, and not out of reach of, the general law of discovery.

Where a bank is a party to civil proceedings, it is subject to the rules of disclosure, such as the Rules of the High Court,[25] just like any other party. For instance, under Order 24 of the Rules of the High Court, the High

---

[23] *Tournier, supra* note 1 at 472 as applied in Hong Kong by the *FDC* case, *supra* note 3.
[24] D. Campbell, *International Bank Secrecy* (London: Sweet & Maxwell, 1992) at para. 16-010.
[25] Cap 4A, Laws of Hong Kong.

Court has the power to order discovery and inspection of documents. Under that power, the court can make an order for the discovery of documents pertaining to a bank customer's account.

Section 20 of the Evidence Ordinance (EO)[26] sets out provisions relating to the admissibility of any entry or matter recorded in a bank's record as evidence in proceedings. Section 21(1) of the EO provides that the court or a judge, on the application of any party to any proceedings, may order that such party be at liberty to inspect and take copies of entries in a bank's record for the purposes of such proceedings. Section 21(4) of the EO provides that an order made pursuant to s 21(1) of the EO against a bank may be enforced as if the bank were a party to the proceedings.

A bank may also be subject to third-party discovery in some cases. For example, the English case of *Norwich Pharmacal Co* v. *Customs and Excise Commissioners*,[27] which has been followed in Hong Kong, established the principle that a person who, through no fault of his own, gets involved in the tortious acts of others so as to facilitate their wrongdoing, comes under a duty to assist the person who has been wronged by giving him full information and disclosing the identity of the wrongdoers. It is therefore possible for a *Norwich Pharmacal* order to be granted against a bank which has, on the instructions of a customer (the wrongdoer), processed funds that have been misappropriated from another person (the victim).

Hong Kong cases that have applied the *Norwich Pharmacal* principle include *A Co* v. *B Co*,[28] *Kensington International Ltd* v. *ICS Secretaries Ltd*[29] and *Evergreen International Storage & Transportation Corp* v. *Hong Kong and Shanghai Banking Corp Ltd*.[30] These cases highlighted that the granting of the order should be subject to certain conditions and restrictions to avoid 'fishing expeditions' by a plaintiff. They further emphasised that the scope of a disclosure order must be properly restricted in its terms in order to be fair to the innocent third party, namely, that it should: (i) be restricted in time; (ii) identify specific classes of documents necessary for discovery or preservation of assets (i.e. no entitlement to general discovery) and (iii) provide for reimbursement of the expenses of compliance on an indemnity basis. In other words, if a disclosure order is to be made against a bank, its terms must be reasonable and must not be unduly wide.

[26] Cap 8, Laws of Hong Kong.
[27] [1974] AC 133.
[28] [2002] 3 HKLRD 111.
[29] [2007] 3 HKLRD 297.
[30] [2008] 5 HKLRD 49.

Further, in the case of *CTO (HK) Ltd* v. *Li Man Chiu*,[31] it was held that the primary purpose of a discovery order in aid of a *Mareva* injunction[32] was to preserve the assets or property which might otherwise be dissipated notwithstanding the injunction. In that case, it was held that though the court would not lightly use its powers to order disclosure of full information touching the confidential relationship of bank and customer, such an order is justified even at the early interlocutory stages of an action where the plaintiff sought to trace funds which, in equity, belonged to it and of which there was strong evidence that it had been fraudulently deprived and delay might result in the dissipation of the funds before trial. In the case of *Wharf Ltd* v. *Lau Yuen How (No 2)*,[33] Poon J repeated the general principles as considered by Barnett J in *Assets Investments PT Ltd* v. *United Islamic Investments Foundation*,[34] which held that an order pursuant to s 21 of the EO (discussed earlier) will not be made in favour of an applicant unless it can be demonstrated that the other party has a bank account and that there is a probability that such account will contain material germane to an issue which is to be tried between the parties (i.e. the test is relevance).

In the *FDC* case,[35] the Hong Kong Court of Appeal recognised that persons opening accounts with local or foreign banks in Hong Kong were entitled to look to the Hong Kong courts to enforce any obligation of confidentiality. In that case, the defendant was a Hong Kong branch of a foreign bank, and had been ordered by the US court to provide information about the plaintiffs' bank records to the US tax authority in connection with its investigations of alleged tax evasion. Each plaintiff successfully applied to the court for an injunction prohibiting the defendant from providing such information.

8.3.1.2   Compulsion by Statute

The statutory provisions in Hong Kong that either require or permit disclosure of confidential information by banks without the consent of the customers concerned can be divided broadly into the following three

---

[31] [2002] 2 HKLRD 875.
[32] According to the *Butterworths Hong Kong Legal Dictionary* (LexisNexis, 2004) at 593, 'a Mareva injunction is an interlocutory court order restraining a party from removing from the jurisdiction of the court, or otherwise dealing with, assets, whether money or goods, which are the subject of the injunction'.
[33] [2009] 1 HKC 479.
[34] HCA 4392/1993, 21 January 1994 (unreported).
[35] *Supra* note 3.

areas: (i) prevention of crime; (ii) prevention of tax evasion and (iii) regulation of the financial services industry. Some examples that are applicable to banks are set out below.

Prevention of Crime

Drug Trafficking (Recovery of Proceeds) Ordinance   Under s 25A(1) of the Drug Trafficking (Recovery of Proceeds) Ordinance (DTO)[36] a person who knows or suspects that any property represents any person's proceeds of drug trafficking, or was used or is intended to be used in connection with drug trafficking, must disclose that knowledge or suspicion to an 'authorized officer' (for example, a police officer) as soon as it is reasonable for him to do so. Section 25A(3)(a) of the DTO allows for an exception to a bank's duty of confidentiality by specifically providing that disclosure under s 25A(1) shall not be treated as a breach of any restriction upon the disclosure of information imposed by contract or by any enactment, rule of conduct or other provision. Section 25A(5) provides for the offence of 'tipping off': a person who, knowing or suspecting that a disclosure has been made under, *inter alia*, s 25A(1), must not disclose to any other person any matter which is likely to prejudice any investigation which might be conducted following the first-mentioned disclosure.

Organized and Serious Crimes Ordinance   Under s 5(1) of the Organized and Serious Crimes Ordinance (OSCO),[37] an authorized officer may, for the purpose of an investigation into: (i) an organized crime; (ii) the proceeds of organized crime of any person who has committed or is suspected of having committed an organized crime or (iii) the proceeds of a specified offence (for example, trafficking in dangerous drugs, robbery or blackmail) of any person who has committed, or is suspected of having committed that specified offence, apply to the Court of First Instance or the District Court for a warrant in relation to specified premises. The court may issue a warrant authorizing an officer to enter and search the premises if it is satisfied that one of the conditions specified in s 5(2) of the OSCO is met. Section 25A(1) of the OSCO requires a person who knows or suspects that any property represents any person's proceeds of an indictable offence, or was used or is intended to be used in connection with such offence, to disclose this knowledge or suspicion to an authorized officer as soon as it is reasonable for

---

[36] Cap 405, Laws of Hong Kong.
[37] Cap 455, Laws of Hong Kong.

him to do so. As in other statutes compelling disclosure for the prevention of crime, s 25A(3)(a) of the OSCO specifically provides that the disclosure of information referred to in s 25A(1) of the OSCO shall not be treated as a breach of any restriction upon the disclosure of information imposed by contract or by any enactment, rule of conduct or other provision. There is also an offence of tipping-off in s 25A(5) of the OSCO.

United Nations (Anti-Terrorism Measures) Ordinance   Under the United Nations (Anti-Terrorism Measures) Ordinance (UNATMO),[38] s 12(1) requires a person who knows or suspects that any property is terrorist property, to disclose to an authorized officer the information or other matter: (i) on which the knowledge or suspicion is based and (ii) as soon as it is practicable after that information or other matter comes to the person's attention. Section 12(3)(a) of the UNATMO provides that a disclosure referred to in s 12(1) of the UNATMO shall not be treated as a breach of any restriction upon the disclosure of information imposed by contract or by any enactment, rule of conduct or other provision. An offence of tipping-off also exists under s 14(6) of the UNATMO.

Police Force Ordinance   Section 67(1) of the Police Force Ordinance[39] gives the Commissioner of Police of Hong Kong certain powers to seek information where there is reasonable cause to suspect that an indictable offence has been committed and it appears expedient to exercise these powers for the purpose of investigating such offence or apprehending the offender. In such cases, under s 67(1), the Commissioner of Police may require any bank or deposit-taking company to notify him whether: (i) any person has or has had an account in Hong Kong with such bank or deposit-taking company or (ii) in the case of a bank, whether such bank provides or did provide a safety deposit box in Hong Kong for such person, or holds or has held in its custody in Hong Kong any property for such person.

Prevention of Bribery Ordinance   Under s 13(1) of the Prevention of Bribery Ordinance (PBO),[40] the Commissioner of the Independent Commission Against Corruption (the 'Commissioner of the ICAC') has certain powers where he or she is satisfied that there is reasonable cause to believe: (i) that an offence under the PBO may have been committed

---

[38] Cap 575, Laws of Hong Kong.
[39] Cap 232, Laws of Hong Kong.
[40] Cap 201, Laws of Hong Kong.

by any person and (ii) that any share account or other specified accounts and any banker's books, company books, documents or other article of or relating to any person identified by the Commissioner of the ICAC are likely to be relevant for the purposes of an investigation of such offence. In such circumstances, the Commissioner of the ICAC may, under s 13(1), for those purposes investigating such offence, authorize any officer to investigate and inspect such accounts, books or documents or other article. The investigating officer may also require from any person the production of such accounts, books, documents, or other article, as well as the disclosure of all or any information relating thereto, and to take copies of such accounts, books or documents or of any relevant entry therein and photographs of any other article. Under s 14(1)(f) of the PBO, where on an application under s 14(1A) of the PBO the Court of First Instance is satisfied that there are reasonable grounds for suspecting that an offence under the PBO has been committed, the court may make an order authorizing the Commissioner of the ICAC by a notice in writing to require the manager of any bank to give to the investigating officer specified in such notice copies of the accounts of such person or of his spouse, parents or children at the bank as shall be named in the notice.

Anti-Money Laundering and Counter-Terrorist Financing (Financial Institutions) Ordinance   Section 9(1) of the Anti-Money Laundering and Counter-Terrorist Financing (Financial Institutions) Ordinance (AMLO)[41] provides that for the purpose of ascertaining a financial institution's compliance with any provision of the AMLO or any notice, licence or other condition issued under the AMLO,[42] an authorized person may at any reasonable time, *inter alia*: (i) enter the business premises of the financial institution and (ii) inspect and make copies or otherwise record details of, any record or document relating to the business carried on, or any transaction carried out, by the financial institution. Under s 12(2) of the AMLO, an investigator may require a person whom he has reasonable cause to believe to be in possession of any record or document that contains, or is likely to contain, information relevant to an investigation under s 11 of the AMLO to produce any record or document that may be relevant to the investigation and is in the person's possession. Section 12(2) also provides that such person may be required to attend before the investigator and

---

[41] Cap 615, Laws of Hong Kong.
[42] Section 9(2) Anti-Money Laundering and Counter-Terrorist Financing (Financial Institutions) Ordinance (Cap 615, Laws of Hong Kong).

answer any question relating to any matter under investigation, and to give the investigator all other assistance in connection with the investigation that the person is reasonably able to give. Under s 13(1) of the AMLO, a person failing, without reasonable excuse, to comply with a requirement imposed on the person under s 12(2) of the AMLO commits an offence.

Mutual Legal Assistance in Criminal Matters Ordinance   The Mutual Legal Assistance in Criminal Matters Ordinance (MLACMO)[43] facilitates and regulates the provision and obtaining of assistance in criminal matters between Hong Kong and places outside Hong Kong. Such assistance includes the making and receiving of requests for search and seizure of, *inter alia*, documents. Section 5 of the MLACMO sets out circumstances in which a request for assistance from another jurisdiction must be refused. These include circumstances where, in the opinion of the Secretary for Justice of Hong Kong: (i) there are substantial grounds for believing that the request was made for the purpose of prosecuting, punishing or otherwise causing prejudice to a person on account of the person's race, religion, nationality or political opinions or (ii) the granting of the request would seriously impair the essential interests of Hong Kong. As of 19 February 2016, Hong Kong has entered into mutual legal assistance agreements with twenty-nine jurisdictions.[44]

Prevention of Tax Evasion   Pursuant to s 51(4)(a) of the Inland Revenue Ordinance (IRO),[45] an assessor or an inspector may, for the purposes of obtaining full information in regard to any matter which may affect any liability, responsibility or obligation of any person under the IRO, give notice in writing to such person, or to any other person whom he considers may be in possession or control of information or documents in regard to any such matter as aforesaid, requiring him to furnish all information in his possession or control respecting any such matter, and to produce for examination, *inter alia*, any relevant books, accounts, bank statements or other documents. Under s 51(4AA) of the IRO, the powers under s 51(4) are also applicable for the purposes of obtaining full information in regard to any matter that may affect any liability, responsibility or obligation of

---

[43] Cap 525, Laws of Hong Kong.
[44] For the full list of jurisdictions, see Department of Justice, 'List of Mutual Legal Assistance Agreements (Legislative References)' (19 February 2016), online: www.doj.gov.hk/eng/laws/table3ti.html
[45] Cap 112, Laws of Hong Kong.

any person under the laws of a territory outside Hong Kong concerning any tax of that territory if: (i) arrangements having effect under s 49(1A) of the IRO are made with the government of that territory and (ii) that tax is the subject of a provision of the arrangements that requires disclosure of information concerning tax of that territory.

Section 51B(1)(a) of the IRO provides that if the Commissioner of Inland Revenue or an authorized officer satisfies a magistrate that there are reasonable grounds for suspecting that a person has made an incorrect return or supplied false information having the effect of understating his income or profits chargeable to tax and has done so without reasonable excuse and not through an innocent oversight or omission, the magistrate may by warrant authorize the Commissioner of Inland Revenue or an authorized officer, *inter alia*, to enter and have access to any land, buildings or place where he suspects there to be any books, records, accounts or documents of that person, or of any other person, which may afford evidence material in assessing the liability of the first-mentioned person for tax, and there to search for and examine any books, records, accounts or documents. The provisions of s 51B(1) also apply, by virtue of s 51B(1AA) of the IRO, to any tax of a territory outside Hong Kong if: (i) arrangements having effect under s 49(1A) of the IRO are made with the government of that territory and (ii) the tax concerned is the subject of a provision of the arrangements that requires disclosure of information concerning tax of that territory.

Section 4(1) of the IRO provides that except in the performance of his duties under the IRO, every person who has been appointed under the IRO or who is or has been employed in carrying out its provisions shall preserve secrecy with regard to all matters relating to the affairs of any person that may come to his knowledge in the performance of such duties. Section 4(1) further provides that this person shall not communicate any such matter to any person other than the person to whom such matter relates or the authorized representative of such person, nor suffer or permit any person to have access to any records in the possession, custody or control of the Commissioner of Inland Revenue. However, s 4(4) of the IRO provides that notwithstanding anything contained in s 4 of the IRO, the Commissioner of Inland Revenue or authorized officer may communicate any matter which comes to his knowledge, including a copy of any return, accounts or other document submitted to him in connection with the IRO, to specified persons such as the Commissioner of Rating and Valuation and the Collector of Stamp Revenue, among others. Additionally, in respect of arrangements for relief from double taxation and exchange of information having effect under s 49 of the IRO, s 49(5) of the IRO provides that the obligation as to secrecy imposed by s 4 of the IRO shall not prevent the disclosure to any authorized officer of the government with which the arrangements are made, of such information as is required to be disclosed under the arrangements.

Under the Inland Revenue (Disclosure of Information) Rules (IRR),[46] s 4 provides that the Commissioner of Inland Revenue must not disclose any information in response to a disclosure request (i.e. a request for disclosure of information that is made by the government of a territory outside Hong Kong under any arrangements made with that government and having effect under s 49 of the IRO) unless the Commissioner of Inland Revenue is satisfied that the information relates to: (i) the carrying out of the provisions of the relevant arrangements in respect of any period that starts after the arrangements have come into operation or (ii) the administration or enforcement of the tax law of the requesting government's territory in respect of any period that starts after the relevant arrangements have come into operation.

To protect the person who is the subject of a disclosure request, s 5(1) of the IRR requires the Commissioner of Inland Revenue, subject to s 5(5) of the IRR, before any information is disclosed in response to a disclosure request and by a notice in writing given to such person: (i) to notify the person of the nature of the information requested and (ii) to notify the person that the person may request a copy of the information that the Commissioner of Inland Revenue is prepared to disclose to the requesting government. Further protection is afforded under s 5(3)(b) of the IRR which provides that where a person has requested a copy of the information that the Commissioner of Inland Revenue is prepared to disclose to the requesting government, that person may request the Commissioner of Inland Revenue to amend the information or any part of the information on the grounds that: (i) the information or that part of the information does not relate to the person or (ii) the information or that part of the information is factually incorrect. However, s 5(5) of the IRR provides that the Commissioner of Inland Revenue is not required to notify the person concerned under s 5(1) of the IRR if the Commissioner of Inland Revenue has reasonable grounds to believe that, for example, the notification is likely to undermine the chance of success of the investigation in relation to which the request is made.

---

[46] Cap 112BI, Laws of Hong Kong.

Regulation of the Financial Services Industry   Under the BO,[47] s 55(1) provides, among other things, that the Monetary Authority may at any time, with or without prior notice to the AI, examine the books, accounts and transactions of any AI. Where the conditions set out in s 55(2) exist in relation to an AI, for example if there is a request from the shareholders holding more than a specified number of its shares, the Monetary Authority shall investigate the books, accounts and transactions of the AI. Pursuant to s 56(1) of the BO, an AI shall, for the purposes of an examination or investigation under s 55 of the BO, afford the person carrying out the examination or investigation access to its books and accounts, to documents of title to its assets and other documents, to all securities held by it in respect of its customers' transactions and its cash and to such information and facilities as may be required to conduct the examination or investigation. The AI shall also produce to the person carrying out the examination or investigation such books, accounts, documents, securities, cash or other information as he may require.

In addition, the Monetary Authority may, pursuant to s 63(2) of the BO, require an AI to submit such further information as the Monetary Authority may reasonably require for the exercise of the Monetary Authority's functions under the BO. Section 68 of the BO permits an appropriate recognized banking supervisory authority of a place outside Hong Kong, with the approval of the Monetary Authority, to examine, *inter alia*, the books, accounts and transactions of the principal place of business in Hong Kong, or any local branch or local office, of an AI which: (i) is incorporated in that place or in respect of which the Monetary Authority is of the opinion that the authority has primary supervisory responsibility or (ii) is incorporated in or outside Hong Kong and is a subsidiary of a company which is incorporated in that place or in respect of which the Monetary Authority is of the opinion that the authority has primary supervisory responsibility.

Under s 117(1) of the BO, if it appears to the Monetary Authority that it is in the interests of depositors of an AI or a former AI or in the public interest that an inquiry should be made into the affairs, business or property of that institution, the Monetary Authority may make a report to that effect to the Financial Secretary of Hong Kong. On receipt of such a report, the Financial Secretary of Hong Kong may, pursuant to s 117(2) of the BO, appoint a competent person to report to him and the Monetary Authority on the state and conduct of the affairs, business and property of the AI or

---

[47] *Supra* note 4.

former AI concerned. Section 118(3) of the BO provides that it shall be the duty of every director, manager, employee or agent of a company whose affairs, business and property is under investigation, and any person who has in his possession books, papers or information relevant to the investigation: (i) to produce to the inspector all books and papers relating to the company concerned which are in his custody or power; (ii) to attend before the inspector when required to do so and (iii) to answer any questions which may be put to him by the inspector and which are relevant to the investigation.

Section 120(1) of the BO provides that, except as may be necessary for the exercise of any function under the BO or for the carrying into effect the provisions of the BO, any person who is or has been, *inter alia*, a public officer, a person authorized by the Monetary Authority or a person appointed under s 117(2) of the BO shall preserve and aid in preserving secrecy with regard to all matters relating to the affairs of any person that may come to his knowledge in the exercise of any function under the BO. Further, such person shall not communicate any such matter to any person other than the person to whom such matter relates; and shall not permit any person to have access to any records in the possession, custody or control of any person to whom s 120(1) of the BO applies. However, there are a number of gateways of disclosure. Pursuant to s 120(5) of the BO, such duty of secrecy does not apply, for example: (i) to the disclosure of information with a view to the institution of, or otherwise for the purposes of, any criminal proceedings; (ii) in connection with any other legal proceedings arising out of the BO; (iii) to the disclosure of information to the police or the Independent Commission Against Corruption, at the request of the Secretary for Justice of Hong Kong, relevant to the proper investigation of any criminal complaint or (iv) to the disclosure of information to the Anti-Money Laundering and Counter-Terrorist Financing (Financial Institutions) Review Tribunal. The duty of secrecy also does not apply to the disclosure of information by the Monetary Authority to certain Government officials (such as the Chief Executive of Hong Kong and the Financial Secretary of Hong Kong) and a person holding an authorized statutory office (such as the Securities and Futures Commission (the SFC)) where, in the opinion of the Monetary Authority: (i) it is desirable or expedient that information should be so disclosed in the interests of depositors or potential depositors or the public interest or (ii) such disclosure will enable or assist the recipient of the information to exercise his functions and it is not contrary to the interests of depositors or potential depositors or the public interest that the information should be so disclosed.

Additionally, under s 121(1) of the BO, the Monetary Authority may disclose information to an authority in a place outside Hong Kong where that authority exercises functions in that place corresponding to the functions of the Monetary Authority or an authorized statutory office (such as the SFC) and in the opinion of the Monetary Authority: (i) that authority is subject to adequate secrecy provisions in that place; and (ii) it is desirable or expedient that information should be so disclosed in the interests of depositors or potential depositors or the public interest or (iii) such disclosure will enable or assist the recipient of the information to exercise his functions and it is not contrary to the interests of depositors or potential depositors or the public interest that the information should be so disclosed. However, where any disclosure of information made pursuant to s 121(1) of the BO relates to the affairs of any individual customer of an AI or a local representative office, the Monetary Authority is obliged pursuant to s 121(3)(b) of the BO to attach a condition that neither: (i) the person to whom the information has been disclosed nor (ii) any person obtaining or receiving the information (whether directly or indirectly) from the person referred to in (i), shall disclose that information to any other person without the consent of the Monetary Authority.

8.3.2   Duty to the Public to Disclose

Instances of this qualification to the duty of confidentiality would occur in cases where a public duty to disclose outweighs the private right to confidentiality, though it has been suggested that the dividing line between a state or public duty and a private duty is hard to define.[48] Whilst the qualification 'may have been thought to have a relatively narrow compass when originally formulated in *Tournier*', Proctor suggests that the qualification may be invoked to deal with a number of situations arising in a cross-border context and to which the 'compulsion by law' qualification does not necessarily apply (for example, major cases of corruption, terrorism and money laundering in connection with which a reputable bank might not wish to be seen to be withholding relevant information even though there may not be a positive obligation to disclose information).[49]

In *Libyan Arab Foreign Bank* v. *Bankers Trust Co*,[50] the defendant bank disclosed payment instructions from the plaintiff customer to, and at

---

[48] *Paget's Law of Banking, supra* note 15 at para. 8.4.
[49] C. Proctor, *The Law and Practice of International Banking* (Oxford University Press, 2016) at paras. 42.49-55.
[50] [1989] QB 728.

the request of, the Federal Reserve Bank of New York. It should be noted that the court specifically rejected the arguments that such disclosure could be justified by reference either to the interests of the bank or the implied consent of the customer. Staughton J was prepared to reach a tentative conclusion that the duty to the public qualification applied. However, he did not find it necessary to reach a final conclusion on the point as he held that 'any breach of confidence there may have been caused [the plaintiff] no loss'.[51]

In the case of *Pharaon* v. *Bank of Credit and Commerce International SA (in liquidation)*,[52] as part of the discovery process in litigation proceedings in the United States, a subpoena was issued in New York against an audit firm based in the United Kingdom for the production of documents in connection with its involvement in the group audits of Bank of Credit and Commerce International SA (BCCI) before BCCI entered into liquidation. In balancing the clear public interest in upholding the duty of confidentiality owed by the audit firm to customers of BCCI and 'the public interest in co-operating with the US courts in their effort to see that justice is done in the US proceedings . . . involving as those proceedings do, allegations . . . of serious wrongdoing, and being proceedings which, if successful, will result in significant further recoveries for the benefit of the hapless BCCI depositors',[53] the court held that the latter outweighed the public interest in preserving confidentiality, provided that the disclosure 'goes no further than is reasonably necessary to achieve the purpose of that public interest in disclosure'.[54]

In the Hong Kong case of *Lai Mei Chun Swana* v. *Lai Chung Kong*[55] in 2011, the court considered that it is always a balancing exercise between the confidentiality which the courts wish to protect and the interest of the public not to allow anyone to hide behind the protection of confidentiality to commit crime and create insecurity in society.[56] On the facts of that case, the court was not convinced that because of some missing information in an affidavit used in a dispute between private individuals, it was in the interest of the public to allow a person to breach his duty of confidence by disclosing a bank statement relating to another person.

---

[51] *Ibid.* at 771D.
[52] [1998] 4 All ER 455.
[53] *Ibid.* at 464.
[54] *Ibid.* at 465.
[55] [2011] HKEC 545.
[56] *Ibid.* at para. 70.

8.3.3   In the Interest of the Bank to Disclose

On the face of it, Bankes LJ's formulation of this qualification in *Tournier* (i.e. 'where the interests of the bank require disclosure')[57] seems to be so widely expressed that it may cover any disclosure that is to the bank's advantage. However, the formulation given by Atkin LJ[58] and Scrutton LJ[59] and the example given in that case (i.e. suing on an overdraft)[60] do not appear to support such a wide interpretation. Where disclosure is justified under this qualification, it must be limited strictly to information necessary to protect the bank's interest.[61] In *Sunderland* v. *Barclays Bank Limited*,[62] the bank had dishonoured the plaintiff's cheque. The plaintiff complained to her husband who, during a conversation with the bank, was told that most cheques passing through the plaintiff's account were in favour of bookmakers. The plaintiff regarded this disclosure by the bank as a breach of the bank's duty to maintain confidentiality concerning her affairs. The plaintiff lost in her claim for bank confidentiality because it was held that the interests of the bank required disclosure (as an explanation was demanded for what the husband thought to be discourteous conduct on the part of the bank) and that it might be said that the disclosure was made with the customer's implied consent since the husband joined the conversation that the plaintiff had with the bank.

As seen from the example given in *Tournier* (i.e. suing on an overdraft), disclosure will be necessary and permissible under this qualification if there is litigation between the bank and its customer, in which case the bank has to disclose in the pleadings the state of the customer's account and the amount owed by the customer to the bank. It has been suggested that it could be permissible to disclose information under this qualification in the situation where a customer borrows money on a guarantee given by another.[63] In that situation, the bank may wish to disclose certain

---

[57] *Tournier, supra* note 1 at 473 (Bankes LJ).

[58] In *Tournier*, Atkin LJ (at 486) described this qualification as follows: 'the bank [has] the right to disclose such information when, and to the extent to which it is reasonably necessary for the protection of the bank's interests.'

[59] In *Tournier*, Scrutton LJ (at 481) described this qualification as follows: 'the bank may disclose the customer's account and affairs to an extent reasonable and proper for its own protection.'

[60] *Ibid.* at 473 (Bankes LJ) and 481 (Scrutton LJ).

[61] F.W. Neate and G. Godfrey, *Neate and Godfrey: Bank Confidentiality*, 5th edn (London: Bloomsbury Professional, 2011) at para. 11.7.

[62] (1938) 5 LDAB 163.

[63] *Bank Confidentiality, supra* note 61 at paras. 2.31 and 2.33.

information containing the customer's account to a guarantor or prospective guarantor.

This qualification has been considered in the *FDC* case.[64] In that case, each plaintiff (being a customer of the Hong Kong branch of the defendant bank) applied for and obtained in Hong Kong an interim injunction against the bank to restrain it from disclosing bank records of that plaintiff to the United States Internal Revenue Service in compliance with a court order of the United States Federal District Court compelling production of those records. The bank applied to the High Court of Hong Kong to have those injunctions discharged and argued that it was in the interest of the bank to disclose the information as it would otherwise be in contempt of the court in the United States. This argument was rejected by the Hong Kong Court of Appeal on the ground that the bank's interest in disclosure was of a different character to that contemplated in *Tournier*. The court held that this qualification to bank confidentiality applied only in respect of the interests of ordinary banking practice which are narrow in nature, such as when it is 'necessary to sue upon an overdraft or matters of that kind'.[65]

8.3.4   Disclosure with Consent

A customer's consent may be express or implied and it may be given to disclose the general state of the customer's account or only such information as is specified by the customer. If a bank were to notify its customer and state clearly what it proposed to disclose, to whom and why, and actually receive the customer's consent, then there would be no breach of the duty of confidentiality if the customer's information were disclosed pursuant to that consent. However, if the notice of proposed disclosure given by a bank to a customer is not replied to, the bank cannot be entitled to assume that the customer has impliedly consented. Moreover, a customer is entitled to withdraw his consent at any time prior to the bank making disclosure.[66]

An instance of such qualification is where the customer authorises his bank to provide a reference. In *Turner v. Royal Bank of Scotland plc*,[67] it was held that the defendant bank was in breach of its duty of confidentiality as it had given an unfavourable credit reference to another bank without its customer's express consent. The court held that the bank could not

---

[64] *Supra* note 3.
[65] *Ibid.* at 292 (Silke JA).
[66] *International Bank Secrecy, supra* note 24 at para. 16-007.
[67] [1999] 2 All ER (Comm) 664.

simply rely on the implied consent of the customer to the general practice of banks to give information on their customers' credit-worthiness in response to status inquiries from other banks given when the customer opened its bank account. It was held that the customers were entitled to have the state of their accounts treated as confidential by banks and that the customers could not be deprived of that right by banks establishing a practice among themselves.

Given that implied consent can be difficult to prove and may easily be argued to have been withdrawn, a practical solution would be for banks to require their customers to give express consent in writing prior to any disclosure by the banks of any confidential information.

In Hong Kong, the PCPD has issued a code of practice entitled 'Code of Practice on Consumer Credit Data'[68] (Credit Data Code) pursuant to the PDPO to provide practical guidance to data users in Hong Kong in the handling of consumer credit data. It deals with collection, accuracy, use, security and access and correction issues as they relate to personal data of individuals who are, or have been, applicants for consumer credit. The Credit Data Code covers, on the one hand, credit reference agencies, and on the other hand, credit providers (including banks) in their dealing with credit reference agencies and debt collection agencies. For example, where consumer credit data is collected in relation to a mortgage loan, under the Credit Data Code,[69] a credit provider shall not provide the mortgage account general data[70] of any account relating to an existing mortgage loan or mortgage application data[71] to a credit reference agency unless the credit provider has obtained the prescribed consent[72] of the individual to whom the data relates for disclosure of the relevant data to the credit

---

[68] See the Office of the Privacy Commissioner for Personal Data, 'Code of Practice on Consumer Credit Data' (January 2013), online: www.pcpd.org.hk/english/ordinance/files/CCDCode_2013_e.pdf

[69] *Ibid.*, cl. 2.4.4A.2(i).

[70] Under cl. 2.4.4A of the Credit Data Code, 'mortgage account general data' means the following information: name of the individual; capacity of the individual (i.e. whether as borrower, mortgagor or guarantor); Hong Kong Identity Card Number or travel document number; date of birth; address; account number; type of the facility; account status (active, closed, write-off, etc.) and account closed date.

[71] Under cl. 2.4.4B of the Credit Data Code, 'mortgage application data' means the fact that the individual has made an application for mortgage loan.

[72] Under cl. 1.24 of the Credit Data Code, 'prescribed consent' means the express consent of an individual given voluntarily but does not include any consent which has been withdrawn by notice in writing served on the person to whom the consent has been given (but without prejudice to so much of that act that has been done pursuant to the consent at any time before the notice is so served).

reference agency. A breach of the Credit Data Code by a data user will give rise to a presumption against the data user in any legal proceedings under the PDPO. Aside from legal proceedings, a failure to observe a code of practice by a data user will weigh unfavourably against the data user in any case brought before the PCPD.

8.4   Recent Developments in Hong Kong

To a significant extent, it is not an option for the customer to dictate how much or how little personal information he gives to his bank. As a result of the international focus on transparency in the area of bank confidentiality for the purpose of combatting crimes, it is difficult, if not impossible, in many jurisdictions not to provide considerable amounts of personal information before obtaining banking services.

As part of its efforts in the global fight to combat tax evasion and maintain the integrity of tax systems, Hong Kong entered into a Tax Information Exchange Agreement (TIEA) with the United States on 25 March 2014, and the Inland Revenue (Exchange of Information relating to Taxes) (United States of America) Order[73] which gave effect to that TIEA came into operation on 20 June 2014. Subsequent TIEAs were entered into with Denmark, the Faroes, Greenland, Iceland, Norway and Sweden on 22 August 2014.[74] The TIEAs provide for the effective exchange of information between Hong Kong and its TIEA partners and also enhance Hong Kong's ability to administer and enforce its domestic tax laws. Apart from such TIEAs, Hong Kong has also concluded over forty comprehensive double taxation agreements (CDTA) with various jurisdictions[75] to prevent double taxation and fiscal evasion, and foster cooperation between Hong Kong and other international tax administrations by enforcing their respective tax laws.

The signed TIEAs and CDTAs provide the legal basis for Hong Kong to implement the international standard on automatic exchange of financial account information in tax matters (AEOI) pursuant to a newly established legislative framework under the IRO which came into effect in

---

[73] Cap 112CK, Laws of Hong Kong.
[74] See Inland Revenue Department, 'Tax Information Exchange Agreements concluded' (Revised on 2 March 2016), online: www.ird.gov.hk/eng/tax/dta_tiea_agreement.htm.
[75] See Inland Revenue Department, 'Comprehensive Double Taxation Agreements concluded' (Revised on 17 January 2017), online: www.ird.gov.hk/eng/tax/dta_inc.htm

June 2016. Under the new legal framework, financial institutions are required to identify financial accounts held by tax residents of reportable jurisdictions (i.e. tax residents who are liable to tax by reason of residence in the jurisdictions with which Hong Kong has entered into an AEOI agreement) in accordance with prescribed due diligence procedures. They are required to collect the reportable information of these accounts and furnish such information to the Inland Revenue Department which will exchange the information with the tax authorities of relevant AEOI partner jurisdictions on an annual basis.[76]

In terms of the US Foreign Account Tax Compliance Act (FATCA) which has garnered much international and domestic attention recently, Hong Kong and the United States signed an intergovernmental agreement on 13 November 2014 (HKIGA).[77] Hong Kong has opted for a 'Model II' intergovernmental agreement and under the HKIGA, financial institutions in Hong Kong will need to register and conclude separate individual agreements with the US Internal Revenue Service. Under those individual agreements, the financial institutions will need to seek the consent of their account holders who are US taxpayers for reporting their account information to the US Inland Revenue Service annually.

These recent arrangements in Hong Kong have been made (and undoubtedly similar future developments in Hong Kong will take place) with the aim of cultivating a more comprehensive legal and regulatory environment for the banking industry in Hong Kong. Views have been expressed that these changes might adversely affect banking business in Hong Kong, such as potentially causing a decrease in the number of high-net-worth individuals using private banks in Hong Kong to avoid disclosure.[78] However, it is suggested that regardless of the challenges, a more robust regulatory regime which complements developments in the international arena will serve only to strengthen and consolidate Hong Kong's role as a leading international financial centre.

Despite the changes and challenges in the area of bank confidentiality and the increased focus on cross-border information exchange, Hong

---

[76] See Inland Revenue Department, 'Automatic Exchange of Financial Account Information' (Revised on 30 December 2016), online: www.ird.gov.hk/eng/tax/dta_aeoi.htm

[77] See the press release of the Hong Kong Government, 'HK and US sign agreement to facilitate compliance with FATCA by financial institutions in HK (with photos)' (13 November 2014), online: www.info.gov.hk/gia/general/201411/13/P201411130432.htm

[78] Toh Han Shih, 'Data exchange to combat tax evasion seen affecting Hong Kong private banks' (7 July 2014), online: South China Morning Post, www.scmp.com/business/banking-finance/article/1548288/data-exchange-combat-tax-evasion-seen-affecting-hong-kong

Kong has increased its ranking to come second among other jurisdictions in the 2015 Financial Secrecy Index (compared to third in 2013 and fourth in 2011) published by the Tax Justice Network,[79] even with a slight drop in its 'secrecy score' from 73 in the 2011 index[80] to 72 in the 2013 and 2015[81] indexes. This indicates that Hong Kong has managed to maintain an exceptionally high level of financial confidentiality, exemplified by the enactment of safeguards and protections on information disclosure discussed earlier. In other words, bank confidentiality in Hong Kong has been maintained hand in hand with, rather than at the expense of, Hong Kong fulfilling its international obligations in the fight against financial crime and tax evasion.

In terms of Hong Kong's anti-money laundering regime, following the enactment of the AMLO in April 2012 and the issuance of a revised guideline entitled 'Guideline on Anti-Money Laundering and Counter-Terrorist Financing' by the Monetary Authority in July 2012,[82] the Financial Action Task Force (FATF) in October 2012 recognised that Hong Kong has made significant progress in addressing the deficiencies identified in its 2008 Mutual Evaluation Report and agreed that Hong Kong should report on any further improvements to its anti-money laundering/combating the financing of terrorism system to FATF biennially rather than under the previously applicable regular follow-up process.[83] The Monetary Authority attaches great importance to maintaining effective anti-money laundering controls and has significantly strengthened resources dedicated to anti-money laundering supervision. The Monetary Authority is strongly committed to Hong Kong's continuing efforts to strengthen its anti-money laundering regime to meet international standards and obligations.

Looking ahead, Hong Kong can therefore be expected to continue to focus on both cross-border cooperation in relation to tax matters, as well as anti-money laundering and counter-terrorist financing. Although

---

[79] See Tax Justice Network, 'Financial Secrecy Index' (2015), online: www.financialsecrecyindex.com/introduction

[80] See Tax Justice Network, 'FSI Rankings 2011' (2011), online: http://financialsecrecyindex.com/Archive2011/FSI-2011/FSI-Rankings.pdf

[81] See the 2015 index at Tax Justice Network, 'Financial Secrecy Index – 2015 Results' (2015), online: www.financialsecrecyindex.com/introduction/fsi-2015-results

[82] See Hong Kong Monetary Authority, 'Guideline on Anti-Money Laundering and Counter-Terrorist Financing' (Revised in March 2015), online: www.hkma.gov.hk/media/eng/doc/key-information/guidelines-and-circular/guideline/g33.pdf

[83] See Financial Action Task Force, '4th Follow-up report to the Mutual Evaluation of Hong Kong, China' (19 October 2012), online: www.fatf-gafi.org/media/fatf/documents/reports/Follow%20up%20report%20MER%20Hong%20Kong%20China.pdf

the focus on, and anticipated changes in, these areas will have implications for the banking industry and bank confidentiality in Hong Kong, past indications show that Hong Kong will be unlikely to neglect the importance of appropriate bank confidentiality in the process.

8.5   Future Challenges for Banks in Hong Kong

The recent development and conclusions of bilateral agreements between various jurisdictions around the world and the United States on the exchange of tax information in compliance with FATCA have added to the obligations of banks to disclose information to foreign jurisdictions. Banks in Hong Kong, as with banks elsewhere around the world, therefore face increasing cross-border challenges in the area of bank confidentiality and must be prepared for the changes to and effects of laws and regulations.

Concurrent with the development and changes in the laws and regulations in this area, financial institutions face increasing regulatory compliance obligations for themselves, such as compliance with anti-money laundering requirements and FATCA regulations. To further complicate matters for financial institutions, the constant evolution and espousal of international standards necessitate compliance with ever-changing regulatory developments and requirements.

However, it is worth noting that the banking industry in Hong Kong has embraced such changes and has proactively worked with the relevant Hong Kong regulators in managing them. For example, the HKAB has worked closely with the PCPD in reflecting the banking industry's views and making recommendations[84] on the PCPD's guidance note entitled 'Guidance on the Collection and Use of Personal Data in Direct Marketing'.[85] In early 2014, the HKAB issued a public statement on behalf of the banking industry in Hong Kong supporting the principles of the voluntary Privacy Management Programme launched by the PCPD to further promote sound practices for the protection of personal data privacy. The HKAB stated that the banking industry 'endeavours to demonstrate a high level of accountability and transparency in personal data protection,

---

[84] See the press release of the HKAB, 'Banking Industry Responds to Guidance on the Collection and Use of Personal Data in Direct Marketing' (20 October 2010), online: www .hkab.org.hk/DisplayWhatsNewsAction.do?ss=1&id=1230

[85] See Office of the Privacy Commissioner for Personal Data, 'Guidance on the Collection and Use of Personal Data in Direct Marketing' (Revised in November 2012), online: www .pcpd.org.hk/english/publications/files/DM_e.pdf

as part of our concerted efforts to maintain Hong Kong as an international financial centre.'[86] In its public statement, the HKAB said that individual banks will take necessary steps having regard to their own privacy protection framework to implement the principles of the Privacy Management Programme, which include, *inter alia*, obtaining top management support, appointing or designating a data protection officer, establishing reporting mechanisms, putting in place policies for the collection, retention, use and security of personal data and assessing and revising such programme controls where necessary on an ongoing basis.

In October 2014, in the light of the developments of the banking industry and technologies over the past several years, the Monetary Authority issued a circular concerning customer data protection[87] (Circular) to all AIs to update guidance set out in an earlier circular issued in July 2008 to remind AIs of the importance of protecting the confidentiality of customer data and some key control measures for customer data protection. The Circular reminded AIs to ensure a high degree of alertness among staff members in protecting customer data and to implement 'layers' of security controls (covering both IT and non-IT controls) to prevent and detect any loss or leakage of customer data. In particular, the Circular provided elaboration of the following control measures for preventing and detecting the loss or leakage of customer data: (i) data classification and risk assessment; (ii) data security policies and awareness; (iii) logical access controls of customer data; (iv) controls over transmission of consumer data; (v) controls over storage of customer data; (vi) controls over personally owned computing devices; (vii) physical security controls over and office environment related to customer data; (viii) periodic audits over customer data protection and (ix) other controls over service providers.

Given the importance of protecting customer data, the Monetary Authority expects AIs to complete a critical review of the adequacy of their existing controls for customer data protection by Q1 2015, having regard to the guidance set out in the Circular as well as other relevant Supervisory Policy Manual modules and circulars issued by the Monetary Authority. Where the outcomes of their reviews reveal any discrepancies or areas for

---

[86] See the press release of the HKAB, 'Privacy Management Programme (PMP)' (18 February 2014), online: www.hkab.org.hk/DisplayWhatsNewsAction.do?ss=1&id=2276
[87] See Hong Kong Monetary Authority, 'Customer Data Protection' (14 October 2014), online: www.hkma.gov.hk/media/eng/doc/key-information/guidelines-and-circular/2014/20141014e1.pdf

improvements, the Monetary Authority expects AIs to implement appropriate measures promptly to strengthen the relevant controls.

8.6 Conclusion

This chapter argues that Hong Kong has effective and robust safeguard measures for protecting the privacy of bank customers. The banking industry in Hong Kong is highly aware of the need to maintain the confidentiality of customers' affairs and to demonstrate a high level of accountability and transparency in personal data protection. In that regard, the banking industry has proactively worked with authorities on the developments in this area.

Such safeguards are however balanced by Hong Kong's international obligations to assist in the fight against financial crime, demonstrated by the recent enactment of the AMLO and the conclusion of recent tax agreements with various overseas jurisdictions incorporating tax evasion provisions. In this area, Hong Kong continues to monitor international developments and consider local reforms.

It is submitted that the maintenance of bank confidentiality on the one hand and the combat against financial crime on the other is not a zero-sum game. Transparency is clearly necessary and is part of regulatory efforts worldwide to combat financial crime, from which banking customers, the banking industry and society in general in Hong Kong benefit. Despite the increased gateways for the disclosure of tax or banking information, the gain in terms of transparency will help to prevent Hong Kong from being used in the commission of international financial crime and has ensured that Hong Kong stays on par with its peers in this regard. Further, Hong Kong has ensured that there are inbuilt limitations to maintain an appropriate level of confidentiality in relation to the customer's relationship with his bank.

Japan

REIKO OMACHI

9.1 Introduction

Like many other countries, in Japan, the principle of bank secrecy means the bank's obligation not to leak or disclose customer information, and, at the same time, it means a kind of privilege to keep customer information confidential against the national authority. By asserting that a bank has the duty of keeping customer secrecy, the bank is exceptionally allowed to refuse orders to submit customer information to the national authority. Therefore, it can be considered that bank secrecy is meaningful to maintain a good relationship between a bank and its customers and to protect the bank's know-how on credit accommodation. However, on a practical level, bank secrecy has not been legislated in Japan, and there have been only a few cases in which a bank has opposed the national authority for the disclosure of customer information.[1]

In recent decades, influenced by the international anti-money laundering movement or exchange of information (EOI) for tax collection, the national authority has had more opportunities to request banks to disclose customer information. Considering that bank secrecy includes the right and duty of a bank to keep customer information confidential against the

I would like to express thanks to my colleagues Akihiro Wani and Yosuke Unami.

[1] Generally speaking, there have been many cases in Japan where corporations, hospitals or municipal governments, etc. were sued by its customer claiming compensation for damage arising from the leakage of customer information. However, before the enactment of the Personal Information Protection Act (see Section 9.4.4), such cases were much fewer than today. Before the enactment of the Personal Information Protection Act, the alleged claims were usually based on the general principle of tort under the Civil Code and if the bank leaked the customer information, the principle of 'bank secrecy' might have been referred to in such cases but it was not common. Enactment of the Personal Information Protection Act has greatly contributed to the increase in cases where customers claim compensation for the damage arising from the leakage of customer information.

national authority, the legality of the requests made by the national authority could be doubted from the perspective of bank secrecy. In fact, however, such requests for disclosure seem to have been addressed smoothly without any attempt to question their legality.

There are two reasons for this. The first reason is that as long as there is a domestic law requiring the disclosure, such disclosure has long been accepted as an exception to bank secrecy. With respect to the implementation of new domestic laws or treaties requiring disclosure from banks for anti-money laundering or taxation purposes, generally speaking, there has been no major movement of resistance. Now there is domestic law requiring the disclosure for these purposes, and banks do not have to fear a customer-claim for damages arising from the disclosure; there is no need to rely on bank secrecy in these circumstances.

The second reason is that, since around 2000, the principle of bank secrecy itself has not been discussed much in Japan. The national authority has regulated the management of customer information strictly since 2000, affected by the international movement for the protection of personal information. The Personal Information Protection Act and other relevant laws and guidelines have provided for the proper management of customer information clearly, specifically, and in detail. These laws and regulations enacted in the 2000s have restricted banks from disclosing customer information to a third party, and a 'third party' herein can be considered to include the national authority. There is a crossover between the laws regarding personal information protection and the principle of bank secrecy in that the bank is obliged under both to keep customer information secret. For this reason, since around 2000, banks' interest has shifted from bank secrecy to the requirements under the Personal Information Protection Act and other regulations established in the 2000s.

Obviously, many banks in Japan have a considerable interest in the management of customer information for compliance with laws and regulations. The management of customer information has become an important and unavoidable issue for banks and, in fact, banks have invested a lot of time and cost to secure and improve the management of customer information. However, it is evident that there has not been as much discussion of bank secrecy in recent years.

This chapter examines the reason why the principle of bank secrecy has not been topical recently even though banks are very conscious of customer information management. For this purpose, first this chapter provides an overview of the banking system in Japan and an outline of the principle of bank secrecy, together with relevant judicial precedents. Secondly, this chapter discusses the laws and regulations that were recently enacted for the implementation of a new protection system of privacy and which have influenced banks in regard to the management of customer information. Then, looking at such recent legislation concerning the management of customer information, this chapter attempts to consider the meaning of the principle of bank secrecy and the relationship between bank secrecy and such legislation.

9.2   Overview of the Banking System in Japan

The traditional banking system in Japan is a commercial banking system, which means that a bank accepts deposits, extends loans to businesses and deals in transfers of funds. Most banks are corporations that have been established under the Companies Act[2] and have a license to conduct banking business in accordance with the Banking Act.[3] Banks in Japan can be divided into several categories, based on their business function or historical background. According to the Japanese Bankers Association, there are 5 city banks, 105 regional banks, 16 trust banks, 51 foreign banks and 13 other banks including internet banks which are full members or associate members of the Japanese Bankers Association as of 1 November 2016.[4]

Businesses permitted to operate as banks are defined primarily in the Banking Act. Typical banking activities stipulated in the Banking Act[5] are (i) taking deposits and instalment savings, (ii) lending and discounting bills and notes and (iii) transferring funds. In addition, ancillary activities are permitted under the Banking Act, such as (i) guarantees and bill acceptance, (ii) trading securities and securities derivatives, (iii) securities lending, (iv) underwriting government bonds, (v) factoring and ceding of monetary claims, (vi) arranging private placements and (vii) subscription agency services for local government, corporate and other bonds.[6]

In Japan, the Financial Services Agency (FSA) serves as the regulatory authority of financial institutions including banks. The Banking Act empowers the Commissioner of the FSA to demand reports and materials

---

[2] Act No. 86 of 2005.
[3] *Ginko Ho* [Banking Act], Act No. 59 of 1981. English translation available online: www .japaneselawtranslation.go.jp/law/detail/?id=1870&vm=04&re=02
[4] The Japanese Bankers Association publishes the number and names of member banks: Japanese Bankers Association, 'List of Members' (1 November 2015), online: www .zenginkyo.or.jp/en/outline/list-of-members/
[5] Banking Act, *supra* note 3, Art. 2, para. 2.
[6] *Ibid.*, Art. 10, para. 2.

concerning the business or financial condition of a bank, to conduct on-site inspections at bank premises, to issue an administrative order, to penalise misconduct and to order a bank to maintain a certain amount of assets within Japan. The Banking Act delegates detailed provisions for its enforcement to the Cabinet Order and the Cabinet Office Ordinances.[7] Furthermore, the FSA issues guidelines and supervisory policies in order to show its interpretation of the Banking Act.

The most important guidelines are the Comprehensive Guidelines for Supervision of Major Banks, etc.[8] (the 'Guidelines for Supervision'). The purpose of these Guidelines for Supervision is to prescribe specific points for officials involved in the administrative evaluation or supervision of major banks in order to achieve fair evaluation and supervision and to promote proper operations by major banks. The Guidelines for Supervision list requirements that a bank should satisfy for orderly banking transactions, sufficient protection for depositors and appropriate financing activities.

The Inspection Manual for Deposit-Taking Institutions[9] (the 'Inspection Manual') is another important guideline formulated as a handbook for the FSA inspectors who inspect financial institutions.

The Guidelines for Supervision and the Inspection Manual are very useful in understanding the FSA's interpretation of the Banking Act, although it is important to keep in mind that both assume that the fundamental policy of the FSA is to encourage that each bank formulate its own rules voluntarily for effective self-assessment and risk management. As a whole, the FSA aims to move from a rules-based regulatory style to a principles-based style under the banner of 'Better Regulation'.[10]

---

[7] *Ginko Ho Seko Rei* [Order for Enforcement of Banking Act], Cabinet Order No. 40 of 1982 and *Ginko Ho Seko Kisoku* [Ordinance for Enforcement of the Banking Act], Ordinance of the Ministry of Finance No. 10 of 1982. A Cabinet Order or a Cabinet Office Ordinance is an order that is enacted by the Cabinet (including Ministries constituting the Cabinet) to implement the Act and/or the Cabinet Order.

[8] *Shuyoko Tou Muke no Sogoteki na Kantoku Shishin* [Comprehensive Guidelines for Supervision of Major Banks, etc.], Financial Services Agency, online: www.fsa.go.jp/common/law/guide/gaigin.pdf. For smaller or regional banks, the FSA also has issued the Comprehensive Guidelines for Supervision of Regional Financial Institutions.

[9] *Yokin Tou Ukeire Kinyu Kikan ni Kakaru Kensa Manyualu ni Tsuite* [Inspection Manual for Deposit-Taking Institutions], Financial Services Agency, online: www.fsa.go.jp/en/refer/manual/yokin_e/y-all.pdf

[10] See Financial Services Agency, 'Better Regulation: Improving the Quality of Financial Regulation' (2016), online: www.fsa.go.jp/en/policy/iqfrs

9.3   General Principles of Bank Secrecy

9.3.1   Traditional and Conventional Views on Bank Secrecy

9.3.1.1   The Legal Basis for Bank Secrecy

In Japan, it has generally been understood that banks and other financial institutions are not allowed to provide any information obtained in connection with transactions or other business relationships with a customer, to a third party unless there are justifiable grounds.[11] Although this obligation of financial institutions has not been legislated in statutory law, there are a number of judicial precedents[12] which have held that banks or other financial institutions are responsible for keeping customer information confidential from third parties. There exists no view that is inconsistent with the banks' responsibility as indicated by those precedents, and this principle is known as 'ginko himitsu' or 'bank secrecy' in Japan.

Usually, a customer who is entering into a contract with a financial institution expects and trusts that a financial institution will not provide the customer's information to a third party. Therefore, it is widely held that such expectations and trust should be protected by making financial institutions take legal responsibility for maintaining secrecy. It may be said that not only financial institutions but also any persons engaging in business should not provide information learned in the course of its business to a third party. However, the information obtained by a financial institution frequently relates to financial standing or financial credibility of the customer, which is valuable information that customers do not want others to know. For this reason, the responsibility of financial institutions for keeping secrecy has been established as a legal duty, and not merely a moral obligation. At the same time, this obligation means financial institutions have a right to keep customer information confidential. By asserting that a bank has the duty of keeping secrecy, the bank is exceptionally allowed to refuse orders to submit customer information to the national authority. Such rights and responsibilities of the bank constitute 'bank secrecy'.[13]

---

[11] Kanichi Nishihara, *Kinyuho* [Finance Law], Yuhikaku, 1968 at 76. Masafumi Yamane, *Ginko no Himitsu Hoji Gimu to Rippoka no Doko* [The Principle and the Enactment of Bank Secrecy], 1257 Kinyu-homu Jijo 7 (1990).

[12] Supreme Court, 11 December, 2007, 61 Minshu 3364.

[13] Shozo Yoshihara, Toshiaki Hasegawa and Shohei Dozono, *Minji Tetsuduki ni Okeru Ginko no Shuhi Gimu* [Bank Secrecy in Civil Procedures], 1482 Kinyu-homu Jijo 27 (1997). Junta Utsumi, *Kinyu Kikan no Shuhi Gimu* [The Responsibility of Financial Institutions for Secrecy]. 1802 Kinyu-homu Jijo 8 (2007).

As stated earlier, these rights and obligations of financial institutions have not been specifically set out in any legislation. There have been different views of their legal basis:

- Customary law: There is a long-standing custom that financial institutions keep customer information confidential, and such custom has become legally binding.
- Duty of loyalty: A financial institution is required to be loyal to customers because it has to act as a good manager of customer assets under Japanese law, which includes the duty of a financial institution to keep customer information confidential.
- Contractual duty: A financial institution naturally has an obligation to keep customer information confidential based on a contract between itself and its customer regardless of whether that obligation is expressed in the contract or implied.[14]

The legal basis for bank secrecy has not been discussed very much recently, because, whatever legal basis is taken, it is broadly understood that a bank is liable in tort or for breach of contract if it breaches the duty of secrecy and must compensate for the damages caused.[15] For this reason, courts do not attempt to explain or establish the definition, the scope or the legal basis of bank secrecy in their rulings because they can reach a conclusion without them. Rather, courts tend to determine whether a bank was responsible on a case-by-case basis by examining whether the customer had given an approval or whether there were any other sufficient reasons for the disclosure.

9.3.1.2   Scope of Bank Secrecy

A wide range of customer information is protected by bank secrecy, including financial condition, credit standing, the presence and the terms of deposits or other transactions, business status and personal matters. While it is clear that banks or other financial institutions are generally not allowed to disclose such information to a third party, this obligation has been neither specifically set out in any Japanese legislation, nor frequently pronounced on by the courts. This means that the boundaries and scope of Japanese bank secrecy are unclear. As described earlier, bank secrecy tends

[14] Chifumi Ibe and Nobuhiko Sugiura, *Kinyu Torihiki no Shuhi Gimu ni Tsuiteno Hikaku-ho Teki Kosatsu* [Consideration on Financial Institutions' Duty to Keep Secrecy from the Perspective of Comparative Law], FSA Research Review in 2006 (2007).
[15] There is no criminal sanction that is derived from the principle of bank secrecy.

to be evaluated on a case-by-case basis with reference to the contractual or business relationship with a customer.

9.3.1.3   Exclusion from Bank Secrecy

It is understood that the obligation of financial institutions for maintaining secrecy may be excluded in the following cases:

(i) Customer consent

If and to the extent that a customer has given consent, banks are exempt from the obligation of maintaining secrecy, and thus a financial institution is allowed to deliver customer information to a third party. The consent may be made in writing or orally, and expressly or impliedly.

(ii) Disclosure required by the law

Where the disclosure of customer information is required by the law, a financial institution is considered to be allowed or obliged to provide a third party with customer information obtained by the financial institution in the course of business without the consent of the customer.[16] Typical examples are cases in which a bank is asked to respond to an inquiry or referral from the police or tax offices. In such cases, it is basically agreed that public interest takes priority over bank secrecy. A bank may be penalised for failing to make disclosure in these cases. Whether the penalty is criminal or administrative depends on the purpose of each law and the public interest at stake.

More specifically, a bank's obligation of secrecy is exempted and its rights are restricted in the following cases:

- Investigation power of the Diet (e.g. Art. 62 of the Constitution, Art. 104 of the Diet Act).
- Examination or inspection of evidence in judicial proceedings (e.g. Arts. 128 and 143 of the Code of Criminal Procedure, Arts. 180 and 197 of the Code of Civil Procedure; see Section 9.3.2).
- Search or seizure by an investigating authority pursuant to a warrant issued by a court (e.g. Arts. 99 and 102 of the Code of Criminal Procedure).
- Investigation by the Prime Minister or a legitimate supervisory authority (e.g. Arts. 24 and 25 of the Banking Act).

---

[16] However, there was an opposing opinion. Tsuneo Otori, Akira Yonekura, Hitoshi Maeda *et al.*, *Zadankai, Yokin Torihiki* [Round Table Discussion – Deposit], 910 Kinyu-homu Jijo 35 (1979).

- Inquiry or inspection by the tax agency or taxation bureau for imposition or collection of tax (e.g. Arts. 74-2 to 74-6 of the Act on General Rules for National Taxes).
- Report to the FSA under the Act on Prevention of Transfer of Criminal Proceeds (see Section 9.5).

(iii) In the following cases, a bank may be exempt from the obligation to maintain secrecy if, and to the extent, deemed necessary for the public interest. Such cases are different from (ii) above in that no penalty is imposed on a bank even if the bank does not provide any information.

- Requests by the Bar Association (Art. 23-2, para. 2 of Attorney Act).[17]
- Bank references.[18]

(iv) If it is necessary for a bank to protect its own rights, typically in a lawsuit filed by a customer against a bank, the bank is basically considered allowed to disclose the customer information to a third party to the necessary extent. However, it is difficult to determine when and whether the right to make such disclosure takes precedence over the confidentiality.[19]

9.3.2   Judicial Precedents with Respect to Bank Secrecy

Article 197, para. 1, item 3 of the Code of Civil Procedure[20] provides for the right of refusal to testify in civil proceedings when the witness is examined on matters concerning professional secrets (see Section 9.3.1.3(ii)).[21]

---

[17] According to Art. 23-2 of the Attorney Act, an attorney may request the Bar Association to make inquiries to public offices or other organisations (including banks) for information which will be necessary to resolve a case to which he/she has been retained. If the Bar Association finds the attorney's request appropriate, the Bar Association may request the relevant public offices or other organisations to provide the necessary information for the attorney.

[18] In Japan, there is a reference system under which a credit bureau collects information on creditworthiness from financial institutions and gives a response to an enquiry about such information. Currently, there are four credit bureaus designated by the Ministry of Economy, Trade and Industry of Japan pursuant to the Personal Information Protection Act. After the enactment of the Personal Information Protection Act, it is clear that the customer's consent is required for a bank to provide such information to credit bureaus.

[19] Utsumi, *supra* note 13 at 9.

[20] *Minji Sosho Ho* [Code of Civil Procedure]. Act No. 109 of 1996. English translation available online: www.japaneselawtranslation.go.jp/law/detail/?id=2092&vm=04&re=02

[21] On the contrary, Art. 4 of the Act for Oath, Testimony, etc. of Witnesses at the Diet or Art. 105 of the Code of Criminal Procedure does not provide for the right of refusal to testify for the reasons of professional secrets, with some exceptions.

In civil proceedings, the right to keep customer information confidential needs to be respected under the Code of Civil Procedure, but the scope of the right to confidentiality that needs to be protected by law has not been clear. With respect to this issue, there are several judicial precedents in Japan. Although judicial precedents relating to bank secrecy are few, there are several cases about the right of refusal to testify under the Code of Civil Procedure as below.

9.3.2.1   Refusal to Testify by a Witness
(Art. 180 of the Code of Civil Procedure)

Under the Code of Civil Procedure, when a court has determined to examine any person as a witness, the witness has the duty of appearance, duty of oath and duty of testimony,[22] provided, however, that if the matter relates to 'professional secrets' the witness may refuse to testify.[23]

In this respect, it is possible for an employee of a bank to refuse to testify with respect to its customer information for reasons of bank secrecy, as a type of professional secret. In practice, however, the documents held by the bank are considered more valuable as evidence than witnesses, and thus bank employees are rarely examined as witnesses. Therefore, the scope of 'professional secrets' (bank secrecy) has been discussed more in the context of court's order to submit documents as described in the following section.

9.3.2.2   Court's Order to Submit Documents
(Art. 220 of the Code of Civil Procedure)

In Japanese civil procedure, there is a rule that a party may request the court to order the holder of a document to submit it so that it may be examined by the court. Any holder of a document receiving such an order from the court cannot refuse to submit the document, except in limited cases listed in Art. 220 of the Code of Civil Procedure. The types of documents subject to the submission order are (i) documents cited in the suit,[24] (ii) documents that a party offering evidence is able to request to receive or inspect, (iii) documents prepared for the purpose of proving the interest of the party offering evidence,[25] (iv) documents concerning the legal rela-

---

[22] Code of Civil Procedure, *supra* note 20, Art. 190.

[23] *Ibid.*, Art. 197, para. 1, item 3.

[24] It is agreed that if a party has cited a document to support that party's claim, the opposing party should be able to inspect the cited document and make a rebuttal argument.

[25] For example, a last will and testament that can prove the party's entitlement for inheritance, medical records relating to the party, a contract, a receipt, a written consent or an identification card that has been connected with any right or interest of the party.

tionship between the party offering evidence and the document holder[26] and (v) any other documents that are not listed as exceptions in the Code of Civil Procedure.[27]

Notwithstanding the foregoing, Art. 220, item 4 (*ha*) of the Code of Civil Procedure provides that in cases where a document includes 'professional secrets'[28] set forth in Art. 197, para. 1, item 3 thereof, the holder of the document may refuse to submit that document (see Section 9.3.2.1). Furthermore, Art. 220, item 4 (*ro*) thereof provides that if the document has been prepared exclusively for the use of the holder, the holder of that document may refuse to submit it.[29] The court may have the holder present the document and may review it in-camera if the document is necessary for the court to determine whether such refusal can be admitted by the law.[30]

With respect to this issue, the Supreme Court[31] has ruled that even if the document contains professional secrets, the holder may not refuse to submit it unless such confidential information needs to be legally protected, and that whether the confidential information needs to be legally protected shall be decided by considering the pros and cons of disclosure based on the content and type of information, disadvantage to the holder caused by the disclosure of information, content and type of the civil case and how necessary the confidential information is to the case.[32]

---

[26] For example, documents relating to a contractual relationship, email correspondences at the stage of negotiation, a letter of intent, a claim for damage, an application, an acceptance and a termination notice. The documents referred to at *supra* notes 25 and 26 overlap each other.

[27] This type (v) means the general duty to submit any and all documents except when the document falls under certain categories. Documents that fall under exceptional categories to this duty are, for example, a document including 'professional secrets', a document relating to public officer's duties or public interests and a document relating to a record of a criminal case or a juvenile case (see the following paragraph).

[28] In the banking context, the professional secret that is being protected here is that of the bank, namely its business know-how.

[29] The purpose of this exemption is to protect privacy and the right of any individual or organisation to make a decision. A holder may also refuse to submit any document concerning a criminal procedure or a record of a juvenile case.

[30] Code of Civil Procedure, *supra* note 20, Art. 223, para. 6. This procedure has been introduced by the amendment to the Code of Civil Procedure in 1996.

[31] The Supreme Court is the highest court in Japan. A party to a legal dispute will be usually entitled to a decision by a district court and two instances of appeal to the High Court and the Supreme Court.

[32] See the Supreme Court's rulings on 3 October 2006 and on 25 November 2008: 60 Minshu 2694 and 62 Minshu 2507. Professor Makoto Ito criticises this ruling for the reason that the method of looking at the pros and cons is inherently incompatible with the nature of the right of refusal to testify and that such method will make it impossible for the party to estimate the scope of the right of refusal. See Makoto Ito, *Minji Sosho Ho* [The Code of the

Based on the principle of the Supreme Court's ruling earlier, there are several precedents about whether the holder may refuse to submit the document for the reason that it needs to be legally protected as a professional secret or that it was created for internal use only.

(i) Transaction history

The Supreme Court has ruled that a bank statement describing the transaction history between a bank and a customer basically constitutes 'professional secrets'.

At the same time, the Supreme Court also stated that while a bank is responsible for keeping secrecy of customer information regarding the customer's transactions or credit, the bank takes such responsibility only with respect to the customer in his capacity as a customer. Therefore, when the customer, acting in the capacity of a party to the civil procedure, is required to disclose the information in the civil procedure, the bank may not refuse to disclose information of such customer in the civil procedure unless the bank needs to protect its own interest in relation to such information.[33]

(ii) Request for internal approval for a loan (*Ringi-sho*)

For most Japanese banks, there is a way of making decisions called *Ringi*. *Ringi-sho* is the documentary process that implements *Ringi*. *Ringo-sho* is circulated internally for the purpose of obtaining approval by the bank for certain transactions. *Ringi-sho* for a loan usually contains information regarding the name of the borrower, the loan amount, the purpose of the funds, a security or a guarantee, the maturity date, the estimated profit for the bank, the credit condition of the borrower, the evaluation of the borrower, the opinion of the bank officer in charge of the loan and the opinion of the bank officer who has the authority to give approval (e.g. the manager or the vice manager of the department).

With respect to the *Ringi-sho*, the Supreme Court[34] has stated that the *Ringi-sho* is created to be used internally in order to make an appropriate and rapid decision for extending a loan, and includes

---

Civil Procedures], rev. 4th edn., 2014 at 419. Although some academics and practitioners support his view, the method following the ruling of the Supreme Court has been already established in the civil procedures.

[33] See the Supreme Court's ruling on 11 December 2007, *supra* note 12.

[34] Supreme Court, 12 November, 1999, 53 Minshu 1787: Where a plaintiff (the successor of the borrower) claimed damages for excessive lending by the bank to the borrower, the plaintiff filed a petition for the court's order to submit the *Ringi-sho*.

frank and straightforward opinions on the loan before the final decision. As a result, the Supreme Court ruled that the bank may refuse to submit the *Ringi-sho*, because requiring the disclosure of such documents may interfere with free discussion within the bank. Likewise, in a subsequent case,[35] the Supreme Court stated that the *Ringi-sho* basically[36] is the document which was prepared exclusively for the bank's internal use, and thus the Supreme Court dismissed the petition for the order to disclose the *Ringi-sho*.

(iii) Internal notification (*Shanai Tsutatsu*)

Internal notification (*Shanai Tsutatsu*) is a document from a bank's headquarters addressed to each branch manager or relevant departments in order to let them know the final decision of the bank regarding its business.

With respect to the *Shanai Tsutatsu*, the Supreme Court[37] has stated that although the notification document is created for internal use, the document is created for the purpose of notifying employees of the bank's final decision and not for the purpose of making the decision. The notification document usually includes neither customer information nor the bank's know-how, while certain business strategy or information concerning business outcomes is described. The Supreme Court ruled that disclosure of the document would not cause an adverse effect on the decision-making of the bank and thus the bank was not allowed to refuse to disclose the *Shanai Tsutatsu*.

(iv) Documents regarding self-valuation (*Jiko Satei Shiryo*)

Documents regarding self-valuation mean documents regarding the classification of debtors for the purpose of preparing an asset

---

[35] Supreme Court, 14 December, 2000, 54 Minshu 2709.

[36] See the Supreme Court's ruling on 7 December 2001 that acknowledged the exceptional circumstances: 55 Minshu 1411. In this case, a liquidation procedure had been commenced with a financial institution and the *Ringi-sho* of the financial institution was, upon the commencement of the liquidation proceeding, transferred to the Resolution and Collection Corporation (RCC) that was in charge of the collection of loans under the liquidation procedure of the financial institution. RCC filed a suit against the borrower to repay the loan, and the borrower filed a petition to submit the *Ringi-sho*. According to the ruling of the Supreme Court, this case had involved the special circumstance that RCC handled collection business only and did not handle the business of new financing, and therefore RCC was not allowed to refuse to submit the *Ringi-sho*. In this case, the Supreme Court considered that the compelling disclosure of the *Ringi-sho* would not interfere with the free discussion inside RCC.

[37] Supreme Court, 17 February, 2006, 60 Minshu 496. In this case, the borrower alleged that the loan agreement was invalid and asked the bank to submit the *Shanai Tsutatsu* in order to prove that the loan agreement was combined with variable life insurance agreement and the bank solicited the loan jointly with an insurance company.

valuation, which the bank is obliged to do under the Banking Act.[38] Banks usually retain those documents for future inspections.[39]

With respect to *Jiko Satei Shiryo*, the Supreme Court[40] has ruled that such documents are basically for internal use, but may also be reviewed by a third party such as an inspector of the regulatory authorities to see the background of the asset valuation and, therefore, the bank may not refuse to disclose the documents.

Without prejudice to the above, the ruling by the Tokyo High Court on 26 February 2010 stated that although a bank cannot refuse to submit the documents regarding self-valuation as long as the customer had given consent,[41] if the document contains information regarding know-how for credit risk management or asset assessment, the bank may refuse to disclose part of such information because such information needs to be legally protected as 'professional secrecy'.[42]

9.4   Implementation of the Protection Scheme of Privacy in the 2000s

Affected by the 1980 OECD Privacy Guidelines, the right to privacy came to be more recognised in Japan and the protection of customer information has become more important to all companies in operating their

---

[38] Articles 14-2 and 26 of the Banking Act, and the Section of Risk Management of the Inspection Manual.

[39] Kohei Yamaya, *Ginko no Jiko Satei Shiryo Chu no Kokyaku no Zaimu Jokyo, Gyomu Jokyo ni Taisuru Bunseki Hyoka Joho no Uchi Knowhow ni Kakawaru Bubun no Shokugyo Himitsu Gaitosei* [Bank Secrecy and Know-how on Self-Asset-Valuation Described in the Section Concerning Customer and Credit Information in the Document of Self-Asset-Valuation], 725 Ginko-homu 21 (2011) at 30.

[40] Supreme Court, 30 November 2007, 61 Minshu 3186.

[41] The ruling did not consider the position if the customer has not consented to the disclosure.

[42] This ruling acknowledged that the information in the case constitutes 'professional secrecy' because the bank had duties to maintain the confidentiality of the computer system regarding self-valuation to a third party which helped to develop the system, and the bank profited by selling the computer system to other banks. However, some experts, including Kohei Yamaya (*supra* note 39) are critical of this ruling because banks also need to be protected even if they do not have a duty to maintain confidentiality to a system developer and do not offer the system for profit. They consider that, generally speaking, it is important for banks to conceal know-how on the method of classification of debtors or the credit rating of customers and that the relevant system needs to be kept confidential regardless of whether the computer system had been developed by the bank or a third party or whether the bank offered the system to other banks.

businesses. The government enacted the Personal Information Protection Act[43] in 2003 (and came into force in 2005). Although the Personal Information Protection Act itself covers only personal information with respect to individuals, the FSA amended some financial regulations and guidelines in order to require a financial institution to manage customer information (with respect to both individual and corporate customers) appropriately for the protection of privacy.

The interpretation of these privacy enactments, set out below, has become important to evaluating whether a bank manages its customer information properly. Theoretically, they overlap with the principle of bank secrecy discussed in Section 9.3 but they are not coextensive with it. Therefore, the bank's responsibility for maintaining secrecy in civil proceedings set out in Section 9.3 continues to merit consideration. However, since the passing of the privacy enactments, they have become the focus of attention rather than the principles governing bank secrecy. In other words, whether or not a bank handles customer information in a proper way tends to be judged by whether or not the bank satisfies the requirements of the privacy enactments without reference to bank secrecy.

9.4.1 Ordinance for Enforcement of the Banking Act

The Ordinance for Enforcement of the Banking Act[44] was amended in 2005 to require that, if a bank outsources the management of information on individual customers or employees to a third party (including the bank's agents), the bank must take appropriate measures to prevent leakage, loss or damage of said information and must manage risks arising from the outsourcing.

9.4.2 Guidelines for Supervision

The Guidelines for Supervision[45] published by the FSA in 2005 have several provisions relating to the management of customer information in III-3-3-3.

---

[43] *Kojin Joho no Hogo ni Kansuru Horitsu* [Personal Information Protection Act], Act No. 57 of 2003. English translation available online: www.japaneselawtranslation.go.jp/law/ detail_main?id=130&

[44] The Japanese title is *Ginko Ho Seko Kisoku*. See *supra* note 7. See the translation at www.japaneselawtranslation.go.jp/law/detail/?id=2424&vm=04&re=02 See Arts. 13-6-5 to 13-6-7.

[45] See *supra* note 8.

The Guidelines for Supervision declare that customer information forms the foundation of financial transactions and therefore a bank needs to take steps to manage such information appropriately. The Guidelines for Supervision consider it essential for a bank to disseminate the appropriate method of customer information management to directors, officers and employees, in order to establish and maintain a system to (i) monitor customer information management and (ii) make a report to the FSA when any information leaks or any other issue occurs. If the FSA finds and confirms a critical problem with the information management of a bank, the FSA may issue a business improvement order and take other appropriate action against the bank pursuant to Art. 26 of the Banking Act.

9.4.3   Inspection Manual

The Inspection Manual[46] published by the FSA in 1999 provides for an 'Inspection checklist for the management of customer protection, etc.' and lists many points that inspectors should check at the time of the inspection. According to the checklist regarding the customer-information-management system (see II-3 and II-4 therein), the inspectors must examine whether a bank has implemented and follows the so-called Plan-Do-Check-Action cycle (PDCA cycle).

9.4.4   Personal Information Protection Act

9.4.4.1   Enactment of the Personal Information Protection Act

In 2003, the Personal Information Protection Act[47] was enacted as domestic legislation of the 1980 OECD Privacy Guidelines adopted by Japan. The purpose of the Personal Information Protection Act is to protect the rights and interests of individuals, and it sets forth the core principles for handling personal information and for the basic policies to be established by the government or local government.

The Personal Information Protection Act specifies the general obligations with which business operators receiving personal information must comply.[48] Aiming to achieve proper handling and to give adequate protection of personal information, the authority to determine detailed regulations for

---

[46] See *supra* note 9.
[47] See *supra* note 43.
[48] With respect to violations of the Personal Information Protection Act, imprisonment, fines or administrative penalties may be imposed.

enforcement has been delegated to each ministry that supervises each business operator. Thus, guidelines for each business field under the Personal Information Protection Act will be or have been established by the relevant ministry for each domain. In the case of the financial field, the FSA has published the 'Guidelines for Personal Information Protection in the Financial Industries'[49] and the 'Practical Guidelines for the Security Policy Regarding Personal Information Protection in the Financial Industries'.[50]

At the time of enforcement of the Personal Information Protection Act in 2005, the Ordinance for Enforcement of the Banking Act[51] was also amended to improve the effectiveness and transparency of management measures against leakage of personal information.

<h4 style="text-align:center">9.4.4.2   Relationship between the Personal Information Protection Act and Bank Secrecy</h4>

There is a crossover between the Personal Information Protection Act and the bank's obligations to keep customer information confidential under the principle of bank secrecy. However, bank secrecy and the Personal Information Protection Act are different and separate from each other as discussed below.[52]

(i) Scope of customer information
  Under the Personal Information Protection Act, on the one hand, only 'personal data' is protected by obligating a business operator (including a bank) to set up its own 'safety management measures', to monitor that employees and outsourcees do not provide its customer's personal information to third parties. The term 'personal data' is defined in the Personal Information Protection Act. Basically, only information pertaining to individuals and stored on databases

---

[49] The Japanese title is *Kinyu Bunya ni Okeru Kojin Joho Hogo ni Kansuru Guideline*. English translation available online: www.fsa.go.jp/frtc/kenkyu/event/20070424_02.pdf. It has been published for the purpose of supporting business operators in the financial field in handling personal information in a proper way. These guidelines interpret the Personal Information Protection Act and set forth actions that need to be strictly implemented by business operators in terms of characteristics of the financial field.

[50] The Japanese title is *Kinyu Bunya ni Okeru Kojin Joho Hogo ni Kansuru Guideline no Anzen Kanri Sochi Tou ni Okeru Jitsumu Shishin*. These practical guidelines are allowed to be amended rapidly and flexibly and are considered suitable to keep pace with continuously developing technology, making the Guidelines for Personal Information Protection in the Financial Industries referred to at *supra* note 49 more effective for the protection of personal information.

[51] See *supra* note 44.

[52] See Chapter 2 for a general comparison of bank secrecy and data protection.

under the protection of the Personal Information Protection Act[53] is protected; information about an entity or organisation is not protected.

On the other hand, the principle of bank secrecy covers any customer information, including information of an entity or organisation, regardless of whether it has been stored in a database.

(ii) Relationship with customers

Irrespective of the view on the legal basis of bank secrecy (see Section 9.3.1.1), on the one hand, a bank is generally considered to be obliged to keep customer information confidential because customers will make or have made an agreement with the bank.

On the other hand, the Personal Information Protection Act requires that the personal data of any individual be protected appropriately even if there is no agreement between the customer and the business operator.

(iii) Provision of customer information to a third party

The Personal Information Protection Act stipulates that personal data may be provided to a third party when such provision is necessary for the protection of another's life, body or property, for improving public health, for promoting the sound growth of children or when it is difficult to obtain customer consent. On the whole, the Personal Information Protection Act has a broader array of exceptions, compared to bank secrecy as described in Section 9.3.1.3. In addition, the Personal Information Protection Act clearly provides for a so-called 'Opt-out Rule'[54] under certain conditions, although it had been generally understood that any business operator (including a bank) always had to obtain customer's prior consent for disclosure (Opt-in Rule).

As stated earlier, even after the enforcement of the Personal Information Protection Act, banks need not only comply with the Personal Information

---

[53] The term 'database' herein means a set of information including personal information (a) which is structurally organised to enable a computer to be used to retrieve certain personal information from it or (b) any set of data of which a predetermined rule is applied to arrange the personal information so that it is structurally organised to enable personal information to be easily retrieved from it by using a table of contents, an index, etc. See Art. 2.2.

[54] The Opt-out Rule means that if (a) a person has been informed of the provision of personal data to a third party and (b) the business operator appropriately offers the person an opportunity to request the suspension of the provision, the personal data may be provided to the third party unless the person requests the suspension. In this respect, the outsourcee in the case of outsourcing, the successor in a merger or in other similar event or someone who is identified to the affected person is not deemed a third party, and therefore a business operator is allowed to deliver the personal data to such a party.

Protection Act, but also to fulfil the obligation to keep customer information confidential under the principle of bank secrecy. However, after the enforcement of the Personal Information Protection Act, banks tend to focus on compliance with the Act, and the principle of bank secrecy is not discussed as much as before, because the Personal Information Protection Act provides clearer requirements and guidelines to banks, compared to the principle of bank secrecy, which is determined on a case-by-case basis. When a dispute regarding customer information has arisen for a bank, it usually tries to prove that it has been compliant with the Personal Information Protection Act because that will support the bank's argument that it has complied with its obligations regarding the handling of customer information. As a result, after the enforcement of the Personal Information Protection Act, arguments regarding the conventional principle of bank secrecy as described in Section 9.3 have not been heard as much as before.

9.4.5 Financial Instruments and Exchange Act

9.4.5.1 Information Sharing among Affiliates

In Japan, the so-called 'firewall regulations' separating different kinds of financial institutions (securities, banking and insurance businesses) from each other have been introduced because if banks engage in securities business, (a) securities business may damage the soundness of the bank and may affect the maintenance of customer deposits, (b) a bank's dual business may cause conflicts of interest and (c) the risk of the abuse of the dominant position of banks may arise. Japan has adopted a Glass–Steagall style separation which means that banks are exclusively engaged in banking business, insurance companies are exclusively engaged in insurance business and securities firms are exclusively engaged in securities business.

However, the financial system in Japan is gradually undergoing conglomeratisation and other new developments. More specifically, through the financial reform of 1993, the ban on mutual business entries through subsidiaries in the relevant business field was partly lifted,[55] and through the Financial System Reform Law in 1998, the ban on financial holding companies was lifted. Furthermore, in 2008, the firewall regulation was relaxed for the convenience of customers; a financial group is now able to offer broad financial services across the banking/insurance/securities spectrum. Also,

---

[55] By this amendment, a bank has become allowed to enter into securities business through its subsidiaries and a security company has become allowed to enter into banking business through its subsidiaries.

in order to enhance the integral management of a united financial group, the new rules basically allow sharing of corporate customer information within a financial group,[56] subject to the restrictions set out below.

In response to the movement of financial system reform, the regulation on information sharing within the financial group has been reinforced and requires proper information management for customer protection. Currently, certain financial institutions[57] are prohibited from providing to, or receiving from, its affiliates any 'nonpublic' information on all customers. They are further prohibited from soliciting for a financial transaction by using 'nonpublic' information on customers acquired by affiliates,[58] provided, however, that if the customer has given prior written consent to the provision of information, or solicitation based on nonpublic information on the customer, such prohibition will not be applied.[59]

---

[56] Yuichi Ikeda, Hidenori Mitsui and Naohiro Masuda, *Chikujo Kaisetsu, 2008 Kinyu Shohin Torihiki Ho Kaisei* [Commentary on the Amendment to the Financial Instruments and Exchange Act in 2008], Shoji-homu, 2008 at 67.

[57] The registered 'Financial Instruments Business Operator' operating 'Type I Financial Instruments Business' (securities-related business), and the 'Registered Financial Institutions', which are defined in the Financial Instruments and Exchange Act. If a bank has made a registration under the Financial Instruments and Exchange Act, the bank is the Registered Financial Institution.

[58] Article 44-3, para. 1, item 4 of the Financial Instruments and Exchange Act, and Art. 153, para. 1, items 7 and 8 and Art. 154, items 4 and 5 of the *Kinyu Shohin Torihiki Gyo To ni Kansuru Naikakufu Rei* [Cabinet Office Ordinance on Financial Instruments Business, etc.], Cabinet Office Ordinance No. 52 of 2007. English translation available online: www .ffaj.or.jp/en/regulation/data/fi.pdf

[59] Provided further, however, that if the financial institution appropriately offers a corporate customer an opportunity to request a suspension of the provision of nonpublic information on the customer to affiliates, the customer is deemed to have given a written consent to the provision of the nonpublic information until the customer requests the suspension (Opt-out Rule) (Art. 153, para. 2 of the Cabinet Office Ordinance on Financial Instruments Business, etc.) The Opt-out Rule does not apply to solicitation for a financial transaction by using 'nonpublic' information on the customer.

The amendment to the Financial Instruments and Exchange Act in 2008 amended the regulations on the sharing of nonpublic customer information among affiliates. By this amendment, the following rules have been introduced:

(a) Individual customers: Opt-in Rule (Prior customer's consent required)
(b) Corporate customers: Opt-out Rule (Information sharing restricted when customers do not approve)
(c) Customer information sharing for internal management: Customer's consent is not required.

In addition to the above, the amendment in 2014 introduced new rules on the 'written' consent in the case of the 'foreign' corporate customers. With respect to the requirement that the customer give 'written' consent for information sharing among affiliates: (i) if the

9.4.5.2 Relationship between the Financial Instruments and Exchange Act and the Personal Information Protection Act

A bank needs not only to comply with the Personal Information Protection Act, but also to satisfy the requirements under the Financial Instruments and Exchange Act[60] if the bank has been registered thereunder.

As stated earlier, the Financial Instruments and Exchange Act sets forth the rules from the perspectives of relaxing the firewall and tightening the protection of customer information. From these perspectives, the Financial Instruments and Exchange Act has stricter rules compared to the Personal Information Protection Act with respect to the management of customer information. Information obtained by a financial institution usually relates to financial standing and financial credibility of customers, and therefore, customers usually do not want others to know such information. Thus, the Financial Instruments and Exchange Act requires a financial institution to provide extra protection for customer information, such that the Financial Instruments and Exchange Act employs a narrower scope of the Opt-out Rule (see Section 9.4.4.2(iii); see also *supra* note 59).

9.4.5.3 Relationship between the Financial Instruments and Exchange Act and Bank Secrecy

The Financial Instruments and Exchange Act maintains and does not contradict the conventional principle of bank secrecy that a bank must keep customer information confidential unless there is customer consent or other justifiable grounds for disclosure. Therefore, the principle of bank secrecy described in Section 9.3 remains relevant to banks; however, banks tend to pay more attention to the rules under the Financial Instruments and Exchange Act, compared to the principle of bank secrecy, for the same reason stated in Section 9.4.4.2 regarding the Personal Information Protection Act: the principles under the Financial Instruments and Exchange Act are clearer and therefore easier to adhere to.

---

customer gives its consent by electromagnetic record or (ii) if there are reasonable grounds to believe that the customer's consent has been given from the perspective of the agreement with the relevant customer or the business customs of the country of the customer, the customer will be deemed to have given written consent (Art. 153, para. 1, item 7(i) of the Cabinet Office Ordinance on Financial Instruments Business, etc.).

[60] *Kinyu Shohin Torihiki Ho* [Financial Instruments and Exchange Act], Act No. 25 of 1948. English translation available online: www.japaneselawtranslation.go.jp/law/detail/?id=2355

9.5   New Restrictions on Bank Secrecy

9.5.1   Anti-money Laundering and
Counter-terrorism Financing

In coordination with international society, Japan has enhanced and developed legal systems to prevent and detect money laundering and terrorism financing.

In Japan, the following Acts stipulate the criminalisation of money laundering and the deprivation of illegal profits: the Anti-Drug Special Provisions Act,[61] the Act on Punishment of Organized Crimes and Control of Crime Proceeds[62] and the Act on Punishment of Financing to Offences of Public Intimidation.[63] Furthermore, the Act on Prevention of Transfer of Criminal Proceeds[64] creates the obligation for business operators (including financial institutions) to implement the preventive measures.

9.5.1.1   The Anti-Drug Special Provisions Act

The Anti-Drug Special Provisions Act is a domestic law implementing the UN Convention Against Illicit Traffic in Narcotic Drugs and Psychotropic Substances and the 40 FATF Recommendations,[65] and came into force in July 1992. The Anti-Drug Special Provisions Act criminalises money laundering activities connected with drug crime and provides penalties for concealing or receiving proceeds of drug crimes. Also, the system of confiscation and forfeiture has been significantly reinforced. Under the Anti-Drug Special Provisions Act, property obtained in exchange for

---

[61] The full title is *Kokusaiteki na Kyoryoku no Moto ni Kisei Yakubutsu ni Kakaru Fusei Koi wo Jochou Suru Koi Tou no Boshi wo Hakaru Tame no Mayaku Oyobi Ko-Seishinyaku Torishimari Ho To no Tokurei Tou ni Kansuru Horitsu* [Act Concerning Special Provisions for the Narcotics and Psychotropics Control Act, etc. and Other Matters for the Prevention of Activities Encouraging Illicit Conducts and Other Activities Involving Controlled Substances Through International Cooperation], Act No. 94 of 1991.

[62] *Soshikiteki na Hanzai no Shobatsu Oyobi Hanzai Shueki no Kiseitou ni Kansuru Horitsu* [Act on Punishment of Organized Crimes and Control of Crime Proceeds], Law No. 136 of 1999.

[63] The full title is *Koshu to Kyohaku Mokuteki no Hanzai Koi no Tame no Shikin no Teikyo to to no Shobatsu ni Kansuru Horitsu* [Act on Punishment of the Financing of Criminal Activities for the Purpose of Intimidation of the General Public and of Governments], Act No. 67 of 2002.

[64] *Hanzai ni Yoru Shueki no Iten Boshi ni Kansuru Horitsu* [Act on Prevention of Transfer of Criminal Proceeds], Act No. 22 of 2007. English translation available online: www.npa.go.jp/syokanhourei/hansyuu.pdf

[65] The first FATF Report on the extent and nature of the money laundering process and the FATF Recommendations to combat money laundering: 'Financial Action Task Force on Money Laundering – Report' (1990) online: www.fatf-gafi.org/media/fatf/documents/reports/1990%20ENG.pdf

the proceeds of drug crimes may be subject to confiscation or forfeiture (as well as the proceeds of drug crimes themselves), and a court has the power to issue a provisional order prohibiting the disposal of property with a view to preserving the proceeds to be confiscated. Additionally, the Act has provided for a reporting system under which a financial institution is obliged to report suspicious transactions.[66]

9.5.1.2 The Act on Punishment of Organized Crime and Control of Crime Proceeds

After the enactment of the Anti-Drug Special Provisions Act, the FATF pointed out that it was difficult for a financial institution to check if a suspicious transaction related to drug crimes, and as a result the reporting system did not work efficiently. To rectify this issue, by the Act on Punishment of Organized Crime and Control of Crime Proceeds that came into force in February 2000, the scope of crimes constituting money laundering has been expanded to include other serious crimes in addition to illegal drug crimes, and the scope of crimes subject to a suspicious transaction report or confiscation has also been expanded.[67]

The Act on Punishment of Organized Crime and Control of Crime Proceeds designated the FSA as an FIU (financial intelligence unit) of Japan, which is responsible for collecting, arranging and analysing information relating to money laundering, or delegating such functions to the investigative authorities.

9.5.1.3 The Act on Punishment of Financing to Offences of Public Intimidation

The Act on Punishment of Financing to Offences of Public Intimidation came into force in July 2002 as a domestic law to implement 'The International Convention for the Suppression of the Financing Terrorism'. The Act has criminalised the financing and receipt of terrorist funds. Concurrently with the enactment of the Act on Punishment of Financing to Offences of Public Intimidation, the Act on Punishment of Organized Crime and Control of Crime Proceeds (Section 9.5.1.2) was also amended so that the financing and receipt of terrorist funds would be within the

---

[66] This reporting system was taken over by the Act on Punishment of Organized Crime and Control of Crime Proceeds and further by the Act on Prevention of Transfer of Criminal Proceeds.

[67] See *supra* note 66.

scope of the crimes subject to prohibition of concealing or receipt, and subject to a suspicious transaction report.

Around the same time, to establish a new regime for ensuring customer identification and maintaining transaction records based upon the above-mentioned Convention and the 40 FATF Recommendations,[68] the Act on Customer Identification by Financial Institutions, etc.[69] was enacted (and came into force in January 2003). For the purpose of preventing fund transfers through financial institutions, this Act requires a financial institution to confirm customer identification because a financial institution can examine transactions beforehand and trace them after execution. Almost at the same time, the Foreign Exchange and Foreign Trade Act[70] was also amended and similar provisions have been added for cross-border transactions including foreign exchange.

9.5.1.4   The Act on Prevention of Transfer of Criminal Proceeds

Corresponding to the revision of the 40 FATF Recommendations to bind more business operators (beyond financial institutions) to the obligation to confirm customer identification, the Act on Prevention of Transfer of Criminal Proceeds[71] was enacted in February 2007. By this amendment, the FIU described in Section 9.5.1.2 has been transferred from the FSA to the National Public Safety Commission. With respect to a financial institution, its obligations under the Act on Customer Identification by Financial Institutions and the Act on Punishment of Organized Crimes and Control of Crime Proceeds have been superseded by the Act on Prevention of Transfer of Criminal Proceeds.

Under the Act on Prevention of Transfer of Criminal Proceeds, a financial institution is required to verify customer identification data, prepare customer identification records and make transaction records when

---

[68] See *supra* note 65.
[69] *Kinyu Kikan ni Yoru Kokyaku to no Honin Kakunin to ni Kansuru Horitsu* [Act on Customer Identification by Financial Institutions, etc.], Act No. 32 of 2002. The title of this act was amended to *Kinyu Kikan ni Yoru Kokyaku to no Honin Kakunin to Oyobi Yokin Kouza to no Fusei na Riyo no Boshi ni Kansuru Horitsu* [Act Concerning Confirmation of Identification of Customers, etc. by Financial Institutions, etc. and Prevention of Unauthorized Use of Deposit Accounts] enforced in December 2004 and abolished in March 2008 by the enforcement of the Act on Prevention Transfer of Criminal Proceeds.
[70] *Gaikoku Kawase Oyobi Gaikoku Boeki Ho* [Foreign Exchange and Foreign Trade Act], Act No. 228 of 1949.
[71] Act on Prevention of Transfer of Criminal Proceeds, *supra* note 66.

entering into certain specified transactions, including when a customer opens a new account with a bank and performs large cash transactions, domestic money transfers of more than 100,000 yen and any overseas remittances, etc. If a financial institution finds that funds or assets provided by the customer are suspected of being criminal proceeds or that the customer is suspected of having committed crimes, the bank shall promptly report its suspicions to the FSA.

9.5.1.5   Relationship with Bank Secrecy

The suspicious transaction report is a legal requirement under the Act on Prevention of Transfer of Criminal Proceeds. As stated in Section 9.3.1.3(ii), with respect to cases where the disclosure of customer information is required by law, a financial institution is allowed to provide a law enforcement authority with customer information even without the customer's consent. Thus, the reporting obligations of banks for the purpose of anti-money laundering and counter-terrorism override bank secrecy in Japan.

9.5.2   Tax Affairs (Exchange of Information for Foreign Taxation)

A nation establishes its own taxation system and conducts a compulsory process in order to secure a tax declaration and payment from its citizens. For the imposition of fair and proper tax, the nation needs to acquire information about overseas assets or overseas income of its taxpayers. From this perspective, tax treaties that enable the EOI on foreign assets or income of taxpayers between countries have become a familiar feature. Further, the OECD has issued and continuously updated the Model Tax Convention.

Japan has executed about 60 bilateral tax conventions for this purpose, including tax treaties with many tax havens such as Bermuda and the Cayman Islands. In addition to those bilateral tax treaties, Japan participated in the Convention on Mutual Administrative Assistance in Tax Matters taking effect in October 2013. In this way, Japan has established a legal network of tax treaties to acquire such information.

With respect to the Foreign Account Tax Compliance Act (FATCA) of the United States, Japanese financial institutions were strongly concerned at first. The reason was that the burden on financial institutions would increase and it was uncertain whether the bank was eligible to withhold taxes or to close an account based on the FATCA (in the absence of any domestic law of Japan). Rather, the Personal Information Protection Act (see Section 9.4.4) seemed not to allow a financial institution to report customer information to the US Internal Revenue Services (IRS).

After some time for consideration, in June 2013, Japan signed the FATCA intergovernmental agreement (IGA)[72] following the Treasury Department's Model 2 structure. Under this IGA, the Ministry of Finance of Japan is responsible for enabling and directing certain Japanese financial institutions to register with the IRS and to fulfil the requirements under the FFI Agreement pursuant to FATCA. Participating Japanese financial institutions have to obtain the consent of accountholders for such reporting. Annually, the participating financial institution has to report the account information to the IRS directly, but with respect to non-consenting accountholders, the financial institution has to report information only about the aggregate number and total amount of those accounts. Subsequent to receiving direct reports from the participating Japanese financial institutions, the US government may make requests to the Japanese government for information on recalcitrant accountholders (non-consenting accounts and reportable amounts paid to nonparticipating financial institutions) based on the IGA.

Apart from the above, Japan is expected to adopt the new OECD/G20 standard on the automatic EOI (AEOI) portal, following the Treasury Department's Models for FATCA, by 2018.

With respect to the FATCA, a bank is required to report customer information to the US IRS only when the customer gives consent. Thus, the reporting obligation of banks does not conflict with bank secrecy in Japan. In the case of the EOI based on the Convention or other EOI agreement, the relationship between the EOI for taxation and bank secrecy has not yet been well figured out. However, it is highly likely that the government will establish domestic legislation to implement the cross-border agreement or otherwise the bank will be obliged to provide customer information only when the customer has given consent. As long as the reporting obligation is required by domestic law, or as long as the customer has given consent, the principle of bank secrecy can be maintained and does not conflict with EOI for taxation.

---

[72] Ministry of Finance Japan, 'Statement of Mutual Cooperation and Understanding between the US Department of the Treasury and the Authorities of Japan to Improve International Tax Compliance and to Facilitate Implementation of FATCA' (11 June 2013), online: www .mof.go.jp/tax_policy/summary/international/250611fatca.htm

9.6 Conclusion

In recent years, Japan has enacted several new laws and regulations affecting the management of customer information provided to financial institutions as presented in Sections 9.4 and 9.5. Each law has a different purpose, such as the protection of personal information of individual customers, anti-money laundering and the exchange of customer information for taxation. The enforcement of these laws has not caused serious conflict with the conventional principle of bank secrecy because the conventional principle of bank secrecy allows broad exemptions including when disclosure is required by law or when the customer has given consent. These laws have become more important than the rules governing bank secrecy because they are more explicit and detailed than the bank secrecy laws.

In general, the Japanese government adopts a positive stance on promoting collaboration with the international community in many fields. With this background, in order to promote international cooperation, it can be considered that the government will have more opportunities to request banks to disclose or report customer information held by them in the future, which may not be limited to cases of anti-money laundering or tax collection. Still, it is unlikely that government policy will be questioned or affected from the perspective of the principle of bank secrecy.

On a practical level, the relationship between these laws and bank secrecy has not been a serious problem for a bank. What is noteworthy, however, is that several recently enacted laws on customer information increased the regulatory burden on the bank regarding both knowledge of the laws and implementing them. A bank needs to pay more attention to rules under these Acts. For the enhancement of the competitiveness and attractiveness of the Japanese financial market, these Acts regarding customer information should be integrated or organised more simply. However, it does not seem easy to improve the current situation. The global standards relating to the management of banks' customer information are always being updated and changing, and the ministry that would be responsible for adopting such updated global standards in Japan would be different depending on the purpose of the regulations. In addition, the laws regarding the management of customer information are becoming more and more complex and will not be easy to integrate. For these reasons, it seems unlikely that these several Acts regarding customer information will be integrated or organised more simply. Banks still need to continuously maintain their understanding of the current complicated laws and pay attention to possible future revisions.

10

Singapore

SANDRA BOOYSEN

10.1 Introduction

An important principle governing the bank–customer relationship in Singapore is that the customer's financial affairs will be kept confidential or secret. At the same time, it is recognised that a bank's obligation of secrecy to its customer is subject to limitations. The last decade or more has seen a proliferation of international cooperation initiatives to counter tax evasion and other transnational crime such as money laundering and terrorism financing. A common feature of this cooperation is the exchange of information (EOI) between jurisdictions. The 9/11 attacks on the United States and the global financial crisis have given added impetus to clampdowns on cross-border crime. Singapore has supported international trends to combat cross-border crime, pursuant to which it has subscribed to various EOI initiatives. Its protection of customer information has, accordingly, seen numerous changes.

In this chapter I offer a portrait of the bank secrecy regime that applies in Singapore, with particular regard to recent developments. What started as an implied term in the bank–customer contract has developed into a detailed statutory duty of secrecy contained in the Banking Act, s 47.[1] My introductory sections offer a brief history of this development as well as an overview of the regulatory landscape in which banks operate in Singapore. Some thoughts on the relationship between Singapore's data protection legislation and its bank secrecy rules come next. In the main body of this

---

For helpful comments on earlier drafts, I am grateful to: Lam Chee Kin, my colleagues Dora Neo and Helena Whalen-Bridge, the audience to whom I presented my research at the Annual Conference of the Society of Legal Scholars, University of Nottingham, 9–12 September 2014, and participants in the Bank Secrecy Symposium, organised by the Centre for Banking and Finance Law at the National University of Singapore on 4–5 December 2014.

[1] Banking Act (Cap 19, 2008 Rev Ed Sing), s 47 [Banking Act].

chapter, I analyse key features of the bank secrecy rules and highlight contentious aspects before moving on to discuss the incursions of recent years. It cannot be denied that these incursions have eroded, to some extent, the customer's right to bank secrecy. I argue, nevertheless, that these developments are consistent with the rationale of bank secrecy in Singapore. As such, Singapore's position as a financial hub is enhanced by these developments. And, while I express some reservations about the EOI initiatives in the tax context, I acknowledge that they reflect a worldwide trend and are therefore, the 'new normal'.

As regards terminology, the term 'secrecy' is used in the heading of s 47 although, as a result of a 2016 amendment, it will be replaced with the phrase 'privacy'. The change has probably been prompted by the negative connotations that 'secrecy' came to acquire in this context. Be that as it may, in keeping with the title of this book, the term 'secrecy' will be used in this chapter, as it is in numerous others.

10.2   History and Rationale of Bank Secrecy in Singapore

Owing to its British colonial history, Singapore received and adopted the leading English authority on a bank's obligation of secrecy[2]: *Tournier* v. *National Provincial and Union Bank of England* (*Tournier*).[3] In *Tournier*, the Court of Appeal (England) recognised that the bank had an implied contractual duty, based on the parties' presumed intentions, to keep the customer's banking affairs confidential.[4] For decades, however, the *Tournier* rule has been supplemented in Singapore's banking legislation.[5] For example, the Banking Act of 1970 prohibited bank officers from dis-

---

[2]   See e.g. *Susilawati* v. *American Express Bank Ltd* [2009] 2 SLR (R) 737 at paras. 66–7; M. Soe, *The Banking Law of Singapore and Malaysia* (Singapore: Law Book Company of Singapore and Malaysia, 1975), chapter V; D. Campbell (General Editor) *International Bank Secrecy* (London, Sweet & Maxwell, 1992) at para. 31-001; G. Griffiths (gen. ed.) *Neate and Godfrey: Bank Confidentiality*, 6th edn (England: Bloomsbury, 2015) at para. 33.2, 33.5.

[3]   [1924] 1 KB 461 [*Tournier*]. For a discussion of Singapore's legal ancestry and background, see W. Woon, 'The Applicability of English Law in Singapore' in K. Tan (ed.), *The Singapore Legal System* (Singapore University Press, 1999); G.W. Bartholomew, 'The Singapore Legal System' in R. Hassan (ed.), *Singapore: Society in Transition* (Oxford: Oxford University Press, 1976), chapter V.

[4]   *Ibid.* at 471–2, 480, 483. Surprisingly, until the *Tournier* decision in 1924, an English bank's duty of secrecy had received little judicial attention, see *ibid.* at 471, 479; also H. Hart, *The Law of Banking* (London: Stevens & Sons Limited, 1904) at 205.

[5]   See Soe, *supra* note 2; E.P. Ellinger, 'Bank Secrecy under the Banking Act of Singapore', *BFLR*, 1 (1986–7), 385; S.A. Booysen, 'Bank Secrecy in Singapore and the Customer's Consent to Disclosure', *JIBLR*, 10 (2011), 501 (Booysen, 'Bank Secrecy in Singapore').

closing account information to nonresident persons and foreign governments.[6] These provisions were replaced in 1983 by more comprehensive
provisions which were further refined in 1984.[7] A major development
came in 2001 when the precursor of the current bank secrecy regime was
introduced.

The reason for the overhaul in 2001 was that the then existing provisions were apparently proving to be unduly restrictive for banks and were
hindering, for example, the outsourcing of operations and securitisation
of loans.[8] In *Ching Mun Fong* v. *Standard Chartered Bank*, the Singapore
Court of Appeal said that the 2001 reform sought to 'loosen the previously
tight banking secrecy laws to the benefit of banks and to strike a better
balance between operational requirements of banks and the need to preserve customer confidentiality'.[9] The 2001 scheme prohibited disclosure of
customer information subject to a list of exceptions. This scheme has since
seen revisions although it retains its 2001 character.

The authors of *Ellinger's Modern Banking Law* explain the bank's duty
of secrecy as an incident of the law of agency, without which the bank–
customer relationship is unlikely to flourish.[10] The rationale for the duty
of secrecy, as explained by Bankes LJ in *Tournier*, is that the customer's
credit depends on it.[11] This rationale is consistent with the duty arising as
an implied term in the contract, breach of which entitles the customer to
damages.[12] Another, perhaps additional, rationale appears to have motivated the scheme introduced by Singapore in 2001. Parliament was told
that 'banking secrecy is important to maintaining the confidence of customers in our banking system.'[13] In other words, bank secrecy helps to

---

[6] Act 41 of 1970, s 42(2)(a) and s 42(2)(b). This prohibition was subject to exceptions including the customer's permission.

[7] Banking (Amendment) Act 1983 (Act 6 of 1983), s 2 and Banking (Amendment) Act 1984
(Act 2 of 1984), s 10. See also Ellinger, 'Bank Secrecy under the Banking Act of Singapore',
supra note 5.

[8] See the statement in Parliament on the second reading of the Banking (Amendment) Bill,
Singapore Parliamentary Debates, Official Report (16 May 2001) vol 73 at col 1689 (BG Lee
Hsien Loong, Deputy Prime Minister) [BG Lee Hsien Loong, Banking (Amendment) Bill
Debate].

[9] [2012] 4 SLR 185 at para. [45]. See BG Lee Hsien Loong, Banking (Amendment) Bill
Debate, *supra* note 8.

[10] E.P. Ellinger, E. Lomnicka and C. Hare, *Ellinger's Modern Banking Law*, 5th edn (Oxford
University Press, 2011) at 171–2 [*Modern Banking Law*].

[11] *Tournier, supra* note 3 at 474.

[12] See the view expressed by Stanton in Chapter 12, that bank secrecy in the United Kingdom
today should not be seen as simply a contractual duty.

[13] See BG Lee Hsien Loong, Banking (Amendment) Bill Debate, *supra* note 8.

attract customers and promote Singapore as a financial centre.[14] Section 47, like its predecessors, makes breach of the secrecy obligation an offence.[15]

Bank secrecy is discussed in this chapter as it pertains to commercial banks. There are numerous other financial intermediaries operating in Singapore,[16] including merchant banks,[17] finance companies (which engage in a similar business to banks but on a smaller scale),[18] trust companies[19] and moneylenders.[20] Most financial intermediaries in Singapore are regulated by the Monetary Authority of Singapore (MAS),[21] each pursuant to its own statute or rules.[22] Merchant banks and trust companies are subject to the same or a similar secrecy regime as applies to commercial banks.[23] In other cases,[24] if not specifically provided for, it is arguable that an implied duty of secrecy resembling *Tournier* arises, or that equity will recognise a duty of confidentiality.

10.3   Bank Secrecy, Data Protection and Outsourcing

The Personal Data Protection Act 2012[25] (PDPA) is the first comprehensive piece of legislation to tackle the collection, use and disclosure of personal data in Singapore.[26] Professor Simon Chesterman has noted that the PDPA 'is clearly focused on the management of information', rather than

---

[14] Similar reasons motivated the passing of Singapore's data protection legislation, as noted by S. Chesterman, 'After Privacy: The Rise of Facebook, the Fall of Wikileaks, and Singapore's Personal Data Protection Act 2012', *Sing JLS*, [2012], 391 at 402.

[15] Banking Act, *supra* note 1, s 47(6); see also Banking Act of 1970, *supra* note 6, s 42(4).

[16] Such as financial advisers, moneylenders, moneychangers, pawnbrokers and remittance agencies.

[17] Merchant banks are regulated via the Monetary Authority of Singapore Act (Cap 186, 1999 Rev Ed Sing), s 28 [MAS Act].

[18] See the Finance Companies Act (Cap 108, 2011 Rev Ed Sing).

[19] See Trust Companies Act (Cap 336, 2006 Rev Ed Sing).

[20] See MAS Act, *supra* note 17.

[21] See MAS Act, *supra* note 17, s 28.

[22] Moneylenders, and pawnbrokers, are under the purview of the Ministry of Law, see: Ministry of Law, 'About Us: What We Do' (18 November 2015), online: www.mlaw.gov.sg/content/minlaw/en/about-us/what-we-do.html

[23] For trust companies, see Trust Companies Act, *supra* note 19, s 49; for merchant banks, see Banking Act, *supra* note 1, s 47(10).

[24] Moneylenders are, for example, required to maintain confidentiality as a condition of their moneylending licence. See: Ministry of Law, 'Registrar's Conditions for the Grant of Moneylender's Licence' (1 October 2015), online: www.mlaw.gov.sg/content/dam/minlaw/rom/Moneylenders/Licence%20Conditions.pdf

[25] No. 26 of 2012 [PDPA].

[26] Chesterman, *supra* note 14 at 400.

on the protection of privacy.[27] Personal data is data from which an individual is identifiable.[28] Business contact information (i.e. an individual's name and work/business contact details)[29] is generally not covered by the Act.[30] The Act permits the collection, use and disclosure of personal data only with the consent (actual or deemed) of the individual concerned, or where required or authorised by the PDPA or another written law.[31]

The main ways in which banks are affected by the PDPA include the need to obtain consent for the collection and use of personal data, and to provide information about its purpose and use[32]; customers can seek information about how their data has been used[33] and there are now restrictions on sending customers marketing messages as a result of the establishment of a 'Do Not Call' Register.[34] While the PDPA undoubtedly affects banks in their operations,[35] it does not offer special protection for particularly sensitive data such as financial records,[36] and the PDPA is subject to other written laws,[37] such as the bank secrecy rules in the Banking Act. The MAS has made it clear to banks (and other financial institutions (FIs)) that their obligations to combat money laundering, for example by performing customer due diligence, override any restrictions imposed by the PDPA. The PDPA has affected bank secrecy in one particularly notable way: prior to the PDPA, banks were allowed to disclose the names and contact details of their customers to other FIs in Singapore for the purposes of marketing financial products and services in Singapore. This exception to the duty of secrecy was removed by the PDPA.

A bank's duty of secrecy and the obligations imposed on banks by the PDPA operate alongside each other. As discussed by Greenleaf and Tyree in Chapter 2 on banks and data protection,[38] there are differences in the ambits

---

[27] *Ibid.* at 403–5; see also PDPA, *supra* note 25, s 3.
[28] PDPA, *supra* note 25, s 2.
[29] *Ibid.*
[30] *Ibid.*, s 4(5).
[31] *Ibid.*, s 13.
[32] *Ibid.*, Part IV.
[33] *Ibid.*, Part V.
[34] *Ibid.*, Part IX.
[35] For a broader insight into how banks are affected by data protection legislation, see Greenleaf and Tyree, Chapter 2. See also: Association of Banks in Singapore, 'Code of Banking Practices – The Personal Data Protection Act' (8 August 2015), online: www.abs.org.sg/docs/library/abs-code-banking-practices-pdpa.pdf
[36] Chesterman, *supra* note 14 at 406.
[37] PDPA, supra note 25, s 4(6) says that Parts III–VI, which set out key provisions of the PDPA, are subject to other written laws.
[38] Greenleaf and Tyree, Chapter 2.

of bank secrecy and data protection regimes, as well as areas of overlap. For example, bank secrecy in Singapore applies to customers while data protection obligations can arise in respect of persons having nonbanking dealings with banks; bank secrecy in Singapore is focused on limiting disclosure of customer information, while the data protection rules are broader and affect the collection, storage and use of personal data. Despite the differences, a breach of bank secrecy may also be a breach of the PDPA.

As noted earlier, Singapore's bank secrecy rules were amended in 2001 to facilitate, inter alia, outsourcing and the Banking Act specifically permits disclosure of customer information for the purposes of a bank's operational needs.[39] The PDPA imposes minimal obligations on so-called data intermediaries,[40] with the primary responsibility for compliance lying with those who contract with them.[41] In this respect, banks are also subject to the obligations set out in MAS Notice 634 which predates the PDPA.[42] For example, banks must conduct due diligence on the suitability of outsourcing service providers,[43] if customer information is sent out of the jurisdiction the bank must satisfy itself that the legal system of the foreign jurisdiction will generally respect the confidentiality of the information,[44] only the minimum information necessary to obtain the service sought should be provided,[45] and outsourcing agreements must include various clauses aimed at securing the confidentiality of the information.[46] In June 2015, the Association of Banks in Singapore announced industry guidelines that outsourcing service providers and their subcontractors, operating in Singapore, are expected to meet.[47] Among other things, outsourcers must have the soundness and suitability of their systems audited annually.[48]

---

[39] Banking Act, *supra* note 1, Third Schedule, Part II at para. 3.

[40] PDPA, *supra* note 25, s 4(2). For example, reasonable steps must be taken to ensure the security of the data – PDPA, s 24; it may not be retained in a form that identifies particular individuals when the purpose for which it was collected has ceased – PDPA, s 25. See also Chesterman, *supra* note 14 at 408–9.

[41] *Ibid.*, s 4(3).

[42] MAS Notice 634, 'Banking Secrecy – Conditions for Outsourcing', revised 25 May 2004 [MAS Notice 634]. See also MAS, 'Consultation Paper: Notice on Outsourcing', P018-2014 (September 2014); MAS, 'Consultation Paper: Guidelines on Outsourcing', P019-2014 (September 2014).

[43] MAS Notice 634, *supra* note 42, Appendix 1 at para. 2.

[44] *Ibid.*, Appendix 1 at paras. 4–5.

[45] *Ibid.*, Appendix 1 at para. 6.

[46] *Ibid.*, Appendix 1 at paras. 8 and 10, see also 13.

[47] Association of Banks in Singapore, 'Guidelines on Control Objectives & Procedures for Outsourced Service Providers' (26 June 2015), online: www.abs.org.sg/docs/library/abs_outsource_guidelines.pdf

[48] *Ibid.*, at 26.

Singapore has seen at least one confidentiality lapse in the outsourcing context. In March 2013, a hacker misappropriated information pertaining to hundreds of Standard Chartered Bank's private banking clients.[49] The information was accessed from the server of a service provider that printed the bank's statements. The MAS took supervisory action and cautioned that it 'takes a serious view on the safeguarding of customer information' and 'reminded all financial institutions to ensure that robust controls are in place'.[50] Details of the supervisory action were not disclosed in the public statement and it is not clear whether it was based on the bank secrecy provisions, MAS Notice 634 or a more general provision in the Banking Act such as s 49, which allows the MAS to take action where, inter alia, it considers that the bank has engaged in conduct that is likely to adversely affect depositors.

10.4   Bank Secrecy Regime in Singapore

The key provision for bank secrecy in Singapore, s 47 of the Banking Act, states that 'Customer information shall not, in any way, be disclosed by a bank in Singapore or any of its officers to any other person except as expressly provided in this Act'.[51] Notably, the statutory obligation of secrecy applies not only to the bank but also to its officers. To fully understand this prohibition, a number of terms require elaboration: 'bank in Singapore', 'customer' and 'customer information'. A 'bank in Singapore' is defined in the Banking Act as comprising banks incorporated in Singapore as well as the Singapore branches of foreign incorporated banks.[52] Both are required to hold a banking licence issued by the MAS.

---

[49] See e.g. L.S. Siow, 'MAS Takes Supervisory Action against Bank', *The Business Times* (12 April 2014); S.S. Lee, 'Standard Chartered Bank Client Statements Stolen from Server', *The Straits Times* (6 December 2013).

[50] See MAS, 'Comment by MAS Spokesperson on the Theft of Bank Statements Belonging to Some Private Banking Clients of Standard Chartered Bank' (11 April 2014), online: www .mas.gov.sg/news-and-publications/media-releases/2014/comment-by-mas-spokesper-son-on-the-theft-of-bank-statements.aspx

[51] Banking Act, *supra* note 1, s 47(1). An officer of a corporation includes its directors, sec-retary and employees, and a 'person' includes a corporation, see Banking Act, s 2. The Interpretation Act (Cap 1, 2002 Rev Ed Sing), s 2 says that a 'person' includes a company, association or body of persons, whether corporate or not.

[52] Banking Act, *supra* note 1, s 2. Banking business (defined as taking deposits, making loans and paying and collecting cheques) may not be conducted in Singapore without a licence, see Banking Act, s 4(1). The MAS distinguishes different types of banking licence, see MAS website, online: www.mas.gov.sg

The notion of a 'customer' is not defined by the Act, save that it includes the MAS and other central banks, and excludes entities engaging in banking business.[53] The common law concept of customer is aligned with having an account with a bank,[54] or an agreement to open an account.[55] The suitability of this test in the bank secrecy context is open to question.[56] On the one hand, if strictly applied, it seems to follow that the prohibition on disclosure will be inapplicable as soon as a person ceases to have a Singapore bank account. The most likely scenario regarding a former customer will involve information obtained during the period that the person was a customer, which information should surely remain protected.[57] Support for this view can be derived from Atkin LJ in *Tournier*,[58] who reasoned that to permit disclosure of a former customer's banking information would be incompatible with the rationale of bank secrecy as articulated in that case. I would argue that to allow disclosure of a former customer's information would equally undermine the statutory rationale of maintaining confidence in the banking system, since customers may be deterred from commencing or continuing a bank–customer relationship with a Singapore bank if the bank is free to disclose their information on the cessation of the relationship.[59] In practice, it seems that Singapore banks operate cautiously and observe s 47 vis-à-vis former customers. On the other hand, secrecy obligations seem to arise when banks transact through an account with counterparties from the shadow banking sector, for example in a foreign exchange transaction; yet if the counterparty engages in banking business,[60] it is not considered a customer, as noted earlier.[61] It is not clear that such different treatment of banks and shadow banks is intended. Legislative clarification of the concept of 'a customer'

---

[53] Banking Act, *supra* note 1, s 40A.

[54] *Great Western Railway Co. Ltd* v. *London & County Banking Company Limited* [1901] AC 414; *Commissioners of Taxation* v. *English, Scottish & Australian Bank Ltd* [1920] AC 683.

[55] *Woods* v. *Martins Bank Ltd* [1959] 1 QB 55. Some texts have queried the necessity for an account: see *Modern Banking Law, supra* note 10, at 116–7.

[56] For a general discussion of the suitability of this definition, see *Modern Banking Law, supra* note 10 at 116–7.

[57] It is noteworthy that under the FCA Handbook in the United Kingdom, former customers are still entitled to the confidentiality of their banking information, see Stanton, Chapter 12.

[58] *Supra* note 3 at 485.

[59] Customers contemplating account closure but wishing to retain maximum confidentiality can always secure their position by maintaining a minimal account presence in Singapore.

[60] 'Banking business' is defined in the Banking Act, *supra* note 1, s 2 as taking deposits, making loans and offering cheque services. See also S.A. Booysen, 'The Meaning of 'Banking Business' in Singapore: Is It Time for an Update?', *JIBLR* [2011], 248.

[61] Banking Act, *supra* note 1, s 40A.

for the purposes of bank secrecy would be welcome since s 47 is rarely the subject of court action and thus an opportunity for future clarification from the courts is uncertain.

'Customer information' is defined in the Banking Act. It embraces information relating to a customer's accounts, deposits, investments and safe custody arrangements.[62] In *PSA Corp Ltd* v. *Korea Exchange Bank*, Woo Bih Li JC noted that the definition of customer information is wide:[63] 'In my view, "information" includes documentary information and so long as the information sought relates to an account of a customer, then, *prima facie* disclosure by the bank is prohibited.'[64] Information that cannot be traced to a named customer is not customer information, as noted by the Court of Appeal in *Teo Wai Cheong* v. *Crédit Industriel et Commercial*: 's 47(1) of the Banking Act does not prohibit the disclosure of "customer information" where the customer cannot be identified.'[65] The court considered, for instance, that disclosure of telephone conversations with customers identified only as A, B or C was not prohibited.

Breach of s 47 is an offence punishable by fine and/or imprisonment.[66] Liability appears to be strict (similar to the *Tournier* duty)[67] although intentional disclosure is likely to be viewed more seriously than inadvertent disclosure. There have been few prosecutions under s 47.[68]

The development of electronic banking has brought with it new vulnerabilities that banks need to safeguard against.[69] MAS Notice 644 requires banks to take reasonable steps to limit system downtime and to implement measures to 'protect customer information from unauthorised access or

---

[62] *Ibid.*

[63] [2002] 1 SLR (R) 871 at para. 24.

[64] *Ibid.*, at para. 25.

[65] [2011] SGCA 13 at para. 23; Banking Act, *supra* note 1, s 40A.

[66] Banking Act, *supra* note 1, s 47(6). An individual may be imprisoned for a term up to three years and/or may be fined up to S$125,000. In other cases, namely corporations, the fine shall not exceed S$250,000.

[67] See the discussion by Stanton, Chapter 12.

[68] No cases are revealed by Singapore's Lawnet search engine. See, however, K. Singh, 'Ex-Bank Officer Jailed', *The Straits Times* (4 June 2010); S. Alkhatib, 'Jail for Relationship Manager Who Sold Details of Bank's Clients', *Today* (24 March 2011). For a more recent incident under investigation, see J. Lee, 'MAS Probes Case of UOB's Unshredded Client Data', *The Business Times* (19 July 2016).

[69] See Chapter 12 in which Stanton draws attention to the cyber risks associated with modern banking. See also Reply to Parliamentary Question on cybersecurity measures to ensure the integrity of our banking system and financial transactions, Question No 385, Notice Paper 234 of 2016, 11 July 2016, online: www.mas.gov.sg/News-and-Publications/Parliamentary-Replies/2016/Reply-to-Parliamentary-Question-on-cybersecurity-measures.aspx

disclosure'.[70] MAS guidelines emphasise bank responsibility at board level for the utilisation of technology and the need to protect systems from disruption and rogue intrusion.[71]

10.4.1 Relationship between the Common Law and Statutory Regimes in Singapore

With the growth of bank secrecy legislation in Singapore, an important question concerns the relationship between the statutory scheme and the common law *Tournier* rule. This question has particular significance for the remedies available for a breach of the secrecy obligation. The remedy for breach of contract (in this case of the implied term to keep information confidential) is damages. Where no actual damage is suffered, a customer is entitled to nominal damages. The statute renders breach of the secrecy obligation a criminal offence and no provision is made for damages to be paid to the customer.

Prior to the wholesale reform of Singapore's bank secrecy regime in 2001, there seemed to be a consensus among authors that the common law and statutory provisions coexisted.[72] After the 2001 overhaul, however, opposing views emerged. One was that the common law and statutory scheme continued to coexist to the extent that they were compatible, failing which the statute prevailed.[73] The other view was that the new statutory rules displaced the common law.[74] The question was finally addressed in 2009 by the Singapore Court of Appeal. It indicated that the 'less sophisticated' common law scheme had not survived the 'more comprehensive' statutory

---

[70] MAS Notice 644, 'Notice on Technology Risk Management', 21 June 2013, at para. 9, online: www.mas.gov.sg/~/media/MAS/Regulations%20and%20Financial%20Stability/Regulations%20Guidance%20and%20Licensing/Commercial%20Banks/Regulations%20Guidance%20and%20Licensing/Notices/Notice%20MAS%20644.pdf

[71] MAS, 'Technology Risk Management Guidelines' (June 2013), online: www.mas.gov.sg/~/media/MAS/Regulations%20and%20Financial%20Stability/Regulatory%20and%20Supervisory%20Framework/Risk%20Management/TRM%20Guidelines%20%2021%20June%202013.pdf

[72] See Soe, *supra* note 2, chapter V; C.C. Poh, *Law of Banking*, 3rd edn, vol I (Singapore: Longman Singapore Publishers (Pte) Ltd, 1995) at 357–9; E.P. Ellinger, 'Disclosure of Customer Information to a Bank's Own Branches and to Affiliates', *BFLR*, 20 (2004/2005) 137 at 137–8 [Ellinger, 'Disclosure of Customer Information']; *Neate: Bank Confidentiality*, *supra* note 2 at para. 33.4.

[73] C.C. Poh, *Law of Banker and Customer*, 6th edn (Singapore: LexisNexis, 2016) at 543–5.

[74] Ellinger 'Disclosure of Customer Information', *supra* note 72 at 137–8.

rules. Thus, in *Susilawati* v. *American Express Bank Ltd* (*Susilawati*), V K Rajah JA said[75]:

> In light of the plain wording of s 47, our current statutory regime on banking secrecy leaves no room for the four general common law exceptions expounded in *Tournier* to co-exist. They have been embraced within the framework of s 47 of the Banking Act, which is now the exclusive regime governing banking secrecy in Singapore.

Prima facie this decision suggests that the common law implied term has been superseded by the statutory rule. If so, no breach of contract arises when the duty of secrecy is breached and hence no damages are recoverable, an outcome that has been criticised for eroding customer rights.[76] It is, however, doubtful that the Court intended such a consequence. One way to understand the *Susilawati* decision is that the common law duty of secrecy remains intact but the common law exceptions have been replaced by the more detailed qualifications in the Act. Some support for the coexistence of the implied contractual duty and the statutory duty can be found in s 47(8) which says that nothing prevents a bank from entering into a higher contractual duty than that owed under s 47. Such reasoning is not, however, without difficulties since despite the legislature's obvious contemplation that an express, higher, contractual duty and the statutory duty can coexist, it is not obvious that there is a residual, implied contractual duty in the absence of an express agreement. An express agreement on bank secrecy would be unusual. This is another respect in which a clarifying amendment to the statute would be welcome.

A customer who has suffered loss from breach of the secrecy obligation may also consider alternative avenues of obtaining redress. There are a number of possibilities, mostly tortious, including breach of statutory duty and defamation. Perhaps the most promising is breach of a duty of confidence.[77] Elaboration of this point is beyond the scope of this chapter but it is noteworthy that some scholars support the view that

---

[75] *Supra* note 2 at para. 67.
[76] See C.C. Poh, 'Banking Law', *SAL Ann Rev*, 10 (2009), 73 at 78–83.
[77] See *X Pte Ltd* v. *CDE* [1992] 2 SLR (R) 575 at paras. 23 and 27; also *PH Hydraulics & Engineering Pte Ltd* v. *Intrepid Offshore Construction Pte Ltd* [2012] 4 SLR 36 at para. 55; *Clearlab SG Pte Ltd* v. *Ting Chong Chai* [2015] 1 SLR 163 at para. 64. See also Chapter 12 in which Professor Keith Stanton discusses the link between the bank's duty of secrecy and confidential relationships.

the equitable duty of confidence has given rise to a new tort of misusing private information.[78]

10.4.2   Permitted Disclosure under the Banking Act

The Banking Act, and *Tournier* before it, recognises that the bank's duty of secrecy is not absolute, and disclosure is therefore permitted in a range of circumstances set out in the Third Schedule to the Act.[79] Where disclosure is permitted by the Third Schedule, it may be subject to conditions. For example, a bank may disclose the cancellation or suspension of a defaulting customer's credit or charge card to other card-issuing 'FIs'.[80] The conditions are that only the customer's name, identity, the amount outstanding and the date of suspension/cancellation may be disclosed.

The Third Schedule is divided into two parts: Part II disclosures may not be disclosed further by the recipient, while Part I disclosures are not so restricted. For example, disclosure with the customer's written consent is in Part I and may therefore be further transmitted by the recipient (unless, presumably, the terms of the consent prohibit it) while disclosure to a professional adviser (such as a lawyer) of the bank is in Part II and may, therefore, not be further divulged by the adviser. Further disclosure by the recipient of the information in Part II cases is also an offence.[81]

Many of the Third Schedule exceptions are specific examples of the more general exceptions recognised in *Tournier*.[82] For example, *Tournier* allowed disclosure where it would be in the interests of the bank to do so whereas the Third Schedule allows disclosure in legal proceedings involving the bank and the customer;[83] *Tournier* allowed disclosure if compelled by law and the Third Schedule allows disclosure in compliance with an

---

[78] See e.g. J. Murphy and C. Witting, *Street on Torts*, 13th edn (Oxford: Oxford University Press, 2012) at 605.

[79] Banking Act, *supra* note 1, s 47(2). The Third Schedule was previously the Sixth Schedule. See also *VisionHealthOne Corp Pte Ltd* v. *HD Holdings Pte Ltd* [2010] 3 SLR 97 at paras. 21–2.

[80] Banking Act, *supra* note 1, Third Schedule, Part II at para. 6.

[81] Banking Act, supra note 1, s 47(5). Where the person receiving the disclosure is outside of the jurisdiction, there are obvious difficulties with enforcement of the prohibition on further disclosure.

[82] *Supra* note 3 at 473, Bankes LJ, namely: (a) disclosure compelled by law, (b) a duty owed to the public to disclose, (c) disclosure in the interests of the bank, (d) disclosure with the customer's express or implied consent. See also the observation of the trial court in *Susilawati* v. *American Express Bank Ltd* [2008] 1 SLR (R) 237 at para. 84 and C.C. Poh, *Law of Banker and Customer, supra* note 73 at 550.

[83] Banking Act, *supra* note 1, Third Schedule, Part I at para. 4(a).

order of the Supreme Court made pursuant to the Evidence Act[84] or for the purposes of a criminal prosecution.[85]

An important question is whether a bank can or must notify the customer of any intended disclosure of customer information.[86] There is no indication in s 47 that a bank must notify its customer of an intended or actual disclosure under the Third Schedule. It stands to reason, though, that such notification cannot be intended in at least some cases, as it could thwart the object of the disclosure, for example in garnishee proceedings or criminal investigations.[87]

Some of the Third Schedule exceptions to the duty of secrecy are very specific and will not be examined here. For example, disclosure is possible: pursuant to a garnishee order,[88] or for the payment of compensation under Singapore's deposit insurance scheme.[89] Bearing in mind that one of the themes of this book is how recent developments targeting tax evasion and other transnational crime have affected bank secrecy, I will elaborate on selected exceptions in the Third Schedule that seem pertinent to disclosure pursuant to a request from a foreign authority.

10.4.2.1   Customer's Written Permission to Disclose

Banks may disclose customer information with the customer's written permission.[90] This is similar to the *Tournier* qualification that banks may disclose information with the customer's express or implied consent. A customer's written permission may be forthcoming, for example, if the customer needs a credit reference. A customer will obviously be reluctant to consent if it is contrary to his interests, for example, if he is under investigation for tax evasion, terrorism or money laundering. The reason for mentioning this exception is that Singapore banks invariably include

---

[84] *Ibid.*, Third Schedule, Part I at para. 7. The object of this exception is to save banks from attending court to produce evidence contained in their records. The exception was applied in *La Dolce Vita Fine Dining Co Ltd v. Deutsche Bank AG* [2016] SGHCR 3 at [85–109]; see also *Wee Soon Kim Anthony v. UBS AG* [2003] 2 SLR(R) 91 at [17].

[85] Banking Act, *supra* note 1, Third Schedule, Part I at para. 5(a).

[86] See *Modern Banking Law*, pp. 188–9; also Broome, Chapter 13.

[87] Some statutes authorising the disclosure of customer information by banks make it an offence to tip off the affected person, see e.g. Corruption, Drug Trafficking and Other Serious Crimes (Confiscation of Benefits) Act (Cap 65A, 2000 Rev Ed Sing), s 48 [CDSA].

[88] Banking Act, *supra* note 1, Third Schedule, Part I at para. 6. For a discussion of some of the exceptions, see *Neate: Bank Confidentiality*, *supra* note 2 at paras. 33.12–33.22.

[89] *Ibid.*, Third Schedule, Part II at para. 10. See S.A. Booysen, 'Deposit Insurance In Singapore: Why Have It, Who Gets It, How Does It Work?', *Sing JLS* [2013], 76.

[90] Banking Act, *supra* note 1, Third Schedule, Part I at para. 1.

some form of consent to disclosure in their standard terms and conditions (T&C).[91] The typical features of 'T&C consent' are that it is given in advance of any contemplated disclosure; it is broadly and generally worded and, therefore, vague and lacking particularity. It signifies 'consent' only in the objective sense that the customer signed a contract incorporating such a clause into his contract. Notably, the customer is invariably unaware of the clause and ignorant of its meaning.

The question that needs to be considered, therefore, is whether banks can rely on such T&C consent to disclose customer information that is not otherwise authorised by the Third Schedule. The answer depends on what the legislature means by 'permission'. I argue that T&C consent should not ordinarily satisfy the kind of permission contemplated by the Third Schedule.[92] Later in this chapter, in the context of the tax cooperation initiatives seen in Singapore, I identify an example of a more circumscribed consent that I consider may qualify under this exception.

My argument is that the primary idea behind the 'written permission' exception is to cover those instances of disclosure that the customer desires in his own interests. It is a cooperative, not an adversarial, exception to bank secrecy and surely means permission that is knowingly given and with a known disclosure in mind. The interpretation of statutes in Singapore must, within the confines of the language of the statute,[93] 'promote the purpose or object underlying the written law'.[94] Since the rationale of bank secrecy in Singapore is to maintain confidence in Singapore's banking system,[95] T&C consent should not qualify as written permission where customers are unaware that broad consents to disclosure have been extracted from them on opening their bank accounts. Such T&C consent denies customers the opportunity to discriminate between favourable and unfavourable disclosure. Support for my restrictive interpretation of the consent provision is that the need for *written* permission was introduced in 1984 to 'tighten up the existing exceptions to banking secrecy'.[96]

---

[91] A similar practice in Australia has been discussed by D. Chaikin, 'Adapting the Qualifications to the Banker's Common Law Duty of Confidentiality to Fight Transnational Crime', *Sydney L Rev*, 33 (2011), 265 at 289–90.

[92] See also Booysen, 'Bank Secrecy in Singapore', *supra* note 5.

[93] See e.g. *PP* v. *Low Kok Heng* [2007] 4 SLR (R) 183 at para. 57.

[94] Interpretation Act, *supra* note 51, s 9A(1).

[95] See BG Lee Hsien Loong, Banking (Amendment) Bill Debate, *supra* note 8.

[96] See the statement in Parliament on the second reading of the Banking (Amendment) Bill, *Singapore Parliamentary Debates, Official Report* (17 January 1984) vol 43 at col 332 (Dr Goh Keng Swee, First Deputy Prime Minister and Minister of Education).

If T&C consent clauses are valid, it will have the unintended effect of relaxing the consent exception and not tightening it. This qualification to the duty of secrecy will then be open to abuse by banks who are the drafters of the T&C. Finally, it is apparent that the Act sets a minimum standard of secrecy that cannot be contracted out of,[97] and allowing broad T&C consent is tantamount to doing just that.

The practice of obtaining T&C consent is also arguably contrary to the Banking Codes to which most Singapore banks subscribe, and it may even constitute an unfair practice under the Consumer Protection (Fair Trading) Act (CPFTA).[98] Singapore's Banking Codes state that banks will observe their secrecy obligations set out in the Banking Act.[99] Although the Banking Act does contemplate written permission, allowing banks to expand the right to disclose without drawing customers' attention to what they are doing, is surely inconsistent with this promise.[100] For similar reasons, banks that use the T&C consent are arguably engaging in an unfair practice under the CPFTA – a statute which sanctions misleading or deceptive conduct, or taking advantage of vulnerable consumers.[101] Since most consumer-customers are unaware of the T&C consent, and many would probably not agree to it if asked overtly, it is arguable that banks are engaging in an unfair practice.

Admittedly, from a bank's point of view, the ability to transmit some information is essential if the bank is to provide the services it offers customers. To the extent that T&C consents are intended to enable banks to fulfil their usual role, I suggest that the solution lies in more informed consent or an addition to the Third Schedule to cover incidental and unavoidable disclosures flowing from the execution of customer instructions.

[97] This view is deduced from Banking Act, *supra* note 1, s 47(8) which allows banks to agree to a higher standard of secrecy than that imposed by the Act; see also C.C. Poh, *Law of Banker and Customer, supra* note 73 at 545.

[98] Consumer Protection (Fair Trading) Act (Cap 52A, 2009 Rev Ed Sing), s 4 [CPFTA].

[99] 'Code of Consumer Banking Practice' (November 2009), cl 3.c.ii.; 'Code of Banking Practice for Small Businesses' (November 2006), cl 16.b. The codes are published by the Association of Banks in Singapore and are available online at: www.abs.org.sg

[100] It is also arguable that an attempt to expand the written permission exception conflicts with the promise in the Banking Codes to act fairly towards the customer, see 'Code of Consumer Banking Practice', *supra* note 99, cl 3.b.i.; 'Code of Banking Practice for Small Businesses', *supra* note 99, cl 3.a.i.

[101] CPFTA, *supra* note 98, s 4.

10.4.2.2 Compliance with an Order/Request for the Purposes of Investigating an Offence or Making a Complaint/ Report on a Suspected Offence under Singapore Law

This exception[102] facilitates disclosure of customer information pursuant to one of eight Singapore statutes,[103] for the purposes of investigating, prosecuting or making a complaint/report about an offence suspected to have been committed under Singapore law.[104] The most significant of the eight statutes is the Criminal Procedure Code under which offences under Singapore law are tried.[105] It makes particular provision for the production of customer information by an FI for the purposes of investigations or proceedings.[106] This exception aligns with the *Tournier* exception that allows for disclosure under legal compulsion and is uncontroversial. Offences such as tax evasion, money laundering and terrorism financing are covered insofar as they are offences under Singapore law and the information is sought under one of the eight stipulated statutes.

10.4.2.3 Disclosure to a Foreign Bank's Parent Supervisory Authority

This exception may appear to offer an indirect route for a foreign authority to obtain customer information, by demanding the information from the parent regulator of a foreign bank operating in Singapore.[107] One of the conditions attached to this exception, however, is that no deposit information may be disclosed. Deposit information covers any deposit, fund management or safe deposit arrangement with a bank. This limitation means, therefore, that there is little scope to obtain detailed information about particular customers via this route.

---

[102] Banking Act, *supra* note 1, Third Schedule, Part I at para. 5.

[103] The term used is 'specified written law' which, under Banking Act, Third Schedule, Part III, refers to one of eight Singapore statutes: the Companies Act (Cap 50, 2006 Rev Ed Sing), the Criminal Procedure Code (Cap 68, 2012 Rev Ed Sing), the Goods and Services Tax Act (Cap 117A, 2005 Rev Ed Sing), the Hostage-Taking Act 2010 (Act No 19 of 2010), the Income Tax Act (Cap 134, 2014 Rev Ed Sing), the Internal Security Act (Cap 143, 1985 Rev Ed Sing), the Kidnapping Act (Cap 151, 1999 Rev Ed Sing), the Moneylenders Act (Cap 188, 2010 Rev Ed Sing) and the Prevention of Corruption Act (Cap 241, 1993 Rev Ed Sing).

[104] The term used is 'written law' which is defined in the Interpretation Act, *supra* note 51, s 2 as embracing any law in force in Singapore.

[105] Criminal Procedure Code, *supra* note 103, s 4.

[106] *Ibid.*, s 20.

[107] Banking Act, *supra* note 1, Third Schedule, Part I at para. 8.

10.4.2.4   Disclosure in the Course of Performing Duties as an Officer or Professional Adviser of the Bank

This exception allows for disclosure of customer information to the bank's officers (including an officer designated by the head office), auditors, lawyers and other professional advisers to facilitate the performance of their duties.[108] This exception does not permit disclosure to a foreign authority. It is possible, however, for the foreign authority to make its request to the bank's foreign parent company or head office outside of Singapore, which could in turn seek the information from the Singapore office with a view to passing it on to the foreign authority. For two reasons, however, this exception is not suitable to allow for disclosure to a foreign law enforcement authority. First, the disclosure by a bank in Singapore under this exception arguably does not satisfy the requirement that the disclosure is made to facilitate the 'performance' of the recipient's duties as an officer or adviser of the bank. Secondly, the officer or adviser receiving the information is not entitled to transmit the information onwards since this exception to the bank secrecy rule is in Part II of the Third Schedule. Although enforcement of this limitation may be problematic if the transgressor is outside of Singapore, if a bank in Singapore is aware that information is to be further disclosed in contravention of the Banking Act, it should surely decline to make the disclosure.

10.5   Other Legislative Exceptions to Bank Secrecy

Some of the most significant qualifications to a bank's duty of secrecy for the purposes of this chapter are set out in legislation other than the Banking Act.[109] These inroads, which centre around the triumvirate of international tax cooperation, anti-money laundering (AML) and countering the financing of terrorism (CTF), bear similar hallmarks and are components of a bigger initiative to combat transnational crime. I will outline the applicable legislative provisions and then, taking them together, comment.

10.5.1   International Tax Cooperation

Since 2013, Singapore's framework for international tax cooperation has been boosted in various ways. The first notable example is the steps taken to facilitate compliance by Singapore FIs with the US Foreign Account

---

[108] *Ibid.*, Third Schedule, Part II at para. 1.
[109] This phenomenon is evident elsewhere, see e.g. Chaikin, *supra* note 91 at 271–2.

Tax Compliance Act (FATCA).[110] FATCA is a US law, designed to limit tax evasion by US citizens, that requires FIs around the world to notify US authorities of offshore account holdings by US persons.[111] FIs failing to comply face a 30 per cent withholding tax on various US sourced payments. In effect, FATCA coerces FIs to assist in the implementation of a US law and harnesses foreign governments to facilitate that objective.[112]

Aside from the substantial economic sanction faced by Singapore's FIs for noncompliance,[113] there were other reasons for Singapore's willingness to facilitate the compliance of FIs with FATCA: 'the importance of the US as a political and economic partner of Singapore and the trend of countries complying with FATCA, it is understandable that Singapore will want to work with the US on this matter.'[114] That being the case, Singapore's response (along with those of a host of other jurisdictions) has been pragmatic. An Inter-Governmental Agreement (IGA) between Singapore and the United States assists Singapore-based FIs to be FATCA compliant,[115] and the Income Tax Act (ITA) reflects the necessary amendments.[116] Banks making disclosure pursuant to FATCA are given immunity from claims for breach of the duty of secrecy.[117] Indeed, a failure to provide the information is an offence.[118]

---

[110] For a more detailed discussion of FATCA, see O'Brien, Chapter 5.

[111] FIs may also be required to withhold 30 per cent of payments made to noncompliant payees, see IRS, 'FATCA Information for Foreign Financial Institutions and Entities' (2 June 2015), online: www.irs.gov/Businesses/Corporations/Information-for-Foreign-Financial-Institutions

[112] See the more detailed discussions in Nakajima, Chapter 4 and O'Brien, Chapter 5; also *AXY v. Comptroller of Income Tax* [2016] 1 SLR 616 at [13].

[113] See R. Cassell and J. McLemore, 'Fear of FATCA', *Financial Instruments Tax and Accounting Review*, 19(8) (2014): 'failure to comply with FATCA would mean exclusion from dollar markets' [Cassell and McLemore, 'Fear of FATCA'].

[114] See the statement in Parliament on the second reading of the Income Tax (Amendment) Bill 2013, *Singapore Parliamentary Debates, Official Report* (21 October 2013) vol 90 (Mr Yee Jenn Jong).

[115] The IGA, on Model 1 form, was signed on 9 December 2014, see the press release issued by the Singapore Ministry of Finance (MOF), 'Singapore and the United States Sign Agreement to Facilitate FATCA Compliance by Singapore Financial Institutions' (2014), online: www .mof.gov.sg/news-reader/articleid/1444/parentId/59/year/2014?category=Press%20 Releases. See also *AXY v. Comptroller of Income Tax* [2016] 1 SLR 616 at [13].

[116] See Income Tax Act, *supra* note 103, Part XXB 'International Agreements to Improve Tax Compliance'. Although FATCA is the genesis of this amendment, allowance is made for similar initiatives by other countries: see s 105K(1)(c).

[117] *Ibid.*, s 105L.

[118] *Ibid.*, s 105M.

Banks are also amending their T&C to obtain customer consent to disclosures made pursuant to FATCA. As pointed out earlier, the Third Schedule permits disclosure of customer information with the customer's written consent. I argued earlier that broad T&C consent to disclosure does not generally constitute the kind of consent envisaged by the Third Schedule. The T&C consent for FATCA compliance may, however, satisfy the requirements of the Banking Act bearing in mind that awareness of the need for this disclosure is probably reasonably high. Problems may arise, however, if information is disclosed in respect of a customer who is not a US person, as defined. The prospects of the consent surviving a challenge would be improved if the T&C are clear about the intended disclosure and customers are given adequate notice. Pertinently, in light of the statutory provisions, T&C consent is not strictly needed for FATCA disclosures although it constitutes good practice from a customer-relationship point of view.

Aside from FATCA, there has been a broader international move spearheaded by the OECD and Global Forum to combat harmful tax practices, including tax evasion.[119] In line with international developments, Singapore has embraced OECD/Global Forum initiatives by establishing, inter alia, a more extensive EOI regime.[120] This has been achieved in part by signing and ratifying the Convention on Mutual Administrative Assistance in Tax Matters. Singapore's press release notifying ratification of the Convention in 2016 reflects its desire to meet internationally accepted norms. At the same time, it reveals concern about losing business to other jurisdictions[121]:

> Ratifying the Convention reflects Singapore's commitment to effective exchange of information based on international standards, but the standards can only work if all financial centres, such as Switzerland, Luxembourg, Singapore and Hong Kong, move together. We will continue to work with our international partners to achieve this and prevent regulatory arbitrage.

In 2013, Singapore's ITA saw amendments to facilitate EOI.[122] These amendments include provisions to allow the Inland Revenue Authority of

---

[119] See O'Brien, Chapter 5; also *AXY v. Comptroller of Income Tax* [2016] 1 SLR 616 at [6–14].

[120] For example, on 14 May 2013, Singapore's MOF, the MAS and the Inland Revenue Authority of Singapore announced a strengthening of Singapore's international EOI framework to combat cross-border tax offences; on 29 May 2013, the MOF announced that Singapore had signed the Convention on Mutual Administrative Assistance in Tax Matters, thereby expanding its EOI network.

[121] See the statement issued by the MOF 'Singapore Strengthens International Tax Co-operation – Ratifies the Convention on Mutual Administrative Assistance in Tax Matters', online www .mof.gov.sg/news-reader/articleid/1577/parentId/59/year/2016?category=Press%20Releases

[122] See Income Tax Act, *supra* note 103, Part XXA 'Exchange of Information under Avoidance of Double Taxation Arrangements and Exchange of Information Arrangements'.

Singapore (IRAS) to obtain information from FIs without a court order.[123] Concerns were aired that the removal of the previous safeguard of a court procedure would undermine the confidence of tax-compliant investors.[124] In the Singapore government's view, the concerns about scrapping the court procedure in 2013 were unfounded despite it having extolled the virtues of the court procedure when EOI for tax purposes was introduced in 2009; the IRAS, it said, was an experienced and effective gatekeeper that can assess the validity of the EOI requests; furthermore, affected persons can make representations to IRAS and, if necessary, seek judicial review of IRAS's decision.[125] As critics have pointed out, judicial review of an administrative decision does not offer the same protection as a right to oppose an application on its merits.[126] Nevertheless, the more efficient procedure dispensing with the need for a court order was approved by Parliament in 2013. As with the ITA provisions dealing with FATCA, the bank's duty of secrecy is overridden.[127]

The OECD took a further step on the EOI trajectory by unveiling a global standard for automatic EOI, to which Singapore signalled its subscription on 6 May 2014. Singapore will begin automatic EOI on the common reporting standard in 2018 and the necessary amendments to the ITA were passed in May 2016. At this time, the Singapore Government reiterated its commitment 'to upholding internationally accepted standards for the exchange of information under the CRS'.[128] After FATCA set the trend, it was inevitable that other jurisdictions would move in the direction of automatic EOI: 'Multinational automatic information exchange is now

---

[123] *Ibid.*, ss 105F, 105N. An example of a case in which a court order was sought under the previous provisions is *Comptroller of Income Tax* v. *AZP* [2012] 3 SLR 690.

[124] See the statement in Parliament on the second reading of the Income Tax (Amendment) Bill 2013, *Singapore Parliamentary Debates, Official Report* (21 October 2013), vol 90 (Ms Foo Mee Har); G. Cua, 'Proposed Changes to Exchange of Information Regime', *The Business Times* (24 August 2013).

[125] See the statement in Parliament on the second reading of the Income Tax (Amendment) Bill 2013, *Singapore Parliamentary Debates, Official Report* (21 October 2013), vol 90 (Mrs Josephine Teo, Senior Minister of State for Finance).

[126] See G. Cua, 'Proposed Changes to Exchange of Information Regime', *supra* note 124. The limitations of the review process are apparent in the case of *AXY* v. *Comptroller of Income Tax* [2016] 1 SLR 616 at [15–16].

[127] See Income Tax Act, *supra* note 103, s 105D(4)(b). See also *AXY* v. *Comptroller of Income Tax* [2016] 1 SLR 616 at [11–12].

[128] See the statement in Parliament on the second reading of the Income Tax (Amendment No. 2) Bill, Singapore Parliamentary Debates, Official Report (9 May 2016), vol 94 (Ms Indranee Rajah, Senior Minister of State for Finance) [Ms Indranee Rajah, Income Tax (Amendment No. 2) Bill Debate]. A public consultation exercise on the regulations that will govern the implementation of the common reporting standards was announced on 11 July 2016.

the future of international tax enforcement.'[129] Notably, in announcing the automatic EOI model, the OECD went so far as to say that the new standard would put 'an end to banking secrecy in tax matters.'[130]

10.5.2   The Fight against Money Laundering and Terrorism Financing

Singapore's primary AML/CFT legislation comprises the Corruption, Drug Trafficking and Other Serious Crimes (Confiscation of Benefits) Act (CDSA),[131] along with the Mutual Assistance in Criminal Matters Act (MACMA),[132] and the Terrorism (Suppression of Financing) Act (TSFA).[133] CDSA criminalises the laundering of funds derived from various offences and facilitates both crime investigation and confiscation of criminal proceeds.[134] MACMA establishes a framework for Singapore to give and receive international assistance in combatting a long list of offences corresponding closely with those identified in CDSA.[135] This list of offences has grown significantly since 1999.[136] MACMA 'signals Singapore's commitment to be part of the wider international network of cooperation in combating crime on a global scale'.[137] Complementing the above measures, TSFA requires persons in possession of terrorist property

---

[129] Cassell and McLemore, 'Fear of FATCA', *supra* note 113. See also *AXY v. Comptroller of Income Tax* [2016] 1 SLR 616 at [14].

[130] See OECD, 'OECD Releases Full Version of Global Standard for Automatic Exchange of Information' (21 July 2014), online: www.oecd.org/tax/oecd-releases-full-version-of-global-standard-for-automatic-exchange-of-information.htm

[131] CDSA, *supra* note 87.

[132] Mutual Assistance in Criminal Matters Act (MACMA) (Cap 190A, 2001 Rev Ed Sing).

[133] Terrorism (Suppression of Financing) Act (TSFA) (Cap 325, 2003 Rev Ed Sing) [TSFA]. See also the statement in Parliament on the second reading of the TSFA Bill, *Singapore Parliamentary Debates Official Report* (8 July 2002), vol 75 at col 77 (Mr Wong Kan Seng, Minister for Home Affairs).

[134] See the statement in Parliament on the second reading of the Corruption, Drug Trafficking and Other Serious Crimes (Confiscation of Benefits) (Amendment) Bill, *Singapore Parliamentary Debates, Official Report* (19 September 2007), vol 83 at col 1966 (Associate Professor Ho Peng Kee, Senior Minister of State for Home Affairs).

[135] See the statement in Parliament on the second reading of the Mutual Assistance in Criminal Matters Bill, *Singapore Parliamentary Debates, Official Report* (22 February 2000), vol 71 at col 980–1 (Professor S. Jayakumar, Minister for Law) [Professor S. Jayakumar, Mutual Assistance in Criminal Matters Bill Debate].

[136] See CDSA, *supra* note 87, Second Schedule which lists the offences by date of introduction.

[137] See Professor S. Jayakumar, Mutual Assistance in Criminal Matters Bill Debate, *supra* note 135.

(covering 'assets of any kind'),[138] or with information about terrorism financing,[139] to notify the police. Under all three statutes, secrecy obligations are overridden and good faith disclosure is protected from criminal or civil recourse,[140] while noncompliance without reasonable excuse is a criminal offence.[141]

Two provisions of CDSA are highlighted here. First, a public prosecutor may apply to the High Court for an order against an FI to disclose 'material' for investigations into a long list of offences under Singapore law, including drug dealing, terrorism financing and tax evasion.[142] 'Material' includes 'any book, document or other record in any form'[143] and is thus broad enough to encompass customer information held by banks. Second, CDSA imposes an obligation on persons (including FIs),[144] to report their knowledge or suspicion that property is derived from or has been/will be used in connection with criminal conduct.[145] Criminal conduct encompasses numerous offences under Singapore law as well as similar offences under a foreign country's laws; tax evasion offences, local and foreign, are covered.[146] Information so reported may be communicated to a foreign authority if certain conditions are met.[147] CDSA requires FIs to keep records of financial transactions for a period of five years.[148]

The international assistance envisaged by MACMA may take various forms including obtaining evidence, such as witness testimony or the seizure of documents. Among other things, MACMA facilitates applications by a prescribed foreign country for the production of 'a thing' in the

---

[138] TSFA, *supra* note 133, s 8; for interpretation, see s 2.

[139] *Ibid.*, s 10.

[140] CDSA, *supra* note 87 ss 31(4)–(5), 39(6)–(8); MACMA, *supra* note 132, ss23(4)(b), 24; TSFA, *supra* note 133, ss 8(5), 10(3).

[141] CDSA, *supra* note 87, ss 33, 39(2); MACMA, *supra* note 132, s 25; TSFA, *supra* note 133, ss 8(3), 10(1).

[142] CDSA, *supra* note 87, s 31, First and Second Schedules.

[143] *Ibid.*, s 2.

[144] The term includes corporates, see the Interpretation Act, *supra* note 51, s 2.

[145] CDSA, *supra* note 87, s 39(1).

[146] *Ibid.*, s 2 defines 'criminal conduct' as a serious offence or a foreign serious offence. The Second Schedule sets out a list of serious offences. A foreign serious offence is basically one that offends the laws of another country and would be a serious offence if committed in Singapore. Foreign tax offences are also foreign serious offences even if not an offence in Singapore. Drug dealing is treated separately and is defined in the First Schedule.

[147] *Ibid.*, s 41.

[148] *Ibid.*, s 37, read with s 36.

possession of Singapore FIs.[149] A 'thing' includes 'any book, document or other record in any form whatsoever',[150] and therefore embraces customer information held by banks.

It is evident that, in promulgating these statutes, the government was conscious of the need to balance competing considerations: the combatting of crime and the right to privacy.[151] To this end CDSA, MACMA and TSFA include safeguards. For example, under CDSA an application by a public prosecutor for disclosure of material held by an FI must be made in camera and the Court must be satisfied, inter alia, that the disclosure appears to be in the public interest.[152] Also, information may, for example, be passed to a foreign authority only if certain conditions are met, including that such disclosure will be reciprocated and undertakings to maintain confidentiality of the information are given.[153] There are similarly limits and controls on the availability of assistance under MACMA to prevent abuse of its facilities. An order permitting information to be obtained from an FI must be made by the Singapore High Court,[154] and a request may be refused in numerous circumstances,[155] for example, if: in the opinion of the Attorney-General, the offence in question is not sufficiently serious[156]; the 'thing' could reasonably be obtained in another way[157]; or if the requesting state does not give an undertaking not to use the 'thing' for any purpose other than that stated in the request.[158]

---

[149] MACMA, *supra* note 132, s 22. Prescribed foreign countries mostly include countries in South/South East Asia, such as India, Indonesia, Malaysia and Thailand. The United States and the United Kingdom are included for some purposes. See also TSFA, *supra* note 133, s 32.

[150] MACMA, *supra* note 132, s 2.

[151] See e.g. the statements in Parliament on the second and third readings of the Drug Trafficking (Confiscation of Benefits) Bill, a predecessor of the CDSA, in *Singapore Parliamentary Debates, Official Report* (20 March 1992), vol 59 at col 1375–6 (Professor S. Jayakumar, Minister for Home Affairs); and (14 September 1992), vol 60 at col 225 (Professor S. Jayakumar, Minister for Home Affairs): it was emphasised that the Government did not wish to adversely impact FIs nor undermine the confidence of customers in the confidentiality of their financial records. See also the second reading of the Drug Trafficking (Confiscation of Benefits) (Amendment) Bill, *Singapore Parliamentary Debates, Official Report* (6 July 1999), vol 70 at col 1736 (Mr Wong Kan Seng, Minister for Home Affairs).

[152] CDSA, *supra* note 87, ss 31(3), 31(6).

[153] *Ibid.*, s 41.

[154] MACMA, *supra* note 132, s 22(2).

[155] *Ibid.*, s 20(1).

[156] *Ibid.*, s 20(1)(g).

[157] *Ibid.*, s 20(1)(h).

[158] *Ibid.*, s 20(1)(j).

The above framework is supplemented in other ways which affect bank secrecy. MAS notices,[159] including Notice 626 to banks,[160] impose obligations on FIs to undertake customer due diligence,[161] maintain records[162] and report suspicious transactions.[163] In April 2015, the MAS Act was amended to boost and expand on existing AML/CTF measures involving FIs. The MAS and foreign authorities can now, in certain circumstances, conduct inspections of FIs for AML/CTF purposes,[164] and the MAS can communicate information relating to AML/CTF to local and foreign authorities.[165] Of these incursions to bank secrecy, Parliament was told they were 'essential in preserving trust and integrity in order to develop the banking sector.'[166] The MAS Act also enables the MAS to issue directions to an FI in order to give effect to decisions of the United Nations Security Council.[167]

10.5.3   Comment

Undoubtedly, the qualifications to bank secrecy in the areas of tax information exchange, AML and CFT represent substantial qualifications to

---

[159] MAS Act, *supra* note 17, s 27B authorises the MAS to give directions to FIs to prevent money laundering and terrorism financing. The MAS has issued Notices in this respect to a range of financial sector intermediaries, including banks, merchant banks, finance companies, money-changers and capital markets intermediaries.

[160] MAS Notice 626 'Notice on Prevention of Money Laundering and Countering the Financing of Terrorism – Banks', 24 April 2015 revised 30 November 2015.

[161] *Ibid.*, at paras. 6–8.

[162] *Ibid.*, at para. 12.

[163] *Ibid.*, at para. 14.

[164] MAS Act, *supra* note 17, s 27C, Part VC including s 30ZG.

[165] *Ibid.*, s 27F, Part VC including ss 30ZA, 30 ZF. A high profile example of AML action taken in Singapore against a bank is the shutting down of the merchant bank, BSI Limited, see 'Investigations into 1MDB-Related Fund Flows through Singapore' Joint Statement by Attorney-General's Chambers, Singapore, Commercial Affairs Department, Singapore Police Force, Monetary Authority of Singapore, 21 July 2016.

[166] See the statement in Parliament on the second reading of the Monetary Authority of Singapore (Amendment) Bill, *Singapore Parliamentary Debates, Official Report* (11 May 2015), vol 93 (Mr Lawrence Wong, Minister for Culture, Community and Youth and Second Minister for Communications and Information); also, more recently, Reply to Parliamentary Question on additional measures to enhance anti-money laundering compliance by FIs, Question No 384, Notice Paper 232 OF 2016, 11 July 2016, online: www.mas .gov.sg/News-and-Publications/Parliamentary-Replies/2016/Reply-to-Parliamentary-Question-on-additional-measures-to-enhance-anti-money-laundering-compliance.aspx

[167] MAS Act, *supra* note 17, s 27A(1). See also: MAS, 'Anti-Money Laundering/Countering the Financing of Terrorism and Targeted Financial Solutions' (4 May 2015), online: www .mas.gov.sg/Regulations-and-Financial-Stability/Anti-Money-Laundering-Countering-The-Financing-Of-Terrorism-And-Targeted-Financial-Sanctions.aspx

the ambit of the duty of secrecy. The motivation underlying these external incursions is similar, and summed up in the words of Singapore's former Attorney-General, Steven Chong: 'Countries must move beyond the traditional notion of individual nations to "a mindset of cooperation between nations".[168] CDSA, MACMA and provisions in the MAS Act give effect to Singapore's obligations as a member of the Financial Action Task Force (FATF) on Money Laundering, TSFA gives effect to the International Convention for the Suppression of the Financing of Terrorism and s 27A MAS Act gives effect to Singapore's obligations as a member of the United Nations. The need to counter money laundering, as articulated in Singapore's Parliament, is equally applicable to other cross-border crimes:[169]

> Unchecked, money laundering can undermine the rule of law and legal systems, erode financial markets' integrity and damage countries' reputations. Money laundering is not only a law enforcement problem, it poses a serious national and international security threat as well.

The Banking Act already provides, uncontroversially, for disclosure of customer information for the investigation or prosecution of a suspected offence under Singapore law.[170] To the extent that CDSA, MACMA and TSFA expand the situations in which disclosure is permitted (and indeed required), I would argue that it is a warranted and rational extension of the principles underlying the exceptions to a bank's secrecy obligations. To the extent that it can apply to offences outside of Singapore's borders, it is a necessary step to avoid criminal elements taking advantage of the gaps that may arise if countries do not club together. It promotes consistency in the treatment of national and international crimes. Even if the crime in question has been perpetrated in a foreign jurisdiction, it is in the interests of all countries adhering to the rule of law for serious crimes to be combatted. Today, cross-border crimes are easier to commit thanks to the ease of international travel and advances in communication technology. From a pragmatic point of view, in order for Singapore to obtain assistance from foreign countries for crimes punishable domestically, it has to be willing to reciprocate. Protecting the integrity of Singapore's financial system and preventing abusive use by criminal elements is also consistent

---

[168] I. Poh, 'As Crime Goes Global, So Must Lawyers', *The Straits Times* (18 January 2014).
[169] See the statement in Parliament on the second reading of the Corruption, Drug Trafficking and Other Serious Crimes (Confiscation of Benefits) (Amendment) Bill, *Singapore Parliamentary Debates, Official Report* (19 September 2007), vol 83 at col 1969 (Associate Professor Ho Peng Kee, Senior Minister of State for Home Affairs).
[170] Banking Act, Third Schedule, Part I, para. 5.

with the 'Core Principles for Effective Banking Supervision' issued by the Basel Committee on Banking Supervision to promote the prudential regulation of banks.[171] For these reasons, I suggest that these qualifications to bank secrecy are consistent with, and indeed true to, the rationale of bank secrecy in Singapore.

Of the triumvirate, the most controversial interference with the duty of secrecy is that which facilitates assistance in foreign tax collection. The argument in favour of EOI has been cogently made by the OECD:[172]

> An open international architecture where taxpayers operate cross-border but tax administrations remain confined to their national borders can only be sustained where tax administrations cooperate. One key aspect of international tax-cooperation is exchange of information.

Tax evasion is undoubtedly a serious problem that needs to be combatted and international cooperation is a necessity if the tax burden is to be shared as various national Parliaments decree. It is unfortunate though, that by its very nature, automatic EOI affects taxpayers generally and not tax evaders only. It is also ironic that obtaining information held by FIs under the AML legislation in Singapore (CDSA and MACMA) requires an application to the High Court while disclosure pursuant to FATCA does not. In other words, disclosure by FIs of information pertaining to persons suspected of committing a serious crime is subject to more stringent oversight than disclosure of information pertaining to the tax liability of potentially compliant taxpayers. If it is any consolation, automatic EOI is apparently effective in enhancing compliance with tax obligations.[173] In choosing to facilitate FATCA compliance by Singapore-based FIs and in choosing to align itself with the OECD/Global Forum initiatives, Singapore has made the only rational choice available to it, to 'act responsibly and uphold EOI standards in line with international norms'.[174] As reflected in the media: 'In today's court of public opinion, it is imperative

---

[171] Basel Committee on Banking Supervision, 'Core Principles for Effective Banking Supervision' (September 2012) at 64, Core Principle 29, online: www.bis.org/publ/bcbs230.pdf

[172] OECD, 'Automatic Exchange of information: What it is, How it Works, Benefits, What Remains to be Done' (2012) at 5, online: www.oecd.org/ctp/exchange-of-tax-information/automatic-exchange-of-information-report.pdf [OECD, 'Automatic Exchange of Information'].

[173] Ibid., at 19–20.

[174] See the statement in Parliament on the second reading of the Income Tax (Amendment) Bill 2013, Singapore Parliamentary Debates, Official Report (21 October 2013), vol 90 (Mrs Josephine Teo, Senior Minister of State for Finance).

to be well perceived in the international community, especially with regard to tax policy.[175]

Inevitably, the question arises as to what this means for the future of Singapore as a wealth management hub. The Singapore Government does not consider that the new EOI culture will damage Singapore's interests as a wealth management centre: 'There is no conflict between high standards of financial integrity and keeping our strengths as a centre for managing wealth. Singapore will continue to be a vibrant wealth management centre, with laws and rules that safeguard legitimate funds and reject tainted money.'[176]

Certainly, to the extent that tainted business has been/will be lost, there should be little regret. Singapore's target should be sustainable clean business; a reputation for harbouring tainted money can harm a jurisdiction by driving away clean money.[177] Far from being a disadvantage, the FATCA IGA with the United States arguably gives Singapore a 'competitive advantage' as one of the first Asian countries to agree an IGA with the United States,[178] and will 'enhance Singapore's status as a financial hub'.[179] In the long run, international pressure and the benefits of conformance will hopefully reduce jurisdictional discrepancies that may lead to arbitrage.[180]

It is possible, of course, that some clean money will also be lost. It has been said, for example, that some banks, including Singapore banks, have turned away US customers in order to avoid the compliance burden of

[175] S.M. Chung-Sim and J. Stuart-Smith, *The Business Times*, 7 August 2013.

[176] See the statement issued by MOF, Monetary Authority of Singapore, Inland Revenue Authority of Singapore: 'Singapore to Significantly Strengthen Framework for International Tax Cooperation' (14 May 2013), online: www.iras.gov.sg/irashome/News-and-Events/Newsroom/Media-Releases-and-Speeches/Media-Releases/2013/Singapore-to-Significantly-Strengthen-Framework-for-International-Tax-Cooperation; see also Ms Indranee Rajah, Income Tax (Amendment No 2) Bill Debate, *supra* note 128; Y. Yahya, 'Eye on the Economy; Bitter Pill to Swallow to Keep Money Clean', *The Straits Times* (21 January 2014); E. Leow and S. Michaels, 'Has Banking Secrecy Come to an End in Singapore?', *The Business Times* (8 June 2010).

[177] See the statement in Parliament on the second reading of the Income Tax (Amendment) Bill 2013 *Singapore Parliamentary Debates, Official Report* (21 October 2013), vol 90 (Ms Tan Su Shan); also Y Yahya, *supra* note 176.

[178] L.S. Siow, 'Singapore Signs Deal with US on American Account Holders' Data', *The Business Times* (7 May 2014).

[179] F.F. Mok, 'US Tax Deal Lifts S'pore as Financial Hub', *The Straits Times* (8 May 2014).

[180] See the statement in Parliament on the second reading of the Income Tax (Amendment) Bill 2013, *Singapore Parliamentary Debates, Official Report* (21 October 2013), vol 90 (Mrs Lina Chiam); also Y Yahya, *supra* note 176. In implementing the Common Reporting Standards, Singapore has also been mindful of regulatory arbitrage, see Ms Indranee Rajah, Income Tax (Amendment No 2) Bill Debate, *supra* note 128.

FATCA – so-called de-risking.[181] With the current trend, however, this reaction may not be sustainable: 'while it may have been possible for foreign institutions to shun American accounts in response to FATCA, such a stand becomes unrealistic if the automatic information exchange that the OECD envisions becomes a global standard.'[182]

EOI does bring its problems.[183] There is understandable concern about illegitimate use of customers' information in some jurisdictions.[184] The OECD/Global Forum has said that EOI is not intended to facilitate fishing expeditions, and information exchanged should be used only for its requested purpose, namely tax assessment.[185] It is hoped that Singapore's IRAS will be vigilant in detecting such abuse, and robust in resisting it. Another negative is the cost of compliance,[186] and inevitable disruption to everyday banking business caused by compliance implementation, for example, delays in opening new accounts because of the due diligence required. An information exchange system does come, literally, at a price and these costs will, presumably, be passed on to customers in the long run. As authorities and FIs become more familiar with the system, and taxpayers become more cooperative, compliance will, however, hopefully operate more smoothly and efficiently. EOI may also affect regulatory coverage by fuelling a trend away from banks to alternative less regulated entities.[187] It is true that banks face competition from operators such as Paypal, apparently even Starbucks,[188] and regulators will have to be vigilant to prevent a dangerous shifting of risk to other sectors.

---

[181] See e.g. Cassell and McLemore, 'Fear of FATCA', *supra* note 113.

[182] *The Business Times*, 'Fatca Compliance: Banks Need to be Vigilant', *The Business Times* (16 May 2014) [*The Business Times*, 'FATCA compliance'].

[183] For a more detailed discussion, see O'Brien, Chapter 5.

[184] Y Yahya, *supra* note 176. See also the recent warning of phishing exercises that masquerade as US IRS enquiries: KPMG, 'IRS Warns of 'Phishing Scams' for FATCA-Related Account Data', *Financial Instruments Tax and Accounting Review*, 19 (2014).

[185] See e.g. OECD, 'The Global Forum on Transparency and Exchange of Information for Tax Purposes Information Brief' (November 2013) at paras. 5 and 7, online: www.oecd.org/tax/transparency/global_forum_background%20brief.pdf; OECD 'Automatic Exchange of information', *supra* note 172 at 6; also Ms Indranee Rajah, Income Tax (Amendment No. 2) Bill Debate, supra note 128.

[186] See 'Fatca Cost and Effect' Money Laundering Bulletin, 23 September 2015 which estimated the cost of compliance to be US$8 billion worldwide.

[187] See the statement in Parliament on the second reading of the Income Tax (Amendment) Bill 2013, *Singapore Parliamentary Debates, Official Report* (21 October 2013), vol 90 (Ms Tan Su Shan).

[188] See Y. Yahya, 'Banks Face Legal Constraints in Cloud Computing', *The Straits Times* (23 November 2013).

A criticism of form, rather than substance, is that it is unfortunate that the Banking Act is not more transparent about the significant provisions affecting bank secrecy that are scattered in statutes such as CDSA, MACMA, TSFA and MAS Act. Section 47 suggests that this and the Third Schedule are comprehensive on bank secrecy in Singapore: 'Customer information shall not, in any way, be disclosed by a bank in Singapore or any of its officers to any other person except as expressly provided in this Act.'[189] The dispersal of significant provisions on bank secrecy in other statutes means that an outsider examining the position under the Banking Act does not get an accurate picture, and it is not apparent from the Banking Act what other statutes he/she must refer to, in order to do so.

10.6 Conclusion

Bank secrecy in Singapore has seen significant legislative inroads from increased international efforts to combat cross-border crime. The message is that bank secrecy should not enable criminal activity to flourish around the world. The recent inroads to bank secrecy discussed here are consistent with the idea that has been present in Singapore's bank secrecy regime since it inherited the *Tournier* principle – that bank secrecy does not shield criminal conduct.[190] Thus, in *Tournier*, it was recognised that disclosure could be made under legal compulsion and when under a duty to the public. The initiatives facilitating EOI for the purposes of money laundering, terrorism financing and other serious crimes are important and necessary to avoid the stigma associated with impregnable bank secrecy rules.

The object of combating tax evasion, while unobjectionable in itself, involves measures that cast the net widely and which impinge on the privacy of tax compliant customers. On the other hand, the tax disclosures envisaged by this new order are probably disclosures that taxpayers are themselves liable to make in any event. Damage to innocent customers will, hopefully, be minimised by the vigilance of the authorities making the disclosures. From a pragmatic viewpoint, this development in tax collection is a worldwide trend and expectations of privacy in the realm of tax are now unrealistic.

There are aspects of the bank secrecy regime in Singapore that would benefit from review and clarification: the customer's right to damages for a

---

[189] Banking Act, *supra* note 1, s 47(1).
[190] The exceptions to bank secrecy recognised in *Tournier* include disclosure under legal compulsion and under a duty to the public.

breach of secrecy, the meaning of 'customer', the protection afforded to the information of former customers, the ambit of the exception pertaining to a customer's written permission and better signposting to significant exceptions not visible in the Banking Act. Overall, though, the rationale of bank secrecy in Singapore remains, I suggest, intact. Maintaining the confidence of customers in Singapore's banking system requires that the bank secrecy rules are not used for purposes that attract international condemnation and suspicion. The *Tournier* rationale, that the customer's credit requires banks to be discreet, is probably also not dented by the new developments. Bank secrecy in Singapore, for legitimate purposes, is alive and well.[191]

---

[191] See e.g. *The Business Times*, 'FATCA compliance', *supra* note 182.

Switzerland

PETER NOBEL AND BEAT BRAENDLI

11.1   Introduction

11.1.1   Bank Secrecy in Switzerland

Bank secrecy is not the secret of the banks, but the secret of their clients. Bank secrecy is in fact a misnomer: it should more appropriately be called bank–client confidentiality as its purpose is focused on the protection by the bank of the confidentiality of its clients' information.[1]

As has long been the case, bank secrecy still exists in Switzerland. However, its operation has changed, in particular in the international context, as it no longer covers tax offences of international clients.

In 1934, the familiar notion of 'bank secrecy' was implemented into the Swiss Banking Act (Swiss BA)[2] as a penal provision that protected something that was, and had long been, understood even before its enactment: the bank's contractual duty of discretion and the client's right of privacy. The introduction of this legislative rule, known as Art. 47, was aimed at protecting the interests and information of foreigners, such as persons of Jewish origin and, in particular, German citizens, from their totalitarian governments. Notably, the latter were thereby protected from exposure in matters related to the breach of exchange control regulations, which was heavily penalised in Germany at that time.[3] Tax avoidance was not an issue then.[4]

Beat Braendli presented a version of this chapter on behalf of Peter Nobel at the Bank Secrecy Symposium on 4–6 December 2014 in Singapore.

[1] See, for example, Thomas Müller, 'Das Geheimnis um das Bankkundengeheimnis' (3 May 2010), online: Jusletter, www.fh-hwz.ch/display.cfm/id/101286/disp_ty; see also Robert Vogler, *Das Schweizer Bankgeheimnis: Entstehung, Bedeutung, Mythos* (Zurich: Verein für Finanzgeschichte, 2005), fn 1.

[2] Swiss Federal Act on Banks and Savings Banks (8 November 1934), SR 952.0 (Swiss BA).

[3] Vogler, *Das Schweizer Bankgeheimnis, supra* note 1 at 15ff.

[4] Müller, 'Das Geheimnis um das Bankkundengeheimnis', *supra* note 1 at 3; Vogler, *Das Schweizer Bankgeheimnis, supra* note 1 at 8.

11.1.2 A Creature of Private Law

The penal provision within Art. 47 of the Swiss BA, commonly known as the 'Swiss Bank Secrecy' provision, has its origin in Swiss private law. Article 47 is in fact nothing more than the imposition of a statutory penalty for breach of the obligation of bank–client confidentiality, which is based upon and formed by private contract law and the law governing the rights of the person (hereinafter referred to as 'the law of personal rights'; this forms a part of the Swiss Civil Code).[5]

It is undisputed that these penal provisions in Switzerland are not autonomous rules. Rather, they serve to protect bank secrecy to the extent that it is established by contract law and the law of personal rights.[6] Consequently, contract law and the law of personal rights also lay out the scope and limits of bank–client confidentiality. This shall be further discussed in the context of the principles surrounding bank secrecy.

11.1.3 Article 47 Swiss BA

The current Art. 47 of the Swiss BA reads as follows:[7]

1. Persons who deliberately do the following will be imprisoned up to three years or fined accordingly:
   a. disclose confidential information entrusted to them in their capacity as a member of an executive or supervisory body, employee, representative or liquidator of a bank, as member of a body or employee of an audit firm or that they have observed in this capacity;
   b. attempt to induce an infraction of the professional secrecy.
2. Persons acting in negligence will be penalised with a fine of up to 250,000 francs.

---

[5] Bank–client confidentiality is part of the individual contract between a bank and its client, and it is an implied duty under Swiss agency law (Art. 398, para. 1 of the Swiss Federal Act on the Amendment of the Swiss Civil Code (30 March 1911), SR 220 (Swiss CO) in connection with Art. 321a, para. 4 CO). Furthermore, the right of personality of the client according to Art. 27 et seq. of the Swiss Civil Code of 10 December 1907, SR 210 (CC) encompasses bank–client confidentiality, as does the Swiss Federal Act on Data Protection (19 June 1992), SR 235.1 (FADP).

[6] Cf. e.g. Bodmer, Kleiner and Lutz, *Kommentar zum Bundesgesetz über die Banken und Sparkassen (Kommentar BankG)* (Zürich: Schulthess Verlag, 2010), Art. 47, Rz 6.

[7] An unofficial translation of the Swiss BA by KMPG can be found online: https://assets .kpmg.com/content/dam/kpmg/pdf/2016/02/ch-banking-act-sr952.0-en.pdf

3. In the case of a repetition within five years of the prior conviction, the fine will amount to a minimum of forty-five daily fines in lieu of jail time.[8]
4. The violation of the professional confidentiality remains punishable even after a bank license has been revoked or a person has ceased his/her official responsibilities.
5. The federal and cantonal provisions on the duty to provide evidence or on the duty to provide information to an authority are exempted from this provision.
6. Prosecution and judgment of offences pursuant to these provisions are incumbent upon the cantons. The general provisions of the Swiss Penal Code are applicable (unofficial translation).[9]

11.2   Scope and Limitations of Swiss Bank Secrecy

11.2.1   Bank Secrecy in Private Law

As mentioned earlier, bank secrecy is derived from both private contract law and the law of personal rights (as part of the law of persons). In other words, the scope and limitation of the secrecy obligation under the penal law is clearly based on private law. Accordingly, a client may also claim damages or bring a (preliminary) injunction because of an asserted breach of the secrecy obligation pursuant to the rules of private law. The duty of secrecy persists after the client has closed his account.

The contractual background between a bank and its client is important, and the terms agreed at the time of contracting determine the scope and limitation of the secrecy duty that the bank owes its client. In practice, however,

---

[8] A daily fine – according to Swiss penal law – ranges between 10 and 3,000 Swiss Francs (CHF) and is fixed by the Court according to the income and wealth level of the convicted person. It can be regarded as a standard unit adjusted to the conditions of the convicted person. Furthermore, the court decides also – within the boundaries of statutory law – about the amount of daily fines a convicted person has to pay according to the severity of the offence/delict. The maximum amount of daily fines that a court can rule (according to Art. 34, para. 2 Swiss Criminal Code) is 360 days (i.e. with a daily fine set at CHF 3,000 the maximum fine is $(360 \times 3,000 = \text{CHF } 1,080,000)$).

[9] With the enactment of the Swiss Federal Act on Stock Exchanges and Securities Trading (24 March 1995), SR 954.1 (SESTA) in 1995, the banks intended to protect themselves and their clients from stock exchanges, and their employees with respect to securities dealings and accounting thereof; therefore, an analogous rule to the one set forth by Art. 47 BA was introduced into the law under the title of 'breach of professional secrecy' (Art. 43, SESTA). This article was analogously replaced by Art. 147 of the Swiss Federal Act on Financial Market Infrastructures and Market Conduct in Securities and Derivatives Trading (June 19, 2015), SR 958.1 (FMIA).

banking contracts are standardised and usually do not leave any room for individual design. Accordingly, such duties and obligations are mostly addressed – if at all – by banks' General Terms and Conditions (GTCs).

The GTCs of Swiss banks have remained largely silent on matters of bank secrecy for a long time, a somewhat curious factor in the light of the importance ascribed to bank secrecy. In more recent times, some banks have introduced new GTC provisions primarily to indicate the limited character of the secrecy obligation that the bank owes its client. The following is a typical excerpt:

> The client hereby releases the Bank from its duty of confidentiality and waives bank client confidentiality insofar as this is necessary to safeguard the legitimate interests of the Bank.[10]

Such wording in the GTC of banks reflects what has always been the legal practice in Switzerland, and in this respect, it only serves as a clarification of what would be implied by courts in case of a dispute between a bank and its client. The wording 'legitimate interests of the Bank' remains, however, broadly undefined and leaves room for legal interpretation.

A client can also waive its right to secrecy. As with all contracts generally, a waiver may be explicit or implicit. However, the courts are unlikely to find an implicit waiver by the client regarding bank secrecy. In the absence of an explicit contractual stipulation, the scope and limitation of the bank's duty of secrecy would extend as far as the client would expect it to in good faith. Good faith is an important principle in Swiss law that is set out in Art. 2 of the Swiss Civil Code. It is the origin of the so-called 'principle of trust' (*Vertrauensprinzip*) developed by the Swiss Federal Court[11] for the general interpretation of contracts.[12] It states that (in case of doubt) the wording of a contract has to be understood such as an honest

---

[10] Credit Suisse, 'General Conditions', edn. 12.13 (June 2009), Art. 16, online: www.credit-suisse.com/media/pb/docs/ch/privatkunden/AGB_en.pdf. The legitimate interests are furthermore concretised *inter alia* as follows:

> [I]nsofar as, in the case of transactions involving foreign securities or uncertificated securities, the applicable provisions demand disclosure. All legal and supervisory obligations imposed upon the Bank to disclose information are expressly reserved.

[11] The Swiss Federal Court is the highest court in Switzerland. Its decisions are of paramount importance for all courts of the country. Even though lower courts are not compulsorily bound by its decisions as in common law countries, it is quite rare that lower courts deviate from the Swiss Federal Court's principles and findings.

[12] See, e.g. BGE 129 III 320 at 326 (BGE stands for 'Bundesgerichtsentscheid' that means Decision of the Swiss Federal Court).

and independent third party would have understood it to the best of his or her knowledge. The principle applies *a fortiori* for banking contracts, as they are usually characterised by a special relationship of trust between the bank and its client.[13] Thus, it seems clear that a waiver of bank secrecy by the client must be sufficiently clearly expressed. At the same time, a client's reliance on the protection of its secrecy, based on the provisions of the contract or the good faith principle, is limited by the existing law. A client cannot expect a bank to infringe its statutory obligations – regardless of whether these are based on national or international law – in order to protect the client's secrecy.

The law of personal rights (as set forth in the law of persons within the Swiss Civil Code) is another source of the client's right to secrecy in the banking relationship.[14] The tortious character of an infringement of such secrecy is set out in the statute.[15] The protection of personal rights (the so-called 'protection of legal personality')[16] operate as limitations on the extent to which parties might contractually vary the duty of bank secrecy. As is the case with the contractual right to secrecy, a client can consent to disclosure and waive its personal right to secrecy. This can be done explicitly or implicitly, but the latter might be difficult to prove. In addition, the right to secrecy does not apply in cases of overriding private or public interests.[17]

Whether a bank can rely on such overriding private or public interests (based on Art. 28, para. 2 Swiss Civil Code) to negate its duty of secrecy without an explicit contractual agreement to this effect is controversial. It can probably do so in cases where the survival of the bank is at stake (without fault on its part). This is supported by the fact that there is a similar justification based on a consideration of interests at stake within penal law

---

[13] This is also referred to as agency law. See, e.g. BGE 4C.53/2000 (13 June 2000).

[14] The general stipulations of personal rights, protecting *inter alia* privacy, can be found in Art. 11 et seq. Swiss Civil Code, *supra* note 5.

[15] Cf. Art. 28, *Ibid.*

[16] Legal personality (a synonym for personal rights) encompasses (in a simplified manner) all the fundamental values of a natural (but to a lesser extent, also of a juridical) person, such as physical and mental integrity, personal freedom, honour, identity (origin, name, picture, voice, etc.), informational privacy, freedom of movement. Legal personality is also a prerequisite for having legal rights and obligations (cf. Art. 11 et seq. *ibid.*). Protection of legal personality is laid out in Art. 27, *Ibid.*

[17] Cf. Art. 28, para. 2, *Ibid.* Overriding private interest: e.g. if the existence of the bank (as a legal entity) is at risk; overriding public interest: e.g. if financial stability in the Swiss Financial Market is at risk.

in cases of necessity.[18] However, under penal law, a bank is usually only allowed to defend higher private interests (the survival of the bank might be one of them) as opposed to assumed higher public ones (as e.g. protection of the stability of the financial system), as the protection of the latter is reserved to the state.[19]

Another area of the law that is potentially relevant to bank secrecy is data protection law,[20] which aims to protect the privacy and the fundamental rights of persons when their data is processed.[21] Data protection law stands cumulatively beside the rules of personal rights in its application to banks, but is less regarded as a source of bank secrecy. This is, on the one hand, because the law was created recently in 1992. On the other hand, obligations such as the economic data of clients (such as information about their bank accounts) whose safekeeping forms the core of bank secrecy is regarded as personal data indeed, but not as sensitive personal data for which the law provides an increased protection under the data protection law.[22] However, the protection of personal data with respect to bank client information is not broader than the rules of personal rights; for enforcement the law even refers to the same procedure.[23] Nevertheless, when processing client data, banks must always comply with data protection law.

11.2.2   Bank Secrecy as a Constitutional Right?

The Swiss Federal Court has always been of the opinion that bank secrecy was not a basic, constitutional, legal principle. It phrased this as follows:

> Meanwhile, banking secrecy is not to be seen in the ranks of a written or unwritten constitutional right that would be granted supremacy in case of a

---

[18]   Article 17, Swiss Criminal Code (21 December 1937), SR 311.0 ('Legitimate act in a situation of necessity') states as follows:

> Any person who carries out an act that carries a criminal penalty in order to save a legal interest of his own or of another from immediate and not otherwise avertable danger, acts lawfully if by doing so he safeguards interests of higher value.

[19]   Moreover, within tort law, an infringement to defend legitimate private interests might not avoid damages but may lead to a reduction of the compensation owed, as in such a case the judge is allowed to determine damages in his or her own discretion (cf. Art. 52, para. 2, Swiss Code of Obligations, *supra* note 5).

[20]   See the Federal Act on Data Protection, *supra* note 5.

[21]   *Ibid.*, Art. 1.

[22]   Cf. Art. 3, paras. a and c, *Ibid.*

[23]   *Ibid.*, Art. 15. For a transnational discussion of the relationship between bank secrecy and data protection laws, see the discussion by Greenleaf and Tyree, Chapter 2.

collision of interest. It has rather to be seen as a legal norm, which may have to be withdrawn in the face of conflicting supranational treaties (unofficial translation).[24]

After the Federal Council[25] decided, on 13 March 2009, to implement the automatic exchange of information (AEOI) among countries according to OECD standards for all tax offences (and thereby effectively abolish bank secrecy in the tax context as discussed later in this chapter), the popular initiative[26] 'Ja zum Schutz der Privatsphäre' (Yes to the protection of privacy) was launched on 17 May 2013.[27] This initiative aims at protecting bank secrecy internally (only for domestic cases) and anchoring it in the constitution. On 26 August 2015 the Federal Council published its dispatch to Parliament, in which it recommended that the initiative be refused. The Swiss Parliament will deliberate upon the recommendation until (not later than) 25 March 2017 and thereafter will hand the question on to the Swiss people for a popular vote. At the end of 2016, one of the two parliamentary chambers, the Swiss House of Representatives, voted surprisingly to support the initiative. In addition, it formulated a simpler counterproposal that would also underpin bank secrecy in the constitution. Even though almost 90 per cent of all popular initiatives are declined in popular votes, the outcome in this specific case especially if the Swiss Parliament gives its placet is very uncertain.

11.2.3   Bank Secrecy and Bank Supervisory Authorities

No secrets may be kept from the Swiss supervisory authority (FINMA).[28] Any attempt to rely on a foreign secrecy provision is disallowed by the following provision:

---

[24] BGE 104 Ia 49, E. 4a; confirmed in BGE 105 Ib 429, E. 6; BGE 115 Ib 68, E. 4b and BGE 137 II 431, E. 2.1.2.

[25] The Swiss Federal Council is the highest executive authority (serving as head of government and state) of Switzerland. It consists of seven members of whom one is the Federal President. The latter function rotates between the seven members on a yearly basis.

[26] In Switzerland, a popular initiative is a political right that allows any Swiss citizen (in general done by several people, i.e. by a popular movement) to gather 100,000 signatures of Swiss citizens within eighteen months after the official publication of their initiative. The initiative contains a draft wording for the amendment of the Swiss constitution. If they succeed to gather the signatures, a popular vote about the initiative (i.e. the whole country votes whether the constitution should be amended accordingly) must be conducted. In case of the above-mentioned initiative, the popular movement was successful and gathered more than 100,000 signatures.

[27] BBl 2013 at 3443ff. (BBl stands for the German Bundesblatt, i.e. Federal Gazette).

[28] Article 29, Swiss Federal Act on the Swiss Financial Market Supervisory Authority (22 June 2007), SR 956.1 (FINMASA).

From the beginning a Swiss bank that chooses to lead a group of corporations, has to organize these in a way that allows the bank, as leader of
the group, to comply with Swiss regulations; in particular, it must maintain possibilities for the Swiss authorities to obtain due information. This
can encompass obtaining the necessary authorization of clients (unofficial
translation).[29]

Furthermore, it has never been disputed that Switzerland can cooperate nationally and internationally in regulatory matters and foreign banks
in Switzerland can give their home regulators any required information
according to the relevant foreign law.[30] For on-site inspections by foreign
regulators in Switzerland, however, certain safeguards are provided for.
For example, in cases where the requested information is related to the
asset management or deposit business of individual clients, FINMA will
conduct the investigation and only thereafter hand it over to the foreign
inspectors.[31]

11.2.4   Implementation of the Financial
Action Task Force Recommendations

Switzerland has in the field of money laundering always been in line with
the Financial Action Task Force (FATF) recommendations. Bank secrecy
has never been a defence for resisting the transfer of information, either
domestically or internationally.[32]

In February 2015, the case against HSBC Switzerland, the largest foreign bank in Switzerland, showed that this bank (among others) was
involved in money laundering.[33] A number of years prior to this, FINMA

---

[29] BGE 108 Ib 513 at 519.
[30] Article 4 quinquies, Swiss BA, *supra* note 2.
[31] Former Art. 23 septies, *ibid.*, repealed by coming into force of the FMIA (SR 958.1) with
effect from January 1, 2016 and replaced by the newly created Art. 43, para. 3bis, Financial
Market Supervision Act (FINMASA, SR 956.1) that contains the same rule (cf. also BBl
2014 7622).
[32] Relevant for international administrative assistance are Art. 30 et seq. of the Swiss Federal
Act on Combating Money Laundering and Terrorist Financing in the Financial Sector (10
October 1997), SR 955.0 (Anti-Money Laundering Act (AMLA)).
[33] From September 2014, around 140 journalists from various parts of the world have analysed client information of the Private Bank HSBC Switzerland under the leadership of the
International Consortium of Investigative Journalists (ICIJ). On 9 February 2015, more
than forty newspapers and news agencies published their findings, including *Le Monde*,
Süddeutsche Zeitung, Guardian, BBC and CBS. The findings of the Swiss newspapers are
summed up in ICIJ, 'Swiss Leaks: Murky Cash Sheltered by Bank Secrecy', online: www.icij
.org/project/swiss-leaks

had already conducted two extensive proceedings and assessed that the bank had infringed Switzerland's anti-money laundering provisions.[34] Such behaviour has never been protected by Swiss bank secrecy laws. The case evinces that even though Switzerland has very strict rules against money laundering and also plays an active part in the ongoing development of such rules on an international level, rules alone are not sufficient and a correct implementation requires effective control.

The revised 2012 FATF recommendations called for further adaptations in the domain of money laundering. Switzerland's Federal Council has implemented these recommendations in its dispatch (*Botschaft*)[35] for the revision of the national anti-money laundering legislation of December 2013.[36] This was adopted by the Swiss Parliament on 12 December 2014 and was put into force completely on 1 January 2016.[37] According to the new legislation, qualified tax offences can now be regarded as predicate offences to money laundering.

11.2.5   *Procedural Right to Refuse to Give Evidence*

Previously, cantonal differences existed within Switzerland with regard to the banker's right to refuse to give evidence due to the old cantonal procedural laws. With the enactment of the federal procedural laws, the Swiss Civil Procedure Code (CPC) and Swiss Criminal Procedure Code (CrimPC), these differences have been minimised. The right to refuse to give evidence has in effect been abolished as it prevails only where the interest of secrecy outweighs the interest of establishing the truth,[38] and not many cases fall into this category. Article 47, para. 5BA also explicitly exempts a bank from its bank secrecy obligations when it has the duty of providing evidence in judicial proceedings. These procedural laws are

---

[34] Cf. Titus Plattner Mario Stäuble, Daniel Glaus and Oliver Zihlmann, 'Die kriminellen Kunden der HSBC Schweiz', 8 February 2015, online: Tagesanzeiger, www.tagesanzeiger.ch/schweiz/swissleaks/Kriminelle-Kunden-einer-Schweizer-Bank-entlarvt/story/22008838

[35] 'Botschaft' (i.e. dispatch) is an official document, drawn by either Parliament or the Federal Council, which accompanies a bill in its parliamentary hearing.

[36] Botschaft zur Umsetzung der 2012 revidierten Empfehlungen der Groupe d'action financière (GAFI) (13 December 2013), BBI 2014 605.

[37] The provisions regarding transparency of juridical persons and bearer shares were already put into effect on 1 July 2015.

[38] Article 166, para. 2, Swiss Civil Procedure Code (19 December 2008), SR 272 (CPC); Art. 173, para. 2, Swiss Criminal Procedure Code (5 October 2007), SR 312.0 (CrimPC).

applied not just internally, but also in the fulfilment of international assistance requests.

11.3   Exceptions to Bank Secrecy in the International Context

11.3.1   Overview

From the discussion earlier in this chapter, it can be seen that there are broadly three bases for the exceptions to bank secrecy: (1) consent, (2) overriding interests (they might be private or public and (3) legal requirements. The third type of exception applies where statutory provisions demand disclosure. Such provisions exist in particular for civil and criminal proceedings where banks as third parties are obliged to give evidence (see Section 11.2.5), e.g. in a fraud case, or in a case involving money laundering (see Section 11.2.4). Furthermore, disclosure is also necessary for supervisory reasons.

This general trio of exceptions to bank secrecy that apply for domestic cases also apply in the international context. If foreign (state) authorities wish to receive information protected by Swiss bank secrecy, they must request it by means of an administrative or legal assistance proceeding.

Legal and administrative assistance in relation to matters involving a client of a bank is regarded as international assistance, and such requests are handled according to international treaties and the relevant Swiss procedural acts (see also Section 11.2.5).[39] It has always been understood in Swiss law that facts which are relevant to criminal activity are not to be hidden behind bank secrecy.[40]

11.3.2   International Controversies: Insider
Trading and Taxation Matters

Most of the international controversies with regard to international assistance to pierce Swiss bank secrecy arose understandably in relation to taxation matters. Already with the passing of the Federal Act on International Mutual Assistance in Criminal Matters[41] (IMAC) in 1981–2, tax fraud

---

[39] Either CPC, CrimPC or the Swiss Federal Act on Administrative Procedure (20 December 1968), SR 172.021.

[40] Walter H. Boss, 'Informationsaustausch unter dem neuen Schweizerisch-Amerikanischen Doppelbesteuerungsabkommen', *Steuer Revue*, 5 (1998) 277; BGer 1A.33/1997.

[41] Swiss Federal Act on International Mutual Assistance in Criminal Matters (20 March 1981), SR 351.1 (Mutual Assistance Act, IMAC).

(in the sense of Art. 14 of the Penal Act on Administrative Matters[42]) was deemed eligible for legal cooperation.[43] The condition required for cooperation was expanded later by a ruling of the Federal Court from just the use of forged documents, to include also the use of a 'web of lies' (fraudulent misdirection).[44] However, in taxation matters that did not fulfil the elements of a crime under Swiss law, i.e. did not amount to tax fraud (discussed further in Section 11.3.3), Switzerland traditionally refused to give legal or administrative assistance.

Yet, the first bank secrecy-related crisis that arose in 1981 did not involve taxes: US insider trading investigations were conducted in relation to an American branch of a Swiss bank, Banca della Svizzera Italiana (BSI). The production of documents from Switzerland was requested but resisted based on the argument that disclosure would be a breach of bank secrecy (as Switzerland did not know the crime of insider trading at that time). The American federal judge, Milton Pollack, of the New York District Court for the Southern District stated:

> It would be a travesty of justice to permit a foreign company to invade American markets, violate American laws if they were indeed violated, withdraw profits and resist accountability for itself and its principals for the illegality by claiming their anonymity under foreign law.[45]

This case was eventually settled, albeit only with the banking client's consent. In 1987, an exchange of notes and messages between Switzerland and the United States[46] occurred and, finally, on 18 December 1987, Switzerland created its first rule on insider trading,[47] which even bears the label 'lex Americana', as described by the Swiss Federal Court.[48] The Swiss insider trading provisions were contained in the Stock Exchange

---

[42] Penal Act on Administrative Matters (VStrR), SR 313.
[43] Article 3, para. 3a IMAC, *supra* note 40.
[44] BGE 111 Ib 242, E. 4b.
[45] *Securities and Exchange Commission* v. *Banca della Svizzera Italiana et al.*, 92 F.R.D. 111 at 119 (S.D.N.Y., 1981); the ruling was partly published in Peter Nobel, *Praxis zum öffentlichen und privaten Bankenrecht der Schweiz, Ergänzungsband* (Bern: Stämpfli, 1984) at 109ff., 117.
[46] Memorandum of Understanding between the United States of America and Switzerland to Establish Mutually Acceptable Means for Improving International Law Enforcement Cooperation in the Field of Insider Trading (10 November 1987), BBl 1988 II 394 at 398ff.
[47] Article 161 Swiss Criminal Code, *supra* note 17, later Art. 40 SESTA, *supra* note 8, today Art. 154 FMIA (*infra* note 8).
[48] BGer Judgment 1A.12/2005 (9 March 2006), E. 4.1.

Act (SESTA)[49] that was recently largely (*inter alia* the insider trading provisions) replaced by the Financial Market Infrastructure Act (FMIA).[50] Already under SESTA, but continuously under FMIA, bank secrecy does not apply for domestic insider trading cases or for international assistance proceedings relating to foreign insider trading cases.

The first Swiss provisions on international administrative assistance were also part of the SESTA under Art. 38. Foreign requests made pursuant to this provision, which were made to FINMA (Swiss Financial Market Supervisory Authority), mostly concerned insider trading relating to Swiss bank accounts and were usually granted, thereby allowing for administrative assistance. Also, appeals against FINMA's decisions in these cases were generally rejected by the court of appeal.[51] Since 1 January 2016, the international administrative assistance is governed by Art. 42 et seqq. of the Financial Market Supervision Act (FINMASA).[52]

11.3.3   Reason for International Controversy in Taxation Matters: Swiss Differentiation between Tax Evasion and Tax Fraud

The reason for international controversies in taxation matters with regard to international assistance to pierce Swiss bank secrecy can be found in the traditional Swiss differentiation between tax evasion and tax fraud.

This sophisticated and most important distinction was made for domestic use. Basically, according to Swiss terminology, tax evasion simply means

---

[49] The relevant article that penalises insider trading and hence allows piercing bank secrecy nationally as well as internationally was Art. 40 SESTA, *supra* note 8.

[50] FMIA (*supra* note 8) came into effect on 1 January 2016. The relevant article that replaced Art. 40 SESTA analogously is Art. 154 FMIA.

[51] Since the enactment of Art. 38 SESTA in February 1997, and until 2007, the supervisory authority has received 653 requests from 36 authorities. These requests concerned 1,600 banking connections. Only 110 cases were filed with the Swiss Federal Administrative Court. Cf. also: Urs Zulauf and Fabian Burckhardt, 'Nachbesserung durch den Gesetzgeber nötig: Internationale Amtshilfe der Eidgenössischen Bankenkommission für ausländische Finanzmarktaufsichtsbehörden unter dem Börsengesetz', in Peter Nobel (ed), *Aktuelle Rechtsprobleme des Finanz- und Börsenplatzes Schweiz*, vol. 11 (Bern: Stämpfli, 2004) at 365ff., 372; FINMA, 'Die internationale Amtshilfe im Börsenbereich' (August 2009) at 22, online: www.finma.ch/de/durchsetzung/amtshilfe/internationale-amtshilfe. With the creation of the Financial Institutions Act (FinIA), the clauses on administrative assistance will be globally revised and become part of the FINMASA, *supra* note 27; cf. Bundesgesetz über die Finanzmarktinfrastrukturen und das Marktverhalten im Effekten- und Derivatehandel (Finanzmarktinfrastrukturgesetz, FinfraG) (3 September 2014), BBI 2014 7647 at 7712.

[52] See *infra* note 27.

the non-declaration of funds, whereas tax fraud signifies an active deception such as lying or using (additional) false documents in order to deceive authorities. While tax evasion is regarded as a minor infringement of the law that is sanctioned by monetary fines and prosecuted by tax authorities (administrative authorities), tax fraud is a criminal offence (crime) penalised also with imprisonment and pursued by prosecutors.

The tax assessment procedure (*Veranlagungsverfahren*), which serves to assess individual taxes in the normal course of reporting on annual income and wealth, relies upon the self-declaration of (natural and juridical) persons. With regard to this procedure, the banks have a duty of certification of bank account information only towards their clients,[53] i.e. Swiss tax authorities are not entitled to request bank account information directly from a taxpayer's bank. On the contrary, within a tax fraud procedure (that is an ordinary criminal procedure) banks are obliged to comply with ordinary criminal procedural rules that allow – with a few exceptions such as for closely related parties and lawyers – for gathering information by the Swiss authorities from any third parties, including banks (cf. Section 11.2.5).[54]

Exceptions to the foregoing differentiation between tax evasion and tax fraud exist where special competences of the federal tax authorities apply that allow them to receive information from banks in cases of suspicion of repeated tax evasion concerning large amounts of money.[55]

Due to the fact that only tax fraud has been regarded as a criminal act under Swiss law while tax evasion has been considered as a minor infringement, Switzerland has always refused to provide international assistance in the latter case. As other countries did not know about such a differentiation, controversies arose, in particular with the United States. As a consequence of international lack of understanding and international developments (tax scandals, but also international disclosure standards), the traditional Swiss differentiation between tax evasion and tax fraud, and Switzerland's reluctance to give assistance in taxation matters (which has long been perceived as an important part of Swiss bank secrecy) were slowly weakened. This will be examined in the remainder of this chapter.

---

[53] Article 127, Bundesgesetz über die direkte Bundessteuer (14 December 1990), SR 642.11 (Act on Direct Federal Taxes, DBG).

[54] Andreas Donatsch, 'Zum Verhältnis zwischen Steuerhinterziehung und Steuerbetrug nach dem Steuerharmonisierungs- und dem Bundessteuergesetz', *ASA Bulletin*, 60 (1991), 289; August Reimann, Ferdinand Zuppinger and Erwin Schärrer, *Kommentar zum Zürcher Steuergesetz* (Bern: Stämpfli, 1963), N2 to s 192; BGE 122 I 257, E. 1c.

[55] Article 190, DBG, *supra* note 52.

11.4   A Slow Farewell

As indicated earlier, Swiss bank secrecy has effectively been abolished in the international tax context. In the remainder of this chapter, we will trace how this development came about.

11.4.1   The Swiss Banks' Code of Conduct

After the Credit Suisse Texon scandal in 1977, whereby the *Schweizerische Kreditanstalt* (the former Credit Suisse) had to cope with a loss of about 2.2 billion Swiss francs because of the actions of three of its senior executives, Swiss banks reached a general agreement, the Agreement on the due diligence of banks (CDB 1977),[56] which prohibited active facilitation of tax evasion and similar acts. However, its wording was limited to incomplete or misleading certificates.

Article 53 CDB 2016 currently states (under the title of 'tax evasion and similar acts'):

> Banks must not provide any assistance to their contracting partners in acts aimed at deceiving Swiss or foreign authorities, particularly tax authorities, by means of incomplete or otherwise misleading attestations.

It is fitting that the provision of incomplete or misleading attestations is prohibited, as attestations are certifications, and such acts would amount to fraud.[57] Although this passage only mentions incomplete or otherwise misleading attestations, it is not, however, to be understood as allowing banks to assist their clients in hiding money in other ways.

11.4.2   Double Taxation Agreement with the United States

An early sign that Switzerland would be willing to give legal or administrative assistance not only in the case of tax fraud was found in the US Swiss Double Tax Agreement 1951, which declared 'tax fraud and the like' as being eligible for legal and administrative assistance in tax matters and

---

[56] The first version of this 'Agreement on the Swiss banks' code of conduct with regard to the exercise of due diligence' was released as a reaction to the Texon Scandal in 1977. A new version is issued every five years by the Swiss Bankers Association. The newest one dates from 2016 (CDB 2016) and is available online at SwissBanking, www.swissbanking.org/en/VSB16_d_SBVg.pdf

[57] In the revised VSB 2016 (online: www.swissbanking.org/vsb16_d_sbvg.pdf), this is also explicitly stated in Art. 54.

thus declared that it entitled the release of information.[58] The further double taxation agreement (DTA) of 1996 was accompanied by a protocol and a sample catalogue of instances where assistance was possible.[59] All tax offences involving the use of false certifications were thus declared eligible for legal assistance.

11.4.3   The OECD Model Tax Convention

Traditionally, the DTAs that Switzerland concluded only led to an information exchange to secure the execution of the respective DTA, i.e. mainly to prevent double taxation, but not to help other states to enforce their domestic tax laws.

Under the auspices of the OECD, a model DTA (the so-called Model Tax Convention) has long been in existence and has undergone periodic revisions. Switzerland made major reservations thereto in the past.[60] These were mainly concerned with information exchange in tax matters, in particular, with the nonavailability of administrative assistance in matters of tax evasion.[61]

On 13 March 2009, the Swiss reservations were withdrawn and the Swiss government went even further to announce the desire to switch to the AEOI as soon as an international standard was put in place to accomplish this.[62]

Under the OECD Model Tax Convention, a requesting government can ask for any client files that it needs for carrying out the provisions of the Convention or for administering or enforcing its domestic tax laws.[63]

---

[58] BGE 96 I 737, E. 3d.

[59] Agreement between the Swiss Confederation and the United States for the avoidance of double taxation with respect to taxes on income (19 December 1997), SR 0.672.933.61.

[60] Amts- und Rechtshilfe in Steuersachen – Gleichbehandlung: Bericht des Bundesrates in Erfüllung des Postulats 08.3244 der Sozialdemokratischen Fraktion vom 26 Mai 2008 (18 December 2013) at 16 (Report of the Federal Council in response to Postulate 08.3244 of the Social-Democratic Fraction from 26 May 2008).

[61] The reservations concerned Art. 26 of the OECD, 'Model Convention with Respect to Taxes on Income and on Capital' (2014), online: www.oecd.org/ctp/treaties/2014-model-tax-convention-articles.pdf (OECD Model Convention). Cf. Report of the Federal Council in response to Postulate 08.3244, *supra* note 59.

[62] Report of the Federal Council in response to Postulate 08.3244, *supra* note 59.

[63] Article 26(1) of the OECD Model Convention states:

> The competent authorities of the Contracting States shall exchange such information as if foreseeably relevant for carrying out the provisions of this Convention or to the administration or enforcement of the domestic laws

Since the withdrawal of the Swiss reservations to the OECD Model Tax Convention, several DTAs with different countries have been revised under the above-mentioned OECD standard.[64]

A new DTA was also concluded with the United States in June 2010 and ratified by Switzerland in March 2012.[65] However, the US ratification has not yet occurred.[66] This treaty, which also allows administrative assistance in tax matters, features a clause that is partially retroactive – i.e. it will be backdated to take effect from the date that the agreement was signed (23 September 2009).[67]

11.4.4   Federal Act on the Unilateral Application of the OECD Standard on the Exchange of Information

Switzerland also wants to complement the OECD system unilaterally by asking for a reciprocal declaration from third countries to commit to information exchange using the OECD standard. To this purpose, the enactment of a statute, called GASI (which is an abbreviation for the Federal Act on the Unilateral Application of the OECD Standard on the Exchange of Information[68]), is being considered.[69]

---

concerning taxes of every kind and description imposed on behalf of the Contracting States, or of their political subdivisions or local authorities, insofar as the taxation thereunder is not contrary to the Convention.

[64] The Federal Department of Finance (FDF) maintains a chart with all relevant double tax agreements. This chart can be found on the homepage of the FDF: www.efd.admin.ch/efd/en/home/themen/wirtschaft--waehrung--finanzplatz/finanzmarktpolitik/avoidance-of-international-double-taxation--dtas-.html. Essentially, Switzerland has in place three types of DTAs: (1) those that are in correspondence with the OECD-standard with fifty-six countries; (2) those that do not yet confirm to the OECD-standard with fifty-nine countries and (3) Tax Information Agreements with ten countries that deal only with the exchange of information and not with the prevention of double taxation.

[65] Federal Decree (Bundesbeschluss) to an amendment of the DTA between the United States and Switzerland (18 June 2010), BBl 2010 4359.

[66] The person responsible for the blocking of the ratification within the US Senate is Senator Paul Rand who generally refuses such treaties as they would infringe the privacy of American people. Nonetheless, on 10 November 2015, the new DTA was approved by the responsible committee of the Senate. However, it is uncertain when the Senate will debate the topic.

[67] Dispatch with request to accept the Protocol amending the Convention between the Swiss Confederation and the United States of America for the Avoidance of Double Taxation with Respect to Taxes on Income (27 November 2009), BBl 2010 235 at 242.

[68] In German: Bundesgesetz über die einseitige Anwendung des OECD-Standards zum Informationsaustausch (GASI).

[69] See press release of the FDF, 'Federal Council Launches Consultation on Unilateral Application of OECD Standard on Exchange of Information upon Request' (22 October

GASI would be temporary in nature and 'will be annulled by the Federal Council as soon as all concerned states and territories are covered by bilateral agreements providing a standards-based exchange of information upon request'.[70]

11.5 Alternative Solutions to Maintain the Protection of Secrecy

11.5.1 Bilateral Approaches

Switzerland has been increasingly aware of the rising international pressure against tax evasion and has reacted by concluding withholding tax agreements with third countries.[71]

These agreements have had the purpose, on the one hand, of regularising the past by making it possible for Switzerland to disclose untaxed assets and to pay a lump sum in respect of those assets, thereby bringing assets of foreign tax subjects in Switzerland to an adequate taxation, albeit anonymously. This is done by a withholding tax on income arising from capital held in Switzerland to be paid by foreign clients (via the banks on an anonymous basis) who refuse to give information about their capital income and their identity to their country of origin.

The conclusion of such treaties with Austria[72] and Great Britain[73] was successful. However, the treaty with Germany failed for political reasons.[74]

2014), online: www.news.admin.ch/message/index.html?lang=en&msg-id=54902. The Federal Council launched the consultation procedure on the Federal Act on the Unilateral Application of the OECD Standard on the Exchange of Information. Cf. Explanatory Report to the Federal Act on the Unilateral Application of the OECD Standards for Information Exchange (GASI) (22 October 2014), online: www.news.admin.ch/NSBSubscriber/message/attachments/36976.pdf

[70] Explanatory Report to GASI, *supra* note 68 at 2.

[71] Peter Nobel, 'Das schweizerische Recht vor den Herausforderungen des internationalen Rechts – Bank- und Finanzmarktrecht', *Zeitschrift für Schweizerisches Recht*, II(1) (2012), 111 at 150.

[72] Abkommen zwischen der Schweizerischen Eidgenossenschaft und der Republik Österreich über die Zusammenarbeit in den Bereichen Steuern und Finanzmarkt (concluded on 13 April 2012, in force since 1 January 2013), SR 0.672.916.33.

[73] Agreement between Switzerland and the United Kingdom of Great Britain and Northern Ireland regarding the Collaboration in Tax Matters (concluded on 6 October 2011, with a protocol for further amendments from 20 March 2012, in force since 1 January 2013), SR 0.672.936.74.

[74] Germany's Federal Council (Bundesrat), overpowered by the states (Länder) governed by the socialist, the green and the left parties, refused to conclude such an agreement. Bundestagsdrucksache 17/12282 (5 February 2013), Bundesratsplenarprotokoll No. 906 (1 February 2013).

However, since Switzerland as well as Austria and Great Britain have decided to implement the new global standard on AEOI of the OECD, the existing withholding tax agreements will become obsolete when the Agreement on the AEOI between Switzerland and the European Union, which was signed on 27 May 2015, enters into force.[75]

11.5.2 Multilateral Approaches

In 2004, two tax-related agreements were concluded with the European Union. These were the Agreement on the Taxation of Savings[76] and the Agreement Against Fraud.[77]

The mechanism under the Agreement on the Taxation of Savings works as follows: a retention tax is applied to all interest payments that are not subject to Swiss anticipatory tax.[78] This is executed by a paying agent located on Swiss territory – for instance a bank – and applied to a natural person whose tax residence is an EU member country. EU tax residents who receive interest can choose to either pay the retention tax or voluntarily declare their interest income to their tax authorities. The retention tax has been increased progressively since it was introduced. It was 15 per cent the initial three years, then 20 per cent for another three years and, since 1 July 2011, it has been 35 per cent.[79] The revenue thus generated is split as follows: Switzerland keeps 25 per cent of it, and 75 per cent is allocated to the EU member state where the individual has his or her tax residency.[80] This agreement has not been too successful for the EU countries as there are many loopholes.

The Agreement on the AEOI between Switzerland and the European Union, concluded on 27 May 2015, will replace the Agreement on the Taxation of Savings. The AEOI is in accordance with the commitment made by almost 100 states, *inter alia* Switzerland and all the EU members, at the

---

[75] This is planned for 1 January 2017.

[76] Agreement between the European Community and the Swiss Confederation providing for measures equivalent to those laid down in Council Directive 2003/48/EC of 3 June 2003 on taxation of savings income in the form of interest payments (concluded on 26 October 2004, in force since 1 July 2005), SR 0.641.926.81 'Swiss–EU Taxation Savings Agreement').

[77] Cooperation Agreement between the European Community and its Member States, of the one part, and the Swiss Confederation, of the other part, to combat fraud and any other illegal activity to the detriment of their financial interests (concluded on 26 October 2004, provisorily applied since 8 April 2009), SR 0.351.926.81.

[78] This is a Swiss withholding tax of 35 per cent on capital income that is received by Swiss debtors, e.g. as dividends from Swiss shares.

[79] Article 1(1), Swiss–EU Taxation Savings Agreement, *supra* note 73.

[80] *Ibid.*, Art. 8(1).

assembly of the Global Forum on 24 October 2014 in Berlin, to implement the OECD's new global standard on AEOI. This new standard was adopted by the OECD Council on 15 July 2014. The AEOI schedules the uniform gathering of account information starting from 2017 and the exchange of such account information between the states starting from 2018.[81]

The Agreement Against Fraud, which established a cooperation between Switzerland and the European Union to fight any kind of fraud in the area of indirect taxes[82] (in particular smuggling), has been criticised for dealing not only with tax fraud but also with cases of pure tax evasion, and thus was considered to be an aberration from the Swiss understanding of bank secrecy already in 2005[83] (and long before the Swiss Government made the fundamental decision to adopt automatic information exchange on 13 March 2009).

11.5.3   QI-Program

As of 2001, Swiss banks were allowed by the US Internal Revenue Service (IRS) to participate in the Qualified Intermediary Program (QI-Program).[84] The QI-Program was replaced in 2010 with the Foreign Account Tax Compliance Act (FATCA, a US federal law[85]). Under the QI-Program, agreements were concluded between the participating banks and IRS, whereby the banks oblige themselves to identify 'US Persons' in possession of US securities, or otherwise, to apply a withholding tax.[86] The fact that the option of applying a withholding tax was available as an alternative to identification suggested that the United States was at the time still tolerant of US persons having unidentified funds abroad.

---

[81] The AEOI is still subject to legislative approval (ratification) in Switzerland.
[82] Taxes where the person taxed are different from the person from which the tax is collected, e.g. customs dues or value-added tax.
[83] Robert Waldburger, 'Amts- und Rechtshilfe in Steuersachen gemäss den sog. Bilateralen II' in Robert Waldburger, Charlotte Baer, Ursula Nobel and Benno Bernet (eds.), *Festschrift für Peter Nobel* (Bern: Stämpfli 2005) 1037–73 at 1045.
[84] This is a programme established by the US IRS pursuant to which Qualified Intermediary Agreements are entered into by (designated) eligible persons with the IRS whereby there is an agreement 'to assume certain documentation and withholding responsibilities in exchange for simplified information reporting for (. . .) its foreign account holders and the ability not to disclose proprietary account holder information to a withholding agent that may be a competitor' (see Merryl Morgan, 'Qualified Intermediary: Frequently Asked Questions', online: www.merrylmorgan.com/faq.php).
[85] See Chapter 5.
[86] Peter Nobel, 'Das schweizerische Recht vor den Herausforderungen des internationalen Rechts – Bank- und Finanzmarktrecht', *supra* note 70 at 147.

This interpretation of the QI-Program was supported by the trial in the United States of Raoul Weil, a former member of the UBS Group's Executive Board who was charged with conspiracy to defraud the IRS.[87] In this case, a particular clause within the QI agreement between the IRS and UBS that allowed UBS to compulsorily liquidate US securities if a client would not agree to disclose them was interpreted as the implicit permission of US tax law that the bank could still manage assets on an anonymous basis (because mechanics of the QI allowed that US clients did not have to declare their accounts).

In a specific dispute between UBS and some of its clients, in which client data was eventually transferred to the IRS based on administrative assistance, there was a disagreement on the question of who was the beneficial owner (either a structure that was built up as a legal entity or a natural person who was a shareholder of this entity) of certain securities based on different declarations the clients made to UBS. The Federal Administrative Court refused the objection of the client and approved the administrative assistance based on fraud. The court concluded, in this regard, that the natural person was the beneficial owner, as a corporate body could only be a beneficial owner to the extent that it complied with the 'Spiel der AG' (literally the game of the limited company), i.e. the rules of the corporation.[88] This means that the principles of corporate governance have to be complied with.[89] In a similar case that went on appeal before the Federal Court, the court confirmed this rationale, also approving administrative assistance (to the United States) because of fraud, stating:

> For a correctly constituted, autonomous corporate body, whose legal construction is respected and that has met the necessary formalities, the dogmatic differentiation between the corporate body on one hand and the beneficial owners on the other hand, has, in principle, to be accepted even by tax legislation. This differentiation has to be ignored in cases where the applicable tax law, despite (civil) autonomy, states that a transparent structure has to be assumed; and, therefore, not the corporate body but a third party has to be qualified as the beneficial owner (unofficial translation).[90]

---

[87] He allegedly offered help to thousands of UBS's US clients who failed to pay their federal income taxes and was tried before the federal district court in Fort Lauderdale, Florida on 16 December 2013 but was found not guilty on 3 November 2014. The case is *US v. Weil*, 08-cr-60322 (S.D. Fla., 2014).

[88] BVGer A-7342/2008 and A-7426/2008 (5 March 2009), E.5.5.2.5.

[89] The most recent Judgment by the Federal Court: BVGer A-737/2012 (5 April 2012), E. 7.5.5.

[90] BGE 139 II 404 at 440, E.9.7.4.

11.5.4   The Case of UBS

The competition for the international business of US clients – who did not pay taxes on their deposits or on their revenues received from these deposits – was raging in the shadows and went unnoticed for a long time. But then, despite the QI-Program, UBS was threatened with an indictment for helping US citizens to evade taxes, and approximately 250 client files were submitted directly to the Americans via FINMA (with the approval of the Swiss Federal Council).

The Federal Court,[91] in contrast to the Federal Administrative Court,[92] deemed this procedure to be lawful and in accordance with the 'Polizeigeneralklausel'[93] (Art. 36 of the Swiss Constitution). It emphasised the potential negative effects of an indictment against UBS:

> If there was an indictment in the US, it would have, with a high probability, existence-threatening consequences for UBS with the stated effects. It is – as the FINMA correctly pointed out – well known that an indictment in the US, regardless of its outcome, leads to irreparable damages in reputation and fortune, which, in the banking world, has devastating effects and can quickly lead to insolvency (unofficial translation).[94]

The UBS case was resolved with a Deferred Prosecution Agreement (DPA) and a payment of US$780 million.[95]

11.5.5   The Case of Credit Suisse

A number of other Swiss banks, as well as a handful of bank employees, were sued in the United States; however, only employees were formally indicted. The banks subjected to lawsuits included the second major bank of Switzerland, Credit Suisse, as well as the Zurich Kantonal Bank and the Basler Kantonal Bank.

---

[91] BGE 137 II 431.
[92] BVGer A-7789/2009 (21 January 2010).
[93] A 'Polizeigeneralklausel' describes a general norm legalising actions without actual legal foundation and applies in case of emergencies – i.e. matters of urgency and importance.
[94] BGE 137 II 431, *supra* note 90 at 447.
[95] Details can be found on the homepage of UBS: UBS, 'UBS settles US Cross-Border Case with the US Department of Justice (DOJ) and the Securities and Exchange Commission (SEC)' (18 February 2009), online: www.ubs.com/global/en/about_ubs/about_us/news/news.html/tchi/2009/02/18/2009_02_18a.html. The DPA can be found on the homepage of the US DOJ: www.justice.gov/sites/default/files/tax/legacy/2009/02/19/UBS_Signed_Deferred_Prosecution_Agreement.pdf

On 21 February 2014, Credit Suisse announced a total payment of US$2,815 billion to the US authorities. This payment[96] was agreed upon as part of a guilty plea, wherein the bank *inter alia*[97] also agreed to cooperate in treaty requests (under the DTA between the United States and Switzerland) for clients' account information (in compliance with Swiss bank secrecy laws for example by the bank obtaining client consent or under other exemptions to bank secrecy).[98]

Even before the arraignment in the United States, FINMA started an enforcement procedure against Credit Suisse, which was only concluded on 21 September 2012. FINMA reprimanded the bank for a severe violation of governance and proper business conduct requirements, finding that it 'had violated its duty to identify, limit and monitor risks relating to its US business'.[99]

11.6   The Smouldering Legal Dispute with the United States

11.6.1   *The UBS-Agreement*

As mentioned earlier under the Case of UBS,[100] on 21 July 2008, the US IRS issued a 'John Doe Summons' to UBS AG seeking information concerning client accounts.[101] In the process of submitting the first client data on 19 August 2009, this case grew to an affair of state and as a solution an agreement was also concluded between representatives of Switzerland and

---

[96] FINMA, 'FINMA Investigation into Business Conducted by Credit Suisse with US clients' (20 May 2014) at 3, online: www.finma.ch/en/~/media/finma/dokumente/dokumentencenter/8news/20140520-br-untersuchung-cs.pdf?la=en

[97] Furthermore, the bank agreed to make a complete disclosure of its cross-border activities, to provide detailed information as to other banks that transferred funds into secret accounts or that accepted funds when secret accounts were closed and to close accounts of account holders who fail to come into compliance with US reporting obligations. The bank also agreed to implement programmes to ensure its compliance with US laws, including its reporting obligations under the FATCA and relevant tax treaties, in all its current and future dealings with US clients.

[98] See press release of the US DOJ: 'Credit Suisse Pleads Guilty to Conspiracy to Aid and Assist US Taxpayers in Filing False Returns' (19 May 2014), online: www.justice.gov/opa/pr/credit-suisse-pleads-guilty-conspiracy-aid-and-assist-us-taxpayers-filing-false-returns

[99] FINMA Credit Suisse Summary Report, *supra* note 95 at 2, 13. Analogous conclusions were found by FINMA in the UBS trial; cf. also: FINMA, 'EBK Investigation of the Cross-Border Business of UBS AG with Its Private Clients in the USA' (18 February 2009) at 14, online: www.finma.ch/en/~/media/finma/dokumente/dokumentencenter/8news/20090218-kurzbericht-ubs-x-border.pdf?la=en

[100] Cf. Section 11.6.4.

[101] Based on its authority under 26 U.S.C. §7602(a).

the United States (UBS-agreement) that obliged Switzerland to deliver about 400 client files (out of the originally asked for 50,000) pursuant to further administrative assistance rules then foreseen in the existing DTA (from 1996) between the two countries. This number was subsequently adjusted to 4,100.[102] This extensive and obligatory declaration was in the following terms:

> The Swiss Confederation declares that it will be prepared to review and process additional requests for information by the IRS under Article 26 of the existing Tax Treaty if they are based on a pattern of facts and circumstances that are equivalent to those of the UBS AG case.[103]

Because of its far reaching consequences, the Federal Administrative Court refused to consider this agreement as a mere enforcement agreement to the DTA-USA 1996 (i.e. an agreement that only implements what the legislature has ruled),[104] and the agreement had to be handed over to the Swiss Parliament for its approval,[105] which was given on 17 June 2010. In view of this development, the declaration was practically superseded.

11.6.2   Unilateral Programme to Come to Terms with Switzerland's Past

Facing a crisis of significant dimension, the Swiss government strove for a global solution, i.e. a possibility to settle the matter of bank secrecy permanently with the rest of the world. This endeavour failed in its entirety. The Swiss parliament was presented with a so-called Lex USA,[106] which had relatively meagre content.[107] As a consequence, the Swiss Parliament

---

[102] Martin Schaub, 'Der UBS-Staatsvertrag und die EMRK', *Aktuelle Juristische Praxis/ Pratique Juridique Actuelle*, 10 (2011) 1294.

[103] Declaration by the Swiss Federation to the Agreement between the United States and the Swiss Confederation on the request for information from the US IRS regarding UBS AG (19 August 2009), SR 0.672.933.612. The text can be found on the Homepage of the IRS: IRS, 'Offshore Tax-Avoidance and IRS Compliance Efforts' (19 August 2009), online: https://www.irs.gov/pub/irs-drop/us-swiss_government_agreement.pdf

[104] BVGer A-7789/2009, *supra* note 91, E. 4.5, 5.5.

[105] Dispatch to the resolution to Parliament for approval to the agreement between the United States of America and Switzerland concerning a request for administrative assistance concerning UBS and the amending protocol (14 April 2010), BBl 2010 2965.

[106] Dispatch to the Federal Act on Measures to Facilitate the Resolution of the Tax Dispute between Swiss Banks and the United States (29 May 2013), BBl 2013 3947.

[107] The dispatch provided for adequate cooperation of banks with the US authorities. According to the dispatch, this essentially comprised two measures: Enabling Swiss banks to provide the US authorities with all the necessary information in order to protect their

rejected this idea in the summer session of 2013 by a refusal to consider. Subsequently, the Federal Council redefined the cornerstones of the cooperation with the United States through a new framework called Plan B. A joint statement between the United States and Switzerland was issued,[108] setting out a programme which allowed Swiss banks, with the permission of the Federal Counsel, to participate in a unilateral programme of the US DOJ to cooperate and settle their past wrongdoing within clear boundaries. Under this programme, banks are divided into four categories:

(i) The first category comprises the fourteen banks against which criminal proceedings had already begun. The new rules are not applicable to these fourteen banks.

(ii) The second category consists of banks which had reason to believe that they had violated American laws by committing tax-related offences. Such banks were obliged to request a 'Non-Prosecution Agreement' by 31 December 2013, and deliver information about their cross-border relations but not the names of clients. They will be confronted with a fine that is based on the amount of untaxed US assets on their accounts and the point of time that these accounts were opened. More than 100 banks belong to this category.

(iii) The third category is composed of banks which believe that they have not violated any law at all.

(iv) The fourth category is made up of banks with at least 98 per cent of their assets held by residents of Switzerland or an EU Member State.[109]

Swiss banks in the third and fourth categories could request a 'Non-Target Letter' between 1 July and 31 December 2014 to obtain assurances that they are safe from prosecution.

The Swiss banks first waited for the Credit Suisse case to be resolved (category 1, above). Proceedings and client data collection (i.e. client files) for banks in category 2 are costly and time consuming. The United States insists on an extensive cooperation without time limitations, and involving information relating to third party countries.[110] Cooperation includes

---

interest and a provision that allowed for the biggest possible protection of bank employees with regard to delivering the information. Cf. BBl 2013 3947, *supra* note 107 at 3952.

[108] 'Joint Statement between the US Department of Justice and the Swiss Federal Department of Finance' (29 August 2013), online: www.news.admin.ch/NSBSubscriber/message/attachments/31815.pdf

[109] 'Program for Non-Prosecution Agreements or Non-Target Letters for Swiss Banks' (29 August 2013), online: www.justice.gov/iso/opa/resources/7532013829164644664074.pdf

[110] The US-Program lists all duties of banks under para. II.D, *Ibid.*

disclosure of information relating to not only internal bank employees, but also third parties, who practically assisted in US tax-relevant business. The disclosure of names of employees and third parties can be seen as controversial with regard to the Data Protection Act[111] rather than the Banking Act. The question is whether the interest of submitting this data is more of a public or a private nature.[112] A large number of court proceedings relating to possible infringement of data protection law have been brought, none of which have led to a conclusive outcome at the time of this writing. They will have to address the question of the actual existence of a sufficient public interest.

Under the IRS's 'Offshore Voluntary Disclosure Program',[113] the US taxpayers with undisclosed foreign financial assets are given the opportunity to get current with their tax returns, and more than 45,000 US persons took advantage of the opportunity to report themselves.[114]

It will take a while to complete all the proceedings.

11.6.3   Position of the Swiss Supervisory Authorities

FINMA has repeatedly maintained (and indeed has had to maintain) that receiving foreign untaxed money is not punishable under the laws of Switzerland:

> Under current Swiss law, accepting untaxed assets, as well as aiding and abetting acts that could have an adverse effect on another country's treasury are generally not criminal unless punishable offences (e.g. forgery of documents) have been committed at the same time.[115]

FINMA has nevertheless imposed the requirement that banks must assess and control (i.e. monitor and limit) their legal and reputational

---

[111] Federal Act on Data Protection, *supra* note 5.

[112] *Ibid.*, Art. 6.

[113] IRS, '2012 Offshore Voluntary Disclosure Program' (10 March 2016), online: www.irs.gov/uac/2012-Offshore-Voluntary-Disclosure-Program

[114] On 26 February 2014, a Senate Hearing was conducted during which the US Deputy Attorney-General James Cole announced that, up till today, over 43,000 persons have reported voluntarily. Cf. Tom Schoenberg and David Voreacos, 'Senate Hearing Likely to Flush Out more US Tax Evaders' (27 February 2014), online: Bloomberg, www.bloomberg.com/news/articles/2014-02-27/senate-hearing-likely-to-flush-out-more-u-s-tax-evaders. On June 2014 the IRS reported more than 45,000 disclosures, see IRS, 'IRS Offshore Voluntary Disclosure Efforts Produce $6.5 Billion; 45,000 Taxpayers Participate' (June 2014), online: www.irs.gov/uac/Newsroom/IRS-Offshore-Voluntary-Disclosure-Efforts-Produce-$6.5-Billion%3B-45,000-Taxpayers-Participate

[115] FINMA Credit Suisse Summary Report, *supra* note 95 at 7.

risks, by adequate means.[116] A failure to do this would violate the principles of sound management and conduct under the 'fit and proper' test. It is also the case that the institution itself, and not just its organs (i.e. its decision-makers such as directors), has to confirm compliance with this requirement. Enforcement proceedings conducted against financial institutions, as far as is apparent, have not led to further sanctions other than a call for improvement of the situation.[117] The FINMA summary report on Credit Suisse states:

> FINMA formally concluded the enforcement proceedings instituted against Credit Suisse with a decree issued on 21 September 2012. FINMA reprimanded Credit Suisse for severe violation of governance and proper business conduct requirements.[118]

A FinIA[119] is currently in parliamentary consultation. This is a uniform Act that will apply to all financial services firms and providers that are subject to authorisation (i.e. that need a state licence) except banks whose rules (for licence, supervision, etc.) will stay in the Banking Act. Worth mentioning here is that the pre-draft of the Act contained a stipulation that financial institutions (including banks) may only accept taxed assets.[120] However, because of criticism in the consultation, the Federal Council decided to refrain from pursuing it.[121]

11.6.4   Group Requests

It is an established principle that a request for legal or administrative aid in tax matters must name the person in respect of whom the request is made.

---

[116] According to Art. 9, para. 2, Banking Regulation (30 April 2014), SR 952.02, a bank must provide a risk management framework as well as regulations or internal directives describing processes and responsibilities for risky business undertakings. Specifically, it must detect, mitigate and monitor market, credit, default, settlement, liquidity, reputational, operating and legal risks.

[117] FINMA Credit Suisse Summary Report, *supra* note 95; FINMA UBS Summary Report, *supra* note 98.

[118] FINMA Credit Suisse Summary Report, *supra* note 95 at 2.

[119] Federal Financial Services Act (FinSA) and FinIA, explanatory report and pre-drafts for parliamentary consultations on 25 June 2014, available online at: www.news.admin.ch/ NSBSubscriber/message/attachments/41734.pdf (FinSA) and www.news.admin.ch/ NSBSubscriber/message/attachments/41750.pdf (FinIA).

[120] Article 11, Pre-Draft FinIA.

[121] The Federal Counsel presented his draft and dispatch for the FinSA and the FinIA on 4 November 2015, 'Bundesrat verabschiedet Botschaft zum Finanzdienstleistungsgesetz und zum Finanzinstitutsgesetz' (4 November 2015), online: www.news.admin.ch/ message/index.html? lang=en&msg-id=59331

This will require the client of the financial institution to be identified by name.

Switzerland has departed from this principle because of international developments, such as the OECD Standards and the BEPS project, which went in another direction. At first, the Federal Administrative Court approved foreign group administrative assistance requests (even if not urgent) that contained no client names or personal data for identification.[122] Later, the Tax Administrative Assistance Act (TAAA)[123] was enacted, which gave statutory authority to this approach, defining group administrative assistance requests as 'administrative assistance requests for information on two or more people with identical behaviour patterns who are identifiable by means of precise details'.[124]

This development opened up the possibility for vastly broad request areas from foreign countries. Fishing expeditions, however, remain prohibited.

11.6.5   US Foreign Account Tax Compliance Act

The underlying intention of FATCA is to tax the incomes of US persons with financial assets located outside the United States by requiring such persons to report their non-US financial accounts, and by requiring non-US financial institutions to search their records for suspected US persons and report their identities and assets. On 14 February 2013, the Swiss government signed the agreement to facilitate the implementation of FATCA.[125] The form of agreement selected was the Model 2 Treaty, whereby foreign financial institutions must submit account information directly to the US tax authority, the IRS. In such cases, the client must provide his consent. Should the client fail to give consent, the client data will be submitted by the bank via a special administrative assistance procedure based on group requests.[126] The FATCA agreement became effective on 2 June 2014.

---

[122] Cf. Robert Waldburger, 'Sind Gruppenersuchen an die Schweiz rechtlich zulässig?', *IFF Forum für Steuerrecht* (2013) 110; BVGer A-7342/2008 and A-7426/2008, *supra* note 87, E. 4.5.

[123] Swiss Federal Act on International Administrative Assistance in Tax Matters (28 September 2012), SR 651.1 (TAAA).

[124] See *ibid.*, Art. 3(c).

[125] Agreement between Switzerland and the United States of America for Cooperation to Facilitate the Implementation of FATCA (14 February 2013), SR 0.672.933.63.

[126] Cf. for the administrative assistance procedure the information given underwww.estv .admin.ch/estv/en/home/internationales-steuerrecht/themen/amts-und-rechtshilfe/ amtshilfe-nach-fatca.html

The Swiss legislation implementing FATCA (the 'Implementation Act')[127] entered into force on 30 June 2014, after a failed referendum to oppose the implementation of the Act. Switzerland is now trying to negotiate a Model 1 agreement based on the AEOI. In February 2014, FINMA issued a bulletin to make the Swiss finance industry aware of the supervisory changes as a result of the implementation of FATCA.[128]

11.7   Conclusion

As discussed, on 13 March 2009, the Federal Counsel announced the implementation of the AEOI among countries according to OECD-standards for all tax offences, thereby effectively abolishing bank secrecy in the tax context. For people who grew up under a veil of secrecy,[129] it is hard to believe what has happened in a short time frame to the long-lasting Swiss tradition of bank secrecy that generally could not have been pierced in taxation matters (except in the case of clearly defined offences, such as tax fraud). At least nobody – neither bankers, nor public authorities, nor politicians or scientists – can say that they did not know anything about it. No one was willing to talk about the inherent dangers[130] because these were believed to be fairly remote. As indicated earlier, banks contract for the right to disclose client information when it is in the legitimate interests of the bank.[131] Such an approach has always signalled a de facto limitation of bank secrecy.[132] Furthermore, as described earlier, a slow farewell to bank secrecy was taking place even before the Federal Counsel's trend-setting decision. Thanks to tax savings, untaxed money produced high interest

---

[127] Bundesgesetz über die Umsetzung des FATCA-Abkommens zwischen der Schweiz und den Vereinigten Staaten (FATCA-Gesetz) (27 September 2013), SR 672.933.6 (Federal Act on the Implementation of the FATCA Agreement between the US and Switzerland).

[128] FINMA, 'Aufsichtrechtliche Konsequenzen des Foreign Account Tax Compliance Act (FATCA)', *FINMA Mitteilung*, 59 (2014), 28 February 2014, online: www.finma.ch/de/~/media/finma/dokumente/dokumentencenter/4dokumentation/finma-mitteilungen/finma-mitteilung-59-2014.pdf?la=de

[129] Enactment of Art. 47, Swiss Banking Act, *supra* note 2 in 1934.

[130] In particular, that Swiss bank secrecy and its differentiation in tax matters were misused and therefore would cease to be acceptable internationally.

[131] See Section 11.3.3.

[132] The situation that bank GTC deal with includes the challenges posed by bank–client confidentiality to the banking group, as disclosure within the group is generally not allowed. Leaving aside the conglomerate structure, other problems in takeovers and similar events arise. This whole area of problems has been discussed for quite some time, cf. the thoughts of Peter Honegger and Thomas Frick, Das Bankgeheimnis im Konzern und bei Übernahmen, in: *SZW* 1/1996, p. 1 ff., p. 1 f.

and was a driving factor in the old business model of banks. Assuming this business model has to be adapted in the future (which is likely to be the case), performance such as the quality of banking products and services will play an important role next to all the other success factors that Switzerland has always accentuated (such as rule of law, stability, international spirit and language skills). In this sense, the future is open, and the exchange of information – in the sense that all-embracing disclosure must be made and secrets can no longer be kept – is open too.

The United Kingdom

KEITH STANTON

12.1 Introduction

My aim in this chapter is to review the current state of the bank's duty of secrecy in UK law.[1] In particular, I attempt to show how the duty has evolved and is evolving. I approach the issue in two ways. First, I summarise the legal structure in which bank secrecy issues arise in the United Kingdom. As will be seen, although there is no doubt that UK law recognises the duty of secrecy as a fundamental component of the banker–customer relationship, there is a degree of complexity in explaining the legal basis of the duty. This complexity is the result of the duty being recognised in a number of ways within the UK's legal and regulatory framework. Second, I review the areas which appear to me to be of greatest significance to bank secrecy today. These areas are divided into two parts. On the one hand, the legislation on money laundering (and the transmission of funds for the purposes of terrorism)[2] and the measures taken to counter tax evasion both make significant inroads into the duty of secrecy. On the other hand, topics such as data protection and cybercrime show that in some areas maintaining customer secrecy remains of vital importance to banks and their customers. This is an area dominated by competing public interests. As will become obvious, the relationship between bank secrecy and the criminal law plays a large part in the modern picture because

I would like to thank my colleagues Ardavan Arzandeh and Holly Powley and the participants in the Bank Secrecy Symposium on 4–5 December 2014 for their helpful comments on earlier versions of this paper. A version of this chapter was presented at the Bank Secrecy Symposium hosted by the Centre for Banking and Finance Law at the National University of Singapore, Faculty of Law on 4–5 December 2014.

[1] I speak throughout this piece of UK law. I am not aware of any differences between English and Scottish law on this subject.

[2] These will be treated together because of the similar legislative framework.

legislation commonly requires banks and others to supply information to bodies charged with enforcing the law. It will also be seen that the modern UK law in this area is strongly influenced by international standards.

This approach of concentrating attention on a limited number of issues involves omitting discussion of a number of statutory and other powers to access bank account information which exist in UK law.[3] I cannot, in the space available, provide a comprehensive description of all aspects of the subject in UK law. In particular, I will not be looking at the issue of the use of customer information for marketing purposes at a time when technology companies such as Apple are moving into the provision of payment services. I will also not be considering any duties which may require banks to notify customers that a secrecy obligation has been broken.

12.1.1   General

There are some important background points to be made.

First, the United Kingdom is the home of one of the world's leading financial centres. It is one which operates globally. It therefore needs to be at the forefront of international developments in banking standards and regulation in order to maintain its reputation and thus its market position. In an era in which the ethics of certain bankers have been widely criticised, the need for banks to be meeting the highest standards of propriety in handling customers' affairs has never been greater.[4] The obligation to keep a customer's affairs secret is undoubtedly one of the fundamental tenets of the bank's relationship with its customers. In the words of a Bank of England Code, '[c]onfidentiality is essential for the preservation of a reputable and efficient market place.'[5]

Second, the challenges faced by all jurisdictions, including the United Kingdom, are often driven by both technological advance and globalisation. Issues such as money laundering and the international moves to

---

[3] The task of producing an accurate list of the statutory incursions into the secrecy principle is a substantial one. In 1989, the Jack Committee (UK, *Banking Services: Law and Practice Report by the Review Committee* (CM 622) (London: Her Majesty's Stationery Office, 1989) [Jack Committee Report]) produced a list of the major items which applied at that time: Appendix Q. But they accepted that this list was not exhaustive. For a recent example of an English case dealing with secrecy in relation to the topical issue of incorrectly keyed electronic transfers, see *Santander UK plc. v. National Westminster Bank plc.* [2014] EWHC 2626 (Ch). Note that the claimant bank was only seeking the identity of the account holders who had received incorrectly directed payments and not the details of their accounts.

[4] Richard Lambert, *Banking Standards Review*, pp. 5–7, 19 May 2014.

[5] Bank of England, *The Non-Investment Products Code* (November 2011) at 18.

combat tax evasion illustrate this. There is also the massive threat to the stability of financial institutions posed by cybercrime. It is against this background that we are currently witnessing modern global technology giants moving into the provision of financial services by monetising the data which they hold on their customers.[6] Apple Pay would have been far more difficult to bring to the market if Apple did not already hold bank account details of 800 million iTunes users.[7]

Third, it must be emphasised that banks do not breach customer secrecy: individuals working in banks do that. Customer data may be released because of intentional misconduct or simple negligence. The issue is therefore part of the ongoing debate in the United Kingdom and elsewhere about professional standards in the banking industry and about managerial responsibility for the conduct of employees. Martin Wheatley, the former Chief Executive Officer of the UK's Financial Conduct Authority (FCA), is quoted as saying in relation to the FOREX case,[8] in which traders had been found to have manipulated foreign exchange rates (in part, by breaching secrecy by revealing to other traders the orders which their clients had placed):

> But this is not just about enforcement action. It is about a combination of actions aimed at driving up market standards across the industry. All firms need to work with us to deliver real and lasting change to the culture of the trading floor. This is essential to restoring the public's trust in financial services and London maintaining its position as a strong and competitive financial centre.[9]

The result is that we see both corporate and, at times, individual responsibility for secrecy breaches being emphasised.

Finally, there is an important legal perspective to be emphasised. The traditional approach to the issue of secrecy has been to consider it as

---

[6] K. Broughton, 'Apple Pay a Systemic Risk? Banker Warns about Nonbank Players' (21 November 2014), online: American Banker, www.americanbanker.com/news/bank-tech nology/apple-pay-a-systemic-risk-banker-warns-about-nonbank-players-1071357-1.html

[7] N. Arora, 'Seeds of Apple's New Growth in Mobile Payments, 800 Million iTune Accounts' (24 April 2014), online: www.forbes.com/sites/nigamarora/2014/04/24/seeds-of-apples-new-growth-in-mobile-payments-800-million-itune-accounts

[8] For brief explanations of the FOREX scandal, see S. Chrispin, 'Forex Scandal: How to Rig the Market' (20 May 2015), online: www.bbc.co.uk/news/business-26526905 and C. Boyle, 'Forex Manipulation: How It Worked' (12 November 2014), online: www.cnbc .com/2014/03/11/forex-manipulation-how-it-worked.html

[9] FCA, 'FCA Fines Five Banks £1.1 Billion for FX Failings and Announces Industry-Wide Remediation Programme' (12 November 2014), online: www.fca.org.uk/news/fca-fines-five-banks-for-fx-failings

creating private law rights and remedies for a customer to use against a bank. Private law claims have not gone away, but the growth of regulation in modern economies has added a new dimension. In the United Kingdom, this centres on the work of the FCA and, to a lesser extent, the Prudential Regulation Authority (PRA) and the Information Commissioner's Office (ICO). There are now a number of ways in which banks that breach secrecy duties may face enforcement action culminating in financial penalties levied by regulators. The truth is that the level of such penalties and the publicity attached to them is likely to be of much greater importance to banks than damages claims brought against them by customers. Regulatory penalties are being set at levels which impact on share prices and capital requirements.[10] A major breach of customer secrecy is nowadays capable of leading to a bank being liable to pay a penalty of millions of pounds.[11]

12.2   The UK Law of Bank Secrecy

UK law tends to speak of confidentiality,[12] not secrecy. There is some writing which attempts to distinguish these concepts.[13] However, I will not attempt to consider this issue because it is clear that issues which are classified in the United Kingdom under the head of confidentiality are the same as those which other jurisdictions treat under the heading of secrecy. For the purposes of this chapter, I speak of secrecy.

There is no statutory statement of the banker's obligation of secrecy in UK law.[14] UK law is a common law system and, as such, is found in an amalgam of case law and statute. The history of the banker's duty of secrecy in UK law can be best summarised as one of ad hoc development. A proposal was made in the late 1980s to codify the subject in

---

[10] And on government borrowing requirements, see J. Treanor, L. Elliott and A. Monaghan, 'Treasury Gains £1.1 bn Windfall from Record Fines on Banks' (12 November 2014), online: www.theguardian.com/business/2014/nov/12/treasury-osborne-bank-fines-fca-foreign-currency-markets

[11] See Section 12.2.5 for a discussion of the Forex cases. On data protection, see the discussion of Bank of Scotland at Section 12.4.1.

[12] Although the Court of Appeal in the leading case of *Tournier v. National Provincial and Union Bank of England* [1924] 1 KB 461 spoke of secrecy.

[13] C. Le Bachelet, *Confidentiality vs. secrecy – What's the difference?* www.rbcwmfiduciarynews.com/getfile.php?id=57. Linguistically, the difference is generally regarded as one of degree with secret information being regarded as more sensitive than that which is confidential.

[14] Cf *Banking Act* (Cap 19, 2008 Rev Ed Sing), s 47. See Booysen, Chapter 10.

statutory form.[15] However, the government of the day firmly rejected this proposal[16] and no further suggestion for legislation of this kind has been made.

The lack of a statute governing bank secrecy has the advantage of making it unnecessary to define which institutions are covered by the duty. This is significant in a world in which we have a great variety of financial institutions, as the UK approach means that there is no need to discuss whether shadow banks, savings institutions, credit unions and all sorts of other institutions are subject to a secrecy obligation. Indeed, in the modern world a wide variety of businesses which are in no way banks hold banking information on their customers and, as has already been said, some are seeking to exploit this data commercially. If we were seeking to construct the law of bank secrecy anew, unencumbered by history, it is likely that the starting point would be the data protection legislation which is, in no way, confined to banks. It applies generally to those who hold other people's personal information. Banks are simply an example of one of the many organisations which do that and, as a consequence, owe a duty of secrecy to their customers.

The lack of a statutory basis does not mean that there is any doubt that an obligation is placed on a bank by UK law to keep a customer's identity and affairs secret. This is regarded as a basic feature of the banker–customer relationship. However, it is difficult to identify the legal basis for the obligation. This is not because the duty is in any doubt: it is because there are a variety of legal rules which express the obligation. The UK law on this subject may best be described as a hotchpotch of remedies doing different, but related, things. The duty of secrecy may be best viewed as a general principle which finds expression in a number of pieces of law and which is subject to detailed rules and exceptions. It is certainly wrong to see it simply as a matter of contract. Furthermore, most of the ways in which the duty is supported, or made subject to an exception, are laws which apply to a range of actors: not simply banks. In the modern world, bank secrecy issues are part of a wider picture. This is not to be decried at a time when banking facilities are being offered by a wide range of organisations: the traditional picture of banking is breaking up.

---

[15] Jack Committee Report, *supra* note 3, Chapter 5.
[16] UK, *Banking Services: Law and Practice The Government's Response* (CM 1026) (London: Her Majesty's Stationery Office, 1990).

12.2.1 The Contractual Duty

The traditional view is that the root principle is enshrined in the words of
Bankes and Atkin LJJ in the English Court of Appeal decision of *Tournier
v. National Provincial and Union Bank of England*.[17] This case recognises
the duty of secrecy as an implied contractual obligation owed by a bank to
its customer.[18]

The Court in *Tournier* placed considerable emphasis on the duty to
maintain secrecy being a qualified, rather than an absolute one. However,
there is no suggestion that the qualifications extend beyond those listed in
the case. This could be important in relation to cyber threats as it is con-
ceivable that a bank might wish to argue in its defence that it had, unsuccessfully, taken all reasonable care to guard customers' data.[19] Such an
argument would be unlikely to succeed. There is no suggestion anywhere
in the UK case law that the contractual duty is anything other than a strict
one, subject to defined exceptions.

Bankes LJ stated the duty as follows:

> I think it may be asserted with confidence that the duty [of secrecy] is a legal
> one arising out of contract, and that the duty is not absolute but qualified.[20]
>
>   In my opinion it is necessary in a case like the present to direct the jury
> what are the limits, and what are the qualifications of the contractual duty
> of secrecy implied in the relation of banker and customer. There appears
> to be no authority on the point. On principle I think that the qualifications
> can be classified under four heads: (*a*) Where disclosure is under compul-
> sion by law; (*b*) where there is a duty to the public to disclose; (*c*) where the
> interests of the bank require disclosure; (*d*) where the disclosure is made by
> the express or implied consent of the customer.[21]

For present purposes, it is the first qualification which is the most important. The scope of much of the modern duty of secrecy exists in the interplay between the basic principle of protecting a customer's confidential
information and the legislation which creates obligations to breach it.

---

[17] *Supra* note 12.

[18] A more modern approach to the subject might be to found the duty on the laws of data
protection or privacy. However, the contractual basis seems perfectly adequate and is the
one conventionally used.

[19] Note that ss 13(3) of the *Data Protection Act 1998* (UK), c 29 provides a defence to a damages claim brought under s 13 by an individual for breach of a requirement of the Act on
proof that the defendant 'had taken such care as in all the circumstances was reasonably
required to comply with the requirement concerned'.

[20] *Tournier, supra* note 12 at 471–2.

[21] *Ibid.* at 472–3.

It should not, however, be thought that all modern statutory developments are reducing the duty of secrecy. The law on data protection and cyber-crime emphasises the continuing importance of the basic principle.

Two important limits to *Tournier* need to be emphasised. First, its contractual nature means that persons who are not parties to the contract will not be subject to the obligation. Second, the fact that this duty is an implied one means that it can be overridden by express contractual terms. The complexity that this can produce in practice is illustrated by the decision of Arnold J in *Primary Group (UK) Ltd* v. *The Royal Bank of Scotland plc*.[22] In that case, the defendant bank had, in order to obtain an industry view of its customer's prospects, disclosed details of the customer's affairs to staff working in a subsidiary company which was a commercial rival of the customer. Express terms and conditions which were held to be wide enough to justify the disclosure were held to apply only to one business account and not to the loan agreements which were at issue in the case. The express terms of the loan facility agreement were held, therefore, not to justify the disclosure which had been made. As a result, the issue ultimately turned on *Tournier*. On that basis, the particular disclosure could not be said to have been in the bank's interests as it was not reasonably necessary to protect the interests which were at issue. An award of damages was made against the bank.

12.2.2 Breach of Confidence and Agency

An alternative explanation for the duty of secrecy is that it derives from the fact that the banker–customer relationship is one of confidentiality, based on there being a relationship of agency. This approach might be regarded as a circular one: that a relationship of confidence creates an obligation of secrecy. However, it is important because it emphasises that a bank's duty of secrecy is simply an example of a wider principle of confidentiality which is applicable to all professional and agency relationships. Both Cranston[23] and Ellinger[24] take this approach in their textbooks. Ellinger states that '[t]he confidential nature of the banker–customer

---

[22] [2014] EWHC 1082 (Ch).

[23] R. Cranston, *Principles of Banking Law*, 2nd edn (Oxford University Press, 2002) at 169–74.

[24] E.P. Ellinger, E. Lomnicka and C. Hare, *Ellinger's Modern Banking Law*, 5th edn, (Oxford University Press, 2011). The authority cited for this is the judgment of Diplock LJ in *Parry-Jones* v. *Law Society* [1969] 1 Ch 1. Both Lord Denning MR and Diplock LJ in that case simply base the duty on contract (Lord Denning cites *Tournier*) and do not mention agency.

contract stems from the fact that that relationship comprises elements of an agency relationship.'[25]

This approach makes equitable remedies[26] available when a bank has broken an obligation of secrecy. The FOREX cases[27] illustrate this possibility. In those cases, traders working for banks were found by FCA to have disclosed client information to other traders in order to manipulate the market to the advantage of the banks they were working for. The situation is, thus, one in which an agent conducting transactions on behalf of a principal permitted a conflict of interest to arise based on an intentional breach of the duty of secrecy. Although the issue has yet to be tested, this would seem to be a classic example of a situation which gives rise to equitable remedies.

Treating the banker–customer relationship as one of confidence means that the privity of contract problems inherent in the contractual approach to the issue can be escaped and remedies sought against third parties who have come into possession of confidential information. The claimants in *Primary Group (UK) Ltd* v. *The Royal Bank of Scotland plc*[28] brought such a claim against the bank's subsidiary (and the claimant's rival) company which had come into possession of confidential information relating to them.[29]

12.2.3   Voluntary Codes

Given that the duty of secrecy functions as a high-level principle, it is not surprising that it has been incorporated into those codes of practice which give guidance to persons working in financial markets.[30]

The *Tournier* principles were reproduced in more modern form in the voluntary Banking Code of practice adopted by the banking industry in the United Kingdom until 2009.[31] The recognition of the duty in this code shows how fundamental it is to this area of law. This code was not legally

---

[25] *Ellinger's Modern Banking Law, supra* note 24 at 171.
[26] For the UK Supreme Court's latest decision on equitable remedies, see *AIB Group (UK) Plc* v. *Mark Redler & Co Solicitors* [2014] UKSC 58.
[27] See Section 12.2.5.
[28] *Supra* note 22.
[29] This part of the claim was unsuccessful on the basis that the recipients reasonably believed that the bank had the right to release the information.
[30] See, for example, *The Non-Investment Products Code, supra* note 5.
[31] 'The Banking Code' (March 2008), online: www.bankingcode.org.uk/pdfdocs/personal_code_2008.pdf

enforceable, but its terms could be taken into account when deciding whether a bank had acted reasonably. This was potentially important in relation to claims brought by customers against the Financial Ombudsman Service (FOS).[32] The Banking Code, which has now been replaced by direct regulation,[33] stated:

11 Your personal information
 Confidentiality.
 11.1 We will treat all your personal information as private and confidential (even when you are no longer a customer)
   We will not make your name and address or details about your accounts known to anyone, including other companies in our group, other than in the following four exceptional cases when we are allowed to do this by law.
   • If we have to give the information by law.
   • If there is a duty to the public to make the information known.
   • If our interests mean we must give the information (for example, to prevent fraud). However, we will not use this as a reason for giving information about you or your accounts (including your name and address) to anyone else, including other companies in our group for marketing purposes.
   • If you ask us to make the information known, or if we have your permission.
 Bankers' references
 11.2 If we are asked to give a banker's reference about you, we will need your written permission before we give it.
 Data protection
 11.3 We will explain to you that, under the Data Protection Act, you have the right to see the personal records we hold about you.
 11.4 We will tell you if we record your telephone conversations with us.

A separate voluntary code directly concerning banking which still remains in force is the Lending Code.[34] Paragraph 15 of that code states that:

Personal information will be treated as private and confidential, and subscribers will provide secure and reliable banking and payment systems.

---

[32] See *R (on the application of Norwich and Peterborough B.S.) v. Financial Ombudsman Service Ltd* [2002] EWHC 2379 (Admin) and pp. 346-7.
[33] See pp. 346-7. The FCA Handbook contains no equivalent reworking of *Tournier*.
[34] Lending Standards Board, 'The Lending Code' (March 2011, revised September 2015), online: www.lendingstandardsboard.org.uk/docs/lendingcoderevised0915.pdf

This is important wording, not only because it moves away from repeating the details of *Tournier*, but also in its recognition that secrecy in modern practice entails running systems which keep customer information secure from cybercrime and other forms of fraud.

12.2.4   Financial Ombudsman Service

There is also a limited, but growing, body of jurisprudence in the United Kingdom which deals with breach of secrecy issues resolved by the FOS. The FOS is an industry-funded alternative dispute resolution mechanism which is free to complainants.[35] Because it is free it is likely to be the best remedy available to a private customer who has been damaged by a breach of the duty of secrecy. These cases tend to be low values ones in which it is alleged that errors or misconduct within a bank have resulted in personal information being released. If a remedy is granted, it will often take the form of an apology and a small award of compensation for distress and annoyance.[36] Cases in this area often concern not only a breach of secrecy but also consideration of the way in which the bank handled the matter.

The duty of secrecy in such a case is not technically founded on the common law as expressed in *Tournier*. Secrecy cases decided by the Ombudsman are determined according to a statutory criterion of what is 'fair and reasonable in all the circumstances of the case'.[37] Breaching customer secrecy is simply regarded as something which a reasonable bank does not do.

A couple of examples of cases decided under this procedure illustrate its effectiveness. In Case Ref: DRN5151001,[38] a woman complained that she had been harassed by her ex-partner who had used his position as a bank employee to discover the address at which she was living. There was no allegation that she had suffered financial loss as a result of this breach of secrecy. The Ombudsman found the bank to be responsible for the act of its employee in accessing the customer's account details for improper purposes. It was also held that the bank's unsatisfactory response to her initial complaint had increased her distress and annoyance. The bank's offer of

---

[35] Decisions made since 2012 are available at FOS, 'Ombudsman Decisions', online: www.ombudsman-decisions.org.uk/

[36] The amount which can be awarded under this procedure is capped at £150,000.

[37] *Financial Services and Markets Act 2000* (UK), c 8, s. 228(2).

[38] Case Ref: DRN5151001, online: www.ombudsman-decisions.org.uk/viewPDF.aspx?FileID =19341

an apology and £400 compensation was regarded as inadequate: £600 was awarded. In another case,[39] A was trading from premises leased from P Ltd. The bank was instructed to send statements to him at 'A c/o P Ltd.' On one occasion, the bank mistakenly addressed a statement to 'P Ltd.' P opened the statement and saw that A had a large overdraft. This information, coupled with the fact that A was in arrears in paying rent, resulted in P Ltd sending in bailiffs and A's business failing. The Ombudsman regarded P Ltd's actions as precipitate, but wholly caused by the bank's breach of secrecy. As the losses were foreseeable, an award of £40,000 was made.

12.2.5 Financial Services and Markets Act 2000

As has already been said, to regard the modern principle of secrecy in UK law as solely based on private law claims in contract and equity would be misleading. It would mean that enforcement is the sole preserve of individuals. In fact, much of the modern UK law is based on the regulation of banks under the *Financial Services and Markets Act 2000*. Under the latest version of this legislation,[40] the PRA and the FCA regulate these issues in so far as they apply to banks.

This regulation is effected by means of handbooks which are legally enforceable.[41] There are no express provisions in the handbooks establishing the right to secrecy. However, it is clear that the FCA's general principles[42] governing all regulated organisations are adequate to support enforcement action in the event of a major breach of the duty: for example, if a security breach permitted third parties to obtain access to customer information.[43] The first three general principles require a firm to conduct business with integrity (Principle 1)[44] and with due skill, care and diligence (Principle 2)[45] and to take reasonable care to organise and control its affairs responsibly and effectively, with adequate risk management

---

[39] Case 45/5 reported in Ombudsman News, Issue 45 (April 2005), online: www.financial-ombudsman.org.uk/publications/ombudsman-news/45/45.pdf. Formal reporting of decisions has only been in place since 2012.

[40] As amended by the *Financial Services Act 2012* (UK), c 21, Part 2.

[41] *Financial Services and Markets Act 2000*, *supra* note 37, Part 9A.

[42] These principles are not actionable in tort by an individual as breach of statutory duty under s 138D.

[43] See pp. 361-6.

[44] FCA, 'Principles for Businesses', PRIN 2.1.1.1, online: www.handbook.fca.org.uk/handbook/PRIN.pdf [Principles for Businesses].

[45] *Ibid.*, PRIN 2.1.1.2.

systems (Principle 3).[46] Principle 10 requires a firm to arrange adequate protection for clients' assets when it is responsible for them.[47] FCA enforcement action against banks is now a familiar element of banking law and penalties are regularly measured in millions of pounds.

Secrecy issues have recently been one of the grounds justifying the imposition by the FCA of penalties totalling £1.1 billion[48] on five banks which had been found to be manipulating the FOREX markets. One of the grounds given by FCA for imposing penalties for breach of Principle 3 was that customer information had been shared among traders working for different banks.[49] This failure concerned traders disclosing to others both the identity of their clients and the orders which they had placed. In addition to the FOREX case, failures to maintain working IT systems[50] and to have adequate measures to counter money laundering (i.e. to decide when it is necessary to breach secrecy) have resulted in penalties.[51]

These regulatory cases show how the focus of the discussion has shifted. The concentration is no longer simply on whether a breach of customer secrecy has occurred: it is now a managerial responsibility to ensure that adequate systems are in place to ensure that the law on this matter is complied with.

12.2.6   Data Protection

An important piece of regulatory legislation which creates obligations of secrecy is the *Data Protection Act 1998*. The Information Commissioner is a third regulator with a significant role in the modern UK law of bank

---

[46] *Ibid.*, PRIN 2.1.1.3.

[47] *Ibid.*, PRIN 2.1.1.10.

[48] The American Commodity Futures Trading Commission imposed an additional US$1.4 billion penalty.

[49] E.g. 'FCA Final Notice 2014: Citibank N.A.' (11 November 2014) at para. 2.6, online: www .fca.org.uk/your-fca/documents/final-notices/2014/citibank-na. The proceedings against the other banks were in the same terms. See 'FCA Final Notice 2014: HSBC Bank Plc' (12 November 2014), online: www.fca.org.uk/your-fca/documents/final-notices/2014/hsbc-bank-plc; 'FCA Final Notice 2014: JPMorgan Chase Bank N.A.' (12 November 2014), online: www.fca.org .uk/your-fca/documents/final-notices/2014/jpmorgan-chase-bank; 'FCA Final Notice 2014: The Royal Bank of Scotland Plc' (12 November 2014), online: www.fca.org.uk/your-fca/ documents/final-notices/2014/royal-bank-of-scotland and 'FCA Final Notice 2014: UBS AG' (12 November 2014), online: www.fca.org.uk/your-fca/documents/final-notices/2014/ubs-ag

[50] The PRA and FCA have imposed a combined penalty of £56 million in relation to the IT failure at RBS Group in 2012 which resulted in customers being unable to access their accounts. See p. 365.

[51] See p. 350ff.

secrecy. This legislation, which has been the ground on which individual bankers have been convicted and fined for improperly accessing customer data, will be considered later in this chapter.[52]

12.2.7   The Influence of Europe

It is also essential to place UK law on bank secrecy in the international context.

12.2.7.1   European Union

As a member state of the European Union, the United Kingdom has been required to incorporate EU legislation on bank secrecy issues into domestic law. It is by this process that many of the modern international standards enter UK law. To pick an important example, the Money Laundering Regulations of 2007 were the result of the European Union's requirement to implement its *Third Money Laundering Directive*,[53] which was itself the European Union's response to requirements specified by the Financial Action Task Force (FATF).[54] The FATF is an intergovernmental body charged with defining standards and promoting effective implementation of measures for combating money laundering and terrorist financing. A further Directive on this subject, which is based on more recent FATF recommendations, is currently under discussion within the European Union.[55]

12.2.7.2   European Convention on Human Rights

The United Kingdom's incorporation of the European Convention on Human Rights into domestic law has also had some relevance to bank secrecy.[56] A challenge to the release of information under money

---

[52] See pp. 359ff.

[53] EC, *Directive 2005/60/EC of the European Parliament and of the Council of 26 October 2005 on the prevention of the use of the financial system for the purpose of money laundering and terrorist financing* [2005] O.J. L. 309/15.

[54] FATF, 'FATF 40 Recommendations' (October 2003), online: www.fatf-gafi.org/media/fatf/documents/FATF%20Standards%20-%2040%20Recommendations%20rc.pdf

[55] EC, 'Proposal for a Directive of the European Parliament and of the Council on the prevention of the use of the financial system for the purpose of money laundering and terrorist financing' (2013), online: http://eur-lex.europa.eu/LexUriServ/LexUriServ.do?uri=COM:2013:0045:FIN:EN:PDF. This is based on the FATF recommendations in FATF, 'International standards on combating money laundering and the financing of terrorism & proliferation' (February 2012), online: www.fatf-gafi.org/media/fatf/documents/recommendations/pdfs/FATF_Recommendations.pdf

[56] For a discussion see R. Stokes, 'The Banker's Duty of Confidentiality, Money Laundering and the Human Rights Act', *Journal of Business Law* (2007), 502.

laundering legislation has been based on an alleged infringement of Art. 6 (the right of access to courts). However, the challenge failed on the grounds that the infringement was an act proportionate to a legitimate policy.[57]

Article 1 of Protocol 1 has also been unsuccessfully mooted as relevant. It states that:

> Every natural or legal person is entitled to the peaceful enjoyment of his possessions.[58] No one shall be deprived of his possessions except in the public interest and subject to the conditions provided for by law and by the general principles of international law.

In practice, it seems unlikely that the Convention will play much of a role in relation to bank secrecy.

12.3   Limiting Bank Secrecy

The laws which qualify bank secrecy tend to be driven by the imperative of crime enforcement. In these areas, the duty to disclose information about a customer's banking activities is required by the law.[59] It also needs to be emphasised that information, when released, does not become public. The recipient will commonly have a duty to keep it secret and to use it only for specified purposes.[60]

The most widely recognised statutory incursion into bank secrecy is the anti-money laundering (AML) legislation.

12.3.1   Money Laundering

The UK claims to have shown global leadership in the fight against money laundering and terrorist financing. It aims to be fully compliant with the standards laid down by the FATF.[61] The United Kingdom is

---

[57] K Ltd v. National Westminster Bank plc [2007] 1 WLR 311 [K Ltd].

[58] In K Ltd, supra note 57, Longmore LJ doubted that a customer's right to have a bank comply with instructions to make a payment could be defined as a possession.

[59] Cranston, supra note 23 at 175 states that it is less an exception to the general rule than a duty which overrides duties which would otherwise obtain.

[60] Ibid., at 177–8. See for example, s. 348 of the Financial Services and Markets Act 2000 which regulates what the PRA and FCA can do with confidential information they have received in the performance of their duties. See also pp. 357-8 and the example given at infra note 99.

[61] HM Treasury, 'Anti-Money laundering and counter terrorist finance supervision report 2012–13' (24 March 2015), online: www.gov.uk/government/publications/anti-money-laundering-and-counter-terrorist-finance-supervision-reports/anti-money-laundering-and-counter-terrorist-finance-supervision-report-2012-13 [HM Treasury Report].

often said to be one of the countries which attracts money laundering, not because it is a country with lax controls, but because the quantity of transactions being conducted in London makes it possible to hide illegal transactions.[62]

There are two prongs to the UK legislation on this subject. The main legislation on the subject is to be found in the *Proceeds of Crimes Act 2002* and the *Money Laundering Regulations 2007*.[63] These measures create for banks and others: first, a regime of 'suspicion-based' reporting which directly overrides the duty of secrecy and, second, a requirement to establish effective procedures to guard against these risks. The provisions are supported by criminal law penalties which can be applied to both banks and bank employees. In practice, however, the policing of these provisions has taken the form of regulatory penalties.[64] In 2014, the FCA imposed a civil penalty of £7.64 million on Standard Bank plc for failing to comply with Regulation 20(1) of the Money Laundering Regulations.[65] This was the result of inadequate controls in its commercial banking operation relating to corporate customers connected to politically exposed persons. It is well known that regulatory penalties concerning the adequacy of measures taken to prevent money laundering are now a major issue for banks. HSBC (a British bank) has reached a settlement under a deferred prosecution agreement with the US Department of Justice under which it has agreed to pay a penalty of US$1.9 billion in relation to money laundering through its US and Mexican subsidiaries.[66]

12.3.1.1   Proceeds of Crimes Act 2002, Part 7/Terrorism Act 2000

The *Proceeds of Crimes Act 2002*[67] produces the 'suspicion-based' reporting regime which is commonly regarded as the UK provision which constitutes

---

[62] *Ibid.*, Lord Deighton, Foreword from the Commercial Secretary to the Treasury: 'Law enforcement agencies believe that many hundreds of billions of pounds of criminal money is laundered through UK banks and their subsidiaries overseas each year.'

[63] SI 2007/2157 [*2007 Regulations*].

[64] SYSC 6.3 is the basis in the FCA Handbook for regulatory action on this subject. However, action has been taken by the FCA in some cases (see Standard Bank, *infra* note 65) directly under the *Money Laundering Regulations 2007*. These Regulations are far more detailed in the requirements placed on banks.

[65] 'FCA Decision Notice: Standard Bank plc' (22 January 2014), online: www.fca.org.uk/static/documents/decision-notices/standard-bank-plc.pdf

[66] As discussed further by Broome, Chapter 13.

[67] (UK), c 29.

the most significant legislative incursion into banker–customer secrecy. Section 330 creates a criminal offence in the following terms:

(1) A person commits an offence if each of the following three conditions is satisfied.

(2) The first condition is that he—
   (a) knows or suspects or
   (b) has reasonable grounds for knowing or suspecting, that another person is engaged in money laundering.[68]

(3) The second condition is that the information or other matter—
   (a) on which his knowledge or suspicion is based or
   (b) which gives reasonable grounds for such knowledge or suspicion, came to him in the course of a business in the regulated sector.

(4) The third condition is that he does not make the required disclosure as soon as is practicable after the information or other matter comes to him.

In such circumstances, a bank which fails to break its obligation of secrecy renders itself liable to prosecution. If the bank makes the disclosure, it is protected from any liability unless it does one of a number of acts which would assist money laundering without the consent of the National Crime Agency (NCA).[69]

For the purposes of this law, UK law specifies a threshold of £250.[70] Transactions conducted by 'deposit-taking' bodies (which will mainly be banks) relating to criminal property below this figure are excluded from the regime. As a result, banks are not required to pay attention to the vast body of low-value transactions which they process.

The definition of suspicion is central to the working of this legislation. The rule which has emerged was stated by the Court of Appeal in *R* v. *Da Silva*:[71]

> the defendant must think that there is a possibility, which is more than fanciful, that the relevant facts exist. A vague feeling of unease would not

---

[68] Defined by s 340(11)(a) as an offence under s 327, 328 or 329. The product of any criminal offence counts as 'criminal property' (s 340(3)). Earlier versions of the legislation applied only to drug trafficking.

[69] The NCA assumed the powers previously held by the Serious Organised Crime Agency in 2013. The UK Financial Intelligence Unit (UKFIU) is the part of NCA charged with responsibility for enforcing the money laundering legislation.

[70] Section 103 of the *Serious Organised Crime and Police Act 2005* (UK), c 15, introducing a new section 339A and amending sections 327, 328 and 329 of the *Proceeds of Crimes Act 2002*.

[71] [2007] 1 WLR 303. See also *K Ltd*, *supra* note 57, *Shah* v. *HSBC Private Bank (UK) Ltd.* [2010] 3 All ER 477.

suffice. But the statute does not require the suspicion to be 'clear' or 'firmly grounded and targeted on specific facts', or based upon 'reasonable grounds'.

The intention here is to ensure that the bank does not take on the role of prosecutor: its role is merely to give information for others to judge.

Section 21A of the amended *Terrorism Act 2000* creates an equivalent regime in relation to the funding of terrorism.[72]

The litigation which has occurred on this subject has centred on the impact which these provisions have had on the banks' contractual duty of secrecy. The majority of claims have involved customers challenging a bank's refusal to comply with an instruction (for example to transfer funds) after the bank has made a Suspicious Activity Report (SAR). I know of no case in which a financial institution has faced a criminal prosecution under these provisions (which are separate from those provisions which permit banks to be fined by regulators for inadequate internal procedures).

The number of SARs made under the UK legislation has increased from 220,484 in 2007 to 354,186 in 2013–14.[73] It is believed that the increase is the result of greater awareness of the legal reporting requirements rather than of an increase in the amount of money laundering.[74] Inevitably banks are at the forefront of this. In 2013–14, 81.2 per cent of SARs were made by banks.[75] To put it in other terms, in 2013–14 there were 291,055 occasions on which a UK bank passed information about a customer to the NCA in compliance with its obligations under the *Proceeds of Crimes 2002 Act*.

---

[72] (UK), c 11, s 21A:

(1) A person commits an offence if each of the following three conditions is satisfied.
(2) The first condition is that he –
    (a) knows or suspects, or
    (b) has reasonable grounds for knowing or suspecting, that another person has committed or attempted to commit an offence under any of s 15 to 18.
(3) The second condition is that the information or other matter –
    (a) on which his knowledge or suspicion is based, or
    (b) which gives reasonable grounds for such knowledge or suspicion, came to him in the course of a business in the regulated sector.
(4) The third condition is that he does not disclose the information or other matter to a constable or a nominated officer as soon as is practicable after it comes to him.

[73] NCA, 'Suspicious Activities Report (SARs) Annual Report 2014' (2014) at 7, online: www.nationalcrimeagency.gov.uk/publications/464-2014-sars-annual-report/file. In the last year, 856 (632 from banks) SARs raised issues of terrorist funding.

[74] *Ibid.*

[75] *Ibid.*, at 8.

Over 14,000 requests for consent to proceed with a transaction were submitted during the year.[76] The refusal rate in such cases was 11.5 per cent.[77]

Two significant recent developments are that HM Revenue & Customs (HMRC) is now accessing SAR data as part of its drive to eliminate tax evasion[78] with the result that two areas in which secrecy can be broken on the basis of statutory authority are becoming interrelated. SARs are also relevant internationally. UKFIU[79] works closely with international partner bodies.[80] Information is now regularly exchanged with these groups.

12.3.1.2   Money Laundering Regulations 2007

The *2007 Regulations* are relevant to the subject in that they create the framework within which a bank decides to break secrecy by making an SAR. The regulations stipulate organisational requirements which a bank must satisfy. A failure to satisfy these requirements is a criminal offence, but it is the regulatory penalties which have been the most significant methods of enforcement. KPMG's Global Anti-Money Laundering Survey 2014[81] expresses the view that compliance with Money Laundering legislation is a major managerial concern:

> In fact, AML has never been higher on senior management's agenda, with regulatory fines now running into billions of dollars, regulatory action becoming genuinely license threatening, and threats of criminal prosecution against banks and individuals.[82]

The *2007 Regulations* impose obligations on banks in a variety of areas. A risk-sensitive approach is adopted in order to ensure that resources are targeted at the areas of greatest risk. At the forefront is an obligation to conduct customer due diligence.[83] A new customer's identity must be verified and, if the customer is not the beneficial owner of the funds the true owner must be identified. Due diligence measures are a continuing obligation,

---

[76] *Ibid.*, at 25.
[77] *Ibid.*, at 26.
[78] *Ibid.*, at 24–5.
[79] See *supra* note 69.
[80] E.g. the Egmont Group, online: www.egmontgroup.org and FIU.Net, online: www.fiu.net (which is EU-based).
[81] KPMG, 'Global Anti-Money Laundering Survey 2014' (2014), online: www.kpmg.com/KY/en/IssuesAndInsights/ArticlesPublications/PublishingImages/global-anti-money-laundering-survey-v3.pdf
[82] *Ibid.*, at 2.
[83] *2007 Regulations, supra* note 63, reg. 5.

not simply one which arises when an account is opened.[84] Enhanced due diligence may be required in some circumstances.[85] It is this requirement, and its reference to dealings with 'politically exposed persons'[86] which led to Standard Bank being subject to a penalty of £7.64 million by the FCA in 2014.[87] The *Regulations* also impose important requirements on banks in terms of: record keeping, the development of appropriate and risk-sensitive policies and procedures and staff training.

The global context of this measure should be noted. As has already been said,[88] these *Regulations* were introduced in the United Kingdom in order to implement the EU's Third Money Laundering Directive.[89] The Directive was introduced by the European Union in order to implement FATF standards.

It should be noted that the provisions of the Regulations are mirrored in the Senior Management Arrangements, Systems and Controls (SYSC) section of the FCA Handbook.[90] SYSC 6.3 on financial crime is of particular relevance. SYSC 6.3.5, which is a guidance provision, states that the FCA:

> [W]hen considering whether a breach of its rules on systems and controls against money laundering has occurred, will have regard to whether a firm has followed relevant provisions in the guidance for the United Kingdom financial sector issued by the Joint Money Laundering Steering Group.[91]

12.3.2   Tax Affairs

Access to bank account information by the UK tax authorities is the second, well-established, statutory inroad into the secrecy principle. Measures to counter tax evasion are very high on the international agenda. The ability to use bank secrecy laws to hide assets from the tax authorities is thus a major issue. It should be remembered that one of the most blatant recent examples of a breach of customer secrecy was that of Hervé Falciani, who is generally regarded as having performed a major public

---

[84] *Ibid.*, regs. 7–8.
[85] *Ibid.*, reg. 14.
[86] *Ibid.*, reg. 14(4)–(5).
[87] See Section 12.3.1.
[88] See Section 12.2.7.
[89] *Supra* note 53.
[90] FCA, 'FCA Handbook: Senior Management Arrangements, Systems and Controls' (March 2016), online: www.handbook.fca.org.uk/handbook/SYSC.pdf [FCA Handbook: SYSC].
[91] This gives detailed industry guidance. Joint Money Laundering Steering Group, 'JMLSG Guidance' (21 November 2014), online: www.jmlsg.org.uk

service by revealing the way in which HSBC's Swiss subsidiary was permitting its accounts to be used by customers to evade tax.[92]

The main focus at present is on the development of international measures aimed at countering tax evasion. UK law has permitted HMRC to access bank account information for many years.[93] What is new is the extent to which such information can now be passed to the authorities in other countries.[94]

In the United Kingdom, HMRC is granted wide powers under Schedule 36 of the *Finance Act 2008* to require the production of information or documents. This requirement can apply to third parties such as banks. Paragraph 2 of the Schedule is in the following terms:

2(1) An officer of Revenue and Customs may by notice in writing require a person –
(a) to provide information or
(b) to produce a document,

if the information or document is reasonably required by the officer for the purpose of checking the tax position of another person whose identity is known to the officer (the taxpayer).[95]

This is a powerful provision which enables HMRC to access information from banks and others even before a taxpayer has made a tax return. It thus enables the Revenue to adopt a proactive approach to possible tax evasion. Several definitions emphasise the width of the provision. First, 'tax position' is defined as including 'past, present and future liability to pay any tax'.[96] Second, 'tax' is defined to include relevant foreign tax.[97] The paragraph thus permits access to information relevant to any reasonably

---

[92] HSBC is currently facing criminal investigation in a number of jurisdictions over the activities of its Swiss subsidiary. See BBC, 'HSBC bank helped clients dodge millions in tax' (10 February 2015), online: www.bbc.co.uk/news/business-31248913

[93] The current legislation is the *Finance Act 2011* (UK), c 11, Schedule 23 and *The Reporting of Savings Income Information Regulations 2003* (SI 2003/3297).

[94] HMRC's powers to disclose to other bodies information which it holds are governed by s 17 to 23 of the *Commissioners for Revenue and Customs Act 2005* (UK), c 11.

[95] *Finance Act 2008* (UK), c 9, Schedule 36, para. 2.

[96] *Ibid.*, at para. 64(1)(a).

[97] Paragraph 63(4) states that:

> In this Schedule, 'relevant foreign tax' means
> (a) a tax of a member State, other than the United Kingdom, which is covered by the provisions for the exchange of information under [Council Directive 2011/16/EU of 15 February 2011 on administrative cooperation in the field of taxation] (as amended from time to time) and

possible liability at any time to UK tax and to tax payable in an EU Member State or a country with whom the United Kingdom has a tax information exchange agreement (TIEA).

This legislation therefore permits access to bank account details in support of the growing number of TIEAs designed to counter tax evasion. Such treaties are given effect by an Order in Council made under s 173 of the *Finance Act 2006*. At the date of writing, seventy-seven Orders had been made under this power.

It is important to see these agreements in the wider context. HMRC states that:

> They broadly follow the Organisation for Economic Co-operation and Development (OECD) Model Agreement on Exchange of Information on Tax Matters.[98] To date the UK has signed a number of bilateral TIEAs based on this OECD model in addition to 9 reciprocal and non-reciprocal TIEAs relating to the EU Directive on the taxation of savings income.[99]
>
> The UK also exchanges information with other countries for tax purposes under the joint Council of Europe/OECD Convention on mutual administrative assistance in tax matters[100] and, with other EU Member States, under the terms of a number of EU Directives and Regulations.[101]
>
> The UK participates actively in OECD work aimed at improving the efficiency of tax information exchange and ensuring that all jurisdictions that have not yet substantially implemented the international standard of fiscal transparency and exchange of information do so as soon as possible.[102]

It should be noted that permitting access to confidential banking information does not mean that that information becomes generally available for all purposes. Information disclosed under TIEAs is generally subject to

---

(b) any tax or duty which is imposed under the law of a territory in relation to which arrangements having effect by virtue of s 173 of FA 2006 (international tax enforcement arrangements) have been made and which is covered by the arrangements.

[98] Online: www.oecd.org/ctp/harmful/2082215.pdf

[99] See EC, *Council Directive 2014/48/EU of 24 March 2014 amending Directive 2003/48/EC on taxation of savings income in the form of interest payments* [2014] O.J. L. 111/50.

[100] OECD, 'Joint Council of Europe/OECD Convention on Mutual Administrative Assistance in Tax Matters' (25 January 1988), online: www.oecd.org/tax/exchange-of-tax-information/Convention_On_Mutual_Administrative_Assistance_in_Tax_Matters_Report_and_Explanation.pdf

[101] For example, under the *European Union Savings Directive* (EC, *Council Directive 2003/48/EC of 3 June 2003 on taxation of savings income in the form of interest payments* [2003] O.J. L. 157/38).

[102] HMRC, 'Tax Information Exchange Agreements: Overview' (29 August 2014), online: www.hmrc.gov.uk/taxtreaties/tiea/overview.htm

a confidentiality agreement under which it can be used only for the purpose of assessing or collecting taxes.[103] This is apparently the reason why HMRC did not disclose to the FCA information which it had obtained from the French tax authorities concerning accounts held at HSBC's Swiss subsidiary.[104]

The United Kingdom is one of a number of European countries which have entered into a 'Model 1' (reciprocal) agreement with the United States concerning the Foreign Account Tax Compliance Act (FATCA).[105] The aim of entering such an agreement is to support the policy of the US legislation while both reducing some of the administrative burden placed upon UK financial institutions and ensuring compliance with domestic data protection legislation (which might render compliance with some aspects of FACTA unlawful). The model adopted routes customer information disclosed by banks via HMRC.[106] As long as UK Financial Institutions are in compliance with the UK legislation, they will not need to enter into a direct agreement with the US Internal Revenue Service (IRS) and will not be subject to any withholding tax on their US income.

12.4   Protecting Secrecy

It should not be thought that all modern developments in the United Kingdom reduce the scope of the customer secrecy duty in the banking industry. Some measures strengthen the secrecy obligation.

---

[103] See, for example, HMRC, 'UK/Bermuda Tax Information Exchange Arrangement' (4 December 2007) at para. 8, online: www.gov.uk/government/uploads/system/uploads/attachment_data/file/330888/bermuda-eol.pdf

[104] See BBC, 'Tax Office Says it was Prevented from Sharing HSBC Tax Data' (10 February 2015), online: www.bbc.co.uk/news/business-31359962

[105] Foreign & Commonwealth Office, 'Agreement between the Government of the United Kingdom of Great Britain and Northern Ireland and the Government of the United States of America to Improve International Tax Compliance and to Implement FATCA' (12 September 2012) Cm 8445, online: www.gov.uk/government/publications/agreement-between-the-uk-and-the-usa-to-improve-international-tax-compliance-and-to-imple ment-fatca [UK–US Agreement].

[106] The governing UK legislation is *Finance Act 2013* (UK), c 29, s 222. This provides HM Treasury with powers to make Regulations to give effect to the UK–US Agreement (and other similar Agreements). The Regulations implementing this are *The International Tax Compliance (United States of America) Regulations 2013* (SI 2013/1962). Guidance notes are available at HMRC, 'Implementation of The International Tax Compliance (United States of America) Regulations 2014 Guidance Notes' (14 September 2015), online: www .gov.uk/government/uploads/system/uploads/attachment_data/file/357542/uk-us-fatca-guidance-notes.pdf

12.4.1   Data Protection[107]

An important piece of regulatory legislation which impacts on the duty of secrecy is the *Data Protection Act 1998*. This legislation is not confined to banks: anyone who processes 'personal data'[108] is subject to it. This statute implements the EU's *Data Protection Directive of 1995*.[109]As this statute does not apply to information held about businesses, it is only relevant in the banking area to cases concerning private customers.

Much of the Act is concerned with the issue of permitting individuals access to data relating to them which is held by organisations. However, it also places obligations on organisations holding personal data to hold it securely. Schedule 1 of this *Act* establishes eight Data Protection principles. In relation to maintaining customer secrecy, Principles 1 and 7 are the most important:

Principle 1 is that:

> Personal data shall be processed fairly and lawfully.

Principle 7 states that:

> Appropriate technical and organisational measures shall be taken against unauthorised or unlawful processing of personal data and against acciden-tal loss or destruction of, or damage to, personal data.[110]

In essence, Principle 7 is a modern statutory obligation to maintain secrecy in relation to the affairs of private customers.

---

[107] For an example of a bank's policy on this matter, see Barclays Bank, 'How Does Barclays Use My Personal Data?' (2015), online: http://ask.barclays.co.uk/help/day2day_banking/data_protection

[108] *Data Protection Act 1998*, *supra* note 19, s 1.

[109] EC, *Directive 95/46/EC of the European Parliament and of the Council of 24 October 1995 on the protection of individuals with regard to the processing of personal data and on the free movement of such data* [1995] O.J. L. 281/31. The Directive is scheduled to be replaced with a Regulation which would apply identical rules throughout Europe.

[110] Information Commissioner's Office, 'Information Security (Principle 7)', online: https://ico.org.uk/for-organisations/guide-to-data-protection/principle-7-security. The Information Commissioner's Office guidance on this is that:

> In particular, you will need to:
>
> • design and organise your security to fit the nature of the personal data you hold and the harm that may result from a security breach;
> • be clear about who in your organisation is responsible for ensuring information security;
> • make sure you have the right physical and technical security, backed up by robust poli-cies and procedures and reliable, well-trained staff and
> • be ready to respond to any breach of security swiftly and effectively.

The Information Commissioner's Office has the power to serve an enforcement notice if it finds that there has been a failure to comply with the principles[111] and can impose a monetary penalty if it finds that a serious breach of the principles has occurred.[112] Criminal offences are created by the *Act* in relation to persons who unlawfully obtain or disclose personal information.[113] These provisions have resulted in successful prosecutions of individual bankers who had accessed account details of colleagues and customers.[114] Section 13 of the *Act* specifies that an individual who suffers damage as a result of a breach of any of the requirements of the *Act* has a right to compensation for the damage suffered.

The Information Commissioner's Office has issued sector guidance for the finance industry which contains specific guidance on reporting information to credit reference agencies and direct marketing.[115] Limited evidence exists of the extent to which UK banks are in breach of their obligations in this area of law. Inadequate security and the disclosure of data to third parties are mentioned, but it is impossible to tell how substantial such problems are.[116] Bank of Scotland was fined £75,000 in 2013 for repeatedly faxing customer information to the wrong recipient.[117] The Information Commission has fined organisations (other than banks) when inadequate website security has allowed hackers to access customers' payment card

---

[111] A failure to comply with such a notice is an offence, *Data Protection Act 1998*, *supra* note 19, s 47(1).

[112] *Ibid.*, s 55A.

[113] *Ibid.*, s 55. For an example of proceedings concerning unlawfully obtained details of a bank account, see *Hughes* v. *Carratu International Plc* [2006] EWHC 1791 (QB).

[114] See Dalvinder Singh in ICO, 'Birmingham Banker Fined for Reading Colleagues' Bank Accounts' (22 August 2014), online: https://ico.org.uk/about-the-ico/news-and-events/news-and-blogs/2014/08/birmingham-banker-fined-for-reading-colleagues-bank-accounts/; WiredGov, 'Barclays Bank Employee Prosecuted for Illegally Accessing Customer's Account (26 September 2013), online: www.wired-gov.net/wg/wg-news-1 .nsf/0/B505BB77BA06218380257BF20045E27E?OpenDocument and Yasir Manzoor, a customer service assistant prosecuted and fined for unlawfully accessing a former partner's account, ICO 'Yasir Manzoor' (12 March 2015), online: https://ico.org.uk/action-weve-taken/enforcement/yasir-manzoor/. Note the ICO's view in the second report that the level of penalties available in such cases is inadequate.

[115] ICO, 'Finance, Insurance and Credit', online: http://ico.org.uk/for_organisations/sector_guides/finance

[116] Although over half of the problems are said to relate to failure to deal correctly with requests to provide customers with details of information that banks are holding on them. See Which, 'Banks Regularly Break Data Protection Rules Says Which?' (25 May 2011), online: www.which .co.uk/news/2011/05/banks-regularly-break-data-protection-rules-says-which-254351/

[117] BBC, 'Bank of Scotland's Fax Blunder Leads to Fine' (5 August 2013), online: www.bbc .com/news/business-23572574

details.[118] In 2013, Sony Computer Entertainment Europe Ltd was fined £250,000 for a breach of Principle 7 as a consequence of its PlayStation Network Platform being hacked. This had resulted in the personal information of millions of customers, including their payment card details, being put at risk.[119] The ICO stated in this case that the security measures Sony had put in place 'were simply not good enough'.

12.4.2   Cybercrime: Defending Customers[120]

The examples mentioned in the previous section show that UK data protection law has developed obligations on those holding personal data, including banks, to guard it against hackers and cybercrime. Data protection laws are, however, not the only way in which the challenge to customer secrecy presented by cybercrime is being addressed.

Cases of security failures in companies as a result of which customers' data has come into the hands of hackers are regularly reported in the press. As is shown by the Sony case, the problem is in no way confined to banks, but it is of particular relevance to them because of the amount of sensitive and valuable information they hold and the practical difficulty of maintaining large IT systems which are connecting with those of many customers. This is not simply a theoretical risk. Press reports are to the effect that millions of US consumers have had credit card details hacked. In the case of JP Morgan, it is now accepted that 76 million accounts were compromised in spite of the bank having spent millions of dollars on its

---

[118] The hotel booking website, Worldview Limited, was fined £7,500 in November 2014 following a serious data breach of this kind. See ICO, 'Worldview Limited' (5 November 2014), online: http://ico.org.uk/news/latest_news/2014/~/media/documents/library/Data_Protection/Notices/worldview-limited-monetary-penalty-notice .pdf and ICO, 'Organisations Must Act Now to Avoid Oldest Hackers' Trick in the Book' (5 November 2014), online: https://ico.org.uk/about-the-ico/news-and-events/news-and-blogs/2014/11/organisations-must-act-now-to-avoid-oldest-hackers-trick-in-the-book-says-ico/. In 2014, the ICO published guidance intended to inform organisations about the measures which are appropriate to safeguard personal data being processed by their computer systems. See ICO, 'Protecting Personal Data in Online Services: Learning from the Mistakes of Others' (May 2014), online: https://ico.org.uk/media/for-organisations/documents/1042221/protecting-personal-data-in-online-services-learning-from-the-mistakes-of-others.pdf

[119] BBC, 'Sony Fined Over "preventable" PlayStation Data Hack' (24 January 2013), online: www.bbc.com/news/technology-21160818

[120] See, generally, British Bankers Association, 'The Cyber Threat to Banking: A Global Industry Challenge' (2014), online: www.bba.org.uk/wp-content/uploads/2014/06/BBAJ2110_Cyber_report_May_2014_WEB.pdf

security systems.[121] Kaspersky Lab is reported to have identified a cyber-crime ring which had stolen up to US$1 billion from over 100 financial institutions over a two-year period.[122] To date, none of this has induced a major loss of faith in the capacity of banks to keep customers' data, and thus their wealth, secure. However, the risk of a collapse of market confidence following a successful cyber attack is very real and presents a very serious modern problem in the sphere of customer secrecy.

It is reported that the United Kingdom is currently suffering more cyber attacks than any other country in Europe.[123] The nature of the problem needs to be appreciated. Banks and their systems now operate in an interconnected world. The issue for banks is not simply one of securing their own systems: it is one of ensuring that their systems are not compromised by means of a vulnerability in a third party system.[124] Furthermore, the nature of the threat is a global one: the JP Morgan hack is generally believed to have originated from Russia. Joseph M. Demarest, Assistant Director of the Cyber Division of the Federal Bureau of Investigation, giving evidence to the US Senate Committee on Banking, Housing and Urban Affairs has summarised the threat as follows:

> [T]oday's cyber actors, from nation states to criminal groups and individuals, find themselves virtually unrestricted in their targets sets and their ambitions, launching attacks from all over the world at literally the speed of light.[125]

---

[121] Jordan Robertson and Michael Riley, 'JPMorgan Hack Said to Span Months Via Multiple Flaws' (29 August 2014), online: Bloomberg Business, www.bloomberg.com/news/2014-08-29/jpmorgan-hack-said-to-span-months-via-multiple-flaws.html

[122] BBC, 'Cyber Bank Robbers Steal $1bn, Says Kaspersky Report' (16 February 2015), online: www.bbc.co.uk/news/business-31482985

[123] Harry Cockburn, 'UK is Europe's Number One Target for Cybercrime' (16 October 2014), online: www.londonlovesbusiness.com/business-news/tech/uk-is-europes-number-one-target-for-cybercrime/9047.article. An impact survey conducted for the Department of Business, Innovation and Skills estimated that the UK's finance industry is currently spending £706.3 million per annum on security: BIS, 'Network and Information Security Directive' (20 September 2013), online: www.gov.uk/government/uploads/system/uploads/attachment_data/file/244978/bis-13-1206-network-and-information-security-directive-impact-assessment.pdf [BIS Impact Assessment]. This figure needs to be compared to JP Morgan's commitment to increase its annual spend on these issues following the breach of its systems in 2014 from US$200 million to US$250 million.

[124] For example, third party apps used to make payments on mobile phones. See Ewan, 'It Gets Worse for Android: IBM Uncovers Android Banking Vulnerability' (8 August 2014), online: Mobile Industry Review,www.mobileindustryreview.com/2014/08/finextra-ibm-uncovers-android-banking-vulnerability-consumers-turned-off-by-security-fears.html

[125] Joseph M. Demarest, 'Statement Before the Senate Committee on Banking, Housing, and Urban Affairs' (10 December 2014), online: www.fbi.gov/news/testimony/cyber-security-enhancing-coordination-to-protect-the-financial-sector

All of these factors call for banks to educate customers in the need to keep their banking details secret and to adopt a collaborative strategy at both national and international level as the only method likely to be able to counter successfully fast-developing cybercrime technology. The practical steps which are being taken consist of national and global collaborative moves to identify and react to threats. The British Bankers Association launched its Financial Crime Alerts Service (FCAS) in April 2015. This coordinates in real-time alerts from a number of law enforcement agencies.[126] This mirrors developments in the United States where The Financial Services Information Sharing and Analysis Center (FS-ISAC) and the Depository Trust & Clearing Corporation (DTCC) have announced a strategic joint venture (Soltra) to develop and market automation solutions that advance cyber security capabilities.[127]

The current UK law on this issue can only be derived from general obligations laid down in the regulatory rulebooks. There is no equivalent of the detailed prescribed conduct that we see in the area of money laundering. However, the Handbook provisions are clearly sufficient to justify regulatory action against a bank which fails to take adequate precautions to protect its customers' information against cybercrime.

The FCA Handbook imposes the following obligations, all of which clearly place banks under an obligation to protect their customers against the risk posed by cybercrime. Principle 2 states that: 'A firm must conduct its business with due skill, care and diligence.'[128] Principle 3 is to the effect that: 'A firm must take reasonable care to organise and control its affairs responsibly and effectively, with adequate risk management systems.'[129] The Conduct of Business Sourcebook (COBS) 2.1.1.(1) imposes a rule that 'A firm must act honestly, fairly and professionally in accordance with the best interests of its client (the client's best interests rule).' The SYSC 4.1.1.(1) goes slightly further and imposes a rule on regulated bodies in the following terms:

> A firm must have robust governance arrangements, which include a clear organisational structure with well defined, transparent and consistent lines

[126] See BBA, 'Banks Team Up with Government to Combat Cyber Criminals and Fraudsters' (23 September 2014), online: www.bba.org.uk/news/press-releases/banks-team-up-with-government-to-combat-cyber-criminals-and-fraudsters/#.VCKd0_ldXVp

[127] See DTCC, 'FS-ISAC and DTCC Announce Soltra, a Strategic Partnership to Improve Cyber Security Capabilities and Resilience of Critical Infrastructure Organizations Worldwide' (24 September 2014), online: www.dtcc.com/news/2014/september/24/fs-isac-and-dtcc-announce-soltra.aspx

[128] Principles for Businesses, *supra* note 44, PRIN 2.1.1.2.

[129] *Ibid.*, PRIN 2.1.1.3.

of responsibility, effective processes to identify, manage, monitor and report the risks it is or might be exposed to, and internal control mechanisms, including sound administrative and accounting procedures and effective control and safeguard arrangements for information processing systems.[130]

Cybercrime would clearly count as one of the greatest risks to which a bank is exposed in the modern world.

Regulation 19(14) of the *Payment Services Regulations 2009*[131] is more explicit.

An authorised payment institution (and any small payment institution which voluntarily safeguards relevant funds) must maintain organisational arrangements sufficient to minimise the risk of the loss or diminution of relevant funds or relevant assets through fraud, misuse, negligence or poor administration.

Under Reg. 120, a contravention of this provision is actionable in tort as a breach of statutory duty by a private person who has suffered loss.[132] Subject to the question of what might constitute 'sufficient arrangements' in this context, a customer who loses money as a result of cybercrime thus has a tort remedy for its recovery. It is, of course, very likely that a situation of this kind would result in regulatory action and either an agreement to compensate or the setting up of a compensation scheme expressly designed to avoid the need for customers to bring individual claims to court or the Ombudsman.

The FCA also expects regulated bodies to report data breaches to it. Under the Supervision section of the Handbook, SUP 15.3.1 requires that:

A firm must notify the FCA immediately it becomes aware, or has information which reasonably suggests, that any of the following has occurred, may have occurred or may occur in the foreseeable future:

(1) ...
(2) any matter which could have a significant adverse impact on the firm's reputation or
(3) any matter which could affect the firm's ability to continue to provide adequate services to its customers and which could result in serious detriment to a customer of the firm.[133]

---

[130] FCA Handbook: SYSC, *supra* note 90.

[131] SI 2009/209.

[132] There is other legislation which might protect the customer in such circumstances. See p. 360.

[133] FCA, 'FCA Handbook: Supervision' (March 2016), online: www.handbook.fca.org.uk/handbook/SUP/15/3.html

SUP 15.3.7 and 15.3.8(2) go further and require a firm to deal with its regulators in an open and cooperative way and to disclose to the regulator anything relating to the firm of which the regulator would reasonably expect notice. Compliance with this requirement is then defined to include 'any significant failure in the firm's systems or controls'.

The penalties imposed by the PRA[134] and FCA on the Royal Bank of Scotland group for the major IT failures which locked many customers out of their accounts for several days in 2012 are a useful example of the likely regulatory response in the United Kingdom to a bank failing to secure its customers' banking details from a cyber attack. The penalty (amounting in total to £56 million) was applied on the basis that shutting customers out of their accounts and thus the banking system generally was the result of a failure to have adequate systems and controls to identify and manage the banks' exposure to IT risk. This was held by the PRA to have created a risk to the stability of the banks and thus to the financial system in general. In para. 3.8 of the Final Notice of its determination, the PRA stated that:

> The PRA considers that properly functioning IT risk management systems and controls are an integral part of a firm's safety and soundness and of particular importance to the stability of the UK financial system.[135]

The FCA held, in a parallel decision, that the failures both damaged customers and threatened the integrity of the financial system.[136] It is difficult to believe that an IT failure which permitted customer information to fall into the hands of criminals would not be regarded in the same way.

---

[134] PRA, 'Final Notice to Royal Bank of Scotland, National Westminster Bank, Ulster Bank' (19 November 2014), online: www.bankofengland.co.uk/pra/Documents/supervision/enforcementnotices/en201114.pdf [Final Notices]. This contains both the PRA and FCA Final Notices issued on 19 November 2014.

[135] The current PRA rule on which to base such a finding is SYSC 4.1.1.(1):

> A firm must have robust governance arrangements, which include a clear organisational structure with well defined, transparent and consistent lines of responsibility, effective processes to identify, manage, monitor and report the risks it is or might be exposed to, and internal control mechanisms, including sound administrative and accounting procedures and effective control and safeguard arrangements for information processing systems.

See also FCA PRIN 2.1.1.3.:

> A firm must take reasonable care to organise and control its affairs responsibly and effectively, with adequate risk management systems.

The actual decisions were made on the Financial Services Authority Rulebook applicable at the time of the failures.

[136] Final Notices, *supra* note 134 at para. 2.18.

There is further legislation in prospect on cyber security which would apply to banks. The proposed EU *Cyber Security Directive*[137] (formerly the *Network and Information Security Directive of 2013*) would (1) create obligations for all Member States concerning the prevention, handling of and response to risks and incidents affecting networks and information systems; (2) create a cooperative mechanism between Member States in order to ensure a uniform application of the Directive within the Union and coordinated and efficient handling of and response to risks and incidents affecting network and information systems and (3) establish security requirements for market operators and public administrations. The current practice of UK banks is said to already be in compliance with many of the Directive's requirements.[138]

12.5 Conclusion

It would be wrong to argue that the obligation of a bank to keep its customer's affairs secret is dying in UK law. Although there are areas in which banks have substantial obligations to pass details concerning their customers to others, the fundamental obligation of secrecy survives and still has an important role to play. This is not just a residual role: in some areas, the obligation to keep customer data secret is central to banking law and practice.

Against this background, the United Kingdom can justifiably claim to be playing a full and leading part in dealing with the real challenges which face bank secrecy in modern practice. The UK banking industry needs to do this if it is to maintain its leading market position in the twenty-first century.

From a legal perspective, the growth of regulation in the financial services industry has revolutionised the subject of bank secrecy. As far as the United Kingdom is concerned, the relationship between banks and regulators on these matters is now far more important, in many ways, than that between bank and customer. But, in contrast, breach of confidence and Ombudsman cases still arise and the obligation to pay compensation for a breach survives and has been supplemented. For example, it is likely that the banks subject to penalties by the FCA for FOREX breaches will face

---

[137] EC, *Proposal for a Directive of the European Parliament and of the Council concerning measures to ensure a high common level of network and information security across the Union* [2013] 2013/0027 (COD).

[138] BIS Impact Assessment, *supra* note 123.

compensation claims brought by their customers based on the findings made by the regulators. The correct position is that the duty to keep a customer's affairs secret has been strengthened by being supported in new ways.

What we can also see is that bank secrecy issues are part of a larger picture of the development of professional standards in the financial services industry. Regulators are adopting a proactive approach to their task and are demanding that management imposes an acceptable culture on those working within firms. In the modern world, a failure to maintain secrecy tends to lead to a regulator responding that systems should have been in place to avoid this happening. From that perspective, the maintenance of secrecy remains a basic requirement placed on those working in the industry, except when legislation requires information to be released. The Information Commissioner's prosecution of individual bankers for breaking secrecy may well be the start of a new way of enforcing banking standards.

However, although the banker's duty of secrecy provides the framework within which developments are taking place, it is difficult to argue that the duty is a predominant factor in driving all of these developments. Law enforcement and systemic risk to the banking system are very important motivators. A realistic view of UK law on bank secrecy is of a basic principle subject to very important exceptions. But, a lot of the discussion which is now taking place has not placed the duty of secrecy at the centre of the debate. The dominant issue is often criminal law enforcement, whether we are talking money laundering, tax evasion or cybercrime.

13

The United States of America

LISSA BROOME

13.1 Introduction

Laws in the United States protecting customer privacy in financial records have been amended and eroded since 1970 by anti-money laundering (AML), countering the financing of terrorism (CFT) and anti-tax evasion legislation. As a result, these bank privacy laws have numerous exceptions that permit or require banks to turn over information about customer accounts to federal and state authorities and to the Financial Crimes Enforcement Network (FinCEN, a bureau in the US Department of Treasury). Recent enforcement actions against domestic and foreign financial institutions have resulted in significant civil money penalties, criminal penalties and deferred prosecution agreements. Many of these actions are joined with claims of violations of US economic trade sanctions laws, which are administered through the Office of Foreign Asset Control (OFAC) in the US Department of Treasury.

The weakening of financial privacy is in stark contrast to other recent initiatives put forward by the US government.[1] On 27 February 2015, for example, the Obama administration proposed a Consumer Privacy Bill of Rights Act. The stated purpose of the Act was to 'establish baseline protections for individual privacy in the commercial arena and to foster timely, flexible implementations of these protections through enforceable codes

Thanks to Jerry Markham and to the participants at the 4–5 December 2014 Bank Secrecy Symposium at the National University of Singapore, Faculty of Law, Centre for Banking & Finance Law. Many thanks also to Rachel Brunswig (UNC Law Class of 2016) and Sanghoon Lee (UNC Law Class of 2017) for research assistance with this chapter.

[1] See Omer Tene, 'Privacy Law's Midlife Crisis: A Critical Assessment of the Second Wave of Global Privacy Laws', *Ohio State LJ*, 74 (2013) 1217 for the development of privacy laws in OECD, European Union and the United States.

of conduct developed by diverse stakeholders.[2] Given this seemingly heightened concern for consumer privacy, one could ask whether tax evasion, AML and CFT legislation and OFAC sanctions were indeed justified. Answering this question, however, would require a detailed cost/benefit analysis, which is beyond the scope of this chapter.[3]

The aim of this chapter is to provide an understanding of US bank secrecy law with particular attention to the recent developments in this area.

This chapter proceeds as follows. Section 13.2 describes common law rights to customer privacy recognised in some states and the Right to Financial Privacy Act (RFPA) and other federal statutes that deal with customer privacy in bank records upon a request for confidential information by the federal government. Section 13.3 explores the Bank Secrecy Act (BSA) and its specific reporting requirements relating to certain currency transactions and suspicious activities as they have evolved over time, particularly in response to the 11 September 2001 terrorist attacks on the United States. Economic sanctions prohibiting transactions with designated countries or individuals affect not only domestic banks but also foreign banks engaged in clearing US dollar transactions, who must understand the identity of their customers and the parties with whom they are engaging in transactions. As a result, customer privacy in foreign institutions is impacted by US sanctions laws. This section also describes the extraterritorial effect of the Foreign Account Tax Compliance Act (FATCA), which requires foreign financial institutions to aid in preventing US tax avoidance by reporting information on their US account holders to the US Internal Revenue Service (IRS), impinging on the privacy of these customers of offshore banks. The result of this comprehensive enforcement regime is described more fully in Section 13.5 as recent multibillion actions have been settled against BNP Paribas SA for sanctions violations, and HSBC Holdings Plc for sanctions violations and BSA/AML deficiencies. Although sanctions laws and their application may be unique to the United States, AML/CFT is a worldwide concern. Accordingly, in

---

[2] The White House, 'Administration Discussion Draft: Consumer Privacy Bill of Rights Act of 2015' (2015), online: www.whitehouse.gov/sites/default/files/omb/legislative/letters/cpbr-act-of-2015-discussion-draft.pdf

[3] See generally David Zaring and Elena Baylis, 'Sending the Bureaucracy to War', *Iowa L Rev*, 92 (2007) 1359 (arguing that antiterrorism legislation introduced after September 11 fails the cost–benefit test); Shima Baradaran, Michael Findley, Daniel Nielson, and Jason Sharman 'Funding Terror', *U Pa L Rev*, 162 (2014) 477 (conducting an experiment to confirm that setting up an anonymous shell company was not difficult even with enhanced antiterror measures).

Section 13.6, multinational AML/CFT efforts which guide and shape US enforcement are discussed. This chapter concludes that the vigorous enforcement of sanctions laws and FATCA effectively deputized foreign banks as part of the enforcement mechanism for US laws, in disregard of the customer privacy and bank secrecy concerns of the foreign country.

This chapter focuses on commercial banks, although much of the regulatory regime discussed also applies to a broader set of financial institutions. Commercial banks accept customer deposits from consumers as well as commercial entities and are used by their customers to receive and transfer payments to others domestically and globally. The United States has a fragmented structure for regulating commercial banks, in part because bank charters may be obtained from the state where the bank is headquartered (a state bank) or from the US government (a national bank). There are far more state chartered banks in the United States than nationally chartered banks, but the assets of national banks far surpass the collective assets of state chartered banks. There are three different federal regulatory agencies that provide federal regulation of all banks – the Office of the Comptroller of the Currency (OCC) within the Department of Treasury which regulates nationally chartered banks, the Federal Reserve Board (FRB) which regulates state chartered banks that have elected to become members of the Federal Reserve System and the Federal Deposit Insurance Corporation (FDIC) which regulates state chartered non-FRB-member banks and also provides deposit insurance to all banks. Most US bank assets are held by bank holding companies. A bank holding company is a company that controls a bank. The Bank Holding Company Act limits the activities of the affiliates of a bank holding company to banking or activities that are closely related to banking. A subset of bank holding companies – financial holding companies, which have been permitted since 1999 – may engage in a broader array of activities that are financial in nature and that specifically include acting as a securities broker, securities underwriter, insurance agent and insurance underwriter. The non-banking activities of bank holding companies and financial holding companies are overseen by their functional regulator (such as the Securities and Exchange Commission for a securities firm or the state insurance regulator for an insurance firm) and by the FRB.

13.2   Bank Secrecy

Prior to 1970, the common law of some states provided guidance to banks regarding disclosure of confidential customer information to third parties or to the government to assist in law enforcement efforts.[4] The common law rights related to financial privacy for disclosure of information to third parties other than the government remain intact, but financial privacy with respect to requests by the federal government was superseded by two primary US federal statutes. Those statutes are the Currency and Foreign Transactions Reporting Act (referred to as the BSA) enacted in 1970 and the RFPA of 1978.[5]

Although a right to privacy in financial matters was recognised in England in 1923 in *Tournier* v. *National Provincial and Union Bank of England*,[6] the first US case to consider a similar issue was the 1961 Idaho state court decision in *Peterson* v. *Idaho First National Bank*.[7] In that case, an officer of the bank responded to an inquiry from the officer of a company about whether the bank could tell him if any of the company's employees might be engaging in any actions that could discredit the company. The bank officer reported that one employee had a large number of checks returned for insufficient funds and that it was possible that some of the payees on those checks might take legal action against the employee. The bank officer later shared the employee's account information with the company's officer. The court did not find a breach of the employee's privacy since the information was disclosed only to the employer and not to the public. The court held, however, that there was an agency relationship between the bank and its customer, the employee, that created a duty by the bank not to communicate confidential information given to it by the customer and that this implied contract had been breached by the bank under the facts of this case.

Later cases explored whether there was an exception to breach of the implied duty of confidentiality with respect to the customer's financial information when the request for information came from the federal government. One such case, *Indiana National Bank* v. *Chapman*,[8] found that

---

[4] For the common-law development of bank secrecy and duty to disclose, see Robert S. Pasley, 'Privacy Rights v. Anti-Money Laundering Enforcement', *NC Banking Institute*, 6 (2002) 147; Thomas C. Russler and Steven H. Epstein, 'Disclosure of Customer Information to Third Parties: When Is the Bank Liable?', *Banking LJ*, 111 (1994) 258; Carl Edward Ty Williams, 'The Effects of Domestic Money-Laundering Countermeasures on the Banker's Duty of Confidentiality', *Banking & Fin L Rev*, 13 (1997–8) 25.

[5] 12 USC §§ 3401–3422 (2013) [RFPA]. See generally L. Richard Fischer, *The Law of Financial Privacy: A Compliance Guide*, 4th edn (Boston: Warren, Gorham & Lamont, 2013).

[6] [1923] 1 KB 461.

[7] 367 P. 2d 284 (Idaho 1961). See Williams, *supra* note 4 at 32.

[8] 482 NE 2d 474 (Ind Ct App 1985).

an exception to the implied contract to maintain confidentiality was the existence of a public duty. Law enforcement officials investigating arson and potential insurance fraud relating to an abandoned and burned out car contacted the bank where the car owner had a car loan and in response to their request learned from the bank that the car owner was late on the car payments and the bank was preparing to repossess the car. The court found the response by the bank to a request by law enforcement met the public duty test.

The common law's expectation regarding the privacy of financial information may still be present in the United States, but all of the discussion in recent years has been around the federal government's ability to access confidential customer financial information from a financial institution. The first seminal federal statute in these areas was the BSA – its purpose, notwithstanding its name, was to require US financial institutions to assist in creating records and reporting those records to the government that will have a 'high degree of usefulness in criminal, tax, or regulatory investigations or proceedings'. After 11 September 2001, it was expanded to include records with a high degree of usefulness 'in the conduct of intelligence and counterintelligence activities, including analysis, to protect against international terrorism'.[9] Its requirements will be discussed in more detail in Section 13.3.

The second federal statute was focused on protecting financial privacy, the RFPA of 1978. This statute was enacted by Congress in response to a US Supreme Court case, *United States* v. *Miller*.[10] That case held that a customer did not have an expectation of privacy in account records maintained by a bank. The RFPA then imposed some limits on the power of the federal government to obtain customer financial records.[11] Any financial records sought must be 'reasonably described' and either (1) the customer authorised the disclosure, (2) there is an administrative subpoena, (3) there is a search warrant, (4) there is a judicial subpoena or (5) there is a formal written request from a federal government authority.[12] If the government seeks information about a customer's account, the bank must notify the customer so that the customer has the opportunity to challenge

---

[9] 31 USC § 5311 (2013) [BSA].

[10] *United States* v. *Miller*, 425 US 435 (1976) (holding that individuals have no Fourth Amendment expectation of privacy in their financial records while these records are in the hands of a third party like a bank).

[11] 12 USC § 3402.

[12] *Ibid.*

the government's request.[13] A bank that violates RFPA may be subject to civil liability,[14] including actual damages, punitive damages if the violation is wilful or intentional and attorneys' fees.[15]

There are numerous exceptions to the RFPA – some added over time – that permit banks to disclose customer information to the government without first notifying the bank's customer. First, a bank may disclose information related to federal financial agency supervisory activities based on the theory that the financial institution, rather than the customer, is under investigation.[16] For instance, in *Adams v. Board of Governors of the Federal Reserve System*,[17] the court concluded that information about loans a bank had made to Adams and two other individuals could be disclosed to the FRB pursuant to this exception. The proceeds of the loans were to be used to purchase the voting stock of a bank. The FRB must approve the acquisition of control of a bank by any person under the Change in Bank Control Act, and justified its review of the customer's financial information in order to determine whether Adams's high level of debt might induce him to reduce his debt burden by seeking dividends, management fees or other loans from the bank he would gain control over.

A second exception permits a bank to voluntarily notify a government authority about information related to a customer that may indicate a violation of a statute or regulation.[18] In this case, only the name (or other identifying information) of the individual, corporation or account, and the nature of the suspected illegal activity may be disclosed.[19] Moreover, the bank will not be liable to the customer under any US law or regulation for the disclosure of the information or for the failure to notify the customer of the disclosure.[20] A third exception provides that the RFPA does not 'authorize the withholding of financial records or information required to be reported in accordance with any Federal Statute'.[21] The RFPA also contains special procedures if there is a request for disclosure related to foreign intelligence activities, Secret Service protective functions

---

[13] 12 USC § 3405(2), 3405(3).
[14] 12 USC § 3417(a).
[15] *Ibid.*
[16] 12 USC § 3413(b).
[17] 855 F. 2d 1336 (8th Cir. 1988).
[18] 12 USC § 3403(c).
[19] *Ibid.*
[20] *Ibid.*
[21] 12 USC § 3413(d). A bank that files a Suspicious Activity Report (SAR) is insulated from liability and does not notify the customer when a SAR is filed. 31 USC § 5318(g) (2013).

and intelligence activities related to international terrorism.[22] The international terrorism provision was added by the USA PATRIOT Act of 2001, passed in the wake of the 11 September 2001 terrorist attacks on the United States.[23] There is no notification to the customer of the request for information in these cases.[24]

Two additional federal statutes permit banks to share customer information in certain circumstances with non-governmental entities but each sets forth very specific and limited purposes for this information sharing. These statutes are the Fair Credit Reporting Act (FCRA) and the privacy provisions of the Gramm-Leach-Bliley Act (GLBA) of 1999. The FCRA, enacted in 1970, requires fair and accurate reporting of consumers' personal financial information[25] by banks to a consumer reporting agency, such as Equifax, Experian and TransUnion. Those with a reasonable need to review a consumer's credit history, including other creditors, landlords and collection agencies, may have access to this personal financial information, through the consumer credit reporting agency, but others may not. For instance, employers may only view a consumer's credit report with the consumer's permission. The customer is not notified when the customer's information is reviewed, but the FCRA does provide the customer with a right to review the customer's credit report and correct any erroneous information. The GLBA of 1999 allowed certain bank holding companies to expand the scope of their activities from those that are 'closely related to banking' to those that are 'financial in nature', and is thus widely known as the statute that repealed the Glass-Steagall Act's separation of commercial banking and investment banking.[26] It also addressed the ability of financial institutions to share customer information with their affiliates (companies owned by their bank holding company) and with non-affiliates (outside the institution's bank holding company family).[27] It provides that customer nonpublic personal information may be shared by financial institutions

[22] 12 USC § 3414. The international terrorism provision was added by the USA PATRIOT Act of 2001, passed in the wake of the 11 September 2001 terrorist attacks on the United States: 50 USC § 1861(a) (2012).

[23] USA PATRIOT Act is an acronym for Uniting and Strengthening America by Providing Appropriate Tools Required to Intercept and Obstruct Terrorism.

[24] 12 USC § 3414(a)(3)(A) (assuming the government 'certifies that otherwise there may result a danger to the national security of the United States, interference with a criminal, counterterrorism, or counterintelligence investigation, interference with diplomatic relations, or danger to the life or physical safety of any person').

[25] 15 USC §§ 1681–1681x (2013) [FCRA].

[26] Compare 12 USC § 1843(c)(8) (2013) with 12 USC § 1843(k)(1) (2013).

[27] Gramm–Leach–Bliley Act, 15 USC § 6801–6827 (2013) [GLBA].

with their affiliates. Customer information may be shared by financial institutions with non-affiliates only if the customer has been given the opportunity to 'opt-out' of such information sharing and has not opted out. Even if the customer has opted out, information may still be shared with law enforcement agencies and the Secretary of the Treasury (under the BSA) to the extent permitted under RFPA[28] to comply with Federal, State, or local laws; to comply with civil, criminal or regulatory investigation or subpoena or summons by Federal, State or local authorities and to share with regulatory authorities having jurisdiction over the institution for examination, compliance or other purposes.[29]

In summary, the RFPA contains significant exceptions that permit banks to disclose a customer's financial records to the federal government. The FCRA and GLBA permit disclosure of customer financial information for limited purposes to third parties. As discussed in the next section, the BSA – contrary to its name – requires disclosure of some bank customer information to the government.

13.3   The Exceptions that Ate the Rule: Anti-Money Laundering and Countering the Financing of Terrorism

The RFPA has numerous exceptions, as discussed above, that permit disclosure of customer financial information to government authorities. The BSA of 1970,[30] as amended over time, furthers that sharing of bank customer information by requiring that banks file financial reports relating to their customers in various circumstances, two of which are significant for present purposes and will be discussed further. The BSA was originally conceived of as an AML statute but, through the USA PATRIOT Act, countering terrorism financing became another important purpose. The BSA requires financial institutions to assist in reporting and creating records that will have a 'high degree of usefulness in criminal, tax, or regulatory investigations or proceedings' or in the 'conduct of intelligence or counterintelligence activities, including analysis, to protect against international terrorism'.[31] The intelligence, counterintelligence and international terrorism language was added to the BSA by the USA PATRIOT Act of 2001, enacted following the 11 September 2001 terrorist attacks on

---

[28]   15 USC § 6802(e)(5).
[29]   15 USC § 6802(e)(8).
[30]   31 USC § 5311.
[31]   *Ibid.*; 12 USC §§ 1829b(a)(2), 1951.

the United States. The BSA originally did not define money laundering or criminalise it, although money laundering was subsequently criminalised in the 1986 Money Laundering Control Act. The BSA withstood an early challenge to its constitutionality vis-à-vis invasion of privacy when the US Supreme Court held that the US Constitution did not protect the privacy of personal information in records maintained by a business or the government.[32]

The two significant reporting requirements in the BSA for financial institutions relate to Currency Transaction Reports (CTRs) and SARs.[33] Financial institutions are not permitted to notify their customers that a CTR or SAR has been filed.[34] A CTR must be filed for cash transactions (deposit, withdrawal, exchange or other payment or transfer) exceeding a daily aggregate amount of $10,000 by, through or to the financial institution.[35] The Annunzio-Wyle Anti-Money Laundering Act of 1992 amended the BSA to require that banks file SARs. The US Treasury Department may require any financial institution 'to report any suspicious transaction relevant to a possible violation of law or regulation'.[36] A transaction includes a deposit; withdrawal; transfer between accounts; exchange of currency; extension of credit; sale of a stock, bond, certificate of deposit or other monetary instrument or investment security; or any other payment, transfer or delivery by, through or to a bank. Suspicious transactions include criminal violations, potential money laundering and terrorism financing. A bank that files a SAR with FinCEN is not liable 'to the person who is the subject of such disclosure or any other person identified in the disclosure'.[37]

---

[32]　*California Bankers Ass'n v. Schultz*, 416 US 21 (1974).

[33]　Other reports include Reports of International Transportation of Currency or Monetary Instruments (CMIRs) and Reports of Foreign Bank and Financial Accounts (FBARS).

[34]　31 USC § 5318(g)(2) (requiring that notification to 'any person involved in the transaction that the transaction has been reported [in a SAR]' is prohibited).

[35]　A CTR must be filed with FinCEN within fifteen days after the date of the transaction (twenty-five days if filed electronically). The bank must retain copies of CTRs for five years from the date of the report. There is a safe harbour for failure to file a CTR for a transaction in currency by an exempt person unless the bank knowingly provides false or incomplete information or has reason to believe that the customer does not qualify as an exempt customer.

[36]　31 USC § 5318(g)(1).

[37]　31 USC § 5318(g)(3) (providing that the financial institution is not subject to any liability for making a disclosure or for failing to provide notice of such disclosure to the person who is subject to it for a 'voluntary disclosure of any possible violation of law or regulation to a government agency').

Over 1.6 million SARs were filed in 2013, a three per cent increase over the prior year.[38]

In 1986, the Money Laundering Control Act criminalised money laundering and the facilitation of money laundering by financial institutions.[39] The criminal penalties include the greater of two times the value of the property in question or $500,000, and prison terms of up to twenty years. In addition, forfeiture of any property 'involved in a transaction or attempted transaction in violation of section 1956 or 1957 . . . or any property traceable to such property' is permitted.[40] The 1986 Act also prohibited structuring currency transactions,[41] where some transactions were 'structured' to avoid the $10,000 per day limit.

The Annunzio-Wylie Anti-Money Laundering Act of 1992 also provided the Department of the Treasury with the authority to issue regulations requiring financial institutions to maintain an AML programme, now referred to as the 'four pillars' compliance programme.[42] The four pillars of an effective AML programme as set forth in the BSA are: (1) internal policies, procedures and controls, (2) a designated compliance officer, (3) ongoing employee training and (4) an independent audit function to test the programme.[43] A proposed rule from FinCEN issued on 4 August 2014 would add, as what some have called a fifth pillar, an enhanced customer due diligence (CDD) programme that would require banks to identify and verify the beneficial owners of legal entity customers.[44] Thus, individuals who own 25 per cent or more of a legal entity or who control the legal entity must be identified and verified. In some cases, banks may need to 'look through' several levels of ownership to find natural persons who are beneficial owners of the entity.[45]

The BSA was amended by other statutes prior to 2001, but the basic contours of the AML programme it set forth were as outlined above.

---

[38] Financial Crimes Enforcement Network, 'SAR Stats: Technical Bulletin' (July 2014), online: www.fincen.gov/news_room/rp/files/SAR01/SAR_Stats_proof_2.pdf; Rachel Louise Ensign, 'Anti-Money Laundering Reports Don't Fall Into 'Black Hole', Officials Say' (2 October 2014), online: *Wall Street Journal*, http://blogs.wsj.com/riskandcompliance/2014/10/02/anti-money-laundering-reports-dont-fall-into-black-hole-officials-say/

[39] 18 USC §§ 1956, 1957 (2013) [Money Laundering Control Act].

[40] 18 USC § 1956(a), 981(a)(1)(A).

[41] 31 USC § 5324.

[42] 31 USC § 5318(h).

[43] 31 USC § 5318(h)(1).

[44] Customer Due Diligence Requirements for Financial Institutions, 79 FR 45151 (proposed 4 August 2014) (to be codified at 31 CFR Parts 1010, 1020, 1023, 1024 and 1026).

[45] *Ibid.*

On 11 September 2001, the terrorist attacks in the United States changed
the worldview of Americans and by 28 October 2001, the USA PATRIOT
Act was enacted.[46] With the terrorist attacks and the new statute, countering terrorist financing was added to AML, and took centre stage. The statute adopted a 'know your customer' standard for financial institutions in
verifying the identity of new account holders.[47] Just a few years earlier, the
FRB proposed a Know Your Customer Regulation which was withdrawn
because of substantial grass roots opposition based on concerns about violation of customer privacy rights. Post 9/11, concerns of customer privacy
were trumped by the desire to root out terrorists and those financing their
activities. The USA PATRIOT Act also requires enhanced due diligence
regarding foreign accounts and large private banking accounts provided
to non-US persons.[48] The owners of any foreign banks with US domestic accounts must be verified every three months.[49] Information sharing is encouraged among industry participants for limited purposes, so
that other institutions may determine whether to maintain an account or
engage in a transaction.[50]

The USA PATRIOT Act made FinCEN, which was created in 1990, a
separate Bureau within the US Department of the Treasury. FinCEN
receives the CTR and SAR filings in electronic form. It has no independent statutory authority, but assists in coordinating enforcement activities
among other federal agencies. The Treasury Department may make the
information reported in CTRs and SARs available upon request to other
federal agencies or to an agency of a foreign government.[51] The request
must specify not only the particular information requested, but also the
criminal, tax or regulatory purpose for which the information is sought.[52]
Otherwise, the information collected is to be held in confidence[53] and is
not subject to disclosure under the Freedom of Information Act.[54] Bank
regulatory agencies may transfer information they obtain to Treasury
and to the Department of Justice (DOJ) for use in criminal investigations

---

[46] See *supra* note 23. The USA PATRIOT Act included Title III, the International Money
Laundering Abatement and Anti-Terrorist Financing Act of 2001 (IMLAFAT).

[47] § 326, 31 USC §§ 5318(i)(1); 31 CFR chapter X.

[48] § 312, 31 USC §§ 5311–5330; 31 CFR chapter X.

[49] § 319, 31 USC §§ 5311–5330; 31 CFR chapter X.

[50] § 314, 31 USC § 5311 (historical and revision notes); 31 CFR § 1010.540.

[51] 31 CFR § 1010.950.

[52] 31 CFR § 1010.950(b).

[53] 31 CFR § 1010.950(c).

[54] 31 CFR § 1010.960.

related to money laundering.[55] For law enforcement purposes, however, multiple teams review reports filed that relate to their area of responsibility. FinCEN recently reported that approximately ninety-four SAR review teams composed of prosecutors and investigators from a number of different agencies regularly review these reports related to their areas of responsibility.[56]

Two of the largest banking organisations in the United States have recently been the subject of enforcement activities related to AML deficiencies. In January 2014, JP Morgan Chase entered into a $2.6 billion settlement arising from the bank's failure to alert authorities about suspicious activity in Bernie Madoff's account.[57] Moreover, this was then the largest amount paid to settle BSA violations.[58] The DOJ brought criminal charges based on failure to maintain an effective AML programme and failure to file a SAR, which resulted in a deferred prosecution agreement and a $1.7 billion forfeiture to the DOJ. The OCC assessed a $350 million civil money penalty for deficiencies in the bank's BSA/AML compliance programme, and FinCEN assessed a $461 million penalty (satisfied by the forfeiture to the DOJ) for BSA violations for not detecting or adequately reporting these suspicious activities.[59]

This action followed earlier actions against Citigroup which resulted in consent orders with the FRB in March 2013[60] and the FDIC in August 2012, and a Cease and Desist Order by the OCC in April 2012[61] for deficiencies in the bank's BSA/AML compliance programme, including violations of the SARs filing requirements and issues with correspondent banking relationships. Part of the settlement was an FDIC consent order related to deficiencies in the BSA/AML compliance programme of a Citi subsidiary, Banamex USA.

---

[55] 12 USC § 3412(f)(1), 3412(f)(2).

[56] SAR Stats: Technical Bulletin, *supra* note 38 (reporting that over 180,000 SARs were reviewed by these teams in the second quarter of 2014).

[57] Madoff pleaded guilty to multiple federal felonies related to a massive Ponzi scheme by the asset management unit of his investment firm. Thousands of investors were defrauded of billions of dollars.

[58] Aaron R. Marcu, 'Government Scrutiny of AML Compliance Efforts', *Review of Banking & Financial Services*, 30 (2014) 67 at 69.

[59] *Ibid.*

[60] Federal Reserve, Consent Order: Citigroup Inc., No. 13-004-B-HC (21 March 2013), online: www.federalreserve.gov/newsevents/press/enforcement/enf20130326a1.pdf

[61] Federal Reserve, Consent Order: Citibank, NA, No. AA-EC-12-18 (5 April 2012), online: www.occ.treas.gov/news-issuances/news-releases/2012/nr-occ-2012-57a.pdf

As these actions make clear, large US financial institutions are not immune from criminal charges or significant civil money penalties for deficiencies in their BSA/AML programmes. Smaller financial institutions are not immune either and say that BSA examinations by bank regulators as part of their regular bank examination process have become more rigorous than in prior years, with deficiencies resulting in stiffer penalties and more onerous corrective actions.[62] An additional concern, as BSA enforcement activities increase, has been called 'de-risking' where banks will decline to serve customers that may present BSA risks sending them to smaller institutions with less well-developed AML compliance programmes or outside of the regulated financial system altogether. Other banks talk about 'pre-risking' which is not accepting a customer whose business might expose the bank to BSA risks. Money services businesses, medical marijuana businesses and payday lenders, although legal businesses in some states are nevertheless viewed by some as perhaps being used for illegal purposes, are some of the customer types that banks have avoided accepting (pre-risked) or continuing to serve (de-risked) as customers.[63] The existence of vigorous AML/CFT enforcement efforts incentivises financial institutions to err on the side of additional SAR reporting, further eroding customer privacy.

13.4 Additional Tools Extend Outside the United States: Sanctions and FACTA

Although the BSA primarily affects US banks and foreign financial institutions with US branches or agencies, its provisions may affect foreign banks without a presence on US soil. For instance, under the USA PATRIOT Act, US banks may terminate correspondent banking relationships[64] and correspondent banking with a shell bank (a bank without a physical presence) is prohibited. 'Special measures', including prohibiting opening correspondent banking accounts, may also be taken against a country of a

---

[62] John Engen, 'What's Behind the Uptick in BSA Enforcement?' (31 July 2014), online: American Banker, www.americanbanker.com/news/consumer-finance/whats-behind-the-uptick-in-bsa-enforcement-1068937-1.html; Ian McKendry, 'Banks Face No-Win Scenario on AML "De-Risking"' (17 November 2014), online: American Banker, www.americanbanker.com/news/regulation-reform/banks-face-no-win-scenario-on-aml-de-risking-1071271-1.html

[63] Ian McKendry, 'Banks Face No-Win Scenario on AML "De-Risking"' (17 November 2014), online: American Banker, www.americanbanker.com/news/regulation-reform/banks-face-no-win-scenario-on-aml-de-risking-1071271-1.html

[64] § 311, 31 USC §5318A; 31 CFR chapter X.

financing institution that the Department of Treasury, through FinCEN, designates as a primary money laundering concern.[65] In other words, a ruling that designates a foreign bank as a primary money laundering concern can cause severe reputational damage to the foreign institution or foreign jurisdiction so designated.[66]

Other US statutes also have significant impact on foreign banking operations occurring outside the United States. Of special significance are the various sanctions programmes administered by the OFAC, also within the Department of Treasury, and the FATCA of 2010.[67] OFAC administers and enforces economic and trade sanctions against foreign countries, terrorists, narcotics traffickers and others who threaten the national security and economy of the United States. Each sanctions programme represents the implementation of multiple legal authorities. Some authorities are statutes and regulations promulgated pursuant to the International Emergency Economic Powers Act (IEEPA)[68] and the Trading with the Enemy Act (TWEA).[69] Other authorities are in the form of executive orders issued by the President. OFAC may also implement United Nations Security Council Resolutions (UNSCRs). Currently sanctioned regimes include Iran, Ukraine, Syria and Cuba,[70] among others.[71] As described more fully below, foreign banks may be subject to US sanctions if they process transactions in US dollars. Violations of the sanctions can result in significant consequences and enforcement has been combined with efforts under the BSA to punish those who fail to comply with its AML provisions.

---

[65] § 321, 31 USC §§ 5311–5330; 31 CFR chapter X.

[66] See Heidi Mandanis Schooner and Michael W. Taylor, *Global Bank Regulation: Principles and Policies* (Burlington, MA: Academic Press, 2009), 235–8 (describing how a FinCEN notice of proposed rulemaking to designate Banco Delta Asia a primary money laundering concern under s 311 of the USA PATRIOT Act resulted in an immediate loss of reputation for the bank and a run by depositors).

[67] A possible acronym for this statute is Foreign Account Tax Compliance Act of Twenty Ten (FATCATT).

[68] 50 USC § 1701–06 (2012) [IEEPA].

[69] 50 USC App. § 1–44 (2012) [TWEA] (imposing restrictions on trade with Cuba).

[70] Following the President Obama's announcement on 17 December 2014, OFAC amended the Cuban Assets Control Regulations to allow, among other things, travel to Cuba for authorised purposes and opening correspondent accounts at Cuban financial institutions: Cuban Assets Control Regulations, 80 FR 2291 (16 January 2015) (to be codified at 31 CFR Part 515), online: www.treasury.gov/resource-center/sanctions/Programs/Documents/31cfr515_new.pdf

[71] OFAC, 'Sanctions Programs and Country Restrictions' (6 October 2016), online: Department of the Treasury, www.treasury.gov/resource-center/sanctions/Programs/Pages/Programs.aspx

FATCA became effective 1 July 2014.[72] Its purpose is to counter known US tax evasion strategies using offshore banks.[73] It requires foreign financial institutions to report information on their US account holders (potentially in violation of the foreign country's bank secrecy regime) either to the foreign government (which in turn reports the information to the US IRS) or directly to the IRS.[74] Which model for reporting on US account holders that is employed is negotiated by the United States and the host country in an Intergovernmental Agreement (IGA).[75] The IGA proves whether the US account holder must consent before the foreign bank may provide information to the IRS.[76] If foreign banks do not report this information as required by FATCA, then US financial institutions are required to impose a 30 per cent withholding tax on payments they make to those foreign banks.[77] FATCA has been described as 'the most important and controversial development in decades in the international fight against tax evasion'.[78] As a result of FATCA, some US citizens have renounced their citizenship.[79] It has been criticised for turning foreign banks into enforcement arms of the US IRS, which has resulted in some foreign banks dropping their US account holders.[80] Moreover, the statute was not subject to any formal cost–benefit analysis. It is hard to imagine that costs of American firms added to the costs of foreign financial firms will outweigh the additional US tax collections, particularly because many

[72] IRS extended the effective date for certain accounts to 1 January 2015: IRS Notice 2014-59, IRB 2014-44, online: www.irs.gov/pub/irs-irbs/irb14-44.pdf

[73] J. Richard (Dick) Harvey Jr, 'Offshore Accounts: Insider's Summary of FATCA and Its Potential Future', *Vill L Rev*, 57 (2012) 471. For a discussion of tax evasion in the UBS case, see Laura Szarmach, 'Piercing the Veil of Bank Secrecy – Assessing the United States' Settlement in the UBS Case', *Cornell Int'l LJ*, 43 (2010) 409.

[74] Nathan Newman, 'International Banking – New Individual Accounts Under FATCA Intergovernmental Agreements', *BNA Banking Reports* (25 November 2014).

[75] Alison Bennett, 'Hong Kong, US Sign FATCA Agreement in Move Awaited by Financial Community' (14 November 2014), online: BNA, www.bna.com/hong-kong-us-n17179911765 (reporting that the United States and Hong Kong IGA requires financial institutions in Hong Kong to report directly to the IRS).

[76] *Ibid.* (pointing out that Hong Kong banks must get US account holders' consent before reporting to the IRS).

[77] Dylan Griffiths, 'Americans Give Up Passports as Asset-Disclosure Rules Start' (7 August 2014), online: BNA, www.bloomberg.com/news/articles/2014-08-06/americans-give-up-passports-as-asset-disclosure-rules-start

[78] The Economist, 'Dropping the Bomb' (28 June 2014), online: www.economist.com/news/finance-and-economics/21605911-americas-fierce-campaign-against-tax-cheats-doing-more-harm-good-dropping

[79] Griffiths, *supra* note 77.

[80] *Ibid.*

US citizens with foreign accounts will owe no US tax since they are entitled to a credit against US taxes for taxes paid abroad.[81]

13.5 A New Era of Vigorous Sanctions Enforcement – Foreign Banks in the Crosshairs

Recent enforcement actions in the United States against domestic banks and foreign banks have been significant in their size and severity, with penalties and fines of close to $9 billion against a single institution and criminal proceedings resulting in guilty pleas or deferred prosecution agreements. Some cases blend sanctions actions with AML violations under the theory that transactions conducted in the United States in a manner to evade compliance with the sanctions restrictions may trigger a duty to file a SAR or suggest noncompliance with a customer identification programme.[82] Additionally, the wrongdoer has attracted the attention of a number of separate US agencies and offices each demanding their own role in the proceedings and seeking monetary as well as nonmonetary sanctions.[83] These actions illustrate the challenges for a global compliance programme by an institution attempting to understand the rules and norms of each country in which it operates.[84] Foreign banks have been particularly vulnerable to sanctions enforcement.

The BNP Paribas guilty plea announced on 30 June 2014 is the most recent and the most extreme example illustrating these new trends in enforcement actions. In terms of severity, this marked the first time a non-US bank pled guilty in settlement of criminal charges of sanctions violations.[85] Of the twenty-two total sanctions actions since 2009, at least six

---

[81] *Ibid.*

[82] Marcu, *supra* note 58.

[83] Juan C. Zarate, former deputy national security advisor for combating terrorism and author of *Treasury's War* (New York: PublicAffairs Books, 2013), noted these commonalities among recent enforcement actions at a 21 November 2014 panel discussion at The Clearing House Association Annual Conference in New York City.

[84] Paul L. Lee, 'Compliance Lessons from OFAC Case Studies – Part I', *Banking LJ*, 131 (2014) 657. ('[T]hese case studies provide a cautionary tale of the challenges for global compliance with a national regime when political, cultural and legal norms among jurisdictions are not adequately aligned.')

[85] US Department of Justice, 'Press Release: BNP Paribas Agrees to Plead Guilty and to Pay $8.9 Billion for Illegally Processing Financial Transactions for Countries Subject to US Economic Sanctions' (30 June 2014), online: www.justice.gov/opa/pr/bnp-paribas-agrees-plead-guilty-and-pay-89-billion-illegally-processing-financial [DOJ BNP Paribas Press Release].

were criminal matters brought by the US DOJ and all, except that for BNP Paribas, resulted in a deferred prosecution agreement, rather than a guilty plea.[86] None of the US banks subject to sanctions during this period have faced criminal charges.[87] The size of the combined criminal forfeiture and fines was the largest sanctions fine to date at $8.9 billion, dwarfing the largest prior settlement of $1.9 billion which involved HSBC Holdings Plc.[88] The twenty-one other sanctions cases against financial firms since 2009 resulted in combined fines of $4.9 billion, with only $90 million in fines imposed upon US financial firms.[89]

BNP Paribas' violations involved IEEPA and TWEA economic sanctions for transactions processed in dollars violating sanctions programmes for Burma, Cuba, Iran and Sudan.[90] It was charged with conspiring to move about $8.8 billion through the US financial system on behalf of sanctioned entities and in violation of US sanctions.[91] References to Sudan were omitted from messages sent to the United States in transactions in dollars and unaffiliated non-Sudanese banks were used to disguise the connection to Sudan. In addition to attracting the attention of the DOJ for a conspiracy to violate US sanctions laws, the New York Attorney General, OFAC, the FRB and the New York Department of Financial Services (NYDFS) were also part of the proceeding. The $8.9 billion in financial penalties included criminal forfeiture of $8.8 billion and a fine of $140 million.[92] BNP Paribas also pled guilty to a charge by the New York Attorney General that BNP Paribas falsified and conspired to falsify business records.[93] The OFAC fine of $963 million was the largest settlement in its history, although it was deemed satisfied by the criminal forfeiture to the DOJ.[94] The FRB assessed a civil money penalty of $508 million – its largest ever civil money penalty in a sanctions case.[95]

---

[86] Tom Schoenberg, 'BNP Paribas Fine Seen Eclipsing Past US Sanctions Cases' (5 June 2014), online: BNA, www.bloomberg.com/news/articles/2014-06-05/bnp-paribas-fine-seen-eclipsing-past-u-s-sanctions-cases

[87] Ibid.

[88] Ibid.

[89] Ibid.

[90] See Paul L. Lee, 'Compliance Lessons from OFAC Case Studies – Part II', Banking LJ, 131 (2014) 717 at 748–62 [Lee, Pt II] (discussing the 30 June 2014 BNP Paribas guilty plea and settlement).

[91] DOJ BNP Paribas Press Release, supra note 85.

[92] Ibid.

[93] Ibid.

[94] Ibid.; Lee, Pt II, supra note 90 at 748.

[95] Lee, Pt II, supra note 90 at 748.

This amount was also credited against the criminal forfeiture amount. The NYDFS received a civil money penalty of $2.24 billion, credited against the forfeiture amount and imposed nonmonetary sanctions including a mandate that thirteen employees be fired, that a limited suspension of the dollar-clearing privileges of BNP Paribas be imposed, and that a monitoring requirement put in place in 2013 be extended for two years.[96] The magnitude of the forfeiture and penalties was justified by the federal and state authorities based on what they characterised as an elaborate cover-up, lack of full cooperation by BNP Paribas and the length of time the misconduct occurred.[97]

A second example of a foreign bank settling sanctions charges involved HSBC Holdings Plc (HSBC), which also was issued civil money penalties for BSA/AML deficiencies. HSBC was charged with laundering $881 million in drug proceeds from Mexico for two drug cartels. The DOJ alleged that payment transfer instructions omitted information that would have identified the sanctioned entities involved in the transactions.[98] The US DOJ made a criminal charge of wilfully failing to establish and maintain an effective AML programme; wilfully failing to establish due diligence for foreign correspondent accounts; wilfully violating TWEA provisions restricting transactions with Cuba and wilfully violating IEEPA restricting transactions with Iran, Libya, Sudan and Burma. The New York District Attorney brought a charge of falsifying business records. The matter was settled in December 2012, in a deferred prosecution agreement, for what was then a record in forfeitures and penalties of $1.9 billion, including forfeiture of $1.25 billion.[99] In addition to the sanctions violations, the FRB assessed $165 million in CMP based on deficiencies in the firm-wide compliance risk management programme and the bank's BSA/AML programme. The OCC issued a $500 million penalty for violations of BSA/AML compliance programmes, SAR requirements and correspondent banking rules. FinCEN issued its own $500 million penalty for BSA/AML violations, but it was concurrent with the OCC penalty. There was an OFAC penalty of $375 million deemed satisfied by the forfeiture amounts. Non-monetary sanctions included installation of a corporate compliance monitor for at least a five-year period, new leadership in the US affiliate

---

[96] DOJ BNP Paribas Press Release, *supra* note 85.
[97] *Ibid.*; Lee, Pt II, *supra* note 90 at 748.
[98] Marcu, *supra* note 58 at 73.
[99] Lee, Pt II, *supra* note 90 at 735–43.

and substantially greater funding for additional compliance personnel and the AML programme.[100]

Furthermore, BNP Paribas claimed that it was acting in accordance with French and European laws, and that US jurisdiction was based merely on the processing of transactions in US dollars.[101] The extraterritorial application of US sanctions laws has not gone unnoticed and may be discussed by the G20.[102]

Efforts to avoid criminal and civil liability for violating sanctions obviously impact the privacy of customer information of foreign banks and for US banks processing transactions for their customers that may be to sanctioned countries. Customer financial transactions must be closely scrutinised by the banks on each side of the transaction to ensure that the US financial system is not used to effect a transaction with a sanctioned entity.

13.6 International Overlay – Multilateral AML/CFT Efforts

AML efforts as well as those to counter terrorism financing must be coordinated globally since money often moves across borders in an effort to disguise the source of the funds or the beneficiary of the funds. US regulators work closely with their international counterparts and international standards guide and inform US laws, regulations and enforcement activities. International efforts, discussed below, have focused on uniform standards and international cooperation in ensuring that the financial institution (1) knows who its customer is, (2) is engaging in ethical conduct in its attempts to deter money laundering and terrorist financing and (3) is cooperating with law enforcement in a manner that is consistent with their customers' legitimate privacy concerns.[103]

The sources of international guidance regarding AML/CFT include the Basel Committee, which issued statements in 1988 on criminal use of the banking system for money laundering,[104] in 2001 on CDD[105] and

---

[100] Marcu, *supra* note 58 at 73; Lee, Pt II, *supra* note 90 at 736.
[101] Tom Schoenberg and Chris Dolmetsch, 'Trade Sanctions – BNP Paribas to Pay $8.9 Billion in Sanctions Investigation Plea Deal', *BNA Banking Reports* (8 July 2014).
[102] Lee, Pt II, *supra* note 90 at 762.
[103] Schooner and Taylor, *supra* note 66 at 226.
[104] Basel Committee, 'Prevention of Criminal Use of the Banking System for the Purpose of Money Laundering (December 1988), online: www.bis.org/publ/bcbsc137.pdf
[105] Basel Committee, 'Customer Due Diligence for Banks' (October 2001), online: www.bis .org/publ/bcbs85.pdf

in 2003 provided additional guidance on customer identification.[106] The European Union has issued a directive on money laundering,[107] also emphasising CDD and incorporating the recommendations of the group most directly involved in international standards and cooperation – the Financial Action Task Force (FATF).[108] The FATF is composed of thirty-six member countries, including the United States and two regional territories.[109] Its purpose is to develop national and international standards to govern money laundering and terrorist financing. The FATF's most recent report is 'International Standards on Combating Money Laundering and the Financing of Terrorism & Proliferation'.[110]

13.7   Conclusion

In the post-9/11 world, the US regulatory thrust has focused on CFT through vigorous AML/CFT enforcement and through an aggressive use of economic sanctions. In addition, the requiring reporting of accounts of US citizens held offshore is designed to avoid US tax evasion. Concerns about privacy in bank records have seldom been raised in either context. Professor Peter Swire has described 'the privacy paradox', wherein there is a long-term concern for privacy but short-term decisions are often made not to respect privacy.[111] Further, he notes that arguments that favour protecting security seem tough and realistic, while those in favour of privacy are sometimes discounted because they seem soft and idealistic.[112] In the United States, it seems clear that the tough security arguments have won out over any long-term ideal of protecting customer privacy. Moreover, the historic BNP Paribas guilty plea, criminal forfeiture and combined

---

[106] Basel Committee, 'General Guide to Account Opening and Customer Identification' (February 2003), online: www.bis.org/publ/bcbs85annex.htm

[107] EC, *Directive 2005/60/EC of the European Parliament and of the Council of 26 October 2005 on the prevention of the use of the financial system for the purpose of money laundering and terrorist financing* [2005] O.J. L. 309/15.

[108] See the website of the FATF, online: www.fatf-gafi.org

[109] FATF, 'FATF Members and Observers', online: www.fatf-gafi.org/pages/aboutus/members andobservers

[110] FATF, 'International Standards on Combating Money Laundering and the Financing of Terrorism & Proliferation: The FATF Recommendations' (February 2012), online: www .fatf-gafi.org/media/fatf/documents/recommendations/pdfs/fatf_recommendations.pdf

[111] Peter P. Swire, 'Financial Privacy and the Theory of High-Tech Government Surveillance', 77 *Washington University L Rev*, 77 (1999) 461.

[112] Peter P. Swire, 'Privacy and Information Sharing in the War on Terrorism', 51 *Vill L Rev*, 51 (2006) 951 at 976.

$8.9 billion penalty against BNP Paribas is the most recent example of the risk to a foreign bank processing US dollar transactions without proper regard for OFAC's sanctions programme. Foreign banks' customer privacy concerns will take a backseat as foreign financial institutions strive to avoid similar penalties. The recently effective FACTA Act illustrates another challenge for foreign banks attempting to protect customer privacy in the light of the requirement to aid US authorities in detecting US tax avoidance by US customers holding accounts in foreign financial institutions.

Financial industry observers long ago noted that US banks have essentially become part of law enforcement in reporting suspicious activities and enforcing AML statutes. Recent sanctions actions against BNP Paribas and HSBC, along with FACTA, seemingly deputize foreign banks with US law enforcement and tax avoidance duties in potential conflict with the views of the foreign banks' home countries on bank secrecy and privacy of customer financial information. The impact of this enforcement regime on the continued use of US dollars in the global economy remains to be seen.[113]

---

[113] Kevin McCoy, 'Banks face intensified sanctions probes in US' (9 July 2014), online: www.usatoday.com/story/money/business/2014/07/09/banks-us-sanctions/12354389

14

Conclusion

SANDRA BOOYSEN

This book is the end product of a two-day Bank Secrecy Symposium held in December 2014 by the Centre for Banking and Finance Law of the National University of Singapore Faculty of Law (NUS Law).[1] The state of bank secrecy in key financial centres and the effect of clampdowns on transnational crime such as tax evasion, money laundering and terrorism financing are the common threads running through the chapters. Initiatives to combat transnational crime are predicated on access to financial information and have prompted the formalisation of channels for exchange of information (EOI). Current EOI programmes and more traditional concepts of bank secrecy find themselves on a collision course, and banks as the holders of this information are caught in the crossfire. The jurisdictional chapters show that bank secrecy gives way to the higher priority of combatting crime, which is unsurprising and largely uncontroversial. This Conclusion reflects on this and other discussions at the Symposium and identifies the themes that emerge from the preceding chapters.

A range of jurisdictions, East and West, have been examined; and civil and common law legal systems are represented. The idea that a customer's banking information should not be disclosed by a bank to third parties is, to a greater or lesser extent, reflected in all the jurisdictions represented here. In a number of jurisdictions, the rule is embedded as an implied term of the contract between bank and customer. Hong Kong (Gannon, Chapter 8) and Singapore (Booysen, Chapter 10) inherited this analysis through their colonial ties with the United Kingdom. In Japan (Omachi,

For helpful comments on this Conclusion, I am grateful to my colleague, Helena Whalen-Bridge, and to fellow contributors to this volume: Christopher Hare, Martha O'Brien and Keith Stanton.

[1] See the symposium flyer at http://law.nus.edu.sg/pdfs/cbfl/events/booysenneo_bss.pdf; also Hu Ying, 'Report of Proceedings', March 2015, available at http://law.nus.edu.sg/cbfl/pdfs/reports/CBFL-Rep-HY1.pdf

Chapter 9), the basis for the bank's duty of secrecy is unclear, although its existence is not in doubt. One explanation is that the duty arises as a term in the bank–customer contract, which is similar to the common law countries. Germany (Hofmann, Chapter 7), like some of the common law countries mentioned, does not have a written bank secrecy law. Rather, the right to secrecy is derived from the Law of Obligations. In this latter respect there is some resemblance between Germany and Switzerland (Nobel and Braendli, Chapter 11) where the right to bank secrecy is found in private law, both contract law and the law of persons, the latter recognising broader privacy rights. The right to bank secrecy in Switzerland has, since 1934, been backed by a statutory criminal sanction in the Banking Act, Art. 47. This aspect of the Swiss position is comparable with Singapore where a criminal penalty accompanies a detailed statutory provision set out in the Singapore Banking Act, s 47.[2] In the United States (Broome, Chapter 13), like Singapore, there has been a move away from the implied term approach to a statutory one. Also in the United Kingdom (Stanton, Chapter 12), Stanton argues that the implied term is only one dimension of the UK's bank secrecy regime which should be seen as a multifaceted scheme shaped by extensive regulatory rules designed to promote financial stability and law enforcement. In China (Wang, Chapter 6), Wang notes that China does not have a tradition of protecting the confidentiality of customer information and bank secrecy in China is generally weak although there are some rules making provision for it. A novel use of bank secrecy highlighted in this chapter is to determine liability for unauthorised transactions via electronic platforms.

In order to promote a deeper understanding of bank secrecy, see it in context and offer insights on related aspects, this book includes five perspective chapters. Starting with a conceptual analysis (Neo, Chapter 1), there is an examination of bank secrecy at a more general level, its rationale and its relationship to privacy in a broader setting. After all, as Neo points out, the banking relationship is not the only one that has a body of rules protecting the information it generates from undue publicity. Neo's chapter also debates the difference between the terms 'secrecy' and 'confidentiality'. Authors were free to use the terms most appropriate for their jurisdiction. Countries following the UK common law approach to bank secrecy tend to use the term 'confidentiality' (for example, Hong Kong, Chapter 8 and United Kingdom, Chapter 12). Stanton has chosen,

---

[2] It is thought to be a coincidence that the section and article numbers are the same.

however, to follow the theme of this book and uses the term 'secrecy' nevertheless. In the United States (Chapter 13), the preferred terminology is 'financial privacy'. In Germany, the European Union and Switzerland (Chapters 7 and 11, respectively), the term is 'geheimnis' which Hofmann considers is best translated as 'secrecy'. Omachi uses 'secrecy' as the translation for the Japanese term, 'ginko himitsu' (Chapter 9), while in China the term 'yinsi' or privacy is found in some laws and 'mimi' or secrecy in others. The term 'secrecy' today may have acquired a negative meaning in the banking context as a result of being associated with tax evasion and the hiding of illicit funds. These negative associations are probably what has prompted Singapore (Chapter 10) to initiate a change from the term 'secrecy' to 'privacy', thereby aligning with the US approach (Chapter 13). In this book, the term 'secrecy' has been used as a neutral alternative to 'confidentiality' or 'privacy'.

Alongside the expansion of EOI, which has eroded bank secrecy, we are ironically also witnessing a mushrooming of data protection legislation around the world. A discussion of the similarities and differences between data protection laws and bank secrecy laws is a pertinent addition to this volume (Greenleaf and Tyree, Chapter 2). The chapter offers an overview of the typical features of data protection legislation and the international standards that have influenced their development. Greenleaf and Tyree show that, with some exceptions, data protection obligations tend to be broader than the bank's duty of secrecy. Omachi (Chapter 9) makes the interesting observation that the scope of the bank's duty of secrecy in Japan is unclear and, as a result, banks tend to focus on their more clearly delineated data privacy obligations as a proxy for complying with their secrecy obligations.

A clear conformity between the various jurisdictions is that there are situations in which customer information can, or must, be disclosed. Aside from crime prevention and enforcement, discussed below, a common exception to the duty of secrecy owed by a bank is where disclosure is made with the customer's consent. What should count as consent is, however, a contentious point. The tension is between formal, objective consent that suffices for contract formation and informed, subjective consent which is more likely to correspond with the ordinary use of the concept of consent. I argue in Chapter 10 that something more than general, advance consent to disclosure is required to satisfy the meaning of consent in Singapore's Banking Act. Until this issue is resolved, bespoke consent in contemplation of a particular disclosure is probably a prudent course for banks to take. In Switzerland, while a customer can consent to waive the right to bank secrecy, Nobel and Braendli indicate that the Swiss principle of good faith, 'Vertrauensprinzip', puts some limits on such waivers by interpreting them as a reasonable person acting in good faith would do. Therefore, any consent to disclosure in the fine print of account Terms and Conditions must be clearly expressed.

Domestic laws have long-established the priority of crime prevention over bank secrecy. Historically, however, that clear domestic priority did not easily translate into a similar position at an international level, and bank secrecy rules have in the past shielded, or been blamed for shielding, transnational crime, including tax evasion, money laundering and terrorism financing. This problem has undoubtedly been exacerbated by the enormous technological advances in travel and communication systems in the last fifty years, which have offered greater opportunities in recent decades to move money around and exploit law enforcement gaps. Factors contributing to this divergence between the domestic and international positions may include the jealousy with which nation states guard their supremacy within their borders, the benefit to recipient countries of revenue inflows and the private international law principle that one country will not assist another in the enforcement of its revenue laws.[3]

However, as the chapters in this book show, the gap between transparency in the domestic and international spheres has been narrowed. The biggest catalysts for change originated in the United States: the 11 September 2001 attacks and the 2007/8 global financial crisis (GFC). The battles against anti-money laundering (AML), terrorist financing and tax evasion are interrelated and have EOI in common. International AML initiatives go back at least to 1989 and have expanded to include terrorist financing particularly after the attacks on the United States in 2001. Tax evasion via undisclosed accounts in foreign jurisdictions was exercising the minds of national states and the OECD prior to 2007, but the severe economic downturn brought by the GFC with its attendant drop in tax revenues and, therefore, national and individual wellbeing, galvanised the United States into action and precipitated the Foreign Account Tax Compliance Act (FATCA).[4] Two chapters offer the domain expert perspective on these driving forces that have affected bank secrecy so significantly in the new millennium. First, the development of the AML campaign spearheaded by the Financial Action Task Force (FATF) on money laundering and the broadening of its focus to include the financing

---

[3] See, e.g. *Government of India* v. *Taylor* [1955] 1 All ER 292 at 295; also O'Brien, Chapter 5.
[4] As noted by O'Brien, Chapter 5. See Broome's suggestion of FATCATT in Chapter 13.

of terrorism (Nakajima, Chapter 4). Nakajima also touches on the global initiative against tax evasion which receives more detailed attention in the following chapter (O'Brien, Chapter 5). O'Brien traces how EOI has progressed from requested disclosure to automatic disclosure. Since FATCA, the OECD has launched a global standard for automatic EOI, to which numerous countries have subscribed and no doubt will continue to do so.[5] FATCA having set the trend, it was inevitable that other jurisdictions would move in the direction of automatic EOI: 'Multinational automatic information exchange is now the future of international tax enforcement.'[6]

A prominent message in this book, and the symposium that preceded it, is the invidious position that multinational banks find themselves in when the legal rules of different jurisdictions are at odds with one another. This problem forms the subject of the chapter on conflicts of law (Hare, Chapter 3). Hare identifies three scenarios in which bank secrecy issues raise a conflicts problem: disputes between a bank and its customer, banks receiving requests for information from parties to a dispute and a jurisdiction using legislation or executive orders extraterritorially to obtain disclosure of information. Each scenario raises different considerations. The first scenario is particularly fertile ground for forum shopping; in the other two scenarios, banks are often unable to comply with one set of laws requiring disclosure, without infringing the other requiring secrecy to be observed. The solution prominent in the AML and tax contexts (Chapters 4 and 5) is international agreements for EOI. An example is the agreements impelled by FATCA in order to avoid the 30 per cent withholding tax on US sourced payments, a sanction which could drive banks out of the US dollar market and severely dent their international operations.[7] Absent government-level agreements to such problems, private international law must fill the gap. Chapter 3 shows that private international law is not well equipped to do so as it is reactive, court-based and largely territorially focused. This inadequacy has prompted the 'global governance' school of thought to debate whether private international law can become more proactive in the absence of international agreements, and offer a

---

[5] See 'OECD releases full version of global standard for automatic exchange of information', 21 July 2014 at www.oecd.org/tax/oecd-releases-full-version-of-global-standard-for-automatic-exchange-of-information.htm

[6] R. Cassell and J. McLemore, 'Fear of FATCA', *Financial Instruments Tax and Accounting Review*, 9 December 2014.

[7] *Ibid.*

solution focused on which state's interests are most directly affected and most deserving of protection in any particular case.

In the absence of a government-level solution, the nature of the sanction for breaching secrecy is likely to significantly affect the choice made by a bank faced with conflicting jurisdictional rules. Where one of the sanctions is a criminal offence, the bank finds itself in a particularly difficult situation. A criminal breach of the duty of secrecy is particularly serious because of the reputational risk and possible imprisonment of bank officers. If the competing sanction is a civil liability of damages or a non-criminal penalty, a bank is likely to elect for the latter. As one participant in the symposium that preceded this book put it, a bank, faced with a stark choice between breaching rules in a country with criminal consequences and one without, will not hesitate to avoid the criminal sanctions. In other words, different sanctions can skew decisions by banks, force them to make difficult choices and lead to undesirable arbitrage. This tension leads to the question of the most appropriate sanction for a breach of bank secrecy. Damages can remedy, so far as money can do it, any loss that a customer has suffered from an unpermitted disclosure. Criminal sanctions or civil regulatory penalties have a stronger deterrent effect but offer no compensatory value to the affected customer. The boundaries of legitimate disclosure have changed significantly since Singapore and Switzerland introduced criminal penalties for breach of the duty of bank secrecy. In this light, these jurisdictions should reconsider whether criminal sanctions remain an appropriate sanction.

An issue that crops up in various chapters, and which we heard much of at the Symposium, is so-called de-risking. De-risking takes different forms and is often prompted by money laundering, terrorist financing or tax evasion concerns. Chapter 13 identifies one manifestation of de-risking in the AML context, namely banks, fearful of an investigation under the US Bank Secrecy Act, turn down customers with profiles that are likely to attract the attention of the authorities, such as payday lenders and legal medical marijuana suppliers. The UK's Financial Conduct Authority (FCA) has identified money remitters, charities and FinTech firms as being 'among the sectors particularly affected by banks derisking'.[8] As noted in Chapter 5, de-risking also involves foreign banks seeking to avoid the cost and hassle of FATCA compliance by declining

---

[8] See Financial Conduct Authority 'Derisking: Managing Money-Laundering Risk', online: www.the-fca.org.uk/money-laundering-and-terrorist-financing/derisking-managing-money-laundering-risk

US customers, or closing the accounts of existing US customers, particularly those of a small, less profitable, nature. There is clear evidence that
FATCA-driven de-risking of US customers is happening, perhaps at a
significant level.[9] Whether it is sustainable is another question. EOI for
tax purposes has spread beyond FATCA to the initiatives of the OECD,
although O'Brien points out that the latter cannot be as effective as
FATCA without the kind of sanctions deployed by FATCA. Bearing in
mind that EOI is also a hallmark of AML measures, it is fast becoming the
norm with significant world coverage.[10] For this reason, on the one hand,
wholesale de-risking such as jettisoning American customers will surely
be unsustainable although customers with small, convenience accounts
may continue to be affected, at least for a while. On the other hand, some
banks may view de-risking as an opportunity to fill any vacuum left
behind, and solicit the business of de-risked customers.[11] A danger of
de-risking, highlighted by Nakajima (Chapter 4), is that rejected customers will seek financial services elsewhere which raises banking accessibility
issues and may cause a shift towards the unregulated sector. It is evident
that regulators are keen for banking accessibility not to be compromised,
revealing the tension between the public, societal role of banks and their
private, profit-driven motive. In the UK FCA's view, 'there should be relatively few cases where it is necessary to decline business relationships
solely because of anti-money laundering requirements.'[12] Furthermore,
they have said that de-risking may raise consumer protection and competition issues.[13] Some industry players have reportedly responded with
indignation: 'On what basis can the FCA force you to make a loss? '[14] This
tension between banking accessibility and regulatory compliance will be
worth watching in the future. Finally, in yet another form of de-risking,

---

[9] 'Fatca Cost and Effect' Money Laundering Bulletin, 23 September 2015: one estimate was
that more than half of UK banks would not accept US customers anymore.

[10] Another development is the Alternative Investment Fund Managers Directive (AIFMD),
a EU law that seeks to regulate the alternative investment fund industry, including hedge
funds and private equity funds. The aim is improved financial stability and investor protection. One feature of AIFMD is increased transparency through disclosure requirements;
see Cassell and McLemore, 'Fear of FATCA', 9 December 2014.

[11] See Cassell and McLemore, 'Fear of FATCA', 9 December 2014.

[12] See Financial Conduct Authority 'Derisking: managing money-laundering risk, *supra* note 8.'

[13] *Ibid.*

[14] 'UK Regulator Issues Thinly Veiled Threat on Derisking', *Money Laundering Bulletin*, 1 May
2015.

it is apparent that some US citizens are engaging in their own de-risking by renouncing US citizenship.[15]

As the dust settles over FATCA, and the new tax EOI world-order gets established, an important issue highlighted in the tax chapter (Chapter 5) is whether the United States will reciprocate with information about foreign account holders in the United States and to what extent. For example, the United States has signed but not, to date, implemented the 2010 protocol to the OECD's Convention on Mutual Administrative Assistance in Tax Matters. The protocol upgrades EOI obligations to the international standard and provides the basis for multilateral automatic EOI. Ninety-eight jurisdictions have implemented the updated Convention, and eighty-three of these have committed to a first multilateral exchange of financial account information by September 2018. The absence of the United States from the multilateral automatic EOI system creates a very significant gap in what should be a comprehensive international mechanism for preventing tax evasion through non-disclosure. O'Brien points to the irony that the imbalance between the disclosure obligations to the United States engineered by FATCA and the lesser disclosure obligations owed by the United States creates the prospect of the United States becoming the world's newest tax haven.[16]

The US discussion by Broome in Chapter 13 ends with the question of whether the US strategy of co-opting foreign banks as US law enforcement agents will affect the US dollar as the currency of choice in the global economy. This closing line provokes the interesting question of whether the US strategies might at some point prompt, or at least contribute to, a shift away from the United States to a rival financial centre. The Global Financial Centres Index, March 2015, ranked New York as the world's number one financial centre and in 2016 it was ranked second.[17] A comprehensive treatment of the makings of a successful financial centre was neither the subject of the bank secrecy symposium, nor is it the focus of this book, but those that have examined the question confirm what we probably would expect: the success of a financial centre is a complex question affected by a range of factors, including a conducive legal system, location, access, critical mass,

---

[15] 'Fatca Cost and Effect' Money Laundering Bulletin, 23 September 2015. A high profile example is the renunciation of US citizenship by UK politician, Mr Boris Johnson.

[16] See also Cassell and McLemore, 'Fear of FATCA', 9 December 2014: 'Now New York is probably a more confidential jurisdiction in which to hold your account than Switzerland.'

[17] Published by the City of London Corporation and Z/Yen Group, available at http://www.zyen.com/research/gfci.html

labour markets, tax rates and infrastructure.[18] The regulatory environment is one of many considerations. Reports of the demise of New York as the world's leading financial centre are undoubtedly premature but as Broome observes, whether the US approach will serve it well 'remains to be seen'.[19]

The Bank Secrecy Symposium hosted by the NUS Centre for Banking and Finance Law was partially driven by the significant international inroads to bank secrecy in the last decade or more which prompted the question: can banks still keep a secret? In tax matters bank secrecy is apparently dead,[20] which raises the question about bank secrecy generally. In Chapter 6, Wang notes that it is premature to discuss the demise of bank secrecy in China since the right to secrecy has never firmly taken root there. Most of the jurisdictional chapters consider that, despite recent inroads, the right of secrecy in the bank–customer relationship remains intact albeit that the exceptions have expanded. Importantly, some authors express the view that countries benefit from implementing the enhanced disclosure measures. For example, Gannon in Chapter 8 argues that Hong Kong's position as an international financial centre is enhanced by aligning itself with the international trends in EOI[21]; furthermore, he points out that the maintenance of confidentiality and combatting financial crime is 'not a zero-sum game'. Looking ahead, Stanton in Chapter 12 flags a vulnerability that banks will increasingly face in meeting their legitimate secrecy obligations: cybercrime. This challenge has already required, and will undoubtedly continue to require, banks to invest in their systems in order to maintain the integrity of their databases against skilled intruders.

The dichotomy identified by Hofmann in Chapter 7 on Germany resonates with most of the jurisdictions discussed here. The law still offers substantial protection to customers from disclosure of their financial information to private entities but there is considerably less protection against disclosure to public authorities. In the Foreword to this book, Peter Ellinger, Emeritus Professor at the National University of Singapore, Faculty of Law, rightly questions the safety of our information in the hands

---

[18] See, for example, C. Youssef, *Capitals of Capital: A History of International Financial Centres, 1780–2005* (Cambridge: Cambridge University Press, 2006), 1–6; also www.gresham.ac.uk/lectures-and-events/what-makes-a-successful-global-financial-centre

[19] Broome, Chapter 13.

[20] Algirdas Šemeta, 'Speaking Points by Commissioner Šemeta at the ECOFIN Press Conference' (14 October 2014), online: European Commission, http://europa.eu/rapid/press-release_SPEECH-14-693_en.htm?locale=en

[21] See also Booysen, Chapter 10.

of these authorities, echoing the cyber security issue mentioned above. The Foreword gives us a valuable historical perspective that reflects on how bank secrecy has gone from relative obscurity to prominence in the last hundred years, and it reminds us that the question of the right balance between the customer's right of privacy and the right of the State to access his/her personal information may still be an appropriate subject for future consideration.

INDEX

Lightning Source UK Ltd.
Milton Keynes UK
UKHW020212220619
344858UK00010B/89/P